Global Trends in Governance and Policy Paradigms

Mahani Hamdan
Universiti Brunei Darussalam, Brunei

Muhammad Anshari
Universiti Brunei Darussalam, Brunei

Norainie Ahmad
Universiti Brunei Darussalam, Brunei

Emil Ali
Universiti Brunei Darussalam, Brunei

IGI Global
PUBLISHER of TIMELY KNOWLEDGE

A volume in the Advances in Public Policy and Administration (APPA) Book Series

Published in the United States of America by
IGI Global
Information Science Publishing (an imprint of IGI Global)
701 E. Chocolate Avenue
Hershey PA, USA 17033
Tel: 717-533-8845
Fax: 717-533-8661
E-mail: cust@igi-global.com
Web site: http://www.igi-global.com

Library of Congress Cataloging-in-Publication Data

Names: Hamdan, Mahani, 1979- editor. | Anshari, Muhammad, 1977- editor. | Ahmad, Norainie, 1980- editor. | Ali, Emil, 1983- editor.
Title: Global trends in governance and policy paradigms / edited by Mahani Hamdan, Muhammad Anshari, Norainie Ahmad, Emil Ali.
Description: Hershey, PA : Business Science Reference, [2024] | Includes bibliographical references and index. | Summary: "The book will make a significant contribution to the field of public policy by providing a comprehensive overview of the different policy paradigms that have shaped global governance in recent years"-- Provided by publisher.
Identifiers: LCCN 2023049097 (print) | LCCN 2023049098 (ebook) | ISBN 9798369317426 (hardcover) | ISBN 9798369317433 (ebook)
Subjects: LCSH: Policy sciences. | Public policy. | International cooperation.
Classification: LCC H97 .G59 2024 (print) | LCC H97 (ebook) | DDC 320.6--dc23/eng/20240209
LC record available at https://lccn.loc.gov/2023049097
LC ebook record available at https://lccn.loc.gov/2023049098

This book is published in the IGI Global book series Advances in Public Policy and Administration (APPA) (ISSN: 2475-6644; eISSN: 2475-6652)

British Cataloguing in Publication Data
A Cataloguing in Publication record for this book is available from the British Library.

For electronic access to this publication, please contact: eresources@igi-global.com.

Advances in Public Policy and Administration (APPA) Book Series

ISSN:2475-6644
EISSN:2475-6652

Editor-in-Chief: Mahani Hamdan, Universiti Brunei Darussalam, Brunei

Mission

Proper management of the public sphere is necessary in order to maintain order in modern society. Research developments in the field of public policy and administration can assist in uncovering the latest tools, practices, and methodologies for governing societies around the world.

The **Advances in Public Policy and Administration (APPA) Book Series** aims to publish scholarly publications focused on topics pertaining to the governance of the public domain. APPA's focus on timely topics relating to government, public funding, politics, public safety, policy, and law enforcement is particularly relevant to academicians, government officials, and upper-level students seeking the most up-to-date research in their field.

Coverage

- Government
- Law Enforcement
- Political Economy
- Politics
- Public Administration
- Public Funding
- Public Policy
- Resource allocation
- Urban Planning

IGI Global is currently accepting manuscripts for publication within this series. To submit a proposal for a volume in this series, please contact our Acquisition Editors at Acquisitions@igi-global.com or visit: http://www.igi-global.com/publish/.

The Advances in Public Policy and Administration (APPA) Book Series (ISSN 2475-6644) is published by IGI Global, 701 E. Chocolate Avenue, Hershey, PA 17033-1240, USA, www.igi-global.com. This series is composed of titles available for purchase individually; each title is edited to be contextually exclusive from any other title within the series. For pricing and ordering information please visit http://www.igi-global.com/book-series/advances-public-policy-administration/97862. Postmaster: Send all address changes to above address.

Titles in this Series

For a list of additional titles in this series, please visit:
http://www.igi-global.com/book-series/advances-public-policy-administration/97862

Soft Power and Diplomatic Strategies in Asia and the Middle East
Mohamad Zreik (School of International Studies, Sun Yat-sen University, China)
Information Science Reference • © 2024 • 386pp • H/C (ISBN: 9798369324448) • US $265.00

Economic and Societal Impact of Organized Crime Policy and Law Enforcement Interventions
Alicia Danielsson (University of Bolton, UK & Hume Institute for Postgraduate Studies, Switzerland)
Information Science Reference • © 2024 • 350pp • H/C (ISBN: 9798369303276) • US $240.00

The Convergence of Traditionalism and Populism in American Politics From Bannon to Trump
Adrian David Cheok (Nanjing University of Information Science and Technology, China)
Information Science Reference • © 2024 • 288pp • H/C (ISBN: 9781668492901) • US $235.00

Regulating Fair Competition Toward Sustainable Development Goals
Siti Fazilah Abdul Shukor (University of Tunku Abdul Rahman, Malaysia) Farahdilah Ghazali (University of Malaysia Terengganu, Malaysia) Nur Yuhanis Ismon (University of Tun Hussien Onn, Malaysia) and Aerni Isa (Taylor's University, Malaysia)
Information Science Reference • © 2024 • 285pp • H/C (ISBN: 9798369303900) • US $275.00

Analyzing Energy Crises and the Impact of Country Policies on the World
Merve Suna Özel Özcan (Kirikkale University, Turkey)
Engineering Science Reference • © 2024 • 283pp • H/C (ISBN: 9798369304402) • US $240.00

Using Crises and Disasters as Opportunities for Innovation and Improvement
Saeed Siyal (School of Economics and Management, Beijing University of Chemical Technology, China)
Information Science Reference • © 2024 • 323pp • H/C (ISBN: 9781668495223) • US $240.00

Cognitive Governance and the Historical Distortion of the Norm of Modern Development A Theory of Political Asymmetry
Renny Rueda (American University in the Emirates, UAE)
Information Science Reference • © 2024 • 254pp • H/C (ISBN: 9781668497944) • US $215.00

Financial Evaluation and Risk Management of Infrastructure Projects
Kleopatra Petroutsatou (Aristotle University of Thessaloniki, Greece) and Constantin Zopounidis (Technical University of Crete, Greece & Audencia Business School, France)
Information Science Reference • © 2024 • 248pp • H/C (ISBN: 9781668477861) • US $225.00

IGI Global
PUBLISHER of TIMELY KNOWLEDGE

701 East Chocolate Avenue, Hershey, PA 17033, USA
Tel: 717-533-8845 x100 • Fax: 717-533-8661
E-Mail: cust@igi-global.com • www.igi-global.com

Editorial Advisory Board

Table of Contents

Detailed Table of Contents

Organizations are under constant pressure. Externally, they face a scenario of intense competition, coupled with a changing environment which is full of uncertainty. Internally, organizations have to deal with limited resources, whilst at the same time comply with increasing requirements and strategic demands. A key to success is the successful management of organizational projects. According to worldwide studies, information systems and information technology (IS/IT) projects have a relatively low success rate. To face these various business challenges, the authors suggest that emphasis should be put on the integration of various and disperse management tools. By combining project management maturity models with benefits management approaches, the authors expect to reinforce support for the drive to use organizational projects to fulfill organizations' strategic plans that will enhance the control techniques of project management, whilst recognizing the need for organizational change and for ensuring the interpersonal skills necessary to orchestrate the successful completion of a project.

The pandemic-induced disruption has created a critical juncture at which the opportunity to experiment with new policy trajectories has widened. Yet, how much public support is there for such an experiment? This chapter addresses this question by studying the Activation (Prakerja) and unemployment protection (Jaminan Kehilangan Pekerjaan, JKP) policies, which served as essential policy responses during the COVID-19 crisis in Indonesia. In this study, the authors analysed 47,916 tweets containing public debates that took place up to three months after the policies' inception. Having performed a set of analyses on sentiments, emotions, and most appealing tweets, the authors argue that different forms of support for Prakerja and JKP emerged not because of the policies' breakthrough traits, but due to citizens' pragmatic-cognitive logic shaped by the urgency and severity of the COVID-19 crisis. It makes the idea of state-centred welfare responsibility (something Prakerja possesses) more desirable than contribution-based insurance, which JKP offers. Discussing the Indonesian case fills in the existing research gap as it facilitates a better understanding of the political legitimacy of welfare state policy institutionalization in developing countries during the COVID-19 catastrophe.

Leadership styles vary as per the context and environment in which the organizations exist. Today's environment for organizations is not the same as it was two decades back. Globalization, ICT convergence, digitalization, multigenerational workforce, and the recent pandemic have completely changed the environment in which organizations operate and exist. To meet this new changing time, there are challenges that leaders face and hence new styles of leadership are merging which will ensure that governance does not take the back seat but is in line with the changing dynamics and expectations. Adopting a qualitative approach, the aim of this chapter is to deliberate on contemporary leadership styles and discuss the challenges therein for better governance.

Governance relates to structures and processes within an organisation to ensure greater accountability, a higher sense of responsiveness, transparency, and rule of law. Corporate governance balances the interests of a company's many stakeholders, such as shareholders, customers, vendors, financiers, the government, the community, and, very importantly, its own employees. While traditionally corporates had one clear agenda—i.e., make more profits and increase the shareholders' wealth—the 21st century saw the corporates turning a new leaf and looking at their growth from a societal perspective, specifically those relating to sustainable development like environmental protection. In the classical case of poor corporate governance, in the year 1984, the city Bhopal in India witnessed the most nightmarish experience, with the death of 16,000 people due to the leakage of a poisonous gas.

Research and development (R&D) are an important issue for companies in a wide range of sectors, as they generate innovation, productivity, and sustainability, which are important factors for competitive advantage. To analyze which corporate governance mechanisms influence R&D investment by B3-listed companies, a fixed effects panel regression analysis was performed from 2010 to 2020. From a universe of 477 companies, a sample of 61 companies that spent at least one year on R&D was drawn. The results show that despite the hypotheses that board independence, ownership concentration, and CEO duality have no positive or negative effect on R&D spending, rejecting the latter hypotheses leads to a negative relationship between the first two factors and R&D spending. Therefore, it can be concluded that some corporate governance mechanisms can explain organizational investment in research and development.

This chapter examines the impact of foreign aid to southeast Asia countries. There are many arguments around the concept of foreign financing for developing countries, especially to the southeast Asia countries.

the Taliban's foreign policy stance, the international status of women under their governance, and the organizational structure of the Islamic Emirate of Afghanistan. Emphasizing the dynamic nature of policymaking influenced by religious legitimacy, the chapter argues that internal dynamics play a pivotal role in shaping the evolving policies of the Taliban. In scrutinizing Afghanistan's security landscape, it investigates the Taliban's efficacy against ISKP, their alignment with Al Qaeda, and their approach to issues with Pakistan and Iran. The study anticipates potential scenarios and provide policy-centric recommendations, urging the international community to actively engage with and fortify Afghan institutions amidst the unfolding dynamics of governance and institutionalization.

Chapter 11
Greening the Guns: How Armed Non-State Actors Can Become a Player in the Fight for a Sustainable Future.. 187
Muhammed Karakuş, Adıyaman University, Turkey

Globalization's inexorable interconnectedness has swept non-state actors onto the stage of global governance, weaving them into its intricate tapestry. Yet, the body of literature is fixated on their ability to sway the levers of state power. This focus overshadows not only their but also the potential contributions, nimbleness, diverse vantage points, and unburdened agility of armed non-state actors (ANSAs) who are known for their most egregious examples. With their sprawling and deftly governance capacities, ANSAs move beyond local issues and incrementally take actions on global policies. States, international organizations, and NGOs look further afield to grow their global clout in shaping, implementing, and accomplishing climate policy while climate change's incipient ascent has taken place. However, too little is still known about conflict areas and ANSAs. By shattering the illusion of ANSA as mere bystanders of environmental concerns, this study asserts that full-fledged environmental protection can be achieved with their engagement.

Chapter 12
How the Productivist Welfare System Frames the Risks of Ageing During the COVID-19 Pandemic: Insights From the Four Asian Tigers 209
Tauchid Komara Yuda, Department of Social Development and Welfare, Universitas Gadjah Mada, Indonesia
Zhen Tian, School of Graduate Studies, Lingnan University, Hong Kong
Zhiming Hu, Department of Sociology and Social Policy, Lingnan University, Hong Kong

COVID-19 presents a systemic social risk for the East Asian welfare system. This chapter focuses on global shocks and its policy responses targeted at older residents, which are East Asia's most pressing social policy issues before and during the COVID-19 pandemic. This review reveals that Taiwan and South Korea seem to combine the developmental-universalist and social democratic welfare state models, whereas Hong Kong and Singapore have followed a typical mix of development-universalist and facilitative approaches. Overall, they have successfully transitioned from an economic-driven preference to a more balanced protective-productive feature, but they have done so through multiple pathways, with the market-conforming role of social policy for the elderly remaining dominant. This study responds to the current debate on policy continuity and adaptation in East Asia and suggests a new perspective.

This chapter reflects on the Ph.D. journey within the Santals of Bangladesh, followed by an ethnographic method at Birganj in Dinajpur, Bangladesh. The Government of Bangladesh formulated diverse forest policies, acts, and rules and either ratified or approved international treaties/documents to preserve, guide, and nurture the forests. However, when the author entered the remote Santals hamlet, they talked about their grief regarding the Sal Forest. Before starting the academic journey, the first author was born and developed in a village where the Indigenous research methodology was embedded informally in his mind as a consciousness part; moreover, as a student spent with Santals neighbours in the agri-field, school, colleges, and even the common playground in the countryside. As a result, it is decorated with field experiences and deals with the "capability approach" while the PhD candidate stayed in the research field for a long time and observed an intricate relationship between Santals and the international legal frameworks to ratify in Bangladesh.

This chapter attempts to explore the interaction between national sovereignty and private security companies, taking Myanmar and Cambodia as examples. After the end of the cold war, some countries are still in the process of State-building. To ensure domestic and international security, the authorities decided to take their security off the border and entrust it to PSC. Among them, the adaptability of shared security sovereignty and the demand for security interests jointly determine the practice of shared security sovereignty of the state over PSC. During the military government period, Myanmar faced significant international pressure, but maintained a certain degree of national stability. the state and PSC had an unstable alliance relationship. After the democratization process began, overall international pressure weakened, and the two parties tended to be stable alliances or potential alliances. As for Cambodia, the lack of national capacity has led it to actively accept international norms and to strengthen cooperation with PSC. After a solid political authority was build, Cambodia began to reduce cooperation with PSC. Whether it is Myanmar or Cambodia, it has been shown that the disembedding of security is a last resort for transitional countries whose state construction has not yet been completed. Once a solid-state authority is established and it meets the needs of international norms, the state will often monopolize security supply. It does not allow private security companies to share security sovereignty.

The purpose of this study is to describe the European Union's (EU) developing approach and governance in the implementation of the sustainable development agenda of the United Nations (UN). UN's

Preface

As editors of *Global Trends in Governance and Policy Paradigms*, we are delighted to present this comprehensive compilation of scholarly works exploring the dynamic landscape of global governance and policy paradigms. This collaborative effort brings together diverse perspectives from esteemed scholars and practitioners to shed light on the evolving nature of governance in response to contemporary challenges and opportunities.

In recent years, the realm of global governance has witnessed significant transformations, shaped by a multitude of factors ranging from rapid technological advancements to shifting geopolitical dynamics and evolving societal expectations. Against this backdrop, understanding the emergence, evolution, and impact of various policy paradigms becomes paramount for scholars, policymakers, and practitioners alike.

This edited volume delves into a wide array of topics, encompassing regulatory policy, evidence-based policymaking, defense and security, AI and public policy, Islamic governance, leadership, and much more. Each chapter offers valuable insights into the complexities of contemporary governance issues, providing analyses, case studies, and recommendations to navigate the intricacies of policy formulation and implementation.

Importantly, this book not only maps the current state of global governance but also paves the way for future discourse and action. By examining the challenges and opportunities associated with emerging policy paradigms, it serves as a guiding beacon for policymakers, international organizations, NGOs, and the private sector in shaping more effective and inclusive governance frameworks.

We extend our gratitude to all the contributors who have enriched this volume with their expertise and dedication. Their invaluable contributions have made this endeavor possible and have ensured that *Global Trends in Governance and Policy Paradigms* serves as a comprehensive resource for scholars, policymakers, and practitioners worldwide.

We hope that this book sparks meaningful dialogue, fosters innovative thinking, and inspires actionable solutions to address the complex governance challenges of our time. May it serve as a catalyst for positive change in the global governance landscape.

Chapter 1: Can ASEAN's Governance of Climate Change Become Participatory?

In "Can ASEAN's Governance of Climate Change Become Participatory?" by Virgemarie Salazar and Jovito Jose Katigbak, the authors delve into the complexities of ASEAN's governance framework concerning climate change. They argue that understanding state interests, institutional dynamics, and global climate ideas is crucial for determining the feasibility of participatory approaches. The chapter provides insights into ASEAN's policies, emphasizing the challenges and prospects of integrating participatory mechanisms within the region's governance framework.

Chapter 2: Challenges of the Digital Transformation—Public Administration

Jorge Gomes and Mário Romão address "Challenges of the Digital Transformation: Public Administration." Their chapter explores the landscape of digital transformation initiatives in the Portuguese Public Administration context. Through a qualitative analysis, they identify critical success factors, challenges, and attributes necessary for evaluating digital transformation projects. The proposed framework aims to enhance strategic alignment, resource allocation, and performance improvement within the public sector.

Chapter 3: Combining Models to Shape Project Success

In "Combining Models to Shape Project Success," Gomes and Romão emphasize the significance of effective project management amidst organizational challenges. They advocate for integrating various management tools, such as project management maturity models and benefits management approaches, to bolster organizational project success. By emphasizing the need for adaptability and strategic alignment, the authors provide valuable insights into enhancing project management practices.

Chapter 4: Comparing Public Support for Two Indonesian Employment Policy Reforms in a Time of COVID-19– Sentiment and Emotion Analysis of Tweets: Public Attitude Towards Indonesian Social Policy Reform

Tauchid Komara Yuda and Fadhli Fauzi analyze public sentiment regarding Indonesian employment policy reforms amidst the COVID-19 crisis in "Comparing public support for two Indonesian employment policy reforms in a time of COVID-19–Sentiment and emotion analysis of tweets." Their analysis of public discourse on social media sheds light on the pragmatic-cognitive logic shaping support for policy initiatives. Through sentiment and emotion analysis, the chapter elucidates the dynamics of social policy legitimation during times of crisis.

Chapter 5: Contemporary Leadership Styles and Challenges for Governance

Neeta Baporikar explores "Contemporary Leadership Styles and Challenges for Governance" in the context of evolving organizational environments. Highlighting the impact of globalization, digitalization, and the recent pandemic, the chapter delves into the emergence of new leadership styles. By adopting a qualitative approach, the author discusses the challenges faced by contemporary leaders and their implications for effective governance.

Chapter 6: Corporate Governance for Sustainable Development

"Corporate Governance for Sustainable Development" by Sridharan A. and Sunita Kumar delves into the evolving role of corporate governance in promoting sustainable development. The chapter elucidates the shift from profit-centric approaches to a more inclusive and socially responsible corporate ethos.

Drawing from historical examples, the authors emphasize the importance of accountability, transparency, and stakeholder engagement in corporate governance practices.

Chapter 7: Exploring the Link Between Corporate Governance and R&D Investments on Brazilian Listed Companies

Yago Teixeira, Lívia Santos, Risolene Araújo, and Adriana Silva investigate the relationship between corporate governance mechanisms and research and development (R&D) investments in Brazilian listed companies. Through panel regression analysis, the authors explore the impact of board independence, ownership concentration, and CEO duality on R&D spending. Their findings provide insights into the factors influencing organizational investment in innovation and sustainability.

Chapter 8: Financing for Development in Southeast Asia Countries

Lili Yulyadi Arnakim, Miranda Tahalele, Hizkia Putra Purnomo, and Muhammad Anshari examine the impact of foreign aid on financing for development in Southeast Asia countries. Their qualitative research explores the perceptions surrounding foreign financing and its role in infrastructure development. By analyzing the successes and challenges of external financing, the chapter contributes to understanding the dynamics of development financing in the region.

Chapter 9: Fostering Inclusivity and a Supportive Workplace for the Hearing-Impaired—Towards Hifz Al-Nafs

Siti Nur Rafhanah Awang Masri and Norainie Ahmad shed light on the importance of fostering inclusivity and supportive workplaces for the hearing-impaired in " Fostering Inclusivity and a Supportive Workplace for the Hearing-Impaired: Towards Hifz Al-Nafs." Through interviews and a focus on Islamic ethics, the chapter advocates for accessible communication and awareness efforts to create a supportive environment for hearing-impaired individuals in the workplace.

Chapter 10: From Insurgents to Custodians—Charting Taliban's Transition Towards 'Governance' and 'Institutionalization' in Afghanistan

Saad Ullah Khan and Sadaf Khan's chapter, " From Insurgents to Custodians: Charting Taliban's Transition Towards 'Governance' and 'Institutionalization in Afghanistan," offers a comprehensive analysis of the Taliban's governance and institutionalization in Afghanistan. By examining internal factionalism, foreign policy stances, and security dynamics, the authors provide policy-centric recommendations for engaging with Afghan institutions amidst evolving governance dynamics.

Chapter 11: Greening the Guns—How Armed Non-State Actors Can Become a Player in the Fight for a Sustainable Future

Muhammed Karakus explores the potential contributions of armed non-state actors (ANSAs) to environmental protection in "Greening the Guns; How Armed Non-State Actors Can Become a Player in the Fight for a Sustainable Future." The chapter challenges conventional perceptions of ANSAs and emphasizes their role in environmental governance. By advocating for their engagement, the study underscores the potential for achieving comprehensive environmental protection.

Chapter 12: How Productivist Welfare System Frames the Risks of Ageing During the COVID-19 Pandemic – Insights From the Four Asian Tigers: Productivist Welfare Regimes and Ageing Risk

Tauchid Komara Yuda, Zhen Tian, and Zhiming Hu analyze the impact of COVID-19 on aging populations and welfare systems in East Asia in "How productivist welfare system frames the risks of ageing during the COVID-19 pandemic." Through a review of policy responses and welfare regimes in Taiwan, South Korea, Hong Kong, and Singapore, the chapter offers insights into addressing the challenges of aging populations amidst global crises.

Chapter 13: Municipal Communication, Governance and the Role to the Local Community—A Case Study in Guimarães (Portugal)

Diana Salgado Pereira, Manuel Fonseca, and Bruno Sousa explore the role of municipal communication in governance and community engagement in "Municipal Communication, Governance and the role to the Local Community: a case study in Guimarães (Portugal)." The chapter highlights the importance of effective communication strategies for territorial management, local development, and enhancing the tourist destination's appeal.

Chapter 14—Navigating the Gap: Protecting Human Rights in the Era of Environmental Migration

Abhinash Mohanta, Akash Bag, Shreya, and Kumud Choudhary discuss the challenges of protecting human rights in the era of environmental migration in "Navigating the Gap: Protecting Human Rights in the Era of Environmental Migration." By evaluating international legal frameworks, the chapter calls for a dedicated mechanism to address the rights of environmental refugees and ensure their protection amidst global migration trends.

Chapter 15: Navigating the Grey Area—Can Cyber Warfare Trigger a State's Right to Self-Defense?

Anirudha Choudhury, Asif Shah, Shrabana Chattopadhyay, and Akash Bag examine the intersection of cyber warfare and the right to self-defense in "Navigating the Grey Area: Can Cyber Warfare Trigger a State's Right to Self-Defense?" The chapter navigates the complexities of cyber operations and defensive actions within the framework of international law, emphasizing the necessity of proportionate responses to cyber threats.

Chapter 16: Pilgrimage Creative Tourism and Sustainable Development Opportunity of Bangladesh

Mohammad Talukder, Sanjeev Kumar, and Fahmida Kaiser explore the potential of pilgrimage as a driver for sustainable development in Bangladesh in "Pilgrimage Creative Tourism and Sustainable Development

Opportunity of Bangladesh." The chapter highlights the role of creative tourism in promoting cultural heritage preservation, economic development, and community engagement within pilgrimage destinations.

Chapter 17: Regulation of Transnational Corporations (TNCs) in International Law-Exploring the Concept of Home and Host State—Transnational Corporations

Krishangee Bhattacharyya, Shaeyuq Shah, Abhilash Sapre, and Shalini Singh delve into the regulation of transnational corporations (TNCs) in international law in " Regulation of Transnational Corporations (TNCs) in International Law-Exploring the Concept of Home and Host State: Transnational Corporations." Through legal analysis and case studies, the chapter examines the balance between promoting economic growth and ensuring responsible corporate behavior in a globalized world.

Chapter 18: Santals, Sal Forest, and Policy of Bangladesh—Reminiscence of Ethnographic Experiences

Parimal Roy reflects on ethnographic experiences with the Santals of Bangladesh and their relationship with forest policies in "Santals, Sal Forest, and Policy of Bangladesh: Reminiscence of Ethnographic Experiences." Drawing from fieldwork and indigenous research methodologies, the chapter provides insights into sustainable community development and the intricate relationship between ethnic communities and legal frameworks.

Chapter 19: State Security Agent—A Study on the Interaction between State Sovereignty and Private Security Companies from the Perspective

Meng Yang and Yuhong LI explore the interaction between national sovereignty and private security companies in "State Security Agent: A Study on the Interaction between State Sovereignty and Private Security Companies." Through a case study of Myanmar's experience with private security companies, the chapter analyzes the dynamics of shared security sovereignty and its implications for national stability and international relations.

Chapter 20: The European Union Development Policy on its Achieving Sustainable Development Goals (SDGs) of the United Nations—EU and its Policy on UN's SDGs

Mukesh Bharti examines the European Union's approach to achieving the United Nations' Sustainable Development Goals (SDGs) in "The European Union Development Policy on its Achieving Sustainable Development Goals (SDGs) of the United Nations." The chapter explores the EU's governance strategies, cooperation initiatives, and contributions to global sustainable development efforts.

Chapter 21: Assimilative Potentials in Planning and Public Policy Analysis—Critical Pragmatic Perspective

Noe John discusses on the argument that assimilative formulas to policy analysis are essential to mending the debate between the technocratic paradigms and the critical approaches to policy analysis. In real-world policy practice at the height of the COVID-19 pandemic, addressing public problems demands an innovative direction to advance policy initiatives that are both inclusive and transformative. The chapter's discussion reimagined the characteristics and role of the assimilative practitioner spanning across issues on social injustices, high inequalities, professionalization, and micropolitics. Critical insight from Chiang Mai City, Thailand suggests that a sound policy analysis goes beyond the hectic technical systems or a messy deliberative process. Lessons direct us to go beyond these boundaries and limitations and seek a creative reimagination of policy analysis that is both assimilative and critically pragmatic.

In closing, Global Trends in Governance and Policy Paradigms stands as a testament to the collective effort of scholars and practitioners committed to advancing our understanding of global governance dynamics. Through the exploration of diverse perspectives and the examination of emerging policy paradigms, this edited volume offers a panoramic view of the evolving landscape of governance in response to contemporary challenges.

As we navigate an increasingly interconnected world, characterized by rapid technological innovation, geopolitical shifts, and evolving societal expectations, the need for effective governance frameworks has never been more pressing. This book serves as a compass, guiding policymakers, international organizations, NGOs, and the private sector towards more inclusive, adaptive, and responsive governance models.

The chapters within this volume not only diagnose the complexities of contemporary governance issues but also prescribe insightful analyses, case studies, and recommendations to navigate these challenges. From climate change governance in ASEAN to the role of armed non-state actors in environmental protection, each contribution offers unique perspectives and actionable insights that contribute to the collective knowledge base.

We extend our deepest gratitude to all the contributors who have enriched this volume with their expertise, dedication, and passion for advancing the field of governance studies. Their contributions have not only shaped this book but have also contributed to the broader discourse surrounding global governance and policy paradigms.

As editors, we hope that this book serves as a catalyst for meaningful dialogue, fosters innovative thinking, and inspires concrete actions to address the complex governance challenges of our time. May it spark collaboration, drive positive change, and contribute to building a more just, sustainable, and prosperous world for future generations.

Editors:

Mahani Hamdan
Universiti Brunei Darussalam

Muhammad Anshari
Universiti Brunei Darussalam

Norainie Ahmad
Universiti Brunei Darussalam

Emil Ali
Universiti Brunei Darussalam

Chapter 1
Can ASEAN's Governance of Climate Change Become Participatory?

Virgemarie Salazar
https://orcid.org/0000-0001-8998-7144
University of the Philippines Diliman, Philippines

Jovito Jose P. Katigbak
https://orcid.org/0000-0002-9291-8251
De La Salle University, Manila, Philippines

ABSTRACT

This chapter argues that state interests and institutions within ASEAN, along with the ideas from the global climate regime to some extent, are important factors that can explain the viability of participatory approaches in ASEAN's governance of climate change. It examines ASEAN's policies on climate change to understand the context defining regional governance and to determine the prospect of enabling participatory mechanisms. This chapter finds that interests, institutions, and ideas can explain the prevailing ASEAN governance framework on climate change. With these factors, integrating participatory approaches to improve the access of non-state actors to governance processes presents a challenge. Intergovernmentalism and ASEAN norms are deeply entrenched in the regional organization's processes and mechanisms. Thus, increasing the participation and inclusion of non-state actors would seem a tall order, although not entirely impossible given ASEAN's initial endeavors.

INTRODUCTION

Relevant studies affirm that ASEAN remains to be a state-centric organization despite its aspiration to be a people-oriented association. Nevertheless, it bears noting that ASEAN has initiated processes to engage non-state actors. ASEAN's region-building has been characterized as a form of soft regionalism (Collins, 2013) given that the interests of member-state governments tend to dominate ASEAN's agenda

DOI: 10.4018/979-8-3693-1742-6.ch001

and decision-making. Thus, ASEAN regionalism grants limited involvement of non-state actors in collectively addressing transnational issues. Pressures to make ASEAN regionalism more participatory stem primarily from democratic forces in Southeast Asian states that have challenged the state-centric structure and norms of sovereignty and non-interference that underpin ASEAN cooperation (Acharya, 2003). The engagement of non-state actors such as civil society organizations (CSOs) fosters participatory regionalism since their inclusion enables them to contribute ideas and other resources to existing mechanisms and allows for their participation in regional governance. Indeed, participatory regionalism entails allowing more space for non-state actors in decision-making processes and developing closer links between government and civil society in managing regional issues (Acharya, 2003).

The extant literature underscores that there are constraints from within and outside the states that make it difficult for ASEAN to enact participatory regionalism. Particularly, there are claims that the regional bloc has retained its corporatist arrangements in spite of its attempt to accommodate interest representation of non-state actors (Rüland, 2014). It has also been observed that ASEAN engages with CSOs to boost the legitimacy of its reform agenda rather than genuinely providing opportunities for CSOs to be involved in regional issues (Gerard, 2015). Moreover, non-state actors perceive that ASEAN policies tend to prioritize markets and profits over peoples' rights and that ASEAN utilizes engagement platforms as a one-way socialization tool for its policies instead of promoting genuine stakeholder participation by gathering inputs from a wide array of actors (Chandra et al., 2017). Thus, the transformation of ASEAN's interest representation to a more pluralist one appears pessimistic since the organization still retains its state-centric decision-making structure (Rüland, 2014).

Accordingly, access to decision-making process has been identified as a causal mechanism that links participatory governance to strong or weak representation of environmental concerns (Newig et al., 2018). Participation allows for a wider representation of actors, particularly those directly affected, to ensure that their concerns are heard before decisions are made. Opening the decision-making process to actors typically outside of restricted policy circles creates opportunities for a broad range of stakeholders to be involved. Hence, this may eventually lead to changes in the distribution of interests, values, and alternatives. Moreover, increased participation of environmental concerns in the decision-making process allows for the inclusion of a diverse set of values, arguments, and knowledge claims that can enhance the environmental quality of outputs (Newig et al., 2018).

To relate participation with climate change governance, this chapter addresses the question: How does ASEAN's governance context determine the access of non-state actors in regional processes on climate change? It argues that state interests and institutions within ASEAN, along with the ideas from the global climate regime, are important factors that can explain the viability of participatory approaches in ASEAN's governance of climate change.

This chapter examines ASEAN's policies on climate change, along with the plans and programs of member states on mitigation and adaptation, to identify the main factors affecting ASEAN's governance context. It is important to peruse the environment wherein governance takes place to ascertain whether conditions enabling participatory processes are present. Thus, this chapter is focused on analyzing the material and ideational realities as well as the institutional landscape that define ASEAN's governance context. Using data extracted from documents available on ASEAN's official website containing the words "climate change," the authors applied content analysis of selected policy statements, declarations, reports, and press releases issued by ASEAN covering the period 2004 to 2020. These materials are collectively referred to as policy documents, which are written records that state the purpose, scope, function, and effectiveness of government actions in response to an issue of public importance. The cited data are supplemented with data from reports that member states submit periodically to the United Nations Framework Convention on Climate Change (UNFCCC). Analysis is centered on the role of interests, institutions, and ideas stated in ASEAN policy documents, and these factors are then used in determining the likelihood of integrating participatory approaches in regional climate change governance.

The chapter is divided into three main sections. The first section provides an overview of the issues that characterize ASEAN's efforts to govern climate change. The penultimate section presents the findings of the content analysis grouped under the main themes of interests, institutions, and ideas, which serve as the factors affecting the governance context. It is worth stressing that the results only apply to the regional grouping's experience in managing climate change-related issues and developments and in advancing relevant objectives. The last section explores the viability of participatory mechanisms in ASEAN's climate change governance. A concluding segment summarizes the key insights of the chapter and outlines considerations for ASEAN, member states, and researchers.

ISSUES IN ASEAN'S CLIMATE CHANGE GOVERNANCE

ASEAN's experience in managing environmental issues depicts mixed results. On the one hand, there has been a growing recognition of the importance of coordinating efforts particularly on transboundary haze and climate change due to the common challenges, shared vulnerabilities, and the promise of mutual gains (Elliott, 2017). To illustrate, ASEAN has formulated regional cooperative frameworks while national governments have instituted policies and agencies to effectively address environmental problems (Anbumozhi, 2017; Koh & Robinson, 2002). However, the regional grouping's efforts to resolve environmental problems have yet to achieve optimal results for effective governance is beset with challenges.

For instance, ASEAN's environmental responses are normatively and materially constrained (Elliott, 2003) since inadequate funding leads to poor monitoring and implementation of commitments. Further, its behavioral and procedural norms, known as the ASEAN Way, have cultivated the soft institutionalism of environmental governance practices thereby discouraging open criticism and the imposition of sanctions when member states fail to deliver on their commitments. Due to ASEAN's emphasis on soft law, there is no concrete instrument for translating regional commitments to domestic-level actions. Barriers to effective regional environmental response include the following: (1) strict adherence to non-interference, which undermines practical cooperative measures; (2) lack of expertise, information, funding, and organizational support within ASEAN; (3) absence of a monitoring system, which limits ASEAN's ability to gather information and respond in a timely manner; and (4) lack of dispute resolution mechanism resulting in conflict avoidance rather than resolution (Koh & Robinson, 2002). Nevertheless, ASEAN has made strides in creating a regional environmental policy framework even without a core bureaucracy overseeing regional environmental efforts.

The role of national agencies should be highlighted. As local grassroots activism and regional networks of non-government organizations (NGOs) grew, ASEAN has responded by exhibiting willingness to work with non-state actors such as experts, think tanks, civil society, businesses, and the like. Policymakers in the region have recognized the advantages of transnational networks in improving knowledge exchanges and capacity-building. However, ASEAN has been slow in integrating non-state actors in its policymaking process. There have been efforts to apply a multi-stakeholder and participatory approach but non-state actors still have a limited capacity to engage and influence ASEAN processes (Allison & Taylor, 2017). In addition, a systematic literature review of climate change governance activities of environmental NGOs in Southeast Asia finds that NGOs are more involved in the implementation of policies, but only bear minimal influence in policy formulation (Haris et al., 2020).

This predicament has reinforced the persistence of a top-down governance structure in addressing sustainability and environmental issues (Anbumozhi, 2017). Specifically, the region's environmental governance structure is still mainly government-driven despite the emergence of new models of regionalism, since ASEAN has failed to offer effective channels of communication and promote democratic representation of stakeholders (Elliott, 2012). Although the organization has ventured into network governance in coordinating environmental policies and managing regulatory tasks by opening opportunities for networks of non-state actors to influence policies through exchanges of policy inputs and knowledge, cooperative arrangements have been less successful in establishing regional standards and prioritizing collective action over national interest (Elliott, 2017).

On climate change, ASEAN has acknowledged the importance of coping with climate-related threats to achieve sustainable development and a resilient region. Notably, all ASEAN member states are signatories to the UNFCCC and the 2015 Paris Agreement on Climate Change. Likewise, the ASEAN Economic and Socio-cultural Blueprints accentuate the need to enhance climate change resilience by strengthening institutional capacity in implementing climate change adaptation and mitigation goals, facilitating the development of comprehensive and coherent responses to climate change, as well as promoting global partnerships, among others. National climate change policies are in place and governments have their respective agencies tasked to pursue mitigation and adaptation goals.

As with any cooperative arrangement under ASEAN, member states are primarily responsible to act on climate change. Although ASEAN appears to have made progress on climate change at the institutional level, it has yet to contend with the issue of aiming to establish cooperative frameworks without clear legal parameters and enforcement mechanisms (Gerstl & Helmke, 2012). Thus, the effectiveness of ASEAN's climate change initiatives suffers from a limited implementation scheme, which is linked to the sovereignty norm and the lack of legally binding agreements (Sahraie, 2011). Even when there is consensus on regional actions, national governments solely decide which measures to take because ASEAN does not interfere with the domestic affairs of member states as a matter of principle.

The adaptive capacity of the region and the member states is also constrained by the scarcity of financial resources, expertise, information, and technology, among others (Sahraie, 2011). This is an important point since funding and technology transfer are needed in research and development to tackle climate change threats. Likewise, major institutional gaps have to be addressed, which include the absence of a coordinating body on regional climate change governance and poor ASEAN leadership in gathering support from Dialogue Partners to assist member states in meeting their pledges under the Paris Agreement (Seah & Martinus, 2021). Another gap is the need for a platform to engage civil society and the private sector on climate change issues given that ASEAN has the means to promote dialogue among various stakeholders (Seah & Martinus, 2021). While ASEAN has made headways in regional responses to environmental issues specifically on climate change, it is expected to step up and sustain its efforts in the long run. Hence, a more in-depth study of ASEAN's governance context can provide insights on future courses of action.

FACTORS SHAPING THE GOVERNANCE CONTEXT

In conducting content analysis of policy documents, particular attention is given to the interests, institutional framework, norms, and ideas that relate to the motivations and understanding of state actors on climate change. Although policy declarations and statements are not binding instruments, these documents represent the consensus among ASEAN member states on a particular issue. Examining these documents can therefore offer insights into the region's prevailing governance milieu on climate change.

In identifying social and material conditions relevant to climate change governance, statements referring to the interests of states are studied. The rationalist perspective suggests that states are utility-maximizing actors. Since states are rational actors, regional integration can be viewed mainly as a process of pursuing common interests. To assume a rational state behavior among ASEAN members on climate change governance is valid since addressing the issue entails costs and benefits, which affects states' preferences during interstate bargaining of collective goals. Thus, the context of ASEAN's governance can be understood through the rational choice of states. This context is also indicative of ASEAN's institutional design, which is to promote common interests. A basic assumption on the rational design of international institutions points to the function of institutions to advance the interests of member states; hence, the design of a particular institution is a product of interactions and interests of states and other actors to solve shared problems (Koremenos et al., 2001).

Other than serving as a venue where states negotiate their interests, regional organizations like ASEAN also provide the environment where socialization of actors occur through dialogue and other forms of interactions that allow for idea exchanges, collective decision making, and norm building from which international institutions are created. Institutions can be defined as enduring rules, norms, and procedures that set expectations, shape interests, and prescribe acceptable behavior; while institutionalization can mean a process of standardizing and harmonizing behavior that make deviations difficult over time (Ba, 2016). Institutions vary ranging from formal to informal ones. Liberal institutionalists argue that cooperation can occur in a world of self-interested actors; thus, institutions are necessary to promote cooperative behavior among states.

Constructivists take the argument up a notch by claiming that identities and interests are endogenous to the process of socialization for these factors can affect institution building. Institutionalization happens when actors begin to internalize a stable set of identities and interests that enables them to abide by rules, norms, and procedures that make cooperation possible. In the case of ASEAN, cooperative activities are achieved even with a low level of institutionalization (Johnston, 2003). As such, statements pointing to ASEAN's rules, norms, processes, and mechanisms related to climate change are assessed to know the institutional components of governance.

Transnational climate change governance is also a product of shifting discourses about prevailing ideas that may transform into a norm, policy, practice, or a widely accepted form of knowledge. Ideas enable the understanding of policy problems, the role of interests in politics, as well as the linkage between institutions and political processes (Béland & Cox, 2010) thereby serving as crucial building blocks to governance. Ideas can be defined as causal beliefs about a phenomenon laden with interpretations of the physical world and the relationships between and among the different facets that exist within the physical world (Béland & Cox, 2016). Ideas matter in governance for causal beliefs can both inform and constrain preferences, along with institutional arrangements, and motivate political action (Rich, 2010). Knowledge, for instance, requires consensus among interested actors before it can create a basis for cooperation and guide policymaking (Haas, 1980). Hence, important ideas and discourses embedded in policy documents that have shaped ASEAN's understanding of climate change are also examined.

This chapter explains that interests, institutions, and ideas are important factors that characterize ASEAN's governance context on climate change. In analyzing these factors, it is important to highlight the points of convergence and divergence to better understand the dynamics among these factors. It is also necessary to accentuate the difference between ASEAN rhetoric and practice concerning its climate change goals. Moreover, this chapter aims to distinguish the gap between ASEAN statements and cooperative goals vis-à-vis the decisions and actions of member states at the national level.

Collective Interests

Data from ASEAN declarations and joint statements on climate change indicate that collective interests of ASEAN member states converge on a number of issues, namely: sustainable economic development, energy security and efficiency, forest management, disaster risk reduction, protection of coastal and marine resources, promotion of biodiversity, linkage between agriculture and food security, water resources management, and facilitation of technical cooperation particularly with developed countries. The national communications of member states from 2000 to 2020, which are submitted periodically to the UNFCCC, also suggest that priorities identified in the national plans of member states are aligned with most issues identified in ASEAN statements. Since ASEAN and UNFCCC are both intergovernmental bodies, representatives from member state governments are the primary interlocutors in these venues. Hence, the collective interests referred to in this sub-section are based on government sources. Although it can be argued that some ASEAN member states conducted consultations with stakeholders in drafting their national plans and programs, these documents remain to be official government sources.

On economic interests, the relevant policy documents note that climate change has negative impacts on socio-economic development. Since majority of ASEAN member states are considered developing countries, ASEAN policy statements often underscore that development and poverty eradication are the main priorities of states together with environmental protection. ASEAN acknowledges that climate change will limit the development options of member states; thus, it aims to address the issue without having to compromise competitiveness or socio-economic development goals. Moreover, policy statements call upon Annex I Parties to the UNFCCC, which are comprised of developed countries, to take the lead in emissions reduction considering their historic responsibility and implement their commitments by providing assistance to developing countries in the form of financial resources, technology transfer, and capacity building.

On energy issues, ASEAN member states agree to improve energy efficiency through capacity building and information sharing. Developing clean energy sources is also a priority, which includes renewable energy and alternative sources. In doing so, ASEAN encourages developed countries to support regional efforts in transitioning to renewable energy and achieving energy efficiency. Member states also acknowledge that their energy mix will still include fossil fuels, and civilian nuclear power remains an option for interested parties complying with international safety standards.

On disaster management, ASEAN recognizes that climate change is intertwined with disaster risk reduction; thus, jointly addressing these issues are important in forging a resilient ASEAN community. In several policy statements, ASEAN affirms that the region is highly vulnerable to disaster risks and that the effects of climate-induced hazards are causing major loss and damage to the region. On forest management, ASEAN regards sustainable forest management to be closely linked to climate change mitigation, transboundary environmental pollution such as haze, and biodiversity. Regional cooperation is centered on initiatives concerning afforestation, reforestation, and reduction of deforestation, forest degradation, and forest fires.

On administering coastal and marine resources, ASEAN strives to protect coral reefs, with the Coral Triangle Initiative as its flagship project, and reduce marine pollution. ASEAN member states also acknowledge the importance of integrating coastal and ocean management in climate change adaptation efforts. Promoting transboundary water cooperation initiatives within ASEAN is important in ensuring that rivers, lakes, and other inland water resources are managed sustainably. On biodiversity, ASEAN calls on developed countries to assist in regional efforts to rehabilitate forest ecosystems, including mangrove and peatland forests, given their critical contributions to mitigation and adaptation strategies. On agriculture, ASEAN's priority is to prevent land degradation to ensure sustainable land management for agricultural needs. Member states are also cognizant that a changing climate has a significant impact on agricultural productivity and food security.

On technical cooperation, ASEAN is of one voice in calling on developed countries to support regional efforts through financing, technology transfer, and capacity building. Moreover, it urges developed countries to participate in international academic partnerships with ASEAN, as well as in joint research projects and exchanges of scientific and technical expertise, to enhance the region's pool of experts.

From analyzing the policy documents, results indicate that there is no shortage of common interests among member states on climate change. It is evident that ASEAN regards climate change as an important issue that requires collective action. More importantly, ASEAN statements and declarations acknowledge that mitigation and adaptation strategies are needed to address climate change. The policy documents also reveal that the interests of member states converge on several issues thereby exemplifying that common interests serve as the foundation of cooperative arrangements. Through consensus-building on collective interests, it can be said that member states have reached a certain level of common understanding on climate change and its adverse impacts on the region. It is also worth noting that many statements and declarations did not explicitly mention the involvement of non-state actors such as civil society groups and international NGOs, although academic partnerships are referred to in efforts to promote technical cooperation.

While consensus among member states seem apparent on climate change, the region continues to lag behind other countries on climate change mitigation and adaptation efforts. The 2022 Environmental Performance Index (EPI), which ranks 180 countries on a number of indicators including climate change performance, places most ASEAN member states at the bottom half of global rankings except for Singapore and Brunei (Table 1) pointing out the need for more stringent emissions reduction schemes. The index measures the performance of countries on climate change mitigation based on several indicators (i.e., adjusted emission growth rates for four greenhouse gases and one climate pollutant, projected emissions in 2050, growth rate in carbon dioxide emissions in 2050, growth rate in carbon dioxide emissions from land cover; greenhouse gas intensity growth rate, and emissions per capita) (Wolf et al., 2022). The EPI ranking of ASEAN suggests that member states have to double their efforts on reducing emissions if they intend to meet their pledged contributions under the 2015 Paris Agreement.

On adaptation efforts, Singapore appears to be an outlier in the region given its low vulnerability score and high readiness score based on the Notre Dame Global Adaptation Initiative Country Index (Table 1), which ranks the vulnerability and readiness scores of each country. Vulnerability refers to

Table 1. Global ranking of ASEAN member states on mitigation and adaptation

ASEAN Member State	EPI 2022 Climate Change Mitigation Ranking*	Notre Dame Global Adaptation Initiative Country Index Ranking**
Brunei Darussalam	78	37
Cambodia	161	149
Indonesia	162	100
Laos	178	137
Malaysia	147	49
Myanmar	174	156
Philippines	175	113
Singapore	63	6
Thailand	106	68
Vietnam	179	97

*Data source: https://epi.yale.edu
**Data source: https://gain.nd.edu/our-work/country-index/

a country's exposure, sensitivity, and capacity to adapt to the adverse effects of climate change, and readiness indicates the country's ability to make use of its investments for adaptation efforts. Of the 10 member states, Myanmar, Cambodia, Laos, and the Philippines have high vulnerability scores and low readiness scores indicating the need for urgent actions to reduce climate risks and prioritize certain investments to improve adaptive capacity.

Similar studies denote the poor performance of ASEAN member states in addressing climate change impacts. Despite the regional bloc's initiatives to establish frameworks and bodies on climate change, most member states underperform in reaching their climate change targets. This underscores the significance of strong government commitment to achieve robust mitigation and adaptation outcomes (Ding & Beh, 2022). Another study finds that ASEAN's mitigation efforts are not commensurate with the threats that the region faces, as evidenced by the member states low proportion of renewable energy sources in their energy mix, slow adoption of electric vehicles, continued fossil fuel subsidies, and expansion of coal power plants, among others (Overland et al., 2021). These studies illustrate that ASEAN declarations and joint statements remain hollow without concrete actions thus emphasizing the gap between what states commit at the regional level and what they actually do at the national and local levels.

Institutional Factors

The analysis of institutional factors centers on finding indicators on the part of ASEAN to include or recognize non-state actors (i.e., experts, think tanks, youth, scientists, women, advocates, civil society, private sector) in regional climate change processes. Of the total 244 documents analyzed, only a handful contained key policy statements, which are mostly ASEAN joint statements on climate change. These joint statements point out the need for ASEAN to step up actions on mitigation and adaptation and call on developed countries to provide financial support to developing countries as they strive to implement their climate change plans. The rest of the documents are press releases and official statements of ASEAN on specific meetings and activities.

Table 2. Percentage of ASEAN policy documents mentioning non-state actors, 2004-2020

ASEAN Process	Count	Percent
Exclusively ASEAN-led	22 of 89	24.72%
ASEAN-Plus	10 of 129	7.75%
ASEAN and other international and regional organizations	3 of 26	11.54%

The analysis of policy documents is grouped into three categories, namely: (1) exclusively ASEAN-led processes; (2) ASEAN-Plus processes; and (3) ASEAN processes with international and regional organizations. The percentage of ASEAN policy documents that mentioned non-state actors in their texts are shown in the table below (Table 2). Only a small percentage of ASEAN statements and press releases include non-state actors, which is an indication that ASEAN processes and mechanisms are still centered among state representatives.

Out of the total 89 documents reviewed under exclusively ASEAN-led processes on climate change from 2004 to 2020, 22 (24.72 percent) referred to or included non-state actors in the documents. With a closer look, the data reveal that references to experts, think tanks, and scientists account for the highest number of mentions followed by stakeholders, the public, and local governments, or cities. The data suggest that ASEAN turns to scientists and policy experts for knowledge-based solutions to climate change challenges. Likewise, there are indications that ASEAN recognizes the need for multi-stakeholder and whole-of-society engagement for effective climate change governance. Nevertheless, the low frequency count of non-state actors demonstrates that ASEAN processes only involve these types of actors occasionally.

While non-state actors are seldom mentioned in the said documents, the data denote that climate change is regularly discussed in ministerial meetings or those attended by minister-level officials from the different executive agencies in government. Climate change is often discussed in ministerial meetings such as the ASEAN Ministerial Meeting on the Environment (AMME), which is a key sectoral body in charge of climate change issues. Environment ministers meet once every two years to provide guidance on policy directions and strategies with regards to environmental cooperation in ASEAN. Of the 89 exclusively ASEAN-led activities, 40 are ministerial meetings which discussed climate change in the agenda. Climate change matters are also addressed in committee-level meetings among senior-level government officials, ASEAN Summits attended by heads of state, and meetings on the ASEAN Chairmanship, as well as events involving the ASEAN Secretary-General. Participation to these activities is often restricted to ASEAN member state representatives and some members of the ASEAN Secretariat.

Likewise, climate change issues are tackled in regional consultations, conferences, symposia, workshops, and webinars organized by ASEAN offices, which often involve participants from outside government such as civil society organizations and other stakeholders. Other relevant activities include film festivals, video launches, award ceremonies for advocates, and science and technology fellowships. The various processes and activities that are open to non-state actors demonstrate ASEAN's efforts to facilitate regional cooperation through awareness-raising, knowledge-sharing, and policy coordination, among others. Although opportunities granted to non-state actors to join ASEAN processes have increased over time, they remain excluded from most processes due to ASEAN's intergovernmental structure.

ASEAN also discusses climate change issues with external partners and/or states. ASEAN confers the formal status of Dialogue Partner, Sectoral Dialogue Partner, and Development Partner to external parties thereby facilitating regular interactions through meetings and other cooperative arrangements.[1] The nature of engagement varies depending on the status of relations, with the Dialogue Partnership being the most extensive. Meetings with Dialogue Partners include regular high-level exchanges and dialogues, ministerial meetings, and summit meetings. The policy documents analyzed often cite climate change as a common area of interest between ASEAN and external partners, which points to the growing recognition to cooperate on climate change issues among state actors participating in ASEAN-Plus processes.

Based on the data citing non-state actors in the policy documents of ASEAN-Plus processes, only 10 out of 129 processes (7.75 percent) can be considered as open to non-state actors. Experts, think tanks, and the academe have been mentioned the most in these sessions followed by civil society organizations. This indicates that ASEAN has established links with experts thereby enabling their participation, which facilitates regular interactions. Further, statements on ASEAN-EU activities contain the most mentions of non-state actors suggesting that the EU endorses the participation of non-state actors in its engagements with ASEAN.

Despite the low frequency of references to non-state actors, climate change is regularly addressed under the ASEAN-Plus processes. For the most part, climate change is tackled in ASEAN meetings with Dialogue Partners (ASEAN+1). Climate change has been identified as a priority area of cooperation in ASEAN meetings with several external partners, including meetings with regional groupings such as the East Asia Summit[2] and ASEAN-Plus Three[3]. For instance, the ASEAN-Plus Three ministers on agriculture and forestry meet regularly to discuss mitigation and adaptation efforts since climate change is a priority agenda under the grouping's cooperation strategy. In 2015, the Philippines hosted the ASEAN-Plus Three Tourism Youth Summit to inform the youth about ASEAN initiatives. One of the objectives of the youth summit was to raise the awareness of young people on environmental protection and climate change. As for ASEAN-EU relations, the two parties have committed to work together on climate change particularly on mitigation, adaptation, long-term strategies, and sustainable finance. Hence, officials from ASEAN and the EU repeatedly hold meetings to enhance cooperation and exchange views on climate change.

In support of multilateralism, ASEAN has also established partnerships with international organizations such as the UN and its specialized agencies along with other regional organizations like the Pacific Alliance, a regional integration initiative involving Chile, Colombia, Mexico, and Peru, and the Gulf Cooperation Council (GCC), a regional, intergovernmental union of Arab States consisting of Bahrain, Kuwait, Oman, Qatar, Saudi Arabia, and the United Arab Emirates. Press releases and statements related to ASEAN activities with these organizations are often about meetings and dialogues to discuss common issues of concern with climate change being one of them. Majority of the documents reviewed under this category are related to ASEAN's activities with the UN and its agencies. The rest of the documents refer to activities between ASEAN and organizations such as the Pacific Alliance, GCC, Forum for East Asia-Latin America Cooperation (FEALAC)[4], the World Bank, and African regional organizations.

Non-state actors are rarely mentioned in these documents pertaining to ASEAN activities with the said organizations on climate change. Unlike the other two categories, the private sector is the non-state actor mentioned the most, followed by women. Only three of the 26 climate change policy documents (11.54 percent) between ASEAN and other international and regional organizations from 2008 to 2019 mentioned non-state actors.

The policy documents reflect some of the priorities of ASEAN and the UN to bring in the private sector and address women's issues in climate change initiatives. The ASEAN-UN relations is guided by a comprehensive partnership framework that includes climate change as a common concern. The two parties have recognized the complementarities between the ASEAN Community Vision 2025 and the UN 2030 Agenda for Sustainable Development and they are committed to step up cooperation to attain shared goals. Climate change, being one of the sustainable development goals under the UN 2030 Agenda, is a priority area of cooperation. The first ASEAN-UN Action Plan on Environment and Climate Change (2016-2020) was adopted in 2017 to promote comprehensive regional solutions. Under the comprehensive partnership framework, the UN affirmed to support ASEAN in strengthening the ability of governments, the private sector, and communities in reducing emissions and adapting to climate change impacts.

In sum, the discussions illustrate that ASEAN conducts regular activities to promote cooperation on climate change among member states, extra-regional states, regional and international organizations, and non-state actors in a wide array of venues such as intergovernmental meetings, dialogues, workshops, conferences, and the like. ASEAN also has established organizational bodies in charge of developing and implementing policies and plans on climate change matters. The said processes and activities enable regular interactions among the different actors. As can be gleaned from the data, these interactions are mostly among state actors consistent with ASEAN's intergovernmental structure. While some activities recognize the participation of non-state actors, the actual number remains very low thereby implying the state-centric nature of these interactions.

More importantly, the finding point to a gap in ASEAN. Despite ASEAN's goals on multisectoral and multistakeholder engagement on climate change, regional mechanisms lack participation from non-state actors (Seah & Martinus, 2021). The 2021 ASEAN State of Climate Change Report also notes the need to strengthen the involvement of experts and practitioners in knowledge sharing to arrive at policy solutions (Arino et al., 2021). The data analyzed in this section reflect the reality presented in related studies that ASEAN falls short in promoting a participatory and inclusive governance of climate change.

Ideational Elements

Analysis on the ideational elements of ASEAN's climate change governance is focused on the flow of ideas between ASEAN and the global climate change regime, along with its effects on governance. The emphasis is on norms and knowledge that are central in shaping ASEAN's understanding of climate change issues and the solutions offered to achieve regional and global targets. ASEAN declarations and joint statements are examined to identify the ideas that are embedded in the policy documents signifying their importance in the governance process. In studying these policy documents, the linkage between ASEAN and global climate change efforts through the UNFCCC regime is evident given that ASEAN regularly cites the UNFCCC and its legal instruments, the principle of common but differentiated responsibilities and respective capabilities (CBDR-RC), as well as the Intergovernmental Panel on Climate Change (IPCC) Assessment Reports, in its statements and declarations. Thus, there are indications of coordination between ASEAN and the UNFCCC regime to cooperate on common goals and benefit from multilateral arrangements that are advantageous to developing countries.

The 2007 Singapore Declaration on Climate Change, Energy and the Environment is an important statement for it affirms the commitment of ASEAN and the participating members of the East Asia Summit to the UNFCCC as the global mechanism for addressing climate change. The Singapore Declaration signals the inclusion of climate change into ASEAN's policy agenda, and it acknowledges ASEAN's participation to the global climate regime. Since then, the ASEAN Working Group on Climate Change (AWG-CC) has organized meetings before the annual UNFCCC Conference of the Parties (COP) session to promote consultation among ASEAN member states on efforts to contribute toward regional and global climate goals. Points of consensus arising from the consultations are summarized into joint statements that are delivered during the UNFCCC COP meetings. Moreover, the joint statements often reflect the collective voice of ASEAN on issues of common interest that are discussed under the UNFCCC process. All parties to the UNFCCC are represented in COP meetings, which function as the supreme decision-making body of the UNFCCC tasked to review the implementation of its legal instruments such as the Kyoto Protocol and Paris Agreement.

ASEAN has repeatedly mentioned the principle of CBDR-RC in its policy statements on climate change highlighting the importance of this principle to ASEAN as a regional organization and its member states. ASEAN urges Annex I Parties to continue taking the lead in substantially reducing emissions given their historic responsibility and economic capabilities. This means that ASEAN's engagement with the UNFCCC is predicated on the notion that state parties must act individually and collectively to address the broad cross-sectoral features of the climate change issue, while reflecting the different social and economic conditions of each state. The principle of CBDR-RC anchors ASEAN's efforts under the global regime along with the standards of equity, universality, and flexibility. ASEAN affirms that CBDR-RC is central to the effective implementation of the Paris Agreement, and it suggests that developing countries require assistance from developed countries to fulfill their nationally determined contributions. The policy documents analyzed emphasize that ASEAN's participation to the UNFCC process is defined by the national circumstance of its member states, its regional priorities, and its discernment of the power politics that underpin the global climate change regime.

Furthermore, ASEAN statements and declarations often cite the IPCC Assessment Reports particularly its finding that climate change leads to disproportionate and adverse effects on marginalized and vulnerable groups. The Fifth Assessment Report released in 2014 finds that climate change can worsen the current conditions of vulnerable groups particularly those communities in low-lying coastal zones and poor populations without adequate access to food and water. Loss of ecosystems poses higher risks to those dependent on agriculture and fisheries for livelihood. Urban dwellers also face threats to their health and well-being as a result of extreme heat and flooding. Despite the steps being taken to build resilience to climate stresses, the report claims that states and communities are falling short of necessary actions to mitigate and adapt to climate impacts.

The policy statements referring to the IPCC reports signify the diffusion of knowledge from IPCC to ASEAN with the IPCC acting as a broker that promotes the diffusion of scientific knowledge on climate change to state and non-state actors through the UNFCCC regime. By participating in the global climate change regime, ASEAN is on the receiving end of knowledge claims from the IPCC through the reports it periodically publishes to disseminate comprehensive assessments of the current state of climate science.

The examination of ideational elements of ASEAN's understanding of climate change governance portray that ASEAN is receptive to the transmission of ideas from the UNFCCC process. The integration of the CBDR-RC norm and IPCC reports in ASEAN's policy documents suggest the influence of the global climate change regime on regional governance mechanisms. Hence, ASEAN's understanding of climate change and the necessary governance schemes to address it can also be explained by the diffusion of ideas from the UNFCCC regime. However, paying lip service these ideas is not enough. The true test of these ideas lies in their implementation on the ground. Although the national communications that ASEAN member states submit to the UNFCCC indicate that states have plans in place and achieved some steady progress in their climate change targets, the global rankings reveal that the region continues to lag behind other countries on climate change mitigation and adaptation efforts.

PROSPECT OF PARTICIPATORY GOVERNANCE IN ASEAN

Governance is a social function of directing collective behavior toward achieving favored results (Young, 2017). It can also be defined as an institutionalized form of social coordination to implement rules binding to a group or to provide collective goods (Börzel & Risse, 2010). The concept of governance acknowledges the participation of different actors apart from states across varying levels of authority. Non-state actors, such as individuals, groups, or organizations that operate independent of government funding or control, have joined the mix of multiple actors involved in governance (Caballero-Anthony, 2018). These actors come from the civil society, businesses, or even government entities but are participating in their private capacity. Governance has also transcended state boundaries. Transnational governance came about as actors working within and outside the state began to focus on functional solutions without heavily relying on existing institutions and processes to avoid the kind of politics that often hinders collective action (Bulkeley & Mol, 2003).

This chapter adopts the concept of participatory governance as the framework of analysis. Participation in this type of governance is applied to widen access to decision making, integrate local knowledge along with the perspectives of diverse actors, and promote acceptance and effective implementation of policy decisions. It is defined as "processes and structures of public decision making that engages actors from the private sector, civil society, and/or the public at large, with varying degrees of communication, collaboration, and delegation of decision power to participants" (Newig et al., 2018, p. 273). Participatory approaches can be utlized as strategies to improve governance outcomes through the following: (1) bridge the gap between scientific knowledge and the lived experiences, values, and practices of actors affected by the problem; (2) clarify different views and interests about an issue; (3) promote learning that can lead to better quality and well-supported decision making; and (4) prevent implementation problems by fostering buy-in and commitment among stakeholders and increasing democratic intent (Bulkeley & Mol, 2003). It is assumed that participation improves the policy system for it enables access of different perspectives and knowledge claims to decision-making processes. To explain the prospect of participatory governance in ASEAN's climate change efforts, the main themes from the content analysis (i.e., interests, institutional framework, and ideas) are used to guide the discussion in this section.

Intergovernmentalism Limits Access

With states being the dominant actors in ASEAN's climate change governance, participation in policy decision-making is kept within a small circle of bureaucrats representing mainly state interests. While ASEAN may have recognized the ability or willingness of non-state actors like NGOs and experts to engage in policy discussions and implementation, their participation depends on the prerogative of state actors. Without a wider access to governance, particularly on collective preference formation, non-state actors remain at the margins. Due to the intergovernmental design of ASEAN, its collective interests, as indicated in the many policy documents on climate change are formed through bargaining and negotiations of state actors. Collective interests are based on the interests communicated by state actors since non-state actors have very little opportunity to participate in collective preference formation. Hence, this chapter confirms that intergovernmentalism is a major factor that leads to the limited, if not restrained, access of non-state actors in regional governance processes on climate change.

Intergovernmentalism is an approach that assumes domestic interests, and the ability of the institution to promote those interests, along with the bargaining power of each state, determine the choices of states (Moravcsik, 1993). Furthermore, this approach is defined by the central role played by state actors embodied through the actions of heads of state and government, ministers, and other high-ranking bureaucrats. Interactions among state actors toward regional integration can be best explained by bargaining particularly during official negotiations, wherein actors are expected to protect and promote state interests as they collectively decide on an issue. Thus, the outcome of the bargaining process often leads to the lowest common denominator or the minimum commitments that actors can agree to. Even if regional bodies and mechanisms are in place, they have little authority over state actors on transnational environmental matters because member states are reluctant to give up their sovereignty in decision making (Schreurs, 2010).

In ASEAN, decision making at the interstate level occurs in meetings with senior officials whose main objective is to represent the interests of their own states. Although there have been efforts to engage with non-state actors such as civil society organizations, they remain on the fringes of the policy formulation process and do not fully participate in decision making. Consequently, regional governance of transboundary environmental issues like haze and climate change is largely determined by state actors guided by a conservative portfolio of interests thereby perpetuating a top-down hierarchical structure of governance (Anbumozhi, 2017). Therefore, the case of ASEAN fits the main assumptions of intergovernmentalism: (1) rational state behavior, (2) inter-state bargaining among senior government officials, and (3) adherence to national interests (Yoshimatsu, 2005).

Since state interest is often associated with economic interest, the region's political structure can also be viewed as a hierarchical corporatist state, where the state strictly controls interest representation to preserve its hold to power (Rüland, 2014). Accordingly, regional governance mirrors the predominant arrangement on interest representation at the state level. This is because many regional issues have an economic dimension to them, and these economic interests are intertwined with state and corporate interests. In ASEAN policy documents on climate change, economic interests are often mentioned when invoking the aim of member states to address the issue without compromising economic competitiveness and development targets. This suggests that environmental goals of member states are secondary to economic goals as demonstrated by ongoing fossil fuel subsidies, coal power plant expansions, and slow progress in curbing deforestation among others (Overland et al., 2021).

Studies have found interests or strategic preferences as important variables in explaining ASEAN's integration process with preserving state sovereignty as a main strategic interest for member states. The strategic preferences of ASEAN states, which are based on sovereignty and domestic regime security, together with economic interdependence, are considered as primary forces that drive ASEAN integration (Kim, 2011). While norms, practices, and identity also support ASEAN's community-building, the pursuit of national interest defines state behavior at the regional level according to the rational approach. Moreover, institutions like ASEAN are considered as vehicles of the integration process for they help reduce transaction costs associated with cooperation involving several states, as well as provide necessary information in resolving collective action problems. Thus, a closer look at the institutional design of ASEAN reveals its brand of regionalism as characterized by strong adherence to state sovereignty and the dominance of self-interests of member states (Cockerham, 2010). Further, ASEAN's intergovernmental character, which is tied to the norm of non-interference, has hampered its attempts to establish a security community or forge a common identity (Jones & Smith, 2007).

Likewise, interactions in ASEAN remain to be driven by state elites despite ongoing efforts to engage non-state actors like civil society groups and think tanks (Collins, 2013). The accreditation of civil society organizations follows a top-down process in which ASEAN expects groups to support ASEAN's objectives and decisions. For instance, ASEAN's Guidelines for Entities Associated with ASEAN issued in 1986 only allow access to NGOs and other associations regarded as cooperative and not critically oriented (Rüland, 2014). Furthermore, Gerard (2014) affirms that participation of civil society in ASEAN is limited in terms of access due to the accreditation system and a range of political activities since ASEAN tends to promote engagement on less contentious issues and exclude other issues from the agenda as state actors see fit. Thus, the sanctioned spaces granted to civil society under ASEAN processes inhibit them from contesting policies. This situation affects the governance of functional areas of cooperation such as environmental issues, which are closely linked to the economic interests of state and corporate actors. As a result, political will is often weak when it comes to collective action on these problems prompting other actors to seek alternatives beyond national and regional arrangements to address governance gaps (Breslin & Nesadurai, 2017).

Accordingly, environmental cooperation is mostly based on agreements and statements to codify common understandings, underscore priority areas of cooperation, and share information, while progress in implementation is often piecemeal and slow. Steps have been taken to promote collective action on regional environmental issues, and more working groups have been set up to foster joint activities over the years. However, the commitment of ASEAN member states to cooperate on shared environmental goals seems limited. ASEAN has made environmental cooperation possible through mechanisms and joint activities that facilitate coordination and collaboration, but more attention is given to the process than achieving substantial outcomes.

ASEAN Way Linked to Low Engagement of Non-State Actors

The findings of the content analysis demonstrate that ASEAN has an institutional framework to support climate change initiatives. ASEAN also has an array of mechanisms involving extra-regional partners and other regional and international organizations that promote cooperation on climate change. In terms of participation, the policy documents show that non-state actors are seldom mentioned, which points out their low engagement in ASEAN processes and mechanism on climate change. This chapter posits that norms like the ASEAN Way is a factor that limits the participation of non-state actors in governance since it privileges the norms of sovereignty and non-interference. These same norms are also the pillars that reinforce ASEAN's intergovernmental structure, which promotes the dominance of state actors and state interests vis-à-vis non-state actors.

To demonstrate, the regional bloc's existence is guided by the Treaty of Amity and Cooperation (TAC) in Southeast Asia, which was signed in 1976. The TAC upholds the fundamental principles of (1) mutual respect for sovereignty, territorial integrity and national identity, (2) freedom from external interference, subversion or coercion, (3) non-interference in the internal affairs of a state, (4) peaceful settlement of disputes, (5) renunciation of threat or use of force, and (6) effective cooperation. The legal-rational norms in the treaty are consistent with the spirit and principles of the United Nations Charter and the Ten Principles adopted at the Asian-African Conference in Bandung in 1955; while the socio-cultural norms have been significant in the development of nascent forms of ASEAN identity, which emerged from incremental socialization as a consequence of regular interaction over time (Acharya, 2014).

It is crucial to emphasize that norms can either restrain the actions of states that run counter to collective goals or create a basis for cooperative action. Regional actors are expected to abide by the norms of informality, consensus decision making, and non-interference, which serve as a shared set of understanding of appropriate behavior (Nesadurai, 2009). Non-interference in internal affairs of states is the single most important principle that underpins ASEAN regionalism that is closely linked to respect for sovereignty (Acharya, 2014). Along with non-interference, seeking consensus is another pillar of the ASEAN Way. Member states engage in informal discussions until decisions are reached unanimously. On the one hand, consensus decision making ensures that all member states are on board thereby increasing the legitimacy of a decision. On the other hand, the process is often slow, particularly when actors disagree or some are resolute on their bargaining positions. Thus, parties that refuse to compromise gain an upper hand.

Those who view the ASEAN Way in a positive light argue that the reluctance of members to commit themselves to rigid rules of conduct has enabled ASEAN cooperation. This is because when members are not strictly bound by rules and are free from coercion, they become more willing to consult with one another and adopt a common position (Acharya, 2014). While the ASEAN Way has promoted cooperation, the firm commitment of member states to these norms creates soft institutionalism since processes are carried out in an informal way of consensus building and consultation and through non-binding agreements (Jones & Jenne, 2016). Consequently, ASEAN's region-building is also characterized as a form of soft regionalism (Collins, 2013) given that the mandate of member state governments tends to dominate ASEAN's agenda and decision making. This makes cooperation more likely when collective action does not undermine national interests since cooperation is based on respecting the sovereignty of every member state (Busse, 1999).

The norms embodied in the ASEAN Way have implications regarding ASEAN's institutional framework and regional governance. For one, it can be said that ASEAN's brand of intergovernmentalism is a product of these norms. The privileging of autonomy and sovereignty has led to a decentralized form of governance wherein member states give the ASEAN Secretariat weak authority to oversee enforcement of regional goals and monitor domestic policies, much less impose sanctions. These norms are mutually constitutive, which play into the state-centric and sovereignty-bound structure of ASEAN thus diminishing its ability to collectively address transnational issues (Acharya, 2003).

The practice of ASEAN Way and its effects have also urged civil society groups to question ASEAN's legitimacy. ASEAN, just like any other international institution, needs the support of civil society, and one way to do so is to include these groups in the governance process (Bierman, 2014; Stubbs, 2019). However, studies claim that ASEAN has not genuinely promoted engagement with civil society for it continues to exert control on their participation (Chandra et al., 2017; Gerard, 2014, 2015). On environmental cooperation, studies have noted the negative impacts of the ASEAN Way resulting in a slow and, at times, unmanageable process that discourages criticisms of member states' harmful practices and undermines efforts to implement solutions to the region's environmental problems (Elliott, 2003; Koh & Robinson, 2002).

Norm Diffusion and Learning Evident Under the Global Climate Regime

As for ideational elements in ASEAN's governance context, the concept of international regimes can explain the dynamics between ASEAN and other multilateral initiatives on climate change. Regimes are a subset of institutions, which means that regimes also embody a set of rules, principles, norms, and decision making procedures pertaining to a specialized topic such as trade and environment or geographically defined areas (Young, 2017). Regimes develop when actors cooperate to pursue interests, gain power, promote norms and values, and generate knowledge (Krasner, 1982). States agree to cooperate since regimes can reduce transaction costs, improve information flows, and raise the costs of noncompliance.

Furthermore, regimes can facilitate the transmission of ideas among the different actors through regular interaction, which can influence the interests and identities of states (Abbott & Snidal, 1998).

International regimes also serve as primary vehicles for the collective legitimation of certain norms. In the area of human rights for instance, the diffusion of norms has largely depended on the networks of domestic and transnational actors that pushed for their advocacies through links with international regimes (Risse & Sikkink, 1999). One core global norm that structures international environmental politics is CBDR-RC. This principle is built on the following arguments: (1) states have the common responsibility to protect the environment; (2) developed countries are accountable for their historical contribution to climate change, thus they should take the responsibility to act; and (3) the different level of economic development, vulnerabilities, and conditions of countries to solve the problem should be considered when negotiating international agreements (Rajamani, 2000). Efforts to introduce this principle began at the 1972 Earth Summit in Stockholm, which set the stage for global environmentalism. The CBDR-RC norm is stated in the Article 3 of the UNFCCC and Principle 7 of the 1992 Rio Declaration, and since then, it has been included in major multilateral environmental agreements giving bargaining power to developing countries (Honkonen, 2009; Stalley, 2018). While all parties have to cooperate on climate mitigation and adaptation efforts according to their respective capabilities, CBDR-RC promotes the notion that developed countries should assume a leadership role in mitigating emissions and in assisting developing countries to adapt to climate change through financing and technology transfer (Rajamani, 2000).

In the case of ASEAN, a study suggests that ASEAN has maintained the UNFCCC interpretation of CBDR-RC since the norm enables member states to consolidate their negotiating positions by holding developed countries responsible for historic emissions, as well as by defending their interests to pursue climate efforts without compromising socio-economic development. Hence, adopting UNFCCC's version of the norm fits ASEAN's internal and external role expectations (Qiao-Franco, 2021). Internally, ASEAN is expected to provide member states with a consultative platform to coordinate national actions through dialogue, knowledge sharing, mobilizing support for initiatives, and developing regional action plans. Externally, member states count on ASEAN to represent their collective views and priorities in international negotiations involving extra-regional states. More importantly, ASEAN's understanding of CBDR-RC is fundamental to the conceptualization of its climate change institutions; thus, transforming its current interpretation requires changes in its role expectations (Qiao-Franco, 2021).

Since all ASEAN member states are parties to the UNFCCC, interactions and discussions on climate change issues occur both at the regional level within the ASEAN process and at the global level under the UNFCCC process. Therefore, participation in climate activities at the regional and global levels offer ASEAN member states multiple opportunities for collaboration and dialogue. The UNFCCC, like any other international body, sets policy agenda, promotes information exchanges, establishes norms, and diffuses lessons, among others. Thus, the UNFCCC can be viewed as a transmitter of norms and information. Socialization of actors through the UNFCCC process provides prospects for learning, which is one way of explaining the formation of consensus among actors with divergent interests. Interactions between UNFCCC and ASEAN, as well as those of ASEAN member states with other UNFCCC parties, enable the flow of innovative ideas that may result in learning.

Learning refers to knowledge acquisition based on experiences, analysis, or social interaction that leads to the updating of causal beliefs among policy actors (Dunlop & Radaelli, 2018). Learning can happen epistemically and from reflection. When uncertainty is high, actors often seek out knowledge and information in trying to solve a problem. The existence of an authoritative epistemic community that is willing and able to interact with policy actors can promote the transfer of ideas and open governance spaces to non-state actors in arriving at policy solutions. Learning from reflection necessitates a dialogue among a diverse group of knowledgeable actors engaging in deliberation of preferences and ideas. Similarly, learning within the purview of international organizations often utilizes knowledge from scientific communities, businesses, NGOs, and other experts, which are imparted to members and converted into programs and activities, under the assumption that the organizations' prevailing institutions can change the behavior of actors through learning (Haas, 2000).

Epistemic communities are considered as important players in building consensual knowledge in international regimes like climate change. Given their ties with international regimes, members of epistemic communities can persuade policymakers to accept certain causal paradigms that are presented as problem-solving ideas to transnational issues. The IPCC is considered as an epistemic community composed of officials and experts representing relevant ministries, agencies, and research institutions from 195 member countries, and observer organizations. In preparing reports on the current state of knowledge on climate change based on peer-reviewed scientific journals and technical publications, the IPCC enlists the participation of leading experts to conduct two review phases. IPCC reports include a summary for policymakers, which is approved in a plenary session where IPCC delegates can dialogue with the authors. The UNFCCC and ASEAN documents often cite the IPCC reports indicating that policy actors acknowledge the legitimacy of the knowledge presented in the reports. However, the IPCC is not without critics. Over the years questions about its disciplinary biases, the type of knowledge assessed, claims of universal authority, and diversity in the selection of experts have come to light (Hulme & Mahony, 2010).

While there are several references to the IPCC Assessment Reports, the mention of traditional and indigenous knowledge has been obviously lacking in ASEAN policy statements despite the strategic goal in the ASEAN Socio-cultural Blueprint to expand regional cross-sectoral platforms to allow for the integration of indigenous and traditional knowledge and practices in developing climate change initiatives. Further inquiry is required to explain this finding, although the under-representation of indigenous issues in IPCC reports can be one explanation. A study finds that IPCC reports have referred to indigenous content; although there remains little evidence of critical engagement with indigenous knowledge systems, which has repercussions to the development of culturally sensitive and community-based adaptation policies (Ford et al., 2016). The absence of explicit references to traditional forms of knowledge both in ASEAN and IPCC documents suggests that these organizations may need to be more inclusive to integrate various knowledge sources and claims in their governance efforts.

Ideational elements embedded in ASEAN's policy documents signify ASEAN's understanding of the climate change issue. Hence, it can be argued that ideas originating from the global climate change regime also shape ASEAN's governance processes. Through the UNFCCC, ideas generated with the help of non-state actors such as IPCC experts become norms and knowledge that can shape ASEAN's own governance processes on climate change. While the access of non-state actors in ASEAN is still limited, the global regime is one pathway for ideas from non-state actors to reach ASEAN, albeit indirectly.

CONCLUSION AND WAY FORWARD

This chapter evidently examines ASEAN's policies on climate change to accurately understand the context defining regional governance and to determine the prospect of enabling participatory mechanisms. Using policy documents as the data source, findings reveal that interests, institutions, and ideas can explain the prevailing ASEAN governance framework on climate change. With these factors, integrating participatory approaches to improve the access of non-state actors to governance processes presents a challenge since intergovernmentalism and ASEAN norms are deeply entrenched in the regional organization's processes and mechanisms that limit the participation and inclusion of non-state actors. Introducing reforms, therefore, to enhance the participation and inclusion of non-state actors seems to be a tall order, although not entirely impossible given ASEAN's initial endeavors.

On interests, intergovernmentalism typifies ASEAN's climate change cooperation since regional bodies such as the ASEAN Secretariat cannot compel states to act on transnational environmental matters. Member states are reluctant to give up their sovereignty in decision-making, and self-interest often dictates the interaction among state actors. With the prevailing intergovernmentalism in the region, ASEAN's governance of climate change largely depends on national actions and plans due to state-centric decision-making that gives regional mechanisms nominal authority over states. The intergovernmental design of ASEAN also limits the participation of non-state actors in governance. ASEAN processes are still restricted to state actors with only minimal participation expected from non-state actors.

On institutional framework, findings show that ASEAN conducts regular activities to promote cooperation on climate change among member states, extra-regional states, international organizations, and non-state actors. However, these activities primarily enable interaction among member states implying that an inclusive and participatory ASEAN remains a work in progress. The low participation of non-state actors is apparent across the various ASEAN mechanisms and processes involved in climate change governance. While ASEAN's diplomatic channels provide opportunities for engagement between state and non-state actors, results of the content analysis affirm that participation of non-state actors in ASEAN processes on climate change remain marginal be it within exclusively ASEAN-led processes, under ASEAN-Plus mechanisms, or those involving regional and international organizations.

On ideas, it is evident that the exchanges between ASEAN and the global climate change regime have contributed to the formation of the region's governance context. Regular coordination between ASEAN and the UNFCCC regime has been ongoing particularly on common goals and multilateral arrangements that member states find beneficial. Interactions have also led to the diffusion of norms and knowledge, which became part of ASEAN's climate change governance mechanisms. From the analysis, it can be gleaned that ASEAN has adopted some norms and knowledge from the UNFCCC and the IPCC. While ASEAN acknowledges the importance of scientific knowledge in climate change governance, the integration of traditional or indigenous knowledge and practices in governance mechanisms is needed to realize a more participatory and inclusive form of governance.

Notwithstanding the abovementioned procedural strides, it is paramount to iterate that ASEAN may still accomplish substantial progress in mainstreaming the effective participation of non-state actors in the agenda-setting and policy formulation stages of the region's climate change governance. Drawing on the principle of incrementalism, the association, through the prodding of member states, may explore the possibility of opening extant platforms for a certain period to a select number of CSOs that are neither handpicked nor co-opted by the state. The latter's involvement may be issue-specific as an initial set-up, which may then be expanded upon review and recommendation of the concerned officials. Another option is the monitoring of shared objectives and/or targets on climate change mitigation and adaptation. ASEAN may hence consider tapping CSOs as third-party auditors in the evaluation of related projects, programs, and activities and subsequent outcomes. CSOs may develop a scorecard to effectively assess the region's climate change governance. When done correctly, this is a crucial step towards fostering deeper collaboration between states and non-state actors. More importantly, it can serve as a testament to ASEAN's resilience and dynamism in the face of wicked problems.

REFERENCES

Abbott, K. W., & Snidal, D. (1998). Why states act through formal international organizations. *The Journal of Conflict Resolution*, *42*(1), 3–32. doi:10.1177/0022002798042001001

Acharya, A. (2003). Democratisation and the prospects for participatory regionalism in Southeast Asia. *Third World Quarterly*, *24*(2), 375–390. doi:10.1080/0143659032000074646

Acharya, A. (2014). *Constructing a security community in Southeast Asia: ASEAN and the problem of regional order* (3rd ed.). Routledge. doi:10.4324/9781315796673

Allison, L., & Taylor, M. (2017). ASEAN's 'people-oriented' aspirations: Civil society influences on non-traditional security governance. *Australian Journal of International Affairs*, *71*(1), 24–41. doi:10.1080/10357718.2015.1135870

Anbumozhi, V. (2017). Ensuring ASEAN's sustainable and resilient future. In A. Baviera & L. Maramis (Eds.), *ASEAN@50 Building ASEAN community: political–security and socio-cultural reflections* (Vol. 4, pp. 309–323). Economic Research Institute for ASEAN and East Asia.

Arino, Y., Prabhakar, S. V. R. K., Lee, Y.-Y., Ikeda, M., & Zusman, E. (2021). *ASEAN State of Climate Change Report*. ASEAN Secretariat.

Ba, A. D. (2016). Institutionalization of Southeast Asia: ASEAN and ASEAN centrality. In A. D. Ba, C.-C. Kuik, & S. Sudo (Eds.), *Institutionalizing East Asia: Mapping and reconfiguring regional cooperation* (pp. 11–34). Routledge. doi:10.4324/9781315709130-12

Béland, D., & Cox, R. H. (2010). Introduction: Ideas and politics. In D. Béland & R. H. Cox (Eds.), *Ideas and politics in social science research* (pp. 3–20). Oxford University Press. doi:10.1093/acprof:oso/9780199736430.003.0001

Béland, D., & Cox, R. H. (2016). Ideas as coalition magnets: Coalition building, policy entrepreneurs, and power relations. *Journal of European Public Policy*, *23*(3), 428–445. doi:10.1080/13501763.2015.1115533

Bierman, F. (2014). Global governance and the environment. In M. Betsill, K. Hochstetler, & D. Stevis (Eds.), *Advances in international environmental politics* (2nd ed., pp. 245–270). Palgrave Macmillan.

Börzel, T. A., & Risse, T. (2010). Governance without a state: Can it work? *Regulation & Governance*, *4*(2), 113–134. doi:10.1111/j.1748-5991.2010.01076.x

Breslin, S., & Nesadurai, H. E. S. (2017). Who governs and how?: Non-State actors and transnational governance in Southeast Asia. *Journal of Contemporary Asia*, *48*(2), 187–203. doi:10.1080/00472336.2017.1416423

Bulkeley, H., & Mol, A. P. (2003). Participation and environmental governance: Consensus, ambivalence and debate. *Environmental Values*, *12*(2), 143–154. doi:10.3197/096327103129341261

Busse, N. (1999). Constructivism and Southeast Asian Security. *The Pacific Review*, *12*(1), 39–60. doi:10.1080/09512749908719277

Caballero-Anthony, M. (2018). *Negotiating governance on non-traditional security in Southeast Asia and beyond*. Columbia University Press. doi:10.7312/caba18300

Chandra, A. C., Abdulrahim, R., & Almuttaqi, A. I. (2017). Non-state actors' engagement with ASEAN: Current state of play and way forward. In A. Baviera & L. Maramis (Eds.), *ASEAN@50 Building ASEAN community: Political–security and socio-cultural reflections* (Vol. 4, pp. 221–246). Economic Research Institute for ASEAN and East Asia.

Cockerham, G. B. (2010). Regional integration in ASEAN: Institutional design and the ASEAN way. *East Asia (Piscataway, N.J.)*, *27*(2), 165–185. doi:10.1007/s12140-009-9092-1

Collins, A. (2013). *Building a People-Oriented Security Community the ASEAN Way*. Routledge. doi:10.4324/9780203104842

Ding, D. K., & Beh, S. E. (2022). Climate change and sustainability in ASEAN countries. *Sustainability (Basel)*, *14*(2), 999. doi:10.3390/su14020999

Dunlop, C., & Radaelli, C. (2018). The lessons of policy learning: Types, triggers, hindrances and pathologies. *Policy and Politics*, *46*(2), 255–272. doi:10.1332/030557318X15230059735521

Elliott, L. (2003). ASEAN and environmental cooperation: Norms, interests and identity. *The Pacific Review*, *16*(1), 29–52. doi:10.1080/0951274032000043235

Elliott, L. (2012). ASEAN and environmental governance: Strategies of regionalism in Southeast Asia. *Global Environmental Politics*, *12*(3), 38–57. doi:10.1162/GLEP_a_00122

Elliott, L. (2017). Environmental regionalism: Moving in from the policy margins. *The Pacific Review*, *30*(6), 952–965. doi:10.1080/09512748.2017.1303534

Ford, J. D., Cameron, L., Rubis, J., Maillet, M., Nakashima, D., Willox, A. C., & Pearce, T. (2016). Including indigenous knowledge and experience in IPCC assessment reports. *Nature Climate Change*, *6*(4), 349–353. doi:10.1038/nclimate2954

Gerard, K. (2014). ASEAN and civil society activities in 'created spaces': The limits of liberty. *The Pacific Review*, *27*(2), 265–287. doi:10.1080/09512748.2014.882395

Gerard, K. (2015). Explaining ASEAN's engagement of civil society in policymaking: Smoke and mirrors. *Globalizations*, *12*(3), 365–382. doi:10.1080/14747731.2015.1016304

Gerstl, A., & Helmke, B. (2012). The Association of Southeast Asian Nations (ASEAN) and climate change: A threat to national, regime, and human security. In B. C. G. Teh (Ed.), *Human security securing East Asia's future* (pp. 135–156). Springer Netherlands. doi:10.1007/978-94-007-1799-2_7

Haas, E. (1980). Why collaborate? Issue-linkage and international regimes. *World Politics*, *32*(3), 357–405. doi:10.2307/2010109

Haas, P. (2000). International institutions and social learning in the management of global environmental risks. *Policy Studies Journal: the Journal of the Policy Studies Organization*, *28*(3), 558–575. doi:10.1111/j.1541-0072.2000.tb02048.x

Haris, S. M., Mustafa, F. B., & Ariffin, R. N. R. (2020). Systematic literature review of climate change governance activities of environmental nongovernmental organizations in Southeast Asia. *Environmental Management, 66*(5), 816–825. doi:10.1007/s00267-020-01355-9 PMID:32893336

Honkonen, T. (2009). The principle of common but differentiated responsibility in post-2012 climate negotiations. *Review of European Community & International Environmental Law, 18*(3), 257–267. doi:10.1111/j.1467-9388.2009.00648.x

Hulme, M., & Mahony, M. (2010). Climate change: What do we know about the IPCC? *Progress in Physical Geography, 34*(5), 705–718. doi:10.1177/0309133310373719

Johnston, A. I. (2003). Socialization in international institutions: The ASEAN way and international relations theory. In G. J. Ikenberry & M. Mastanduno (Eds.), *International relations theory and the Asia-Pacific* (pp. 107–162). Columbia University Press.

Jones, D. M., & Jenne, N. (2016). Weak states' regionalism: ASEAN and the limits of security cooperation in Pacific Asia. *International Relations of the Asia-Pacific, 16*(2), 209–240. doi:10.1093/irap/lcv015

Jones, D. M., & Smith, M. L. (2007). Making process, not progress: ASEAN and the evolving East Asian regional order. *International Security, 32*(1), 148–184. doi:10.1162/isec.2007.32.1.148

Kim, M. H. (2011). Theorizing ASEAN integration. *Asian Perspective, 35*(3), 407–435. doi:10.1353/apr.2011.0005

Koh, K. L., & Robinson, N. (2002). Regional environmental governance: examining the Association of Southeast Asian Nations (ASEAN) model. In D. C. Esty & M. H. Ivanova (Eds.), *Global environmental governance: Options & opportunities* (Vol. 8, pp. 101–120). Yale School of Forestry and Environmental Studies., https://elischolar.library.yale.edu/fes-pubs/8

Koremenos, B., Lipson, C., & Snidal, D. (2001). The rational design of international institutions. *International Organization, 55*(4), 761–799. doi:10.1162/002081801317193592

Krasner, S. (1982). Structural causes and regime consequences: Regimes as intervening variables. *International Organization, 36*(2), 185–205. doi:10.1017/S0020818300018920

Moravcsik, A. (1993). Preferences and power in the European Community: A liberal intergovernmentalist approach. *Journal of Common Market Studies, 31*(4), 473–524. doi:10.1111/j.1468-5965.1993.tb00477.x

Nesadurai, H. E. (2009). ASEAN and regional governance after the Cold War: From regional order to regional community? *The Pacific Review, 22*(1), 91–118. doi:10.1080/09512740802651169

Newig, J., Challies, E., Jager, N. W., Kochskaemper, E., & Adzersen, A. (2018). The environmental performance of participatory and collaborative governance: A framework of causal mechanisms. *Policy Studies Journal: the Journal of the Policy Studies Organization, 46*(2), 269–297. doi:10.1111/psj.12209 PMID:30034065

Overland, I., Sagbakken, H. F., Chan, H.-Y., Merdekawati, M., Suryadi, B., Utama, N. A., & Vakulchuk, R. (2021). The ASEAN climate and energy paradox. *Energy and Climate Change, 2*, 100019. doi:10.1016/j.egycc.2020.100019

Qiao-Franco, G. (2021). ASEAN's role expectations and the diffusion of common but differentiated responsibilities principle in the climate change context. *The Pacific Review*, *34*(6), 1079–1107. doi:10.1080/09512748.2020.1797860

Rajamani, L. (2000). The principle of common but differentiated responsibility and the balance of commitments under the climate regime. *Review of European Community & International Environmental Law*, *9*(2), 120–131. doi:10.1111/1467-9388.00243

Rich, A. (2010). Ideas, expertise, and think tanks. In D. Béland & R. H. Cox (Eds.), *Ideas and politics in social science research* (pp. 191–208). Oxford University Press. doi:10.1093/acprof:oso/9780199736430.003.0010

Risse, T., & Sikkink, K. (1999). The socialization of international human rights norms into domestic practices: Introduction. In T. Risse, S. C. Ropp, & K. Sikkink (Eds.), *The power of human rights: International norms and domestic change* (pp. 1–38). Cambridge University Press. doi:10.1017/CBO9780511598777.002

Rüland, J. (2014). The limits of democratizing interest representation: ASEAN's regional corporatism and normative challenges. *European Journal of International Relations*, *20*(1), 237–261. doi:10.1177/1354066112445289

Sahraie, M. (2011). The ASEAN actions on climate change: Recognizing or pro-actively addressing the issue. *Sustainable development law on climate change: Working paper series.* International Development Law Organization (IDLO) and the Centre for International Sustainable Development Law (CISDL).

Schreurs, M. A. (2010). Multi-level governance the ASEAN Way. In H. Enderlein, S. Wälti, & M. Zürn (Eds.), *Handbook on multi-level governance* (pp. 308–320). Edward Elgar. doi:10.4337/9781849809047.00029

Seah, S., & Martinus, M. (2021). *Gaps and opportunities in ASEAN's climate governance.* ISEAS-Yusof Ishak Institute. doi:10.1355/9789814951609

Stalley, P. (2018). Norms from the periphery: Tracing the rise of the common but differentiated principle in international environmental politics. *Cambridge Review of International Affairs*, *31*(2), 141–161. doi:10.1080/09557571.2018.1481824

Stubbs, R. (2019). ASEAN sceptics versus ASEAN proponents: Evaluating regional institutions. *The Pacific Review*, *32*(6), 923–950. doi:10.1080/09512748.2019.1611627

Yoshimatsu, H. (2005). From distrust to mutual interests?: Emerging cooperation in Northeast Asia. *East Asia (Piscataway, N.J.)*, *22*(4), 18–38. doi:10.1007/s12140-005-0002-x

Young, O. R. (2017). *Governing complex systems: Social capital for the anthropocene.* The MIT Press. doi:10.7551/mitpress/9780262035934.001.0001

ENDNOTES

1 To date, ASEAN has 11 Dialogue Partners (i.e., Australia, Canada, China, European Union, India, Japan, New Zealand, Russia, South Korea, United States, and United Kingdom), four Sectoral Dialogue Partners (i.e., Norway, Pakistan, Switzerland, and Turkey), and four Development Partners (i.e., Chile, France, Germany, and Italy).

2 The East Asia Summit is a regional forum of state leaders from ASEAN together with Australia, China, India, Japan, New Zealand, South Korea, Russia, and the United States.

3 The ASEAN-Plus Three is a cooperation process involving ASEAN with China, Japan, and South Korea.

4 FEALAC is an inter-regional multilateral forum composed of 36 member countries from East Asia and Latin America to promote better understanding, political and economic dialogue, and cooperation in all areas between the two regions.

Chapter 2
Challenges of the Digital Transformation:
Public Administration

Jorge Vareda Gomes
https://orcid.org/0000-0003-0656-9284
Universidade Lusófona, Portugal

Mário Batista Romão
https://orcid.org/0000-0003-4564-1883
ISEG, Universidade de Lisboa, Portugal

ABSTRACT

At a global level, governments are implementing transformation projects and initiatives to respond to a changing society and as part of a drive for efficiency and cost savings. Considering the profile of digital transformation (DT) projects within the context of the Portuguese public administration (PA), the proposal for a framework was developed which contains a set of attributes and criteria to identify the feasibility and adequacy of the projects submitted for evaluation. The study identifies the set of characteristics, critical success factors, challenges, and difficulties of DT projects in this public administration context. A qualitative methodological approach was used, and a single case study strategy was applied. The proposed framework enables a better alignment of strategies, as well as an improved allocation of resources and the consequent improvement of the performance objectives defined by the PA.

INTRODUCTION

Business and government have long recognized the potential of technology and both are strongly committed to ongoing digital transformation programmes. Datta et al. (2020) state that DT is able to bring about various benefits, such as the reduction of corruption and inefficiencies in the PA, as well as increased transparency and increased public confidence in the government resulting from accountability, which leads to an increase in security with regards data privacy and sustainability. Portugal's initiatives also

DOI: 10.4018/979-8-3693-1742-6.ch002

reinforce this topic, examples being the launch of the second phase of the national strategy of Industry 4.0 for the digitization of the economy in 2019, with associated financing of approximately 600 million euros for the two years duration (European Commission, 2020a).

According to Schwab (2016), the impact of Industry 4.0 implies flexible cooperation between the virtual and the physical and also between industries at a global level, which consequently enables product customization and the creation of new operational models. This paper relates the analysis of a case study of the Administrative Modernization Agency (AMA) – a public institute that is responsible for the promotion and development of administrative modernization in Portugal. AMA operates under the auspices of the Secretary of State for Innovation and Administrative Modernization in the areas of administrative modernization, including simplification and electronic administration. The relevance of this study is related to the primordial role played by DT in the Portuguese Administration, as manifested by the development and management of new service models which enable citizens and companies to interact with the State in an innovative and efficient manner. Another relevant reason for this study is the fact that the public sector is part of the Innovation System (Freeman, 2008). The innovation system has now expanded its concept and is starting to be recognized as an innovation process (Godinho, 2013) as it is characterized by collaboration between different actors and the respective interactions among themselves, namely: companies, customers, financiers, and the State. AMA has a department called the Project Management Office (PMO), which is dedicated to project portfolio management, with more than 80 currently active projects.

According to Too & Weaver (2014), when a lot of projects are being carried out simultaneously, the effect is that the associated project management becomes more complex, due to its interdependencies and multiple implementations. The main driver for our proposal is the current absence of an adequate DT model, which is necessary to enable the evaluation as to whether a project meets the conditions to be approved. Accordingly, the objective of the study was to elaborate a proposal for a framework to be used to evaluate whether DT projects meet the necessary conditions to be initiated, based on the characteristics of projects of this nature and the context of the Portuguese PA. This framework needs to be simple to use, with the possibility be tested in the near future. The study is conditional on the following three research questions:

QInv1 - What are the main factors that influence the success of a DT project?

QInv2 - What are the main challenges and difficulties of carrying out a DT project?

QInv3 - How can a framework be built to evaluate the needs of the PA's DT projects?

Another objective of this proposal for a framework is to enable the organization and coherent integration of the diverse range of elements which are considered for the assessment and evaluation of DT projects.

LITERATURE REVIEW

Digital Transformation

Interoperability is a crucial issue for DT in PA, as this is the path that enables the integration of various entities. AMA uses a platform which encourages the development of interoperability which is called iAP. This tool is extendable to the private sector through the means of legal support. Multichannel electronic services are made available on the iAP platform, which are aimed at meeting the needs of citizens and companies alike. Mergel et al. (2019) refers to DT as being a holistic effort to review key government

Figure 1. eGovernment evolution

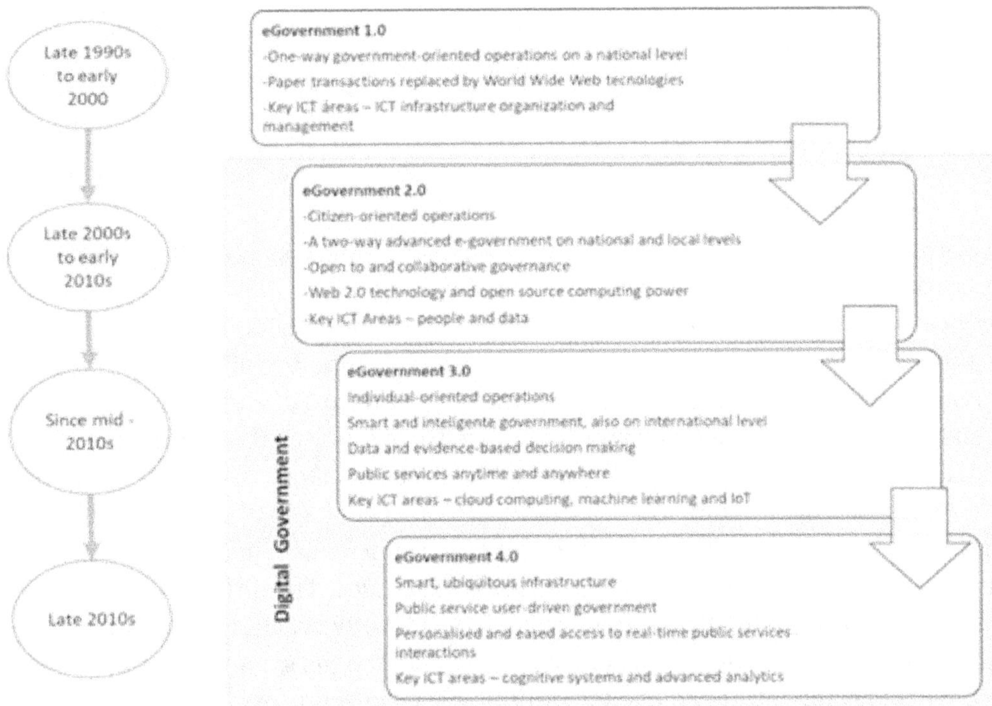

processes and services, in addition to the traditional digitization efforts. Among others, the result of these DT efforts are focused on meeting users' needs, as well as new ways of providing services and expanding the user base. DT is a continuous process, which requires constant adjustments to the entire chain, products, and services offered to the population and most likely leads to better relations between entities and stakeholders, as well as an increase in satisfaction among the population, with the most relevant impact being the promotion of change in a bureaucratic and organizational culture (Mergel et al., 2019). For those responsible for the implementation of DT, the ability to make essential, yet sometimes disruptive changes is a necessity (Iannacci et al., 2019; Pittaway & Montazemi, 2020).

e-Government

According to Barcevičius et al. (2019), the PA took the first steps towards e-government during the late 90s. Based on a broad literature review, these authors conceived a framework which describes the path to date (Figure 1).

Importantly, e-government acquired a new and larger dimension in the early 2000s, called Digital Government. Digital Government refers to the concept of a digital ecosystem which is composed of various actors besides the government, such as non-governmental organizations, companies, and citizens' associations that support the production and access to data, services, and content through interaction with the government (OECD, 2014). According to the report of the Digital Economy and Society Index (DESI) (European Commission, 2020b), Portugal is in 13th place among the 28 Member States with regards the provision of digital public services. Another report that assesses the European digital situ-

Table 1. Performance of PT compared to EC and United Kingdom (UK)

	Penetration	Digitization
EC27 + UK	60%	72%
PT	53%	82%

Source: European Commission (2020b)

ation is the eGovernment Benchmark issued by the European Commission (2020a), which is an annual monitoring instrument (Table 1).

The European Commission report reveals that the innovation process in Portugal was carried out efficiently, although there is an underlying desire to expand the number of users online and to realize all the potential benefits. The country had significant growth from 2017 to 2018 and its performance remained constant in 2019. The same report also concludes that Portugal is within the European average for digitization and when combining relative and absolute indicators, has a better performance than expected. To understand the meaning of 'digitization', Mergel et al. (2019) state that digitization goes beyond migrating a service from the physical to the digital sphere, as it also includes focusing on potential changes which can promote the transformation of processes. The difficulties of PA with regards the digital dimension on a global scale are known, and Weerakkody et al. (2016) state that in most cases the frustrating results are attributed to the technology itself. A significant number of DT projects are implemented without being integrated into the institutional change process, often as a reactive political decision based on the private sector mentality, without due consideration of the complex institutional environment of the PA (Currie & Guah, 2007; Currie, 2012; Janowski, 2015). Situations of competition between public entities are also reported, in the search for power and institutional legitimacy, as well as social and economic adequacy (Cordella & Tempini, 2015). The challenge is not only to introduce digital technologies in the PA, but rather to integrate its use in the modernization of the PA (OECD, 2014).

Successful Strategies, Critical Success Factors (FCS), Challenges, and Difficulties of Digital Transformation

Based on an extensive literature review, García & Pablo (2005) identified a set of strategies which resulted in e-government initiatives being successful, and yet at the same time met the challenges involved. A summary of the main findings of these authors is outline below:

1. Information and data strategies: adopt comprehensive planning, quality assurance and compliance; the involvement of the right partners, common structure, and standards to facilitate iteration, continuous feedback from users.
2. Information technology strategies: useful and easy-to-use information systems; raise awareness of the topic and focus initial efforts on developing prototypes of system and process; project leader with strong technical skills and specialization, as well as at least some team members to create ways to deal with the insufficiency of a qualified technical workforce.
3. Organizational and managerial strategies: clear, realistic and measurable goals; identify the most important stakeholders and insert them in the project's development, especially users; good communication channels and process improvements are extremely important to map out the current

capacities and training needs of developers and users; political skills and experience among its members; and financial resources where managers often need to develop innovative financial schemes and partnerships to implement the initiatives.
4. Legal and regulatory strategies: invest in changes in the regulatory environment which permit or enable the adoption of emerging technologies, policies, and appropriate IT standards to provide a common framework.

Critical success factors (CSF) can be described as the set of situations, factors, or actions which contribute to meeting the success criteria of a project (Gomes & Romão, 2016). Carrasqueiro et al. (2018) concluded that there are three main critical success factors for DT projects:

1. Articulation between the sponsors of the initiative.
2. Federated architecture which implements interoperability through pre-existing components.
3. Existence of governance and management of multilevel structures.

Other CSF can also be cited and can be generalized as the following: the existence of a clear vision and strategy; leadership with a high level of commitment; identifying and engaging stakeholders; clear communication for stakeholders to promote trust; the existence of legal and regulatory framework; adequate project management; the profile of the project; the skills of the technical teams involved; and the existence of adequate infrastructure. Chandler & Thomas (2015) highlight the role played by the sponsor as an influencing factor in the project. For the sponsor can exercise their influence in the following two ways (Crawford et al., 2006, Crawford et al., 2008):

1. Through their governance in coordinating activities, such as taking responsibility for the project plan and obtaining the forecast benefits, guiding and making decisions, critically evaluating the outcome of the project's progress, and being senior enough to be able to represent the project.
2. In the form of their support, through their availability to support, and through their credibility to be able to influence the relationship and leadership network.

According to Bousdekis and Kardaras (2020), interoperability is also considered to be a FCS, and these authors argue that when capacity is limited between the various information systems, then the result is a repetitive and time-consuming processes. They also reinforce the role of Corporate Architecture (CA) as a tool which provides a coherent set of principles, methods, and models used in the design and execution of business processes, information systems, and infrastructure, which contribute to a better alignment between the business domains and TI (Jensen et al., 2011). Through an analysis of 528 articles on DT, Pihir et al. (2019) concluded that the main factors which determine and influence the views of success and challenge are the following:

- Orientation to the strategy and support of senior leadership.
- The customer is the starting point for development through the monitoring of their needs.
- ICT and process infrastructure, where the level of digital maturity of an organization is directly related to the introduction of technology in the execution of processes.
- Strengthening talent and employee capacity through the investment in training human resources.

- Innovation culture and organizational commitment, where employees need to be committed to innovation and the organization, and steps must be taken to ensure that the work environment is conducive to innovation and change.

Still focused on the challenges and difficulties, Datta et al. (2020) describe the experience of DT in Italy:

- The level of adoption of digital services by the population.
- The risk of non-continuity of the projects due to the inconsistency of the objectives of the PA, due to political changes.
- Low level of digital skills, not only for users, but also for public servants, which reveals digital exclusion, even at the labor level.
- The bureaucracy that undermines efficiency increases complexity and costs and also undermines confidence in the government.

Public entities aim to achieve high levels of cooperation between stakeholders to improve the efficiency and quality of public service delivery (Chourabi et al., 2012; Van Veenstra et al., 2011; Kohli & Johnson, 2011; Matt et al., 2015).

Frameworks and Models

Next the construction of the proposal, some frameworks, business models, methods of evaluation and decision making were identified, whose objectives have a greater affinity with the objective of the study (Table 2).

RESEARCH METHODOLOGY

Methodological Approach

The research carried out for this paper used a qualitative approach and its underlying philosophy underlying is the interpretivist approach – which states that reality originates by means of a social construction, where the meanings that social actors attribute to their experiences predominate (Saunders et al., 2019). A survey was carried out for which the respondents were selected from a group of targeted professionals who had experience of acting on and/or deciding about DT projects, who were therefore potentially capable of clearly identifying their points of view according to their own experiences. To analyses the data collected in the research, an inductive approach was used (Saunders et al., 2019) which enables the identification of themes and patterns in the results of the collected data which can somehow be related to the existing literature to improve or build new theories, that is to say, to migrate from the specific to a more general view of the phenomena. Three research questions were defined. The first two research questions and a questionnaire with semi-structured questions were used as a source to answer the third research question. The collection of all the research questions was used to achieve the objective of the work (Figure 2).

Table 2. Frameworks, business models, methods of evaluation, and decision

Montagna (2005)	**A framework to evaluate e-government initiatives regarding the feasibility, benefits and advantages generated by each initiative. Five dimensions were defined: product, time, distance, iteration, and procedures. Each dimension can be assessed by using four criteria: efficiency, effectiveness, strategic benefits, and also transparency and institutional value. According to the author, the dimension-criterion relationship must be viewed from the point of view of the government, the citizen, and the company.**
Chesbrough (2011)	Open Service Innovation – this concept is recognized when the organization uses internal and external knowledge to accelerate internal and market innovation. The framework uses the participation of customers for co-creation, due to the difficulty of describing tacit knowledge and service innovation. This framework encourages consumer appreciation and rewards and uses open innovation to accelerate and strengthen innovation, leading to a less costly, less risky, and faster innovation.
Datta et al. (2020)	Carried out a study on DT projects in the Italian PA, and recommend best practices for managing the projects, including the affirmation of their broad degree of generalization. The key measure identified in the Italian study was the division of large projects into smaller modules to make them more understandable and manageable. According to the authors, modularity allows dealing quickly with any problems from the beginning to control costs and complete projects on time and within budget.
Osterwalder & Pigneur, 2010	Consider an organization's business model to be a tool which creates, delivers, and captures value. It consists of nine blocks which are developed according to the customer's needs. A resource used by Canvas is to establish a Minimum Viable Product that works as a prototype before starting the project and will later be increased. Al-Debei & Avison (2010) recognize that the business model can play an essential role in the face of the complex and turbulent scenario of the current world, because it is versatile, multipurpose, and has high levels of flexibility.
Hanelt et al. (2020)	The multidimensionality of DT projects – where these authors concluded about the existence of three fundamental dimensions for the success of DT projects: (1) Contextual Conditions – which initially act in the definition of DT (Henfridsson and Yoo, 2013) and which result from the material, environmental, and managerial antecedents and the respective interaction; (2) Mechanisms – strategic and operational innovation mechanisms which involve the application of resources, processes, and capabilities that are new to the organization. Integration mechanisms which include their alignment with existing resources, processes, and capabilities (Daniel & Wilson, 2003; Henfridsson & Yoo, 2013; Ranganathan et al., 2003); (3) Results – organizational results resulting from the change caused by DT. Economic results, better performance, and new forms of value which are caused by better service quality or cost reductions. Spillovers – the effect on the organizational environment caused by DT, which has an effect on systems, industry, information security, and individual effects.
Ross et al. (2019)	Accountability framework – which is based on large private sector companies and does not follow a technical approach, but rather adds value. This framework has eight principles: (1) Owner with responsibility for the entire product life cycle instead of project manager; (2) Continuous launches, rather than a scheduled agenda; (3) A mission that guides the team through objectives and limits, rather than a formal organizational structure; (4) Metrics, rather than directives designed to allow teams to define how they intend to achieve their mission; (5) Experiments to perceive the user's response in phases, rather than major launches; (6) Teams which have complete and even multifunctional autonomy and resources, rather than a traditional matrix structure; (7) Collaboration with inter-coordination between teams, rather than a hierarchy; (8) The trust of leaders in teams which results in the team assuming full responsibility, rather than of controlling the team's routine.

The survey was then prepared and subjected to a pre-test. The interviewees were sent an e-mail in which they were informed about the reason for the contact and the estimated duration of the interview. The identifications of the most cited themes in each response to questions were used as a source to define the categories (Yin, 2018) and to answer the research questions. These categories were then used to identify the factors that influence the success of DT projects, which were then used as the basis for constructing the framework (Montagna, 2005; Hanelt et al., 2020). The sampling was shaped by four attributes:

1. Convenience: due to the easy access to the interviewees, as they work in the same organization and have common projects with the researcher.
2. Intentional: the interviewees were chosen on purpose, to make it possible to collect more appropriate data to answer the research questions.

Figure 2. Relationship between investigation and inquiry questions

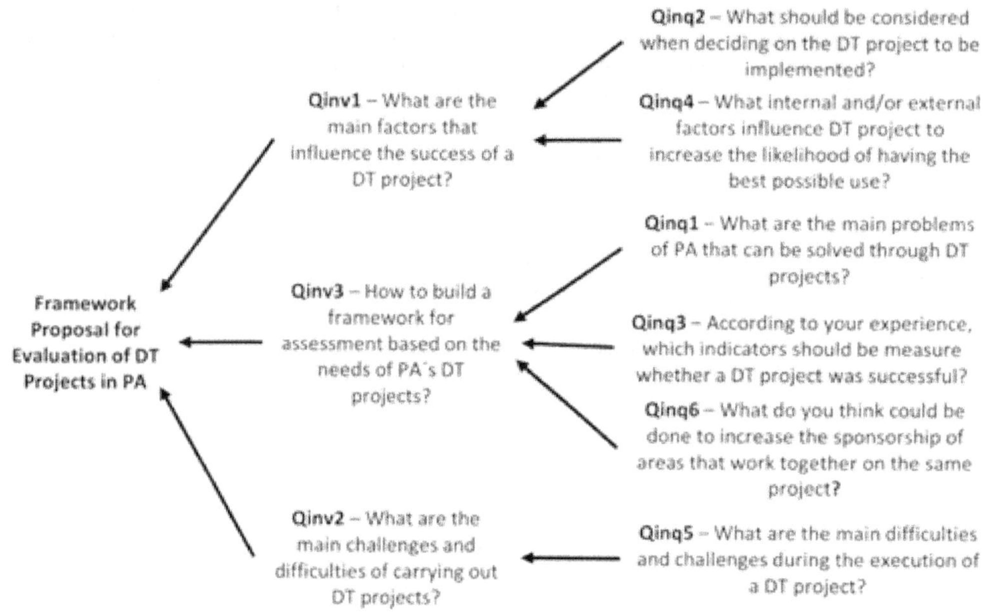

3. Type: is characterized as being homogeneous, as the interviewees occupy managerial and/or leadership positions in the same entity. Additionally, their functions have a direct relationship or influence on DT projects, thus making it possible to explore particular issues more profoundly and, consequently, the small differences that arose would be more easily exposed.
4. Size: the minimum acceptable for a non-probabilistic sample from a homogeneous group – which is 4 to 12 people, according to Saunders et al. (2019).

In the sample, from among the directors and team leaders of AMA who were either directly connected with or had influence on the DT projects, 13 were invited to participate in the survey, although only 11 accepted and were interviewed. As mentioned above, the most-cited themes of each question were used as a source to define the categories for the CSFs (Yin, 2018) and to answer the four research questions. These categories were the critical success factors for the success of TD and were used as the basis for the construction of the framework (Montagna, 2005; Hanelt et al., 2020). An analysis was first made of the consolidation of the responses of all the interviewees, identifying which themes were the most cited and the least cited, after which a second analysis was made of the answers to the other questions if anything was identified as being complementary. The themes which were cited at least three times were transformed into categories. All interviews were conducted individually and remotely, using video and audio communication software. The respondents spontaneously filled out the responses, which were often similar to other interviewees' responses. All the issues were then analyzed and all the complementary contributions were identified as well. At the end, the respondents were also given the opportunity to add any further information or comment that they considered relevant to the study.

Table 3. Identified categories and related survey questions (Qinq)

	Category	Qinq1	Qinq2	Qinq3	Qinq4	Qinq5	Qinq6
01	Citizen at the center	+	+		+		
02	Human resources	+	+		+	+	
03	Clear definition of projects		+		+		+
04	Entities, areas and partners		+		+		+
05	Sponsor		+		+		+
06	Political, strategic, operational and technological alignment		+		+	+	
07	Communication		+		+		+
08	Suppliers		+		+		
09	Product management	+	+			+	
10	Technological Infrastructure and process integration	+	+		+		
11	Stakeholders			+		+	+
12	Monitoring						
13	Legal and regulatory environment					+	

ANALYSIS AND DISCUSSION

The answers to the research questions are presented below, which are based on the analysis of the interviews, the establishment of categories and the literature, as well as the respective transversality between the data (Table 3). The compilation of the survey responses is reproduced in Appendix I.

QInv1: What Are the Main Factors That Influence the Success of a DT Project?

The answers to questions from the Qinq 2 and Qinq 4 questionnaire were used mainly to answer QInv1. Correspondences were found in the literature regarding the responses of Qinq 2 and Qinq 4, for different degrees of intensity. The most common topics were classified into 10 categories (Table 4).

QInv2: What Are the Main Challenges and Difficulties in Carrying Out a DT Project?

As mentioned in QInv1, the factors and elements that influence success can also be seen from the point of view of challenges and difficulties when faced with the reality of the DT project environment. This was confirmed by the responses to the Qinq5 interview. Almost the same categories as QInv1 were found, with the exception of a new category entitled (11) Stakeholders. With regards the other categories already mentioned in QInv1, what occurred was the expansion of the responses of the categories under the view of the challenge and difficulty (Table 5).

Table 4. The most common topics related to the QInv1

	Category	Explanation
01	Citizen at the center	Projects must be designed by taking into consideration the needs of the citizen and/or the company, where they can exercise the role of co-creators of the services and their experiences are monitored, their opinions collected, and prototypes are created before the products are implemented (Ross et al., 2019) and systems should focus on usability.
02	Human resources	Technical qualification and adequate profile to lead, according to the profile of the project (Carrasqueiro et al., 2018). This category was also supported in the literature by Pihir et al. (2019), when they emphasized the importance of investing in the training and management of human resources, and also by Datta et al. (2020) with regards the difficulties derived from the low digital skills of civil servants.
03	Clear definition of projects	Includes the objective, the viability of the final product, the target audience, how performance will be measured, budget control, team responsibilities, priorities, and the justification for carrying out the project. The adoption of Agile methodology. This category was supported by García & Pablo (2005) and Datta et al, (2020) through the recommendation of the roadmap of project deliveries and reverse engineering to meet the planned deadline. Another correspondence is the dimension of the success of projects by Shenhar et al. (2001), as the expected impact for dimension depends on the level of technology required by the project.
04	Entities, areas, and partners	Mentioned the need to map the reality and the business of the partners involved to get to know their capabilities and limitations. Manage the relationship and deal with dependency and competition between entities (Weerakkody et al., 2016; Cordella & Tempini, 2015).
05	Sponsor	The need for the commitment of a representative sponsor throughout the project, as well as in the other entities involved, together with decision-making power and influence (Chandler & Thomas (2015).
06	Political, strategic, operational, and technological alignment	The need to meet the political agenda and whether there is congruence with the master plan of PA, AMA, and the partner entities and the design of projects. Projects fail because they are not integrated into the process of institutional change (Weerakkody et al., 2016)
07	Communication	A communication strategy and plan and the sharing of information in the rendering of accounts during the project up until the results are released. Transparency in the sense of promoting trust through the flow of communication (Datta et al., 2020)
08	Suppliers	Quality is an important point as there is a shortage of specialized ICT labor. The element of the successful strategy (García & Pablo, 2005).
09	Product management	Who will be responsible and how will the final product be managed after the project is completed?
10	Technological infrastructure and process integration	Align expectations concerning availability, technological maturity, integration, network, and data security (Hanelt et al., 2020)

QInv3: How to Build an Assessment Framework Based on the Needs of DT Projects in PA?

The answer to this question is the result of the analysis of the first two research questions and the survey questions that are presented below. In this stage, two final and new categories were identified, in addition to those already mentioned above. From this point onwards the framework proposal was developed. Reducing bureaucracy for citizens/companies and internal PA was one of the most cited points of Qinq1, however it is not considered to be a category, as it is more of an objective, rather than an attribute (Table 6).

Table 5. The most common topics related to the QInv2

	Category	Explanation
02	Human resources	The difficulty of maintaining the best human resources, whether owned or outsourced, is added due to the intense need in the market for professionals with digital skills, high remuneration, and the number of people needed to execute the projects.
04	Entities, areas, and partners	Reinforcing the importance of relationship management
06	Political, strategic, operational, and technological alignment	Decision dependencies and obligation to adjust to political urgencies (Datta et al., 2020)
10	Technological infrastructure and process integration	Measure the performance of projects in general due to data access restrictions, whether for legal or operational reasons, the integration of processes, and also about the interconnection of infrastructures (Pihir et al., 2019; Datta et al., 2020; Rogers, 2016)
11	Stakeholders	The importance of keeping the various stakeholders aligned throughout the project

Framework Proposal for DT Project Evaluation

A matrix structure was designed using the principle that there is an order of categories which are independent of the others, in the sense of being used as a construction base for the others and also as a filter. The framework presents seven layers of filters that should be used in the evaluation of a project. Each layer is an evaluation phase to ascertain whether the project starts, or not. If the sequence of layers does not meet the requirements of the project, the proponent must be advised that their proposal needs to be revised to validate those layers that did not present consistency, and the evaluation should only be resumed again afterwards (Table 7).

As mentioned in the introduction, the framework needs to be tested to verify how it behaves in practice. The ideal would be to also define a specific area for the pilot to be carried out – such as health, education, or social security – as this would facilitate the analysis of the tool's performance by evaluating projects which satisfy similar conditions.

Table 6. The most common topics related to QInv3

	Category	Explanation
03	Clear definition of projects	There is a strict pre-start plan for projects and a clear definition of support requirements in project management, using tools such as a Balanced Scorecard or gamification
07	Communication	Is primarily to maintain a high level of collaboration and make it explicit where it does not exist. Visibility with stakeholders to attract and maintain support (Pihir et al., 2019; Hanelt et al., 2020). Sufficient and easily accessible documentation.
12	Monitoring	Measure the success of a DT project. The following subcategories were also considered in monitoring: the impact produced for society (Panagiotopoulos et al., 2012); adherence to the budget; level of adoption of public services by citizens/companies (Datta et al., 2020 and Panagiotopoulos et al., 2012); time of the execution of the service for both the user and the public servant; saving human and financial resources when migrating the service from physical to digital; level of user satisfaction and level of achievement of objectives; the importance of metrics rather than directives (Ross et al., 2019).
13	The legal and regulatory environment	Legal and regulatory environment in which the project is to be developed (Carrasqueiro et al., 2018; García & Pablo, 2005; Hanelt et al., 2020), which can be considered to be both a success factor and also a difficulty.

Table 7. Framework proposal for DT project evaluation

Layer	Description
First	The project addresses the following categories: *(01) Citizen at the Centre*, including the aspect of participation in the creation of the project (Barcevičius et al., 2019; Chesbrough, 2011; Datta et al., 2020; Garcia & Pablo, 2005; Greve, 2015; Hanelt et al., 2020; Montagna, 2005; Osterwalder et., 2010; Pihir et al., 2019; Ross et ., 2019) and *(03) Clear definition of projects* (Carrasqueiro et al., 2018; Chesbrough, 2011; Garcia & Pablo, 2005; Hanelt et al., 2020; Montagna, 2005; Too& Weaver, 2014; Weerakkody et al., 2016).
Second	Includes *(06) Political, strategic, operational, and technological alignment* during the initial phase (Bousdekis & Kardaras, 2020; Carrasqueiro et al., 2018; Datta et al., 2020; Hanelt et al., 2020) and also whether the conditions of the *(13) The Legal and regulatory environment* have been validated (Carrasqueiro et al., 2018; Datta et al., 2020; Hanelt et al., 2020). Although these categories were not those most frequently present in the study, they can be restrictive factors for categories *(04), (05), (08)*, and *(10)*.
Third	Human Resources are sufficient and have the appropriate skills for the type of project (Carrasqueiro et al., 2018; Datta et al., 2020; Garcia & Pablo, 2005; Hanelt et al., 2020; Pihir et al., 2019), in *(04) Entities, areas, and partners* (Carrasqueiro et al., 2018; Pittaway & Montazemi, 2020; Weerakkody et al., 2016) and *(08) Suppliers* (Carrasqueiro et al., 2018; Datta et al., 2020; Garcia & Pablo, 2005).
Fourth	The mapping plan for *(10) Technological and Process Infrastructure* at AMA, entities and suppliers is planned. Including corporate architecture (Bousdekis & Kardaras, 2020; Carrasqueiro et al., 2018; Chesbrough, 2011; Garcia & Pablo, 2005; Greve, 2015; Hanelt et al., 2020; Pihir et al., 2019; Rogers, 2016; Weerakkody et al., 2016), also *(04) Entities* and *(08) Suppliers*.
Fifth	Who is the *(5) Sponsor* and has leadership power and influence in the relationship network according to the characteristics identified in the previous layers (Carrasqueiro et al., 2018; Chandler & Thomas, 2015; Datta et al., 2020; Pihir et al., 2019)
Sixth	How *(07) Communication* (Carrasqueiro et al., 2018; Datta et al., 2020; Greve, 2015; Montagna, 2005) and *(12) Monitoring* (Garcia & Pablo, 2005; Panagiotopoulos et al., 2012; Ross et al., 2019) will be conducted throughout the project, as the second will be one of the sources of the first, favouring transparency, as well as the relationship with *(11) Stakeholders* (Carrasqueiro et al., 2018; Datta et al., 2020; Hanelt et al., 2020; Pihir et al., 2019) which include the categories *(01), (02), (04), (05)* and *(08)*.
Seventh	What will be the minimum viable product at the end of the project and who will be responsible for managing the product (Montagna, 2005; Osterwalder et al., 2010).

CONCLUSION

The end objective of this research is to create a proposed framework for project evaluation which is customized for DT, taking into consideration the characteristics and complexity of the Portuguese PA in order to confirm whether the project already satisfies the necessary conditions to be started. This objective was partially achieved, in that the framework is capable of identifying those factors that are most relevant to DT for the reality of PA and it presents a matrix structure. In total, thirteen factors were identified. Furthermore, the complexity of the projects was also confirmed, based on the dynamics of the relationship between them and the number of actors involved. The co-creation and co-participation between the State and the citizen were identified as being the most relevant factors for the success of DT in both the interviews and the literature, and accordingly this principle is also applied in the development of the framework proposal. This tool will be presented to the AMA, with the aim that it can be jointly developed by this organization's leaders and teams and will consequently be subject to internal and external criticism and adaptations and later be tested in practice by project decision-makers and managers. After experimentation, this tool can be improved, and if its application is found to promote a positive impact, then it can be adopted by the AMA as a means of support for decision making.

CONTRIBUTIONS, LIMITATIONS, AND FUTURE RESEARCH

The first contribution of this research was to identify those factors that influence the success of a DT project in the specific environment of the PA in Portugal, in alignment with the vision of the AMA's leadership. This identification was corroborated by the correlation with the literature, which added more credibility to the result. A significant part of the objective of the research was achieved, namely the proposal of a personalized tool, which is more likely to succeed in terms of its application, as it was constructed by those who work with and know the reality of the projects in question. A second contribution is the framework structure, which represents a structured and straightforward starting point for leaders and teams who can use and develop it – even if they possess differing levels of knowledge and experience of the project. The simplicity of the tool was another objective of the study, and an additional contribution is the fact that by being a simple and visual tool, it will enable better choices to be made, and assist in achieving better results. Certain limitations exist, such as the lack of information regarding the reasons that lead to the failure of DT projects in the PA and also the fact that there are very few references concerning frameworks for the evaluation or approval of specific projects for the management of DT in the PA. Further research is required to identify how human resources can be trained and developed to manage the complexity of DT better. It would also be relevant to investigate ways of increasing the involvement of the Digital Government ecosystem actors in the creation of public policies, as it is they who are often responsible for the initial creation of programmes and plans. The consequent increased level of involvement would promote both support for the political system and also commitment to the success of the public policy. In turn, this sharing of a certain part of the responsibility for implementing DT would result in the government becoming more experienced in carrying out the process of stakeholder consultation.

REFERENCES

Al-Debei, M., & Avison, D. (2010). Developing a unified framework of the business model concept. *European Journal of Information Systems, 19*(3), 359–376. doi:10.1057/ejis.2010.21

Barcevičius, M., Cibaitė, E., Codagnone, G., Gineikytė, C., Klimavičiūtė, V., Liva, L., Matulevič, G., & Vanini, G. (2019). *Exploring Digital Government transformation in the EU - Analysis of the State of the art and review of literature.* Publications Office of the European Union., doi:10.2760/17207

Bousdekis, A., & Dimitris, K. (2020). *Digital transformation of local government: A case study from Greece.* In Proceedings IEEE 22nd Conference on Business Informatics, Antwerp, Belgium. 10.1109/CBI49978.2020.10070

Carrasqueiro, S., Monteiro, M., Pereira, R., Pereira, C., & Martins, H. (2018). Dematerialization of the medical certificate for driving license in Portugal: a case study of success factors of whole-of-Government e-Government initiatives. In Proceedings of the *11th International Conference on Theory and Practice of Electronic Governance*, Galway, Ireland. 10.1145/3209415.3209510

Chandler, D., & Thomas, J. (2015). Does executive sponsorship matter for realizing project management value. *Project Management Journal, 46*(5), 46–61. doi:10.1002/pmj.21521

Chesbrough, H. (2011). *Open Services Innovation: Rethinking Your Business to Grow and Compete in a New Era* (1st ed.). Jossey-Bass.

Chourabi, H., Nam, T., Walker, S., Gil-Garcia, J., Mellouli, S., Nahon, K., Pardo, T., & Scholl, H. (2012). *Understanding Smart Cities: An Integrative Framework*. In proceedings of the 45th Hawaii International Conference on System Sciences, Maui, HI, USA.

Cordella, A., & Tempini, N. (2015). E-government and organizational change: Reappraising the role of ICT and bureaucracy in public service delivery. *Government Information Quarterly*, *32*(3), 279–286. doi:10.1016/j.giq.2015.03.005

Crawford, L., Cooke-Davies, T., Hobbs, B., Labuschagne, L., Remington, K., & Chen, P. (2008). Governance and Support in the Sponsoring of Projects and Programs. *Project Management Journal, 39*. doi:10.1002/pmj.20059

Crawford, L., Pollack, J., & England, D. (2006). Uncovering the trends in project management: Journal emphases over the last 10 years. *International Journal of Project Management*, *24*(2), 175–184. doi:10.1016/j.ijproman.2005.10.005

Currie, W. (2012). Institutional Isomorphism and Change: The National Programme for IT – 10 Years On. *Journal of Information Technology*, *27*(3), 236–248. doi:10.1057/jit.2012.18

Currie, W., & Guah, M. (2007). Conflicting institutional logics: A national programme for IT in the organizational field of healthcare. *Journal of Information Technology*, *22*(3), 235–247. doi:10.1057/palgrave.jit.2000102

Daniel, E., & Wilson, H. (2003). The role of dynamic capabilities in e-business transformation. *European Journal of Information Systems*, *12*(4), 282–296. doi:10.1057/palgrave.ejis.3000478

Datta, P., Walker, L., & Amarilli, F. (2020). Digital transformation: Learning from Italy's public administration. *Journal of Information Technology Teaching Cases,* 1-18. . doi:10.1177/2043886920910437

European Commission. (2020a). eGovernment Benchmark 2020: eGovernment that works for the people. Luxembourg: Publications Office of the European Union.

European Commission. (2020b). *Digital Economy and Society Index: Digital public services*. EC. https://ec.europa.eu/digital-single-market/en/news/digital-economy-and-society-index-desi-2020

Freeman, C. (2008). Systems of Innovation Selected Essays in Evolutionary Economics. Cheltenham, UK: Edward Elgar Publishing. doi:10.4337/9781035306176

García, J., & Pardo, T. (2005). E-government success factors: Mapping practical tools to theoretical foundations. Government, IT implementation, Information Technology, Relevance, Success factors. *Government Information Quarterly*, *22*(2), 187–216. doi:10.1016/j.giq.2005.02.001

Godinho, M. (2013). Inovação em Portugal. Fundação Francisco Manuel dos Santos.

Gomes, J., & Romão, M. (2016). Improving Project Success: A Case Study Using Benefits and Project Management. *Procedia Computer Science*, *100*, 489–497. doi:10.1016/j.procs.2016.09.187

Hanelt, A., Bohnsack, R., Marz, D., & Marante, C. (2020). A Systematic Review of the Literature on Digital Transformation: Insights and Implications for Strategy and Organizational Change. *Journal of Management Studies*. doi:10.1111/joms.12639

Henfridsson, O., & Yoo, Y. (2013). The Liminality of Trajectory Shifts in Institutional Entrepreneurship. *Organization Science*. doi:10.1287/orsc.2013.0883

Iannacci, F., Seepma, A., Blok, C., & Resca, A. (2019). Reappraising maturity models in e-Government research: The trajectory-turning point theory. *The Journal of Strategic Information Systems*, *28*(3), 310–329. doi:10.1016/j.jsis.2019.02.001

Janowski, T. (2015). Digital government evolution: From transformation to contextualization. *Government Information Quarterly*, *32*(3), 221–236. doi:10.1016/j.giq.2015.07.001

Jensen, C., Cline, O., & Owen, M. (2011). *Combining Business Process Management and Enterprise Architecture for Better Business Outcomes* (1st ed.). IBM Redbooks.

Jones, B., & Baumgartner, F. (2012). From There to Here: Punctuated Equilibrium to the General Punctuation Thesis to a Theory of Government Information Processing. *The Policy Studies Journal*, *40*(1).

Kohli, R., & Johnson, S. (2011). Digital Transformation in Latecomer Industries: CIO and CEO Leadership Lessons from Encana Oil & Gas (USA) Inc. *MIS Quarterly Executive*, *10*(4), 141–156.

Matt, C., Hess, T., & Benlian, A. (2015). Digital Transformation Strategies. *Business & Information Systems Engineering*, *57*(5), 339–343. doi:10.1007/s12599-015-0401-5

Mergel, I., Edelmann, N., & Haug, N. (2019). Defining digital transformation: Results from expert interviews. *Government Information Quarterly*, *36*(4), 101385. doi:10.1016/j.giq.2019.06.002

Montagna, J. (2005). A framework for the assessment and analysis of electronic government proposals. *Electronic Commerce Research and Applications*, *4*(3), 204–219. doi:10.1016/j.elerap.2005.01.003

OECD. (2014). *Recommendation of the Council on Digital Government Strategies*. Public Governance Committee. https://www.oecd.org/gov/digital-government/Recommendation-digital-government-strategies.pdf

Osterwalder, A., & Pigneur, Y. (2010). *Business Model Generation: Handbook for Visionaries, Game Changers, and Challengers*. John Wiley & Sons, Inc.

Panagiotopoulos, P., Al-Debei, M., Fitzgerald, G., & Elliman, T. (2012). A business model perspective for ICTs in public engagement. *Government Information Quarterly*, *29*(2), 192–202. doi:10.1016/j.giq.2011.09.011

Pihir, I., Tomičić-Pupek, K., & Tomičić, M. (2019). Digital transformation playground - literature review and framework of concepts. *Journal of Information and Organizational Sciences*, *43*(1), 33–48. doi:10.31341/jios.43.1.3

Pittaway, J., & Montazemi, A. (2020). Know-how to lead digital transformation: The case of local governments. *Government Information Quarterly*, *37*(4), 101474. doi:10.1016/j.giq.2020.101474

Ranganathan, C., Goode, V., & Ramaprasad, A. (2003). Managing the transition to bricks and clicks. *Communications of the ACM*, *46*(12), 308–316. doi:10.1145/953460.953515

Rogers, D. (2016). *The digital transformation playbook: rethink your business for the digital age*. Columbia University Press. doi:10.7312/roge17544

Ross, J., Beath, C., & Mocker, M. (2019). *Designed for Digital How to Architect Your Business for Sustained Success*. MIT Press. doi:10.7551/mitpress/12188.001.0001

Saunders, M., Thornhill, A., & Lewis, P. (2019). *Research methods for business students* (8th ed.). Pearson Education Limited. ISBN.

Schwab, K. (2016). *The Fourth Industrial Revolution*. Geneve, Switzerland: World Economic Forum.

Shenhar, A., Dvir, D., Levy, O., & Maltz, A. C. (2001). Project success: A multidimensional strategic concept. *Long Range Planning*, *34*(6), 699–725. doi:10.1016/S0024-6301(01)00097-8

Too, E., & Weaver, P. (2014). The management of project management: A conceptual framework for project governance. *International Journal of Project Management*, *32*(8), 1382–1394. doi:10.1016/j.ijproman.2013.07.006

Van Veenstra, A. F., Klievink, B., & Janssen, M. (2011). Barriers and impediments to transformational government: Insights from literature and practice. *Electronic Government. International Journal (Toronto, Ont.)*, *8*(2/3), 226–241. doi:10.1504/EG.2011.039838

Weerakkody, V., Omar, A., El-Haddadeh, R., & Al-Busaidy, M. (2016). Digitally-enabled service transformation in the public sector: The lure of institutional pressure and strategic response towards change. *Government Information Quarterly*, *33*(4), 658–668. doi:10.1016/j.giq.2016.06.006

Yin, R. (2018). *Case Study Research and Applications: Design and Methods* (6th ed.). Sage Publications, Inc.

APPENDIX ONE: COMPILATION OF THE RESULTS OF THE SURVEY RESPONSES

Qinq1: What Are the Main Problems of Public Administration (PA) That Can Be Solved Through Digital Transformation (DT) Projects?

Most cited problems:

- Bureaucracy for citizens and companies.
- PA internal bureaucracy.
- Digital services which are not centered on the citizen and fail to consider the usability and the full range of the facilities of the technology.
- Citizens' access barriers, such as distance and difficulty in moving.
- Interoperability.
- High costs for the citizen.
- Insufficient level of digital skills among the human resources to meet demand and at the requested speed.

Other problems:

- Reduced level of accessibility for citizens with physical or cognitive limitations.
- Failure to meet the State's duty of transparency regarding the results of the government's activity.
- High public costs and difficulty in integrating service procedures that involve more than one entity.
- There is a lack of a consolidated database of government data on project results.
- Difficulty in managing emerging technologies.
- Low level of knowledge of citizens and companies with regards the digital products and services available.

Qinq2: What Should Be Considered When Deciding on the Digital Transformation (DT) Project to Be Implemented?

Most cited issues:

- Know the service or product as well as the business of the entity that will experience a DT process.
- Clear definition of the problem to be solved.
- Clear definition of which stakeholder will benefit from the service.
- The project must have a strong and motivated Sponsor.
- Sufficient human resources who are trained in accordance with the needs of the project.
- Which political impact for citizens and companies is to be promoted and whether this is sufficient to justify implementing the project.
- How will both impact and performance be measured during the project?
- Map in detail the platforms involved (interoperability).
- Political, strategic, operational, and technological alignment.
- Who will be responsible and how the final product will be managed after the conclusion of the project?

Other issues:

- · Context costs.
- · Political will.
- · Lack of necessary information and the need for more planning.
- · Public departments must be provided with visibility to projects.
- · Less ambitious and consequently more feasible objectives.
- · The need for a communication plan.
- · Usability of the services.
- · If the ecological sustainability of resources is considered, then what is the applicable governing legislation?
- · The need for an organizational risk analysis and information security risk analysis at the level of personal data.

Qinq3: According to Your Experience, Which Indicators Should Be Used to Measure Whether a DT Project Was Successful?

Most cited indicators:

- · Compliance with the deadline.
- · The impact produced for society.
- · Adherence to the budget.
- · Percentage of user adoption.
- · Service execution time for both users and civil servants.
- · The number of human resources made redundant by the implementation of the digital service.
- · The cost reduction resulting from the implementation of the digital service
- · The level of user satisfaction and the level of achievement of the objectives

Other indicators:

- · Maintenance of the structure to perform the service after implementation, in accordance with the impact caused.
- · Fulfilments of the function.
- · Measurement of the level of difficulty in performing the service.
- · Level of stakeholder involvement.
- · Reduction of the number of iterations between the citizen and the PA.
- · The achievement of the objective resulting from implementation of the policy measures.
- · Quality, productivity, and return on investment.

Qinq4: Which Internal and/or External Factors Influence the Likelihood of a DT Project Having the Best Possible Use?

Most cited internal factors:

· Communication during all phases of the project.
· Sufficient human resources according to the requirements of the projects.
· Active involvement of the top leadership.
· The projects are focused on citizens' needs.

Other internal factors:

· Clear definition of the problem by the entity or business.
· Clear definition of the target stakeholders.
· Involvement of direct and indirect stakeholders.
· The political relationship between the departments.
· The approach to managing the projects.
· Insufficient and/or inaccessible documentation.
· Feedback on the progress of the project delivery.
· Definition of responsibilities and deadlines.
· Limitations and bureaucracy regarding the public procurement of goods, services, and people,
· Ability to establish alternative scenarios.
· Consumption of resources within the budget cycle,
· Level of services between different areas.
· Clear definition of requirements, the setting of priorities, and carrying out a detailed risk analysis.
Most cited external factors:
· The Sponsor being more senior that the management of the AMA.
· Reconciliation of political interests.
· Dependence on teams from other entities.
· The quality of suppliers due to the limited resources available and the scarcity of technology specialists.
· The relationship between entities during the implementation of the project.

Other external factors:

· Adequate information, especially regarding projects that involve a high degree of integration.
· People with the right skills. in the right places.
· Measuring the impact of the project to ensure that the Sponsor and the steering committee are aware.
· Competition between entities.
· Influences of business, political. and external interests.
· Budget and time available.
· Interoperability, risk analysis. and governance of the PA.

Qinq5: What Are the Main Difficulties and Challenges During the Execution of a DT Project?

Most cited difficulties and challenges:

· External dependence on other entities to carry out the project.
· Dependent on decision and political urgencies.
· Human resources management of the entities.
· Insufficient number of human resources.
· Capture and maintain the best human resources.
· Digital training and planning failures.
· Keeping stakeholders on board and alignment between areas and entities.
· Managing the final product.

Other difficulties and challenges:

· Level and number of technology providers available.
· Alignment between support areas.
· Delay in responding to expert validation.
· Lack of access to available data from other entities' services to measure performance or user satisfaction.
· Lack of a clear definition of requirements and clarity of the project scope.
· Lack of direction for the usability of the services.
· How financial resources are distributed over time.
· Difficulty and delay in hiring consultants.
· Lack of a systematic and integrated process.
· Validation of deliveries and acceptance criteria.
· Impaired performance of long projects and failure to test the solutions.
· Lack of a defined process for suspending or canceling a project.
· Permission to use data from interoperability.
· Sponsorship, communication, and bureaucracy,

Qinq6: What do You Think Could be Done to Increase the Sponsorship of Areas That Work Together on the Same Project?

Most cited suggestions:

· Strict planning during the pre-start phase of projects.
· A greater level of knowledge sharing, which is well documented and easily accessible.
· Continuous communication of progress and results.
· A strong Sponsor and alignment between stakeholders.

Other suggestions:

- Integrated product view and clarity in setting priorities.
- Implement a Balanced Scorecard and Gamification.
- A change in the organizational culture.
- Build trust between teams and permanently involve the teams.
- Reduce dependence on people and areas.
- Bi-weekly meetings with all areas.
- All areas should sign the work plan.
- A plan which involves all stakeholders who are linked to a service level.
- A plan to mitigate damages due to a delay in the schedule.
- Accountability and the elimination of redundancies.
- Leaders who are capable of increasing collaborative logic.
- Tender documents which are written with the strategy in mind.
- Exchange of information between all those involved.
- Lack of collaboration, being a political priority, and project control.

Chapter 3
Combining Models to Shape Project Success

Jorge Vareda Gomes
https://orcid.org/0000-0003-0656-9284
Universidade Lusófona, Portugal

Mário Batista Romão
https://orcid.org/0000-0003-4564-1883
ISEG, Universidade de Lisboa, Portugal

ABSTRACT

Organizations are under constant pressure. Externally, they face a scenario of intense competition, coupled with a changing environment which is full of uncertainty. Internally, organizations have to deal with limited resources, whilst at the same time comply with increasing requirements and strategic demands. A key to success is the successful management of organizational projects. According to worldwide studies, information systems and information technology (IS/IT) projects have a relatively low success rate. To face these various business challenges, the authors suggest that emphasis should be put on the integration of various and disperse management tools. By combining project management maturity models with benefits management approaches, the authors expect to reinforce support for the drive to use organizational projects to fulfill organizations' strategic plans that will enhance the control techniques of project management, whilst recognizing the need for organizational change and for ensuring the interpersonal skills necessary to orchestrate the successful completion of a project.

INTRODUCTION

There is a need to work with faster and more flexible organizational structures, which force companies to operate through projects which help them to successfully achieve their objectives (Gomes & Romão, 2014). Furthermore, in an increasingly competitive business market, it is necessary to ensure that the successful results of one project can be extended to future projects, using standardized procedures. Project management has evolved over the last decades, as have the roles and responsibilities of the project

DOI: 10.4018/979-8-3693-1742-6.ch003

manager (Kerzner, 2022). Organizations have adopted the project form as an important economic and social process on which the emerging knowledge economy has been supported (Cleland and Ireland, 2006; Meredith and Mantel, 2009). Practices and techniques of project management are recognized by many organizations in various industries as being essential skills, which benefit businesses (Anderson & Jessen, 2003). These skills are measured using benchmarking and comparative models Hillson (2003). clarifies that the benchmarking process aims to diagnose strengths and weaknesses, to measure the current capacity and to identify areas for improvement. According to Kwak and Ibbs (2002), most companies consider using practices and support tools which are applicable for project management processes, as they permit them to adapt to changing business environments, yet they need a reference model for the efficient implementation of such tools. Project management has experienced a very important growth and its economic impact is considerable in different sectors, industries and countries (Turner et al, 2010; Winter et al, 2006). Academic literature has paid a considerable attention to the concept of maturity models (Crawford, 2002; Kerzner, 2005: Kwak & Ibbs, 2002, Pennypacker & Grant, 2003). Maturity models represent a structured collection of elements which highlight the characteristics of effective processes at different stages of development (Pullen, 2007). Maturity models approach is the evolutionary progress in demonstrating the specific ability or accomplishment of a target from an initial to a final desired stage (Mettler and Rohner, 2009). Maturity in project management consists of developing repeatable processes and systems which lead to project success (Kerzner, 2019). Project management maturity models emerge which provides companies with the necessary mechanisms to allow them to identify the key areas for opportunity and improvement in project management tasks. Additionally, these models serve to develop comparative indicators for the application of project management practices and techniques across organizations which operate in the same business environment or sector. Maturity has been expressed by organizations as a potential key factor for increasing performance, for achieving goals and for being successful. Organizational project management maturity and competency seem to be promising variables which are both related to project success (Skulmoski, 2001; Suikki et al., 2002). Maturity shows how an organization has progressed in relation to the incorporation of project management as a way of working, thus reflecting its effectiveness in completing projects (Piwowar-Sulej, 2021).

Basically, the purpose of the maturity model is to provide a framework for improving an organization's business result by assessing the organization's project management strengths and weaknesses, by enabling comparisons with similar organizations, and by measuring the correlation between an organization's project management level and its project performance (Gomes & Romão, 2013; Ibbs & Kwak, 2000).

There is a considerable volume of literature dealing with project success, and this tends to fall into three categories: 1) studies that deal primarily with the criteria for measuring project success; 2) studies that are primarily concerned with success factors; and 3) studies that mix both.

The success of the project is a relevant factor in project management, it is one of the most frequently debated topics among academics, and there is no consensus on the criteria by which it can be judged (Volden & Welde, 2022).

Judgev and Müller (2005) identified four stages of project success evolution: 1) the time and cost quality constraints evaluation method; 2) the need for stakeholder satisfaction; 3) the emergence of an organization's specific strategic view; and 4) a more focused, strategically oriented view, in response to increasing globalization and the advent of IS/IT. The notion of success is one of the most controversial topics in the field of project management (Gomes & Romão, 2015; Yu et al., 2005). Cleland and Ireland (2002) claimed that the success or failure of a project can be perceived differently by different stakeholders of the project. A wide range of variables can affect the success of a project. However, these authors emphasize that success factors are dependent on the type of project, thus challenging the idea of a universal set of valid factors for all projects (Berssaneti & Carvalho, 2015).

This paper presents a literature review that covers diverse subjects, such as maturity models, benefits management and project management approaches. We also describe our proposal as to how these approaches can be brought together, with the perspective of delivering a useful integrative tool for managers. We comment on a small example where this integrated model has been applied, and we conclude our paper with the most relevant observations.

BACKGROUND

Changes in technology and in the business environment has meant that greater demands are required from traditional management models, which have difficulty in giving a rapid response to changing markets. Three main key characteristics of modern organizations and society which reflects the increased adoption of project-based work across several industrial sectors are the following (Sydow and Staber, 2002); (1) Rapidly changing environments and markets; (2) The increasing complexity of products and services; (3) The knowledge intensity in production processes.

Project management is the process within organization where temporary endeavours are undertaken for beneficial change and added value (Nokes, 2007), requiring a multi-dimensional set of skills and a professional practice of managerial knowledge (Kerzner, 2022). Organizations have adopted the project form as an important economic and social process on which the emerging knowledge economy has been supported (Cleland and Ireland, 2006; Meredith and Mantel, 2009). Project management has received increasing attention in the business and academic world, as projects are important tools for change and organizational development (Pollack, 2017). In an environment where projects are increasingly becoming the fundamental component of running a business, project management has recently been the subject of much scrutiny (Locatelli et al., 2017). Grant and Pennypacker (2006) report that over the last decades, more businesses are employing project management as a way of developing a competitive advantage, but projects do not always progress as planned. Project performance targets are tied to the well-coordinated control of project activities, with relation to schedule, cost and quality, so that project can be fulfilled within the planned scope of the project (Taderdoost and Keshavarzsaleh, 2016).

According to the literature, organizational growth in respect of the use of IS/IT is described in terms of clearly defined stages of maturity (Sliż, 2018). Various stages of growth models have been presented by researchers to describe the evolution of organizational information systems (Galliers et al., 2008). Maturity has been expressed by organisations as a potential key factor for increasing performance, for achieving goals and for being successful. Several studies recognize the benefits from investments in project management skills in organisations and others have discussed the issue of the correlation between level of maturity and the performance of projects (Mullaly, 2006). The use of maturity models provides an approach for continuous improvement in many areas of business (Brookes & Clarke, 2009). They drive strategically linked continuous improvement and require a prior thorough understanding of an organization's current position and an idea of where it aims to be in the future (Brookes & Clarke, 2009). Maturity models have become an essential tool in assessing organisations' current capabilities and helping them to implement change and improvement in a structured way (Jia et al., 2011). Maturity model is a set of characteristics, attributes, indicators, or patterns that represent progression and achievement in a specific domain or discipline (Caralli et al., 2012). Maturity models aim to integrate, assess and improve project management practices. The concept of process maturity was born out of Total Quality Management, where the application of statistical process control techniques showed that improving the maturity of any technical process leads to a reduction of the inherent variability in the process and to an improvement in the mean performance of the process (Cooke-Davies, 2001). Identifying the maturity model in the change domain suggests that many of the ideas developed to address broader business change are applicable to the project management environment (Sadatsafavi and Walweski, 2011). Project management framework is a good choice for guiding the implementation of a change initiative in a business (Naslund & Norman, 2022). In the area of IS/IT project management, Lee and Anderson (2006) used a Delphi study to research factors not covered by maturity models, which influence project management capability. Ibbs and Kwak (2002) demonstrated no statistically significant correlation between project management maturity and project success, based on cost and schedule performance, whereas Jugdev and Thomas (2002) could not find a correlation between process capability and project success for many maturity models.

Investments in IS/IT are inevitable in today's business world, as they play a fundamental role in creating all forms of business to ensure productivity and efficiency (Koi-Akrofi, 2020). There has been a trend for rising expenditure in IS/IT over the last two decades, which corresponds to the plethora of IS/IT products now available in the market. Well-managed IS/IT investments, which have been carefully selected and which are focused on meeting business needs, can have a positive impact on an organization's performance (Peppard et al., 2008). Essentially, the purpose of investment in IS/IT is to improve the operational efficiency of an organization, to reduce costs and improve levels of profit. Thus, many traditional appraisal techniques are used to evaluate tangible benefits, which are based on direct project costs. Firms in almost every industry rely on investments in IS/IT to realize benefits after their successful implementation. However, many IS/IT projects fail to deliver the desired benefits (Peppard et al., 2008). Although organizations continue to make substantial investments in IS/IT, the successful realization of value, namely, in the form of benefits from such investments, has consistently been reported as a major organizational challenge. The difficulties due to the implementation of IS/IT solutions and assessment of their performance have been acknowledged by several scholars (Lueg and Lu, 2012, 2013). Grounded by theory of competitive strategy, several authors argued that IS/IT can contribute to more profits if it cannot be replicated easily or it can make product differentiation (Mithas et al., 2012). Although many studies have focused on the consequences of IS/IT investments, fewer studies have examined factors that impact the IS/IT capabilities (Devaraj and Kohli, 2003). Studies have found that few organizations have a comprehensive process to ensure that planned benefits are realized and that organizations tend to focus on benefits in the early stages of the project but do not follow a benefits management approach through the project lifecycle (Ward et al., 2007). In the last decades, the relationship between investments in IS/IT and improving organisational performance has been the subject of many studies (Melville et al., 2004). The issue remains controversial, as evidenced by articles in major business magazines. Carr (2003) argues that emergent technologies may offer opportunities to those who can exploit them effectively in the early stages of their development. Organizations are being put under increasing pressure to justify the large number of financial resources spent on IS/IT assets (Madeira, Gomes and Romão, 2017). The decision-making process over IS/IT investments is not as objective and transparent as it is claimed to be, creating significant failures on achievement of the objectives and their related benefits (Berghout et al., 2005).

Organizations seek benefits and value only in monetary terms, which have resulted in a lot of wasted energy, time and money. It is very common that organizations place their focus on the technical aspects such as does it work? rather than the social aspects such as is this adopted successfully? or from a business perspective is this delivering value? (Gomes and Romão, 2017).

To respond to the constraints of the new business environment, successful organizations have basically developed three important strategies (Gomes and Romão, 2012):

1. Training employees in the use of IS/IT, to provide organizations with the knowledge and capacity to respond to the pressures to change.
2. Participating in collaborative platforms which involve all relevant stakeholders in the business process.
3. Finding ways of obtaining superior performance by using frameworks that assist management processes.

Research on benefits management as a comprehensive approach began in the mid-1990s, with an empirical study on industry practices in the UK (Ward et al., 2006). This study found that many organizations were not satisfied with the results of their IS/IT investments. The basic assumption in benefits management literature is that benefits can be realized if they are managed appropriately. Other studies have attempted to develop models and frameworks to manage the entire benefits management process, which includes those of the Cranfield Model (Ward et al., 2006); Benefit Realisation Management (Bradley, 2010); Active Benefit Realization (Reymenyi, et al., 1997) and the Model of Benefits Identification (Changchit et al., 1998). A recent survey of benefits management practices reports that only a minority of responding organizations had adopted a comprehensive approach to managing benefits from their IS/IT investments (Ward et al., 2007). Ashurst et al. (2008) used the example of benefits realization to highlight the frequent gap between management theory and practice. Benefits management follows several phases, namely:

1. Identifying and structure the process: the identification of the correct benefits and classification according to their nature, i.e., in practical terms, the identification of the realistic benefits which are achievable through a project is critical to their actual realization.
2. Planning: the ability to effectively identify the parties responsible for each identified benefit and change. The need to establish the ownership of the benefits and to identify the changes required and the corresponding implications for stakeholders. The tool used in cause-effect logic to connect all the defined activities, interdependencies, timings and responsibilities, is known as the Benefits Dependency Network (BDN) (Ashurst et al., 2008).
3. Execution: The management of change programmes and the review of progress versus the benefits plan (Ward & Daniel, 2006).
4. Measurement and review: the ability to develop suitable measures for each identified change (Peppard et al., 2008). Organizations need to implement effective and ongoing monitorization and evaluation of their project results, to ensure that benefits are being realized as planned (Ward & Elvin, 1999).
5. Further benefits: organizations will only deliver value from IT projects if they can design and execute the organizational change programmes needed to realize all the benefits as planned (Ashurst et al., 2008).

Also important is the identification of additional improvements through business changes, the subsequent initiation of action and the identification of additional benefits originating from further IT investment.

It has been argued that this lack of alignment between IS/IT and business is the reason why incorrect unrealistic benefits are identified, or not identified at all, and why the operationalization of measures is incorrectly specified, activities and resources are improperly planned, and required organizational changes are not carried out (Chan & Reich, 2007). Although the increasing role and importance of IS/IT, the understanding of why, how, and when technology enables the productivity improvement is in its early stages, resulting in a delay in productivity growth (Jorgenson and Stiroh, 2000). The IS/IT is becoming so central to modern organisations that implementation of large projects is synonymous of huge changes within organisations (Kuruppuarachchi et al., 2002). This means that an organization's IS/IT projects are part of deep changes involving business systems, organizational structure, and people. In these cases, customer acceptance rather than technical, time, or budget requirements, more often determines project success.

Traditional appraisal techniques are often unable to capture many of the qualitative benefits that are brought about by IS/IT (Ward et al., 2006). These techniques also ignore the impact that the system may have in human and organizational terms. Some studies suggest that IS/IT investments produce negligible benefits (Strassmann, 1997), while others report a positive relationship between the performance of organizations and IS/IT expenditure (Lee & Barua, 1999). Lin et al. (2005) supports the argument of a generalized inappropriate, or ineffective use of IS/IT methodologies in most organizations. According to Willcocks and Lester (1999), management and financial controllers' attitudes have changed towards IS/IT investment criteria, in the sense that IS/IT is now seen more as a support function, rather than a strategic tool; executives are unsure about how IS/IT may be effectively implemented; most view IS/IT from a technical point of view, rather than from a business approach.

In the past, evaluating a project was largely based on the criteria of the achievement of time, cost and quality. Recently it was realized that success cannot be effectively evaluated by these three criteria alone and many researchers tried to improve the situation by adding new dimensions to these criteria. Success is far more complex than the factors just addressed by these criteria. Projects vary, depending on the subject, and criteria must be developed to evaluate a project's outcome that is specific for each project. Over time, various attempts have been made to either add more dimensions to the basic criteria, or to reduce them to less dimensions (Atkinson, 1999). Although not strongly supported by empirical research, many papers exist which address the issue of project success criteria. These papers tend to agree that there is a lack of agreement concerning the criteria by which success is judged (Baccarin, 1999; Freeman & Beale, 1992; Shenhar et al., 1997;). A review of the literature reveals that there is, in fact, some degree of agreement with the definition provided by Baker et al. (1988), which states that project success is a matter of perception and that a project will be most likely to be perceived as an "overall success". Baker et al. (1988) gave a definition of success which includes several major issues, the most important being technical performance and satisfaction amongst the various key people involved with the project. What is important is the recognition that all people involved need to be satisfied with the outcome of a project. While the achievement of objectives is useful for evaluating the outcome of a project, this is not enough to evaluate a project's success. The criteria used for measuring project success must be established at the beginning of the project, otherwise team members and the project leader will find that they are heading in different directions and the result of the project will not be successfully determined, owing to differences in perception, emphasis and objectives (Baccarin, 1999). Baccarini (1999) agrees with the existence of success-related factors for projects, which can be divided into two groups: 1) Project Success Criteria (PSCs): – which refers to a group of principles or standards used to determine project success; 2) Critical Success Factors (CSFs): – which refers specifically to conditions and circumstances that contribute to project results.

Success factors are those elements that are required to deliver the success criteria (Wateridge, 1995) and can thus be described as the set of circumstances, facts, or influences which contribute to the result or the achievement of success criteria (Lim & Mohamed, 1999). Collins and Baccarini (2004) and Turner (2008) emphasized that PSCs are used to measure success, whilst CSFs facilitate the achievement of success.

What are the influences on project success? Seeking the answer to this question resulted in research into project CSFs. The concept of success factors was introduced by Daniel (1961) as: "usually three to six factors determine success; these key jobs must be done exceedingly well for a company to be successful" (p.116) (Daniel, 1961). This concept has been applied to project environments (Cooke-Davies, 2002) and analysis of the literature found that most studies have focused on deriving CSFs that are applicable to a particular industry, such as construction or IS/IT (Lyer & Jha, 2005). This suggests a need for further study to identify generic CSFs for projects. An outcome which is common to most studies of project CSFs, is a list of factors. It is difficult for project managers to evaluate which key factors impact on performance (Belassi & Turkel, 1996). In response to this difficulty, Belassi and Tukel (1996) proposed the development of frameworks that group CSFs. According to Ward and Griffiths (Ward & Griffiths, 1996), critical success factors enable management to use their judgment in two ways: 1) by assessing the relative importance of systems opportunities in terms of how well they support the achievement of business objectives; and 2) by identifying the information required to manage and plan the information needs of business executives.

CASE STUDY

The P3M3® maturity model gives an opportunity for organizations to use self-assessment to obtain an up-to-date evaluation of the maturity of their project (Sowden, 2010). As an example, we decided to carry out a self-assessment process in a small-medium sized company that has been operating and leading in various fields, in particular the application of technological solutions for the supply of specialized cartographic products, geographical databases and geo-referenced information. The main goal was to collect the information needed to get the correct "picture" of the organization.

The organization under study was assessed to answer the following two questions: "Where are we now?", and "Where do we want to be?". This self-assessment was crucial for providing the data for the strategic analysis needed to endorse the organization's choice of drivers for investment, as well as the identification and structure of benefits beyond those of the objectives.

The result of this self-assessment identifies the maturity stage of the organization in question (Table. 1). It should be noted that the overall assessed maturity level is equal to the lowest score for the process perspectives. In our example, the level attributed to the organization is 1. To stabilize maturity at level 2, it is advisable for top managers, business managers, IS/IT specialists and others relevant stakeholders to agree on an improvement plan which includes the major issues, namely: new processes or the redesign of the old ones; new skills and responsibilities; new methodologies and approaches; organizational changes and technological tools. Maturity level 2 is characterized by basic management practices, such as: tracking expenditure or scheduling resources. Key individuals should be trained and need to demon-

Table 1. Example of P3M3 self-assessment answers

	P3M3 Self-Assessment Model						
	Questions / levels	1	2	3	4	5	level
1	How our organization can be characterized	√					1
2	How our management control is best described		√				2
3	How our benefits management is best described	√					1
4	How our financial management is best described		√				2
5	How our risk management is best described			√			3
6	How our approach to stakeholder management is best described		√				2
7	How our organizational governance is best described	√					1
8	How our resource management is best described			√			3
9	How does the organization go about programme/project management		√				2

strate a successful track record, as it is through them that the organization becomes capable of repeating success. Initiatives are performed and managed according to their documented plans and delivery should be visible to management at defined points. To ensure that the benefits from the investments materialize, the following two questions need to be answered: "What benefits are we seeking?", and "How will achieve them?". Most of the value from IS/IT investments come from the business changes that enable an organization to carry out some of the following actions (Ward & Daniel, 2006): 1) Adoption of new or redefined processes; 2) New roles and responsibilities; 3) Operation of new teams, groups or divisions; 4) New governance arrangements; 5) Use of new measures and metrics; 6) Use of new appraisal and reward schemes; 7) New practices for managing and sharing information.

The achievement of benefits obviously depends on the effective implementation of technology, however evidence from project successes and failures suggests that it is an organizations' inability to accommodate and exploit the capabilities of technology that usually causes a poor return from many investments. While business changes may be considered as being the way that an organization intends to work 'for ever more', it is recognized that organization will also carry out other investments and changes (Ward & Daniel, 2006). Our linking process intends to use benefits management not only as a contained process area, but also as a process that crosses all the process areas. In accordance with the benefits management approach, two internal workshops were organized to facilitate further discussion and the sharing of knowledge and expertise (Gomes et al., 2013; Ward & Daniel, 2006). The ability of all stakeholders to commit the required time and resources for the project must also be ensured. The outputs from the workshops will form the basis of the business case and benefits plan and should become integral components of the overall project plan. The final objective of the workshops is to build a consensus to identify the main objectives and their related benefits, as well as the CSFs and PSCs that could enhance the probability of a project's success. Through the identification of CSFs and PSCs, organizations learn to identify what they need to change to improve their ultimate chances for success. The resulting business plan should provide answers to two different sets of questions:

Figure 1. Example of a benefits dependency network

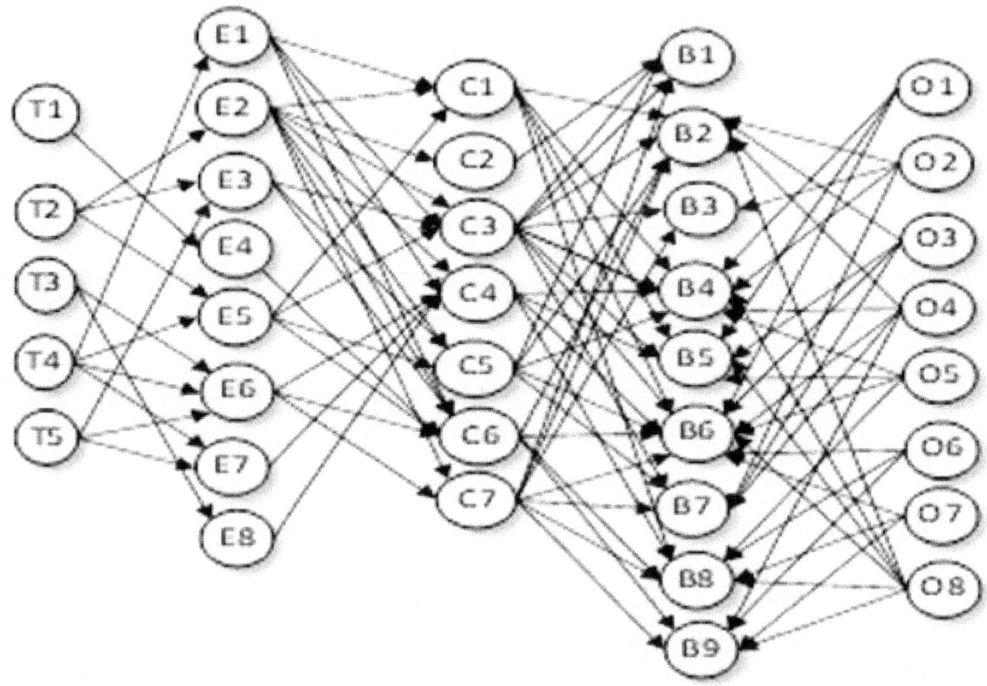

1. Benefits achievement: Why must we improve and what improvements are necessary or possible? What benefits will be realized by each stakeholder if the investment objectives are to be achieved? How will each benefit be measured? Who owns each benefit, and who will be accountable for its delivery? What changes are needed to achieve each benefit, and who will be responsible for ensuring that each change is successfully made? How and when can the identified changes be made? (Ward & Daniel, 2006).
2. Projects strategic alignment: Are all investors' interests considered? Are strategic goals chosen by considering the customers' needs? Is the process perspective directed at objectives related to internal processes? Does the potential perspective refer to the constant improvement of employees' qualifications? (Kaplan & Norton, 1996).

Benefits management proactively encourages stakeholders to explore the multitude of relationships that exist between technology, organizational change and benefits, whilst keeping benefits very firmly on the agenda, facilitating a benefit-oriented communications amongst all the system's stakeholders (Gomes et al., 2013). The BDN is the central technique of this approach and it is designed to ensure that investment objectives and benefits are linked to the business in a structured way (Figure 1).

Building the BDN is recognized as being an important first step towards ensuring that the initiative maintains a clear focus on the delivery of value (Gomes et al., 2013; Ward & Daniel, 2006). The network depicted in Figure 2 provides a framework which explicitly links investment objectives with the required benefits enabled by organizational changes and investments in IS/IT initiatives. BDN has the

Figure 2. Example of benefits stream extracted from the BDN

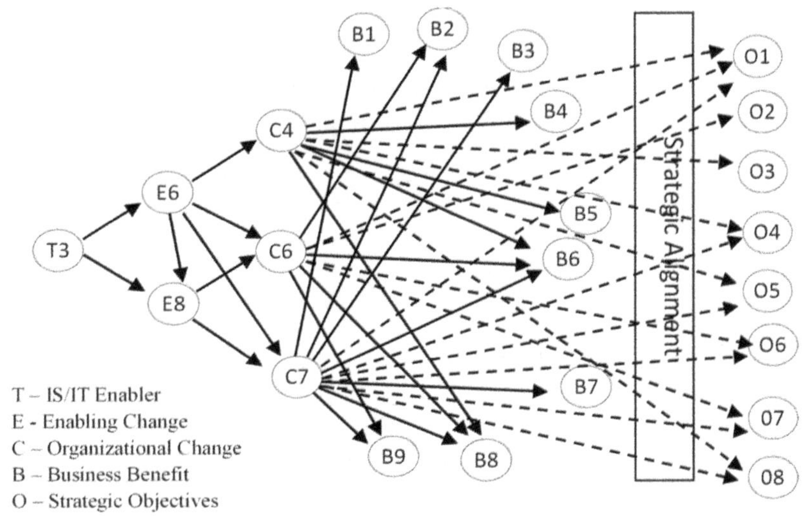

purpose of processing those business activities that are required to deliver the expected benefits and the IS/IT skills and facilities that enhance these changes. CSFs can be defined as a small number of easily identifiable operational goals, which are shaped by different levels and elements such as the industry, the firm, the managers, and the broader environment. Accordingly, CSFs are mostly intended to be used to ensure the success of an organization.

By implementing the benefits management cycle and by designing the BDN from within the organization's core, the achievement of CSFs can be enhanced, performing a cause-effect set of transformations which is leveraged by the change enablers and by the technological assets used (Figure 3).

Several studies based on the analysis of project management skills have shown that the issue discussed can somehow influence the success of a project (Crawford, 2003, 2005; Turner & Müller, 2005). Managers are trained to focus on the fulfillment of short-term criteria, i.e., to comply with time, cost and quality. In general, these constraints are imposed by the organization's top management, and are opposed to the long-term criteria, which typically are more related to the satisfaction of stakeholders' expectations (e.g., better products and/or more efficient services). The major challenge is to deliver an outcome which targets not only the project management objectives and the business improvements, but also promotes an adequate level of organizational change, benefits realization, and, ultimately, the satisfaction of all stakeholders involved in the project, namely: customers, partners, suppliers, project teams and users.

CONCLUSION

Projects are powerful assets which allow companies to translate strategy into results, namely: new products, innovative services, and/or business performance improvements.

Projects often possess a specialized set of critical success factors which, if correctly addressed, will improve the likelihood of their successful implementation. Furthermore, if these factors are not taken seriously, this may lead to a failure of the project management and/or the project itself. Organizations

Figure 3. Example of project success criteria through benefits management cycle

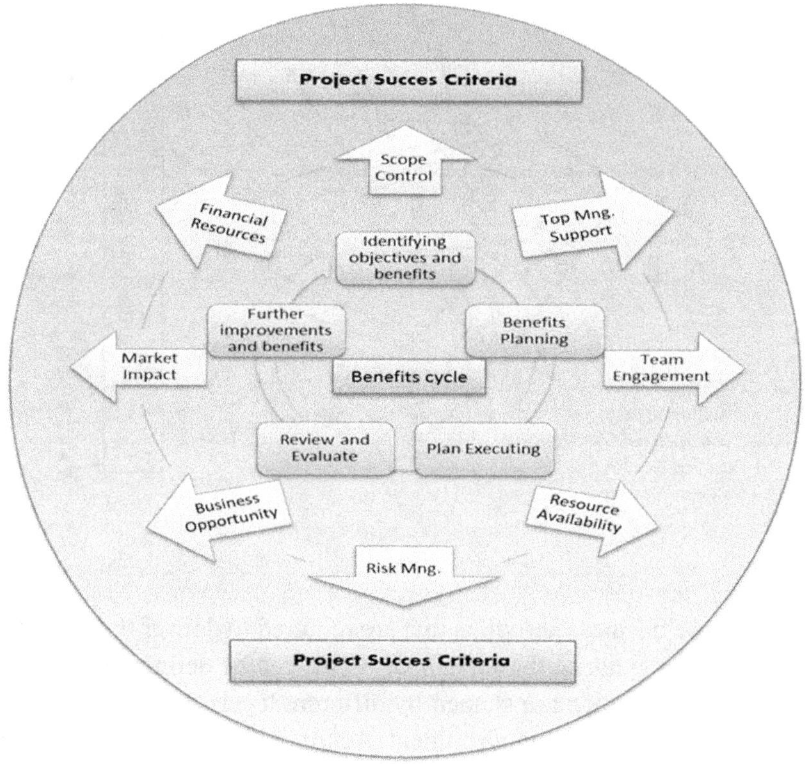

thus need to align their project management practices to the organization's strategy, to increase their sustainability and the probability of success.

The general perception that IS/IT projects continually fail, has forced organizations to seek new ways and approaches to achieve a higher probability of success. To make organizations more profitable, it became necessary to add more value to the business through projects and initiatives that incorporate changes in ways of performing work, as well as changes to support processes and the alignment of skills, or even the acquisition of the right mix of resources.

The benefits management approach promotes the utilization of effective organizational change management capability for the management of all the other factors which are necessary to make effective use of the assets created by projects. These include training and operational support to facilitate the necessary cultural changes within the organization.

By linking maturity, benefits and project management methodologies, we provide a more complete and integrated answer to internal stakeholders' expectations and to the demands of the external market. This combination of approaches allows organizations to assess the strengths of each method and to build a response to the challenging business environments, whilst at the same time keeping the focus on the organization's objectives and benefits, on aligning initiatives with strategy, and on operating faster and more efficiently.

The resulting framework described in this paper can be a useful management tool which is aimed at helping managers and organizations deal more effectively with today´s dynamic business environments.

REFERENCES

Anderson, E. S., & Jessen, S. A. (2003). Project maturity in organisations. *International Journal of Project Management*, *21*(6), 457–461. doi:10.1016/S0263-7863(02)00088-1

Ashurst, C., Doherty, N. F., & Peppard, J. (2008). Improving the impact of IT developments projects: The benefits realization capability model. *European Journal of Information Systems*, *17*(4), 352–370. doi:10.1057/ejis.2008.33

Atkinson, R. (1999). Project management: Cost, time and quality, two best guesses and a phenomenon, it's time to accept other success criteria. *International Journal of Project Management*, *17*(6), 337–342. doi:10.1016/S0263-7863(98)00069-6

Baccarini, D. (1999). The logical framework method for defining project success. *Project Management Journal*, *30*(4), 25–32. doi:10.1177/875697289903000405

Baker, B. N., Murphy, D. C., & Fisher, D. (1998). Factors affecting project success. In D. I. Cleland & W. R. King (Eds.), *Project Management Handbook* (2nd ed., pp. 902–909). Van Nostrand Reinhold.

Belassi, W., & Tukel, O. (1996). A new framework for determining critical success/failure factors in project. *International Journal of Project Management*, *14*(3), 141–151. doi:10.1016/0263-7863(95)00064-X

Berghout, E., Nijland, M., & Grant, K. (2005). Seven ways to get your favoured IT project accepted-politics in IT evaluation. *The Electronic Journal of Information System Evaluation*, *8*(1), 31–40.

Berssaneti, F., & Carvalho, M. (2015). Identification of variables that impact project success in Brazilian companies. *International Journal of Project Management*, *33*(3), 638–649. doi:10.1016/j.ijproman.2014.07.002

Bradley, G. (2010). *Benefit Realization Management: A Practical Guide for Achieving Benefits through Change* (2nd ed.). Gower Publishing.

Brookes, N., & Clark, A. (2009). *Using Maturity Models to Improve Project Management Practice*. In Proceedings of the *20th Annual Conference - Production and Operations Management Society (POMS)*, Orlando, Florida, USA.

Caralli, R., Knight, M., & Montgomery, A. (2012). Maturity Models 101: A Primer for Applying Maturity Models to Smart Grid Security, Resilience, and Interoperability. CERT, Software Engineering Institute, Carnegie Mellon University. doi:10.21236/ADA610461

Carr, N. G. (2003). It doesn't matter. *Harvard Business Review*, *81*(5), 41–49. PMID:12747161

Chan, Y., & Reich, B. (2007). IT alignment: What have we learned? *Journal of Information Technology*, *22*(4), 297–315. doi:10.1057/palgrave.jit.2000109

Changchit, C., Joshi, K. D., & Lederer, A. L. (1998). Process and reality in information systems benefits analysis. *Information Systems Journal*, *8*(2), 145–162. doi:10.1046/j.1365-2575.1998.00031.x

Cleland, D. L., & Ireland, L. R. (2002). *Project Management: Strategic Design and Implementation* (4th ed.). McGraw-Hill.

Collins, A., & Baccarini, D. (2004). Project Success - A Survey. *Journal of Construction Research*, *5*(2), 211–231. doi:10.1142/S1609945104000152

Cooke-Davies, T. (2002). The "real" success factors on projects. *International Journal of Project Management*, *20*(3), 185–190. doi:10.1016/S0263-7863(01)00067-9

Cooke-Davies, T., Schlichter, J., & Bredillet, C. (2001). Beyond the PMBOK® guide. Paper presented at *Project Management Institute Annual Seminars & Symposium*. Newtown Square, PA: Project Management Institute.

Crawford, L. H. (2003). Assessing and Developing the Project Management Competence of Individuals. In J. R. Turner (Ed.), *People in Project Management*. Grower.

Crawford, L. H. (2005). Senior Management Perceptions of Project Management Competence. *International Journal of Project Management*, *23*(1), 7–16. doi:10.1016/j.ijproman.2004.06.005

Daniel, D. R. (1961). Management Information Crisis. *Harvard Business Review*, *39*(5), 111–116.

Devaraj, S., & Kohli, R. (2003). Performance Impacts of Information Technology: Is Actual Usage the Missing Link? *Management Science*, *49*(3), 273–289. doi:10.1287/mnsc.49.3.273.12736

Dvir, D., Lipovetskey, S., Shenhar, A., & Tishler, A. (1998). In search of project classification: A non-uniform mapping of project success factors. *Research Policy*, *27*(9), 915–935. doi:10.1016/S0048-7333(98)00085-7

Freeman, M., & Beale, P. (1992). Measuring Project Success. *Project Management Journal*, *23*(1), 8–17.

Galliers, R. D., & Sutherland, A. R. (2008). Information systems management and strategy formulation; the stages of growth' model revisited. *Information Systems Journal*, *1*(2), 89–114. doi:10.1111/j.1365-2575.1991.tb00030.x

Gomes, J., & Romão, M. (2012). How benefits management helps Balanced Scorecard to deal with business dynamic environments. *Tourism & Management Studies*, *9*(1), 129–138. https://www.tmstudies.net/index.php/ectms/article/view/558

Gomes, J., & Romão, M. (2014). Advantages and Limitations of Performance Measurement Tools: The Balanced Scorecard. In *Proceedings of the 7th IADIS International Conference (IS 2014)*, Madrid, Spain.

Gomes, J., & Romão, M. (2015). *Maturity, Benefits and Project Management shaping Project Success*. Springer. doi:10.1007/978-3-319-16486-1_43

Gomes, J., & Romão, M. (2017). Aligning Information Systems and Technology with Benefit Management and Balanced Scorecard. In S. De Haes & W. Van Grembergen (Eds.), *Strategic IT Governance and Alignment in Business Settings* (pp. 112–131). IGI Global. doi:10.4018/978-1-5225-0861-8.ch005

Gomes, J., Romão, M., & Caldeira, M. (2013). *Linking Benefits to Maturity Models*. In Proceedings of the 15th International Conference of Academy of Management and Business, ISEG, Lisboa.

Gomes, J., Romão, M., & Caldeira, M. (2013). The Benefits Management and Balanced Scorecard Strategy Map: How They Match. *International Journal of IT/Business Alignment and Governance*, *4*(1), 44–54. doi:10.4018/jitbag.2013010104

Grant, K. P., & Pennypacker, J. S. (2006). Project Management Maturity: An assessment of Project Management Capabilities Among and between Selected Industries. *IEEE Transactions on Engineering Management, 53*(1), 59–68. doi:10.1109/TEM.2005.861802

Hillson, D. (2003). *Effective Opportunity Management for Projects.* Marcel Decker. doi:10.1201/9780203913246

Ibbs, C. W., & Kwak, Y. H. (2000). Assessing project management maturity. *Project Management Journal, 31*(1), 32–43. doi:10.1177/875697280003100106

Jia, G., Chen, Y., Xue, X., Chen, J., Cao, J., & Tang, K. (2011). Program management organization maturity integrated model for mega construction programs in China. *International Journal of Project Management, 29*(7), 834–845. doi:10.1016/j.ijproman.2011.03.003

Jorgenson, D. W., & Stiroh, K. J. (2000). Raising the speed limit: US economic growth in the information age. In Jorgenson (eds) Economic growth in the information age, 1-146, Cambridge, Massachusetts: MIT Press

Judgev, K., & Müller, R. (2005). A Retrospective Look at our Evolving Understanding of Project Success. *Project Management Journal, 36*(4), 19–31. doi:10.1177/875697280503600403

Jugdev, K., & Thomas, J. (2002). Project management maturity models: The silver bullets of competitive advantage? *Project Management Journal, 33*(4), 4–14. doi:10.1177/875697280203300402

Kaplan, R. S., & Norton, D. P. (1996). *The Balanced Scorecard: Translating Strategy into Action.* Harvard Business School Press.

Kerzner, H. (2001). *Applied Project Management: Best Practices on Implementation.* John Wiley & Sons, Inc.

Kerzner, H. (2019). *Using the Project Management Maturity Model: Strategic Planning for Project Management* (3rd ed.). John Wiley and Sons.

Kerzner, H. (2022). *Project Management: a systems approach to planning, scheduling and controlling* (13th ed.). John Wiley and Sons.

Koi-Akrofi, G. (2020). Justification of, and benefits realization beyond IT investments: Analysis from literature. *International Journal of Managing Value and Supply Chains, 11*(3), 1–16. doi:10.5121/ijmvsc.2020.11301

Kuruppuarachchi, P., Mandal, P., & Smith, R. (2002). IT project implementation strategies for effective changes: A critical review. *Logistics Information Management, 15*(2), 126–137. doi:10.1108/09576050210414006

Kwak, Y. H., & Ibbs, C. W. (2002). Project management process maturity $(PM)^2$ model. *Journal of Management Engineering, 18*(3), 150–155. doi:10.1061/(ASCE)0742-597X(2002)18:3(150)

Lee, B., & Barua, A. (1999). An integrated assessment of productivity and efficiency impacts of information technology investments: Old data, new analysis and evidence. *Journal of Productivity Analysis, 121*(1), 21–43. doi:10.1023/A:1007898906629

Lee, L. S., & Anderson, R. M. (2006, Fall). An Exploratory investigation of the Antecedents of the IT Project Management Capability. *e-Service Journal*, *5*(1), 27–42. doi:10.2979/esj.2006.5.1.27

Lim, C. S., & Mohamed, M. Z. (1999). Criteria of project success: An explanatory re-examination. *International Journal of Project Management*, *17*(4), 243–248. doi:10.1016/S0263-7863(98)00040-4

Lin, K., Lin, C., & Tsao, H. (2005). IS/IT Investment Evaluation and Benefit Realization Practices in Taiwanese SMEs. *Journal of Information Science and Technology*, *2*(4), 44–71. http://hdl.handle.net/20.500.11937/38113

Locatelli, G., Mariani, G., Sainati, T., & Greco, M. (2017). Corruption in public projects and megaprojects: There is an elephant in the room! *International Journal of Project Management*, *35*(3), 252–268. doi:10.1016/j.ijproman.2016.09.010

Lueg, R., & Lu, S. (2012). Improving efficiency in budgeting: An interventionist approach to spreadsheet accuracy testing. *Problems and Perspectives in Management*, *10*, 32–41. https://ssrn.com/abstract=2156164

Lueg, R., & Lu, S. (2013). How to improve efficiency in budgeting: The case of business intelligence in SMEs. *European Journal of Management*, *13*(2), 109–120. https://ssrn.com/abstract=2463828. doi:10.18374/EJM-13-2.13

Lyer, K. C., & Jha, K. N. (2005). Factors affecting cost performance: Evidence from Indian Construction Projects. *International Journal of Project Management*, *22*(4), 283–295. doi:10.1016/j.ijproman.2004.10.003

Madeira, B., Gomes, J., & Romão, M. (2017). Applying Benefits Management to the Implementation of a Copy Point: A Case Study. *International Journal of Strategic Decision Sciences*, *8*(1), 13–26. doi:10.4018/IJSDS.2017010102

Melville, N., Kraemer, K. L., & Gurbaxani, V. (2004). Information Technology and Organizational Performance: An Integrative Model of IT Business Value. *Management Information Systems Quarterly*, *28*(2), 283–321. doi:10.2307/25148636

Meredith, J., & Mantel, S. J. (2009). *Project Management: A managerial approach* (7th ed.). John Wiley and Sons, Inc.

Mettler, T., & Rohner, P. (2009). Situational Maturity Models as Instrumental Artifacts for Organizational Design. In Proceedings of the *4th International Conference on Design Science Research in Information Systems and Technology (DESRIST'09),* Malvern, PA, USA. 10.1145/1555619.1555649

Mithas, S., Tafti, A., Bardhan, T., & Goh, J. M. (2012). Information Technology and Firm Profitability: Mechanisms and Empirical Evidence. *Management Information Systems Quarterly*, *36*(1), 205–224. doi:10.2307/41410414

Mullaly, M. (2006). Longitudinal Analysis of Project Management Maturity. *Project Management Journal*, *36*(3), 62–73. doi:10.1177/875697280603700307

Nokes, S. (2007). *The Definitive Guide to Project Management: The Fast Track to Getting the Job Done on Time and on Budget* (2nd ed.). Pearson Education Limited.

Peppard, J., Ward, J., & Daniel, E. (2008). Managing the realization of business benefits from IT investments. *MIS Quarterly Executive*, *6*(1), 15–25. https://aisel.aisnet.org/misqe/vol6/iss1/3

Piwowar-Sulej, K. (2021). Organizational culture and project management methodology: Research in the financial industry. *International Journal of Managing Projects in Business*, *14*(6), 1270–1289. doi:10.1108/IJMPB-08-2020-0252

Pollack, J. (2017). Change management as an organizational project capability. In Sankaran, S., Müller, R., Drouin, N. (eds.) Cambridge Handbook of Organizazonal Project Management. Cambridge University Press. doi:10.1017/9781316662243.021

Pullen, W. (2007). A public-sector HPT maturity model. *Performance Improvement*, *46*(4), 9–15. doi:10.1002/pfi.119

Reymenyi, D., Sherwood-Smith, M., & White, T. (1997). *Achieving Maximum Values from Information Systems: A Process Approach*. John Wiley & Sons.

Sadatsafavi, H., & Walweski, J. (2011). Study of organizational change management in project-driven organizations using maturity models. Paper presented at *PMI® Global Congress 2011—North America*. Newtown Square, PA: Project Management Institute

Shenhar, A. J., Levy, O., & Dvir, D. (1997). Mapping the dimensions of project success. *Project Management Journal*, *28*(2), 5–13.

Skulmoski, G. (2001). Project maturity and competence interface. *Cost Engineering (Morgantown, W. Va.)*, *43*(6), 11–18.

Sliż, P. (2018). Concept of the organization process maturity assessment. *Journal of Economics and Management, 33*(3). . oi:10.22367/jem.2018.33.05

Sowden, R. (2010). *OGC´s Portfolio, Programme and Project Management Maturity Model (P3M3): Introduction Guide to P3M3*. AXELOS Limited.

Strassmann, P. (1997). Will big spending on computers guarantee profitability? Maybe. But maybe not. In Paul Strassmann's book The Squandered Computer. Datamation-Highlands Ranch.

Suikki, R., Tromsted, R., & Haapasalo, H. (2002). Project management competence development framework in turbulent business environment. *Tecnovation*, 1-16. doi:10.1016/j.technovation.2004.11.003

Sydow, J., & Staber, U. (2002). The Institutional Embeddedness of Project Networks: The Case of Content Production in German Television. *Regional Studies*, *36*(3), 215–227. doi:10.1080/00343400220122034

Taderdoost, H., & Keshavarzsaleh, A. (2016). *Critical Factors that lead to Projects' Success/Failure in Global Marketplace*. In Proceedings of the 9th International Conference Interdisciplanary in Engineering (INTER-ENG 2015), Tirgu-Mures, Romania.

Turner, J. R. (2008). *The Handbook of Project-Based Management: Leading Strategic Chance in Organisations* (3rd ed.). McGraw-Hill.

Turner, J. R., & Müller, R. (2005). The Project Manager's Leadership Style as a Success Factor on Projects: Literature Review. *Project Management Journal*, *36*(1), 46–61. doi:10.1177/875697280503600206

Volden, G., & Welde, M. (2022). Public project success? Measuring the nuances of success through ex post evaluation. *International Journal of Project Management*, *40*(6), 703–714. doi:10.1016/j.ijproman.2022.06.006

Ward, J., & Daniel, E. (2006). *Benefits Management - Delivering Value from IS & IT Investments*. John Wiley and Sons Ltd.

Ward, J., & Elvin, R. (1999). A New Framework for Managing IT-enabled Business Change. *Information Systems Journal*, *9*(3), 197–222. doi:10.1046/j.1365-2575.1999.00059.x

Ward, J., & Griffiths, P. (1996). *Strategic Planning for Information Systems* (2nd ed.). John Wiley.

Ward, J., Hertogh, S. D., & Viaene, S. (2007). *Managing Benefits from IS/IT Investments: An Empirical Investigation into Current Practice. Proceedings of 40th Hawaii International Conference on Information Systems*, Waikoloa, Big Island, HI, USA. 10.1109/HICSS.2007.330

Ward, J., Taylor, P., & Bond, P. (1996). Evaluation and Realization of IS/IT Benefits: An Empirical Study of Current Practice. *European Journal of Information Systems*, *4*(4), 214–225. doi:10.1057/ejis.1996.3

Wateridge, J. (1995). IT projects: A basis for success. *International Journal of Project Management*, *13*(3), 169–172. doi:10.1016/0263-7863(95)00020-Q

Willcocks, L., & Lester, S. (1999). Information Technology: Transformer or Sink Hole. In L. Willcocks & S. Lester (Eds.), *Beyond the IT Productivity Paradox*. John Wiley and Sons Ltd.

Yu, A. G., Fleett, P. D., & Bowers, J. A. (2005). Developing a value-cantered proposal for assessing project success. *International Journal of Project Management*, *23*(6), 428–436. doi:10.1016/j.ijproman.2005.01.008

Chapter 4
Comparing Public Support for Two Indonesian Employment Policy Reforms in a Time of COVID-19:
Sentiment and Emotion Analysis of Tweets

Tauchid Komara Yuda
Department of Social Development and Welfare, Universitas Gadjah Mada, Indonesia

Fadhli Zul Fauzi
https://orcid.org/0000-0002-0156-6538
Department of Applied Indonesian Politics, Faculty of Politics and Governance, Institut Pemerintahan Dalam Negeri, Indonesia

ABSTRACT

The pandemic-induced disruption has created a critical juncture at which the opportunity to experiment with new policy trajectories has widened. Yet, how much public support is there for such an experiment? This chapter addresses this question by studying the Activation (Prakerja) and unemployment protection (Jaminan Kehilangan Pekerjaan, JKP) policies, which served as essential policy responses during the COVID-19 crisis in Indonesia. In this study, the authors analysed 47,916 tweets containing public debates that took place up to three months after the policies' inception. Having performed a set of analyses on sentiments, emotions, and most appealing tweets, the authors argue that different forms of support for Prakerja and JKP emerged not because of the policies' breakthrough traits, but due to citizens' pragmatic-cognitive logic shaped by the urgency and severity of the COVID-19 crisis. It makes the idea of state-centred welfare responsibility (something Prakerja possesses) more desirable than contribution-based insurance, which JKP offers. Discussing the Indonesian case fills in the existing research gap as it facilitates a better understanding of the political legitimacy of welfare state policy institutionalization in developing countries during the COVID-19 catastrophe.

DOI: 10.4018/979-8-3693-1742-6.ch004

INTRODUCTION

The first of COVID-19 in Indonesia was reported on March 2, 2020. Within a month, nearly 1,800 cases and 117 deaths were confirmed across 32 districts, impacting many economic sectors and and causing many businesses to shut down (Fealy, 2020). These intertwined factors led to layoffs and those affected could not afford to seek any other jobs except for very few employment opportunities. Central Statistics Agency (BPS) reported that the number of unemployed increased by 4.59% in the first wave of the pandemic, with the open unemployment rate increased by 7% compared to 2019.

In the face of mass job cuts during periods of lockdowns, the Indonesian government experimented with a radical approach to employment protection through the Active Labour Market Policy (Prakerja) and Unemployment Protection (*Jaminan Kehilangan Pekerjaan*, JKP), two policy initiatives in focus in this article. In addition, it is worth considering that JKP was the first unemployment protection introduced to the formal sector, which is antithetical to the country's productivist welfare character (Yuda & Kühner, 2022). Meanwhile, Prakerja is an activation policy, which grants cash transfers and a wide range of online job training tailored to the 4.0 industries. Prakerja draws its conceptualization from Balai Latihan Kerja (BLK), a state-driven agency that was mandated with providing job training for low-educated individuals and channelling them to manufacturing industries.

Within academic debates, Prakerja and JKP represent a rare instance of policy dynamics, as they are presenting a 'punctuation process' resembling a path-clearing policy accelerator (Prakerja) and path-creation accelerator (JKP) (see Hogan et al., 2022; Yuda & Qomariyah, 2022). These processes, however, are different from those observed in the OECD countries/welfare states in producing responses to COVID-19, which is characterized by path dependence (Béland et al., 2021; Cantillon et al., 2021; Greve et al., 2021; Hick & Murphy, 2021; Moreira & Hick, 2021; Soon et al., 2021). Based on observations in papers that discussed policy responses to the pandemic, that there is little evidence to suggest that path-breaking changes have been made during the crisis. Policy adaptation is, instead, preferred. The choice to adapt policies can be understood by looking at the fact that these regions are progressively influenced by the global economy, hence national governments could not commit too much to radical changes that would potentially bring about risks to market stability (Yuda et al., 2022).

So far, the studied public support towards social policy during the pandemic supports that argument. As summarized by Ebingghaus et al. (2022), support for welfare in welfare states has not shown any significant variations, except for a few cases in which current preference levels are higher, but only in the short term. The favourable attitude is related to perceptions of vulnerability induced by the first wave of the COVID-19 outbreak, which in turn influences attitudes towards increased support for government intervention (Ares et al., 2021). On the other hand, a stable or slight decline in support (Jørgensen et al., 2021), as clearly found in the Netherlands (Reeskens et al., 2021), is associated with concerns about tax increases. However, the argumentation of these studies needs to be examined in different settings, such as the rare case of Prakerja and JKP, which the current article explores.

Experimental trials with activation and unemployment protection, however, have become the subject of most heavily-criticized social policies but have also been the most persistently favoured—they even became trending topics on Twitter during the pandemic. In particular, criticism was aroused due to the assumption that two policies were merely instrumental in concealing the true nature of the massive labour market deregulation plans the Jokowi administration had been proposing since 2014 to attract more foreign investment to the country (cf. Yuda, forthcoming). As Prakerja and JKP have received increasing attention in public debates and among policymakers, a deeper understanding of public support for these policies has many merits in terms of understanding the character of Indonesians' welfare attitudes in times of crisis.

From the research literature, there has been a little amount of attention paid to the welfare attitudes beyond OECD/European welfare states (e.g. Amoah, 2020, Ng, 2015; Cheng & Ngok, 2020; Kühner & Chou, 2020; Yuda, 2020; Yeh & Ku, 2021 etc.), but understanding support for social policy in a time of COVID-19 cannot be simply extrapolated from this body of literature. Prakerja and JKP are introduced as alternatives for the current pandemic policy response, but the general ideas of such policies are relatively new, which means that people do not have much experience with them and perhaps know little about their potential consequences. Expounding public support towards JKP and Prakerja, therefore, will make a substantive contribution to a better understanding of the political legitimacy of welfare state policy institutionalization that is not limited to Indonesia, but developing countries in general.

In this study, data on public support towards two policies under examination are mined from Twitter, a microblogging social media platform that facilitates two-way communication through the exchange of thoughts, ideas, information, and opinions in 280 characters. The importance of Twitter lies in the likelihood that many individuals tend to share their opinions and experiences on this platform during lockdown conditions. This claim is supported by studies that have also revealed that COVID-19-related issues have gained a great deal of attention on Twitter (Goel & Sharma, 2021). The same trend was observed in Indonesia although Twitter is less popular than Facebook. However, Twitter offers greater access to data for this study than Facebook, which has recently restricted third-party data extraction following the Cambridge Analytica case (Osborne & Parkinson, 2018). In addition, Twitter has also compressed the typing space for netizens. Tweets convey the essence of the message and deliver the necessary information in real time as quickly as possible (Goel & Sharma, 2021).Thus, mining data from Twitter, with a focus on the exploration of sentiment and emotion analysis of tweets, is advantageous for studying social policy legitimation.

The article proceeds by briefly explaining Prakerja and JKP, two distinct policy punctuation models which attracted public attention during the COVID-19 pandemic. After that, this article goes into detail about methods—including the benefits and limitations of sentiment and emotion analysis as a method of capturing welfare attitudes, procedure and process for collecting data, and the data analysis. This paper then continues to the results, brief examination of public attitudes towards respective policies, and to discussion. The final section summarizes the findings and discusses them with a snapshot of theoretical and policy implications.

PRAKERJA AND JKP: INSTITUTIONAL DYNAMICS AND CONTROVERSIES

Periods of uncertainty and instability arising from the COVID-19 outbreak have imposed path-changing disruption to existing policy trajectories (Hogan, et.al., 2022; Kusumasari et.al., 2022). Previously, employment protection and benefits were stuck—compared with other policies domain such as health insurance and cash transfer programs (Aspinall, 2014; Yuda & Pholpark, 2022; Sutiyo, 2022)—but now are engaged in yet another round of reform following the implementation of employment activation policy (Prakerja) and unemployment benefits (JKP) for the first time.

As discussed in the introduction section, Indonesian employment policy responses to crises adopt an approach different from premises related to path dependency in existing literature. It is fairly typical for path dependency to view crises such as COVID-19 as forces that drive policy change, and serve as stabilizing mode without challenging the core institutions of welfare capitalism (Wilsford, 1994; Mahoney & Thelen, 2010; Pierson, 2000; Howlett & Cashore, 2009). Consequently, their arguments centre on the premise that COVID-19 is an exogenous attack to which *policy routines* must respond, as extensively documented in established welfare state countries (Béland et al., 2021; Cantillon et al., 2021; Greve et al., 2021; Hick & Murphy, 2021; Moreira & Hick, 2021; Soon et al., 2021). However, the different accounts outlined in Prakerja and JKP make them representatives of two alternative policy processes; Prakerja represents a *path-clearing policy accelerator* (Hogan et al., 2022), while JKP is a *path-creation accelerator* (Yuda & Qomariyah, 2022).

Path-clearing policy accelerators demonstrate the significance of COVID-19 as an event that has removed administrative and political barriers, at least temporarily, but allowing policymakers to speed up the sequence of events along the pathway (Hogan et al., 2022). Under this premise, policy responses to COVID-19 must be viewed as part of an ongoing reform plan rather than necessarily as a continuation of existing practices (Yuda et al., 2022). In a slightly different manner from path-clearing accelerators, path-creation accelerators view COVID-19 as an opportunity to accelerate the adoption of new policy ideas through the permissive opportunity provided by shocks. In this sense, policy responses to COVID-19, are presented as a new program (Yuda & Qomariyyah, 2022), for which JKP is representative of the path-creation accelerator premise.

The pandemic operating mainly as a path-clearing policy accelerator is evident in Prakerja announced on 20 April 2020. It collectively takes the ideas of activation policies which promote work and protect labour by encouraging and requiring beneficiaries to find paid employment (Ingold & Stuart, 2015; Jordan, 2018; Skjold & Lundberg, 2022). It has been a topic of parliamentary discussion since 2016, and President Joko Widodo reiterated it during the 2019 campaign, but it had not been implemented (Yuda & Rezza, 2021).

In its grand vision design, Prakerja was designed to support the medium-term economic policies as a measure to increase the number of entrepreneurs in Indonesia to 4% by 2030. More broadly, this activation policy is in line with the ongoing economic liberalization process that began in the late 1990s (London, 2018).

The cornerstone of Prakerja was the creation of the *Balai Latihan Kerja* (BLK) in 1953 to provide low-skilled and unemployed workers with training programs that required direct skills in the furniture and manufacturing industries. Despite sharing many ideas with the BLK administration, Prakerja is not associated with it. Instead, it was developed as part of the labour ministry's activation policy.

In more detail terms, Prakerja consists of two features: a cash transfer (at US$250) and a variety of online job training aimed at improving the skills of the unemployed and those who were laid off during the pandemic. However, since its inception, Prakerja has drawn many criticisms in Indonesia. There have been no additional measures such as facilitation to match supply and demand, gathering of information about job vacancies and potential applicants for both employers and job seekers, as well as management and coordination of labor resources.

JKP, rolled out in February 2022, is an example of a path-creation accelerator. It is the first unemployment benefits in this country that would supercharge the safety net for those unemployed. In its current form, the JKP is implemented on the principle of social insurance and is managed by BP-Jamsostek, a single administrative body in charge of employment-related social insurance programs.

JKP, originally designed to address the impact of COVID-19 on employment, has now been institutionalized, signalling a potential leap in welfare regimes in the near future (Yuda et al., 2022; see also Yuda & Kühner, 2022). In particular, the program provided laid-off formal workers with limited benefits, equalling to 45% of their previous salary for the first three months and 25% for the following three months. To qualify for JKP benefits, employees must have contributed for at least 12 consecutive months to BP-Jamsostek and have paid the least premiums at least six consecutive months before they were let go. In cooperation with the ministry of labour, recently, JKP is integrated into voluntary work-training programs that allow beneficiaries to return to work.

Taken collectively, the nature of changes of Prakerja and JKP as policy responses tend to be political and administrative in character rather than directly related to the substance of policies (Ramia & Perrone, 2021). Many argue that both policies, especially JKP, has been used as a tool to soften the blow of criticism towards the gradually implemented grand scenario of labour market flexibility. This labour market flexibility would affect the minimum wage and contract workers, as well as reduce severance costs—all of which could negatively affect workers and lead to job insecurity. Those in favour of Prakerja and JKP, on the other hand, claim that the implementation of these two policy was timely to help mitigate the job cuts as well as provide social safety nets for the unemployed in times of uncertainty. Here, we can see that changes in structures of risks have provided cognitive manipulation among the citizens for supporting the JKP and Prakerja (cf. Yuda, *forthcoming*).

Overall, the presence of Prakerja and JKP has a particularly strong divisive effect on netizens. This is obvious in the increasingly sharp rift between political spectrums in many districts. Such divisions reduce the chances of promoting the expansion of COVID-19 social risk policies (Choi et.al., 2022), particularly, because conceptualization of COVID-19 risks is subject to the different views.

In light of the persistent controversy, it is extremely relevant to study further the public support for Prakerja and JKP in order to understand citizens' preferences and demands on the welfare state idea directions (Taylor-Gooby & Leruth, 2018).

Researching Welfare Attitude Using Sentiment and Emotion Analysis: Advantages and Limitations

Over the past few decades, attitudes have become an increasingly prominent component of social policy studies—usually discussed in studies concerning public support for welfare state provisions—and their analysis involves numerous methods (Arts & Gelissen, 2001; Blekesaune & Quadagno, 2003; Muuri, 2010; Taylor-Gooby & Leruth, 2018). Welfare attitudes are multidimensional, covering a wide range of perceptions, such as funding, government responsibility, redistribution preferences, and benefits and satisfaction (Taylor-Gooby et al., 2019). Moreover, a study on welfare attitudes primarily helps us to assess support for the current policy or system—including trust in government—as well as extend it to describe different characteristics of welfare regimes from the welfare attitude dimension (Amoah, 2020; Yuda, 2021; Valarino et al., 2018). However, the evidence from the Global South, such as Indonesia, is meagre and indicates the need for further research, particularly concerning COVID-19.

One drawback of the studies on attitudes towards social policy has been the lack of an explicit focus on sentiment and emotion analysis, which might be challenging to identify with existing research tools. This is because much research focuses on clear and quantifiable aspects, such as people's support for welfare state goals, which is paired with the two major hypotheses shaping attitudes: self-interest and welfare ideologies.

More specifically, the self-interest approach argues that beneficiaries of welfare reforms who perceive themselves as vulnerable will support the reforms compared with those in privileged positions. Meanwhile, in the welfare ideology theory, it is assumed that individual ideological preferences have resulted in different stances to support particular welfare settings. Comparative social policy literature has identified three dominant welfare ideologies influencing individual attitudes. First, social democracy emphasizes equality and promotes redistribution and universalism. Second, the conservative ideology categorizes the welfare of individuals based on their corporate/occupational divisions of labour and their status. Third, the liberal ideology advocates equality of opportunity and the idea that each individual is responsible for their well-being (Blekesaune & Quadagno, 2003; Muuri, 2010; Taylor-Gooby & Leruth, 2018). Finally, in East Asian contexts, a fourth welfare ideology is incorporated, namely familism, which concerns the importance of intergenerational solidarity and filial devotion (Kühner & Chou, 2020). Meanwhile, Indonesia, which is leaning towards universalism as found in healthcare research, is associated with common Abrahamic teachings, especially Islamic teachings (Yuda, 2020).

The advantage of researching welfare attitudes using sentiment and emotion analysis is outlined. On social media, people freely express their feelings, arguments, and opinions on a wide range of topics, including employment policy dynamics that this study addresses. Such big data, once analysed, may help researchers better understand the participants' stance towards Prakerja and JKP at a low cost and with a larger sample size than regular research.

In addition, sentiment analysis and emotion identification for this research also have a great potential to document depictions of people's attitudes (including emotion detection) in real time during and after implementation of the two policies, which may be difficult to capture using a standard research strategy. The real-time feature of the study of welfare attitudes in this research is an essential component since it allows us to offer data that represents public opinions relevant to crisis situations. Such opinions have not been adequately explored in existing research on welfare attitudes. More extensive benefits include people's active feedback, which is not limited to citizen satisfaction and monitoring program legitimacy but is also related to their trust in the government, which is discussed in the final section of this article.

Despite this strategy's exceptional features, it lacks the ability to identify whether ideologies, familial relationships, self-interest, and religious beliefs affect netizens' political support towards the programs. This limitation arises as detailed information related to individual identity is restricted for privacy.

Similarly, this strategy is subject to the same limitations as regular surveys, including the possibility that an individual's sentiment and emotion towards policies may be influenced by one or more indirect causes. For instance, it is possible that a person is experiencing a difficult time and tweets a negative comment on a subject on which they normally express neutrality. To overcome this drawback, we mined a large and relevant sample covering 35,223 tweets for Prakerja and 12,693 tweets for JKP. With a large sample size, outliers became harder to spot.

Another drawback is sentiment and emotion very likely changes over time according to a person's mood, world events, and so forth. The study, therefore, considers a specific time for data mining to coincide with the timing of implementation and the intensity of news reporting on the policy in order to minimize this drawback. This will be discussed in detail in the next section.

METHODS

Data Collection and Data Cleaning Process

Materials for analyzing sentiment and emotion data towards JKP and Prakerja are generated from Twitter. It is based on the results of previous studies which found that social media is a widely used platform among Indonesian people, including both youth and adults. Government policies and performance often become headlines in existing discussions on social media (Nurmandi et al., 2018; Safitri et al., 2021). Indonesia has one of the most active Twitter user bases with over 29 million users (with a gender ratio of around 53% male and 47% female), and this platform has become an effective medium for discussing government policies or activities (Kusumasari et al., 2023; Machmud et al., 2024). Social media is currently identified as a platform that young people often use; however, Twitter is a medium that adults also use to have conversations and comment on problems around them (almost 40% of Twitter users in Indonesia are aged 25 to 34 years). Moreover, in the context of Indonesia, government officials or members often use Twitter as a medium for socialization and communication in every government activity (Kamaludin & Nurmandi, 2022; Rasyid et al., 2021). The various economic backgrounds of Twitter users are the reason why Twitter is often used as a communication medium by the government and society in general (Safitri et al., 2021). The intense communication carried out on this platform regarding government policies and programs in Indonesia then became a strong basis for its use in this research.

To generate the Twitter data we then used Tweepy, a Python library that allows us to collect large volumes of conversation data from social media platforms. A number of other similar studies have also utilized this application and generated the desired data quality (for instance, Goel & Sharma, 2021; Lacatus & Meibauer, 2022)..

With the help of Tweepy, researchers can view and track basic metrics regarding public tweets in real time from Twitter (Goel & Sharma, 2021). This advantage in turn allows us to observe reactions and patterns in public conversations and debates regarding the two policies under investigation (Binsar & Mauritsius, 2020; Rasyid et al., 2021).

It is important to note that access to Tweepy requires additional procedures, namely submitting a request to the developer for academic purposes. The developer then provides the Twitter streaming application programming interface (API) key and bearer token required for data pre-processing.

Conversation data was collected for Prakerja from 2020-03-11 to 2020-06-15 and for JKP from 2021-12-01 to 2022-03-31—the periods in which controversial policy reforms were continuously discussed on various social media platforms, especially Twitter. These processes were facilitated using pre-defined keywords, such as "*prakerja* (pre-employment)", "*pelatihan online* (online training)" and, "*pelatihan kerja* (job training)" for the **Prakerja data**, and "*jaminan kehilangan kerja* (job loss guarantee)", "*Jaminan Kehilangan Pekerjaan* (Unemployment Benefits, JKP)", "*PHK/pemutusan hubungan kerja* (termination of employment)" for **JKP data**.

In total, 47,916 tweets were collected from those processes, with 12,693 tweets for JKP and 35,223 tweets for Prakerja. In accordance with standard procedures, the data collected was then stored in the JSON format to facilitate parsing and analysis and then cleaned in order to remove some forms of data that were not necessary for the research analysis.

Adopting the same procedure commonly used by studies using similar strategies (see Goel & Sharma, 2021 for an overview), we pre-processed the stored tweet dataset. All tweets were subjected to lowercase and URLs were removed since they had no useful content. Emojis, emoticons, numbers, mentions (@), and hashtags (#) were excluded from tweets because of their specific semantics in tweets and overall text. To understand a tweet's context, all slang text was converted to its true meaning.

Sentiment and Emotion Analysis

This article uses sentiment and emotion analysis to identify public support towards the investigated policies. Literature defines sentiment analysis as extracting meaningful information and semantics from text using natural processing techniques to determine the public or individual attitude (Nandwani & Verma, 2021; Kothari et al., 2021; Ortiz & Oubiña, 2021).

The analysis process in this study began with identifying polarity and categorizing opinionated texts in Twitter using the Narrative Fiction Corpus (NFC), a sub-feature of the Rstudio application that can analyse a collection of literary texts annotated with information about their structure and content, such as characters and themes. With NFC, researchers can also build computational models for analysing and comprehending the narrative elements of a text. It is an excellent tool for researchers interested in the structure and meaning of literary texts.

In the present study, we analysed the collected dataset about JKP and Prakerja by using two suggested and identical steps (Goel & Sharma, 2021; Nandwani & Verma, 2021). The first was sentiment analysis, which was expressed through positive and negative signals. However, sentiment analysis can only indicate levels of support, lacking the depth of information to draw meaningful conclusions. To address this issue, emotion analysis was conducted as the second step. The analysis displayed a variety of emotions, such as “anger”, “fear”, “sadness”, “trust”, “disgust”, “anticipation”, “surprise” and “enjoyment” (further explanation in Table 1). Each collected conversation was distilled into a collection of words and categorized according to the sentiments and emotions associated with each phrase (Lain, 2019; Raj & Balachandran, 2020). This is presented in the figure 1, which we will see in the findings section.

The third strategy, which served as complementary step for this study, was performing an analysis of the dominant emotions displayed in the number of likes, retweets, quoted tweets, and replies (comments) on certain opinions. These elements, especially the content of opinions, are an essential metric to pay attention to on social media as it provides a better indicator of public engagement.

The last but not least is pattern matching and explanation building. Informed by the sentiment and emotion analysis, and supplemented by the most attentive tweets, we continually refined the commonalities and variations across cases to develop an analytically generalizable logical framework.

RESULTS

Attitudes Towards Prakerja

This section presents results on the different data processing analyses. Figure 1 provides the results of the sentiment analysis about Prakerja, which shows that the majority of tweets express positive sentiments towards the examined policy. The results of this study support the claim that concerns about insecurity are increasingly important in shaping welfare support and may be of considerable relevance as far as income replacement is concerned.

However, as indicated above, studies contend that sentiment analysis can only reveal people's level of support because there is insufficient information to capture deeper dynamics of expressions in order

Table 1. Interpretation of emotions representing public reactions to examined policies

Emotion	Original Meaning	Contextualised meaning
Trust	A set of values, beliefs, or experiences that foster a sense of belonging	A sense of satisfaction with a government policy, either at the decision-making stage or during its implementation
Anger	Disappointment or resentment caused by deliberately negative behavior	Disappointment or resentment toward a policy
Fear	The feeling of being threatened or persecuted	Pessimistic expectations about the possible outcomes of a policy, or the belief that the said policy will bring adverse effects to beneficiaries
Sadness	Symptoms of emotional states that include disappointment, grief, and hopelessness	Grieving and feeling hopeless when they see the negative effects of a policy on others (or themselves)
Anticipation	Feeling of anxious suspense when unsure whether the outcome of a particular event will occur as expected	Feeling of anxious suspense when unsure whether the outcome of an implemented policy will play out as expected
Enjoyment	An individual's happiness, satisfaction, and compatibility with an event or other people's response to what they expected	An individual's sense of happiness, satisfaction, and compatibility with the expected policy outcome
Disgust	An intense emotion that causes a feeling of repulsion	A sense of exclusion/alienation from a policy's benefits, leading to a lack of interest in policymakers or regimes
Surprise	A positive or negative emotional state after an unexpected event	Astonishment at the existing policy in a positive or negative manner, indicating neutrality

Source: Plutchik, 2003 (modified). We modified the figure by updating some features based on current updates on Twitter analysis.

to indicate meaningful attitudes and achieve general understanding. To address this issue, a subsequent test was performed on shared tweets with some different emotions is to help us disentangle sentiment results. The results, as displayed in Figure 2, are dominated "trust" emotions. Consistent with the sentiment analysis results, this finding indicates the level of satisfaction with Prakerja among the general public. In addition, the "trust" dominance also implies that the public has the assumption that the activation program—which provides cash benefits with online job training attendance as a requirement—is an expected policy response in the first round of the COVID-19 outbreak in Indonesia.

However, other negative-oriented emotions, particularly "anger" and "sadness", also demand attention as they demonstrate general disappointment reaction to important issues concerning policy content.

Our further exploration of the most appealing tweets found that criticisms towards Prakerja were not directed at its policy feature. They were made to the appointed partner startup company to run the Prakerja program, as expressed by the following most retweeted and liked tweets (Table 2).

Several criticisms were made regarding the government's alleged scheme to benefit a companies that facilitate online training; the company is owned by some high-level officials. Furthermore, the large profits achieved by some of these companies have also been highlighted by the tweets, showing a sense of cynicism because the majority of society was experiencing a drastic decline in their earnings. This demonstrates the *importance of the equality frame* in the distribution of Prakerja. Given the result, there is an opportunity to respond to public criticism to minimize negative attitudes that may erode the legitimacy of the program while paying attention to the feelings of "fear", "disgust", "anticipation" "and surprise". Negative-coded emotions have potential to be altered through sufficient improvement in policy, resulting in a more positive outlook.

Figure 1. Public sentiment toward Prakerja

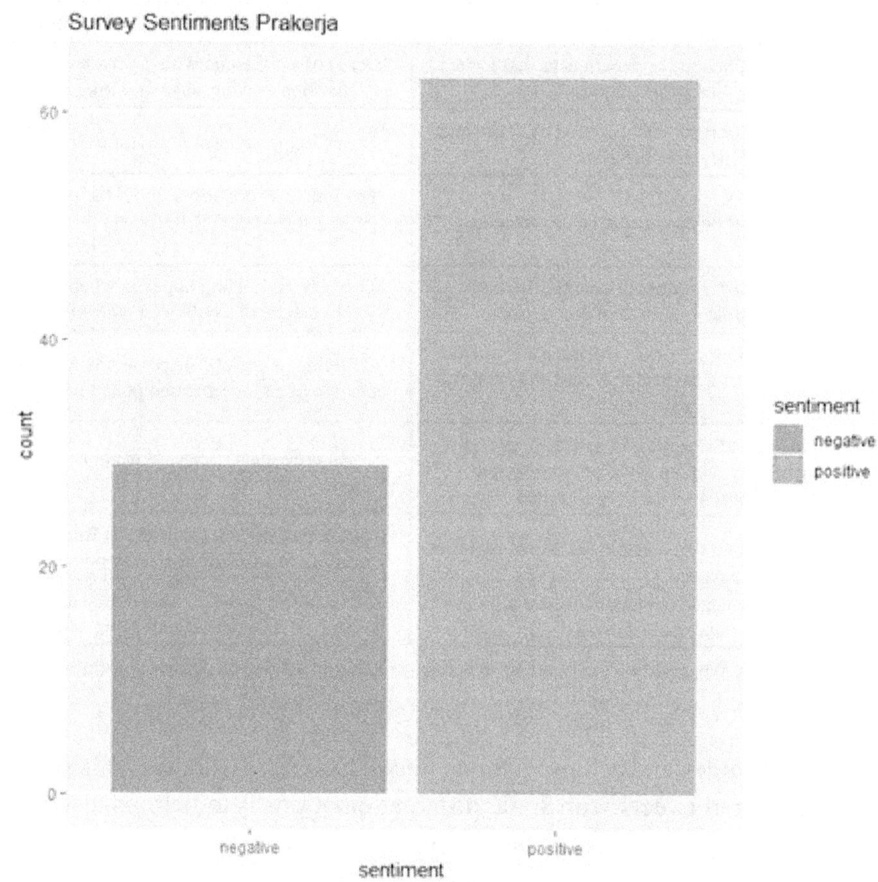

Attitudes Towards JKP

JKP showed a different trend than what was observed in the Prakerja, though it was received favourably. This is chiefly because the negative sentiments towards supporting JKP are somewhat higher than that for Prakerja (Figure 3), indicating that societal support for JKP is intensely divided.

However, when digging deeper into emotional responses, we found the results to be inconsistent with those of the sentiment analysis (Figure 4). The main reason is that ominously oriented expressions, such as "fear", "sadness" and "anger" show a dominant trend, while "trust" is little found in the tweets. As informed by Table 1, these three emotions confirm that JKP, based on the social-insurance model, was associated with weaker public support due to perceived dissatisfaction over the benefits and low expectations of the program in the long run.

To gain further understanding of this result, we identified most retweeted and liked tweets. The quoted tweet below (Table 3) indicates that this policy is viable for this country given the massive layoffs, but the timing of its introduction makes it unfeasible.

Taken collectively, these results imply that contributory-based initiatives in uncertain times have not fully received public support compared with non-contributory schemes. The latter received more sup-

Figure 2. Emotion analysis toward Prakerja

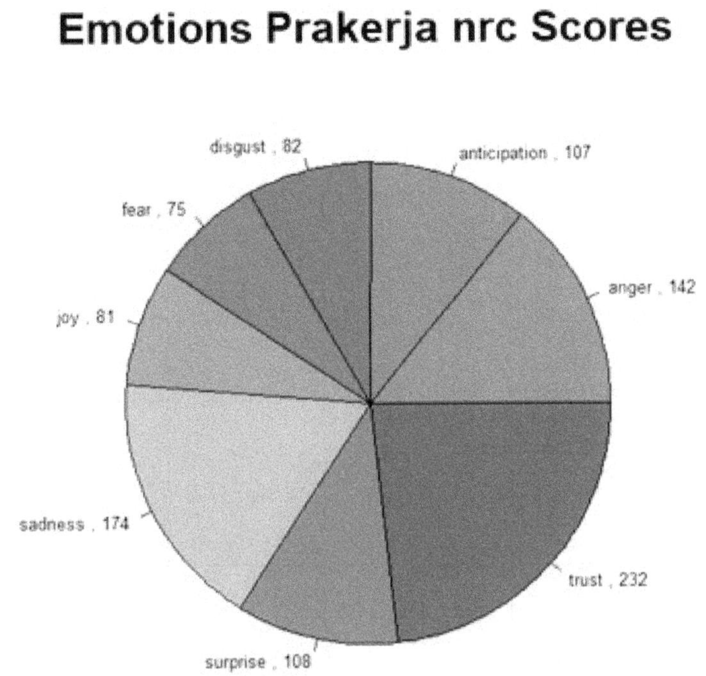

port, as we have seen in the case of Prakerja. In addition, people might be poorly informed the concept of contributory unemployment benefits, given that it is a new initiative to this country. It might prevent them from trusting the government in managing the system.

DISCUSSION

Indonesia prioritised reforming two employment protection and benefits systems during the COVID-19 pandemic. However, there is no evidence of public support for the reform options, making this article relevant to welfare attitude studies in Global South in general and Indonesia in particular.

The results show a widespread preference for supporting employment protection ideas as a viable alternative to economic hardship. This phenomenon can be explained in several ways. ***First***, the COVID-19 pandemic and its risk seemed to have complicated existing social risks and even produced new social risks (Choi et al., 2022), making perceived state responsibility more and more desirable and arousing public support for the ability of the government to provide support the individuals. This argument is particularly evident in the case of Prakerja—a new form of activation providing cash transfers and mandatory online training for laid-off workers and the unemployed; the positive sentiments surrounding this program are significantly high. This finding led us to argue that positive support might be shaped by the urgency and the scale of the crisis (Ramia & Perrone, 2021), particularly in the first wave of the

Table 2. Prakerja issues' most appealing tweet

No	Time	Tweet	Count of Retweet	Count of Like	Count of Quote Tweet	Count of Replies
1	2020-05-08 06:08:32+00:00	Here are some examples of government pranks: Electricity is discounted, but the bill is going up... [and now is] Prakerja for the unemployed and layoff victims, but start-ups and venture capital benefit more.	12785	23484	582	484
2	2020-05-18 11:30:15+00:00	Prakerja programs only enrich a handful of companies.	5085	7771	848	346

COVID-19 outbreak, which brought about cleavage period resulting in a critical juncture, for which reform is politically acceptable (Collier & Munck, 2022).

However, in the case of JKP, the trend is different. Despite the fact that positive sentiments dominate the public's support for the program, there is no meaningful difference between the positive and negative sentiments. The emotion analysis also reveals that negative-oriented expressions are more prevalent than favourable ones—the result is consistent throughout most retweets, comments, and like quotes concerning the program's implementation timing. It indicates that contribution-based insurance is unpreferable for most people who might be poorly informed about this unemployment benefit. Another relevant explanation is that public debates on JKP arose after the controversial decision of a flexible labour market to attract foreign investment had been announced a few months before. Therefore, the attitudes shown against JKP were arguably shaped not only by insecurity brought upon by COVID-19 calamities, but also widespread suspicion against the government for using JKP to pave the way for a more extensive liberalization agenda.

In addition, negative sentiments towards JKP can also be associated with potential consequences of labour market flexibility, which allows employers to escape their responsibilities of providing severance pay benefits. A new JKP initiative based on joint contributions from employers and employees would supersede the regular severance system, and this would lead to higher labour costs.

A ***second*** explanation is derived from an institutionalist perspective, which contends that exogenous factors only become significant in influencing the political support of reform once the cumulative process of minor adjustments within the original course has begun (Palier & Martin, 2007; see also Varjonen,

Figure 3. Public sentiment toward JKP

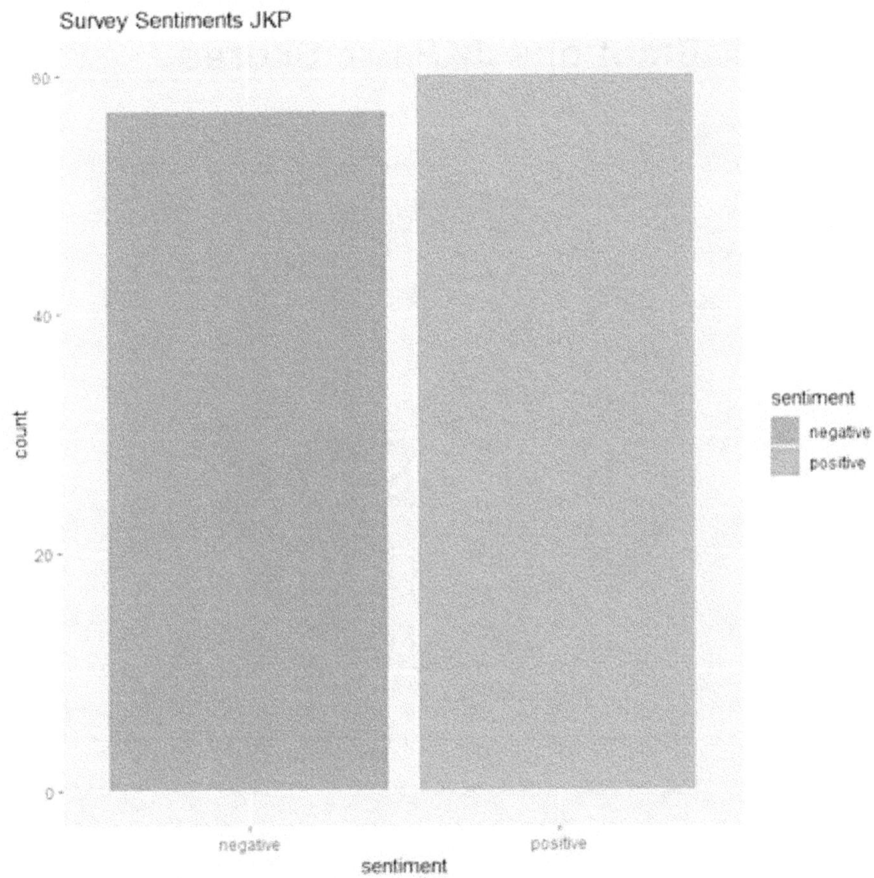

2020). We observe from the case of Prakerja that positive sentiment analysis, along with trust-related emotions, dominated the results. Anchored in institutionalist arguments, we extend this public support reasoning towards Prakerja by connecting it with previous cumulative adjustments of activation policy in its original form known as BLK, which has undergone some modifications since it was initiated in 1953 (cf. Yuda et.al., 2022). The existence of BLK and its historical development undeniably provide a cognitive reference for the public to support Prakerja. In addition, the renewal of the activation policy by adding Prakerja has been extensively discussed since 2016 and was used as part of the political campaign of President Joko Widodo in 2019. COVID-19 thus only served as a path policy-clearing accelerator (Hogan et al., 2022), which removed administrative and political blockages and sped up the ongoing proposal of Prakerja.

The conclusion is that Prakerja's ideas become more effective and politically legitimate when the emphasis on policy is given during a crisis. Furthermore, the argument lends weight to ideational scholarship (Béland & Cox, 2011; Campbell, 2004; Daigneault, 2014; Padamsee, 2009; Parsons, 2007; Schmidt, 2011), which shows that specific policy ideas may evoke more excellent emotional responses when presented at the right time, and, therefore, contribute to more significant policy impact through their emotional impact.

Figure 4. Emotion analysis toward JKP

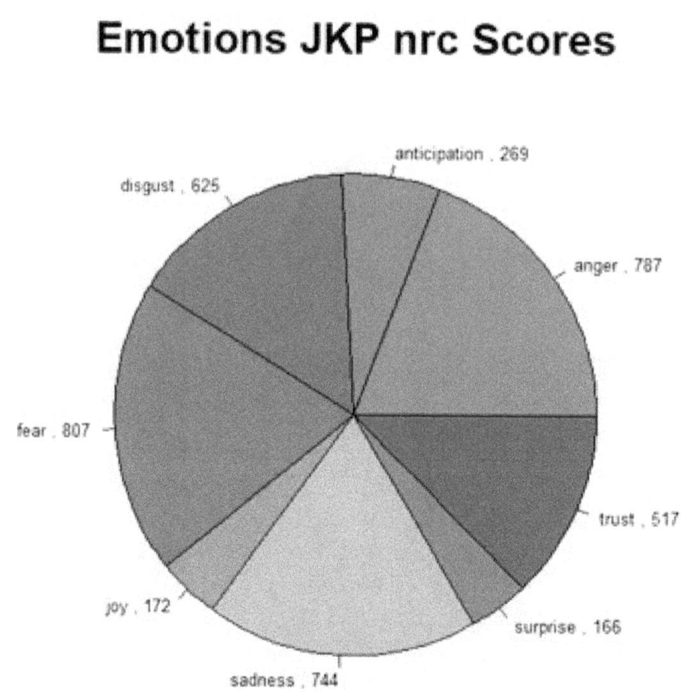

Meanwhile, the lack of 'meaningful' political support for JKP can be attributed to the opposite explanation of Prakerja. The absence of institutional routines for making temporary changes in advance has an unfavourable effect on the construction-making of collective cognition. This fact confirms Torfing's point of view (2019) about the importance of institutional changes in advance as an antidote to amplifying the predominance of "risk-aversive voices" on novel initiatives. An empirical study by Weisstanner (2022) about the lack of practically implemented Universal Basic Income (UBI) schemes in European

Table 3. JKP issues' most appealing tweet

No	Time	Tweet	Count of Retweet	Count of Likes	Count of Quote Tweet	Count of Replies
1	2022-02-11 16:39:12+00:00	OK, after reading the rules... [of] Unemployment Protection (JKP). My take is that the policy may be right, but the timing isn't right.	3205	1199	93	44

countries supports our argument. Despite the pandemic, the result indicates that the support pattern has not been fundamentally altered by retaining traditional welfare policies instead of UBI.

Finally, we should note there are stark divisions of support for JKP; therefore, prospects for eroding lukewarm political support for this policy after the pandemic remain uncertain.

We could further regard the public support in this study as a representation of the ideal image of egalitarian preferences and state-centred support. Contributory schemes, which are practiced in conservatives welfare regimes, are excluded from such an image.

CONCLUSION, LIMITATION, AND FUTURE RESEARCH

Social policy literature has extensively examined public support to asses welfare state legitimacy. However, literature on this topic has primarily focused on the welfare states in OECD/Europe, thus missing out on cases in the Global South, such as Indonesia, particularly during the COVID-19 pandemic. This article, therefore, aims to make a substantive contribution to welfare attitude scholarship by expounding on the analysis of the Indonesian case, of which the welfare system has progressively evolved through several fascinating phases (Hort & Kuhnle, 2000; Kusujiarti, 2012; Kühner, 2015; Sumarto, 2017; Murphy, 2019; Yuda & Kühner, 2022). In this regard, two policy responses to the COVID-19 turmoil, Prakerja and JKP, are studied.

Based on an algorithm-based sentiment and emotion analysis of 47,916 tweets, this article argues that different support for Prakerja and JKP emerged not because of the breakthrough traits of policies but due to citizens' pragmatic-cognitive logic shaped by the urgency and severity of the COVID-19 crisis. It makes the idea of state-centred welfare responsibility (something Prakerja possesses) more desirable than contribution-based insurance, which JKP offers.

Such an argument is supported by our results revealing that most tweets express positive sentiments towards the two policies. However, the share of negative sentiments towards JKP is larger than that of Prakerja, which indicates that societal support for JKP is starkly polarized. Emotion tests were thus performed and surprisingly showed that disappointment towards JKP has a dominant trend, with trust at the minimum. Prakerja, on the other hand, consistently indicates positive sentiments and a significant predominance of trust/legitimation.

Taken collectively, the most important logic to the support that Prakerja received is that it would offer more temporary income security and training benefits in a time of insecurity due to the COVID-19 crisis. Meanwhile, JKP, which relies on contribution-based insurance, is not preferable, though it received a majority of positive sentiment. The disappointment towards JKP in the first term of launching was exacerbated by concerns about future uncertainty that might arise from abrupt decisions on labour market deregulation. However, other studies found that escalating assumptions that JKP would replace severance pay, which is derived from joint contributions by employers and employees, contributed to the public's hostility.

Our study promises a fruitful avenue for understanding policy feedback (Pierson, 1994; 1996) to social policy institutions in developing countries' point of view (Béland et al., 2018; Foli et al., 2018). It explains how new policies generate constituencies in which egalitarian preferences, as well as state-centred support, shape the welfare imagination of citizens rather than contributory schemes as usually found in conservative welfare systems. Specifically, this study provides an empirical foundation for understanding the nature of the political legitimacy of welfare state institutionalization in times of crisis.

Finally, a number of important limitations need to be considered. Our study relies on rapid and real-time assessment, which allows us to provide a snapshot of support in areas more visibly and adversely affected during the initial crisis and for the short term. Consequently, we are unable to provide evidence on medium- or long-term trends that lend themselves to the theory of welfare attitudes. Generally, this is also due to limited statistics and qualitative information available. Making use of a variety of indicators to conceptualize and measure welfare state development in evolutionary terms is not currently possible. As a future research agenda, we need more studies on public attitudes to analyse whether the expectations of the Indonesian population on JKP and Prakerja have changed. The discouraged support for JKP also suggests that future studies should be conducted to better understand worker willingness and ability to contribute to the contributory-based welfare system in general along various avenues.

REFERENCES

Amoah, P. A. (2020). Examining attitudes towards welfare in an in/security regime: Evidence from Ghana. *Social Policy and Society, 19*(4), 1–16. doi:10.1017/S1474746420000172

Ares, M., Bürgisser, R., & Häusermann, S. (2021). Attitudinal polarization towards the redistributive role of the state in the wake of the COVID-19 crisis. *Journal of Elections, Public Opinion, and Parties, 31*(sup1, S1), 41–55. doi:10.1080/17457289.2021.1924736

Arts, W., & Gelissen, J. (2001). Welfare states, solidarity and justice principles: Does the type really matter? *Acta Sociologica, 44*(4), 283–299. doi:10.1177/000169930104400401

Aspinall, E. (2014). Health care and democratization in Indonesia. *Democratization, 21*(5), 803–823. doi:10.1080/13510347.2013.873791

Béland, D., Cantillon, B., Hick, R., & Moreira, A. (2021). Social policy in the face of a global pandemic: Policy responses to the COVID-19 crisis. *Social Policy and Administration, 55*(2), 249–260. doi:10.1111/spol.12718 PMID:34230721

Béland, D., & Cox, R. H. (Eds.). (2011). *Ideas and Politics in Social Science Research.* Oxford University Press.

Béland, D., Foli, R., & Kpessa-Whyte, M. (2018). Social Policy as Nation-building: Identity Formation, Policy Feedback, and Social Citizenship in Ghana. *Canadian Journal of African Studies / Revue Canadienne des études Africaines, 52*(1), 19 - 36.

Binsar, F., & Mauritsius, T. (2020). Mining of Social Media on Covid-19 Big Data Infodemic in Indonesia. *Journal of Computational Science, 16*(11), 1598–1609. doi:10.3844/jcssp.2020.1598.1609

Blekesaune, M., & Quadagno, J. (2003). Public Attitudes toward Welfare State Policies: A Comparative Analysis of 24 Nations. *European Sociological Review, 19*(5), 415–427. doi:10.1093/esr/19.5.415

Campbell, J. L. (2004). *Institutional Change and Globalization.* Princeton University Press. doi:10.1515/9780691216348

Cantillon, B., Seeleib-Kaiser, M., & van der Veen, R. (2021). The COVID-19 crisis and policy responses by continental European welfare states. *Social Policy and Administration, 55*(2), 326–338. doi:10.1111/spol.12715 PMID:34230722

Cheng, Q., & Ngok, K. (2020). Welfare Attitudes Towards Anti-poverty Policies in China: Economical Individualism, Social Collectivism and Institutional Differences. *Social Indicators Research, 15*(2), 679–694. doi:10.1007/s11205-020-02313-y

Choi, Y. J., Kühner, S., & Shi, S. J. (2022). From "new social risks" to "COVID social risks:" the challenges for inclusive Society in South Korea, Hong Kong, and Taiwan amid the pandemic. *Policy and Society, 41*(2), 260–274. doi:10.1093/polsoc/puac001

Collier, D., & Munck, G. L. (Eds.). (2022). *Critical Juncture and Historical Legacies: Insights and Methods*. The Rowman and Littlefield Publishing Group, Inc.

Daigneault, P.-M. (2014). Reassessing the concept of policy paradigm: Aligning ontol- ogy and methodology in policy studies. *Journal of European Public Policy, 21*(3), 453–469. doi:10.1080/13501763.2013.834071

Ebbinghaus, B., Lehner, L., & Naumann, E. (2022). Welfare state support during the COVID- 19 pandemic: Change and continuity in public attitudes towards social policies in Germany. *European Policy Analysis,* 1–15. https://doi.org/. doi:10.1002/epa2.11523118

Fealy, G. (2020). Jokowi in the Covid-19 Era: Repressive Pluralism, Dynasticism and the Overbearing State. *Bulletin of Indonesian Economic Studies, 56*(3), 301–323. doi:10.1080/00074918.2020.1846482

Foli, R., Béland, D., & Fenwick, T. B. (2018). How Instrument Constituencies Shape Policy Transfer: A Case Study from Ghana. *Policy and Society, 37*(1), 108–124. doi:10.1080/14494035.2017.1377987

Goel, R., & Sharma, R. (2021). Studying leaders & their concerns using online social media during the times of crisis - A COVID case study. *Social Network Analysis and Mining, 11*(46), 1–12. doi:10.1007/s13278-021-00756-w

Greve, B., Blomquist, P., Hvinden, B., & van Gerven, M. (2021). Nordic welfare states – still standing or changed by the COVID-19 crisis. *Social Policy and Administration, 55*(2), 295–311. doi:10.1111/spol.12675 PMID:33362319

Hick, R., & Murphy, M. (2021). Common shock, different paths? Comparing social policy responses to COVID-19 in the UK and Ireland. *Social Policy and Administration, 55*(2), 312–325. doi:10.1111/spol.12677

Hogan, J., Howlett, M., & Murphy, M. (2022). Re-thinking the coronavirus pandemic as a policy punctuation: COVID-19 as a path-clearing policy accelerator. *Policy and Society, 41*(1), 40–52. doi:10.1093/polsoc/puab009

Hort, S. E. O., & Kuhnle, S. (2000). The coming of east and south-east Asian welfare states. *Journal of European Social Policy, 10*(2), 162–184. doi:10.1177/a012488

Howlett, M., & Cashore, B. (2009). The dependent variable problem in the study of policy change: Understanding policy change as a methodological problem. *Journal of Comparative Policy Analysis*, *11*(1), 33–46. doi:10.1080/13876980802648144

Ingold, J. O., & Stuart, M. (2015). The demand-side of active labour market policies: A regional study of employer engagement in the work programme. *Journal of Social Policy*, *44*(3), 443–462. doi:10.1017/S0047279414000890

Jordan, J. D. (2018). 'Welfare grunters and workfare monsters? An empirical review of the operation of two UK 'work programme' centres'. *Journal of Social Policy*, *47*(3), 583–601. doi:10.1017/S0047279417000629

Jørgensen, F., Bor, A., Lindholt, M. F., & Petersen, M. B. (2021). Public support for government responses against COVID-19: Assessing levels and predictors in eight Western democracies during 2020. *West European Politics*, *44*(5–6), 1129–1158. doi:10.1080/01402382.2021.1925821

Kamaludin, N. K., Nurmandi, A., & Salahudin. (2022). How Does the Local Government Provide Official Website and Twitter Quality? Case Study of Three Local Governments of Indonesia. *Lecture Notes in Networks and Systems*, *216*, 137–147. doi:10.1007/978-981-16-1781-2_14

Kothari, A., Foisey, L., Donelle, L., & Bauer, M. (2021). How do Canadian public health agencies respond to the COVID-19 emergency using social media: A protocol for a case study using content and sentiment analysis. *BMJ Open*, *11*(4), e041818. doi:10.1136/bmjopen-2020-041818 PMID:33888527

Kühner, S. (2015). Analysing the productive and protective dimensions of welfare in the Asia-Pacific: Pathways towards human development and income equality*? Journal of International and Comparative Social Policy*, *31*(2), 151–173. doi:10.1080/21699763.2015.1047395

Kühner, S., & Chou, K. (2020). The Politics of MPF Reform: Lessons from Public Attitudes in Hong Kong. *Social Policy and Society*, *19*(3), 414–430. doi:10.1017/S1474746420000020

Kusujiarti, S. (2012). Pluralistic and informal welfare regime: The roles of Islamic institution in the Indonesian welfare regime. In T. Keskin (Ed.), *The sociology of Islam: Secularism, economy, and politics* (pp. 419–452). Itacha Press.

Kusumasari, B., Fauzi, F. Z., & Santoso, A. D. (2023). Amplifying Local Leadership: A Twitter Analysis of Indonesian Responses to the COVID-19 Pandemic. *BISNIS & BIROKRASI: Jurnal Ilmu Administrasi Dan Organisasi*, *30*(1). doi:10.20476/jbb.v30i1.1385

Kusumasari, B., Munajat, M. E., & Fauzi, F. Z. (2022). Measuring global pandemic governance: How countries respond to COVID-19. *The Journal of Management and Governance*, *0*(0), 1–27. doi:10.1007/s10997-022-09647-4

Lacatus, C., & Meibauer, G. (2022). 'Saying it like it is': Right-wing populism, international politics, and the performance of authenticity. *British Journal of Politics and International Relations*, *24*(3), 437–457. doi:10.1177/13691481221089137

Lain, T. (2019). A picture is worth a thousand words: the evidentiary promise of emoji-based sentiment analysis. 1–14.

Machmud, M., Fatimah, J. M., Sultan, M. I., & Farid, M. (2024). Social media as communication tools for anti-corruption campaign in Indonesia. *International Journal of Data and Network Science*, *8*(1), 357–368. doi:10.5267/j.ijdns.2023.9.018

Mahoney, J., & Thelen, K. (2010). A Theory of Gradual Institutional Change. In J. Mahoney & K. Thelen (Eds.), *Explaining Institutional Change: Ambiguity, Agency, and Power* (pp. 1–37). Cambridge University Press.

Murphy, J. (2019). The historical development of Indonesian social security. *Asian Journal of Social Science*, *47*(2), 255–279. doi:10.1163/15685314-04702005

Muuri, A. (2010). The Impact of the Use of the Social Welfare Services or Social Security Benefits on Attitudes to Social Welfare Policies. *International Journal of Social Welfare*, *19*(2), 182–193. doi:10.1111/j.1468-2397.2009.00641.x

Nandwani, P., & Verma, R. (2021). A review on sentiment analysis and emotion detection from text. *Social Network Analysis and Mining*, *11*(1), 1–19. doi:10.1007/s13278-021-00776-6 PMID:34484462

Ng, I. Y. H. (2015). Welfare Attitudes of Singaporeans – Ambiguity in Shifting Socio-Political Dynamics. *Social Policy and Administration*, *49*(7), 946–965. doi:10.1111/spol.12107

Nurmandi, A., Almarez, D., & Roengtam, S. (2018). To what extent is social media used in city government policy making? Case studies in three asean cities. *Public Policy and Administration*, *17*(4), 600–618. doi:10.13165/VPA-18-17-4-08

Ortiz, S. L., & Oubiña, C. P. (2021). The informative coverage of tragic events into television channels. A case study: The Pedrógão Grande fires in Portugal and the disappearance of Julén Roselló in Spain. *Observatorio (OBS*)*, *15*(4), 19–39. doi:10.15847/obsOBS15420211963

Osborne, H., & Parkinson, H. (2018, March 22). Cambridge Analytica scandal: The biggest revela- tions so far. *The Guardian*. https://www.theguardian.com/uk- news/2018/mar/22/cambridge-analytica-scandal-the-biggest-revelations-so-far

Padamsee, T. (2009). Culture in connection: Re-contextualizing ideational processes in the analysis of policy development. *Social Politics*, *16*(4), 413–445. doi:10.1093/sp/jxp018

Palier, B., & Martin, C. (2007). From a 'frozen landscape' to structural reforms: The sequential transformation of Bismarckian welfare systems. *Social Policy and Administration*, *41*(6), 535–554. doi:10.1111/j.1467-9515.2007.00571.x

Parsons, C. (2007). *How to Map Arguments in Political Science*. Oxford University Press. doi:10.1093/oso/9780199286676.001.0001

Pierson, P. (1994). *Dismantling the Welfare State? Reagan, Thatcher, and the Politics of Retrenchment*. Cambridge University Press. doi:10.1017/CBO9780511805288

Pierson, P. (1996). The new politics of the welfare state. *World Politics*, *48*(1), 143–179. doi:10.1353/wp.1996.0004

Pierson, P. (2000). Increasing returns, path dependence, and the study of politics. *The American Political Science Review*, *94*(1), 251–267. doi:10.2307/2586011

Raj, H. W., & Balachandran, S. (2020). Future emoji entry prediction using neural networks. *Journal of Computational Science*, *16*(2), 150–157. doi:10.3844/jcssp.2020.150.157

Ramia, G., & Perrone, L. (2021). Crisis Management, Policy Reform, and Institutions: The Social Policy Response to COVID-19 in Australia. *Social Policy and Society*, *0*(0), 1–15. doi:10.1017/S1474746421000427

Rasyid, S. B. A., Nurmandi, A., Suswanta, Mutiarin, D., & Salahudin. (2021). Public Communication of Local Government Leaders: A Case Study of Three Major Governors in Indonesia. *Advances in Intelligent Systems and Computing*, *1352*, 487–497. doi:10.1007/978-3-030-71782-7_43

Rasyid, S. B. A., Nurmandi, A., Suswanta, Mutiarin, D., & Salahudin. (2021). Public Communication of Local Government Leaders: A Case Study of Three Major Governors in Indonesia. *Advances in Intelligent Systems and Computing*, *1352*, 487–497. doi:10.1007/978-3-030-71782-7_43

Reeskens, T., Muis, Q., Sieben, I., Vandecasteele, L., Luijkx, R., & Halman, L. (2021). Stability or change of public opinion and values during the coronavirus crisis? Exploring Dutch longitudinal panel data. *European Societies*, *23*(sup1, S1), S153–S171. doi:10.1080/14616696.2020.1821075

Ritchie, J., Spencer, L., & O'Connor, W. (2003). Carrying out qualitative analysis. In J. Ritchie & J. Lewis (Eds.), *Qualitative research practice* (pp. 219–262). Sage Publications.

Safitri, Y., Angeline, M., & Wibowo, D. (2021). *Tweeps and their tweeting behavior during natural disaster. 729*(1). doi:10.1088/1755-1315/729/1/012083

Schmidt, V. A. (2011). Reconciling ideas and institutions through discursive institu- tionalism. In D. Béland & R. H. Cox (Eds.), *Ideas and Politics in Social Science Research* (pp. 47–64). Oxford University Press.

Skjold, S., & Lundberg, K. (2022). Accountability in personalised Supported Employment-based activation services. *Journal of Social Policy*, 1–17. doi:10.1017/S0047279422000915

Soon, S., Chou, C. C., & Shi, S. J. (2021). Withstanding the plague: Institutional resilience of the East Asian welfare state. *Social Policy and Administration*, *55*(2), 374–387. doi:10.1111/spol.12713 PMID:33821059

Sutiyo, S. (2022). A neo-institutional analysis of social protection: Insights from Indonesia. *Global Social Policy*, *0*(0), 1–18.

Taylor-Gooby, P., Chung, H., & Leruth, B. (2018). The contribution of deliberative forums to studying welfare state attitudes: A United Kingdom study. *Social Policy and Administration*, *52*(4), 914–927. doi:10.1111/spol.12405

Torfing, J. (2009). Rethinking path dependence in public policy research. *Critical Policy Studies*, *3*(1), 70–83. doi:10.1080/19460170903158149

Valarino, I., Meil, G., & Rogero-García, J. (2018). Family or state responsibility? Elderly- and child-care policy preferences in Spain. *The International Journal of Sociology and Social Policy*, *38*(11/12), 1101–1115. doi:10.1108/IJSSP-06-2018-0086

Weisstanner, D. (2022). COVID-19 and welfare state support: The case of universal basic income. *Policy and Society*, *41*(1), 96–110. doi:10.1093/polsoc/puab015

Wilsford, D. (1994). Path dependency, or why history makes it difficult but not impossible to reform health care systems in a big way. *Journal of Public Policy*, *14*(3), 285–309. doi:10.1017/S0143814X00007285

Yeh, C.-Y., & Ku, Y. W. (2021). Welfare attitude and economic developmentalism in new democratic developmental welfare state: An examination of the Taiwanese case. *Journal of Asian Public Policy*, *14*(1), 13–29. doi:10.1080/17516234.2020.1790729

Yuda, T. K. (2022). Who should care? Exploring the views and experiences of individuals in negotiating solutions for health security. *The International Journal of Sociology and Social Policy*, *42*(11-12), 1109–1128. doi:10.1108/IJSSP-09-2021-0246

Yuda, T. K. (forthcoming). Comparing Social Policy Responses Between Separate Crises: Taking the Case of Indonesia. In C. Aspalter (Ed.), *The Covid-19 Pandemic: Problems Arising* (pp. xx–xx). Springer Verlag.

Yuda, T. K., Kim, M., Pholpark, A., & Bin Aedy Rahman, H. N. (2022). Unmasking the social policy responses of COVID-19 in four southeast Asian nations: Institutional patterns and policy adjustment. *Asia Pacific Journal of Social Work*, *0*(0), 1–22. doi:10.1080/02185385.2022.2136234

Yuda, T. K., & Kühner, S. (2022). Bringing Indonesia into the global welfare regime debate: A literature review and future research agenda. *Asian Social Work and Policy Review*, *0*(0), 1–12.

Yuda, T. K., & Pholpark, A. (2022). Healthcare expansion in Indonesia and Thailand: A causal mechanism and its implications for welfare regimes. *Journal of International and Comparative Social Policy*, *38*(2), 111–129. doi:10.1017/ics.2022.6

Yuda, T. K., & Qomariyah, N. (2022). Ideas and Policy Response to the COVID-19 Crisis: Evidence from Jakarta, Indonesia. *Social Policy and Society*, *0*(0), 1–20. doi:10.1017/S1474746422000616

Yuda, T. K., & Rezza, M. (2021). The forms of decommodification and (de)familisation measures during COVID-19: What is the impact on female's welfare? *Public Administration and Development*, *41*(3), 135–141. doi:10.1002/pad.1955 PMID:34539025

Chapter 5
Contemporary Leadership Styles and Challenges for Governance

Neeta Baporikar
https://orcid.org/0000-0003-0676-9913
Namibia University of Science and Technology, Namibia & SP Pune University, India

ABSTRACT

Leadership styles vary as per the context and environment in which the organizations exist. Today's environment for organizations is not the same as it was two decades back. Globalization, ICT convergence, digitalization, multigenerational workforce, and the recent pandemic have completely changed the environment in which organizations operate and exist. To meet this new changing time, there are challenges that leaders face and hence new styles of leadership are merging which will ensure that governance does not take the back seat but is in line with the changing dynamics and expectations. Adopting a qualitative approach, the aim of this chapter is to deliberate on contemporary leadership styles and discuss the challenges therein for better governance.

INTRODUCTION

Tone-at-the-top is established by management and the Board of Directors and is critical for creating and maintaining a corporate governance framework (Andreou, Antoniou, Horton, & Louca, (2016). Corporate governance is the basis for the company's internal control environment and for maintaining effective business processes (Andreou et al., 2016). A robust internal control environment with effective business processes is crucial because it aids management in protecting shareholder welfare (Andreou et al., 2016). Management establishes internal controls and operating procedures that protect company assets and minimize the risk of fraud or abuse (Gao & Zhang, 2019). As evidenced by a robust internal control environment, corporate governance establishes acceptable employee behavior and allows an organization to have consistent process activities. To meet this new changing time there are challenges that leaders face and hence new styles of leadership are merging which will ensure that governance does not take the back seat but is in line with the changing dynamics and expectations. Adopting a qualitative approach the aim of this chapter is to deliberate contemporary leadership styles and discuss the challenges for better

DOI: 10.4018/979-8-3693-1742-6.ch005

governance. The content of this chapter includes a discussion of leadership styles and the challenges for governance. In the process, agency theory, the internal audit function, and the accounting and financial reporting processes as operating aspects in governance and significance of the Board of Directors as they are in leadership role, are also looked into. The results of this study expand the understanding of the leadership styles and the role from the Board of Directors plays in governance and specifically the internal controls governing the accounting and financial reporting processes.

LITERATURE REVIEW

Leadership

The goal of leadership is to direct or persuade others to obtain a stated goal (Afsar, Badir, & Saeed, (2014). Dinh, Lord, Gardner, Meuser, Liden, & Hu, (2014) completed an exhaustive 12-year study of leadership theory and identified several current and emerging leadership models that focused on micro-processes at the individual level, such as knowledge and emotion, and macro-processes such as social and team oriented leadership styles. The idea is for these processes to work together to achieve established goals and objectives. Leaders influence team performance, and each leader's style of leadership has a direct correlation to the effectiveness of the organization's operations (Dal Mas & Barac, 2018). Dryer (2018) defined leadership as a complex process of self-mentoring and coaching others to work together to achieve personal and organizational goals. Meuser, Gardner, Dinh, Hu, Liden, & Lord, (2016) studied leadership and concluded that leadership includes two continua locus and process and locus is described as the initiation of a leadership activity that results in action by a follower, and process is described as an influence to inspire new behavior. Leadership locus and process are developed through learning and experiences that enhance a leader's ability to influence and motivate others. Dryer (2018) also suggested that leadership is intended to drive performance and suggested that leadership is complex and multifaceted.

Avolio (2007) completed a study of the first 100 years of leadership and concluded that leadership theory dates back to the great man theory. Spector (2016) traced the great man leadership theory which implies that specific individuals were sent or ordained by God to be change agents to enlighten the world to new theory. While the great man theory represents the history of leadership, Dinh et al. (2014) concluded that the foundation of leadership is traced to the history of trust and loyalty. Dinh et al. (2014) completed a study of leadership theory by analyzing ten of the top-10 leadership journals over 12 years starting in 2000 and found many established and emerging leadership theories such as transformational, transactional, inspirational, strategic, and team leadership. Leadership is a topic with a deep history. There are many established leadership styles, but the leadership discipline continues to emerge with new styles that challenge leaders to be agents of change. Transformational leadership principles were critical to this study because it focuses on the achievement of higher levels of improvement. Bass (1985) became the theorist of transformational leadership and argued that transformational leadership theory increases goal consciousness and how to achieve each goal. Transformational theory allows the leader to transcend self-interest for the greater good of the team. Leading is complex and multifaceted, and while there are many definitions and theories, the goal of leadership is to mentor and coach oneself and others to attain higher goals through ongoing learning and personal development (Baporikar, 2023a; 2023b). Krog and Govender (2015) stated that leadership is less about an individual's role in the company and more about a person's ability to influence others. The Board of Directors and the Chief Audit Executive are

Figure 1. Conceptual framework
Source: Self-Developed

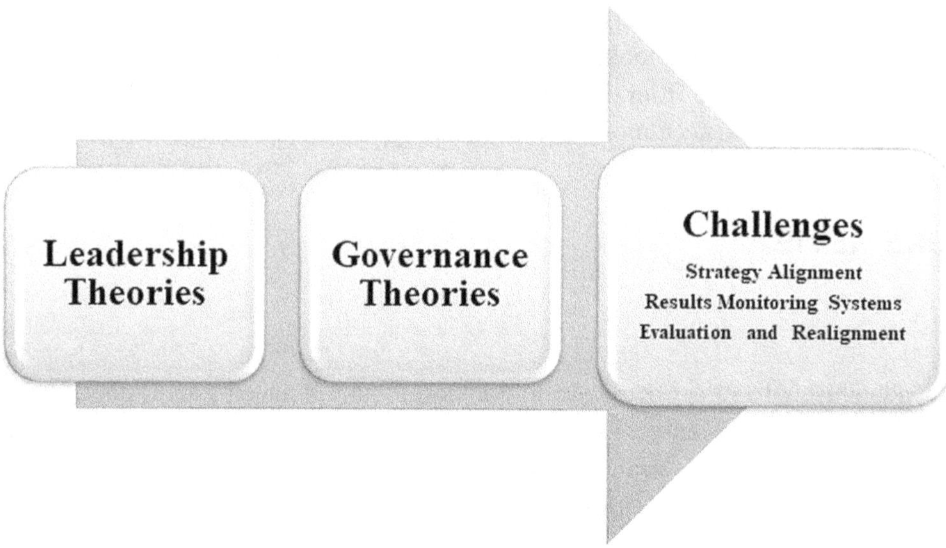

important roles in an organization, but collaborative leadership establishes a strong corporate culture that influences employee behavior. The focus or goal of governance is to establish a robust internal control culture and collaborative leadership, regardless of organizational position, to influence others to comply with policies and procedures and leadership over governance enhances the accounting and financial reporting processes through a robust internal control environment (Dănescu, Prozan, & Prozan, 2015).

Figure 1 gives the conceptual framework.

Leadership Theories

Leadership theory is a dynamic phenomenon and continues to change over time (Benmira & Agboola, 2021). The history of leadership theories began with the Great men theory. The theory states that not everyone can be a leader or even aspire to be a leader as leadership is divine and comes as a gift from God. The Great Man Theory centers on two main assumptions: great leaders are born possessing certain traits that enable them to rise and lead and great leaders can arise when the need for them is great. Examples were often drawn from popular historical figures such as Julius Caesar, Mahatma Gandhi, Abraham Lincoln and Napoleon Bonaparte. It was believed that these individuals were natural born leaders with innate characteristics of leadership, which enabled them to lead individuals while they shaped the history (Figueiredo, 2022).

Trait Theories

From the limitations of the great men theory birthed the trait theory of leadership in the 20th century. Trait theories ignored the assumptions about whether leadership traits were genetic or acquired and identified two traits; emergent traits (those which are heavily dependent upon heredity) as height, intelligence, attractiveness, and self-confidence and effectiveness traits (based on experience or learning), including charisma, as a fundamental component of leadership.

Behavioral Theories

According to behavioral theories, leaders are not born. What makes a leader can be identified and learned, and for a leader to be effective, he or she must be trained. The three different leadership styles introduced then were: democratic, autocratic and laissez faire leaders. The employees working with democratic leaders displayed a high degree of satisfaction, creativity, and motivation; they worked with great enthusiasm and energy irrespective of the presence or absence of the leader; they also maintained better connections with the leader in terms of productivity, whereas autocratic leaders mainly focused on greater quantity of output. Laissez faire leadership was only considered relevant while leading a team of highly skilled and motivated people who excelled track-record in the past.

Contingency Theories

The theories of contingency recommends that no leadership style is presented as a stand-alone style, as it is reliant upon a variety of factors such as the quality and situation of the followers or a number of other variables. Overall assumptions of the contingency theories are that there is no standard leadership style. That different situations demand different leadership approaches. The theories of contingency are a category of behavioral theories that challenges the idea that there is no one finest way of leading or organizing and that the style of leadership that is operative in some circumstances may not be effective in others. Three well-known contingency theories include contingency model of leader effectiveness aimed to incorporate situational variables when looking at leader effectiveness. The model predicts that leaders who are task oriented will be more successful in situations in which leaders have either high or low control, whereas leaders who are relationship orientated will be more effective in situations which offer them moderate levels of control; situational approach proposed that effective leaders must understand their followers and apply the correct balance between directive and supportive leadership, depending on the situation and path-goal approach has been used to help explain how leaders influence their followers' motivation and behavior towards achieving desired outcomes. The role of the leader in path-goal theory is to increase follower goal attainment.

Process Theories

Process leadership theories suggest that the work of leaders is to contribute to the well-being of others with a focus on some form of social responsibility. Leadership theories with a process focus include servant leadership, principal centered leadership and charismatic leadership. One of the most studied models is the servant leadership theory which focuses on the needs of the followers and helps them to become more autonomous, freer and knowledgeable. Servant leadership became popular recently by emphasizing the importance of followers. Servant leaders seek to support their team members and are most concerned with serving people first (Eliot, 2020).

Governance

Berle and Means pioneered governance theory, which was described as a separation of ownership and control (Pande & Ansari, 2014). Duit and Galaz (2008) defined governance theory as exceedingly dynamic and nonlinear by identifying four types of governance: rigid, robust, fragile, and flexible. Rigid governance is slow to change and provides stability but little exploration or innovation. A robust corporate governance program enhances continuous improvement through development and expansion. Fragile governance results in weaknesses and failures because it lacks support and sustainability. Flexible governance allows for exploration but fails to transform the governance environment. Governance theory is critical to studying the role leadership plays in corporate governance because effective internal controls are designed to achieve business objectives and strategy by controlling an organization's business processes, information systems, and company culture (Werner & Gehrke, 2019). Governance may be rigid, robust, fragile, or flexible, but the goal of governance is to separate ownership and control (Baporikar, 2021).

Effective governance theory or corporate governance includes internal controls, monitoring, and oversight roles from the Board of Directors, management, and the CAE (Cullen & Brennan, 2017). Essen et al. (2013) defined corporate governance as a process of maintaining an effective Board of Directors, a management leadership team with requisite training and experience, and alignment of processes and activities designed to meet employee and stakeholder needs. Mathew, Ibrahim, & Archbold, (2018) researched corporate governance and governance theory and concluded that the Board of Directors' composition, leadership structure, and processes are critical to governance success. While oversight of corporate governance is a critical role for the Board of Directors, the process used to establish and maintain a governance program can vary by organization. Figure 2 gives the basic elements of good governance.

OPERATIONALIZING LEADERSHIP

Regardless of the leadership theory used, leadership principles are only effective if operationalized and used to influence others. Hazy and Uhl-Bien (2015) concluded that the operationalization of leadership requires looking beyond the person and considering the complexities of the leadership process in conjunction with corporate governance needs. This distinction involves more than studying and learning leadership methods but requires the leader to evaluate the leadership process and organizational goals to apply the leadership principles to achieve maximum results. This section evaluates Operationalizing leadership and the complexity of leadership by evaluating the role of the Board of Directors, the role of management including the CAE, alignment of strategy between the Board and management, and monitoring of results.

Role of the Board

Bajra and Cadez (2018) concluded that corporate governance includes leadership from the Board of Directors that focuses on strengthening the accounting and financial reporting function by reducing the risk of earnings management. Nahum and Carmeli (2019) stated that involving the Board of Directors in strategic decision-making enhances the overall success of the organization's ability to achieve strategy

Figure 2. Basic elements of good governance
Source: Self-Developed

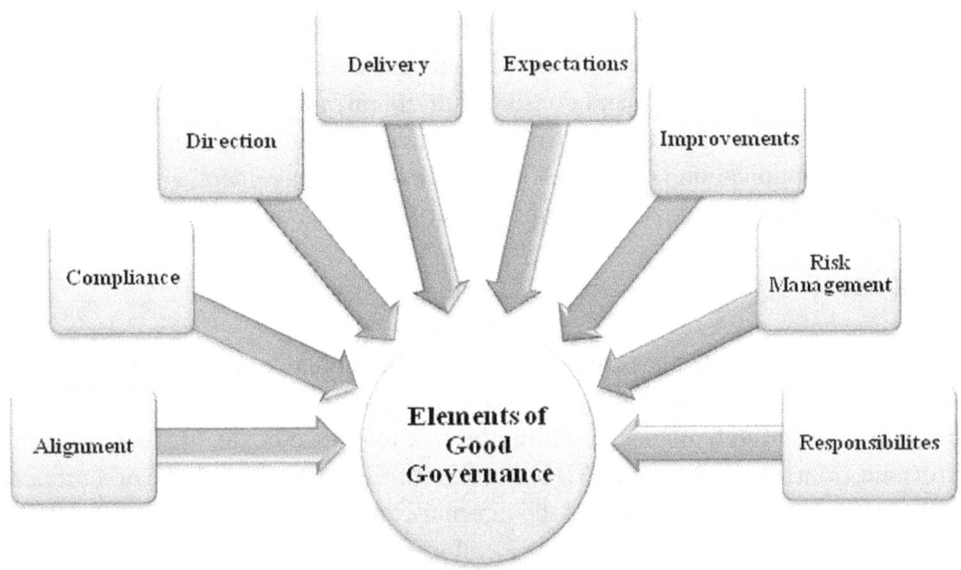

and is frequently becoming a core contribution expected of Board members. Corporate governance, including the strategy over the accounting and financial reporting processes, is enhanced by including the Board of Directors in planning and oversight activities. This conclusion demonstrates the importance of leadership at the Board of Directors level and implies that Board members demonstrate leadership when they draw upon their expertise when fulfilling their responsibilities.

Nahum and Carmeli (2019) also concluded that drawing on individual expertise is beneficial to corporate strategy and demonstrated that Board members participate at different levels depending on the make-up and personal characteristics of the entire Board. This conclusion draws attention to the importance of the holistic Board and the individual members' background and experience. Baysinger and Hoskinsson (1990) stressed the importance of Board composition as a work-sharing and risk-sharing initiative. Work sharing describes how the Board of Directors divides responsibilities. Risk-sharing describes how the Board of Directors divides the responsibility for risk management. Creating a Board composed of diversified leaders enhances overall leadership within the organization and allows each member to play to his or her strength while collectively addressing the organization's workload and risk profile on a holistic basis.

Role of Management

Operationalization of corporate governance leadership is defined as a sustained culture of excellence that creates a corporate governance program to detect and prevent costly operational inefficiencies (Ferdowsian, 2016). Management uses a strong and well-defined corporate governance program to create a control structure established on ethics and excellence, two critical variables for consistency in operational performance (Ferdowsian, 2016). Menz and Barnbeck (2017) identified corporate strategy development as an essential executive management activity since the strategy development process affects operating decisions. Due to the significance of management's decisions, the executive team must embrace leadership principles and build and maintain a strong corporate governance program to correctly identify and mitigate critical risks to the organization. Dal Mas and Barac (2018) identified leadership as a core competency for the CAE and the internal audit department. The internal audit staff utilizes leadership skills to collaborate and consult with organizational peers. While internal audit has the authority to investigate risk and test controls, most internal audit department personnel prioritize behavior skills like communication conflict resolution, change management, and problem-solving over technical audit skills to increase audit effectiveness (Dal Mas & Barac, 2018).

Board of Directors

The Board of Directors and the CAE have a responsibility to enhance the organization's strategic and corporate governance success by evaluating the risk within the organization, preparing an audit plan to assess if the risk is appropriately managed within the risk tolerance of the organization, and reporting on work performed (Martino, D'Onza, & Melville, 2019). Since the Board of Directors and the CAE play a vital role in corporate governance and the internal controls governing the accounting and financial reporting processes, a review of the role leadership plays in corporate governance is valuable to current and future Board members and CAEs. This section evaluates the Board of Directors' oversight role, including a focus on strategy and vision and corporate governance as the Board of Directors is responsible for oversight of the organization's strategy and the executive management team, and Mathew, Ibrahim, & Archbold, 2018) concluded that a lack of oversight and leadership from the Board of Directors increased organizational risk.

- *Strategy and Vision:* Corporate strategy is intended to develop organizational goals and objectives so the influence and oversight of the Board of Directors are paramount to balancing the goals of management and shareholders (García-Sánchez, Rodríguez-Domínguez, & Frías-Aceituno, 2015). The Board of Directors' role in influencing and guiding management is enhanced by the composition and independence of the Board of Directors (García-Sánchez et al., 2015). The conclusion is that the Board of Directors' composition includes a broad representation of skills and experiences and that independence enhances objectivity, both of which improve the team's decision-making process. Masli, Sherwood, & Srivastava, (2018) agreed with the importance of independence and stressed that the "rubber stamp" process of the past Board of Directors is no longer acceptable and that independence is a necessity in corporate governance. Moghaddam, Massihabadee, Shorvarzi, & Mehrazeen, (2018) agreed with the importance of independence and said that increased independence resulted in increased oversight and supervision of executive management.
- *Corporate Governance:* The Board of Directors' involvement and influence in setting and overseeing strategy and company activities is important to maintaining the Board's legitimacy and power, including the ability to recommend or influence changes that protect or enhance the shareholder's investment (Nahum & Carmeli, 2019). Moghaddam et al. (2018) identified efficient governance as the primary role of the Board of Directors, which included the alignment of goals between executive management and the shareholders of the organization. Andreou et al. (2016) agreed with the importance of corporate governance and tied corporate governance to stock prices by suggesting that attributes like institutional investors, CEO stock options, directors that own stock, and other

factors act as an indicator of negative future stock prices. Governance begins with the Board of Director oversight but continues with accountability and supervision from the Board of Directors over the executive management team.

LEADERSHIP STYLES AND CHALLENGES FOR BETTER GOVERNANCE

Leadership is the process of influencing others to understand and agree about what needs to be done and how to do it, and the process of facilitating individual and collective efforts to accomplish shared objectives Leadership is a process whereby an individual influences a group of individuals to achieve a common goal (Northouse, 2019). A leader is an individual who accompanies people on a journey, guiding them to their destination and by implication holds them together as a group while steering them in the right direction. A leader is an individual who rules, guides or inspires others and fully understands how to deploy their strengths and compensate their weaknesses to ultimately achieve a common goal.

Defining leadership as a process means that it is a transactional event that happens between leaders and their employees but on a continual basis. However it is a bidirectional process, an interactive event between leaders and employees rather than a linear, one-way event in which the leader only affects the followers (Baporikar, 2023c). Leadership is about influence, without influence it will be impossible to be a real leader. Figure 3 gives the contemporary leadership styles followed by the discussion on leadership styles and challenges for better governance.

Authoritative

Authoritative leadership was accepted as a critical leadership style, but authoritative leadership is of the past and outdated leadership styles are no longer effective in motivating employees that seek collaboration, teamwork, and social interactions (Fang, Chen, Wang, & Chen, (2019). While authoritative leaders can drive employee behavior by exerting authority, the instantaneous employee response provides short-term compliance and cannot drive long-term change. Holm and Fairhurst (2018) concluded that authoritative leadership enhances governance and compliance through hierarchical roles based on expertise that drives employee behavior. This highlights the importance of leadership from the Board of Directors and the Chief Audit Executive (CAE) as hierarchical positions of expertise over corporate governance shared with employees to ensure compliance with internal controls. Lawrence (2017) agreed with the definition of authoritative leadership as hierarchical governance and referred to this control style as a system of dominance to drive a behavior of compliance. Pynnönen and Takala (2018) referred to authoritative leadership as leadership by fear and noted that a focus on controls by dominance decreases employee motivation. This style of leadership can lead to negative results, such as increased turnover or decreased morale. Employees seeking coaching and development are less motivated by the authoritative leadership style, so effective leaders must go beyond leading from authority positions.

While leadership is a crucial element to driving employee behavior and compliance with company policies, management desires to obtain more than employee compliance. Fang et al. (2019) suggested that effective interaction with employees, also called inclusive leadership, creates new era workers who use new concepts, techniques, and social rules, resulting in increased innovation, commitment, and employee flexibility. Kanwal, Lodhi, & Kashif, (2019) built on this concept when they concluded that authoritative leadership increases workplace ostracism where employees feel isolated and excluded

Figure 3. Contemporary leadership styles
Source: Self-Developed

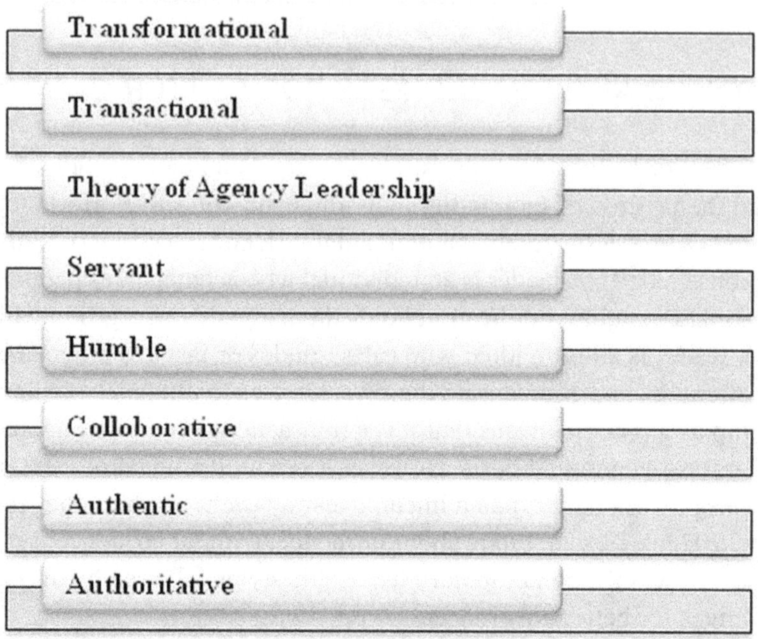

from the team as it lacks a relationship with the employee because the manager and staff interactions are more transactional than caring or personal. Hence, more preferred are current leadership styles like humble, servant, and transformational leadership focus on building relationships with employees and investing in a mentee's success. Based on this overview, one may consider if authoritative leadership is useful or if the outcome of authoritative leadership is so negative that it should be discouraged. Joshi and Jha (2017) suggested that authoritative leadership might be relevant in special situations such as implementing decisions that are critical to the company's survival, including corporate governance with regulatory requirements. This example can be expanded to include situations where worker safety is at risk or emergencies where immediate compliance or completion of a task is critical to the organization. While these examples indicate that authoritative leadership may be appropriate in specific situations, current leadership research concludes that authoritative leadership is not the desired leadership style for long-term innovation, motivation, and commitment from employees and is not the ideal leadership style for corporate governance.

Authentic

Authentic leadership describes a leadership style where leaders remain true to themselves by living values versus following along with the norm (Leroy, Anseel, Gardner, & Sels, (2015). Example of an authentic relationship is between the accountant and the accounting staff which results in enhanced governance. Steckler and Clark (2019) described the authentic leader as sincere and congruent in holding to one's beliefs. An example may be a whistleblower or a member of management that refuses to overlook accounting wrongdoing. However, Leroy et al. (2015) suggested being true to self is an authentic leadership style that admits mistakes, shortcomings in knowledge or experience, communicating the truth to others when giving feedback, or working to avoid the group norm by speaking up and providing a diverse opinion. It also includes follower authenticity in the definition of authentic leadership because followers must also be authentic to themselves and others, which lead to a feeling of self-endorsement, autonomy, and increased motivation. From these, one can conclude that authentic leadership is successful when both the leader and the team embrace authenticity, truthfulness, and genuineness to enhance corporate governance and the internal control environment.

Ling, Liu, & Wu, (2017) linked authentic leadership and servant leadership, because authentic leadership invests in others by providing honest feedback and by expanding and growing new skills to attain goals and in true sense servant leadership principles, is about putting others before self, are relevant and connected to authentic leadership. Hence, servant leadership starts with authenticity, which is the foundation for authentic leadership. The simplistic goal for leadership is to create change that results in achieving a stated objective (Conger & Kanungo, 1994). Multiple leadership styles can be used to achieve corporate governance. However, Braun and Peus (2018) suggested that authentic leadership is a person-oriented leadership style and focuses on authenticity to self and creates the motivation and work-life balance to create sustainable, long-term governance through the health and well-being of the employee.

Collaborative

Collaborative leadership includes the principles of teamwork and partnership. Lawrence (2017) defined collaborative leadership as a transformative and experiential learning process that involves the whole team to achieve corporate governance. The accountability for collaborative leadership under this definition includes the entire team to maximize success, and collaborative leadership requires willing participants that share and learn together. Corporate governance and collaborative leadership focus on a shared vision, consistent values, mutual respect, empathy, vulnerability, and open communication and collaborative leadership includes a degree of ambiguity that allows a free flow of information and experimentation to enhance governance and performance and also promotes creativity and innovation that allows for an improved governance environment (Lawrence (2017; Otter and Paxton, 2017).

This diversity of thought enhances individual creativity and increases innovation. These factors enhance team performance related to corporate governance through the discovery of new ideas and concepts. Calvert (2018) viewed collaborative leadership as a team of individuals from different hierarchical or departmental reporting units that work across organizational silos to form cross functional teams focused on compliance with common goals. This cross-functional team concept expands the definition to include team projects where an appointed leader or manager does not exist. A peer group or a team pursues compliance with common goals by working together to accomplish a stated task, and each member shares responsibility and accountability to the greater team. Since, collaborative leadership establishes a shared vision, effective communication, and team trust, all of which are required for governance this style of leadership utilizes the skills and experiences of the team to establish internal controls through compromise and collaboration, but it requires effort to succeed. Corporate governance leads to financial sustainability and operational success, and is defined as the ability to deliver goods and services to clients and stakeholders (Kim, 2018). Collaboration is a plural activity, so collaborative leadership requires participation from multiple leaders and followers to deliver consistent performance. When an organization delivers value for compensation, financial performance improves but without each team member contributing, the risk of inconsistent corporate governance increases. Collaborative leadership facilitates the implementation and acceptance of agency performance and organizational change. An increase in collaboration and the subsequent acceptance of change results in less allocation of time and resources to change management and a rapid increase in operational efficiency leading to decreased cost and increased margin, thereby increased business growth and long-term success (Randa, & Baporikar, 2022; Hsieh & Liou, 2018).

Humble

A humble leader reflects more on his or her weaknesses and opportunities for improvement and surrounds self with strong supporters that bring additional strengths to bear on the leadership team. According to Ashford, Wellman, Sully de Luque, De Stobbeleir, & Wollan, (2018), humble leaders reflect less on being the greatest leader, the leader that knows everything, or the leader that can do everything, while the humble leader openly shares limitations. When leaders share limitations, they create an opportunity for others to rise to the occasion. Humble leaders are more effective when they have a formal feedback system and a strong vision, but between the two attributes, the formal feedback system demands priority. Thus leaders who embrace formal feedback can overcome challenges related to organizational vision because they consistently receive feedback from others to compensate for individual weaknesses. These examples demonstrate that formal feedback among leaders allows for the team's strength to offset a leader with less organizational vision. A humble leader overcomes a personal weakness by capitalizing on the team's strength by allowing others to create a corporate governance vision. While collaborative leadership increases participation from the team through trust, shared vision, and teamwork, humble leadership exploits each person's strength by recognizing the leader is human and has knowledge, skill, or experience limitations. Collaborative leadership focuses on the team where a leader may or may not exist, but humble leadership focuses on the leader and the leader's need for his or her management team to bring complementary strengths to the leadership ranks.

Humble leadership enhances collaboration among leaders and empowers each leader to be more proactive in the governance role. Humble leaders engage in egalitarian-based leadership that increases governance through increased accountability between the accountant and the accounting staff. Showing mutual respect for each person enhances trust and increases collaboration. The proactive leader uses psychological empowerment, which implies that leadership creates respect through empowerment resulting in leadership participation and an increased focus on performance (Chen, Liu, Zhang, & Qian, (2018). This distinction is important because a manager focuses on implementing and complying with organizational directives versus creating and developing a vision and strategy that drives performance. After all an empowered leader is more likely to take the initiative, solve problems, improve governance effectiveness, and be innovative. Further, humble leadership increased innovation and improves an individual's core self-evaluation, which is defined as a person's belief in himself or herself and is directly related to value and commitment as humble leaders actively seek to disclose personal weaknesses and empower others on the leadership team to open up, be proactive and fill the leadership void, creating more balance within the leadership team and success from their decisions. According to Aziz (2019), the good news is that humility can be coached, and humble leadership can be learned and practiced. Many of the leadership attributes identified in this research are innate, but these attributes are also learned or enhanced through practice. For example, leaders can be authoritative when needed, but conversely, most leaders also know how to adapt to the current occasion. Humility can be learned and practiced.

The leader who adopts humble leadership learns to apply humility and teach the team to be proactive and participative as corporate governance leaders versus compliance managers.

Servant

Servant leadership is traced to the 1970s and focuses on others' interest over oneself to provide opportunities or support for someone to learn, grow, and develop (Krog & Govender, 2015). The servant leader's goal is to sacrifice opportunities for recognition and reward so others grow and receive recognition for their contributions and success. The term servant is relevant since the difference between servant leadership and other leadership styles is the desire to serve others. Newman, Schwarz, Cooper, & Sendjaya, (2017) referred to servant leadership as a means to increase organizational citizenship behavior. Corporate governance and organizational citizenship behavior are synonymous, and servant leadership increases employee governance behavior, including compliance with internal controls.

Krog and Govender (2015) identified five servant leadership dimensions: altruistic calling, emotional healing, wisdom, persuasive mapping, and organizational stewardship. Each of these characteristics is tied to the mentee and his or her behavior. Altruistic calling is the deliberate decision to lead others using a servant mentality. As the name implies, emotional healing addresses the mentee's emotional state and healing from past challenges or failures. Wisdom occurs as the mentor and mentee forge a relationship that allows the mentor to identify future growth areas and create self-awareness with the mentee. Persuasive mapping puts wisdom into action by creating a map or plan of action for growth and change. Lastly, organizational stewardship focuses on creating organizational commitment and collaboration to improve the organization as a whole. Conger and Kanungo (1994) suggested that servant leadership focuses on people and creates a greater level of development for a mentee versus a leadership style focused on organizational rules or processes. However, organizational rules and processes measure performance. Rules and processes create an organizational structure and maintain accountability among employees. Striking a balance in individual learning between structure, compliance, and investments define servant leadership and demonstrate why the servant leadership style impacts corporate governance. However, the research is clear that servant leadership, especially persuasive mapping, is important to influence employee action and support of corporate governance (Krog & Govender, 2015). Thus, servant leadership creates a team commitment that results in team effectiveness and this can be maximized by serving others and helping others succeed, which drives improved performance and long-term achievement through compliance with established controls and process policies.

Theory of Agency Leadership

Leadership can take on many forms and there are many definitions, but leadership based on agency theory recognizes the relationship between the manager or the principal and the employee or the agent (Franco-Santos, Nalick, Rivera-Torres, & Gomez-Mejia, (2017). Agency theory leadership is about balancing the roles and responsibilities of the principal and agent and is seen as the balance of leadership between the Board of Directors and various roles occupied by management and the CAE's oversight role, including the monitoring of risks and controls by the internal audit department. The agency theory is exemplified in leadership when the agent becomes a change agent by trusting, respecting, and following the principal and a leader creates agents that act as change agents that facilitate transformation or serve as an intermediary between the principal and the end goal (van Aarde, 2017).

Transactional

Transactional leadership and transformational leadership are often compared to each other, but remain very different in principle. Megheirkouni, Amaugo, & Jallo, (2018) compared the two leadership styles and defined transactional leadership as an exchange between the leader and a follower, and transformational leadership as a relationship or connection focused on transforming the follower. Using these definitions, transactional leadership's primary focus is to focus on the immediate goal or transaction that needs to be addressed or completed. Transformational leadership focuses on influence, inspiration, and individualized coaching, while transactional leadership focuses on management through rewards or management by exception, and focuses on compliance activities. Conger and Kanungo (1994) referred to transactional leadership as task-oriented leadership because it lacks inspiration and individualization, while transformational leadership creates sustained change through influence.

However, both leadership styles increase innovation and idea generation but also examined research that both leadership styles failed to create lasting change. The conflict between innovation and lasting change was resolved by further comparison. For example, transformational leadership includes a relationship between the employee and the leader based on trust, respect, and a mutual value system (Deichmann & Stam, 2015). Transformational leadership invests in the employee's success. Transactional leadership also includes trust and respect between the employee and the leader but relies on assigned roles and responsibilities. Both leadership styles can be successful, but transactional leadership focuses on a contingent reward and emphasizes on management by exception, so the relationship between the leader and employee results from outcomes-based versus personal change and individualized development.

Deng, Zhao, Lio, Chen, Ma, Liang, & Feng, (2019) agreed with this focus on rewards and concluded that a positive relationship exists between transactional leadership and employee motivation when the focus is on promoting employees' self-efficacy. Megheirkouni et al. (2018) suggested that leaders should carefully consider governance assignments because unqualified leaders damage the organization's culture. If the governance process leaders are not qualified, internal control compliance does not create a lasting change or focus on risk management. Transactional leadership focuses on helping employees develop an awareness of corporate governance and realize their capacity to improve long-term success (Deng et al., 2019).

Transformational

Like servant leadership, transformational leadership gained recognition in the 1970s. Transformational leadership focuses on transforming individuals to achieve new personal and professional success through motivation and encouragement (Ghasabeh, Soosay, & Reaiche, (2015). As the name implies, the mentor or leader's goal is to help a mentee or employee increase success through a transformation over time. Governance from the Board of Directors enhances cultural transformation in the accounting and financial reporting processes and the auditors and the accounting staff play an equal role to the Board of Directors in transforming an organization's governance environment. Transformational leadership takes time and is not a discipline that is implemented to achieve results overnight. Ghasabeh et al. (2015) suggested that effective transformational leadership comprises four characteristics:

1. Idealized guidance, the characteristic of idealized guidance focuses on the ideal state, which creates a vision of the future achieved by developing a strategy to guide the individual from the current state to a future state.
2. Consideration focused on the individual, is the tactical development and implementation of the ideal strategy that focuses on the specific weaknesses, opportunities, and gaps that an individual has identified to achieve new success.
3. Intellectual motivation includes intellectual motivation, which comprises a plan for training and development through knowledge enhancement and augmentation of experience.
4. Inspirational incitement when applied to a mentee, the evidence of these characteristics is inspirational incitement that results in sustained behavioral change.

Mesu, Sanders, & van Riemsdijk, (2015) referred to transformational leadership as visionary leadership with individualized development stimulation resulting in increased commitment to organizational governance. The transformational leader seeks to develop a vision of each mentee's future that can be obtained through coaching and leadership support. Transformational leadership benefits are best characterized by the individualized plan designed to address a person's growth area, including personal and professional transformation. Transformational leadership also increases an employee's innovation and interdependency with others and achieves the greatest success or sustained improvement over time. Thus, transformational leadership aims to customize leadership coaching to the individual so a customized coaching plan is developed to address and improve the area's most impactful on achieving governance improvement and is beyond academic training or theoretical studies and applies leadership through a customized plan that creates change and improves performance.

SOLUTIONS AND RECOMMENDATIONS

The below solutions and recommendations are to ensure that leadership styles adopted can minimize the challenges of governance if not totally eliminate them. These include:

- *Strategy Alignment:* Alignment of strategy and organizational structure as a critical determent in strategy implementation and organizational success. Each organization consists of various individuals with unique talents, strengths, and weaknesses. While brainstorming and thinking about the future are important to strategy development, the alignment of goals and ambitions must align to organizational capabilities for effective strategy execution (Srivastava & Sushil, 2017). The alignment of strategic and organizational goals is not easy and requires leaders capable of managing complex challenges and the complexities in leadership as administrative, adaptive, and enabling exist (Hazy and Uhl-Bien, 2015). Moreover, the alignment of strategy and organizational goals positively affects governance and internal controls hence there is need to do strategy alignment by planning, training, and empowering staff to enable behaviors and actions that drive change and achieve governance goals.
- *Result Monitoring Systems:* Ineffective internal controls over financial reporting fail to identify and mitigate accounting risks, but corporate governance can strengthen accounting controls and reporting accuracy (Bajra & Cadez, 2018). To enhance internal controls, the Board of Directors and management, including the CAE, should ensure alignment between operational and leader-

ship constructs and this requires an isometric alignment with operational constructs. Such an alignment allows accounting and financial reporting controls to be evaluated, monitored, and adjusted as needed to maintain compliance with regulations and company policies. In addition to the alignment of operational and leadership constructs, Ashford et al. (2018) identified employee feedback as a valuable tool for managing and monitoring results. Employees are in the details of the business and know the day-to-day activities that work and the activities that do not work. Often monitoring of results can begin by asking employees what is working and what is not working because upward feedback often does not occur or lacks the completeness to allow management to understand what is happening at the operational level. Avolio (2007) agreed and described the leader-follower link as a relationship that allows the leader to be more transparent about strategic or operational needs, and the employee is more open and productive. Once the leader-follower link is established, increased communication provides monitoring feedback that enhances the operationalizing of corporate governance leadership. Hence, efforts and systems must be in put in place to establish this link with proper monitoring systems.

- *Evaluation and Realignment:* Chiarini and Vagnoni (2017) concluded that ineffective quality management leads to ineffective internal controls and that both issues result from leadership failure. A lack of quality leads to ineffective operations, which is counter to organizational improvement. When operational processes are not appropriately designed and are ineffective, the controls designed to monitor process risks are also ineffective. If management activities are not properly executed, they create additional risks for the organization. By categorizing and rating leadership activities according to risk and complexity, the high risks and highly complex activities are evaluated and realigned more frequently, which leads to operationalizing leadership and an enhanced probability of organizational success. Thus implementing evaluation and realigning on a continual basis in accounting and financial reporting processes increase the likelihood of accuracy in financial reporting. While evaluation and realignment appear to be straightforward, human nature does not quickly recognize and evaluate control changes until forced to implement a change. However, once a needed change is recognized, leaders are more likely to respond and proceed with evaluation and realignment. The challenge is that most individuals do not proactively identify the need for change, which results in lost time between the initial signals of change and realignment. Hence there is need to have effective evaluations systems and realignment procedures in place.

Thus there is a direct and moderating effect of leadership style on the relationship between governance and organization performance which provides direction on managers to ensure adoption of the appropriate leadership styles that drives performance of the organization.

FUTURE RESEARCH DIRECTIONS

Leadership theory is viewed at the micro or individual level and the macro or team level (Dinh et al., 2014). Leadership, regardless of leadership style, focuses on the leader using his or her skills and knowledge to lead others at the team level. This process is defined as a complex activity focused on self-mentoring and coaching of others to work together to achieve personal and organizational goals (Dyer, 2018). The perception of leadership theory is leadership is based on personal growth and development that is then transferred to others through training and motivation to achieve organizational goals and objectives but there is need to investigate how these various theories, approaches and perception about leaders and leadership promote better governance and ensure ethical practices. Governance theory aims to ensure the shareholders or owners of the organization are represented and a governing authority supervises management's control and actions. Governance can be rigid, robust, fragile, or flexible depending on the degree of change and exploration (Duit & Galaz, 2008). The goal of governance is to be responsive to the situation and to allow for the exploration of new ideas and innovations. The perception of governance theory is that oversight and control are necessary, but the two activities are independent to ensure the owner's rights are represented fairly and accurately. There is need to review how these aspects of influence and impact leadership roles in the organizations and these studies can be undertaken sector wise or region wise.

Another interesting area to investigate is how the contractual relationship between leaders and organizations work in principle, regarding the aspect of commitment, which needs honesty, trust, and loyalty. The perceptions of agency theory demonstrate the alignment with governance theory and that the principal is responsible for the development and oversight of the agent. The principal provides governance over the agent as the Board of Directors provides oversight of management through a governance framework. Leadership shortcomings serve as the source of organizational inefficiency due to misalignment of objectives or the pursuit of personal interests (Kastberg & Siverbo, 2016). This conclusion demonstrates the need to study about interconnectivity of leadership, governance, and agency theory, and the need for effective leadership and oversight of management.

Alvesson (2019) identified four leadership scenarios including high-alignment, value misfit, construction misfit, and multiple breakdowns. High-alignment reflects a shared sense of position or goal congruence between the leader and the follower. Value misfit is a dissimilar assessment or conclusion between the leader and the follower. Construction misfit is defined as the leader and follower having a different interpretation of a situation or assessment of fact. Studies on how this affects governance in different regions and emerging economies would be useful in this interdisciplinary field. Another interesting area for research is on designing models and frameworks' on how high-alignment can be achieved by understanding leadership styles and governance principles to develop oversight strategies and enhance organizational performance and efficiency in the reporting processes.

CONCLUSION

No doubt that leadership style has a positive and significant effect on the relationship between governance and performance of organizations. The role of leadership style in organizations is crucial in terms of creating a vision, mission, determination and designing strategies, policies, and procedures to achieve the objectives effectively and efficiently along with directing and coordinating the efforts and activities.

Organizations and individuals at the helm of affairs need to embrace appropriate leadership style in order to improve performance and excellence (Baporikar, 2018; 2017). The overall objective of this research was to analyze how leadership style has influence on the governance and the challenges therein. It is absolutely clear leadership style must be effective as its influence is not only on the corporate sector but also the society at large. Effective leadership and appropriate style dependent on the needs of the organizations should lead to better governance, which ultimately leads to better and productive organizations. Better governance would also ensure the corporate social responsibilities (CSR) which encourages working for welfare of people (Baporikar, 2021). Thus, it clearly means that leadership, governance and corporate social responsibilities are interrelated with each other. The influence of leadership does not end here as result displays that it also put strong influence on small and medium enterprises, which are considered as backbone of any economy. Effective inter-action and proper working methodology by leadership with governance mechanisms in place can save the organizations from financial crisis, and run the economy towards productivity and sustainable economic development and growth.

Successful leaderships and executives must have strong vision to specify and strong motivation to pursue the goals which leads towards economic prosperity and community development (Baporikar, 2018). Corporate sector and non-governmental organizations (NGOs) are working jointly with Governments on different projects like health, education and business policy and planning, which always ensure best results. The concept of collaborative work of public and private sector is most important discussion now days as a fruit for the joint work by both parties have always been got by the different stakeholders in the shape of better living standard and economic prosperity, hence participatory style of leadership with collaborative governance is also gaining importance. This study therefore advocates that leadership style be taken seriously by the managers in organizations. The findings of the study are a useful guide for developing training programs for the leaders on the need for good governance and mechanisms of improving performance through creating competitive advantage.

Funding

This research received no specific grant from any funding agency in the public, commercial, or not-for-profit sectors.

REFERENCES

Afsar, B., Badir, Y. F., & Bin Saeed, B. (2014). Transformational leadership and innovative work behavior. *Industrial Management & Data Systems*, *114*(8), 1270–1300. doi:10.1108/IMDS-05-2014-0152

Andreou, P. C., Antoniou, C., Horton, J., & Louca, C. (2016). Corporate governance and firm specific stock price crashes. *European Financial Management*, *22*(5), 916–956. doi:10.1111/eufm.12084

Ashford, S. J., Wellman, N., Sully de Luque, M., De Stobbeleir, K. E. M., & Wollan, M. (2018). Two roads to effectiveness: CEO feedback seeking, vision articulation, and firm performance. *Journal of Organizational Behavior*, *39*(1), 82–95. doi:10.1002/job.2211

Avolio, B. J. (2007). Promoting more integrative strategies for leadership theory-building. *The American Psychologist*, *62*(1), 25–33. doi:10.1037/0003-066X.62.1.25 PMID:17209677

Aziz, K. (2019). Why is humility so relevant for leaders and can it be developed through coaching? *Strategic HR Review*, *18*(1), 30–33. doi:10.1108/SHR-10-2018-0088

Bajra, U., & Cadez, S. (2018). The impact of corporate governance quality on earnings management: Evidence from European companies Cross-listed in the US. *Australian Accounting Review*, *28*(2), 152–166. doi:10.1111/auar.12176

Baporikar, N. (2017). Corporate Leadership and Sustainability. In Collective Creativity for Responsible and Sustainable Business Practice (pp. 160-179). IGI Global. doi:10.4018/978-1-5225-1823-5.ch009

Baporikar, N. (2018). Critical success factors for executives in global economy. In *Geopolitics and Strategic Management in the Global Economy* (pp. 40–56). IGI Global. doi:10.4018/978-1-5225-2673-5.ch003

Baporikar, N. (2021). Innovative Systems Structure for Real Corporate Governance. [IJSDA]. *International Journal of System Dynamics Applications*, *10*(4), 1–20. doi:10.4018/IJSDA.20211001.oa1

Baporikar, N. (Ed.). (2023a). *Leadership and Governance for Sustainability*. IGI Global. doi:10.4018/978-1-6684-9711-1

Baporikar, N. (2023b). Millennial Leadership in Global Society and Future Prospects. In T. Graham (Ed.), *Considerations and Characteristics of the Millennial Leader in Today's Global Society* (pp. 1–21). IGI Global. doi:10.4018/978-1-6684-4711-6.ch001

Baporikar, N. (2023c). Leadership for Sustainable Development in Emerging Economies. In B. Dutta & P. Chaudhuri (Eds.), *EDUCATION IN SUSTAINABLE DEVELOPMENT* (pp. 1–16). MTC Global.

Bass, B. M. (1985). Leadership: Good, better, best. *Organizational Dynamics*, *13*(3), 26–40. doi:10.1016/0090-2616(85)90028-2

Baysinger, B., & Hoskisson, R. (1990). The Composition of Boards of Directors and Strategic Control: Effects on Corporate Strategy. *Academy of Management Review*, *15*(1), 72–87. doi:10.2307/258106

Benmira, S., & Agboola, M. (2021). Evolution of leadership theory. *BMJ Leader*, *5*(1), 3–5.

Braun, S., & Peus, C. (2018). Crossover of work–life balance perceptions: Does authentic leadership matter? *Journal of Business Ethics*, *149*(4), 875–893. doi:10.1007/s10551-016-3078-x

Calvert, K. (2018). Collaborative leadership: Cultivating an environment for success. *Collaborative Librarianship*, *10*(2), 79.

Chen, Y., Liu, B., Zhang, L., & Qian, S. (2018). Can leader "humility" spark employee "proactivity"? The mediating role of psychological empowerment. *Leadership and Organization Development Journal*, *39*(3), 326–339. doi:10.1108/LODJ-10-2017-0307

Chiarini, A., & Vagnoni, E. (2017). TQM implementation for the healthcare sector: The relevance of leadership and possible causes of lack of leadership. *Leadership in Health Services*, *30*(3), 210–216. doi:10.1108/LHS-02-2017-0004 PMID:28693393

Conger, J. A., & Kanungo, R. N. (1994). Charismatic leadership in organizations: Perceived behavioral attributes and their measurement. *Journal of Organizational Behavior*, *15*(5), 439–452. doi:10.1002/job.4030150508

Cullen, M. M., & Brennan, N. M. (2017). Differentiating control, monitoring and oversight. *Accounting, Auditing & Accountability Journal*, *30*(8), 1867–1894. doi:10.1108/AAAJ-12-2015-2345

Dal Mas, L. O., & Barac, K. (2018). The influence of the chief audit executive's leadership style on factors related to internal audit effectiveness. *Managerial Auditing Journal*, *33*(8-9), 807–835. doi:10.1108/MAJ-12-2017-1741

Dănescu, T., Prozan, M., & Prozan, R. D. (2015). Perspectives regarding accounting – corporate governance – internal control. *Procedia Economics and Finance*, *32*, 588–594. doi:10.1016/S2212-5671(15)01436-7

Deichmann, D., & Stam, D. (2015). Leveraging transformational and transactional leadership to cultivate the generation of organization-focused ideas. *The Leadership Quarterly*, *26*(2), 204–219. doi:10.1016/j.leaqua.2014.10.004

Deng, G., Zhao, D., Lio, J., Chen, X., Ma, X., Liang, L., & Feng, C. (2019). Strategic elements of residency training in China: Transactional leadership, self-efficacy, and employee orientation culture. *BMC Medical Education*, *19*(1), 1–8. doi:10.1186/s12909-019-1792-7 PMID:31521148

Dinh, J. E., Lord, R. G., Gardner, W. L., Meuser, J. D., Liden, R. C., & Hu, J. (2014). Leadership theory and research in the new millennium: Current theoretical trends and changing perspectives. *The Leadership Quarterly*, *25*(1), 36–62. doi:10.1016/j.leaqua.2013.11.005

Dryer, C. (2018). Leadership. *Teaching and Learning in Nursing*, *13*(3), A7–A8. doi:10.1016/j.teln.2018.04.002

Duit, A., & Galaz, V. (2008). Governance and Complexity – Emerging issues for governance theory. *Governance: An International Journal of Policy, Administration and Institutions*, *21*(3), 311–335. doi:10.1111/j.1468-0491.2008.00402.x

Eliot, J. L. (2020). Resilient Leadership: The Impact of a Servant Leader on the Resilience of their Followers. *Advances in Developing Human Resources*, *22*(4), 404–418. doi:10.1177/1523422320945237

Fang, Y., Chen, J., Wang, M., & Chen, C. (2019). The impact of inclusive leadership on employees' innovative behaviors: The mediation of psychological capital. *Frontiers in Psychology*, *10*, 1803. doi:10.3389/fpsyg.2019.01803 PMID:31447740

Ferdowsian, M. C. (2016). Total business excellence – a new management model for operationalizing excellence. *International Journal of Quality & Reliability Management*, *33*(7), 942–984. doi:10.1108/IJQRM-08-2014-0109

Figueiredo, P. C. (2022). Leader Competence Effectiveness. In F. Ince (Ed.), *International Perspectives and Strategies for Managing an Aging Workforce* (pp. 115–143). IGI Global. doi:10.4018/978-1-7998-2395-7.ch006

Franco-Santos, M., Nalick, M., Rivera-Torres, P., & Gomez-Mejia, L. (2017). Governance and Wellbeing in academia: Negative consequences of applying agency theory logic in higher education. *British Journal of Management*, *28*(4), 711–730. doi:10.1111/1467-8551.12249

Gao, P., & Zhang, G. (2019). Accounting manipulation, peer pressure, and internal control. *The Accounting Review*, *94*(1), 127–151. doi:10.2308/accr-52078

García-Sánchez, I., Rodríguez-Domínguez, L., & Frías-Aceituno, J. (2015). Board of directors and ethics codes in different corporate governance systems. *Journal of Business Ethics*, *131*(3), 681–698. doi:10.1007/s10551-014-2300-y

Ghasabeh, M. S., Soosay, C., & Reaiche, C. (2015). The emerging role of transformational leadership. *Journal of Developing Areas*, *49*(6), 459–467. doi:10.1353/jda.2015.0090

Hazy, J. K., & Uhl-Bien, M. (2015). Towards operationalizing complexity leadership: How generative, administrative and community-building leadership practices enact organizational outcomes. *Leadership*, *11*(1), 79–104. doi:10.1177/1742715013511483

Holm, F., & Fairhurst, G. T. (2018). Configuring shared and hierarchical leadership through authoring. *Human Relations, 71*(5), 692–721. doi:10.1177/0018726717720803

Hsieh, J. Y., & Liou, K. T. (2018). Collaborative leadership and organizational performance: Assessing the structural relation in a public service agency. *Review of Public Personnel Administration, 38*(1), 83–109. doi:10.1177/0734371X15623619

Joshi, M., & Jha, S. (2017). Choice of an authoritative style when implementing a survival urgency-based strategic change. *Journal of Strategy and Management, 10*(2), 168–186. doi:10.1108/JSMA-06-2014-0041

Kanwal, I., Lodhi, R. N., & Kashif, M. (2019). Leadership styles and workplace ostracism among frontline employees. *Management Research Review, 42*(8), 991–1013. doi:10.1108/MRR-08-2018-0320

Kastberg, G., & Siverbo, S. (2016). The role of management accounting and control in making professional organizations horizontal. *Accounting, Auditing & Accountability Journal, 29*(3), 428–451. doi:10.1108/AAAJ-03-2014-1632

Krog, C. L., & Govender, K. (2015). The relationship between servant leadership and employee empowerment, commitment, trust and innovative behaviour: A project management perspective. *SA Journal of Human Resource Management, 13*(1), 1–12. doi:10.4102/sajhrm.v13i1.712

Lawrence, R. L. (2017). Understanding collaborative leadership in theory and practice. *New Directions for Adult and Continuing Education, 17*(156), 89–96. doi:10.1002/ace.20262

Leroy, H., Anseel, F., Gardner, W. L., & Sels, L. (2015). Authentic leadership, authentic followership, basic need satisfaction, and work role performance: A cross-level study. *Journal of Management, 41*(6), 1677–1697. doi:10.1177/0149206312457822

Ling, Q., Liu, F., & Wu, X. (2017). Servant versus authentic leadership: Assessing effectiveness in China's hospitality industry. *Cornell Hospitality Quarterly, 58*(1), 53–68. doi:10.1177/1938965516641515

Martino, P., D'Onza, G., & Melville, R. (2019). The relationship between CAE leadership and the IAF's involvement in corporate governance. *Journal of Accounting, Auditing & Finance, 34*(4), 1–19.

Mathew, S., Ibrahim, S., & Archbold, S. (2018). Corporate governance and firm risk. *Corporate Governance (Bradford), 18*(1), 52–67. doi:10.1108/CG-02-2017-0024

Megheirkouni, M., Amaugo, A., & Jallo, S. (2018). Transformational and transactional leadership and skills approach: Insights on stadium management. *International Journal of Public Leadership, 14*(4), 245–259. doi:10.1108/IJPL-06-2018-0029

Menz, M., & Barnbeck, F. (2017). Determinants and consequences of corporate development and strategy function size. *Strategic Organization, 15*(4), 481–503. doi:10.1177/1476127017711070

Mesu, J., Sanders, K., & van Riemsdijk, M. (2015). Transformational leadership and organisational commitment in manufacturing and service small to medium-sized enterprises: The moderating effects of directive and participative leadership. *Personnel Review, 44*(6), 970–990. doi:10.1108/PR-01-2014-0020

Meuser, J. D., Gardner, W. L., Dinh, J. E., Hu, J., Liden, R. C., & Lord, R. G. (2016). A network analysis of leadership theory: The infancy of integration. *Journal of Management*, *42*(5), 1374–1403. doi:10.1177/0149206316647099

Moghaddam, A. T., Massihabadee, A., Shorvarzi, M., & Mehrazeen, A. (2018). Board of directors and general manager role in organization governance and attention to board of directors' characteristics components. *International Journal of Organizational Leadership*, *7*(2), 143–152. doi:10.33844/ijol.2018.60213

Nahum, N., & Carmeli, A. (2019). Leadership style in a board of directors: Implications of involvement in the strategic decision-making process. *The Journal of Management and Governance*, *7*(19), 1–29.

Newman, A., Schwarz, G., Cooper, B., & Sendjaya, S. (2017). How servant leadership influences organizational citizenship behavior: The roles of LMX, empowerment, and proactive personality. *Journal of Business Ethics*, *145*(1), 49–62. doi:10.1007/s10551-015-2827-6

Northouse, P. G. (2019). *Leadership, theory and practice* (8th ed.). SAGE.

Otter, K., & Paxton, D. (2017). A journey into collaborative leadership: Moving toward innovation and adaptability: A journey into collaborative leadership. *New Directions for Adult and Continuing Education*, *2017*(156), 33–42. doi:10.1002/ace.20248

Pande, S., & Ansari, V. A. (2014). A theoretical framework for corporate governance. Indian. *Journal of Corporate Governance*, *7*(1), 56–72.

Pynnönen, A., & Takala, T. (2018). The discursive dance: The employee co-operation negotiations as an arena for management-by-fear. *Journal of Business Ethics*, *147*(1), 165–184. doi:10.1007/s10551-015-2991-8

Randa, I. O., & Baporikar, N. (2022). Collaborative Governance Contribution for Improving Post-Crash Responsiveness at Motor Vehicle Accident Fund. [IJSEM]. *International Journal of Sustainable Economies Management*, *11*(1), 1–25. doi:10.4018/IJSEM.304875

Spector, B. A. (2016). Carlyle, Freud, and the great man theory more fully considered. *Leadership*, *12*(2), 250–260. doi:10.1177/1742715015571392

Srivastava, A. K., & Sushil. (2017). Alignment: The foundation of effective strategy execution. *International Journal of Productivity and Performance Management*, *66*(8), 1043–1063. doi:10.1108/IJPPM-11-2015-0172

Steckler, E., & Clark, C. (2019). Authenticity and corporate governance. *Journal of Business Ethics*, *155*(4), 951–963. doi:10.1007/s10551-018-3903-5

Van Aarde, A. (2017). 'By faith alone' (undivided loyalty) in light of change agency theory: Jesus, Paul and the Jesus-group in Colossae. *Hervormde Teologiese Studies*, *73*(3). Advance online publication. doi:10.4102/hts.v73i3.4355

Werner, M., & Gehrke, N. (2019). Identifying the absence of effective internal controls: An alternative approach for internal control audits. *Journal of Information Systems*, *33*(2), 205–222. doi:10.2308/isys-52112

KEY TERMS AND DEFINITIONS

Business: Pertains broadly to commercial, financial, and industrial activities.

Challenges: Something that by its nature or character serves as a call to make special effort, a demand to explain, justify, or difficulty in a undertaking that is stimulating to one engaged in it.

Core Competences: Knowledge based technical and human abilities and skills.

Decision-Making: A rational and logical process of choosing the best alternative or course of action among the available options.

Individual Competence: Refers to the capacity of individuals/employees to act in a wide variety of situations. It's their education, skills, experience, energy and their attitudes that will make or break the relationships with the customers and the products or services that are provided.

Leader: Head, superior, a person who rules, guides, motivates, encourages, stimulates, and inspires others.

Management: Any act by an individual member on the behalf of a group, with the intent to get the group to better meet its goals. It includes acts or activities or the process of looking after and making decisions about something.

Motivation: The act or an instance of motivating, arousing desire to do, creating interest or drive by incentive or inducement. It is also a psychological that arouses, sustains, and regulates human behavior.

Policy: Refers to guidelines as issued by the governance.

Stakeholder: A person with an interest or concern in something, especially in an organization or institution. A stakeholder is a member of a type of organization or system in which a member or participant seen as having an interest in its success.

Strategies: Method chosen and plans made to bring about a desired future, achievement of goals or solutions to a problem. Strategies are a result of choices made. It is that set of managerial decisions and actions that determine the long-term performance of a business enterprise.

Chapter 6
Corporate Governance for Sustainable Development

A. Sridharan
https://orcid.org/0000-0002-0753-3585
Christ University, India

Sunita Kumar
https://orcid.org/0000-0002-0628-1873
Christ University, India

ABSTRACT

Governance relates to structures and processes within an organisation to ensure greater accountability, a higher sense of responsiveness, transparency, and rule of law. Corporate governance balances the interests of a company's many stakeholders, such as shareholders, customers, vendors, financiers, the government, the community, and, very importantly, its own employees. While traditionally corporates had one clear agenda—i.e., make more profits and increase the shareholders' wealth—the 21st century saw the corporates turning a new leaf and looking at their growth from a societal perspective, specifically those relating to sustainable development like environmental protection. In the classical case of poor corporate governance, in the year 1984, the city Bhopal in India witnessed the most nightmarish experience, with the death of 16,000 people due to the leakage of a poisonous gas.

INTRODUCTION

Corporate Governance

The responsibilities of corporate managers guard the rights of the shareholders through policies and control structures called corporate governance (Kurawa & Abdulrahman, 2014). According to Duztas (2008), Corporate Governance is an instrument to ensure the well-being, impartiality, transparency and responsibility of shareholders

DOI: 10.4018/979-8-3693-1742-6.ch006

Figure 1. Tangible and intangible assets of the organisation

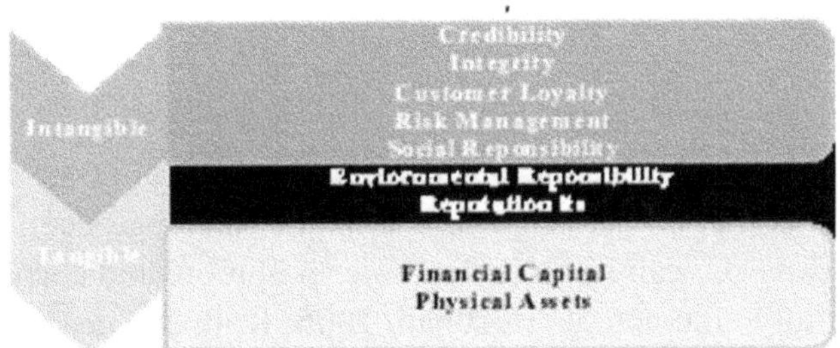

There is a direct relationship between business governance and public trust, confidence and faith in the organisation. This actually leads to goodwill in the organisation. While governments worldwide pass legislation to protect societies from threats and challenges from occurring or recurring, corporates have higher responsibilities and accountability to stakeholders – the public, governments, shareholders, and their employees. In spite of various legislations, the public does have their own concerns about organisations due to various scandals hitting corporations now and then.

An organisation is judged by both its tangible and intangible assets:

The aims of Corporate Governance are to provide a holistic framework to the organisation in order to ensure it remains meaningful to its stakeholders:

- It is to operate and self-govern itself within the regulatory framework set by governments.
- All its economic activities are to be environmentally beneficial to society
- The textile industry at Tiruppur, India, lets the waste into the Cauvery Rivulet, whose water is also used for agricultural purposes. Instead, the industry could have set up an ETP to treat the dyeing material.
- Business houses are to realise that they protect human rights and have huge social responsibilities like supporting the underprivileged, equal pay, sports promotions, building hospitals, etc.

Conventionally, corporate governance protects shareholders' interests from the pressures of unprincipled executives (Roberts & Van den Steen, 2000). However, in recent years, governance has encompassed much more areas and activities, including the environment. Indeed, sustainability is progressively becoming an important part of the strategies followed by organisations (Iansiti & Levien, 2004),

The Brundtland Report of 1987 of the World Commission on Environment and Development defined sustainability as a concept integrated with environmental, economic and social dimensions. This report helped sensitise governments and business houses to take constructive steps for developing emerging nations, as the members felt that growth could happen only through integrating sustainability with social responsibility.

Scholars have repeatedly demonstrated that corporate governance structure should ensure growth in monetary performance and sustainable performance by backing up larger stakeholder partaking (Rao & Tilt, 2016; Carter et al., 2010; Naciti, 2019).

Also, governments and financial institutions are more than willing to support organisations that show greater sensitivity to sustainable initiatives. The role of the board is not only to maximise the wealth of shareholders but to look beyond the organisation to support and establish an ethical approach. (Burke and Mattis 2013).

Sustainability

The popularity of sustainability among firms is evolving and growing for three reasons. First, all are highly conscious of the fact that climate change is a major challenge due to extreme heat or massive floods. These are either caused by air pollution or water pollution, and corporates have a huge responsibility to reduce, if not fully eliminate it (Hoffman, 2005; Kolk & Pinske, 2005; Lash & Wellington, 2007). Second, worldwide investment managers look at the organisations in their commitments to social and environmental performance, suggesting that economic performance is not the sole criterion for firm valuations (Mercer et al., 2006). Lastly, sustainability is being viewed by scholars and society as the new battleground for competitive advantage, one in which firms try to achieve a balance between economic, social and environmental strategies. (Porter and Kramer, 2006).

When most of the firms focused only on corporate social responsibilities and had very little impact on sustainability challenges, extensive work by researchers (Wolfe & Aupperle 1991; Waddock & Graves 1997; Hillman & Keim 2001; Waldman et al. 2006) viewed sustainability as a composite, complete and multidimensional concept apprehending "a business organisation's outline of philosophies of social responsibility, methods of social responsiveness, policies, programmes and noticeable outcomes as they relate to the firm's connectivity to society (Wood 1991: p.693). An important understanding of this definition is that the sustainability performances of the firms incorporate three distinct concepts: (1) why a firm engages in some activities like principles, (2) the firm idea of an organisation to generate an intended outcome, like policies and procedures, and (3) the results themselves, like greenhouse gas emissions.

Over a period of time, companies have been revising their stand and approach and started to show interest and intent to increase investments in sustainability practices. Among these are the necessity to adapt to the regulatory norms, the importance of producing quality products and, at the same time, reducing production costs, and energy costs, leading to lesser pollution – air and water, and these will go a long way to improve the goodwill of the organisation in the minds of customers and which will lead to growth potential in new markets (Poddar et al., 2019). Thus, firms have started to realise the increasing association between sustainable activities and organisational accomplishment (Fernando et al., 2019). Thus, corporate sustainability has broadened its borders from being a mere environmental issue to covering the firm's overall business model.

In the name of increasing shareholder wealth and in pursuit of economic growth, organisations supersede concern about the environment and society. **4.**8 million acres of the Amazon rainforest were lost in 2021. In the last ten years, 400 square miles of forest had been destroyed in one Brazilian state to sow soy.

This massive destruction of forest cover could cost a staggering US $ 422 million in annual loss to agriculture

. The following will highlight the need for sustainable business growth:

- Better environment for current and future generations
- Internal stakeholders get the benefit of a safer and healthier working environment
- This would eventually lead to improvement in the company's bottom line
- More importantly, such a sustainable movement will bring a competitive advantage to businesses due to a better image of the organisation in the minds of end consumers.

Figure 2. Major decrease in primary forest loss in 2023 compared to both last year, 2022 and the recent peak Year, 2020, in the western Amazon

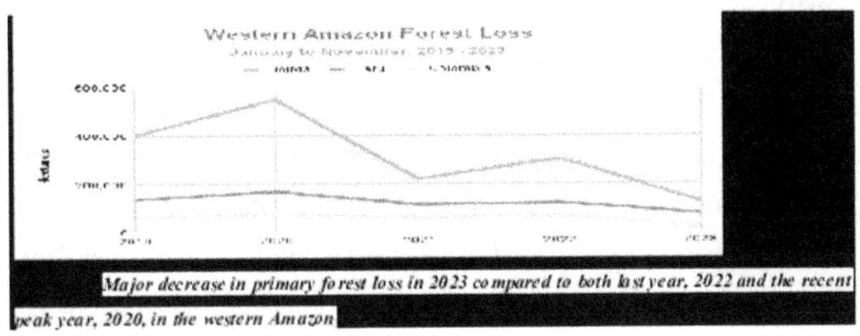

Based on the research conducted by Bansal (2001:48), he says firms "almost certainly face extinction" if they do not follow the path of sustainability. Corporate sustainability relates to a firm's ability to produce fiscal, social and ecological performance simultaneously (Elkinton, 1997; Bansal, 2001; Wilson & Lombardi, 2001; Steurer *et al.,* 2005).

Methodology

The researchers have undertaken the study of corporate governance and sustainability from two perspectives, one analysing the situation based on inputs from various research literature and two based on case studies pertaining to sustainability goals and achievements of organisations.

Literature Reviews

Maier (2005) mentioned, "Corporate governance states the relationship between the company, its board and its shareholders and stakeholders.

While Brand, effective management, innovative ideas and quality principles drive the economic prosperity of an organisation, it is also important to remember that this bottom-line principle also depends on corporate governance principles. This governance definitely improves the internal effectiveness and efficiency of the firms in advanced economics. (Tadesse, 2004)

However, lack of transparency and the effort not to give out full information about the health of the organisation reduce the effectiveness of corporate governance and thus have a huge impact on the lasting performance and sustainability of the organisation. (Ehikioya, 2009)

Gompers, Ishi, and Metrick (2003) stated in their research report that firms that have been listed on the New York Stock Exchange showed a low expenditure level but a significantly higher market valuation due to their better governance.

Corporate Sustainability is an enduring strategic approach. The onus of responsibility lies with corporates to reverse their own negative impacts by making valuable contributions to society and thus create stakeholder value (Stuart Hart, 2003)

Corporations with a high focus on sustainability have a strong competitive advantage, relatively lower share price volatility, and improved brand image. While this forced corporations to publish their reports on sustainability, it also prepared them to be future-ready for any external environmental impact. (Siew et. al.2014).

Organisations have become highly conscious of the linkage between sustainable green practices and accomplishment (Fernando et al., 2019). Thus, sustainability is not just an environmental issue to organisations; it now encompasses its overall business model.

The concept of sustainability has been evolving over a period of time, and organisations' adaptation to sustainability programmes are also taking different shapes at different times. Organisations for an elongated period of time believed that sustainability and environmental challenges are more of social responsibility with legal, moral and ethical consequences than the firm's business model, and consumers do expect from the organisation green goals and achievements. Companies have now realised that their sustainability programmes help in getting increased investments. The sustainability practices include producing good quality products for end consumers and sourcing raw materials from vendors who adopt green practices at their production units. Consumers and investors also look at organisations that reduce production costs at their own factories and adopt green production methods, like installing Effluent Treatment Plants (ETP) to recycle precious water (Poddar et al., 2019).

Therefore, the sustainability report has dual value for the organisation to provide information on organisation policies by providing safeguards to human and natural resources. (Schaltegger & Wagner, 2006). This report helps consumers and investors to make a judgement on an organisation's social responsibility and its sustainable policies. (Aras & Crowther, 2009). It also helps to boost the image of the business that has public consent. (Kolk, 2008). Thus, a good sustainability policy and programme helps to promote its reputation, which in turn helps to build community faith in the organisation. (Zadek, 2001).

The continued interest of researchers in corporate governance and sustainability shows the increasing importance of not only sustainability but also the recognition of the role to be played by organisations in such social programmes. (Naciti, Valeria, et. al., 2021)

Scholars argued that some organisations could have better access to market funds than other firms because of their sustainability efforts. (Cochran & Wood, 1984; Waddock & Graves, 1997), enticing and retaining higher talented personnel (Turban & Greening, 1997; Greening & Turban, 2000), helping them to market their products and services in a more efficient and effective way (Moskowitz, 1972; Fombrun, 1996), generating prospects that were not there or hidden (Fombrun et al., 2000), and gain greater social acceptability (Hawn et al., 2011).

More importantly, sustainability helps firms to get better advertising mileage without actually spending any amount, and it helps to increase the demand for the products of such firms and in fact, may help to reduce consumer price sensitivity towards its products (Dorfman & Steiner, 1954; Navarro, 1988; Sen & Bhattacharya, 2001; Milgrom & Roberts, 1986). It also helps firms to develop intangible assets like goodwill (Gardberg & Fomburn, 2006; Hull & Rothernberg, 2008; Waddock & Graves, 1997).

PURPOSE IN CORPORATE GOVERNANCE - PATH TOWARDS A MORE SUSTAINABLE WORLD

9.4 of United Nations Sustainability Development Goal

UN SDG has urged all countries and organisations to upgrade their infrastructure and refit, re-engineer and revalue their processes by 2030 to make sustainable through increased resource-efficient materials and methods and greater adoption of environmentally sound techniques and technologies and industrial processes based on their capabilities.

Figure 3. Purpose in corporate governance
(Ricart, J. E., & Rey, C. (2021).

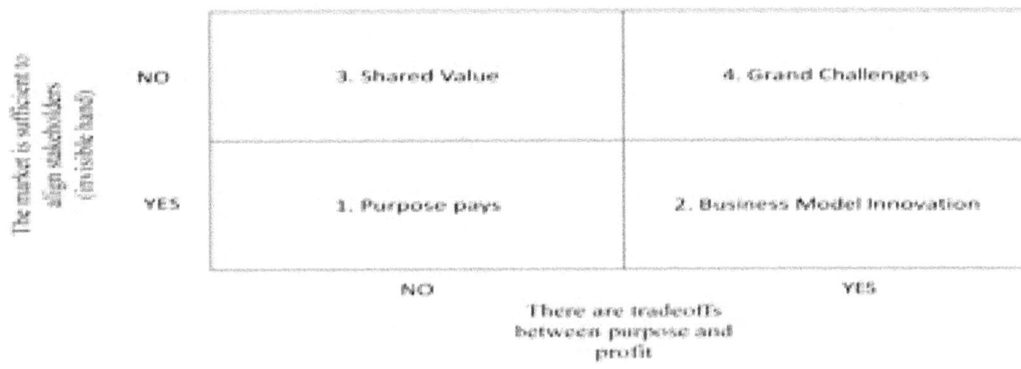

Organisation Trade-Off Between Societal Good and Profit

The intersection of trade-offs and market incentive, create four responses in which corporate governance plays a vital role. There are no trade-offs in 'purpose pays', and the market is adequate to align stakeholders' interests. In the second model of 'business model innovation', though there is a trade-off, this can be resolved through the innovation of the business model. The 'shared value' considers that market mechanisms are not enough to align stakeholders' interests for a common purpose. The fourth scenario. 'Grand challenge' considers trade-offs cannot be resolved by market mechanisms, and hence, it is necessary for organisations to go beyond the mere innovation of the business models.

The four scenarios are not exclusive but illuminate the changes the businesses need to make. This model brings out the importance of values of equity, inclusion, sustainability, and suppleness that already prevail in society and need to be integrated into the corporate governance of business. If these values are integrated into governance, it will impregnate the whole organisation and make the organisation one of the guardians of society through its sustainability programmes. Corporate Governance should spread these demands from society, encouraging management to tackle the challenges of change. When there are public goods and common values at work, corporate governance must explore systems of public-private collaboration to prevent the exhaustion of community resources. This will help to develop shared-value business models easily.

There has been increasing pressure on companies to evince greater concern over social and environmental challenges. This has led companies to actively pursue sustainability goals with greater vigour and leave a green footprint (Adams & Frost, 2008). There has been quite a large research effort directed towards the integration of ethical, social, environmental and economic performances of organisations (Adams & Frost, 2008). According to Güler and Crowther (2008), organisations need to have corporate governance based on the principles of (1) transparency, (2) accountability, (3) responsibility, and (4) fairness.

In order to have a better governance of the organisation, corporates need to take a hard look into the following factors and consider them and implement them effectively to ensure governance is not only on paper but also in spirit:

a. Impact on Society: Today, organisations have to implement environmental management systems like the materials that cannot be used like toxic, hazardous materials, the amount of energy that can be used and better waste management. Their sustainability programmes also include the use of green energy like solar or wind power, moving from traditional fossil fuels like petroleum.

Buysse and Verbeke (2003) developed a classification of natural competencies that create a competitive advantage through engagement and commitment and promise to align businesses with environmental factors.

While it is true that such an implementation of environmental policies will benefit society, there is also no denying that these practices can also result in a better working atmosphere for internal players. In cases of industries where they produce toxic materials, if organisations can reduce or implement safeguards for employees, it will positively impact employees' mental and physical health conditions. This, thus, in a way, is also a contribution to the society as employees are part of the society. (de Giovanni, 2012; Gimenez et al., 2012).

Corporates are to realise that they take all resources from society – men or materials for which they need to pay back either through salaries or replenishment of raw materials through better soil conservation, water conservation, pollution control, etc.

b. Environmental Impact: Sustainability is defined as "development that meets the needs of the present without compromising the ability of future generations to meet their needs". The authors of this research paper focus on sustainability through the ESG concept of environmental, social, and governance (ESG) (Manescu, 2011; Galbreath, 2013; Ortas et al., 2015).

During the last few decades, there has been constant search and increased awareness of ESG at the corporate level (Ortas et al., 2015; Chams & Garcıa-Blandon, 2019a).

The above clearly indicates that companies look into environmental and social factors and governance very seriously. (Manescu, 2011; Galbreath, 2013; Fu & Su, 2020). This refers to using environmental management systems and policies for better energy usage and reducing environmental waste (Montabon et al., 2007; Husted & de Sousa-Filho, 2017).

Corporates are to save Mother Earth for longer sustainability and need to have internally better planning on wastage of water, recycling of used water through ETP (effluent treatment plant) and STP (sewage treatment plant), regular energy audits, to prevent energy waste, paper/stationery waste (as millions of trees are cut to make papers globally) Governance relates to a formal structure of senior managers and board members who operate the organisation on behalf of its shareholders. They need to exhibit a sense of responsibility in all their dealings with society, stakeholders and financial matters. They must show a high amount of ethical value system in all their dealings without compromising their moral responsibility. Thus, corporate governance principles are based on transparency, accountability and fairness.

The above four enlisted principles operate as a control mechanism for the company so as to increase the value to society in general and improve and enhance the satisfaction of shareholders and stakeholders in particular.

As per the authors, sustainability is focused on the future and is not to be inhibited by the pronouncements taken in the present. This essentially means investing in new technologies and concepts in production and distribution, like renewable resources minimising pollution. Thus, good environmental protection and performance by a firm in the present is an investment in the future. (Waddock and Graves, 1997).

Figure 4. Model of sustainable development
(Aras, Guler, & Crowther, 008)

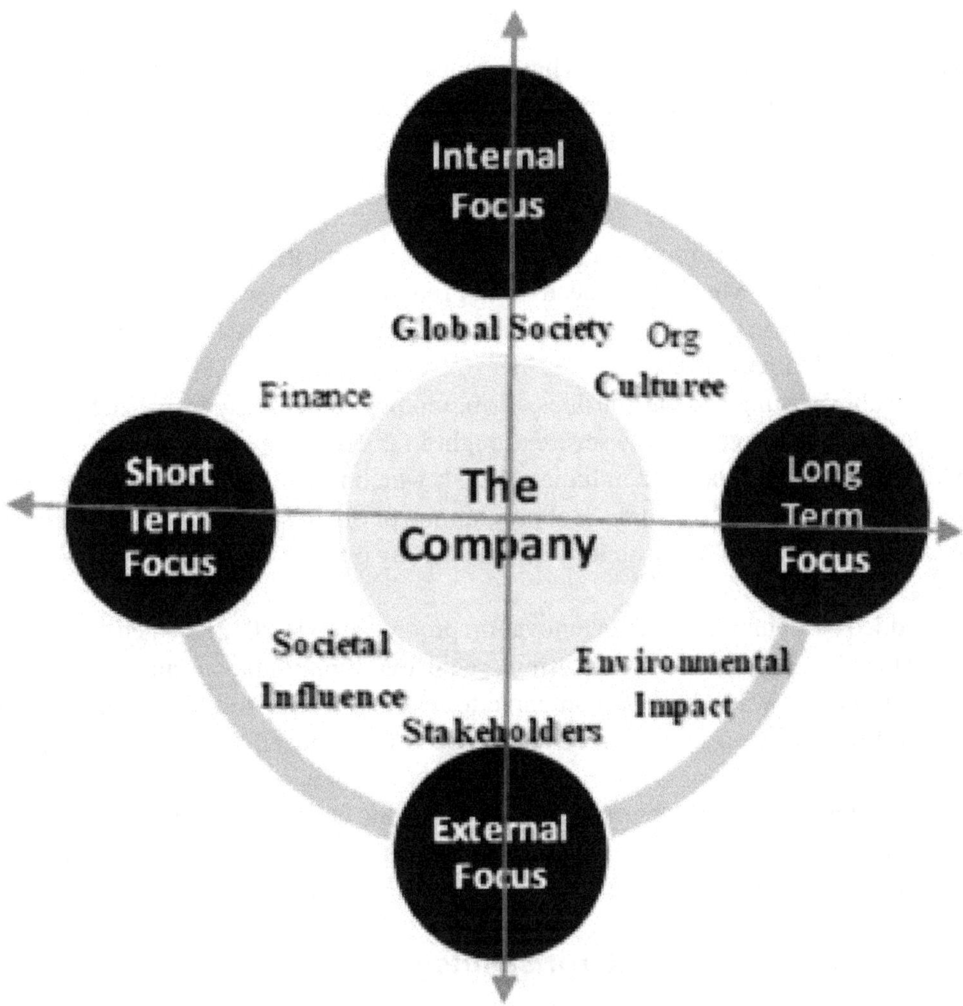

This is achieved through value-creation methods in sustainable procurement and production activities. This internal value creation will ultimately lead to humanity's augmented welfare.

Corporate Sustainability

According to Güler & Crowther (2009), *"Sustainable development is a development that meets the needs of the present without compromising the ability of future generations to meet their own needs."* Their research emphasised the importance and urgency of making concerted efforts toward economic development that could be sustained without depleting natural resources or harming the environment. Their research gave insight into sustainability that helps the organisation work in harmony with people and the planet.

Historically, traditional business models created values for shareholders, ignoring the interests of other stakeholders. The corporate ecosystem is now redefined through new sustainable models, creating a value system for people and the planet.

Thus, sustainable practices of the organisation should include the following

- ❖ The least the organisation can do is not to harm people or the planet through bad commercial practices
- ❖ Efforts should be on to improve environmental, social, and governance performance
- ❖ Practice social responsibility consistently and voluntarily rather than doing it based on government mandates.

The importance of sustainability can be understood through the supply chain disruptions. Supply Chain depends on vendors, who, in turn, need clean groundwater, clean air and climate. If good climatic conditions like monsoon or good air are not available, their production of raw materials will be affected and push up prices of commodities.

To illustrate above, Bunge, an agribusiness firm, reported a quarterly loss of US $ 56 million in its sugar and bioenergy segments due to a severe drought in 2010.

Coca-Cola faced a water shortage in India in 2004, which forced it to shut down one of its plants.

"Pollution Prevention Pays" is a universal programme of organisations today. Organisations reap the rewards through new business opportunities by redesigning products that conform to society's environmental norms.

Nike embedded sustainability into its innovation process and, in 2012, created a US $ 1 billion-plus Flyknit line. This uses a specialised yarn system, requiring minimal labour and generating large profit margins. Flyknit reduces waste by 80% compared to regular cut-and-sewn footwear. This helped Nike to reduce 3.5 million pounds of waste, and it also helped the organisation to move from yarn to recycled polyester.

With better water and energy management, organisations can bring about internal operational efficiency and reduce waste. GE reduced greenhouse gas emissions by 32% and water use by 45% in 2013 compared to 2004 and 2006 baselines, respectively, resulting in US $ 300 million in savings.

Sustainable Business: 1.0: Enterprise Integration

Enterprise sustainability is about balancing the three pillars of sustainability in all business activities and performance as firms look to create sustainable values today. (Edrisi Munoz et al., 2013). Organisations began to balance between three pillars of sustainability, economic, environmental, and social priorities, more as a compulsion than a requirement to provide support to society. In order to have continuous business growth and success, business houses intertwine sustainable development into their business processes of supplier management, customer management, planning, production, sales, and marketing of their products.

Customer Requirements

Millennial customers consider "ethical consumption" in their purchase decisions. Hence, organisations will have to go beyond their vendors and look at their purchases of inputs to ensure the sustainability chain is maintained in the entire supply chain operations.

Stakeholders' Requirements

While maximising business value, the sustainability factor is not just a requirement from the outside but is actually an important and essential tool to improve corporate governance, which would lead to better and bigger competitiveness of the organisation.

Good or bad, market pressures bring sustainability to business. To bring in the example of the insurance sector, the sustainability pressures on the firm become one of the risk managements. When pressure is due to competition, it gives a strategic direction to the firm. When the pressure is exerted by the banks and inventors, it is an issue of capital acquisition. When vendors and customers exert pressure, it is a supply chain management question. The issue of market demand arises when the customers give pressure.

If it is to remain successful and meaningful in the business, a company needs to integrate sustainability into its structure and strategies.

Sustainable Business: 1.0: Market Transformation

Businesses today are entering an area of responsible business by taking a broader role of "serving society ".

Businesses use some signposts like "greenwashing," "blue washing," and "sustainable development goals washing" to market their positive contributions so that their products and services can do better in the market; they are to go a long way to address environmental and social challenges. (Gabriel 2019; Nieuwenkamp 2017; Parguel, Benoît-Moreau, and Larceneux 2011),

Corporate governors today, without reactive action of accepting market rules, move to carbon neutral and, more importantly, look for carbon negative, thus changing the planet's key performance indicators.

To sustain the planet, businesses today move to manufacture electrical vehicles – both two-wheelers and four-wheelers and shut down plants that manufacture petrol/diesel vehicles.

Business houses like Uber made mobility easier and more convenient for customers, but more importantly, it reduced the number of cars that run on roads, thereby reducing air pollution.

As an innovative idea, Coca-Cola and Pepsi operate reverse logistics for its bottle requirements. The trucks that deliver filled bottles bring back empty bottles, thereby reducing the supply of bottles, which means there is a considerable reduction in energy requirements to produce bottles, which also results in lesser usage of depletable raw materials like silica sand.

Sustainability Provides Success and Continuity to Businesses

While sustainability efforts like reduction in pollution, lesser water usage, and going green with paperless offices positively impact the profitability of the organisation, it is also to be borne in mind that it has a huge concrete impact on the minds of consumers, thereby making the brand of the business highly successful through recall value.

Sustainable vs. Not-so-Sustainable Practices of Organizations

While organisations have embarked upon a concerted to support society through their sustainable programmes, the stakeholders and investors do have apprehensions on the true intentions of such programmes and activities.

CASE STUDIES: ORGANISATIONS EMBARKED ON SUSTAINABILITY

The following companies are demonstrating their commitment to sustainability through their deeds rather than words and paperwork:

A. **Disney:** While constantly expanding its horizon throughout the world, it also ensures that it contributes to Mother Earth through its best sustainable practices. For example, in 2019, they purchased a 270-acre solar facility outside Orlando. With this and their other initiatives, they can reduce their net carbon emissions by 47% and are hopeful that they will go fully green soon.
B. **Target:** While they had invested only US $ 802,440 in 2017 in green chemistry innovations, in 2022, they have invested US $ 5 million and continue to invest more and more in green energy without any mandate or pressure.

THOSE WHO TRY TO IMITATE/CLONE BUT HAVE NO ACTUAL SUSTAINABILITY PROGRAMME:

Oil and Gas Industry

Firms are increasingly under pressure to reach out to society to resolve social challenges. (Augilera *et al.*, 2007), Mahon & Waddock, (1992). While general examples range from AIDs to Poverty and obesity, these can also be very specific to firms operating in a particular industry, and these could be working conditions, product manufacturing safety, equal rights, etc. (Dobbin & Sutton, 1998).

Carroll (1979) argues that firms have huge responsibilities to the communities in which they operate by volunteering and contributing money to various social and cultural activities. Capturing this agenda, Donaldson and Dunfee (1994, 1995, 1999), in their research papers, emphasise that firms have obligations of responsible behaviour to all stakeholders, whether they are inside or outside the organisation, thus making social responsiveness an important milestone of sustainability. (Elkinton, 1997).

(1) BP's *Deepwater Horizon* Oil Spill (2010)

While oil companies face many hardships in extracting oil from the sea bed, they are also responsible for marine life and people dependent on the sea, like fishermen and those living in coastal areas.

While accidents do happen regularly, the largest accidental oil spill in human history happened in the Gulf of Mexico on April 20, 2010, after a surge of natural gas blasted through a cement well cap to seal a well drilled by the Deepwater Horizon Oil Platform. The gas travelled up the rig's riser to the platform, where it ignited, killing 11 workers and injuring 17. The oil platform capsized and sank two days later. Before the well was capped much later, some 134 million gallons of oil were released (according to the findings of U S District Court), and about 2,100 km of the U S Gulf Coast from Texas to Florida were coated with oil. While the company paid compensation of US $ 65 million to people who relied on the gulf for their livelihoods, it created a permanent catastrophe in the sea bed for the marine life and the people.

(2) Bhopal Gas Tragedy, India: It was waiting to happen:

On December 3, 1984, about 45 tons of dangerous gas, methyl isocyanate, escaped from a poorly maintained insecticide plant owned by the Indian subsidiary of the American firm Union Carbide Corporation. The gas drifted over the city and killed more than 20,000 children, adults, men and women who were sleeping in their houses that night. The after-effect of poisonous gas still has a huge effect on human beings as thousands live with cancer, respiratory problems, and blindness. Many were later awarded a poor compensation of a few thousand rupees (a few hundred dollars). Investigations by the Government, private agencies and the court clearly established that the company did not have any safety norms and was operating with substandard materials and processes to make maximum profit for the shareholders without any concern for society. Above all, neither Union Carbide nor Dow Chemicals (who later took over the company) did not own any responsibility for the poor maintenance of the factory. Even after 40 years of disaster, the land surrounding the factory cannot be used due to the seepage of chemicals into the earth.

Volkswagen

The international automobile company Volkswagen is a classic case of 'greenwashing". While the company was advertising that their cars emit fewer emissions, the fact remained contrary. The car manufacturer fitted in various vehicles with a defect device with software that could detect when it was undergoing an emission test and alter the performance to reduce the emissions level. In reality, these engines emit up to 40 times the norms for nitrogen oxide pollutants.

Plastic Bottle Water Companies

A more subtle form of greenwashing is being done by water bottle manufacturing companies like Evian, Pepsi's Aqua Fina, and Parle India's Bisleri, as all of them show nature on their labels to signify they contribute to the sustainability programmes. This, possibly is the worst form of misleading the public on sustainability as water bottles are plastic in nature for single-use and are the major contributor to the massive plastic waste on the planet.

Fast Fashion Brands

Zara and H&M are among the fashion brand manufacturers who were caught greenwashing over the years. These brands contribute to a massive amount of textile waste produced by clothing companies. According to the fashion non-profit organisation ReMake, 80% of discarded textiles globally are incinerated or landfill-bound, with just 20% being reused or recycled. Fashion brands are habitual offenders and habitually advertise their brands as "green", though it forms only a tiny part of their operations. For example, in 2019, H&M launched its own "green" clothing line titled "Conscious". The company claimed that it used "organic" cotton and recycled polyester. However, this is only a marketing tactic to show that they are environmentally friendly. The advertising line was "Shop our selection of sustainable fashion pieces that make you both look and feel good". H&M was criticised by the Norwegian Customer Authority for a "misleading" marketing campaign because "the information given by the company on sustainability is not sufficient, especially as the fabric "conscious." is advertised as a collection with environmental benefits.

CONCLUDING THOUGHTS ON CORPORATE GOVERNANCE AND SUSTAINABILITY

Good corporate governance is built on three premises – economic development, social progress and environmental progression. Good governance ultimately leads to sustainable values, which helps companies achieve greater progress and better profitability. It also helps businesses attract new investors and shareholders and increase their equity.

Today, all the organisation's stakeholders are better informed about its governance and sustainable activities. Hence, robust, transparent and well-connected corporate governance and sustainability will ensure that the consumers become closer to the organisation.

Governance, Sustainability and social responsibilities are high on the agenda of corporates; many of them turn to external agencies for training their employees, including board members, which will ensure the fullest transparency in all their activities.

Environmental Quality

Economic activities of organisations will naturally have an impact on the environment – air, water or noise and lead to detrimental effects on biodiversity, ozone depletion, greenhouse gas emissions, waste by-products and deforestation (as already mentioned in an earlier paragraph of the destruction of Amason Forest) (Doering *et al.*, 2002).

All commercial firms contribute (negatively!) towards environmental degradation, ranging from lighting and air-conditioning of offices, air pollution through spewing of poisonous gases and affecting Mother Earth through irresponsible waste disposal (Hart, 1995; Russo & Fouts, 1997).

Klassen and Whybark (1999) suggest that firms take measures through innovative uses of processes and technologies in production so that the environment will be less affected and, in fact, lead to cost controls by firms, leading to their becoming cost-competitive players in the marketplace. The waste material can be recycled through an Effluent Treatment Plant (ETP), and thus, such treated water can be ritualised, if not in production, but for growing plants inside the factory or in the washrooms.

However, organisations will have to kill their inner demons to become responsible organisations through sustainability programmes to sustain their businesses long-term.

Inner Demon #1: Structure and Governance

Even today, organisations consider sustainability as a mere marketing tool or a way to advertise to the world and make sustainability into an ad hoc function. As a result, it is siloed away by employees and kept away from key corporate strategies and business operations. With little support from top management, sustainability has not percolated down the organisation. While there have been some improvements in the recent past, either by choice or by pressure, there is still a disconnect between what organisations say and do.

Inner Demon #2: Processes and Metrics

In the pre-sustainability era, profit-making was the only consideration, along with price, costs, market shares, earnings per share and wealth maximisation for shareholders. The corporate achievements were also directed towards outperforming the competition. Firms did not consider people and the planet, and sustainability was not embedded into the business.

With strong procedures, rules and metrics anchored in the traditional approach, as mentioned above, corporate bureaucracy always neutralises sustainability initiatives. For example, Environmental Social and Governance (ESG) reports often contain inaccurate, unverifiable, contradictory data without any accounting rigour of conventional financial metrics.

Inner Demon #3: Culture and Leadership

For almost all firms of the 20th century, putting sustainability at the heart of the business requires a huge cultural transformation. It is not simply a recalibration of the mission statement or a new manifesto of values. Employees will have to have a change of heart and mind, and this has to start from top management. However, most business executives built their careers based on the profit-only paradigm, fighting against competitors. Sustainability programmes are different ball games where these executives need to have empathy, openness, collaboration and trust. While changing the narrative is a first toddler step, it will backfire on the organisation if it is not implemented with an observable change of heart by top management.

Inner Demon #4: Methods and Skill

While the current business executives are very well versed with business tools like Net Present Value (NPV) or Porter's supply chain or marketing model, too often, they lack in-depth knowledge of sustainability tools and techniques. If sustainability methods are not practised daily, it will become difficult for organisations to decide on sustainability goals.

Fighting and Winning over the Inner Demons

The internal demons of sustainability are very strong as they are deeply and widely ingrained inside the organisation but need to be banished. They inhibit the progress of transformational initiatives of organisations, which results in failed ambitions and pledges. However, the important question is how to defeat these internal demons and make organisations embrace good initiatives of sustainability.

The following will answer how business leaders can eliminate these demons for the betterment of society.

a. **Organisation is to build a community of practice**: bring in a team of experts as catalysts (or ambassadors) to percolate down sustainability practices within the organisation. Tata Sons in India, led by effective leadership, has a very efficient and effective sustainability practice. While ensuring adequate profitability to shareholders, they also guarantee the stakeholders in the society are not harmed. All their factories, including their largest steel plant in Rourkela, has all modern technologies and safety standards so that the poisonous fumes do not either affect internal customers – employees or the society by the air pollution.

   1. Some companies take a bigger leap by changing the entire organisation's design. For example, Enel, a world leader in renewable energy, created a corporate unit called "innovability", a term which combines innovation and sustainability, as the organisation firmly believes that

any new innovation will have to have a sustainable goal to benefit society. Coco Cola in India recycles its bottle inventory 8 to 10 times, so the wastage of natural resources is minimised.

b. Embed sustainability by design into every process and trade-off decision-making.
   1. Mahindra Group manufactures automobiles in India and created sustainability checkpoints under the "Rise for Good" to reduce emissions through eco-friendly technologies. They have started the "Cut the Crap" Project, under which 11 facilities of their have gone for zero waste generation through recycling, reusing and composting waste. They have also made their offices plastic-free.
   2. Indian Railways has requested its top executives to utilise the services of railways rather than travel by air to cut down CO2 emissions. While it also reduced the cost burden to the organisation, it also ensured that the government contributes in its own way to the sustainability of Earth.

c. Agree on new Social Contract: Walk the Talk with Employees and stakeholders:
   1. Sustainability efforts are not a one-time affair and need to be continuous. For example, HDFC Bank in India scored high due to its responsible lending policies, encouraging green housing and integrating employees into the climate strategies. Empathy and trust are foundational to connecting to authenticity of sustainability with all stakeholders, including employees.

All said and done, changing minds is a difficult proposition, especially as the organisations during the last 200 years since industrialisation focused only on profits and wealth maximisation of shareholders. There is now an urgent need for organisations to change themselves to embrace sustainability programmes, more out of necessity and compulsion than voluntarily. Organisations will have to embark upon various measures like

A. Include all stakeholders, internal and external, to create a conscious effort on sustainable programmes being pursued by the firms
B. Care about people planet and process and receive continuous feedback to improve themselves
C. Co-create knowledge workshops and learning seminars with partners, especially vendors, define the sustainability problem, and provide solutions through organic materials and sustainable packaging developments, like permanently removing one-time-use plastic materials as has been achieved by biscuit company Britannia India.
D. Even if a project is profitable, drop the idea because it does not conform to Environmental, Social and Governance (ESG)

The sustainable farming ecosystem, orchestrated by the BASF Agricultural Division to provide holistic solutions to farmers, goes beyond the traditional BASF model of selling crop protection products. The BASF strategists have gone beyond a product-centric business model to a more holistic and sustainable business model.

Sustainability is a new buzz in businesses, and corporates must embrace it more willingly as an imperative measure rather than being brushed aside by society as a non-entity.

As mentioned earlier, firms will have to kill the internal demons as early as possible, or they will never be able to achieve sustainability at scale.

Defeating the internal demons is simple and swift, as shown earlier in the examples of various companies, but it needs honest and concerted efforts from organisations.

The integrated governance and sustainability framework will show the world and customers their ethical value system, responsibility towards society, long-term value creation, and regulatory compliance. This will enhance the company's reputation, resilience, and long-term societal commitment.

REFERENCES

Adams, C. A., & Frost, G. R. (2008). Integrating sustainability reporting into management practices. *Accounting Forum*, *32*(2), 1–15. doi:10.1016/j.accfor.2008.05.002

Aguilera, R. V., Rupp, D. E., Williams, C. A., & Ganapathi, J. (2007). Putting the S Back in Corporate Social Responsibility: A Multi-Level Theory of Social Change in Organizations. *Academy of Management Review*, *32*(3), 836–863. doi:10.5465/amr.2007.25275678

Aras, G., & Crowther, D. (2009). Corporate sustainability reporting: A study in disingenuity? *Journal of Business Ethics*, *87*(1), 279–288. doi:10.1007/s10551-008-9806-0

Bansal, P. (2001). Building Competitive Advantage and Managing Risk through Sustainable Development. *Ivey Business Journal*, *66*, 47–52.

Brundtland, G. H., Khalid, M., Agnelli, S., Al-Athel, S., & Chidzero, B. J. N. Y. (1987). *Our common future*. New York. https://sustainabledevelopment.un.org/content/documents/5987our-common-future.pdf

Burke, R. J., & Mattis, M. C. (Eds.). (2013). *Women on corporate boards of directors: International challenges and opportunities* (Vol. 14). Springer Science & Business Media.

Buysse, K., & Verbeke, A. (2003). Proactive environmental strategies: A stakeholder management perspective. *Strategic Management Journal*, *24*(5), 453–470. doi:10.1002/smj.299

Carroll, A. B. (1979). A Three-Dimensional Conceptual Model of Corporate Performance. *Academy of Management Review*, *4*(4), 497–505. doi:10.2307/257850

Chams, N., & Garcıa-Blandon, J. (2019). Sustainable or not sustainable? The role of the board of directors. *Journal of Cleaner Production*, *226*, 1067–1081. doi:10.1016/j.jclepro.2019.04.118

Cochran, P., & Wood, R. (1984). Corporate social responsibility and financial performance. *Academy of Management Journal*, *27*(1), 42–56. doi:10.2307/255956

De Giovanni, P. (2012). Do internal and external environmental management contribute to the triple bottom line? *International Journal of Operations & Production Management*, *32*(3), 265–290. doi:10.1108/01443571211212574

Dobbin, F., & Sutton, R. C. (1998). The Strength of a Weak State: The Rights Movement and the Rise of the Human Resources Management Divisions. *American Journal of Sociology*.

Doering, D. S., Cassara, A., Layke, C., Ranganathan, J., Revenga, C., Tunstall, D., & Vanasselt, W. (2002). *Tomorrow's Markets: Global Trends and their Implications for Business*. World Resources Institute.

Donaldson, T., & Dunfee, T. W. (1994). Toward a Unified Conception of Business Ethics: Integrative Social Contract Theory. *Academy of Management Review*, *19*(2), 252–284. doi:10.2307/258705

Donaldson, T., & Dunfee, T. W. (1995). *Integrative Social Contracts Theory*. Economics and Philosophy. doi:10.1017/S0266267100003230

Donaldson, T., & Dunfee, T. W. (1999). *Ties That Bind. A Social Contracts Approach to Business Ethics*. Harvard Business School Press.

Dorfman, R., & Steiner, P. O. (1954). Optimal Advertising and Optimal Quality. *The American Economic Review*, *44*, 826–836.

Düztaş, S. (2008). *Corporate governance: The effects of board characteristics, information technology maturity and transparency on company Performance*.

Edrisi Muñoz, E., Capón-García, E., Laínez, J. M., Espuña, A., & Puigjaner, L. (2013). Considering environmental assessment in an ontological framework for enterprise sustainability. *Journal of Cleaner Production*, *47*, 149–164. doi:10.1016/j.jclepro.2012.11.032

Ehikioya, B. I. (2009). Corporate governance structure and firm performance in developing economies: Evidence from Nigeria. *Corporate Governance (Bradford)*, *9*(3), 231–245. doi:10.1108/14720700910964307

Elkington, J. (1997). *Cannibals with Forks: The Triple Bottom Line of the 21st Century Business*. Capstone Publishing.

Fernando, Y., Jabbour, C. J. C., & Wah, W. X. (2019). Pursuing green growth in technology firms through the connections between environmental innovation and sustainable business performance: Does service capability matter? *Resources, Conservation and Recycling, 141*, 8–20.

Fombrun, C., & Shanley, M. (1990). What's in a Name? Reputation Building and Corporate Strategy. *Academy of Management Journal*, *33*(2), 233–258. doi:10.2307/256324

Fu, W., & Su, H. C. (2020). Take actions or outsource? An empirical examination of strategic environmental options of greenhouse gas emissions. *International Journal of Operations & Production Management*, *40*(6), 753–776. doi:10.1108/IJOPM-02-2020-0088

Gabriel Marcelo, L. D. (2019). Sustainability as a Key Component of Marketing Strategy. In P. Atul & S. Rajendra (Eds.), *Handbook of Advances in Marketing in an Era of Disruptions – Essays in Honour of Jagdish N. Sheth* (pp. 119–124). Sage.

Galbreath, J. (2013). ESG in focus: The Australian evidence. *Journal of Business Ethics*.

Gardberg, N. A., & Fombrun, C. J. (2006). Corporate Citizenship: Creating Intangible Assets Across Institutional Environments. *Academy of Management Review*, *31*(2), 329–346. doi:10.5465/amr.2006.20208684

Gompers, P., Ishii, J., & Metrick, A. (2003). Corporate governance and equity prices. *The Quarterly Journal of Economics*, *118*(1), 107–155. doi:10.1162/00335530360535162

Güler, A., & Crowther, D. (2009). *The Durable Corporation: Strategies for Sustainable Development*. Gower.

Güller, A., & Crowther, D. (2008). Governance and sustainability: An investigation into the relationship between corporate governance and corporate sustainability. *Management Decision*, *46*(3), 433–448. doi:10.1108/00251740810863870

Hart, S. L. (1995). *A Natural-Resource-based View of the Firm.* Academy of Management Journal. doi:10.2307/258963

Hart, S. L., & Milstein, M. B. (2003). Creating sustainable value. *The Academy of Management Perspectives, 17*(2), 56–67. doi:10.5465/ame.2003.10025194

Hawn, O., Chatterji, A., & Mitchell, W. (2014). *How Firm Performance Moderates the Effect of Changes in Status on Investor Perceptions: Additions and Deletions by the Dow Jones Sustainability Index.* (Working paper).

Hillman, A. J., & Keim, G. D. (2001). Shareholder Value, Stakeholder Management, and Social Issues: What's the Bottom Line? *Strategic Management Journal, 22*(2), 125–139. doi:10.1002/1097-0266(200101)22:2<125::AID-SMJ150>3.0.CO;2-H

Hoffman, A. J. (2005). Climate Change Strategy: The Business Logic behind Voluntary Greenhouse Gas Reductions. *California Management Review, 47*(3), 21–46. doi:10.2307/41166305

Hull, C. E., & Rothenberg, S. (2008). Firm performance: The interactions of corporate social performance with innovation and industry differentiation. *Strategic Management Journal, 29*(7), 781–789. doi:10.1002/smj.675

Husted, B. W., & de Sousa-Filho, J. M. (2017). The impact of sustainability governance, country stakeholder orientation, and country risk on environmental, social, and governance performance. *Journal of Cleaner Production, 155*, 93–102. doi:10.1016/j.jclepro.2016.10.025

Iansiti, M., & Levien, R. (2004). Strategy as ecology. *Harvard Business Review, 82*(3), 68–81. PMID:15029791

Klassen, R. D., & Whybark, D. C. (1999). The Impact of Environmental Technologies on Manufacturing Performance. *Academy of Management Journal, 42*(6), 599–615. doi:10.2307/256982

Kolk, A. (2008). Sustainability, accountability and corporate governance: Exploring multinationals' reporting practices. *Business Strategy and the Environment, 17*(1), 1–15. doi:10.1002/bse.511

Kurawa, J. M., & Abdulrahman, S. (2014). Effect of corporate governance on corporate social responsibility of listed firms in the Nigerian petroleum marketing industry. In *Proceedings of International Conference on Humanities, Science and Sustainable Development.* Research Gate.

Mahon, J. F., & Waddock, S. A. (1992). Strategic Issues Management: An Integration of Issue Life Cycle Perspectives. *Business & Society, 31*(1), 19–33. doi:10.1177/000765039203100103

Maier, S. (2005). *How global is good governance?* Ethical Investment Research Services.

Manescu, C. (2011). Stock returns in relation to environmental, social and governance performance: Mispricing or compensation for risk? *Sustainable Development (Bradford), 19*(2), 95–118. doi:10.1002/sd.510

Mercer Investment Consulting. (2006). *Fearless Forecast.* Mercer Investment Consulting.

Milgrom, P., & Roberts, J. (1986). Price and Advertising Signals of Product Quality. *Journal of Political Economy, 94*(4), 796–821. doi:10.1086/261408

Montabon, F., Sroufe, R., & Narasimhan, R. (2007). An examination of corporate reporting, environmental management practices and firm performance. *Journal of Operations Management, 25*(4), 998–1014. doi:10.1016/j.jom.2006.10.003

Moskowitz, M. (1972). Choosing socially responsible stocks. *Business and Society Review, 1*(1), 71–75.

Naciti, V., Cesaroni, F., & Pulejo, L. (2021). Corporate governance and sustainability: A review of the existing literature. *The Journal of Management and Governance, 26*(1), 1–20. doi:10.1007/s10997-020-09554-6

Navarro, P. (1988). Why do corporations give to charity? *The Journal of Business, 61*(1), 65–93. doi:10.1086/296420

Nieuwenkamp, R. (2017). *Ever Heard of SDG Washing? The Urgency of SDG Due Diligence.* OECD Development Matters. https://oecd-development-matters.org/2017/09/25/ever-heard-of-sdg-washing-the-urgency-of-SDG-due-diligence/

Ortas, E., Álvarez, I., Jaussaud, J., & Garayar, A. (2015). The impact of institutional and social context on corporate environmental, social and governance performance of companies committed to voluntary corporate social responsibility initiatives. *Journal of Cleaner Production, 108*, 673–684. doi:10.1016/j.jclepro.2015.06.089

Parguel, B., Benoît-Moreau, F., & Larceneux, F. (2011). How Sustainability Ratings Might Deter "Greenwashing": A Closer Look at Ethical Corporate Communication. *Journal of Business Ethics, 102*(1), 15–28. doi:10.1007/s10551-011-0901-2

Poddar, A., Narula, S. A., & Zutshi, A. (2019). A study of corporate social responsibility practices of the top Bombay Stock Exchange 500 companies in India and their alignment with the Sustainable Development Goals. *Corporate Social Responsibility and Environmental Management, 26*(6), 1184–1205. doi:10.1002/csr.1741

Porter, M. E., & Kramer, M. R. (2006). Strategy and Society: The Link between Competitive Advantage and Corporate Social Responsibility. *Harvard Business Review, 84*, 78–92. PMID:17183795

Rao, K., & Tilt, C. (2016). Board composition and corporate social responsibility: The role of diversity, gender, strategy and decision making. *Journal of Business Ethics, 138*(2), 327–347. doi:10.1007/s10551-015-2613-5

Ricart, J. E., & Rey, C. (2021). Purpose in Corporate Governance: The Path towards a More Sustainable World. *Sustainability (Basel), 14*(8), 4384. doi:10.3390/su14084384

RobertsD. J.Van den SteenE. (2000). Shareholder interests, human capital investment and corporate governance. Stanford GSB Working. doi:10.2139/ssrn.230019

Russo, M. V., & Fouts, P. A. (1997). A Resource-Based Perspective on Corporate Environmental Performance and Profitability. *Academy of Management Journal, 40*(3), 534–559. doi:10.2307/257052

Schaltegger, S., & Wagner, M. (2006). Integrative management of sustainability performance, measurement and reporting. *International Journal of Accounting. Auditing and Performance Evaluation, 3*(1), 1–19. doi:10.1504/IJAAPE.2006.010098

Sen, S., & Bhattacharya, C. B. (2001). Does Doing Good Always Lead to Doing Better? Consumer Reactions to Corporate Social Responsibility. *JMR, Journal of Marketing Research*, *38*(2), 225–243. doi:10.1509/jmkr.38.2.225.18838

Siew, R. Y. J. (2014). Evaluating and enhancing the impact of sustainability reporting tools (SRTs) [Doctoral dissertation, Ph. D. thesis, School of Civil and Environmental Engineering, University of New South Wales, Sydney].

Steurer, R., Langer, M. E., Konrad, A., & Martinuzzi, A. (2005). Corporations, Stakeholders and Sustainable Development I: A Theoretical Exploration of Business-Society Relations. *Journal of Business Ethics*, *61*(3), 263–281. doi:10.1007/s10551-005-7054-0

Tadesse, S. (2004). The allocation and monitoring role of capital markets: Theory and international evidence. *Journal of Financial and Quantitative Analysis*, *39*(4), 701–730. doi:10.1017/S0022109000003185

Turban, D. B., & Greening, D. W. (1997). Corporate social performance and organizational attractiveness to prospective employees. *Academy of Management Journal*, *40*(3), 658–672. doi:10.2307/257057

Waddock, S. A., & Graves, S. B. (1997). The corporate social performance-financial performance link. *Strategic Management Journal*, *18*(4), 303–319. doi:10.1002/(SICI)1097-0266(199704)18:4<303::AID-SMJ869>3.0.CO;2-G

Waldman, D. A., Siegel, D. S., & Javidan, M. (2006). Components of CEO Transformational Leadership and Corporate Social Responsibility. *Journal of Management Studies*, *43*(8), 1703–1725. doi:10.1111/j.1467-6486.2006.00642.x

Wilson, M., & Lombardi, R. (2001). Globalisation and its Discontents. *Ivey Business Journal*, *66*, 69–72.

Wolfe, R., & Aupperle, K. (1991). Introduction to Corporate Social Performance: Methods for Evaluating an Elusive Construct. *Research in Corporate Social Performance and Policy*, *12*, 265–268.

Wood, D. (1991). Corporate Social Performance Revisited. *Academy of Management Review*, *16*(4), 691–718. doi:10.2307/258977

Zadek, S. (2001). *Third-generation corporate citizenship*. The Foreign Policy Centre.

Chapter 7
Exploring the Link Between Corporate Governance and R&D Investments on Brazilian Listed Companies

Yago da Silva Teixeira
Federal University of Rondônia, Brazil

Lívia Maria da Silva Santos
Federal University of Rondônia, Brazil

Risolene Alves de Macena Araújo
https://orcid.org/0000-0001-6423-6299
Federal University of Pará, Brazil

Adriana Rodrigues Silva
https://orcid.org/0000-0003-1538-6877
Polytechnic Institute of Santarém, Portugal & CICF-Research Centre on Accounting and Taxation, Portugal

ABSTRACT

Research and development (R&D) are an important issue for companies in a wide range of sectors, as they generate innovation, productivity, and sustainability, which are important factors for competitive advantage. To analyze which corporate governance mechanisms influence R&D investment by B3-listed companies, a fixed effects panel regression analysis was performed from 2010 to 2020. From a universe of 477 companies, a sample of 61 companies that spent at least one year on R&D was drawn. The results show that despite the hypotheses that board independence, ownership concentration, and CEO duality have no positive or negative effect on R&D spending, rejecting the latter hypotheses leads to a negative relationship between the first two factors and R&D spending. Therefore, it can be concluded that some corporate governance mechanisms can explain organizational investment in research and development.

DOI: 10.4018/979-8-3693-1742-6.ch007

INTRODUCTION

In today's world, where competition and the need for constant innovation are a reality, organizations are giving greater importance to investments in Research and Development (R&D) (Lv et al., 2019). Such investments enable technological innovation, as well as the improvement of a given product or service, improving its quality and reducing costs to benefit users.

According to Honoré et al. (2015), the financing and generation of efforts in R&D by companies are crucial pillars for the launch of new products and fundamental to sustainability and productivity. These initiatives are, therefore, seen as essential components for organizational advancement (Muhammad et al., 2022). Fortunato et al. (2012) supplement this perspective by emphasizing the continuous need for companies to invest. These investments are essential not only to expand production and meet the excess market demand but also to innovate in cost reduction or achieve productivity improvements, replace obsolete equipment, or even create barriers to the entry of new competitors into the market.

However, the decision-making process regarding these investments is strategic, which makes assessing the associated risks crucial (Lee, 2015). According to Lee (2015), there is a divergence in expectations between investors and organizational managers. Investors tend to favour investments in R&D for their potential high returns and risks. At the same time, managers may prefer more cautious approaches to minimize personal risks, such as job loss, since such investments may prove unprofitable. The uncertainty of returns, the complexity of their assessment, and the possibility of being indeterminate for a significant period, along with the potential inefficiency of the productivity of such expenses, especially when there are failures in internal control systems, are relevant factors in decision-making (Jensen, 1993; Chan et al., 2015; James & McGuire, 2016).

Cordis and Kirby (2017) warn about market imperfections, which make deeper analyses necessary regarding the impacts brought by investments, as these may not add value when seeking, for example, to meet managers' interests, which characterizes a problem of agency (Fama, 1970; Jensen & Meckling, 1976). From this perspective, Baysinger et al. (1991) justify that divergence between market participants can generate a conflict in decisions about R&D investments, which can result in the so-called agency problem. According to Eisenhardt (1989), the agency problem is related to the difference in behaviour and objectives between managers and shareholders.

In this context, investment in R&D is rooted in Agency Theory, as it is a decision that can lead to conflicts of objectives since managers are averse to risk and have a preference for short-term gains, with a strategy of search for efficiency because their efforts are directed only at the company they manage, that is, they take a more cautious stance on risk to protect their employment, which can harm long-term gains and innovation. At the same time, shareholders tend to be risk-neutral, as they have opportunities to invest in several companies, thus diversifying their investments (Honoré et al., 2015).

As an attempt to solve agency problems, corporate governance stands out, which, based on a set of restrictions on managers' actions, seeks to reduce the inadequate allocation of investors' resources (Corrêa et al., 2015). Ratifying, La Porta et al. (2000) and Toigo et al. (2018) report that these are mechanisms through which external investors protect themselves against expropriation by those internal to the organization. In other words, corporate governance concerns the set of controls, internal and external, that aim to minimize the conflict of interests related to the agency problem (Baysinger & Hoskisson, 1990). Therefore, governance practices positively affect R&D investments (Honoré et al., 2015; Rodrigues et al., 2020).

According to Honoré et al. (2015), a more significant portion of investment in R&D comes from large publicly traded companies, and it is essential to know the influence of corporate governance on their R&D spending. Given the above, the following question is proposed: **Which Corporate Governance mechanisms influence investments in R&D of companies listed on B3?** Therefore, the objective of this work is to analyze which Corporate Governance mechanisms affect investments in R&D of companies listed on B3.

The significance of this research stems from the fact that, despite the existence of studies investigating the relationship between Research and Development (R&D) investments and corporate governance (Chan et al., 2015; AlHares, 2020; Muhammad, et al., 2022; Muhammad et al., 2024), empirical evidence remains ambiguous with conflicting opinions (Honoré et al., 2015). Furthermore, we identified a gap in the literature regarding the absence of studies addressing this relationship within the Brazilian context as of the completion date of this research. This gap underscores the importance of this study, particularly considering the crucial role that R&D investments play in the productivity growth and sustainability of companies, aspects that are widely recognized and documented in the literature (Driver & Guedes, 2012; Honoré et al., 2015; Pindado et al., 2015).

THEORETICAL FRAMEWORK

Agency Theory

Agency theory, according to Eisenhardt (1989), is a topic of study used by various fields, with both defenders and critics, but still surrounded by controversy. The explanation of this theory stems from the so-called "pervasive agency relationship", in which one party, called the principal, delegates a function to another party, called the agent, who performs the task. To describe this relationship, the metaphor of a contract is used.

In summary, this theory states that two conflicts can arise between managers and shareholders, consequently affecting investment in research and development. This conflict can be caused firstly by divergent objectives and secondly by information asymmetry, as it would be difficult and costly for shareholders to understand and verify what managers are doing (Honoré et al., 2015).

Also, according to Honoré et al. (2015), it is traditionally linked to the literature on R&D investment, as this decision can lead to conflicts between managers and shareholders. According to the theory, it can be assumed that the shareholders' goal is to maximize the value of their investment, while for managers, the goal is to keep their job and be well paid.

The result is the agency problem, which leads to a decrease in the efficiency and value of R&D research and conveys uncertainty about the value of R&D investment (Chu et al., 2016). Therefore, firms with this problem tend to conduct less R&D (O'Connor et al., 2013).

In this scenario, according to Rodrigues et al. (2020), several studies have been conducted on the relationship between R&D and agency problems, which can be mitigated by corporate governance mechanisms in the firm. In support of this idea, Driver and Guedes (2012) state that corporate governance is an institutional form that addresses the problem above.

Corporate Governance

Corporate governance involves controlling the activities of managers, who in this case represent one of the actors in the agency problem, and also represent an incentive to take risks, which minimizes the self-interested behaviour of the manager (Driver & Guedes, 2012). According to Baysinger and Hoskisson (1990), corporate governance is a set of mechanisms through which investors protect themselves against expropriation by insiders.

For Baysinger and Hoskisson (1990), it represents internal and external mechanisms that limit agency problems. The internal mechanisms represent the internal environment of the company. They can be represented by the ownership structure, the capital structure and the board of directors, for example, while the external environment means the market in general, represented by the legal and regulatory environment, accounting rules, and shareholder activism, among others (Driver & Guedes, 2012).

Silva (2006) states that corporate governance in Brazil became more important with the socio-economic changes of the 1990s, such as the Real Plan, foreign investments and privatizations, and the entry of national companies into the foreign market.

Corporate governance is directly related to governance mechanisms, as it is an institutional form that addresses the problems of agency theory, and the cost of creating the tools is part of the agency cost, which includes a monitoring system or, more generally, incentives to encourage the manager to take risks (Driver & Guedes, 2012).

However, Baysinger et al. (1991) state that excessive monitoring, which leads to decreased managerial autonomy, can be dangerous in this scenario. For Driver and Guedes (2012), the benefits of alignment between owners and managers would be contradictory, and they state that it is an empirical question of whether governance supports R&D spending, for example, through transparency, or depresses it through reduced autonomy and excessive caution (Driver & Guedes, 2012).

Investments in Research and Development

In Brazil, around 90% of R&D investments are made with companies' resources, that is, private resources, according to a survey by the National Confederation of Industry (CNI) in 2020. There was an increase in the number of companies that invested in R&D, and the total that this investment represented in the national GDP, which was 1.21%, was about 2019 (Portal da Industria, 2022).

Investment in Research and Development is essential for product and process innovation (Pindado et al., 2015). Furthermore, Mata and Woerten (2013) report that companies that invest in R&D are more profitable than those that do not invest. However, it is not so simple because, when making this investment assessment, the literature suggests that some governance characteristics must be considered at the company and country level (Pindado, 2015).

According to Lv et al. (2019), one of the factors that generate some reservations regarding R&D expenditure is that it requires a lot of resources and has a high failure rate, leaving short-term gains aside. Driver and Guedes (2012) justify that R&D has specific characteristics: (i) its assets are intangible (often irreversible); (ii) the return will hardly be entirely appropriate, except for some means of protection, such as patents; and (iii) long-term cash flow and unusual returns.

As discussed previously, corporate governance mechanisms can play an important role when deciding on investments related to R&D. In this study, we investigated which of these mechanisms are influential, including the board of directors, which, according to Srivastav and Hagendorff (2015), plays an important role. Another point addressed will be the duality of the CEO, in which there is the possibility of the CEO also serving as chairman of the board, and, finally, the ownership structure, which plays an important role in investment decisions in R&D (Rodrigues et al., 2020).

Development of Research Hypotheses

Corporate governance mechanisms can be categorized as internal, developed within the organization, and external, associated with the various markets in which the organization operates. This research focuses on internal mechanisms due to their relevance to innovation. These mechanisms include, on the one hand, the ownership structure and, on the other, the board of directors, encompassing its structure and operational dynamics, such as the size and composition of the board. These are considered critical measures for the oversight of corporate management and strategic decisions, directly impacting the performance and competitiveness of the organization (Asensio-López et al., 2019; Salas, 2022).

The board of directors plays a crucial role in representing the interests of shareholders and other stakeholders. In this context, the Brazilian Institute of Corporate Governance (IBGC), in its 2023 Best Practices of Corporate Governance Manual, provides specific guidance for the composition of boards of directors. These guidelines emphasize the importance of the board as a guardian of the organization's purposes, values, mission, and governance system. Furthermore, it highlights its responsibility in defining and monitoring corporate strategy, ensuring alignment between executive management and shareholders, and protecting business interests, thus reinforcing its essential role in corporate governance.

Among the guidelines proposed by the Brazilian Institute of Corporate Governance (IBGC) for 2023, the emphasis on board members' independence stands out. This independence is crucial for impartial and effective action, essential to ensuring the integrity of the corporate governance system and contributes significantly to the creation and protection of the organization's value. In this context, it is recommended that the board composition preferably includes a majority or a substantial portion of independent members, reinforcing the commitment to best governance practices (IBGC, 2023).

The main function of the board of directors can be compromised if there is no independence in carrying out its functions, which, according to the literature, are guaranteed by the following attributes: the CEO does not hold the presidency of the board, emphasis given by regulators to external directors, not employees or affiliates of the company, and finally, an independent advisor who is not linked to the CEO (Lu & Wang, 2015).

Independence positively impacts the board's actions and, as studies (Kor, 2006; Osma, 2008) suggest, independent boards help to visualize short-sighted cuts in R&D, which can reduce the company's long-term value. This is because internal, non-independent directors tend to align themselves with managers' desires, which is why they have more qualified and significant information (Rodrigues et al., 2020).

As recommended by the Code of Best Corporate Governance Practices (2015), independent directors do not have a family, business or any other type of relationship with partners with significant participation, controlling groups, executives, service providers or non-profit entities that influence or that may influence, in a considerable way, your judgments, opinions, decisions or compromise your actions in the best interests of the organization.

External directors are better positioned to represent the interests of shareholders, who are more prone to risk. Therefore, this relationship favours higher-risk investments, such as investments in R&D (Sánchez et al., 2017). Thus, independent members of a board are likely to make decisions that favour the organization and not personal agendas, even in the long term. Thus, the more independent members, the greater the propensity to invest in R&D. Based on this, the following research hypothesis is formulated:

H1: The independence of the Board of Directors positively influences R&D investments.

Another aspect highlighted in the literature is the greater efficiency conditioned by the fact that a company has a CEO who is not, at the same time, the chairman of the board since, in the case of duality, this individual could maximize his utility to the detriment of value of the company (Lu & Wang, 2015). In other words, duality could cause the CEO to become entrenched due to greater formal power and more significant influence over the board, and, as a consequence, they would be more inclined to avoid debt and risk (Huang & Gao, 2022), resulting in a lower expenditure on research and development.

On the other hand, separating the positions of CEO and chairman of the board can promote improvements in board effectiveness, positively influence the board's actions and the selection of strategies to maximise results, and increase the breadth of strategic decisions, such as investments in R&D (Kor, 2006; Kim et al., 2009; Rodrigues et al., 2020). In this sense, investments in R&D increase when the CEO and the chairman of the board are different people (Lu & Wang, 2015). From this, the following hypothesis was formulated:

H2: CEO duality negatively influences R&D investments.

Furthermore, the literature shows that the configuration of the ownership structure can influence R&D investments (Góis et al., 2015). According to Gul et al. (2010), the greater concentration of ownership impacts managers' decisions regarding investments in R&D.

According to Belloc (2012), it is very likely that large owners are more concerned with the organisation's market value and more motivated to invest in projects that generate value. In addition, large shareholders may prefer to make long-term investments in R&D to increase the stability of the company rather than focusing on their own profits (Asensio-López et al., 2019).

As stated by Rodrigues et al. (2020), the ownership structure has been studied and has an inference regarding R&D investments and points to a positive relationship between ownership concentration and more significant investment in R&D, also verified in the studies by Kim et al. (2008), Nekhili et al. (2012) and Brossard et al. (2013). In this way, the following hypothesis was arrived at:

H3: Ownership concentration positively influences R&D investments.

METHODOLOGY

The present study, in terms of objectives, is descriptive, as it sought to describe the characteristics of corporate governance that influence investments in R&D. Regarding procedures, it is documentary, considering the use of explanatory notes and registration and reference forms for B3 companies. As for the approach to the problem, it is characterized as quantitative, regarding the use of statistical analysis instruments, which will validate or not the literature on the topic.

The universe of this study is made up of publicly traded companies, with shares traded on Brasil, Bolsa, Balcão (B3), Brazilian stock exchange, which is one of the leading financial market infrastructure companies in the world, operating in an exchange environment and over-the-counter (B3, 2022), and which published their Standardized Financial Statements, during the period from 2010 to 2020, resulting, therefore, in a total of 477 companies, according to the B3 sectoral classification, as of November 12, 2021.

Table 1. Sectors of companies that made up the research sample

B3 Sectors	Number of Companies
Oil, Gas and Biofuels	5
Mining	1
Steel and Metallurgy	2
Chemicals	1
Transport material	3
Machines and equipment	4
Miscellaneous services	2
Processed foods	1
Personal use and cleaning products	1
Construction	2
Clothing and footwear fabrics	2
Housewares	1
Cars and motorcycles	2
Business	1
Equipment	1
Commerce and distribution	2
Medical-hospital analysis and diagnostic services	2
Computers and equipment	2
Programs and services	2
Electricity	24

Source: Research Data, 2022.

To construct the sample, companies that did not spend on investment in R&D during the period studied were excluded. Those that presented R&D investment data for at least one year of observation were maintained. Therefore, a sample of 61 companies was obtained, distributed across 20 sectors, as shown in Table 1.

The research variables, as well as the expected relationships, based on the literature, how they are calculated and where they will be collected, are presented in Table 2.

As shown in Table 2, R&D Expenses were collected in the Explanatory Notes of the companies studied, and the value of Sales in the Economática database. The other variables related to Corporate Governance had data collected in the Comdinheiro database. Regarding the control variables, these were collected in the Economática database, except the AGE and CG variables, which were collected in the registration forms and on the companies' websites, respectively. Finally, the SECTOR variable was compiled based on B3's sectoral classification.

To obtain the results, the panel data regression model was used, which, according to Mesquita et al. (2021), has some advantages, such as the detection of casual relationships between X and Y, the possibility of individually analyzing different indicators, more excellent reliability in variable changes, measurement gains, increased sample size, and, finally, it allows the control of omitted variables.

Thus, the model used for estimation is presented in Equation 1:

Table 2. Research variables

Variables	Type	Description	Expected Signal	Calculation	Data collect
R&D	Dependent	R&D intensity		Natural logarithm of the ratio 'Expenditure on R&D and Sales' (Expenditure on R&D/Sales)	Explanatory Notes
INDEPCONS	Independent	Independence of the Board of Directors	+	Percentage of the number of independent members of the Board about the total number of Board members	ComDinheiro
DUAL	Independent	CEO duality	-	Dummy variable – (1) if the CEO is also the chairman of the Board of Directors; (0) otherwise	ComDinheiro
CONCENT	Independent	Ownership Concentration	+	Percentage of shares held by the largest shareholder	ComDinheiro
SIZE	Control	Company size	+	Natural logarithm of Total Assets	Economática
AGE	Control	Company Age	+	Number of years since the company was founded	Registration forms available on the B3 website
SECTOR	Control	Sector	+	Dummy variables, each representing a specific sector - (1) when companies belong to one of the particular sectors; (0) for companies belonging to other sectors	The data was collected based on the B3 Sector Classification
CG	Control	Corporate governance	+	(1) If the company is included in one of the differentiated levels of CG; (0) otherwise	The data was collected on the B3 website

Source: Research Data, 2022.

$$P\&D_{it} = \beta 0_{it} + \beta 1INDEP_{it} + \beta 2DUAL_{it} + \beta 3CPROP_{it} + \beta 4SIZE_{it} + \beta 5AGE_{it} + \beta 6SECTOR_{it} + \beta 6CG_{it} + \varepsilon$$

Where the dependent variable is Research and Development (R&D); the independent ones are Board Independence (INDEPCONS), CEO Duality (DUAL) and Ownership Concentration (CONSENT); and the control ones are Company Size (SIZE), Age (AGE), Sector (SECTOR) and, finally, Corporate Governance (CG).

PRESENTATION AND DISCUSSION OF RESULTS

To test the research hypotheses, econometric tests were carried out to determine the best model to be considered, as shown in Table 3.

Table 3. Result of econometric tests: Panel model identification

Test	Hypotheses	Results
Chow	H0: Pooling Model	Prob>F = 0,0000
	H1: Fixed Effects Model	
Hausman	H0: Random Effects Model	Prob>F = 0,0000
	H1: Fixed Effects Model	
Breusch Pagan	H0: Pooling Model	-
	H1: Random Effects Model	

Source: Research Data, 2022.

The Chow test, according to Carvalho Júnior et al. (2010), aims to guide the choice of estimators for the pooling and fixed effects model. The question test resulted in Prob>F = 0.0000, showing that the most appropriate model is the fixed effects model, to the detriment of the pooling model.

According to Cruz and Lima (2010), the Hausman test is used to decide between fixed and random effects models. With a result of Prob>F = 0.0000, H0 is rejected, and it is concluded that the best model to be used is the fixed effects model. The Breusch-Pagan test was not used, considering it aims to choose the most appropriate between the pooling and random models.

Subsequently, to test the presence of heteroscedasticity in the fixed effects model, the Wald test was applied, which resulted in the rejection of the null hypothesis of absence of heteroscedasticity, with a result of Prob>chi2 = 0.0157. Thus, a heteroscedastic model was shown. The Wooldridge test was also performed, where it was noted that there is the presence of autocorrelation, as the null hypothesis was rejected (Prob>chi2 = 0.0000). To solve these problems, the Driscoll and Kraay (1998) correction test was carried out. In Table 4, the regression model with panel data, with robust fixed effects, is presented after the heteroscedasticity and autocorrelation correction test.

$$P\&Dit = \beta 0it + \beta 1INDEPit + \beta 2DUALit + \beta 3CPROPit + \beta 4SIZEit + \beta 5AGEit + \beta 6SECTORit + \beta 6CGit + \varepsilon$$

From Table 4, the GC (Corporate Governance) and SECTOR (Company Sector) variables were omitted from the model since they are dummy variables; that is, they only take on two values: 1 and 0, which remained constant in the panel data regression and, for this reason, it was not possible to estimate their coefficients.

It is also noted that the variables INDEPCONS, CONCENT and SIZE were statistically significant at the 1% level. In contrast, in the independent variable DUAL and the control variable AGE, no statistical significance was observed. Therefore, based on these results, the research hypotheses were rejected or not, as discussed below:

H1: The independence of the Board of Directors positively influences R&D investments.

The INDEPCONS variable presented statistical significance (p-value = 0.002) at a level of 1%, with a negative relationship about R&D. Therefore, hypothesis H1 was rejected since, in the present study, the evidence shows that the greater the independence of the board, the lower the volume of investment in Research and Development. An explanation for this result may be related to the need for external financing to conduct R&D investments in the Brazilian context.

Table 4. Regression results with panel data

P&D	Coeficiente	Std. Err.	t	P>ltl
INDEPCONS	-568617	139143.6	-4.09	0.002
DUAL	-10408	15525.09	-0.67	0.518
CONCENT	-4531,764	1303.051	-3.48	0.006
SIZE	76884.18	17604.53	4.37	0.001
AGE	811.5465	2949.609	0.28	0.789

n° 534 observações Prob>F = 0,0000

Caption: R&D: Research and Development; INDEPCONS: Independence of the Board of Directors; DUAL: CEO duality; CONCENT: Concentration of Ownership; SIZ: Company Size; AGE: Company Age.

Source: Research Data, 2022.

In this case, advisors would be unlikely to make such investments, as verified in the study by Hsu et al. (2009). The authors explain that a possible reason would be the financial constraints of companies; that is, investment behaviour is encouraged by independent advisors if external financing needs are not a barrier. In this way, it is believed that a solid and independent board has a positive influence on corporate investment in a situation with few financial restrictions (Rodrigues et al., 2020).

H2: CEO duality negatively influences R&D investments.

The variable DUAL (CEO Duality) did not present statistical significance (p-value = 0.518); therefore, the hypothesis that the CEO also holds the position of Chairman of the Board and exerts influence on the company's R&D expenditure is rejected. This result corroborates the research by Rodrigues et al. (2020), who states that a high level of investment in R&D can occur regardless of the presence or absence of duality. This is because R&D investments generate growth in productivity and sustainability (Driver & Guedes, 2012; Honoré et al., 2015; Pindado et al., 2015), essential factors in strong competitiveness at the national and global level.

H3: Ownership concentration positively influences R&D investments.

The CONCENT Variable (Concentration of Ownership) presented statistical significance (p-value = 0.006) at a significance level of 1% and a negative coefficient (-4531.764). As a result, hypothesis H3 is rejected, thus showing that the greater the concentration of ownership, the lower the investment in R&D, as found in the study by Di Vito et al. (2010), who concluded that ownership concentration is negatively associated with R&D intensity.

A possible explanation for this finding may be related to the search for private gains by the largest shareholders to the detriment of minority shareholders. This takeover, according to La Porta et al. (2000), would be more decisive in countries with an emerging economy, such as Brazil. This way, these large shareholders would not be inclined to spend heavily on R&D to the detriment of personal gains.

Another possible cause, according to Di Vito et al. (2010), would be the profile of these large shareholders, since when large shareholders are family members of the company, they tend to be more prone to investments in R&D, as they have long-term investment horizons. Still, when there is no such profile, the relationship ends up being negative, and this could be the possible profile of investors in the companies studied.

CONCLUSION

The present research aimed to analyze which Corporate Governance mechanisms influence investments in R&D of companies listed on B3 from 2010 to 2020. Based on the results found, through the rejection of the hypotheses explored, it was found that all tested hypotheses were rejected, being related to board independence (INDEPCONS), CEO duality (DUAL) and ownership concentration (CONCENT).

Although the research hypotheses were rejected, the variables board independence (INDEP) and ownership concentration (CONCENT) proved to be significant, signalling, therefore, that they exert influence on R&D investments, however, in a way contrary to what was expected. It is important to note that the CG and SECTOR variables were omitted since they did not vary over time, and therefore, it was impossible to estimate their coefficients.

From this, it can be concluded that, due to the institutional and cultural characteristics of the countries, as recommended in the literature, there may be mixed relationships between corporate governance variables and realised R&D investments. The results suggested that, when considering corporate governance mechanisms and their relationship with investment in R&D, Brazilian companies left something to be desired in terms of innovation and increases in production processes, as expected in the context of developing countries, mainly because most nations in the world offer tax incentives to companies to invest in fixed assets.

However, the economic slowdown experienced in the last decade may have led some economic segments that are sensitive to a decrease in demand, thus affecting the development of their innovation projects and the continuity of investments in R&D. Furthermore, corporate governance can function to reduce excessive bad investments by managers and inhibit agency conflict. In this case, the reduction in R&D investments mitigates the effects related to market imperfections, especially in periods of instability. In other words, corporate governance contributes to the assertiveness of management decisions in the most diverse situations.

This research allows us to fill a gap regarding the influence of corporate governance on investments in R&D in the context of companies listed on the Brazilian stock exchange to contribute to the literature on the topic. As well as expand reflections on the relevance of investments in R&D for companies in the global context.

For further work, a study with other variables is suggested to investigate possible factors that can explain investments in R&D. Furthermore, verify the possibility of field research to explore, in more detail, the barriers that prevent companies from making such investments.

REFERENCES

AlHares, A. (2020). Corporate governance mechanisms and R&D intensity in OECD courtiers. *Corporate Governance (Bradford)*, *20*(5), 863–885.

Asensio-López, D., Cabez-García, L., & González-Álvarez, N. (2019). Corporate governance and innovation: A theoretical review. *European Journal of Management and Business Economics*, *28*(3), 266–284.

Institucional. (2022). Uma das principais empresas de infraestrutura de mercado financeiro do mundo. Disponível em: <https://www.b3.com.br/pt_br/b3/institucional/quem-somos/>. Acesso em: 7 Ago. 2022.

Baysinger, B., & Hoskisson, R. E. (1990). The composition of boards of directors and strategic control: Effects on corporate strategy. *Academy of Management Review*, *15*(1), 72–87.

Baysinger, B. D., Kosnik, R. D., & Turk, T. A. (1991). Effects of board and ownership structure on corporate R&D strategy. *Academy of Management Journal*, *34*(1), 205–214.

Belloc, F. (2012). Corporate Governance an Innovation: A Survey. *Journal of Economic Surveys*, *26*(5), 835–864.

Brossard, O., Lavigne, S., & Erdem Sakinç, M. (2013). Ownership structures and R&D in Europe: The good institutional investors, the bad and ugly impatient shareholders. *Industrial and Corporate Change*, *22*(4), 1031–1068.

Carvalho Júnior, V. D. O. C., de Araujo, M. B. V., Lima, V. S., Corrar, L. J., & de Lima, G. A. S. F. (2010). Representatividade do valor de marcas no valor de mercado da empresa no Brasil. In Anais do Congresso Brasileiro de Custos-ABC.

Chan, K., Chen, H., Hong, L., & Wang, Y. (2015). Stock market valuation of R&D expenditures—The role of corporate governance. Pacific-Basin finance jornal, 31(1), 78-93.

Chu, W. K., Yang, N. T., & Yang, S. Y. (2016). Corporate governance'impact on research and development. *Journal of Business Research*, *69*(6), 2239–2243.

Código das Melhores Práticas de Governança Corporativa. (2023). 6. ed. São Paulo: Instituto Brasileiro de Governança Corporativa (IBGC).

Cordis, A. S., & Kirby, C. (2017). Capital expenditures and firm performance: Evidence from a cross-sectional analysis of stock returns. *Accounting and Finance*, *57*(4), 1019–1042.

Corrêa, E. D. L., Silva, W. A. C., Pinheiro, J. L., & Melo, A. A. O. (2015). Estrutura de propriedade e criação de valor em companhias brasileiras. *Tourism & Management Studies*, *11*(2), 130–137.

Cruz, C. V. O. A., & de Lima, G. A. S. F. (2010). Reputação corporativa e nível de disclosure das empresas de capital aberto no Brasil. *Revista Universo Contábil*, *6*(1), 85–101.

Di Vito, J., Laurin, C., & Bozec, Y. (2010). R&D activity in Canada: Does corporate ownership structure matter?. Canadian Journal of Administrative Sciences/Revue Canadienne des Sciences de l'Administration, 27(2), 107-121.

Driscoll, J. C., & Kraay, A. C. (1998). Consistent covariance matrix estimation with spatially dependent panel data. *The Review of Economics and Statistics*, *80*(4), 549–560.

Driver, C., & Guedes, M. J. C. (2012). Research and development, cash flow, agency and governance: UK large companies. *Research Policy*, *41*(9), 1565–1577.

Eisenhardt, K. M. (1989). Agency theory: An assessment and review. *Academy of Management Review*, *14*(1), 57–74.

Fama, E. F. (1970). Efficient capital markets: A review of theory and empirical work. *The Journal of Finance*, *25*(2), 383–423.

Fortunato, G., Funchal, B., & Motta, A. P. (2012). Impacto dos investimentos no desempenho das empresas brasileiras. *Rev. Adm. Mackenzie*, *13*(4), 75–98.

Góis, A. D., Parente, P. H. N., & Ponte, V. M. R. (2015). Estrutura de Propriedade e Investimentos em P&D: uma análise nas companhias abertas do Brasil. Revista Base (Administração e Contabilidade) da UNISINOS, 12(1), 2-14.

Gul, F. A., Kim, J. B., & Qiu, A. A. (2010). Ownership concentration, foreign shareholding, audit quality, and stock price synchronicity: Evidence from China. *Journal of Financial Economics*, *95*(3), 425–442.

Honoré, F., Munari, F., & de La Potterie, B. V. P. (2015). Corporate governance practices and companies' R&D intensity: Evidence from European countries. *Research Policy*, *44*(2), 533–543.

Hsu, C. Y., Hsiao, H. F., & Li, C. A. (2009). Effect of board monitoring on corporate investment and firm performance: Taiwan evidence. *Investment Management and Financial Innovations*, *6*(3), 84–93.

Huang, Z., & Gao, W. (2022). The effects of formal and informal CEO power on debt policy persistence. *The North American Journal of Economics and Finance*, *62*, 101748.

James, B. E., & McGuire, J. B. (2016). Transactional-institutional fit: Corporate governance of R&D investment in different institutional contexts. *Journal of Business Research*, *69*, 3478–3486.

Jensen, M. C. (1993). The modern industrial revolution, exit, and the failure of internal control systems. the Journal of Finance, 48(3), 831-880.

Jensen, M. C., & Meckling, W. H. (1976). Theory of firm – managerial behaviour, agency costs and ownership structure. *Journal of Financial Economics*, *3*(4), 305–360.

Kim, B., Burns, M. L., & Prescott, J. E. (2009). The Strategic Role of the Board: The Impact of Board Structure on Top Management Team Strategic Action Capability. *Corporate Governance*, *17*(6), 728–743.

Kor, Y. Y. (2006). Direct and interaction effects of top management team and board compositions on R&D investment strategy. *Strategic Management Journal*, *27*(11), 1081–1099.

La Porta, R., Lopez-de-Silanes, F., Shleifer, A., & Vishny, R. (2000). Investor protection and corporate governance. *Journal of Financial Economics*, *58*(1-2), 3–27.

Lee, M. (2015). Impact of corporate governance on research and development investment in the pharmaceutical industry in South Korea. *Osong Public Health and Research Perspectives*, *6*(4), 249–255.

Lu, J., & Wang, W. (2015). Board independence and corporate investments. *Review of Financial Economics*, *24*, 52–64.

Lv, D. D., Chen, W., Zhu, H., & Lan, H. (2019). How does inconsistent negative performance feedback affect the R&D investments of firms? A study of publicly listed firms. *Journal of Business Research*, *102*, 151–162.

Mata, J., & Woerter, M. (2013). Risky innovation: The impact of internal and external R&D strategies upon the distribution of returns. *Research Policy*, *42*(2), 495–501.

Mesquita, R., Fernandes, A. A. T., & Figueiredo Filho, D. B. (2020). Uma introdução à regressão com dados de painel. *Revista Política Hoje*, *29*(1), 434–507.

Muhammad, H., Migliori, S., & Consorti, A. (2024). Corporate governance and R&D investment: Does firm size matter? *Technology Analysis and Strategic Management*, *36*(3), 518–532.

Muhammad, H., Migliori, S., & Mohsni, S. (2022). Corporate governance and R&D investment: The role of debt financing. *Industrial and Corporate Change*, *31*(3), 628–653.

Nekhili, M., Boubaker, S., & Lakhal, F. (2012). Ownership structure, voluntary R&D disclosure and market value of firms: the French case. International journal of business, 17(2), 126.

O'Connor, M., Rafferty, M., & Sheikh, A. (2013). Equity compensation and the sensitivity of research and development to financial market frictions. *Journal of Banking & Finance*, *37*(7), 2510–2519.

Osma, B. G. (2008). Board independence and real earnings management: The case of R&D expenditure. *Corporate Governance*, *16*(2), 116–131.

Pindado, J., de Queiroz, V., & De la Torre, C. (2015). How do country-level governance characteristics impact the relationship between R & D and firm value? *R & D Management*, *45*(5), 515–526.

Portal da Industria. (2022). Apenas 10% das empresas usam recursos públicos para inovação, diz sondagem da CNI. agência de notícias da indústria. Disponível em: <https://noticias.portaldaindustria.com.br/noticias/inovacao-e-tecnologia/apenas-10-das-empresas-usam-recursos-publicos-para-inovacao-diz-sondagem-da-cni/#:~:text=Apenas%2010%25%20das%20empresas%20usam%20recursos%20p%C3-%BAblicos%20para,entrevistados%20disseram%20usar%20apenas%20recursos%20pr%C3%B3prios%20para%20inovar>. Acesso em: 31 Jul. 2022.

Rodrigues, R., Samagaio, A., & Felício, T. (2020). Corporate governance and R&D investment by European listed companies. *Journal of Business Research*, *115*, 289–295.

Salas, V. (2002). El gobierno de la empresa: Presentación. Ekonomiaz. *Revista Vasca de Economía*, *50*, 10–27.

Sánchez, L. P. C., Guerrero-Villegas, J., & Hurtado Gonzalez, J. M. (2017). The influence of organizational factors on board roles. *Management Decision*, *55*(5), 842–871.

Silva, A. L. C. (2014). *Governança corporativa e sucesso empresarial: melhores práticas para aumentar o valor da firma* (2nd ed.).

Srivastav, A., & Hagendorff, J. (2016). Corporate governance and bank risk-taking. *Corporate Governance*, *24*(3), 334–345.

Toigo, L. A., Hein, N., & Kroenke, A. (2018). Características predominantes dos mecanismos de governança corporativa e desempenho pós-fusões e aquisições no Brasil. Enfoque. *Reflexão Contábil*, *37*, 85–104.

Chapter 8
Financing for Development in Southeast Asian Countries

Lili Yulyadi Arnakim
Binus University, Indonesia

Miranda Tahalele
Binus University, Indonesia

Hizkia Putra Purnomo
Binus University, Indonesia

Muhammad Anshari
https://orcid.org/0000-0002-8160-6682
Universiti Brunei Darussalam, Brunei

ABSTRACT

This chapter examines the impact of foreign aid to southeast Asia countries. There are many arguments around the concept of foreign financing for developing countries, especially to the southeast Asia countries. Some believe foreign aid is detrimental for infrastructure development, while many also believe that foreign aid is one the key factors for the development. This research is qualitative research that uses descriptive analysis research and secondary data collection. Despite of the many arguments, foreign aid has shown a positive impact for their recipient country infrastructure development. Moreover, the most developed countries for the ASEAN countries member use external financing as a method to finance their huge project infrastructure, other than relying on government funding and private sectors or public private partnerships. It is found that most foreign aid failures are caused by internal shortcoming itself, rather than the external financing.

INTRODUCTION

Infrastructure is one of the most important aspects for a country's economic development. This statement can be proven by the reported correlation between an improved infrastructure and the economic rise of a country. By their definition, what is meant by infrastructure is water supply, sewage, housing, roads

DOI: 10.4018/979-8-3693-1742-6.ch008

and bridges, ports, power, airports, railways, urban services, communications, oil and gas production, and mining which serves to help the running of a country. Several studies concluded that infrastructure has a great influence on national economic growth and has become a major factor in economic development. Therefore, in order to maintain a high quality infrastructure, a huge number of funds is needed for infrastructure to be constructed, operated and used for its development.

Southeast Asia countries are very diverse. The differences can be seen from various aspects of a country such as the military, culture, and also economy sectors which are different with one and another. The diversity of Southeast Asia countries causing them to face various economic problems as well. Most of countries income per capita differences are being counted on from the low total factor productivity (TFP) in poor countries (Klenow and Rodr´ıguez-Clare, 1997; Hall and Jones, 1999). Based on the TFP, poor countries tend to be more unproductive in the production of tradables and investment goods. Although some countries in Southeast Asia have developed, some of them are still struggling to build their economy sectors. This situation shows the importance for other countries to help those that are still developing (Hamdan et al., 2021).

External financing is a necessity for developed and developing countries (Rosli et al., 2022). A successful economic development and net financial flows are built upon external financing (Anshari et al., 2022; Firmansyah et al., 2024). Thus, it is very important for Southeast Asia countries to maximize the benefits of external financing, which can have done through cooperation, investment, loan, or in the form of bilateral, regional, or international trade to improve their country infrastructure development. However, it is believed that the external financing would actually be detrimental and increasing the burden of the recipient countries. This research has the purpose to reveal the impact of external financing in Southeast Asia, by conducting in-depth observations of its countries.

Theoretical Framework

The theory of foreign aid and the theory of general growth and development have the same fundamental principles. Despite of the same basis, these are two different separated theories. However, development economic did not acknowledge the independent existence of the theories, whereas the criticism of the foreign aid theory is range and suit to the growth and development theory. There are three approaches of the foreign aid theory. One, savings-investment gap approach. two, foreign exchange earning expenditure gap approach, and three capital absorptive capacity approach with all of them are focused to made a positive impact to the recipient country growth and the development in infrastructure or economy.

Foreign aids have an important role for global development dialogue and International economic order. Based on the Harrod-Domar growth model, it is explained that capital is one of the most important factors in the growth and development of a country, in accordance with foreign aid. This model emphasizes the function of foreign aid, especially in a developing country. After the second world war, foreign aid significantly impacts the third world countries development experiences and forming a south-north relation. Foreign aid is capable to remove three major deficiencies of a developing countries, that is capital, foreign exchange, and technical knowledge.

METHODOLOGY

This paper use qualitative research for its research methodology. In opposite with quantitative research, a qualitative research collect data in the form of text, video, or audio. A qualitative research is more focused on understanding human being experience or reflection to a situation, rather than setting a finite question to the speaker. State (1995) emphasize 3 major differences of qualitative and quantitative researches. Firstly, the distinction on understanding and explaining the purpose if an inquiry. Secondly, the distinction between the role of personal and impersonal of the researcher. Thirdly, a distinction between discovered knowledge and constructed knowledge. Despite of the many varieties to the qualitative research approaches, most of them are flexible and more focused on keeping the rich meaning of a situation while processing a data.

Data Collection and Data analysis

This paper is a descriptive analysis research that use secondary data collection. A descriptive analysis research paper aim to explain a situation of an ongoing event. This data analysis is essentials in delivering an insight to the readers in a meaningful way. a descriptive analysis paper is not responsible to predict future outcome and explain the background of a situation, but is useful for further research material. A secondary data collection is a data collection method that collect data in the form of text, video, audio, and images. This method is commonly being used when a researcher doesn't have the ability to access a data of a population first hand. A secondary data collection can be done through search for information that has been collected by the government or research organizations via internet, documents, manuscripts, or record from the libraries.

LITERATURE REVIEW

The People Republic of China (PRC) recently carried out a movement in order to aid developing countries. In the form of development aids, loans, technical assistance, and state sponsored investment, the China economic assistance is intended to help countries that are located in Africa, Latin America, and Southeast Asia (Lum, 2009). China's diplomatic movement reaped various reactions from the public, which some people believe that this movement is aimed to increase China's influence as the world's greatest power. The journal aims to study the impact of China's government supported foreign assistance in these three regions (Lum, 2009).

China's economic assistance played a huge role for Southeast Asia infrastructure development (Lum, 2009). The financial aid however, are not carried out with economic purposes, but are focused on to build long-term regional diplomacy instead. In recent years, China has provided a total of $2 billion dollars of loans for Southeast Asia energy, agriculture, and mining infrastructure development (Lum, 2009). Yet, various public opinions have emerged that the economic assistance rather disadvantages Southeast Asia countries. The "no conditions" assistance of the Chinese government would actually burden developing countries with debt and influence another democratic country's ability to donate. The ongoing assistance is also believed to be one of the Chinese government ways to rival the influence of the United States to become the world's greatest power (Lum, 2009).

Within his journal, Yong (2017) discusses the many reasons why Malaysia has the highest quality of infrastructure among other ASEAN countries. Based on a study from Goldman Sachs Global economics, Malaysia infrastructure is ranked as one of the highest, alongside South Korea, Thailand, and India. The journal clearly describes the taken topic, however, the writer's data collection considered is not fairly accurate to explain the existing infrastructure development. (Yong, 2017)

There are many factors that push Malaysia infrastructure development. Yong (2017) stated that the government's strong commitment to the five years' economic plan (Malaysia Plans) are one of the biggest reasons for the quality infrastructure. Though, beside the government, foreign investment is also one of the main sources of Malaysia infrastructure financing. Under the Chinese investment, Malaysia successfully ran various large scale projects. One of the example are the HSR (Kuala Lumpur – Singapore High Speed Rails) projects which are formed under the cooperation with China Railway Engineering Crop (CREC) that cover a total of 60% needed funds and creates more than 20,000 km of rails for the HSR projects (yong, 2017). The synergy between government and foreign aid significantly improved Malaysia infrastructure, which made it important for the Malaysian government to fully support the development of their citizens' quality of life (Yong, 2017).

Thailand has suffered major shocks to their sovereignty, internally and externally. Several ways have been done by Thailand to recover from this situation, one of them is by creating a large industrial base. The journal aimed to analyse the significance of Thailand intra-regional trade, physical connectivity, trade facilitation, energy cooperation, and the importance of infrastructure funding to the country. Within this journal, the various ways for the government to restore the economy stability are being explained in full, while they still conclude the importance of infrastructure development for the country (Chirathivat, Cheewatrakoolpong, 2015).

Thailand has many infrastructure projects that are being constructed, or want to be constructed. In the recent project called the Greater Mekong Subregion Highway expansion, Thailand received a total of $77.1 million from the ADB (Tanaka, 2013). Several large scale projects like the Trilateral Highway and the Dawei Deep-Sea Port are also one of many Thailand important projects that are expected to operate in 2023 (Chirathivat, Cheewatrakoolpong, 2015). However, a discrepancy exists between large projects funded by foreign countries and small projects funded by PPPs (Public Private Partnerships). From the current ongoing projects, the PPP only contributed not more than 5% of the total funds, whereas the domestic organization that involved foreign investors provided almost 30% of the needed funds (Chirathivat, Cheewatrakoolpong, 2015). This statistic showed that the private sector under the government does not have a more impact in comparison with the foreign assistance (Chirathivat, Cheewatrakoolpong, 2015).

Key Discussion

Infrastructure development requires a huge amount of funds. Within 2010-2020, the ADB (Asian Development Bank) estimated a minimum of $3.6 trillion infrastructure investment was needed by South Asia and Southeast Asia to meet the required funds for their growing populations (Bhattacharyay 2012). However, financial shortages are not the issue for Southeast Asian countries. Southeast Asia countries had enough excess liquidity for reliable long term returns, but, on the other hand, their current framework and instruments are incapable of bridge the gap. Most of the Southeast Asia government is being faced by increasing budget pressure that made the role of private funding crucial to fund and finance infrastructure projects (Anshari et al., 2020; Fithtriyah et al., 2022). Although bank finance is more available in Southeast Asia, it is becoming more scarce and expensive compared to other regions (Anshari et al., 2019; Hamdan & Anshari, 2020).

In the year below 2010, Southeast Asia countries only did a few intra-regional trades. Based on statistics from ADB, it is found that Southeast Asia countries only did a total of 1%-5% intra-regional trade with neighboring countries, compared to the global average of 25%. This situation is caused by infrastructure shortfalls. The immaturity of the capital and financial markets are one of the main reasons for the slow infrastructure development. In addition, most of the Southeast Asia countries are heavily reliant on bank loans for expansions that cause the lack of the long term yield curve and market marking, illiquidity in the regional bond markets, and the low plausibility of the financial report that keeps foreign investors away from financing a project (Firmansyah et al., 2022; Anshari et al., 2021).

Originally, most of the Southeast Asia foreign investors were US banks and large Europeans. However, the provider country investment began to decline after the economic crisis in the last 4 years. The financial crisis also impacted Southeast Asia countries by increasing their dependence on bank loans and foreign capital. This situation has developed the needs for Southeast Asia countries to improve their regional financing capabilities. To prevent any future financial crises, each country in Southeast Asia needs to upgrade their own financing and risk management abilities by strengthening their regional financial cooperation within the support of international organizations and more developed countries.

The first approaches of Foreign aid theory stated that poor saving and investment rate are the major constraint for less developed countries. Based on the savings-investment approach, extra savings in the form of foreign aid is an important variable for countries' economic growth. The proposed foreign capital would help developing countries to have an optimum level of operation and production for their economic sectors. Vice versa, a capital shortage is the equivalent for a country's poor performance. Within the support of foreign aid, the receiving country will possibly sustain a higher growth rate because of the high saving rate that is provided.

Foreign Exchange Earning Expenditure Gap Approach argued that foreign aid would have much more impact to the development of developing countries if the received funds are being used to purchase goods and services that are not produced domestically. This approach believes that the experienced difficulty for their development is caused by goods and services deficiencies and weak foreign exchanges, whereas a structural limitation such as primary commodity secular decline and inelastic domestic supply is the main reason for the slowed down foreign exchanges earnings. Prebisch opined that developing countries should rely more on the massive import substitution with the help of foreign aid rather than focusing on primary commodity production which implies the significance of external help.

A capital absorptive capacity approach defends the concept of non-economic foreign aid. This approach is being used for economists and policy makers to determine the amount and nature of foreign aid if they did not confine themselves only to the other foreign aid approaches. The capital absorptive capacity approach assumes that non-economic factors such as the lack of entrepreneurship, low education, and rapid population growth are the major constraints of the development of a country. Also, this approach believes that the investment on education and technical institutions are beneficial for developing countries to overcome deficiency in the early phase of development.

Some argued that foreign aid is actually detrimental for the recipient country. These arguments are based from the perspective that believe foreign aid is used as a tool for the provider country to promote countries national interest. The development theory distinguishes the argument of foreign aid by a clear polarization of pro-aid and anti-aid arguments. The anti-aid argued that the foreign aid did not contribute to the development of a country, moreover worsened the current situation by increasing their country savings or foreign exchange constraints. On the other hand, pro aid believe that foreign aid would help the underdeveloped country by generating the required resource that can be formed by internal economic structure. This research aims to get know the impact of the foreign aid in Southeast Asia region by conducting an analysis to four (Singapore, Thailand, Philippines, Myanmar) Southeast Asia countries within the most to the least developed one.

Singapore

Singapore is the most developed country in Southeast Asia. Compared to another Southeast Asia countries, Singapore infrastructure project did not fully dependent to foreign aid, with most of the infrastructure projects financing are done by their own government. Because of the unavailability of natural resources, Singapore heavily relied on their trade, capital and labor flows. The development of foreign capital and labor has been fundamental for Singapore economy sectors. At the meantime, over 5,000 foreign and multinational companies have been established to operate and manufacture bases on the island.

Singapore had one of the most developed infrastructure. The strategic location of Singapore builds this country to become the world best international airlines and shipping hub. These infrastructures alone won Singapore multiple international awards consistently. With the infrastructure that they have now, a huge amount of funds is spent for the purpose to set up and operates their projects, where the role of foreign aid is very important in this situation. The development of Singapore airport and railroads construction is one of several examples of foreign country involvement to Singapore infrastructure projects.

The Singapore MRT (Mass Rapid Transit) system development was discussed in 1970. This project was made by the Singaporean government to develop a healthy and vibrant public transportation. Unlike their bus system, the proposed concept of the MRT is wished to become a public transportation system that did not drain government funds continually. The development of this project are being funded by several international agencies, namely, the UNDP (United Nation Development Program), the World Bank, Harvard University team, and Wilbur Smith and Associates private sector consultants. The failure to the MRT development would made a chain impact to the reduced demands of Singapore workers to reduced real earnings. With some argument roam around the development of this project, the MRT finally operate 4 years later with a total cost of S$5 billion.

Despite of the several foreign financing, the viabilities of Singapore infrastructure are in the hand of the government. The MRT infrastructure (tunnels, viaducts, and station) and the first set of operating assets (trains and signaling systems) were all funded by the government. The Singapore government are consistent with their beliefs regarding to the financing of infrastructure projects. The government always allocate the generated revenue from the MRT fare to be used to cover MRT maintenance and operation costs, including to the replacement of their operating assets, which are also being implemented to Singapore any other infrastructure projects.

Thailand

Thailand infrastructure experience massive growth in the past few decades. Compared to their foreign aid, Public sector has much bigger contribution to Thailand infrastructure planning, construction and operation, and infrastructure investment. Given the magnitude of their impact, most of Thailand's future projects are financed around the PPP sectors. Thailand's share of trade scope has always been larger to the mainland of Southeast Asia, which are more or less the same as the characteristics of their external infrastructure financing. Despite of their dependence to foreign aid, most of the cooperation only made with ASEAN member countries.

Thailand's economic development goes hand in hand with their infrastructure development. With the uptrend of their economy sectors, Thailand mostly focused their infrastructure development project to energy and transportation sectors. Several attempts were done by the government to turn state enterprises of power generation into private companies in purpose to encourage private investment to the mentioned sector. Based on 2012 fiscal budget statistic however, it can be found that most of Thailand fiscal budgets are being used to finance internal debts of US$129,304 million dollars, which are far apart if being compared to US$6,825.7 million of external financing.

Most of Thailand foreign aid are being used to finance transportation sectors. The loans that Thailand made to international agencies and foreign country consist a total of US$1,485.4 million external debt to the government and US$5,340.3 million external debt to the state enterprises. Thailand state enterprises such as Mass Rapid Authority, State Railways of Thailand, and Airport of Thailand Plc were all getting funded by International agencies or foreign countries. These financing however, does not cover half of the amount of Thailand state enterprises which is supported by the PPP.

Philippines

As a country with a developing economy, Philippines infrastructure still considered poor and unfair to access. The under-investment of the infrastructure is the one that resulted this situation. Compared to other Southeast Asia Countries, the available statistic showed that Philippines infrastructure quality are still left behind. some of the existing infrastructure showed the obvious underdevelopment, especially their transportation sector. the Philippines' transportation sector is lacking in terms of international population mobility of its airports and seaports. The underdevelopment of the infrastructure has led Philippines seaport to reduce the operational number of their ferries, while also causing the Philippines international airport to accommodate more flights than the accepted provisions.

Official Development Assistance (ODA) played a huge part for Philippines infrastructure development. These multilateral agencies focused on a different part of the country, which can be separated within their function. The Asian Development Bank (ADB) prioritize to support transportation, energy, agriculture infrastructure, and water supply projects. The United Nation (UN) focused on the he attainment of the Millennium Development Goals. While the bilateral foreign agencies provide infrastructure investment promotion, Public Private's Partnerships (PPP), tourism infrastructure support, and infrastructure for peace and development in Mindanao.

The received aid from international agencies and foreign country mostly are focused to improve country's Infrastructure development. Philippines ODA partners has consistently encouraged the development of the country's infrastructure within the recent the years. With the total amount of US$8.82 billion loans received, 78% or US$ 6.89 billion of loans are used to finance infrastructure projects, while the rest are used for program development. Within all the funds received throughout the years, Japan contributed the most for Philippines infrastructure development at 48% accounted loans which then followed by France and the World Bank at 23% and 15% respectively.

Regional sources also had a major impact for Philippines infrastructure development beside the ODA. As of the year of 2020, the ASEAN infrastructure fund has lent Philippines a total of US$4 billion, while also being expected to provide loans of US$300 million per year. Still classified as an external financing methods, the ASEAN infrastructure funds were collected throughout 9 Southeast Asia countries in with its implementation alone already leveraged 1.5 times of the Southeast Asia US$335.2 million equity.

Despite of the foreign aid, Philippines infrastructure quality still unable to compete with other Southeast Asian countries. The Philippines was ranked as the seventh among nine ASEAN countries regarding of their infrastructure quality based from World Economic Forum statistic in 2018. there are several reasons why the funds provided are still insufficient in encouraging the development of Philippine infrastructure. The Philippines government did not spend the given fund correctly to improve their country infrastructure quality. Thus, there are still many internal factors from the country that might cause the utilization of existing funds to be not optimal. It is important for the state to organize country's other sectors to make it not bother the mobility of infrastructure and economic financing, whereas the implementation of foreign aid was not completely at fault.

Myanmar

Infrastructure financing problem has been an issues for Myanmar in a long time. this country are the least developed among other Southeast Asia countries, which implies the urgency of any kind of assistance for the country. The prolonged infrastructure financing issues is commonly being related to the macroeconomic fundamentals and the level of infrastructure lending of the country. Based by several surveys that was done in major city of Myanmar, it can be concluded that the inability to access formal sector is one of the major constraint for Myanmar private sectors.

Most of Myanmar firms did not take the advantage of external financing into their start up. A 2003 survey revealed that only 30 out of 167 firms that are located in Yangon and Mandalay borrowed funds from the private and state-owned bank. A similar survey that was done in 2007 also concluded that more than half of the firm that is surveyed, most of them did not avail to the outside source financing, thus, these firms relied on their own money for the planned expansion and startup. Based by the mentioned surveys, it can be concluded that Myanmar infrastructure development are being limited by the lack of access to the formal financing sources and their reluctant to use foreign aid as one of the steps for infrastructure funding.

There are several reasons why most of Myanmar enterprise and industry did not want to implement foreign aid as a way to finance their startup and infrastructure projects. Most of Myanmar citizen believe that foreign aid is complex in the term of banking procedures which oblige a tight collateral requirement for its recipient. They also believe that foreign aid is only beneficial for short term basis and cannot be relied for business expansion. The Myanmar business owner rather expand their business to the level of their own finance allowed, without the support of external financing in any kind. With the lack of assistance that are coming from external sources, there is not much information about foreign aid in Myanmar

CONCLUSION

Foreign aid impact is differing in each Southeast Asia countries. Depend on the economic situation of the recipient country, the impact of foreign aid will also vary to each of them. However, this research has found an interesting characteristic that distinguish the influence of the external financing to Southeast Asia countries. Based by the World Economic Forum of ASEAN countries infrastructure ranking, most of the high-ranked countries such as Singapore and Thailand did not fully rely their infrastructure development to foreign aid. Although many big projects are in the aid of external financing, the majority of the infrastructure viabilities, Infrastructure planning, operating assets, and operating cost are getting funded by the government and Public Private Partnership (PPP). Compared to the underdeveloped countries of the Southeast Asia, they are not utilizing or unable to utilize the funds from foreign aid optimally. The negative assumptions of the external financing and the inability of the government to manage the fund Are the most common factor that caused this situation.

Many assumptions have roam around the concept of external financing. The most common assumption believed that the foreign aid is done because of the donor country wanted to promote their own national interest, rather than helping other country economy sectors. With their complexity of bank procedures, lots of people believed that the foreign aid only provide short termed benefits and are not suitable for countries infrastructure development. Despite of their questioned credibility however, it is uncontested that foreign aid is one of the determining factor for the development of a country. Moreover, International agencies such as the Asian Development Bank, United Nation, and World Bank considerably will not be taking advantages over a developed nor a developing country. The foreign aid itself are underutilized in an underdeveloped country for the positive impact to be felt. This research is still incomplete, with the lacking of financing impact example to the Southeast Asia countries. But, it is safe to say that the cooperation of the private sectors, government and the foreign aid will made a very positive impact for a country infrastructure development.

REFERENCES

Anshari, M., Almunawar, M. N., & Masri, M. (2020). An overview of financial technology in Indonesia. *Financial technology and disruptive innovation in ASEAN*, (pp. 216-224). IEEE.

Anshari, M., Almunawar, M. N., & Masri, M. (2022). Digital twin: Financial technology's next frontier of robo-advisor. *Journal of Risk and Financial Management, 15*(4), 163. doi:10.3390/jrfm15040163

Anshari, M., Almunawar, M. N., Masri, M., & Hamdan, M. (2019). Digital marketplace and FinTech to support agriculture sustainability. *Energy Procedia, 156*, 234–238. doi:10.1016/j.egypro.2018.11.134

Anshari, M., Almunawar, M. N., Masri, M., & Hrdy, M. (2021). Financial technology with AI-enabled and ethical challenges. *Society, 58*(3), 189–195. doi:10.1007/s12115-021-00592-w

Buera, F. J., Kaboski, J. P., & Shin, Y. (2011). Finance and development: A tale of two sectors. *The American Economic Review, 101*(5), 1964–2002. doi:10.1257/aer.101.5.1964

Carr, T (2018). *Supporting the Transition: Understanding Aid to Myanmar Since 2011.*

Firmansyah, E. A., Masri, M., Anshari, M., & Besar, M. H. A. (2022). Factors affecting fintech adoption: A systematic literature review. *FinTech, 2*(1), 21–33. doi:10.3390/fintech2010002

Firmansyah, E. A., Masri, M., Anshari, M., & Besar, M. H. A. (2024). Innovation in finance: A bibliometric and content-analysis study. *Nankai Business Review International.* Advance online publication. doi:10.1108/NBRI-08-2023-0071

Fithriyah, M., Masri, M., Almunawar, M. N., & Anshari, M. (2022). Financial Inclusion and Mobile Payment to Empower Small and Medium-Sized Enterprises: Post-COVID-19 Business Strategy. In FinTech Development for Financial Inclusiveness (pp. 50-59). IGI Global.

Hamdan, M., & Anshari, M. (2020). Paving the Way for the Development of FinTech Initiatives in ASEAN. In *Financial technology and disruptive innovation in ASEAN* (pp. 80–107). IGI Global. doi:10.4018/978-1-5225-9183-2.ch004

Hamdan, M., Besar, M. H. A., Salleh, N. A. H., & Anshari, M. (2021, December). Small and Medium Enterprises & International Financial Reporting Standards (IFRS): Evidence from Emerging Economy. In *2021 International Conference on Sustainable Islamic Business and Finance* (pp. 109-118). IEEE. 10.1109/IEEECONF53626.2021.9686347

Ketkar, S., & Ratha, D. (Eds.). (2008). *Innovative financing for development*. World Bank Publications. doi:10.1596/978-0-8213-7685-0

Komatsuzaki, T. (2019). Improving public infrastructure in the Philippines. *Asian Development Review*, *36*(2), 159–184. doi:10.1162/adev_a_00135

Kregel, J. A. (2004). *External financing for development and international financial instability* (Vol. 32). Geneva: UN.

Kumari, A. Sharma, A. (2016). *Infrastructure financing and development: A bibliometric review*.

Morgenthau, H. (1962). A political theory of foreign aid. *The American Political Science Review*, *56*(2), 301–309. doi:10.2307/1952366

Navarro, A., & Llanto, G. M. (2014). Financing infrastructure in the Philippines: Fiscal landscape and resources mobilization. *Philippine Institute for Development Studies.*

Ongkittikul, S. (2014). Thailand country report. *Financing ASEAN Connectivity: ERIA Research Project Report FY2013, 15*, 355-400.

Pankaj, A. K. (2005). Revisiting foreign aid theories. *International Studies*, *42*(2), 103–121. doi:10.1177/002088170404200201

Phang, S. Y. (2003). Strategic development of airport and rail infrastructure: The case of Singapore. *Transport Policy*, *10*(1), 27–33. doi:10.1016/S0967-070X(02)00027-6

Ray, S. (2015). *Infrastructure finance and financial sector development*. Research Gate.

Rillo, A. D. (2017). *Public financing of infrastructure in Asia: In search of new solutions*. Research Gate.

Rosli, S. N., Anshari, M., Almunawar, M. N., & Masri, M. (2022). Digital wallet ecosystem in promoting financial inclusion. In *FinTech development for financial inclusiveness* (pp. 31–49). IGI Global. doi:10.4018/978-1-7998-8447-7.ch003

Chapter 9
Fostering Inclusivity and a Supportive Workplace for the Hearing Impaired: Towards Hifz Al-Nafs

Siti Nur Rafhanah Awang Masri
Universiti Brunei Darussalam, Brunei

Norainie Ahmad
https://orcid.org/0000-0001-7800-232X
Universiti Brunei Darussalam, Brunei

ABSTRACT

In contemporary society, there exists a growing recognition of the imperative to integrate individuals with hearing disabilities into all aspects of social life, including the realm of employment opportunities. The theory of equal capability and workforce integration emphatically asserts that individuals with hearing impairments inherently possess the same capacity and abilities as their hearing peers to perform tasks and excel in various professional fields. This belief finds substantial support in the growing number of hearing-impaired individuals actively participating in the workforce. However, despite the progress in inclusion, hearing-impaired individuals are still confronted with significant career-related obstacles. These challenges encompass communication barriers, feelings of isolation and misunderstanding, and the persistent presence of stigmas and stereotypes. These hurdles have the potential to affect their mental and emotional well-being adversely. When viewed through the lens of Maqasid Al Shariah, it becomes evident that fostering inclusivity and cultivating a supportive work environment is essential and inherently aligns with the principles of Islamic ethics and the core objectives of Maqasid Al Shariah itself. The central focus of this study is on the principle of hifz al nafs, or preservation of life, as it pertains to fostering inclusivity and establishing a workplace that fully supports individuals with hearing impairments. This study draws evidence from six hearing-impaired individuals working for two chosen organisations in Brunei. The organisations represent a government department, and a private company respectively. Semi-structured in-depth interviews sought to gather insights into the participants' personal working experiences alongside their able-bodied (hearing) colleagues. Findings show that various workplace or organisational-level policies and measures are imperative to achieve a truly inclusive and supportive working environment. These policies include the implementation of accessible communication methods, awareness-raising, and sensitization efforts, all of which are needed in the establishment of a society conducive for the worship of Allah.

DOI: 10.4018/979-8-3693-1742-6.ch009

INTRODUCTION

Working Experiences of Hearing-Impaired Employees

In today's diverse and inclusive workforce, the experiences of employees with hearing impairments have gained increased attention and significance. As a hub of social interaction and productivity, the workplace presents unique challenges and opportunities for individuals with hearing disabilities. Understanding and addressing the specific needs and experiences of hearing-impaired employees is essential for fostering an inclusive work environment and unlocking their full potential and contributions.

Employees with hearing impairment often face communication barriers at work. Social interactions are essential in the workplace, promoting a productive environment where employees connect with colleagues. Workplace discourse, as defined by Koester (as cited in Trisha H, 2018), encompasses interactions in various work settings, ranging from formal discussions like negotiations and meetings to informal chats about personal interests, such as favorite sports teams during breaks. Hearing-impaired employees actively participate in these interactions but typically have fewer opportunities for both formal and informal engagement compared to their hearing colleagues. Foster & MacLeod, (2003), Luft (2000) and Shuler et al. (2014) highlighted the detrimental effects of these barriers on job performance and social integration where communication challenges significantly affect their interactions with co-workers, supervisors, and customers, particularly in environments with speechreading difficulties or background noise, leading to potential feelings of isolation and hindered job performance.

Despite their capabilities, hearing-impaired individuals often encounter lower employment rates and barriers to career advancement. Studies by Frasier, Hansmann & Saladin (2009), Haynes (2014), Rosengreen & Saladin (2010) and Shuler et al. (2014) underscore the pervasive nature of communication challenges in the workplace. For instance, participating in meetings can be tough or daunting for hearing-impaired employees due to the inability to discern speech or navigate distracting environmental stimuli. These barriers not only hinder job performance but also to broader issues of employment inequality and economic disparities.

The working experiences of hearing-impaired individuals are further complicated by negative stereotypes, societal attitudes and discrimination. McCaughey and Strohmer (as cited in Farber, 2015) highlight the detrimental impact of these attitudes on identity, well-being and social integration as these negative stereotypes and societal attitudes lead to unfair biases against the hearing impaired. Jones (2002) elucidates hoiw individuals with hearing impairment are often dehumanized and perceived through a lens of deficiency rather than as individuals with diverse strength and qualities. To tackle this problem, people with hearing impairments have tried to think positively about their situation, as supported by Barnes et al. (1999) and Linton (1998), yet Munyi (2012) emphasizes the importance of resilience in the face of persistent stigma.

Furthermore, there is also impact on Social Integration. Negative stereotypes not only affect the perceptions of hearing-impaired individuals but also influence their interactions within social networks. Thomas & Gilholme-Herbst (1980) highlight how these stereotypes contribute to feelings of isolation and disconnection from mainstream society. Lane (1992) discusses the phenomenon of social distancing; wherein hearing-impaired individuals may withdraw from societal engagement due to perceived differences. This withdrawal, exacerbated by societal stigma, perpetuates a cycle of exclusion and marginalization.

Addressing the challenges faced by hearing-impaired employees requires a multifaceted approach encompassing policy advocacy, organizational change, and societal education. Initiatives aimed at fostering inclusive environments, such as workplace accommodations and awareness campaigns, play a crucial role in promoting equity and diversity. Additionally, advocacy efforts led by hearing-impaired individuals and their allies serve to challenge stereotypes, dismantle barriers, and promote social inclusion.

In conclusion, the working experience of hearing-impaired employees is a topic of paramount importance that calls for our attention and commitment. Throughout this exploration, we've delved into the challenges and barriers that hearing-impaired individuals often face in the workplace, from communication obstacles to feelings of isolation and the enduring weight of stigmas and stereotypes.

RESEARCH PROBLEM AND GAP

Despite growing awareness of the importance of inclusivity and accommodation for individuals with hearing impairment in the workplace, there remains a significant gap in understanding the practical challenges, barriers, and opportunities in achieving these objectives within the context of Islamic principles, specifically *Hifz al-Nafs* (Preservation of Life). This research seeks to address this gap by investigating the specific challenges, communication dynamics, and support mechanisms that can lead to a more inclusive and supportive work environment for hearing-impaired individuals, aligning with the principles of *Hifz al-Nafs* in Islamic ethics. In essence, the research problem centers on how to effectively implement inclusivity and support for the hearing-impaired workforce while taking into account the Islamic concept of *Hifz al-Nafs*, considering the unique challenges that arise from the intersection of cultural and religious values with the specific needs of hearing-impaired individuals in the workplace.

Furthermore, while there is a growing body of literature addressing workplace inclusivity and accommodation for individuals with disabilities, including hearing impairment, there is a noticeable dearth of research that systematically explores the practical implementation of these principles within an Islamic cultural and ethical framework, specifically through the lens of *Hifz al-Nafs* (Preservation of Life). Existing studies primarily focus on Western, secular contexts and often lack the nuanced understanding of the unique challenges and opportunities presented by Islamic values in fostering an inclusive and supportive workplace for hearing-impaired individuals. The research gap lies in the need to bridge the knowledge divide between general inclusivity practices and the application of Islamic principles in supporting the hearing-impaired workforce. This gap pertains to understanding how Islamic values can inform workplace policies, communication strategies, and accommodations, and how these principles can contribute to a more holistic and culturally sensitive approach to inclusivity. The research will address this gap by investigating the specific challenges, cultural considerations, and best practices that can create a workplace environment that not only accommodates but also empowers hearing-impaired individuals within the context of *Hifz al-Nafs*.

MAIN AIM AND OBJECTIVES

In light of the specific challenges faced by hearing-impaired employees in Brunei, this research aims to delineate fundamental principles grounded in the principles of *Hifz al-Nafs,* or Preservation of Life, within the context of promoting inclusivity and nurturing a supportive workplace environment for individuals living with hearing impairment. This exploration aims to uncover insights that can guide policies, accommodations, and cultural shifts, ensuring that the workplace becomes a sanctuary for every individual, regardless of their hearing ability, where their safety, well-being, and dignity are meticulously safeguarded. To achieve this aim, some objectives are identified:

1. To gain a comprehensive insight into workplace experiences through the exploration deeply the professional journeys of hearing-impaired employees, unearthing a nuanced understanding of the unique hurdles and obstacles they face within the work environment.
2. To assess the dynamics of communication by exploring the modes of communication employed by both hearing-impaired and hearing employees, evaluating its efficiency and its impact on overall workplace cohesion.
3. To address a discernible information void by highlighting the employment experiences of hearing-impaired individuals, contributing valuable insights to a currently underrepresented body of knowledge in this domain.

SIGNIFICANT CONTRIBUTIONS

This research is positioned to make a significant contribution to the expanding body of literature on the impairment, with a particular focus on the distinctive context of Brunei Darussalam. In this region, there exists a noticeable scarcity of data and knowledge regarding hearing impairment, underscoring the paramount importance of this research endeavor. The ultimate aim of this study is to benefit policymakers with invaluable insights and tools, equipping them to effectively govern and support the hearing-impaired population. This endeavor aligns harmoniously with Brunei's overarching vision, the Whole of Nation Approach which is designed to achieve the ambitious goals of *Wawasan Brunei 2035*. Furthermore, it resonates deeply with Islamic principles, in accordance with Brunei's identity as a Zikir Nation or *Negara Zikir*, steadfastly upholding the values of Islam according to *Ahli Sunnah Wal-Jemaah, Mazhab Shafie*.

This study primarily focus on the principle of *Hifz Al Nafs*, emphasizing the preservation of life. Consequently, it holds the potential to make a meaningful contribution to the broader framework of *Maqasid Al-Shariah*. It does so by focusing on the promotion of inclusivity and the creation of a workplace environment that offers comprehensive support for individuals with hearing impairments, thus safeguarding their well-being and aligning with Islamic values and objectives.

While it is acknowledged that the study's sample size is limited, comprising only six hearing-impaired employees, the empirical data collected is poised to have far-reaching implications for the hearing-impaired community in Brunei. By offering a comprehensive exploration of their lived experiences, this research will empower individuals and institutions alike with a profound understanding of the challenges and triumphs faced by the hearing-impaired population. Moreover, the study will proffer practical recommendations for fostering inclusivity within the workplace through the implementation of evidence-based policies. As the findings of this research become an integral part of the Islamic literature pertaining to the hearing-impaired, they will serve as a wellspring of inspiration and ideas for future research endeavors in this critical domain.

Hearing Impaired and Stigma

The hearing-impaired community has long grappled with the burden of negative stereotypes and misconceptions, which have cast a pervasive shadow over the lives of those affected by this condition. These entrenched misbeliefs, whether perpetuated by individuals with or without hearing impairments, serve as a formidable barrier to the comprehensive development of an individual's identity, exerting profound influence over their physical and emotional well-being, social integration, academic attainment, and professional accomplishments. This stigmatization eventually results in discrimination, isolation, and negative attitudes towards those who are hearing-impaired.

The societal perception of hearing-impaired individuals diverges significantly from attitudes directed toward individuals with other disabilities, such as blindness. Jones (2002) argued persuasively that hearing-impaired individuals are often unfairly regarded as lacking typical human attributes, largely due to the prevailing notion that hearing loss is synonymous with impairment or disability. This is further by supported by Munyi (2012) that individuals with hearing disabilities must actively distance themselves from the pernicious effects of stigmatization. Like their counterparts, they too yearn for acceptance, the opportunity to partake in life's myriad experiences, and the chance to demonstrate that they possess a multitude of positive attributes transcending the confines of their disability, as underscored by Linton (1998). Consequently, these negative social attitudes and stereotypes have given rise to pessimistic biases against the non-hearing community, resulting in the imposition of disparate standards and expectations as highlighted by McCaughey and Strohmer (cited in Farber, 2015).

Moreover, negative stigmatization extends to the belief that non-hearing individuals are more likely to experience depression, loneliness, workplace dissatisfaction, and difficulty adapting to mainstream society. As stated by Lane (1992), many non-hearing individuals feel distanced from the majority due to a lack of full integration into mainstream society. For example, Easterbrooks (1999) highlighted the tendency of hearing individuals to assume that non-hearing individuals can hear to some extent, which can result in unintentional overcompensation. This can lead to disappointment and frustration for non-hearing individuals, prompting some to conceal their deafness to achieve a sense of belonging within society. Therefore, challenging these misconceptions and promoting greater awareness and understanding of the experiences of deaf individuals is essential in breaking down the barriers that perpetuate stigmatization and isolation, ultimately leading to a more inclusive and accepting society for all.

Navigating Social Interactions in the Workplace for Hearing-Impaired Employees

The workplace is not merely a site for completing tasks; it's a dynamic environment where social interactions play a crucial role in shaping relationships, collaboration, and overall job satisfaction. These interactions, whether formal or informal, are the lifeblood of organizational culture, providing avenues for connection, collaboration, and camaraderie among colleagues. However, for hearing-impaired employees, these interactions are fraught with unique challenges that demand urgent attention and concerted efforts to address. For instance, imagine a team meeting where colleagues are brainstorming ideas for an upcoming project. For hearing-impaired employees, this seemingly routine interaction presents significant challenges. As the discussion unfolds, multiple voices overlap, making it difficult to discern who is speaking. Background noise from nearby conversations further complicates matters, rendering lip-reading virtually impossible. Despite their best efforts to follow the conversation, hearing-impaired employees struggle to keep up, leading to feelings of frustration and isolation. In this scenario, the unique challenges faced by hearing-impaired employees demand urgent attention and concerted efforts to address. Without appropriate accommodations, such as captioning services or sign language interpreters, hearing-impaired employees may be sidelined in crucial discussions, depriving them of the opportunity to contribute their insights and expertise. Moreover, the inability to fully participate in team meetings can erode their sense of belonging and undermine their confidence in their abilities, ultimately impacting their job satisfaction and performance. By recognizing and proactively addressing these challenges, organizations can create more inclusive work environments where all employees, regardless of their hearing status, can fully participate and thrive. This may involve implementing accessibility measures, providing communication training for colleagues, and fostering a culture of respect and understanding. Through concerted efforts, organizations can ensure that hearing-impaired employees are empowered to contribute their unique perspectives and talents to the workplace.

Koester's (as cited in Trisha H, 2018) definition of workplace discourse underscores the breadth of communication within professional settings, spanning from formal meetings to casual conversations during breaks. While hearing-impaired employees participate in these interactions like their hearing counterparts, their access to both formal and informal communication channels is often curtailed. This limitation stems from various factors, including inadequate communication infrastructure, lack of accessibility accommodations, and societal attitudes that undervalue the communication needs of hearing-impaired individuals.

Communication barriers present formidable obstacles for hearing-impaired employees when engaging with colleagues, supervisors, and clients. The severity of these challenges is exacerbated in environments with poor communication infrastructure, leading to feelings of isolation and impeding job performance (Foster & MacLeod, 2003; Luft, 2000; Shuler et al., 2014). Moreover, these barriers contribute significantly to the persistently lower employment rates and hindered career advancement opportunities for hearing-impaired individuals (Frasier, Hansmann & Saladin, 2009; Haynes, 2014; Rosengreen & Saladin, 2010; Shuler et al., 2014).

Rosengreen and Saladin's (2010) study underscores the critical importance of effective communication in the workplace, with all respondents highlighting its significance. However, despite recognizing its importance, hearing-impaired employees often grapple with participation in meetings due to speechreading difficulties or environmental distractions, such as the rustling of papers. Even when utilizing sign language, hearing-impaired individuals encounter additional hurdles, including limited access to interpreters and challenges in interpreter adaptation to the workplace context (Compton as cited in Luft, 2000). The scarcity of interpreters and logistical complexities further exacerbate communication barriers, impeding the seamless exchange of information and hindering collaboration and productivity (Foster & MacLeod, 2003).

In conclusion, acknowledging and addressing the multifaceted challenges faced by hearing-impaired employees is imperative for fostering an inclusive workplace culture. Beyond mere recognition, proactive measures are needed to mitigate communication barriers, enhance accessibility accommodations, and cultivate deeper understanding and empathy among colleagues. By embracing diversity and investing in inclusive practices, organizations can create environments where all employees, regardless of their hearing status, feel valued, supported, and empowered to thrive and contribute their fullest potential.

BRIDGING THE CONTEXT OF MAQASID AL SHARIAH, HEARING-IMPAIRED AND WORKPLACE

Islamic jurisprudence, known as "Fiqh" in Arabic, is the body of Islamic legal principles and rules that govern various aspects of the lives of Muslims. It is derived from the Quran, the Hadith (the sayings and

Figure 1. The hierarchy of the Maqasid of the Shariah (Levels of necessity)

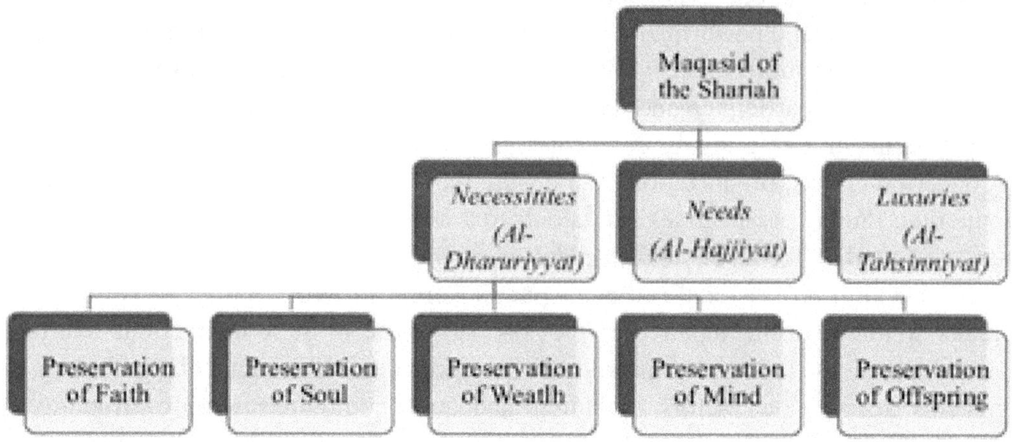

actions of the Prophet Muhammad), consensus among Islamic scholars (ijma), and analogical reasoning (qiyas). Islamic jurisprudence guides on matters such as worship, family law, contracts, commerce, and ethics. *Maqasid Al Shariah* holds a pivotal role in Islam, guiding individuals on distinguishing between virtuous and wrongful actions, urging the practice of righteousness while discouraging wrongdoing, and encouraging thoughtful contemplation in all aspects of daily life. The main objectives of the *Shariah* are explained in Surah Al-Anbiya, verse 107,

"And We have sent you (O Muhammad SAW) not but as a mercy for the exists)"

After the Companions' era, the theory and classifications of *maqasid* started to evolve. However, ma*qasid*, as we know them today, was not developed until the later *usulis* of the fifth to eighth Islamic century by some scholars such as Abd al-Malik al-Juwayni, Abu Hamid al-Ghazali, Al Izz Ibn Abd al-Salam and many others.

The term "*maqsid*" (plural "maqasid") encompasses a wide array of meanings, including purpose, objective, principle, intent, goal, and end. The concept of *Maqasid al-Shariah* is the branch of Islamic knowledge, in particular, refers to the higher objectives, purposes, intents, ends, and principles inherent in Islamic law. This *maqasid* of Islamic law represent an alternative expression for the concept of "people's interest" or "*masalih.*" They serve as the overarching goals and principles that form the foundation of Islamic legal rulings and ethical guidelines. These objectives provide a framework for the interpretation of Islamic law in a manner that fosters justice, mercy, and the well-being of both individuals and society at large.

The figure above illustrates the levels of *Maqasid al Shariah. Maqasid al Shariah* can be understood in three levels: necessities, needs, and luxuries. Necessities include five categories: protecting one's faith (*Hifz al-Din*), life (*Hifz al-nafs*), wealth *(Hifz al-Mal),* mind (*Hifz al-'aql),* and offspring (*Hifz al-Nasl).* These are crucial for human well-being, like the prohibition of alcohol in Islam, which safeguards minds and souls. Needs, like marriage, are less critical but still important. If a need becomes widespread, it can become a necessity. Luxuries, like stylish clothing and perfumes, enhance aesthetics and are signs of Allah's generosity, but they should have lower priority compared to necessities and needs in one's life.

Hearing impairment, on the other hand, is another type of disability. Through the lens of Al-Qur'ān and prophetic traditions, Islam has a positive way of looking at disability. Unlike the medical model, which perceives disability as an illness or a condition that needs to be treated and as a problem belonging to the individual, Islam promotes equal rights between normal people and disabled/differently-abled people. Al-Qur'ān and the Hadith of Prophet Muhammadﷺ have declared disability as a natural part of being a human, and disability should not be misinterpreted as it should not be perceived as Allah's punishment. However, it is a means for the sins to be forgiven. Furthermore, Islam gives a great deal of attention to all groups within society; each has its rights, including individuals with a disability. Way before the enaction of the UN Convention on the Rights of Persons with Disabilities, Prophet Muhammadﷺ was the advanced initiator and defender of disability rights. Prophet Muhammadﷺ had already given greater attention to ensuring that disabled people were given their rights and privileges to live their lives just like anyone else. This is justified in the Al-Qur'ān, Surah Al Hujurat, verse 11;

"O you have believed, let not a people ridicule (another) people; perhaps they may be better than them; nor let women ridicule (other) women; perhaps they may be better than them. And do not insult one another and do not call each other by (offensive) nicknames. Wretched is the name of disobedience after (one's) faith. And whoever does not repent- then it is those who are the wrongdoers"

Furthermore, disabled people should be given support about self-esteem as the Prophet Muhammad ﷺ emphasized in a hadith narrated by Muslim and Ibnu Majah;

"Indeed, Allah never judges you based on your appearance and property, but on your heart and actions."

Hence, from the hadith above, it is clear that those with disabilities such as the hearing impaired or blindness deserve similar honor and status as others. In fact, after the era of Rasulullahﷺ, there are some vivid examples of how people with disabilities were treated. One of the examples is Omar Ibn Al Khattab provided a blind man with housing near the mosque after the father of the disabled boy complained to Omar that his son could not reach the mosque to have congregation prayer.

Furthermore, those with physical disabilities, such as the hearing impaired, deserve similar honor and status as others. Narrated that one day, the Prophetﷺ was occupied preaching to the Quraysh leaders, then came a blind man asking about Islam named Abdullah bin Ummu Maktum. Seeing Abdullah, the Prophetﷺ turned away the blind man to prioritize the Quraysh leaders. Upon this occasion, Allah reprimand the Prophetﷺ through the verse 1-3 in Surah Abasa;

'He [the Prophet] frowned and turned away because there came to him a blind man, but what would make you perceive, [O Mohammed], that perhaps he might be purified, or be reminded and the remembrance would benefit him?'

Although the occasion above is about a visually impaired person, it can be generalized to those with other disabilities. The revelation above clearly illustrated that individual whether disabled or not disabled, must be treated equally. Especially for Muslim-deaf, there is no exception from the obligation to seek knowledge, understand the religion, and perform religious practices as mentioned in the Quran. The sunnah supports the notion of the roles of society in providing assistance and facilitating those who are in need. This is because, in the hadith narrated by Sahih Muslim stated that;

'The similitude of believers in regard to mutual love, affection, feeling, is that of one body; when any limb aches, the whole-body aches, because of sleeplessness and fever'

Today, it is apparent there exists a growing recognition of the imperative to integrate individuals with hearing disabilities into all aspects of social life, including the realm of employment opportunities. The Theory of Equal Capability and Workforce Integration emphatically asserts that individuals with hearing impairments inherently possess the same capacity and abilities as their hearing peers to perform tasks and excel in various professional fields. This belief finds substantial support in the growing number of hearing-impaired individuals actively participating in the workforce. However, despite the progress in inclusion, hearing-impaired individuals are still confronted with significant career-related obstacles. These challenges encompass communication barriers, feelings of isolation and misunderstanding, and the persistent presence of stigmas and stereotypes. These hurdles have the potential to affect their mental and emotional well-being adversely. When viewed through the lens of *Maqasid Al Shariah,* it becomes evident that fostering inclusivity and cultivating a supportive work environment is essential and inherently aligns with the principles of Islamic ethics and the core objectives of *Maqasid Al Shariah* itself.

RESEARCH DESIGN AND METHODOLOGICAL APPROACH

The central focus of this study is on the principle of *Hifz Al Nafs*, or Preservation of Life, as it pertains to fostering inclusivity and establishing a workplace that fully supports individuals with hearing impairments. This study draws evidence from six hearing-impaired individuals working for two chosen organisations in Brunei. The organisations represent a government department, and a private company respectively. Semi-structured in-depth interviews sought to gather insights into the participants' personal working experiences alongside their able-bodied (hearing) colleagues.

To facilitate effective communication and data collection, the research has collaborated with a qualified interpreter from the government agency. This interpreter played a pivotal role in bridging the gap between spoken language and sign language, facilitating the translation of spoken questions posed by the researcher into sign language and vice versa, ensuring seamless communication throughout the research process. The facilitation of this research project was greatly aided by a mutual contact who played a crucial role in securing the services of the sign language interpreter. This accessibility to professional interpretation services significantly enhanced the research's ability to effectively translate spoken inquiries into sign language. Furthermore, the interpreter's involvement provided valuable insights into the experiences of non-hearing employees, enriching the overall depth of this research study.

Prior to their involvement in the study, respondents were fully informed about the research's objectives. In adherence to ethical principles, the researcher adopted multiple strategies to convey the study's purpose comprehensively. These strategies included presenting written objectives on paper and engaging the services of a sign language interpreter to ensure that each respondent had a complete understanding of the research's goals. Consent procedures encompassed the use of two distinct documents, namely, an informative letter outlining the study's objectives and procedures, and a consent form signed by the respondents. Throughout the research process, strict measures were in place to maintain the confidentiality of the non-hearing respondents, preserving the integrity of their personal and sensitive information.

Preceding to the transcription of the interview results, the researcher engages in an initial phase of immersing themselves in the data. This immersion serves the dual purpose of gaining familiarity with

Table 1. Tabulated details of the participants in the study

Participant (Pn)	Age	Gender	Brief Description of Work
P1	32	Female	IT Services
P2	31	Female	Finances - Debt Recovery
P3	36	Female	Administrator - Endorsement Services
P4	39	Female	Administrator - Issuance Services
P5	40	Female	Administrator - International Services
P6	45	Male	Administrator - Renewal Services

the content and actively searching for underlying themes and intricate relationships within the dataset, which in turn enhances its comprehensibility. Following this immersive phase, all the gathered findings are transcribed and subjected to comprehensive analysis. This rigorous examination of the data aims to yield refined and equitable results. Thematic analysis is a pivotal tool employed for identifying and extracting the pivotal elements from the transcriptions, streamlining the data analysis process.

WORKING EXPERIENCE OF SOME HEARING-IMPAIRED EMPLOYEES IN BRUNEI

A study conducted by Rosengreen and Saladin (2010) found that all their respondents mentioned a major challenge related to workplace interactions. This confirms that one of the main issues for most hearing-impaired employees in the workplace is difficulties in interacting with others. The research also shows that hearing-impaired employees have fewer interactions with their hearing colleagues at work. Just like in other countries, hearing-impaired employees in Brunei Darussalam face significant challenges in their workplaces. Many hearing-impaired employees' express frustration because their hearing colleagues usually engage in work-related discussions and rarely include casual conversations or humor when talking to them. Earlier research established valuable insights and context into the modes of interaction between hearing and hearing-impaired employees in the workplace in Brunei (Masri, 2020). These interactions predominantly rely on sign language and alternative forms of communication, including written exchanges. However, the limited proficiency in sign language among hearing employees has notably shaped the dynamics of their social interactions with their hearing-impaired colleagues, which then contribute to a noticeable decline in workplace interactions for hearing-impaired employees. This reduction in interaction occurs not only during breaks but also throughout regular working hours. Consequently, despite their strong enthusiasm for their work, hearing-impaired employees frequently find themselves grappling with feelings of isolation within the workplace, due to limitations in communication skills, as observed in the following interview response:

*"I generally feel comfortable working alongside my hearing colleagues, but my interactions with them are somewhat limited." (***P2, aged 31***).*

Furthermore, lack of proficiency in sign language did not just isolate the participants, they also led to a feeling of time being wasted:

"Sometimes, interactions with my hearing colleagues become less stimulating because, firstly, they are not proficient in sign language, and secondly, the fact that they have to use alternative methods to communicate with me, such as writing on paper, leads to delays. This can be quite time-consuming." *(***P3, aged 36***).*

P4, aged 39, expressed:

"Most of the people here are not proficient in sign language; their knowledge is limited to basic signs like 'salaam' or simple gestures, like when they guide us to the restroom by making a fist with their thumb stopped by their index finger and moving it up and down. That's about it. That's why they often resort to writing their messages on paper or typing them on their phones, which I find quite tedious and time-consuming. It would be helpful if they could at least learn how to spell words using sign language."

P5, aged 40, shared:

"They do try to communicate with me using sign language, but sometimes they use incorrect signs, which can be confusing. Eventually, my colleagues resort to other means of communication, like writing the conversation on paper, and I find this uncomfortable and less engaging. I hope they can invest in learning sign language to make our interactions more enjoyable."

P6, aged 45, shared:

"I've been employed for nearly 21 years, primarily stationed at the license collection counter where my workload can be quite substantial. As a result, my interactions with hearing colleagues are relatively limited. Once my tasks are completed, I often find myself sitting there, observing people coming and going. Unfortunately, my colleagues rarely engage with me even when they are aware that I've finished my work. They typically only initiate interaction when it's related to work matters, like when the boss calls or they require my assistance. Their method of getting my attention is by nudging my elbow, which I've found to be somewhat inappropriate."

The result illustrates a notable disparity in the frequency of interactions between non-hearing and hearing employees within the workplace. It is contended that a significant source of frustration among non-hearing employees stems from the perception that their hearing colleagues primarily engage in work-related discussions and seldom indulge in light-hearted banter or humor in their presence. This phenomenon can be attributed to the limited use of sign language by hearing employees, thereby complicating communication and reducing the likelihood of informal exchanges and jests.

However, only respondent **P1** expressed a positive sentiment regarding their interactions through alternative means and stated that while some of her colleagues do know sign language, there are times when they opt for different communication methods. She, however, feels at ease using diverse means of interaction, including writing on paper or typing out conversations on her phone.

On the contrary, during the interview sessions, a noticeable contrast emerged in interaction dynamics when non-hearing respondents engaged with interpreters using proficient sign language. In these instances, interactions became notably more vibrant, with hearing-impaired employees displaying greater enthusiasm and a heightened inclination to articulate their thoughts compared to their interactions with hearing colleagues. Additionally, it was evident that their rapport with the interpreters was considerably stronger, even when their meetings were infrequent or, for some, their initial encounter. This phenomenon resonates with Hauser et al.'s analogy (as cited in Montgomery, 2018), which likens the relationship between Deaf employees and interpreters to a "marriage," highlighting the role of interaction as a conduit to a flourishing partnership. It becomes evident that proficient sign language can foster increased interaction among non-hearing employees, imbuing these interactions with vibrancy. Furthermore, it was observed that most non-hearing respondents exhibited a better comprehension of information when conveyed through sign language.

The findings of this research align with the observations made by Rosengreen and Saladin (2010), highlighting that social interactions between hearing and hearing-impaired employees are infrequent and often challenging. Consequently, this impacts the well-being of hearing-impaired employees, leading to feelings of isolation and frustration when their anticipated smooth interactions with hearing colleagues do not materialize as expected.

IDENTIFYING THE PRESERVATION OF LIFE AT THE WORKPLACE

This paragraph discusses the application of Islamic principles, particularly the concept of preservation of life in addressing the challenges faced by hearing-impaired employees in the workplace. It highlights the importance of preserving life and protecting the mental well-being of individuals, regardless of their hearing status, in line with Islamic teachings. Furthermore, it emphasizes the need for organizations, particularly in Islamic countries like Brunei, to uphold these principles and ensure the welfare and support of all citizens, including the hearing-impaired community.

Life is the most fundamental quality in Islamic law, regardless of socioeconomic status, religious beliefs, or other differences, it must be safeguarded without exception. Preserving the lives of all individuals is a fundamental obligation and holds immense significance for both individuals and society as a whole. Allah had emphasized this point in Surah Al Isra, verse 33,

"And do not kill anyone who Allah has forbidden, except for a just cause. And whoever is killed (intentionally with hostility and oppression and not by mistake), We have given his heir the authority [(to demand Qisas, Law of Equality in punishment or to forgive, or to take diyah (blood money)]. But let him not exceed the limits in the matter of taking life (i.e. he should not kill anyone except the killer only). Verily, he is helped (by the Islamic Law)"

The application of Hifz al Nafs or preservation of life in the workplace context involves implementing specific policies and initiatives to address the unique challenges faced by hearing-impaired employees. These include providing sign language classes for all employees, instituting mentoring programs, and ensuring the physical workspace is universally accessible. By adopting a comprehensive approach that promotes social interaction, enhances communication accessibility, and fosters professional development opportunities, organizations can create an inclusive and supportive environment for hearing-impaired employees.

Moreover, the paragraph emphasizes the importance of diversity and inclusion training for all employees to cultivate a culture of understanding, respect, and inclusivity within the workplace. This training should cover various topics, including effective communication strategies, awareness of diverse needs, and the promotion of equal opportunities for all employees.

Overall, the discussion underscores the significance of aligning organizational practices with Islamic principles to ensure the well-being and dignity of hearing-impaired employees in the workplace. By embracing the concept of Hifz al Nafs, organizations can create environments that prioritize the safety, mental health, and equitable treatment of all individuals, contributing to a more inclusive and harmonious workplace culture.

Since work directly impacts the mental health and well-being of employees, it is imperative that the mental health and overall well-being of every individual, particularly hearing-impaired employees must be protected under all circumstances. For an Islamic country such as Brunei, the welfare and support system provision should reach all levels of citizens including the Muslim and Non-Muslims, particularly the hearing-impaired community. Hence, in pertaining to fostering inclusivity and establishing a workplace that fully supports individuals with hearing impairments, it inherently aligns with the principle of *Hifz Al Nafs*. *Hifz al Nafs* is a fundamental concept in Islamic ethics and jurisprudence, it can be applied to various aspects of life, including the workplace. As cited in W.M.A, & Desa, R. (2022), Al Bustani (1956) give definition to Hifz as to preserve, while Ibn Manzur (1993) al-Nafs derived from the Arabic language which means soul or life.

As previously mentioned, hearing-impaired employees encounter various workplace challenges, including obstacles in communication, feelings of isolation, and the enduring presence of stigmas and stereotypes. These issues have the potential to negatively impact their mental and emotional well-being. Therefore, organizations can implement specific policies aligned with the concept of *Hifz al-nafs* to address these challenges. These policies may include providing sign language classes for all employees, instituting a buddy system, and ensuring accessible facilities. The research findings underscore the crucial role of promoting social interaction between hearing and hearing-impaired employees in creating an inclusive and supportive workplace environment. To facilitate such interaction, organizations should adopt a comprehensive approach, which involves offering sign language classes to all employees, not exclusively those with hearing impairments. Initiatives like these can encourage hearing employees to acquire sign language skills, thereby enhancing inclusive and accessible communication. Hearing-impaired employees may face challenges when it comes to engaging in larger meetings or group discussions, particularly those that are fast-paced and lack proper moderation. Therefore, the adoption of inclusive communication tools, such as video captions, text alternatives for audio messages, and accessible virtual meeting platforms, becomes essential. These tools help break down communication barriers and ensure that everyone, regardless of their hearing ability, can participate fully in discussions and meetings.

Other than promoting social interaction via the enhancement of sign language skills to foster inclusivity and a supportive workplace for the hearing-impaired, the introduction of mentoring initiatives that match hearing-impaired employees with their hearing colleagues could be a valuable strategy. These programs not only support career growth but also foster strong professional connections, contributing to the overall cohesiveness of an inclusive work environment.

Another essential aspect of creating an inclusive and supportive work environment that caters to the needs of all employees is to ensure that the physical workspace is universally accessible, accommodating both hearing and hearing-impaired individuals. This encompasses various features such as clear and appropriate signage, the installation of hearing loops, and the availability of assistive technologies. Assistive technology designed for deaf individuals falls into three primary categories: hearing technology, alerting devices, and communication technology. Hearing technology includes devices like hearing aids, assistive listening devices, and personal sound amplification products (PSAPs). Alerting devices, on the other hand, are specifically designed for individuals who are deaf or hard of hearing and do not rely on residual hearing. These devices use visual or tactile signals, such as lights or vibrations, to alert individuals about specific events or situations, like incoming phone calls or alarms. (Assistive Technologies for People with Disabilities Part II: Current and Emerging Technologies Study Science and Technology Options Assessment, 2018)

Preserving mental well-being is a fundamental element of *Hifz al Nafs*, emphasizing the importance of ensuring that hearing-impaired employees do not face discrimination, harassment, or exclusion in their workplace solely because of their hearing condition. Any form of discrimination or workplace barriers that obstruct their progress can have a profoundly negative impact on their overall well-being. Therefore, it becomes essential to provide equal opportunities for hearing-impaired employees, not only to safeguard their mental well-being but also to facilitate their professional growth and career advancement. To foster such an environment, organizations should incorporate diversity and inclusion training into the onboarding process for all employees. This comprehensive training should cover a range of topics, including effective communication, a deep understanding of diverse needs, and the active promotion of inclusivity within the workplace.

To conclude, within the context of hearing-impaired employees, *Hifz al Nafs* guarantees their safety, mental health, equitable opportunities, and the preservation of their dignity within the workplace. It highlights the significance of establishing a workplace that is inclusive and considerate, ultimately safeguarding their overall well-being and quality of life.

CONCLUSION

In conclusion, this study has shed light on the critical issue of fostering inclusivity and support for individuals with hearing impairments in the workplace, within the context of Islamic ethics, specifically Hifz al-Nafs. While the findings provide valuable insights into the challenges faced by hearing-impaired individuals, the study is not without limitations.

First, the research was conducted within the specific cultural and institutional framework of Brunei, which may limit the generalizability of its findings to other regions and cultural contexts. The extent to which Islamic principles, such as *Hifz al-Nafs*, can be applied in workplaces with different cultural norms and legal systems remains an open question. Second, the small sample size of six participants, while providing rich qualitative data, may not represent the diversity of experiences among hearing-impaired individuals in different work settings. Future research should aim to include a more extensive and diverse participant pool to enhance the study's external validity. Moreover, the involvement of a government-provided interpreter raises questions about potential biases in translation and interpretation. The interpreter, while a vital link for communication, may inadvertently introduce subjectivity or misinterpretations. A critical examination of this aspect should be considered in future research.

Furthermore, the study's focus on individual experiences may not fully capture the broader organizational dynamics that influence workplace inclusivity. Factors such as organizational culture, policies, and the role of management in promoting inclusivity warrant deeper investigation. Despite these limitations, the research underscores the importance of considering Islamic ethics, like Hifz al-Nafs, in discussions about inclusivity for hearing-impaired employees. It suggests that the principles of compassion, understanding, and support found in Islamic ethics can offer a valuable framework for addressing the challenges faced by hearing-impaired individuals in the workplace. Nevertheless, the applicability of these principles on a global scale requires further exploration and adaptation to diverse contexts.

In essence, this study opens the door to a more critical conversation on how cultural and ethical values can intersect with practical inclusivity efforts, and it lays the groundwork for future research that can bridge the gap between theory and practical implementation, striving for more inclusive and supportive workplaces worldwide.

REFERENCES

Duthey, B. (2013). *Hearing Loss*. World Health Organization. https://www.who.int/medicines/areas/priority_medicines/BP6_21Hearing.pdf

Foster, S., & Macleod, J. (2003). Deaf people at work: Assessment of communication among deaf and hearing persons in work settings. *International Journal of Audiology, 42*(sup1), 128–139. doi:10.3109/14992020309074634

Hankins, R. (2015). *Social Interaction Between Deaf And Hearing People*. CORE. https://core.ac.uk/download/pdf/148695046.pdf

Rafhanah, M. (2020). *Social Interaction Between Non Hearing and Hearing Employees in the Workplace* [Unpublished thesis, Universiti Brunei Darussalam].

Royal National Institute for Deaf People. (n.d.). *Persons with a hearing loss in the Workplace*. RNID. https://rnid.org.uk/wp-content/uploads/2020/05/Employers-Guide.pdf

Science and Technology Options Assessment. (n.d.). *Assistive technologies for people with disabilities Part II: Current and emerging technologies STUDY*. European Parliament. https://www.europarl.europa.eu/RegData/etudes/IDAN/2018/603218/EPRS_IDA(2018)603218(ANN2)_EN.pdf

Swanepoel, D. W., & Laurent, C. (n.d.). *Open Access Guide to Audiology and Hearing Aids for Otolaryngologists' Classification of hearing Loss*. Research Gate.

Wan Halim, W. M. A., & Desa, R. (2022). Analysis of Hifz al-Nafs' (Protection of Life) Achievements on the Shariah Criminal Offenses Enactment in Malaysia Based on the Fuzzy Delphi Method. *International Journal of Academic Research in Business & Social Sciences, 12*(5). doi:10.6007/IJARBSS/v12-i5/13239

Chapter 10
From Insurgents to Custodians: Charting Taliban's Transition Towards 'Governance' and 'Institutionalization' in Afghanistan

Saad Ullah Khan
https://orcid.org/0000-0002-3392-7844
Amity University Rajasthan, Jaipur, India

Sadaf Khan
https://orcid.org/0009-0005-1348-0386
IEC College of Engineering and Technology, Greater Noida, India

ABSTRACT

This chapter centered on Taliban's governance and institutionalization, conscientiously examines the intricate dynamics of internal factionalism and their impact on key aspects of governance, including education, women's rights, foreign policy, security, and constitutional order. The inquiry extends to the Taliban's foreign policy stance, the international status of women under their governance, and the organizational structure of the Islamic Emirate of Afghanistan. Emphasizing the dynamic nature of policymaking influenced by religious legitimacy, the chapter argues that internal dynamics play a pivotal role in shaping the evolving policies of the Taliban. In scrutinizing Afghanistan's security landscape, it investigates the Taliban's efficacy against ISKP, their alignment with Al Qaeda, and their approach to issues with Pakistan and Iran. The study anticipates potential scenarios and provide policy-centric recommendations, urging the international community to actively engage with and fortify Afghan institutions amidst the unfolding dynamics of governance and institutionalization.

INTRODUCTION

In the ever-shifting landscape of contemporary geopolitics, the Taliban in Afghanistan stands out as a focal point of global attention and curiosity. Rooted in insurgency and driven by a distinctive interpretation of Islamic law fused with tribal codes, the Taliban has undergone a noteworthy transformation, sparking inquiries into its journey from 'insurgents' to 'custodians'. The ascent of the Taliban in Afghanistan's

DOI: 10.4018/979-8-3693-1742-6.ch010

political arena has unfolded through a series of developments characterized by insurgency, governance attempts, and external interventions (D'Souza, 2016). This transition, from a belligerent insurgent force to a quasi-governing entity, presents a multifaceted puzzle. Understanding this transition entails a systematic exploration into the ideological foundations shaping the Taliban's worldview, the historical context influencing its identity, and the complex webs of power propelling it towards governance. The elevation of the Taliban is not a straightforward linear progression; instead, it involves a complex interweaving of historical, ideological, and geopolitical factors.

A crucial aspect of the Taliban's evolution revolves around its relationship with governance structures and the challenges faced in establishing and sustaining institutions. The transition from insurgency to governance requires a delicate balance, with the Taliban grappling with the demands of statecraft while adhering to its ideological foundations. Scrutinizing the Taliban's efforts at institutionalization provides a lens to assess the group's capacity to navigate governance complexities and analyse the socio-political implications of its policies. To navigate this labyrinthine transformation, engagement with diverse academic disciplines is imperative for a holistic understanding of the multifaceted factors influencing the Taliban's evolution.

From macro point of view, this chapter employs a methodical descriptive approach to analyse the Taliban's governance model, documenting its transition from insurgency to governance. Utilizing the descriptive research method, it provides essential factual insights for policymakers (Nassaji, 2015). Key domains such as education, women's rights, and foreign policy etc. are examined, highlighting the dynamic nature of the Taliban's policy articulation. Historical research complements this, identifying pivotal turning points crucial for understanding the Taliban's evolution into custodians of governance in Afghanistan. Additionally, the discussion includes an in-depth analysis of Afghanistan's security landscape, acknowledged as a significant threat by the United Nations (Singh, 2023). Furthermore, the research focuses on the Taliban's developing policies and their global repercussions, examining potential scenarios for future engagements.

The study concludes with the proposal of policy-centric recommendations aimed at fostering and strengthening crucial institutions for the effective functioning of the country. These recommendations seek to establish a constructive framework for addressing the challenges posed by the Taliban's governance and promoting stability in Afghanistan. Undertaking this intellectual exploration into the heart of the Taliban's metamorphosis requires adopting a dispassionate analytical lens. The research does not seek to pass judgment but rather aims to illuminate the complex process with implications not only for Afghanistan but also for the broader global landscape. Exploring the strategic trajectories forged by the Taliban, this research adds valuable insights towards understanding of the complex dynamics that unfolds when insurgent movements undertake the formidable journey towards establishing governance and institutional structures.

FROM INSURGENTS TO RULERS: UNDERSTANDING THE STATE OF AFFAIRS WITH REGARDS TO POLITICS, POLICY, AND DIPLOMACY

Following the collapse of the Afghan Republic in August 2021, the Taliban adeptly asserted control over a nation beleaguered by the repercussions of war and ensnared in a web of economic challenges (Ameyaw-Brobbey, 2023). Post their triumph, the Taliban's emir, not only reaffirmed his stature as the 'supreme leader' but also orchestrated a deliberate shift in the trajectory of domestic policies towards an unmistakably conservative orientation (Dawi, 2023). This calculated manoeuvre has laid bare profound schisms within the echelons of the Taliban's leadership, notably pertaining to the prospective course of Afghanistan's future and the intricate dynamics of power distribution among themselves. In the face of these internal discordances, the Taliban has steadfastly prioritized the preservation of unity within their movement and governing framework (Glinski, 2022). This emphasis, however, has attracted censure from Western nations, prompting a circumspect global approach in dealing with the Taliban. In response to international pressures, the Taliban, propelled by a staunch aversion to foreign influence, has adamantly rebuffed demands from the global community (Krishnankutty, 2023). As the Taliban approaches the two-and-a-half-year mark in governance, their domestic agenda has become intricately interwoven with the impasse in foreign relations. The condemnations emanating from Western states and the worldwide hesitancy to engage with the Taliban have only fortified their resolve to chart an independent course, underscoring the complex interplay between their domestic imperatives and international standing (Malejacq & Terpstra, 2023).

Since the fall of Kabul, Haibatullah Akhundzada has held the esteemed position of emir, leading the Taliban's Islamic Emirate. Collaborating with him are three distinguished deputies, namely Sirajuddin Haqqani, scion of the Haqqani Network progenitor Jalaluddin Haqqani; Mohammad Yaqoob, offspring of Taliban's founding father, Mullah Omar; and Abdul Ghani Baradar (Wheeldon, 2021). These deputies played pivotal roles in the current Taliban regime. Notably, Yaqoob previously presided over the influential Military Commission, overseeing the nomination of shadow governors and officials throughout Afghanistan's 34 provinces. Conversely, Abdul Ghani Baradar helmed the Political Commission headquartered in Doha, Qatar, shouldering responsibilities for negotiations with the United States and regional diplomatic affairs (Yusufzai, 2019). Beyond the Military and Political Commissions, the Taliban systematically upheld 14 additional commissions, spanning diverse sectors such as the judiciary, media, health, agriculture, and antiquities.

The hierarchical framework further incorporated a Leadership Council, also known as Rahbari Shura, comprising the emir, his deputies, an approximate cohort of 26 individuals approximately (Guler, 2021). This council, alternatively acknowledged as the Quetta Shura, derived its nomenclature from the Pakistani city where certain members were situated alongside their families. Evidently, it purportedly wielded authority over Taliban forces and operational endeavours in the southern and western provinces. In addition, the Peshawar Shura took charge of responsibilities concerning other provinces, particularly those in the east (Franco & Giustozzi, 2016). The Miran Shah Shura, predominantly constituted of Haqqani Network fighters and led by them, fulfilled a distinctive role within the comprehensive organizational structure (Ishfaq, 2019).

On September 07, 2021, Zabihullah Mujahid, the spokesperson for the Taliban, formally disclosed a roster comprising 33 individuals designated as 'acting' ministers, constituting a provisional cabinet tasked with overseeing the governance of the nation. This ad hoc assembly, characterized as a 'caretaker cabinet', operates under the umbrella of what the Taliban have historically denominated as the Islamic Emirate of Afghanistan ("Taliban announces new government", 2021). The nomenclature and organizational structure of this nascent government hark back to the group's self-identification over the past several decades. The intricacies surrounding the potential replacement of these designated ministers and the underlying rationale governing such transitions remain shrouded in uncertainty. Furthermore, the distinction between these caretaker roles and their ostensibly more permanent counterparts remains elusive, demanding an intricate exploration of the Taliban's strategic governance approach ("Taliban Government in Afghanistan", 2021).

Comparisons with the Taliban's governance paradigm during the 1990s reveal a historical precedence wherein their administration was ostensibly categorized as 'nominally interim'. This historical context sheds light on the transient nature of their earlier rule, prompting inquiries into the temporal considerations and underlying motives inherent in their current designation of certain positions as 'caretaker'.

Notably, the Taliban has articulated its intention to implement the '1964 constitution' of the former Afghan monarchy (Gul, 2021). However, this commitment is qualified by the stipulation that such implementation will occur without any content that contradicts Islamic law and the principles of the Islamic Emirate. This proclamation raises significant questions about the Taliban's broader strategy, particularly concerning how they plan to reconcile this intent with the existing 2004 constitution, the institutional framework of Afghanistan's parliament, and other facets of the post-2001 political system.

The composition of the interim cabinet is characterized by a conspicuous prevalence of former Taliban functionaries and steadfast loyalists, constituting an overwhelmingly homogeneous group. Notably, the gender dynamics within this assembly are marked by an exclusive male representation. Furthermore, a substantial majority of these individuals hail from the ethnic Pashtun community, predominantly originating from the southern regions of Afghanistan (Graham-Harrison & Makoii, 2021).

An intriguing facet of this caretaker cabinet is the prominence of individuals who have a historical association with the Taliban and, in several instances, have been subjected to punitive measures, including U.S. and/or U.N. sanctions. Among these figures, the acting Interior Minister, Sirajuddin Haqqani, stands out prominently. Haqqani, who leads the Haqqani Network, an entity designated as a Foreign Terrorist Organization (FTO) by the United States, has been subject to a longstanding reward offer of up to $10 million by the U.S. Department of State for information leading to his apprehension (Dawi, 2022). The inclusion of Haqqani and others affiliated with the Haqqani Network within the ranks of the Taliban's interim government has sparked discussions and raised concerns. Some assert that their notable presence is indicative of their substantial military significance within the broader Taliban framework (Raghavan, 2021). This contention posits that their role could potentially complicate collaborative efforts between the United States and the Taliban, given the contentious history and designated terrorist status associated with the Haqqani Network.

This confluence of historical allegiances, ethnic demographics, and the complex interplay of designated individuals within the caretaker cabinet underscores the intricate dynamics shaping the current political landscape in Afghanistan. As observers grapple with the implications of these appointments, the potential ramifications for diplomatic engagements and the broader geopolitical context warrant cautious scrutiny.

Following the collapse of the First Emirate (1996-2001), the Taliban engaged in a retrospective examination of their past deficiencies. However, the articulation of a specific vision for the Second Emirate remained notably absent. Despite the return of prominent Taliban figures to Afghanistan post-2001, efforts to establish a moderate Taliban political faction within the emerging political framework faced hindrance from the United States and Karzai. This opposition manifested prominently during the Bonn Conference in December 2001, leading to the exclusion of the Taliban. The exclusionary stance drew criticism from Afghan peace negotiator Masoom Stanekzai and former UN special advisor Steve Brooking, who respectively deemed it a 'historic mistake' and the 'original sin' (Sen, 2022). It is noteworthy that former Taliban Foreign Minister Wakil Ahmad Muttawakil faced detention upon returning to Afghanistan in 2005, after an unsuccessful attempt to establish a Taliban party.

Despite encountering various challenges, the Taliban vehemently maintains the perpetuity of the First Emirate by characterizing it as in a state of abeyance rather than facing complete collapse. This narrative strategically situates the Islamic Emirate of Afghanistan (IEA) as an uninterrupted extension of previous

Figure 1. Key officials in the Taliban's interim government
Source: Anadolu Agency Türkiye. Published on 08.09.2021. Retrieved on 12.01.2024.

Emirate. The Taliban's dissatisfaction with the 2004 constitution is grounded in two fundamental contentions, specifically its Western origin and its perceived association with foreign invaders (Zelin, 2015). Moreover, from the perspective of Pashtun ethnonationalism, the constitution is construed as emblematic of corrupt political leadership and an illegitimate system imposed during the NATO occupation.

The Taliban critically assesses the 2004 constitution, arguing that it lacks adherence to Islamic principles. They contend that the constitution fails to establish God's commands as the foundational basis for laws, potentially promoting secularism (Lombardi & March, 2022). In 2022, Taliban leader Hibatullah affirmed their commitment to Islamic principles, even in the face of potential nuclear threats from the West (Hakimi & Fair, 2022). Despite numerous challenges, the Taliban recognizes the necessity of a constitution, referencing their own drafted constitution during the First Emirate in 1998. This historical document integrated classical and modern constitutional concepts within an overarching Islamic framework. The acknowledgment of this intricate historical and ideological backdrop underscores the Taliban's nuanced stance on governance and constitutional principles in Afghanistan.

Several experts posit the possibility of the Taliban pursuing a hybrid political system that amalgamates medieval Islamic ideals with a Western-style state akin to the Islamic Republic of Iran. Drawing parallels with the Iranian model, where a top cleric assumes the role of supreme leader with authority over both state and religious matters, in Afghanistan, this position could be occupied by the emir. Under such a framework, the presidency might be retained by the opposition, provided it operates under the oversight of a clerical body, akin to Iran's Guardian Council (Bezhan, 2020). In contrast, some political analysts suggest the likelihood of the Taliban adopting the Saudi model—a theocratic kingdom led by a king with lifelong tenure, exercising both legislative and executive powers. Presently, given Hibatullah's inclination towards centralization, a 'one-leader' system appears more feasible (Nelson, 2021).

In the realm of economic governance, the Taliban has effectively demonstrated their adeptness by showcasing successes in taxation and currency stabilization, underscoring their capacity to administer the nation. The third quarter of 2023 witnessed the Afghani currency emerging as the top-performing currency, attributed to a combination of humanitarian aid inflow and strategic currency control measures implemented by the Emirate, as highlighted by Bloomberg (Sankranti, 2023). The most recent Afghanistan Economic Monitor, a publication by the World Bank, further substantiates positive trends in specific economic metrics. Particularly noteworthy is the eight percent upswing in revenue collection during the initial five months of 2023 when compared to the corresponding period in 2022 ("Afghan Economic Monitor", 2023). These favourable macroeconomic indicators are strategically utilized by the Taliban to legitimize their governance and dispel apprehensions regarding the precarious state of the Afghan economy. However, despite these encouraging macroeconomic signals, the tangible benefits have not trickled down to the Afghan populace. Persistent concerns revolve around the equitable distribution of revenue and the prioritization of specific sectors, issues that are likely to persist without resolution in the immediate future.

It is notably intriguing that the Taliban predominantly functions within the pre-existing state structures and institutions inherited from the previous Republic. While preserving the fundamental structure of the prior regime, particular entities, ironically, the Ministry of Women's Affairs and the Afghanistan Independent Human Rights Commission, underwent dissolution, with offices devoted to parliamentary affairs similarly shuttered (Ghosh, 2021).

In the sphere of education, the Taliban administration voices reservations regarding the prospective enrolment of female students in educational institutions, spanning from primary schools to universities. Despite assurances from the de facto authorities of the Taliban that constraints, particularly those related to educational access, would be of a transitory nature, the prevailing circumstances on the field have brought to light a swift and systematic execution of a framework marked by deliberate marginalization, persecution, and segregation (Ahmadi, 2023). The expressed apprehension of the Taliban administration centres on the potential ramifications of allowing girls to enrol in schools and universities, with a notable concern being the conceivable alienation of their predominantly rural support base (Gannon, 2022). Simultaneously, there exists a palpable anxiety about the susceptibility of this rural support base to exploitation by extremist factions, exemplified by the apprehension that groups such as the Islamic State-Khorasan Province (ISKP) could exploit these circumstances to their advantage.

In response to these apprehensions and perceived threats, the Taliban has taken the initiative to re-establish the Ministry of Vice and Virtue. This ministry is expressly tasked with the oversight of moral considerations, encompassing the regulation of women's roles, the imposition of prohibitions on musical expression, and the enforcement of stringent dress codes. This re-establishment reflects a strategic move by the Taliban to fortify ideological and moral controls amidst a backdrop of heightened concerns and potential challenges to their established power dynamics (Kakar, 2022).

In the realm of the Taliban's judicial governance, their approach to dispensing justice is intricately tied to Islamic law, embodying a system wherein discernible evidence of a robust judiciary or an explicit penal code is notably scarce. Instead, the predominant focus lies on adjudications grounded in morality, orchestrated by the Ministry of Vice and Virtue. This strategic orientation has led to substantial curtailments of personal freedoms and individual rights, thereby shaping the contours of the justice landscape under the Taliban's sway. The involvement of the Taliban in local dispute resolution has elicited a spectrum of responses among the Afghan populace. Some perceive it as a mechanism of fostering expeditious and efficacious resolutions, appreciating the potential for swift justice (Dawi, 2023). Conversely, there exists a cohort harbouring apprehension concerning the latent proclivity for power abuse and human rights transgressions within this distinctive Islamic justice paradigm.

Examining the governance model and institutionalization adopted by the Taliban necessitates a thorough investigation into specific dimensions. Foremost among these is the formidable challenge of crafting a more inclusive government. The Taliban's adeptness in negotiating internal power dynamics and establishing an administration that reflects broader representation holds profound implications for their global reputation and the stability of the domestic socio-political milieu.

Simultaneously, lingering concerns pertain to the group's justice delivery approach, characterized by an ongoing reliance on morality-based resolutions. This prompts pertinent inquiries into the alignment of such a framework with contemporary standards of justice and human rights, bringing into focus the compatibility of the Taliban's judicial practices with prevailing international norms.

In the economic sphere, uncertainties persist regarding the equitable distribution of resources and the just allocation of benefits arising from augmented revenue collection. The Taliban's approach to addressing these economic intricacies will decisively mould the socio-economic well-being of the Afghan populace, marking a critical juncture in their ability to foster prosperity and mitigate disparities.

On the diplomatic front, the international community is positioned to seek the Taliban's de facto engagement, particularly concerning terrorism-related issues and regional dynamics (Mir, 2023). The way Taliban negotiates and meets these diplomatic expectations will wield substantial influence in shaping their global reception and determining the extent of their integration into the international community. The convergence of these multifaceted challenges underscores the inherent complexity of the Taliban's governance framework, highlighting the intricate array of considerations they must navigate to secure both national and international legitimacy.

DECIPHERING THE FRAMEWORK: TALIBAN'S GOVERNANCE, INSTITUTIONAL DYNAMICS, AND STATECRAFT

In the wake of the Taliban's resurgence and return to power in Afghanistan, the details of their governance, institutional dynamics, and statecraft have become subjects of intense scrutiny and analysis. The framework through which the Taliban governs, the structures that shape their institutions, and the strategies they employ in statecraft are pivotal aspects that demand a closer examination. This section delves into the multifaceted dimensions of the Taliban's rule, aiming to decipher the complexities that define their governance model and shed light on the evolving nature of their presence on the global stage. As the world navigates the challenges posed by this new era of Taliban leadership, understanding the nuances of their governance becomes crucial for policymakers, scholars, and the global community at large. Several distinct vignettes emblematic of the Taliban's governance and statecraft are examined, shedding light on their unique characteristics and practices through a lens informed by extensive research.

(1) **Centralization**: The present rule of the Taliban is characterized by a pronounced centralization of authority, with decision-making concentrated in a hierarchical structure (Ibrahimi, 2022). This centralized approach has significant implications for governance and state institutions, as power is tightly controlled at the top echelons of the leadership. In terms of governance, the centralized structure of the Taliban rule allows for swift decision-making but may limit inclusivity and representation. Decisions and policies are often formulated by a select few, potentially leading to a lack of diverse perspectives and stakeholder input. This concentration of power could contribute to challenges in addressing the complex needs and aspirations of a diverse population. The impact on state institutions is noteworthy, with a centralized system potentially resulting in a more streamlined but authoritarian functioning. State agencies may find themselves subordinate to the central leadership, potentially diminishing their autonomy and ability to act independently. This can lead to a reduction in the effectiveness of institutions, as they may become instruments of centralized control rather than entities capable of responsive and adaptive governance.

Furthermore, the centralization of power may contribute to a lack of checks and balances, increasing the risk of potential abuses and a decrease in accountability. This concentration of authority might lead to challenges in addressing the demands and grievances of various societal groups, potentially fostering discontent, and opposition. In short, the current centralized nature of Taliban rule has significant repercussions on both governance and state institutions. While it may facilitate quick decision-making, the potential drawbacks include limited inclusivity, reduced institutional autonomy, and challenges in maintaining accountability and responsiveness to diverse societal needs. Understanding these dynamics is crucial for comprehending the broader implications of the Taliban's governance model.

(2) **Ethnic Dominance**: The contemporary Taliban's governance structure is characterized by a pronounced framework of ethnic dominance, notably with a concentration of power and influence within specific ethnic groups, particularly the Pashtuns (Durrani and Ghilzai tribes). This phenomenon is evident in the composition of leadership, where key positions are predominantly held by individuals from the dominant ethnic background, fostering a perception of exclusion among other ethnic communities (Lieven, 2021). Decision-making processes and policy formulation reflect biases in favour of the dominant ethnicity, potentially marginalizing the concerns and perspectives of minor-

ity groups. The distribution of resources, opportunities, and institutional roles tends to favour the dominant ethnic group, contributing to socio-economic disparities and hindering the development of inclusive and representative institutions. This framework of ethnic dominance raises concerns about the equitable representation of diverse ethnicities, social cohesion, and the potential for inter-ethnic tensions within the complex fabric of Afghan society under Taliban rule.

(3) **Governance Structure**: The governance structure within the Taliban's regime is a complex amalgamation of Shariah law and Pashtunwali, the traditional code of conduct among Pashtun tribes. Rooted in a commitment to Islamic principles, Shariah law is the bedrock of the Taliban's governance, influencing legal, political, and social dimensions. Concurrently, Pashtunwali, with its emphasis on hospitality, justice, and honour, shapes the tribal dynamics that play a crucial role in decision-making (Nagamine, 2015). The interplay of these two elements creates a unique governance framework where religious principles and cultural traditions intertwine. The recent formation of the interim cabinet reflects the delicate balance between these influences, showcasing the Taliban's attempt to integrate Shariah law and Pashtunwali into a cohesive governance structure. As the Taliban navigates both internal dynamics and international expectations, understanding the interplay between these two forces provides critical insights into the complexities of their rule and the challenges they face in achieving legitimacy on a broader scale.

(4) **Institutionalization:** The interim government, functioning as a caretaker administration, has embarked upon a process of institutionalization, albeit predominantly through superficial modifications. This strategic shift is exemplified by the selection of accomplished individuals such as Dr. Qalandar Ibad as the Minister of Public Health and entrepreneur Nooruddin Azizi as the Minister of Commerce and Industry. Taliban spokesperson Zabihullah Mujahid contends that these appointments serve to fortify and standardize the structural framework of the Islamic Emirate of Afghanistan (Khan, 2021). Notably, the immediate emphasis on projecting a veneer of professionalized governance is evidenced by the issuance of uniforms to police and security forces patrolling the streets. The painstaking revival of functionality within numerous ministries took months, a process hampered by the exodus or concealment of former civil servants and stringent policies surrounding women's employment, as highlighted by the UN Secretary-General's observations in 2022. Drawing from Weber's bureaucratic theory (1930), the Taliban's governance structure exhibits traits of bureaucracy with its myriad rules, standardized processes, meticulous division of labour, and hierarchical clarity. However, a glaring limitation arises from the leadership's constrained comprehension of technical state affairs. To bridge this knowledge gap, former Taliban fighters residing in refugee camps in Pakistan and officials from the prior government have been enlisted, as the Taliban leaders themselves acknowledge their limited governance expertise. The emir, Hibatullah, candidly admitted, "While I do not have much knowledge of governance, we should govern ourselves." Despite the evident shortfall in achieving complete bureaucratization, the Taliban's governance performance, given these circumstances, remains noteworthy.

(5) **Economy**: In their bid to assert control over Afghanistan's economy and currency, the Taliban have implemented a series of measures with notable implications. First, the prohibition of foreign currencies, specifically the US dollar and Pakistani rupees in local transactions, seeks to solidify the Afghani's prominence as the primary currency. Concurrently, stringent outflow restrictions on US dollars aim to curb capital flight, ensuring a degree of economic stability. Moreover, the Taliban has taken an assertive stance against online currency trading, criminalizing such activities, and imposing severe penalties, including imprisonment, for violators.

In February 2023, Afghanistan's Ministry of Finance reported a historic milestone, collecting 100 billion Afghanis (approx. US$1.1 billion) in customs revenue for the fiscal year, attributed to robust anti-corruption measures. This surpassed previous ceilings, marking a significant financial shift. The Taliban notably boosted exports to a record US$1.085 billion in the first half of 2022. In May 2023, the Ministry reduced the value-added tax from 4% to 2%, signalling support for commerce. The Taliban's Ministry of Finance presented a comprehensive mini-budget (Dec 2021-Mar 2022) totalling 634 million USD, allocating almost half to key ministries. Notably, the Ministry of Interior received 105 million USD, Defence got 101 million USD, and Education was allocated 97 million USD. In August 2022, the Ministries disclosed personnel figures of 200,000 and 150,000, indicating the Islamic Emirate of Afghanistan possesses a larger armed force than the former Republic's 300,000 personnel, despite foreign funding (Clark & Shapour, 2023). As the Taliban transitions to a state actor, their governance aligns with the Weberian model, justifying a significant budget for the defence sector within this state-building context.

(6) **Judicial Institutions**: Amidst the Taliban's ascendancy in Afghanistan, a profound transformation characterizes the status of the judiciary, exemplifying the group's interpretation of Islamic law and their governance strategy. At the core of this transformation is the pivotal role played by the Taliban's judicial system in shaping the legal landscape and social order within their controlled territories. Functioning as an integral component of the governance structure, the judiciary operates across multiple tiers, engaging in organizational structuring, legal legitimization, and the imposition of a conservative social agenda. Entwined with the broader administration, the judicial system incorporates formal state principles, with judges acting as enforcers of hierarchy in the absence of a dedicated police force, relying on combatants to execute rulings.

Furthermore, the Taliban's assertion of being the legitimate Afghan state is intricately connected to their judicial system. The courts contribute significantly to the Taliban's narrative, cultivating influence in previously hostile regions. Despite their non-recognition, the Taliban strives to establish a legal framework aligned with their interpretation of Islamic law, presenting themselves as a governing authority. Locally, the legitimacy of Taliban courts is bolstered by their perceived effectiveness and accessibility compared to the former governmental counterparts. This perception is reinforced by the swift and stringent justice meted out by the Taliban, providing a sense of predictability in daily life.

Moreover, the Taliban's judiciary plays a pivotal role in constructing an alternative social order characterized by social conservatism and moral rigour. Advocating a conservative agenda, the judicial system imposes restrictions on various aspects of daily life, particularly concerning gender roles and cultural practices (Backzo, 2023). While some flexibility may exist in specific areas, such as technology usage, the Taliban remains steadfast in enforcing stringent measures related to gender issues, reinforcing patriarchal dominance. In essence, under Taliban rule, the judiciary functions as a crucial instrument for governance, organizational control, and the assertion of authority. The Taliban's approach to the judiciary serves as a manifestation of their broader vision for an Afghan state governed by their interpretation of Islamic law, with far-reaching implications for legal practices, social norms, and the overall governance structure in the regions under their influence.

(7) **Education:** Since assuming control in Afghanistan, the Taliban have instituted substantial modifications to the education system, particularly in higher education, grounded in an exceedingly conservative interpretation of Sharia. Among their most impactful decisions was the sweeping

prohibition of secondary education for young girls in 2021 (Ahmadi & Ebadi, 2022). This unprecedented measure, deemed temporary by the Taliban, has singularly positioned Afghanistan as the exclusive country globally where girls and women encounter a categorical denial of access to secondary education. The rationale behind this restriction, as articulated by the Taliban, is the perceived necessity to harmonize female uniforms and curricula with their interpretation of 'Islamic values.' This policy represents a marked regression from the educational advancements of the past two decades, during which significant progress, especially in the education of girls and women, had been accomplished with international backing. The (former republic) era witnessed an enrolment surge to 9.5 million students, with girls comprising 39 percent of the student body.

(8) **Women Rights:** Since assuming control in August 2021, the Taliban has professed a commitment to safeguarding women's rights under the auspices of Sharia. However, scepticism arises regarding the veracity of these statements in quelling concerns about an imminent erosion of women's rights and addressing rumours of pre-takeover actions. Despite initial calls for women government employees to resume work with the condition of wearing the hijab, subsequent directives advised women to remain at home temporarily, citing concerns over the inadequately trained Taliban forces. While the Taliban's rule is commonly associated with the oppression of Afghan women, it's crucial to recognize that prevailing societal attitudes predate the group, particularly in rural areas. For some, the Taliban's ascension may bring respite from ongoing violence, especially in conflict-ridden rural zones. Nonetheless, apprehensions persist among women concerning sexual violence, reprisals, and forced displacement. The reinstatement of the Ministry of Propagation of Virtue and Prevention of Vice by the Taliban raises apprehensions. Despite assertions of reopening girls' education, scepticism lingers, prompting foreign agencies to advocate for girls' education during diplomatic encounters with the Taliban (Vale, Margolin & Akbari, 2023).

(9) **Religious and Ethnic Minorities**: The Taliban's treatment of ethnic and religious minorities exhibits a nuanced perspective, departing from their more rigid stance on women's rights. Despite the absence of formal policy directives from senior Taliban leaders, their handling of minorities, particularly the Hazaras, reveals a complex scenario (Mohammadi, 2024). The Hazaras, predominantly Shia Muslims comprising 10-15% of Afghanistan's population, have historically confronted persecution. Although reports indicate massacres and forced displacement in Hazarajat, the Taliban's official position appears relatively more accepting in urban settings. Noteworthy instances include the appointment of a Hazara to the Taliban's cabinet and the safeguarding of Shia commemorations by Taliban fighters (Raghavan, 2021). Nevertheless, conflicting actions, such as reported forced evictions and executions of Hazara civilians, contribute to a fluid situation, prompting observers to speculate on the Taliban's pragmatic approach for control. Afghanistan's Hindu and Sikh communities, previously numbering in the tens of thousands, have dwindled, with remaining individuals seeking to depart post the Taliban's 2021 takeover. Interactions between the Taliban-appointed mayor of Kabul and Hindu-Sikh representatives suggest a more tolerant stance; however, instances of vandalism underscore persisting concerns about safeguarding religious minorities.

(10) **Foreign Policy**: Since assuming power in August 2021, the Afghan Taliban's foreign policy exhibits a cautious strategy involving intricate regional engagement, diplomatic initiatives, and endeavours to attain global recognition. Leveraging historical affiliations, the Taliban has solidified ties with pivotal regional actors, emphasizing robust relationships with Pakistan and China, while concurrently addressing security concerns through engagement with Iran, India, and Russia. Diplomatically, the Taliban has actively pursued for recognition through dialogues with nations like Qatar and Turkey,

alongside engagements with international bodies like the Shanghai Cooperation Organization. Seeking acknowledgment on the world stage, the Taliban has provided assurances concerning counterterrorism measures to prevent Afghanistan from serving as a sanctuary. Nonetheless, formidable challenges persist, notably in the domain of human rights, where apprehensions regarding the treatment of women and minorities impede widespread international acceptance. Amid economic challenges, the Taliban's adept navigation of geopolitical intricacies and cultivation of global partnerships will significantly influence the trajectory of their foreign policy (Hazoori, 2022).

(11) **State Security & Counterterrorism Measures**: Under Taliban rule, Afghanistan's security landscape undergoes a complex transformation, exhibiting a semblance of tranquillity amidst localized instances of violence. Noteworthy is the Taliban's recalibration of force posture, evident in the dismantling of numerous checkpoints, driven by manpower constraints and a perceived absence of threats from previously supportive rural areas. Despite these adjustments, the Taliban grapples with urban policing complexities and internal dissent management, encountering impediments in realizing their vision for a robust security apparatus (Demirjian & Schmitt).[45] Concurrently, insurgencies from the Islamic State-Khorasan Province in the east, northern challenges from former army factions, and nuanced measures to oversee dormant militant groups like al-Qaeda further complicate the security scenario. In responding to security challenges, the Taliban's initial approaches involve categorical denials, particularly regarding al-Qaeda's presence, accompanied by coercive measures.

Recognizing adverse repercussions, the Taliban experiments with new strategies, including relocating security personnel, disarmament efforts, and leveraging religious scholars' soft power. Despite ongoing anti-Taliban violence, the regime faces potential risks such as internal fractionalization and a jihadist uprising. The prospect of regional and Western powers arming proxies or resorting to unilateral actions against foreign militants introduces unpredictability. The international community expresses concern over the Taliban's leniency towards jihadists, emphasizing uncertainties within the evolving geopolitical landscape.

(12) **Diplomacy and International Engagement:** The Taliban's assumption of governance has sparked significant changes in diplomacy and international engagement. Acknowledging global concerns rooted in historical ties to terrorism, the international community scrutinizes the Taliban's conduct on the world stage. To secure international recognition and support, the Taliban has actively pursued diplomatic initiatives, engaging with various nations and international organizations. Their diplomatic endeavours include outreach to regional stakeholders, neighbouring nations, and global entities, strategically projecting an image of political stability and a commitment to addressing issues such as counterterrorism, human rights, and women's rights. Despite these efforts, the international community remains vigilant, assessing the Taliban's adherence to diplomatic norms. The endorsement of the Taliban government by foreign nations and international bodies hinges on tangible actions, especially in governance, human rights, and counterterrorism. The diplomatic landscape under Taliban governance involves a delicate balancing act as the group seeks international legitimacy while navigating global expectations. The Taliban's effectiveness in integrating into the international diplomatic arena depends on adeptly addressing concerns and demonstrating an unwavering commitment to inclusive and accountable governance. In the dynamic geopolitical landscape, the diplomatic engagements orchestrated by the Taliban will wield substantial influence,

Figure 2. Comparative database of violent incidents in Afghanistan: Pre- and post- Taliban takeover (September 2020-July 2022)

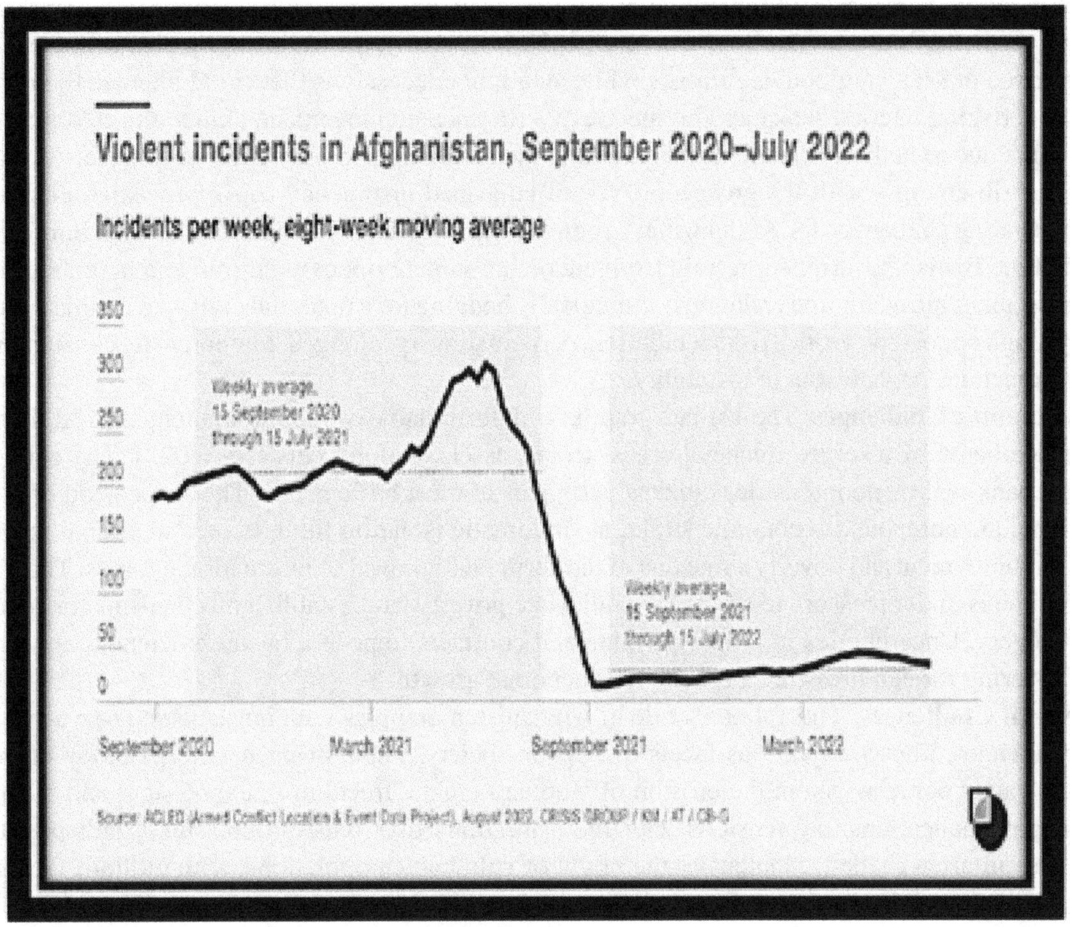

shaping the trajectory of their relationship with the international community. The delicate interplay between global expectations and the Taliban's diplomatic actions is pivotal in determining their standing on the world stage (Faheem & Khan, 2022).

CRACKS IN THE FAÇADE: THE UNFOLDING CHALLENGES TO TALIBAN'S RULE

In the aftermath of the Taliban's resurgence in Afghanistan, the governance landscape is besieged by an array of intricate challenges that transcend the mere exercise of authority. The Taliban's incumbency faces a formidable array of hurdles, encompassing political, economic, social, and humanitarian dimensions, each constituting a discrete menace to their efficacy in governance.

(1) **Political Challenges**: The primary challenge facing the Taliban involves deftly navigating a complex political landscape, both domestically and globally. Their assumption of power has been met with

widespread scepticism and international criticism, fuelling concerns about human rights, inclusivity, and the potential resurgence of Afghanistan as an extremist hub. The lack of broad international recognition hampers the Taliban's ability to engage in diplomatic and economic initiatives, hindering the nation's overall development (Gul, 2022). Internally, the Taliban grapples with the delicate balance of seeking global legitimacy while avoiding concessions that could alienate their support base, risking internal schisms. The spectre of a fragmented movement, akin to the 1990s civil war, looms due to authoritarian leadership, ethnic factionalism, and external interference. A troubling scenario emerges with the prospect of a unified armed insurgency backed by external sponsors, presenting challenges for Afghanistan's future. Despite calls for support, the Biden administration, and the British government refrain from endorsing violent opposition. Iran and neighbouring nations maintain ambiguous relations, strategically hedging for a potential civil war. Military pressure through opposition groups risks retaliation, perpetuating a prolonged, low-intensity conflict, further entrenching Afghanistan in instability.

(2) **Economic Challenges**: The Taliban grapple with formidable economic challenges in Afghanistan, exacerbated by a severe financial crisis, frozen assets, and aid cuts (Ng, 2023). The collapse of the banking system intensifies citizens' struggles to meet basic needs. The suspension of international aid compounds economic strain, as diplomatic isolation limits access to crucial resources. Unemployment and poverty surge due to the abrupt withdrawal of international forces. The Taliban regime is under pressure to create jobs, alleviate poverty, and establish mechanisms for economic recovery. Uncertainties in property rights and contracts impede a business-friendly atmosphere, hindering foreign investment crucial for economic growth.

(3) **Social Challenges**: The Taliban's rule in Afghanistan grapples with intricate and pervasive social challenges, impacting various facets of Afghan society. Their stringent interpretation of Islamic law raises concerns about the erosion of women's rights, freedom of expression, and inclusivity in governance, creating tensions with the aspirations of a once-progressing youth population. Humanitarian challenges intensify the plight of vulnerable populations, with millions facing food shortages and displacement, demanding prompt, and effective action from the Taliban to avert a catastrophe. Internal strife, armed resistance groups, and tribal rivalries pose threats to social stability. The authoritarian leadership style, ethnic factionalism, and repressive measures contribute to an environment of tension. The social fabric, once diverse and pluralistic, strains under Taliban rule. Balancing traditional values with evolving expectations requires a nuanced approach to foster inclusivity, protect human rights, and mitigate crises for Afghanistan's social stability and cohesion.

(4) **Security Challenges**: The Taliban's evolution from insurgency to governance raises critical questions about their capacity to ensure security, a fundamental state function. Transitioning from perpetrating attacks to governance underscores the dichotomy they confront establishing stability for legitimacy after years of destabilization attempts. The appointment of former suicide attack commanders to key security roles and affiliations with groups like Al-Qaeda raises concerns about ongoing instability. Since the Taliban's Kabul takeover, a surge in suicide attacks, including at Kabul Airport and Shiite sites, indicates a volatile security situation. Daesh (ISIS-Khorasan's) responsibility underscores ideological differences and territorial competition. The dilemma lies in the Taliban prioritizing security while others, like Daesh, exploit insecurity. Short- and medium-term security scenarios involve a Taliban struggle with ex-affiliates, sustaining insecurity, or Taliban dominance for stability. Outcomes depend on intricate factors such as power dynamics and ideological motivations (Sakhi, 2022).

(5) **Humanitarian Challenges:** The influx of refugees from Pakistan poses formidable humanitarian challenges for the Taliban in Afghanistan (Tastan, 2023). The return of Afghan refugees and internal displacement strain resources, pressuring infrastructure and exacerbating existing challenges. Reintegrating returnees into Afghan society, amid economic and security concerns, presents hurdles to rebuilding lives. The sudden population increase strains the job market, heightening unemployment, and economic instability. Navigating these complexities is crucial for the Taliban, facing economic challenges, to prevent social and economic strains. Collaborative efforts between the Taliban, international organizations, and neighbouring countries are vital to address essential needs, support economic opportunities, and foster social harmony. Managing this situation significantly influences the Taliban's legitimacy and governance effectiveness.

CONCLUSIVE POLICY CENTRIC RECOMMENDATIONS FOR EMPOWERING INSTITUTIONS AND STRENGTHENING GOVERNANCE

Navigating the complex governance landscape of Afghanistan, the Taliban can strategically implement a spectrum of policy measures to fortify governance structures and institutions. This imperative undertaking is pivotal for not only establishing stability but also catalysing economic growth and securing international recognition.

(1) **Inclusive Political Representation**: Prioritizing the construction of an inclusive political framework reflecting Afghanistan's diverse ethnic and cultural mosaic stands as a cornerstone. By incorporating representatives from various groups, the government can address historical grievances and promote national unity. Research underscores that inclusive governance diminishes the risk of internal conflict and nurtures social cohesion. A World Bank study accentuates the positive correlation between inclusive institutions and sustained economic development (Das, Fisiy & Kyte, 2013).

(2) **Human Rights Protection**: Gaining international legitimacy necessitates a steadfast commitment to upholding human rights. The Taliban can institute policies safeguarding the rights of women, minorities, and vulnerable populations. Various studies substantiate that societies staunchly devoted to human rights not only attract foreign investment and aid but also uphold an economic and diplomatic imperative (Garriga, 2016).

(3) **Economic Reforms**: Addressing Afghanistan's financial challenges mandates the implementation of sound economic policies. The Taliban should pivot towards economic diversification, attracting foreign investment, and fostering employment opportunities. Insights from institutions like the International Monetary Fund (IMF) underscore the pivotal role of economic reforms in post-conflict nations. A stable and burgeoning economy not only enhances the populace's well-being but augments the government's service delivery capacity.

(4) **Counter-Corruption Measures**: Eradicating corruption is paramount for instilling public trust in the government. Transparent and accountable institutions must be established to combat corruption at all levels. Transparency International's data accentuates a strong negative correlation between corruption and economic development, emphasizing that nations with lower corruption levels exhibit superior economic prospects and higher standards of living (Wang & Rosenau, 2001).

(5) **Investment in Education**: Prioritizing scientific education is essential for Afghanistan's enduring progress. The Taliban can strategically invest in establishing a comprehensive education system that integrates both traditional and vocational elements. Insights from reputable organizations highlights the constructive influence of education on social and economic development, empowering an educated populace to actively participate in the workforce and civic affairs (Adams & Adams, 1968). Swift action is imperative to lift the embargo on girls' education, emphasizing the crucial need for the Taliban to acknowledge that girls rightfully belong in schools, not confined to their homes.

(6) **Infrastructure Development**: Revitalizing infrastructure, spanning roads, energy, and telecommunications, assumes pivotal significance for economic growth and connectivity. The Taliban can harness international assistance and forge private partnerships to embark on crucial infrastructure projects. Studies by the World Bank emphasize infrastructure's pivotal role in fostering economic development by enhancing productivity, reducing transportation costs, and attracting investment ("World Development Report", 1994).

(7) **Diplomatic Engagement**: Active engagement with the international community is instrumental for garnering recognition and support. The Taliban can initiate diplomatic overtures, participate in regional forums, and showcase a commitment to peaceful coexistence. It is to be remembered that diplomatic recognition is closely entwined with a government's ability to access international aid and partake in global economic activities.

(8) **Security Sector Reforms**: Bolstering the security sector assumes a fundamental role in preserving stability. The Taliban should prioritize the professionalization of the military and police forces, ensuring their alignment with the interests of the entire population. A well-functioning security sector is prerequisite to overall governance and stability.

(9) **Public Health Initiatives**: Enhancing public health infrastructure and services, with a specific focus on addressing malnutrition and achieving polio eradication, is an imperative requirement. Collaborating with reputable international organizations to augment healthcare delivery has the potential to portray the Taliban as proactive and responsible stewards of public health. The World Health Organization (WHO) bears a significant responsibility in this context, necessitating its active and just recognition of its duty towards the impoverished citizens of a war-torn nation.

(10) **Legal and Judicial Reforms**: Implementing comprehensive legal and judicial reforms is imperative for the establishment of the rule of law. The Taliban should endeavour to forge a fair and transparent legal system that guarantees justice for all citizens. Research accentuates that a robust legal framework is pivotal for attracting foreign investment and fostering economic growth, with investors gravitating towards countries with reliable and transparent legal systems.

In conclusion, the Taliban finds itself at a pivotal juncture in Afghanistan's governance landscape, standing on the precipice of a transformative era. The successful execution of these cautiously devised policy measures, rooted in research-oriented sagacity and bolstered by empirical validation, possesses the inherent potential to elevate governance frameworks and fortify the edifice of public institutions. The efficacy of these measures is inexorably tied to the Taliban's resolute dedication to an all-encompassing governance paradigm, an unwavering commitment to the tenets of human rights, and a collaborative overture with the international community. Furthermore, the international community, particularly with a focal lens on Afghanistan's neighbouring nations, bears an ethical obligation to actively participate in initiatives aimed at normalizing relations with the Taliban. It is paramount to acknowledge that the marginalization of the Taliban regime yields deleterious repercussions for the ordinary Afghans, who have borne the brunt of global political vicissitudes and hegemonic struggles spanning the last four decades.

Limitations of the Study

Given that the addressed matter pertains to an ambitiously expansive field of study, demanding significant investments of time, energy, and financial resources, the policy-centric recommendations are predominantly derived from secondary sources. Crafting essential policy directives entails researchers primarily extrapolating insights from political, economic, social, health, and educational databases, prioritizing these domains over other intrinsic variables.

REFERENCES

Adams, D., & Adams, J. (1968). Education and Social Development. *Review of Educational Research, 38*(3), 243–263. doi:10.2307/1169396

Ahmadi, B. (2023, December 07). *How the Taliban Enables Violence Against Women*. United States Institute of Peace. https://www.usip.org/publications/2023/12/how-taliban-enables-violence-against-women

Ahmadi, B., & Ebadi, A. (2022, April 01). *Taliban's Ban on Girls' Education in Afghanistan*. United States Institute of Peace. https://www.usip.org/publications/2022/04/talibans-ban-girls-education-afghanistan

Ameyaw-Brobbey, T. (2023). THE U.S. WITHDRAWAL, TALIBAN TAKEOVER, AND ONTOLOGICAL (IN)SECURITY IN AFGHANISTAN. *World Affairs, 186*(1), 105–134. doi:10.1177/00438200221125800

Backzo, A. (2023, November 14). *The Taliban Courts in Afghanistan: Waging War by Law.* Oxford Academic.

Bezhan, F. (2020, October 02). *Is The Taliban Seeking A 'Sunni Afghan Version' Of Iran?* Radio Liberty. https://www.rferl.org/a/is-the-taliban-seeking-a-sunni-afghan-version-of-iran-/30870998.html

Clark, K., & Shapour, R. (2023). *WHAT DO THE TALEBAN SPEND AFGHANISTAN'S MONEY ON? Government expenditure under the Islamic Emirate*. Afghanistan Analyst Network. https://www.afghanistan-analysts.org/en/reports/economy-development-environment/what-do-the-taleban-spend-afghanistans-money-on-government-expenditure-under-the-islamic-emirate/

Congressional Research Service. (2021, November 02). *Taliban Government in Afghanistan: Background and Issues for Congress*. CRS. https://crsreports.congress.gov/product/pdf/R/R46955

D'Souza, S. M. (2016). Taliban: The Rebels Who Aspire to be Rulers. *Journal of Asian Security and International Affairs, 3*(1), 20–40. https://www.jstor.org/stable/48602132. doi:10.1177/2347797015626043

Das, M. B., Fisiy, C. F., & Kyte, R. (2013, October 18). *Inclusion Matters: The Foundation for Shared Prosperity*. New Frontiers of Social Policy Washington, D.C.: World Bank Group. https://documents1.worldbank.org/curated/en/114561468154469371/pdf/Inclusion-matters-the-foundation-for-shared-prosperity.pdf

Dawi, A. (2022, August 04). *Will US Hit Most-Wanted Haqqanis in Afghanistan?* VOA. https://www.voanews.com/a/will-us-hit-more-most-wanted-haqqanis-in-afghanistan-/6687402.html

Dawi, A. (2023, March 28). *Unseen Taliban Leader Wields Godlike Powers in Afghanistan*. VOA. https://www.voanews.com/a/unseen-taliban-leader-wields-godlike-powers-in-afghanistan-/7026112.html

Dawi, A. (2023, September 28). *Taliban Undertake Speedy Overhaul of Afghanistan's Justice System*. VOA. https://www.voanews.com/a/taliban-undertake-speedy-overhaul-afghanistan-justice-system/7289101.html

Demirjian, K., & Schmitt, E. (2023, April 25). Taliban Kill Head of ISIS Cell That Bombed Kabul Airport. *The New York Times*. https://www.nytimes.com/2023/04/25/us/politics/isis-leader-killed-kabul-airport-bombing.html

Faheem, M., & Khan, M. M. (2022). Recognition of the Taliban Government in Afghanistan and International Community. *Strategic Studies, 42*(1), 81–96. https://www.jstor.org/stable/48732345

Franco, C., & Giustozzi, A. (2016). Revolution in the Counter-Revolution: Efforts to Centralize the Taliban's Military Leadership. *Central Asian Affairs, 3*(3), 249–286. doi:10.1163/22142290-00303003

Gannon, K. (2022, March 24). Taliban Break Promise on Higher Education for Afghan Girls. *The Diplomat*. https://thediplomat.com/2022/03/taliban-break-promise-on-higher-education-for-afghan-girls/

Garriga, A. C. (2016). Human Rights Regimes, Reputation, and Foreign Direct Investment. *International Studies Quarterly, 60*(1), 160–172. https://www.jstor.org/stable/43868314. doi:10.1093/isq/sqw006

Ghosh, P. (2021, September 17). Afghanistan had a ministry for women affairs. Taliban replace it with 'vice and virtue'. *Hindustan Times*. https://www.hindustantimes.com/world-news/afghanistan-had-women-ministry-taliban-replace-it-with-vice-and-virtue-101631887569231.html

Glinski, S. (2022, February 28). Taliban Struggle to Maintain Unity Six Months into Their Reign. *Foreign Policy*. https://foreignpolicy.com/2022/02/28/taliban-divisions-afghanistan-government-resistance/

Graham-Harrison, E., & Makoii, A. M. (2021, September 07). Taliban name all-male Afghan cabinet including minister wanted by FBI. *The Guardian*. https://www.theguardian.com/world/2021/sep/07/taliban-name-afghanistans-new-government

Gul, A. (2021, September 28). *Taliban Say They Will Use Parts of Monarchy Constitution to Run Afghanistan for Now*. VOA. https://www.voanews.com/a/taliban-say-they-will-use-parts-of-monarchy-constitution-to-run-afghanistan-for-now/6248880.html

Gul, A. (2022, June 18). *Taliban Say US Is 'Biggest Hurdle' to Diplomatic Recognition*. VOA. https://www.voanews.com/a/taliban-say-us-is-biggest-hurdle-to-diplomatic-recognition/6623070.html

Guler, B. (2021, August 24). *6 major figures to lead Taliban through critical process*. Anadolu Agency. https://www.aa.com.tr/en/asia-pacific/6-major-figures-to-lead-taliban-through-critical-process-/2343771

Hakimi, S., & Fair, C. (2022, September 09). *The Taliban's Amir on the "Victory" in Afghanistan*. Hudson Institute. https://www.hudson.org/node/45218

Hozoori, S. (2022). Comparing the Foreign Relations of Emirate I and Emirate II: Has Anything Changed? *India Quarterly*, *78*(4), 585–601. doi:10.1177/09749284221127806

Ibrahimi, S. Y. (2022). False negotiations and the fall of Afghanistan to the Taliban. *International Journal (Toronto, Ont.)*, *77*(2), 168–187. doi:10.1177/00207020221135299

Ishfaq, S. (2019, December 31). South Asia's Most Notorious Militant Groups. *The Diplomat*. https://thediplomat.com/2019/12/south-asias-most-notorious-militant-groups/

Kakar, A. W. (2022, April 25). In Afghanistan, Vice and Virtue Are Front and Center. *New Lines Magazine*. https://newlinesmag.com/reportage/in-afghanistan-vice-and-virtue-are-front-and-center/

Khan, S. K. (2021, September 21). *Taliban bring new faces to fill Cabinet positions in Afghanistan*. Anadolu Agency. https://www.aa.com.tr/en/asia-pacific/taliban-bring-new-faces-to-fill-cabinet-positions-in-afghanistan/2370524

Krishnankutty, P. (2023, June 10). UN report says Taliban showing no signs of 'bending' to pressure for reform, has split leadership. *The Print*. https://theprint.in/world/un-report-says-taliban-showing-no-signs-of-bending-to-pressure-for-reform-has-split-leadership/1622069/

Lieven, A. (2021, May 15). An Afghan Tragedy: The Pashtuns, the Taliban and the State. *Survival*, *63*(3), 7–35. doi:10.1080/00396338.2021.1930403

Lombardi, C., & March, A. (2022, February 28). *Afghan Taliban Views on Legitimate Islamic Governance*. United States Institute of Peace. https://www.usip.org/publications/2022/02/afghan-taliban-views-legitimate-islamic-governance

Malejacq, R., & Terpstra, N. (2023, July 30). *Why International Leverage Has Failed with the Taliban*. Lawfare. https://www.lawfaremedia.org/article/why-international-leverage-has-failed-with-the-taliban

Mir, A. (2023, August 15). *Two Years Under the Taliban: Is Afghanistan a Terrorist Safe Haven Once Again?* United States Institute of Peace. https://www.usip.org/publications/2023/08/two-years-under-taliban-afghanistan-terrorist-safe-haven-once-again

Mohammadi, G. H. (2024, January 24). The Plight of Hazaras Under the Taliban Government. *The Diplomat*. https://thediplomat.com/2024/01/the-plight-of-hazaras-under-the-taliban-government/

Nagamine, Y. (2015). *The Legitimization Strategy of the Taliban's Code of Conduct*. Palgrave Macmillan. doi:10.1007/978-1-137-53088-2

Nassaji, H. (2015). Qualitative and descriptive research: Data type versus data analysis. *Language Teaching Research*, *19*(2), 129–132. doi:10.1177/1362168815572747

Nelson, M. J. (2021, November 03). *Taliban Constitutionalism in Comparative Perspective*. Berkeley Center for Religion, Peace, and World Affairs https://berkleycenter.georgetown.edu/responses/taliban-constitutionalism-in-comparative-perspective

Ng, K. (2023, April 18). *Afghan economic hopes threatened by Taliban – UN*. BBC. https://www.bbc.com/news/world-asia-65307858

Raghavan, S. (2021, September 11). The U.S. branded the Haqqanis terrorists and issued $5 million bounties. Now they're in power in the Taliban government. *The Washington Post.* https://www.washingtonpost.com/world/asia_pacific/haqqanis-afghanistan-taliban/2021/09/10/71f82620-123b-11ec-baca-86b144fc8a2d_story.html

Raghavan, S. (2021, November 01). The Taliban is trying to win over Afghanistan's Shiites with a 33-year-old Hazara emissary. But many question the group's sincerity. *The Washington Post.* https://www.washingtonpost.com/world/asia_pacific/taliban-afghanistan-hazaras/2021/11/01/096c9690-3775-11ec-9662-399cfa75efee_story.html

Sakhi, N. (2022). The Taliban Takeover in Afghanistan and Security Paradox. *Journal of Asian Security and International Affairs*, *9*(3), 383–401. doi:10.1177/23477970221130882

Sankranti, S. (2023, September 28). *Under Taliban, Afghan currency tops global rankings amid turmoil.* WION. https://www.wionews.com/business-economy/under-taliban-afghan-currency-tops-global-rankings-amid-turmoil-640145

Sen, A. K. (2022, October 27). *Missteps and Missed Opportunities for Peace in Afghanistan.* United States Institute of Peace. https://www.usip.org/publications/2022/10/missteps-and-missed-opportunities-peace-afghanistan

Singh, Y. (2023, February 15). Afghanistan remains primary source of terrorist threat for Central and South Asia UN report. *The Week.* https://www.theweek.in/wire-updates/international/2023/02/15/fgn9-un-afghan.html

Taliban announces new government in Afghanistan. (2021, September 07). Al Jazeera. https://www.aljazeera.com/news/2021/9/7/taliban-announce-acting-ministers-of-new-government

Tastan, N. (2023, November 15). *Afghan refugees returning from Pakistan in 'very bad condition,' says UN official.* Anadolu Agency. https://www.aa.com.tr/en/asia-pacific/afghan-refugees-returning-from-pakistan-in-very-bad-condition-says-un-official/3054109

Vale, G., Margolin, D., & Akbari, F. (2023). *Repeating the Past or Following Precedent? Contextualising the Taliban 2.0's Governance of Women.* International Centre for Counter - Terrorism. https://www.icct.nl/sites/default/files/2023-01/Taliban%202.0%E2%80%99s%20Governance%20of%20Women%20-%20Vale%2C%20Margolin%20Akbari%20final.pdf

Wang, H., & Rosenau, J. N. (2001). Transparency International and Corruption as an Issue of Global Governance. *Global Governance*, *7*(1), 25–49. https://www.jstor.org/stable/27800285. doi:10.1163/19426720-00701005

Wheeldon, T. (2021, August 19). Who are the Taliban leaders ruling Afghanistan? *France 24.* https://www.france24.com/en/asia-pacific/20210819-who-are-the-taliban-leaders-ruling-afghanistan

World Bank. (2023, August 31). *Afghan Economic Monitor.* World Bank. https://thedocs.worldbank.org/en/doc/8cd4001da4ac981a9d239f5536b173ea-0310012023/original/Afghanistan-Economic-Monitor-31-August-2023.pdf

World Development Report 1994. (1994). Oxford University Press. https://documents1.worldbank.org/curated/en/535851468336642118/pdf/131840REPLACEMENT0WDR01994.pdf

Yusufzai, A. (2019, January 25). Taliban appoint Mullah Baradar as head of political office in Doha. *Arab News*. https://www.arabnews.com/node/1441536/amp

Zelin, A. (2015). *Full Text Statement Delivered By the Delegation of the Political Office in the International Pugwash Research Conference*. Jihadology. https://jihadology.net/2015/05/05/new-re-lease-from-the-islamic-emirate-of-afghanistan-full-text-of-statement-delivered-by-the-delegation-of-the-political-office-in-the-international-pugwash-research-conference

ADDITIONAL READINGS

Cordesman, A. H., Gold, B., & Hess, A. (2013). *The Afghan War in 2013: Meeting the Challenges of Transition: The Challenges of Leadership and Governance (CSIS Reports)*. Centre for Strategic & International Studies.

Jalalzai, M.K. (2021). *Afghanistan: Militias Governance and their Disputed Leadership (Taliban, ISIS, US Proxy Militias, Extrajudicial Killings, War Crimes and Enforced Disappearances)*. VIJ Books (India) Pvt. Ltd.

Karlekar, H. (2012). *Endgame in Afghanistan: For Whom the Dice Rolls*. SAGE India.

Levi-Sanchez, S. (2016). *The Afghan-Central Asia Borderland: The State and Local Leaders (Central Asian Studies)*. Routledge. doi:10.4324/9781315691718

Maloney, S. M. (2007). *Enduring the Freedom: A Rogue Historian in Afghanistan*. Potomac Books Inc.

Mgbeke, D. (2009). *Public Policy Implementation in a Democratic Governance Society: A Roadmap to Empowering Citizen Participation: An Empirical Study*. Author House.

O'Connell, A. B. (2017). *Our Latest Longest War: Losing Hearts and Minds in Afghanistan*. The University of Chicago Press. doi:10.7208/chicago/9780226265797.001.0001

Schroeder, U. (2015). *Building Security in Post-Conflict States: The Domestic Consequences of Security Sector Reform*. Routledge.

Singh, A. P., & Murari, K. (2018). *Governance: Issues and Challenges*. Pearson Education.

Singh, S. (2016). *Governance*. Sage Publications India Private Limited.

KEY TERMS AND DEFINITIONS

Daesh: An alternative term for ISIS (Islamic State of Iraq and Syria), used to delegitimize the group by its opponents.

Diplomacy: The art and practice of conducting international relations and negotiations between states, aiming to resolve conflicts, establish agreements, and foster cooperation.

Ethnicity: A social construct based on shared cultural traits, language, ancestry, and history, influencing group identity and relations within diverse populations.

Governance: The systematic process of decision-making, implementation, and management within an organization or state, ensuring effective and accountable administration based on established principles.

Institutionalization: The establishment and formalization of institutions within a society or organization, embedding enduring structures, norms, and practices to ensure stability and continuity.

Pashtunwali: The traditional ethical code and way of life followed by the Pashtun people, emphasizing hospitality, honor, and community values.

Political Inclusivity: The incorporation of diverse perspectives, groups, and individuals into political processes and decision-making, fostering representation and participation for a comprehensive and equitable governance approach.

Refugee: An individual forced to flee their home country due to persecution, conflict, or natural disasters, seeking safety and asylum in another nation.

Shariah Law: Islamic legal principles derived from the Quran and Hadith, governing various aspects of life, including morality, justice, and personal conduct.

State: A politically organized entity characterized by defined borders, a government system, and sovereignty over its territory, exercising authority and providing public services.

Chapter 11
Greening the Guns: How Armed Non-State Actors Can Become a Player in the Fight for a Sustainable Future

Muhammed Karakuş
https://orcid.org/0000-0003-0078-8603
Adıyaman University, Turkey

ABSTRACT

Globalization's inexorable interconnectedness has swept non-state actors onto the stage of global governance, weaving them into its intricate tapestry. Yet, the body of literature is fixated on their ability to sway the levers of state power. This focus overshadows not only their but also the potential contributions, nimbleness, diverse vantage points, and unburdened agility of armed non-state actors (ANSAs) who are known for their most egregious examples. With their sprawling and deftly governance capacities, ANSAs move beyond local issues and incrementally take actions on global policies. States, international organizations, and NGOs look further afield to grow their global clout in shaping, implementing, and accomplishing climate policy while climate change's incipient ascent has taken place. However, too little is still known about conflict areas and ANSAs. By shattering the illusion of ANSA as mere bystanders of environmental concerns, this study asserts that full-fledged environmental protection can be achieved with their engagement.

INTRODUCTION

As environmental problems proliferate and deepen, the borderless nature of the problems has been realised. Thus, various frameworks have emphasized the need for sustainable human-environmental relationships, including endangerment of flora and fauna, migratory species, air and marine pollution, hazardous wastes, ozone depletion and climate change. (Young, 1997) In this regard, governance scholars are grappling with assessing the efficacy of international environmental regimes such as The Kyoto Protocol, Copenhagen Accord and the Paris Agreement.[1] Their assessments covered the interactions and

DOI: 10.4018/979-8-3693-1742-6.ch011

interconnections among international institutions to acclimatise and ensure ambitious actions against climate change and its impacts.

The dominant paradigm in international relations for a protracted period, the Realist school, traditionally highlighted state security within a narrow military lens. It considered environmental concerns, international migration, and economic issues to be a secondary tier of importance. However, it has been realized that this limited understanding needs to be revised to address the increasingly global and growing environmental problems we face today.

The 1972 Stockholm United Nations Conference on the Human Environment marked a pivotal turning point, propelling environmental issues to the forefront of the international political agenda. With the changing concept of security, environmental problems are emerging as primary policy areas with which states should increasingly concern themselves. Among various environmental problems, the effects of climate change are one of the issues that attract the most attention and interest. To address and tackle the mounting complexities posed by climate change, similar to other states, Sub-Saharan African countries have actively participated in international climate negotiations as Ethiopia has operationalised the "Climate Resilient Green Economy" strategy, with a focus on enhancing resilience in critical sectors such as agriculture and water resources (Feliciano et al., 2022; Paul & Weinthal, 2019).

On the other hand, diverse and far-ranging international organisations (I.O.s), non-state organisations (NGOs), companies, and advocacy groups have also wielded considerable influence on climate policy. Their impact goes beyond the efforts of traditional state actors like governments. Functioning as watchdogs, ensuring governments are held accountable for their climate commitments, these I.O.s and NGOs engage in public awareness campaigns and lobbying endeavours, galvanising public opinion and exerting pressure on policymakers for more palpable, ambitious and divaricated climate actions (Pandey, 2015). Additionally, by using diverse channels, with advocacy and mobilisation, these organisations contribute technical expertise and innovation to climate policy (Rödder, 2020). Moreover, while academic institutions, think tanks, and research organisations coalesce pertinent research and analysis on climate science, corporations invest and foster innovation in the renewable energy sector and climate-friendly technologies (de Coninck et al., 2008; Fischer et al., 2012). At the same time, I.O.s and NGOs collaborate with government actors (to develop and finance renewable energy or projects to reduce carbon emissions) in these policies, usually known as public-private partnerships (Pandey, 2015).

As we strive to tackle the issue of climate change, states and organizations are expanding their reach to increase their global influence in shaping, implementing and achieving climate policies. However, we need to gain a better understanding of areas affected by climate change that are also experiencing conflicts, and are ill-equipped to adapt. Additionally, we need to pay attention to the role of Armed Non-State Actors/Groups (ANSAs) and how they exert their influence in the policymaking process in areas under their control. It is important to understand their impact and how it differs from their growing influence in governance areas. In terms of legal perspective, even the early legal principles (i.e. the Protection of the Environment in Relation to Armed Conflict -PERAC[3]) addressed environmental degradation; however, its orientation was primarily directed towards states.

The following chapter begins by demystifying the world of armed groups and their evolving role in global governance. It then delves into the environmental dimensions of conflicts while highlighting the link between climate change and security. Subsequent sections explore the debate on how environmental problems, due to their borderless feature, transcend traditional actors such as states, I.O.s and NGOs and encompass a broader spectrum, including societal and armed non-state actors/groups. The exact section analyses the international legal framework and the position of the actors having an impact on the environment. The final sections of this chapter outline how ANSAs, across different regions, can contribute to environmental protection within the territories they either govern or control.

ANSAS AND ENVIRONMENT

Armed Non-State Actors (ANSAs)[4] have a mixed - and mostly negative - impact on the environment. Indeed, self-sufficient ANSAs resort to exploiting natural resources and engaging in illicit and environmentally harmful activities like logging, mining, or operating refineries (Le Billon, 2001a; Ross, 2004b, 2004a). Contemporary instances can easily be seen in almost every part of the country, including the diverse array of ANSAs in the Democratic Republic of the Congo, the Kachin Independence Army in Myanmar, and the Movement of Democratic Forces of Casamance in Senegal. On the other hand, it is not possible to mention any ANSAs solely having a negative effect during and after armed conflict. However, research on how these commitments translate into concrete policy outcomes and their contribution to global climate goals still needs to be completed.

Nevertheless, identifying ANSAs can be a complex task. These are individuals or groups that employ violence to achieve their objectives, but they are not affiliated with the regular armed forces or state institutions. ANSAs may operate across borders, utilizing neighbouring territories for protection or material mobilization. When the state is unable to address evolving security challenges or when parts of the security sector collude with these armed groups, the risk of violence is heightened. This is particularly true when the state lacks complete control over its territory or when porous borders facilitate the illicit transit of armed groups. Literature's diverging categorisation may reflect a lack of consensus even for a single armed group, which has different characteristics such as organisation types, political, economic, ideological objectives, military tactics, and many other specifications. The toll of armed groups is cumulative; new ones appear faster than old ones disappear (Rapoport, 1992). According to the estimation of the U.N. Assistance Mission in Afghanistan (UNAMA), 1800 armed groups are operating in Afghanistan alone. The crucial point is that most armed groups would not meet the narrow definitions below.[5]

Harvard Law School Program on International Law and Armed Conflict's (HLS PILAC) research states that the U.N. Security Council described nineteen armed groups depending on the circumstances and context (Burniske et al., 2017). On the other hand, Non-State Actors Working Group (NSAWG), a unit of ICBL, published a list of armed actors as rebels, liberation movements, insurgents, militias, guerrillas, irregular armed groups, dissident armed forces, and de facto territorial governing bodies (Ferrer, 2000). Caroline Holmqvist offered six categories: "Rebel opposition groups; Local militias (ethnically, clan or otherwise based); Vigilantes; Warlords; Civil defence forces and paramilitary groups (when such are clearly beyond state control); Private companies that provide military and security services (Holmqvist, 2005)." Lastly, Thomas (2005) classified ANSAs under six categories: warlords with private armies, transnational criminal organisations, militant religious organisations, ethnic-nationalist groups, emergent set of eco-warriors and anti-globalisations, and anarchists. As it is seen, the categories above (and many other categorisations) are subjective. Depending on their composition and various goals, people unite to get their will but use violence either initially or as a reaction.

Despite controversy over their definition, extensive literature concerns these armed groups. Studies state that armed groups control vast territories (Jabareen, 2015; M. A. Rubin, 2019; ZELIN, 2016) use violence (Carey et al., 2013; Schlichte, 2009; Zhukov, 2012), seeks legitimacy (McCullough, 2015; Podder, 2013; Terpstra & Frerks, 2017), establish governance system (Arjona et al., 2015; Furlan,

2020; Karakuş, 2022a; Kasfir et al., 2018; Loyle et al., 2021), provides healthcare (Lillywhite, 2015) and education (Fortin, 2015; Huang & Sullivan, 2020), cooperate with state (Phillips, 2009, 2014) and international actors (Eleftheriadou, 2020), use cyberspace (Theohary & Rollins, 2011; U.N., 2021) and have various economic initiatives (Bojicic et al., 2018; Weinstein, 2003).

According to statistics shared by the International Committee of the Red Cross (ICRC), more than 200 million people reside in territories governed by these armed groups (Mia, 2023), and 160 million are under the direct control of these groups (Munive, 2023a). Collaboration with these groups in climate adaptation efforts probably yields profound impacts since these groups often control significant territories rich in natural resources. These armed groups function as state-like actors in governing territories and populations with established institutions and rules (Podder, 2014). Literature about armed group behaviour and resource governance tends to be found mainly in studies on shadow, quasi, parallel or areas of limited governance practices (Lochard, 2008; Pegg, 1998; Peters, 2010; Stanislawski, 2008). The absence of a one-size-fits-all approach underscores the need to tailor engagement strategies based on context-specific risks.

On the other side, researchers and policymakers have focused on the growing recognition of the nexus between climate change and security. As Lietzman and Vest (1999) defined, the relationship between environmental stress and conflict can be characterised by multi-causality (interaction with other political, social and economic factors), reciprocity and feedback effects (environmental stress can lead to conflict; conversely, conflict can lead to more environmental stress) and complex consequences of environmental stress (including poverty, food shortages, migration and refugee movements, which can contribute to conflicts against the background of unfavourable socio-economic conditions). Depending on socio-economic and political context factors (including perception patterns, economic vulnerability and resource dependence, institutional and technological capacities for action, and cultural and ethnopolitical factors), environmental stress factors represent structural, conflict-accelerating or triggering factors but do not necessarily lead to conflicts.

In other words, the relationship between climate change and conflict is not predetermined yet; in the absence of proactive preventive strategies, there may be multiple pathways that climate-related issues interact with political, social and environmental stresses (frequency and severity of droughts and floods, food and resource scarcity) to heighten pre-existing vulnerabilities and tensions and diminish livelihood options for the populace while compound existing vulnerabilities (particularly affecting marginalised communities). The relationship between climate change, peace, and security can be delineated through four interrelated pathways (NUI, 2021): (1) deterioration of livelihoods, (2) migration and mobility, (3) involvement of military and armed actors, and (4) political and economic exploitation.

The notion of "deterioration of livelihoods" pertains to a state wherein the resources within an environment are diminishing as the result of the mismanagement or excessive utilisation of these resources, a decline in either quantity or quality, adverse climatic conditions, and pollution (Lenshie et al., 2021). Regarding "migration and mobility," as an adaptive strategy for groups facing threats, climate-induced migration is increasingly common in areas less affected by adverse climate conditions. Migration and shifts in mobility patterns carry the potential to heighten the risk of violent conflict through two interconnected mechanisms. First, in regions grappling with resource scarcity, a substantial influx of people may strain the economic resource base, increasing the likelihood of local resource conflicts. Second, migration and altered mobility patterns are closely associated with violent conflict between communities lacking shared institutions for conflict resolution (Gordon, 2022a). Although most environmentally driven mobility observed thus far has occurred within countries, significant cross-border migration

Figure 1. Climate and conflict: A cyclical dilemma
Center for strategic and international studies

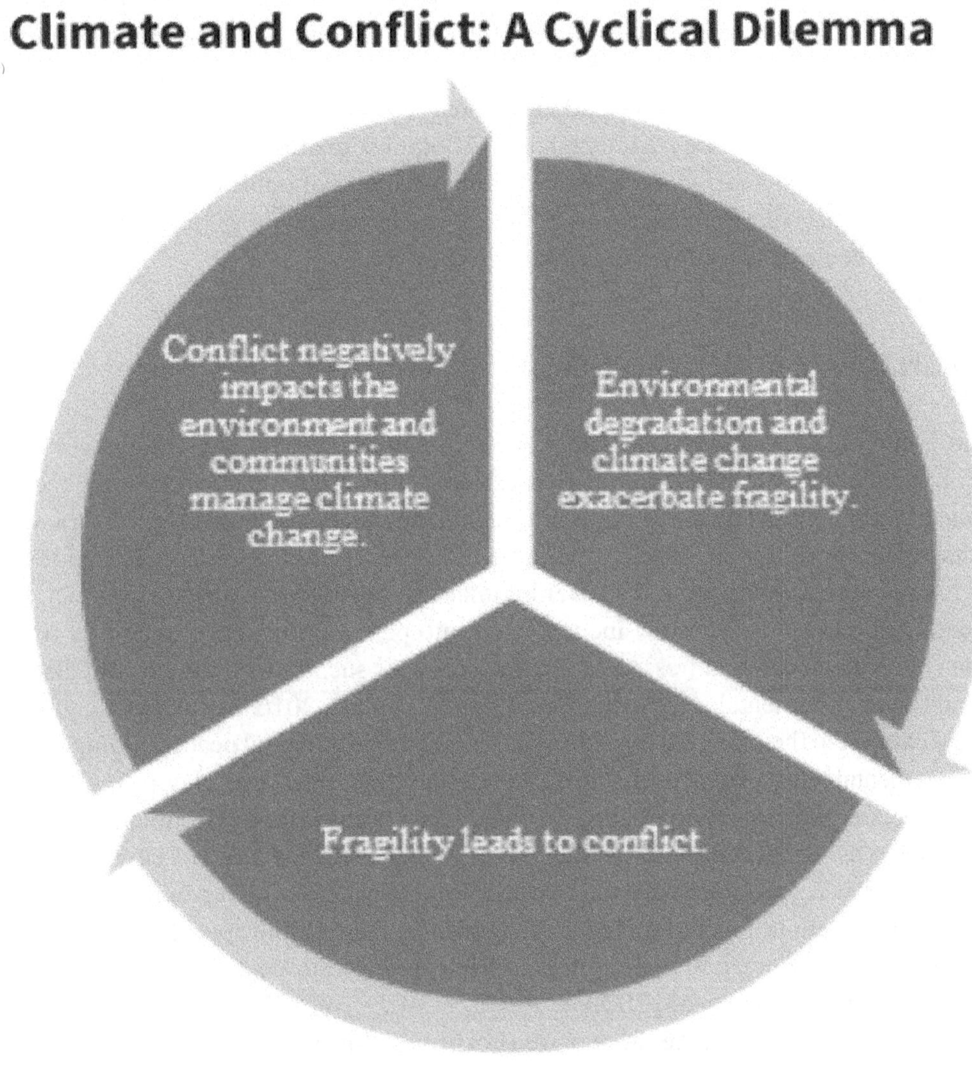

in response to climatic changes, particularly towards areas less affected, has become a notable focus, spurred by even recent large-scale international migration events (NUI, 2021). Concerning "political and economic exploitation," instead of civil wars, local conflicts are a more probable consequence of environmental degradation caused by climate change (Pham, 2011). Nevertheless, these small-scale tensions may escalate into broader conflicts when manipulated by elites—individuals or groups possessing relative wealth, privilege, power, or influence. Political factions can exploit grievances arising from weather-related losses and conflict experiences within the population (NUI, 2021).

One and most significant risk -from climate change, fragility, and conflict - is the emergence or flourishing of ANSAs. These armed groups not only benefit from the weakness of the state but also exacerbate the overall adverse effects such as compelling civilians to migrate, deforestation and resource extraction (Ross, 2004b; Vinci, 2007; Walch, 2018). According to the Environment of Peace initiative, the environmental crisis heightens security and peace risks globally, particularly in nations characterised by pre-existing fragility. Climate change progressively contributes to this fragility, primarily by intensifying conflicts related to natural resources and livelihood insecurity. Similarly, the heightened vulnerability of affected populations amplifies the adverse effects of climate change and makes them more susceptible to recruitment by ANSAs (Gates & Nordås, 2015; Kubota, 2013).

Environmental peacebuilding aims to understand the complex relationship between conflicts and the environment and to find ways to address the environmental aspects of conflicts. This approach seeks to identify the underlying causes of conflicts and develop long-term strategies for managing them, rather than just addressing the immediate cessation of hostilities.

ENVIRONMENTAL PEACEBUILDING

As the realisation deepens that environmental degradation has posed both resource challenges and security risks, its rank in the global political agenda is rising. Today, this problem is increasingly recognised as a primary concern, unlike what classical realists thought since it is underscored by historical facts that many conflicts or wars have stemmed from the competition over natural resources. This type of conflict is inclined to relapse at a rate of twice and shorter in timelapse than other conflicts. This fact, in contrast to environmental provisions, is seldomly incorporated into peace agreements, but since 2005, almost all major peace agreements have addressed ecological concerns such as inequitable land distribution or livelihoods and the environmental aftermath of conflicts (Bartolini, 2016a; Bruch et al., 2019).

The primary catalyst in the emergence and progression of environmental peacebuilding resulted from extensive environmental issues that steadily impacted conflict zones over time. Having roots in KenConca and Geoffrey Dabelko's works, environmental peacebuilding became an Environmental Peacebuilding Association (EnPAx) as a knowledge platform in 2013. Within the framework of environmental peacebuilding to resolve today's most interconnected issues, violent conflict and adverse environmental change. According to Ide et al., "environmental peacebuilding comprises multiple approaches and pathways by which management of environmental issues integrated into and can support conflict prevention, mitigation, resolution and recovery (Ide et al., 2021)."

In situations where conflict resources have driven hostilities, this policy strives to identify and resolve the underlying causes and cultivate alternative livelihoods or to foster lasting peace, encouraging them to collaborate and act in pursuit of common goals. Characterised mainly by its meta-framework nature and twinned with resilience (Johnson et al., 2023), environmental peacebuilding integrates a diverse array of themes and practices ranging from climate security, environmental cooperation, conflict-sensitive programming and sustainable livelihoods (Medina et al., 2023).

The environmental problem is a worldwide issue that affects all societies and their future. As it is borderless in nature, it requires interdependence to solve. The search for a solution to this problem has resulted in a need for a different type of institutionalization at the global level. In other words, the issues that go beyond the scope of sovereignty are no longer within the solution possibilities of nation-states that are limited by the concept of sovereignty.

In a world where problems have become global, politics should also be globalised, and global responsibility should be taken. The reorganization of existing institutions or the creation of new global structures is recommended to address this issue (Lenschow et al., 2016). Global environmental governance is also in this context; it is a collective and alternative solution to eliminate these critical deficiencies of traditional, local and national governments that are insufficient to address cross-border issues (Benedict, 2001). Similarly, global governance may entail the exercise of authority across national borders justified concerning common goods or transnational problems (Zürn, 2018, p.138). It is claimed that global governance is a multi-level system (possessing autonomy) that has no reliance on consensual decision-making. The system is structured on the interplay of various levels of actors (Zürn, 2010). In other words, global governance extends beyond traditional actors such as states and NGOs and encompasses societal and non-state actors/groups. Under the umbrella of reflexive authority, global governance is not a fixed and top-down regime but rather a dynamic and contingent system. Without a government capable of managing the country, enduring political, economic, and military challenges, forming geopolitical configurations and the complexity of civil war, these armed groups may exhibit distinct governance profiles, characterised by varying degrees of strength, ranging from robust to feeble.

Despite its swift evolvement domain in both research and practical applications, it has hitherto bestowed limited attention on ANSAs in the realms of conflict and collaboration. Although administrating large swaths of territories and controlling millions of people, these armed groups have largely been neglected.

This study claims that engaging in environmentally destructive practices to create a working system of environmental peacebuilding requires multifaceted engagement with these armed groups since they may struggle to safeguard the environment and biodiversity. Early literature rarely addresses the role of armed groups, opting instead for umbrella terms like conflict parties; however, contemporary studies have gradually identified the causal mechanism linking them. The subsequent sections cover the legal and policy framework governing their engagement in safeguarding the natural environment.

IHL AND ENVIRONMENT POLICY

As frequently observed, the scorched earth tactics being used by most of the belligerents not only entail substantial human suffering and the destruction of infrastructure but also contribute to the degradation of the natural environment (explosions, destruction, shelling, detonation of mines and other types of hostile actions). This environmental repercussion has been appropriately labelled as the "silent victim" of these circumstances, such as in Iraq by ISIL, Russians in Ukraine or Israel in Gaza (Bartolini, 2016b; Repez & Atanasiu, 2020). It is manifested through the "destruction of oil depots, plants, factories, warehouses, mines, infrastructure facilities – water pipelines, gas pipelines, water purification stations, water supply stations, the destruction of numerous buildings, which is accompanied by powerful fires, emissions of dangerous substances into the atmosphere, spills of fuel and lubricants, entry of untreated sewage into rivers life (EPL, 2023)." However, the destruction and its direct and indirect effects (stretch far beyond the conflict zones) linger well beyond the actual period of the war. Nevertheless, it is possible to mention that scrutinised bilateral or multilateral agreements aim to protect the environment during armed conflicts, but the position of the ANSAs is relatively recent. However, as part of the belligerency during the conflict, ANSAs with an Islamic orientation frequently cited Islamic law sources as integral to their military doctrine. The very reference is the teachings of Abu Bakr al-Siddeeq, emphasising principles such as "do not cut down and burn date palms" and "do not cut trees that bear fruit," alongside directives on the judicious use of livestock, underscoring that such resources should only be slaughtered for sustenance purposes (ReliefWeb, 2014).

Figure 2. Proposed actors of environmental governance
(Prepared by Author)

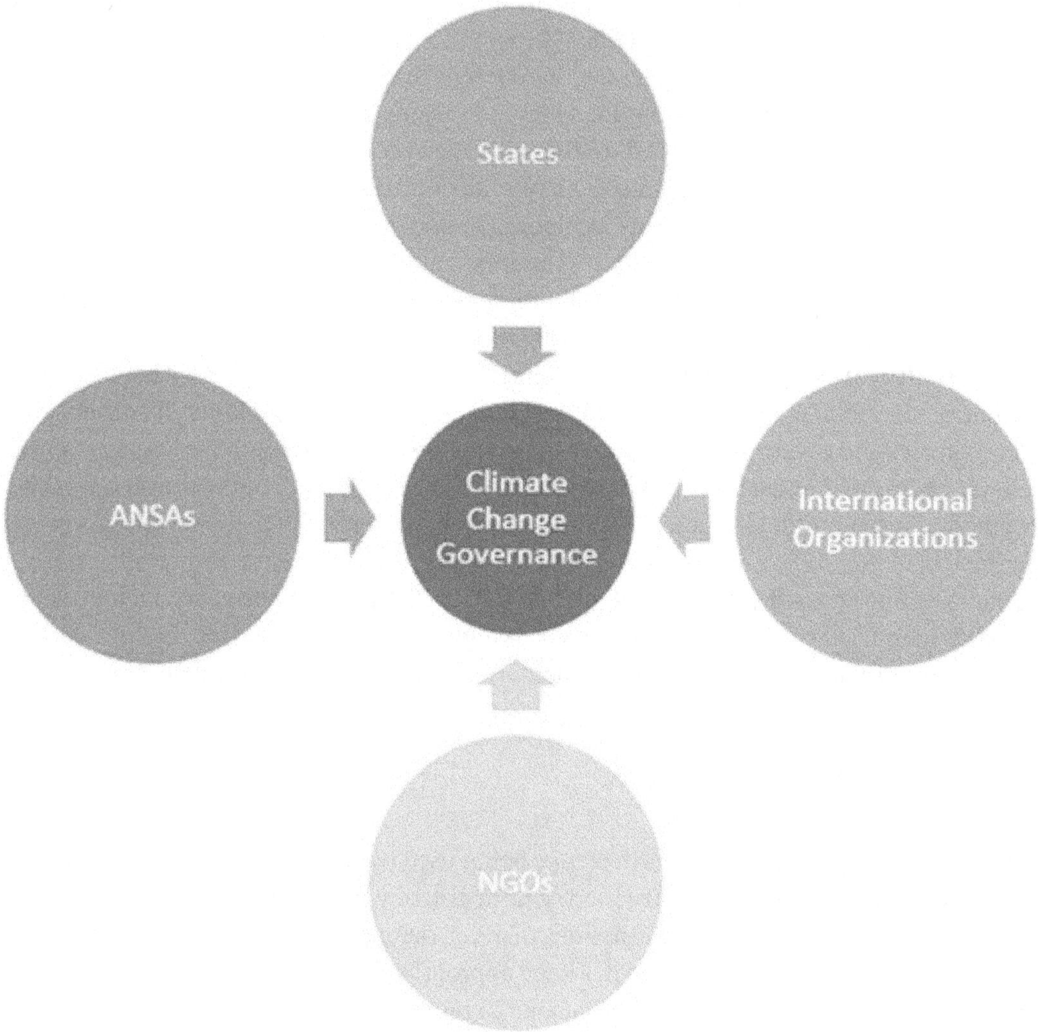

Over the years, due to the consequences of long-term conflicts, accessibility of dirty weapons, state failures, climate change and scarcity of resources, International Humanitarian Law (IHL) has incorporated obligations (Mouratidi, 2022) related to the environment for ANSAs that control territory and wield de facto authority. In these territories, they exploit natural resources like oil, timber, or gems as a substitute for diminishing Cold War sponsorship, in certain instances, served as motivations for conflicts, influencing power strategies rooted in the commercialisation of armed conflict and the establishment of sovereignty around valuable resource areas and trading networks (Le Billon, 2001b).

According to the United Nations Environment Programme (UNEP), natural resources have been linked to at least 40% of intrastate conflicts in the past 60 years. Countries like the Democratic Republic of Congo, Côte d'Ivoire, Liberia, Sierra Leone, Angola, Somalia, Sudan, Indonesia, and Cambodia have all been affected by conflicts that are related to natural resources (UNEP, 2009; p.8-9).

As a contemporary example, in western Syria, over 36% of forested areas experienced the impact of unregulated logging and intense forest fires from 2018 to 2020, which resulted in the felling of nearly 60% of trees (PAX, 2023). Moreover, in places like Palmyra, over 52% of fruit trees were lost due to intense fighting between regime forces and armed groups (PAX, 2023).

Besides the exploitation of natural resources, the conduct of hostilities by using landmines,[6] and explosive weapons,[7] Particularly in urban areas, which are of notable concern for the environment. I.S., during its retreat from Iraq in 2016, set ablaze nineteen oil wells near Mosul, releasing vast toxic fumes that polluted the surrounding environment (BBC, 2016). Another example is Boko Haram, which has utilised Lake Chad's wetlands for shelter and launched attacks, thereby contaminating water sources like wells and streams (ICRC, 2011, p. 43A).

From the facts above, from a legal perspective, traditional human rights tools have been inadequate in protecting ecological balance and solving environmental problems. Therefore, multilateral environmental agreements, which find the legal expression of environmental rights at a universal level, aim to establish an international social order based on the collective right to life. The doctrine defined in the Handbook on International Rules Governing Military Operations published -and updated in 2020- by ICRC sheds light on their position regarding the environment, and even if the doctrine employed by ANSAs does not fully align with their legal obligations regarding the environment, it still provides an opportunity to initiate engagement with them. The doctrine prohibits direct targeting of the environment as "no part of the natural environment may be attacked unless it is a military objective (ICRC, 2011, n. 43. A)." Customary IHL Rule 43. C, based on the principle of "proportionality," prohibits launching attacks that may cause incidental environmental damage even during legitimate military operations. However, this rule obligates ANSAs to plan to conduct their attack and employ all the available means to minimise or lessen environmental damage. However, this raises serious questions regarding its practical applicability and effective control of this principle during an armed conflict.

Besides the regulation of means of warfare (the use of poisonous, biological, or chemical weapons (ICRC, 2011, n. 148), prohibitions on environmental damage during armed conflict extend to cases where it would effectively lead to the displacement of civilian populations. This underscores the recognition in international law that environmental harm, mainly if it results in the forced displacement of civilians, is not permissible during armed conflicts (ICRC, 2011, n. 164).

While International Human Rights Law's (IHRL) application in armed conflict is firmly established, whether and to what extent it is legally binding on ANSAs remains fiercely contested. Recent practices indicate a growing recognition that armed groups exercising territorial control and performing government-like functions incur responsibilities under IHRL. However, the precise legal parameters and obligations binding ANSAs under IHRL remain subject to ongoing debate and clarification within the international legal community (Rodenhäuser, 2018).

To sum up, at a minimum, ANSAs must operate within the frameworks in accordance with IHRL and International Environmental Law (IEL), serving as a supplementary framework to IHL rules. This integration is essential for enhancing environmental protection measures. State-like ANSAs are expected to conduct thorough environmental impact assessments of their activities to realise environmental and human rights. ANSAs that lack territorial control or possess limited control that does not enable them to safeguard and fulfil human rights are nonetheless expected to respect human rights. In such cases, these groups must abstain from violating human rights (Knox, 2018).

In their very nature, ANSAs can possess the potential for positive environmental outcomes through dedicated policies and practical initiatives. Particularly, ANSAs with explicitly articulated political goals, especially those intricately connected to specific territories and the natural environment—often observed in ethnic ANSAs—can establish institutions to manage the sustainable use of limited resources like water, forests, and wildlife.

The next part is detailed with concrete examples of how armed groups actively protect the environment, from wildlife conservation efforts to conflict-sensitive resource management.

How ANSAs Protect the Environment

As explained earlier, awareness of the links between climate change and security has increased radically due to the perception of threats. Despite the classification of the U.N., the E.U., and the G7, the links between climate change, conflict, and fragility are not simple and linear. Climate change is frequently perceived as a 'threat multiplier in contexts marked by fragility and the impact of conflicts.' This perception stems from its tendency to exacerbate challenges to international stability, manifesting through increased migration, conflicts over resources, and heightened recruitment efforts for non-state armed actors.

It is crucial to underscore that the motivations of armed groups are typically intricate and frequently influenced by political or military considerations. Information regarding the willingness of armed groups to support climate adaptation exhibits variability. Certain armed groups may acknowledge the necessity of safeguarding the environment or mitigating the adverse effects of climate change in areas under their influence or control. So, to analyse how ANSAs take a proactive stance against climate change or take an active role in protecting the environment, this study will use the identification of the Danish Institute for International Studies report in which Munive and Finn (2023) categorised them as *unintended forest protection*, *environmental protection for recruitment and legitimacy* and *environmental protection as political vision*.

Unintended Forest Protection

Unintended Forest Protection is about how the actions of ANSAs can inadvertently alleviate pressure on forest resources by rendering extensive areas inaccessible to national armies, settlers, or extraction companies. Despite some exceptions, non-state actors generally exhibit a tendency to safeguard and conserve the natural environment in the regions from which they originate and upon which they depend. The isolation of the companies contributes to an awareness of the limited and finite resources available to them, prompting a recognition of the costs associated with unsustainable exploitation.

In Columbia, Latin America's best-equipped insurgency group, the Revolutionary Armed Forces of Colombia (FARC), as a social revolutionary organisation with Marxist-Leninist ideological foundations, aimed to overthrow the government, which caused a 53-year civil war. In terms of environmental policy, the group ran roughshod over the environment in several ways, but it tended to restrict deforestation in the regions where it operated. It is stated that the reason for this policy is to prevent aerial surveillance by the state (Collins, 2023).

Environmental Protection for Recruitment and Legitimacy

The second category concerns certain ANSAs that have incorporated provisions for environmental protection within their doctrines. These provisions include a commitment to minimising the use of weapons or actions that could cause harm to the environment, thereby adhering to the principle of proportionality outlined in IHL. The 1995 ELN Code of War states a qualified obligation to minimise environmental damage during acts of sabotage, irrespective of their legal status. This echoes "feasible measures" provisions in IHL but notably excludes a specific threshold at which such actions would be outrightly prohibited. On the other side, although lacking a specific timeframe, the CNF Guidelines on the Code of War strongly advocate for avoiding weapons and technologies capable of inflicting long-term ecological devastation. While this directive solely addresses one of IHL's three cumulative threshold limits, its inspiration from the broader IHL framework is highly probable. The examples of the armed groups in this category are PYD (ANNS), HTS, ONLF, EMC, Taliban, and al-Shabaab.

During a period when the internal conflict was intensifying significantly, ISIS expanded its control, the Syrian government consistently lost territory to the opposition, and the PKK-affiliated PYD/YPG in Turkey began strengthening and taking control of the region, while the United States and Russia were still in the indirect intervention phase. The Kurdish Autonomous Administration of North-East Syria declared an "eco-socialist" initiative that aligns with the Charter of the Social Contract and is centred on the Environmental Protection Law issued by the Autonomous Administration in July 2022. This mentality dictates the complete prohibition of incendiary weapons, including napalm, lava, and phosphorus. This proscription encompasses weapons capable of inflicting undue ecological devastation or jeopardising the delicate balance of life among humans, plants, and animals. The administration also prohibited timbering, harvesting and arbitrary grazing in the forest areas. It compels financial penalties for those who breach it (al-Jeratli et al., 2024).

On the other side, in the Northern side of Syria, the Ministry of Agriculture and Irrigation in the Salvation Government, established by the initiative of Hayat Tahrir al-sham (HTS), enacted State Property Law No. 35 in 2020. It is to protect forests and forested areas, and by virtue of the law, cutting and grazing, ploughing, and planting these areas or urban expansion by the locals were prohibited with the inspection of the Department for Forestry and Forestry Stations. The administration also launched "an afforestation campaign that included planting 2,112 trees in al-Atareb, Sarmada, Harem, Kafr Takharim, Idlib, Ariha, and Jisr al-Shughour, while in the next phase, it plans to activate a nursery for the production of forest seedlings (al-Jeratli et al., 2024)."

The Ogaden National Liberation Front (ONLF) in Ethiopia advocated for self-determination until the peace accords 2018 and exhibited a robust ideological stance toward environmental protection.[8] With self-determination aspirations, the armed group actively opposed oil exploitation and perceived intrusions that detrimentally affected grazing lands (Abdullahi, 2007). Highlighting their commitment to protecting the environment, the ONLF pledged to confront all initiatives with negative environmental consequences as a national duty.

The other armed group is known as Estado Mayor Central (EMC), led by a FARC commander named Ivan Mordisco since 2016. EMC began to expand in power and territory. The group issued a communique on May 15, 2022, from large swaths of Amazonian regions under its control, presenting a "Manual of Coexistence." In this announcement, the group declared a fine of 1 million pesos (approximately US$250) for every hectare (2.47 acres) of forest cleared. Additionally, the communication prohibited the sale of uncultivated land without explicit permission from its leadership. (Collins, 2023).

Islamist Non-State Armed Groups operating in regions susceptible to climate change and desertification utilise environmental narratives for recruitment and to establish legitimacy. These groups often attribute environmental degradation to the West and may implement reforestation initiatives, as seen with the Taliban (BBC News, 2017). In Somalia, al-Shabaab has banned plastic bags, which are particularly harmful in the pastoral areas where the group garners support. It also fines individuals $1,500 for cutting down trees, which makes deforestation too costly to pursue (Brennan, 2018). That said, it is essential to emphasise that armed group motives are typically complex and often politically or militarily influenced—for example, tree cover shields al-Shabaab fighters from detection and airstrikes. In essence, the Code encourages environmental awareness and prioritises minimising collateral harm to the ecosystem, even within the context of potentially unlawful actions (Noriega, 2023).

Environmental Protection as a Political Vision

The last category defines the armed groups that have developed political visions that centre on environmental protection. The armed groups in this category include KNU, ULMWP, LTTE, NDFB, SPLM, MNLA, MEND and EZLN.

Myanmar has the largest forest area in mainland Southeast Asia, but its forest area decreased from 60% in 1990 to 43% by 2020 (Gupta, 2023). However, a militant separatist group, the Karen National Liberation Army, is serious about protecting the natural environment. The Karen National Union (KNU), recognised as Myanmar's oldest ethnic armed organisation, has substantial expertise in natural resource management, implementing its policies and departments for land, forestry, and the environment (Htoo et al., 2023; Prescott et al., 2017). The KNU, in collaboration with civil society organisations and communities, conducts environmental protection based on customary practices and the concept of indigenous sovereignty within KNU-controlled territories. Notably, the KNU has engaged with international NGOs like the Worldwide Fund for Nature (WWF) to "cooperate on projects to enhance forestry conservation, build the capacity of forest rangers, raise awareness amongst residents, hold workshops and conduct research in the forests (KIC, 2016)" efforts before the 2021 military coup.

West Papua constitutes half of the island of New Guinea – which hosts the world's third-largest rainforest. Since the 1960s, the indigenous inhabitants of West Papua have been under a harsh military occupation imposed by Indonesia. Extractive industries under the administration of Indonesia caused deforestation, pollution and human rights abuses. Due to the developments, the United Liberation Movement for West Papua (ULMWP) was formed, and political independence for Western New Guinea (West Papua) was sought from Indonesia. Moreover, indigenous peoples of West Papua formed their united government-in-waiting, and ULMWP has decided to take more proactive environmental action and published a statement presenting its Green State Vision at Glasgow at the COP26: "This Vision is our offer to the world. We have the just solution to the global climate crisis. My people have looked after New Guinea's green land for thousands of years. Our rainforests are the world's lungs, and we are its best guardians. The Indonesian government and multinational corporations are destroying our forest and killing our people... The Green State Vision[9] means peace, it means self-determination and independence. It means life and the preservation of survival of beings… If we become independent, we make these promises to the world. The newly independent government will immediately introduce an international ecocide standard into our country's legal framework (Chivers, 2021; Early, 2021)."

In the Philippines, an archipelagic country in Southeast Asia, the government is unable to control and develop large parts of the country due to a longstanding insurgency that has strong roots in the different regions. New People's Army (NPA), a rural-based guerrilla group and the military wing of the Communist Party of the Philippines- and the National Democratic Front of the Philippines - the umbrella group representing the rebels- declared that "environmentally destructive operations of big business and multinational corporations make them valid military targets." Moreover, Madlos, spokesperson of the NDF in Mindanao, added that "banning, disabling and dismantling these large, environmentally-destructive operations are still the best ways we could avert the disastrous impact on people's lives and livelihood of calamities such as this… and prevention is still better than curing the aftermath damages of these calamities (Ellorin, 2011)."

On the other hand, The Liberation Tigers of Tamil Eelam (LTTE) in Sri Lanka, while primarily known for their armed conflict, also implemented some measures related to environmental conservation in the areas under their control. They imposed restrictions on logging and engaged in reforestation efforts.

In Assam, India, the National Democratic Front of Bodoland (NDFB) has advocated a protracted conflict for an independent Boroland homeland for the Bodo people. Through seeking autonomy, their actions against illegal logging in Bodo areas picture a concern for environmental issues (B. R. J. Rubin, 2008).

On the other side of the world, the various armed forces across Sudan have been implicated in cases of "ivory poaching and trafficking, commercial bushmeat poaching and trafficking, illegal logging, gold mining and charcoal production. As they declared in their 1991 resolution, Sudan People's Liberation Movement (SPLM), a Sudanese national movement that seeks to change the policies of the centre, declared "shall do everything to…protect and develop [our wildlife resources] for us and posterity." Through this policy, they declared to safeguard and cultivate the region's wildlife resources for future generations.

The National Movement for the Liberation of Azawad (LIBYA) (Mouvement National de Libération de l'Azawad, MNLA) has demonstrated a positive step in safeguarding the environment during armed conflict. Stipulated in their "Organic Text for the Organization and Regulation of MNLA Armed Forces" explicitly mandates regional commanders and senior officers to uphold IHL during military operations, emphasising a specific mention of environmental protection (Gordon, 2022b).

The Niger Delta, a region abundant in oil, is presently grappling with multiple security challenges. A decentralised armed group, the Movement for the Emancipation of the Niger Delta (MEND), targeted the oil and gas infrastructure of the oil corporations in partnership with

the federal government. The MEND exemplifies the resource curse phenomenon and violent conflicts in developing nations. Using methods including kidnapping oil workers, assaults on production sites and pipeline destruction, besides attacking Niger security personnel. Similarly, the campaign against copper mining in Bougainville, Papua New Guinea, in the late 1980s was fuelled by a combination of concerns regarding profit control and resentment over environmental degradation (Gordon, 2022b).

Again, on the other side of the world, in Mexico, the Zapatista Army of National Liberation (EZLN) revolted in a region of Chiapas and fought for Land and Liberty. Besides its religious and ethnic overlays, the movement was essentially an ecological struggle. The armed group seeks the protection of tropical forests and to save the benefits of Chiapas rather than giving to other regions of Mexico (Nations, 2010).

This modest preliminary study highlights the diverse environmental approaches adopted by ANSAs. Their approaches are shaped by factors such as military might, territorial control and resource wealth within it, geographic location, political ideology, organisational structure and governance skills, as well as external rivalries. As it demonstrates, a standardised method lacks; however, a shared focus on "Restrict Deforestation", "Taking Declared Actions", and "Raising Awareness" stands out. Interestingly, these armed groups demonstrate, at times, a state-like ability to make environmental decisions.

Figure 3. Policies of ANSAs RD

	FARC	ELF	AANS	HTS	ONLF	EMC	Taliban	Al-Shabaab	KNU	ULMWP	NPA	LTTE	NDFB	SPLM	MNLA	MEND	EZLN
RD	*	*	*	*	*	*	*	*		*	*	*	*	*	*		*
RA			*	*	*	*	*	*	*	*	*	*	*	*	*	*	*
SIL				*	*				*	*	*	*	*	*			*
SMO					*						*					*	
CMUW		*	*							*				*	*		
TDA	*	*	*	*	*	*	*	*	*	*	*	*	*	*	*	*	*
FP			*			*		*									
PLS						*											*
R			*	*			*					*		*			*
POM			*					*		*							
IR			*	*	*	*		*	*	*	*	*	*	*	*		*
CCS									*	*							
SEO		*	*	*	*						*			*	*		
IHL															*		

CONCLUSION

This study aimed to examine the climate-related position from the perspective of Armed Non-State Actors/Groups. However, we know relatively little about what position armed non-state actors take place in climate change and its environmental effects. In regions where state authority is weak or absent, these armed groups create new forms of governance. Globalisation processes have rendered these armed actors an integral part of global governance. As a result, growing numbers of armed actors participate actively in different steering activities, such as healthcare, schooling, trade, peacebuilding, justice, and law-making. However, more information is needed regarding the environmental attitudes of ANSAs in various contexts. As the previous chapters presented, armed groups are responsible for destroying environmental resources, hindering adaptation efforts, and undertaking various measures—intentional or unintentional—that worsen the impact of climate change. Armed groups active in Afghanistan, Colombia, Ethiopia, Iraq, Mali, Myanmar, Somalia, and Syria revealed predominantly adverse outcomes in terms of their environmental impact.

The state (or governments) needs more commitments concerning climate change and its ferocious effects. In this process, the inadequacies arising from the matter concerning states and the international community have given rise to problems related to international law. Additionally, the impact of climate change on human rights debates has introduced a new dimension, highlighting the need for a climate change governance model. Governance is a concept that finds its roots in the beginning of humanity and throughout different eras, and humanity has established governance systems based on their respective periods and conditions. Because of this fact, with the advancement of political, economic, social and legal changes driven by the winds of globalisation, non-state actors are expected to play a predominant role. However, they have represented a challenge to state power.

This study conceptualises armed groups as autonomous agents with sufficient authority that is capable of influencing the course of events. As exemplified in Table 1, ANSAs have proactively implemented various autonomous environmental policies. Additionally, certain groups have initiated and are in the process of enhancing their measures to protect the environment depending on their political goals. Accordingly, many armed groups --aspiring to achieve statehood or other forms of legitimacy-- attempt to adhere to international norms to gain positive international recognition. The designed model in Figure 2 indicates the sum of this study, encompassing the activities of the state, International Organizations, Non-governmental Organizations and Armed Non-State Actors. As explained, when considering approximately 200 million individuals reside in regions governed by armed groups, collaborating with these armed groups on issues of climate adaptation, climate change, and environmental degradation efforts could yield profound impacts.

This issue may become an opportunity for international interaction with ANSAs regarding environmental issues, and the newly introduced U.N. Principles for the Protection of the Environment in Relation to Armed Conflict offer a framework for such engagement. Previous humanitarian engagements with ANSAs indicate their responsiveness to adopting international norms, such as the landmine ban. States may be hesitant to enter into treaties with ANSAs due to concerns about recognition, but positive experiences have been observed with unilateral declarations by ANSAs.

However, it has its practical and ethical dilemmas. First of all, in instances where ANSAs incorporate principles of any international laws into their doctrines and commit to fulfilling responsibilities like conducting environmental impact assessments, it raises the question of whether it should be assumed that all ANSAs can and should follow suit. The lack of authority that may enforce these obligations lets armed groups take a different level of interaction, knowing well enough that they will not be held accountable. Secondly, engaging politically with armed groups might confer legitimacy or recognition concerning the state-based international system. Alternatively, it could be grouped that might manipulate the recruitment of Nel. Thirdly, it is not logical to expect much more involvement from armed groups that need more technical capacity to comprehend the ecological complexities and financial adequacy. Fourthly, most states have laws that prevent the collaboration of states with these groups. Lastly, despite their initiatives in terms of forest protection, the same group may continue timbering as NDFB, MEND, and NPA do. Alternatively, The Democratic Union Party (PYD) in Syria, which has been trying to portray itself as a legitimate actor on the international stage, and the Kurdistan Workers' Party (PKK), which has been operating in Turkey for many years, have been responsible for many forest fires in recent years.

Still, when viewed positively, climate change governance is multi-stakeholder and multi-level. Different actors are involved in the global, national, and local process. Of course, different actors at different levels have different interests. Governance is used as a tool to manage these differences and reach a consensus basis. However, when the current contributions of NGOs and I.O., which were once opposed to the process, are evaluated, the positive or negative contribution of ANSAs can also be understood over time. Of course, the most crucial obstacle blocking the process is not internalising governance and participation. Therefore, willingness is the precondition for climate change governance to be realised at all levels. Lastly, as initiatives gather momentum towards policy-based resolutions to enhance environmental safeguards before /during and after the armed conflict, the emphasis on participatory engagement becomes a compelling argument for the inclusion of ANSAs. A deeper understanding of these organisations may contribute to developing international engagement strategies concerning environmental issues during and after armed conflicts.

REFERENCES

Abdullahi, A. M. (2007). The Ogaden National Liberation Front (ONLF): The Dilemma of Its Struggle in Ethiopia. *Review of African Political Economy*, *34*(113), 556–562. https://www.jstor.org/stable/20406430

al-Jeratli, K., Fansa, M., & Khattab, B. (2024, January 19). *Who stops the destruction of vegetation in Syria?* Enab Baladi. https://english.enabbaladi.net/archives/2024/01/who-stops-the-destruction-of-vegetation-in-syria/

Andonova, L. B., Betsill, M. M., & Bulkeley, H. (2009). Transnational climate governance. *Global Environmental Politics*, *9*(2), 52–73. doi:10.1162/glep.2009.9.2.52

Arjona, A., Kasfir, N., & Mampilly, Z. (2015). Rebel governance in civil war. In *Rebel Governance in Civil War*. Cambridge University Press., doi:10.1017/CBO9781316182468.009

Bartolini, G. P. M. (2016a, November). *The work of the ILC on the environment and armed conflicts: Enhancing protection for the 'silent victim of warfare'?* Questions of International Law.

BBC. (2016). *I.S. oil wells set on fire as Iraqi troops approach Mosul - BBC News*. BBC News. https://www.bbc.com/news/av/world-middle-east-37891389

BBCNews. (2017). *Taliban leader urges Afghans to plant more trees*. BBC. https://www.bbc.com/news/world-asia-39094578

Benedict, K. (2001). Global Governance. In N. J. Smelser & P. B. Baltes (Eds.), *International Encyclopedia of the Social & Behavioral Sciences* (pp. 6232–6237). Pergamon. doi:10.1016/B0-08-043076-7/04499-5

Bojicic, V., Turkmani, D., & Turkmani, R. (2018). War economy, governance and security in Syria's opposition-controlled areas. *Stability*, *7*(1), 1–17.

Brennan, D. (2018). *Al-Shabab Bans Plastic Bags to Protect People and Livestock*. Newsweek.

Bruch, C., Jensen, D., Nakayama, M., & Unruh, J. (2019).. . *The Changing Nature of Conflict, Peacebuilding, and Environmental Cooperation.*, *49*, 10134–10154.

Burniske, J. S., Modirzadeh, N. K., & Lewis, D. A. (2017). *Armed Non-State Actors and International Human Rights Law: An Analysis of the Practice of the U.N. Security Council and U.N. General Assembly*. Research Gate.

Carey, S. C., Mitchell, N. J., & Lowe, W. (2013). States, the security sector, and the monopoly of violence: A new database on pro-government militias. *Journal of Peace Research*, *50*(2), 249–258. doi:10.1177/0022343312464881

Chivers, D. (2021). *West Papua: A Green State Vision*. New Internationalist. https://newint.org/features/2021/11/04/west-papua-green-state-vision-cop26

Collins, J. (2023). Armed Groups as Forest Protectors in Colombia: A Risky Dynamic. *Sierra*.

de Coninck, H., Fischer, C., Newell, R. G., & Ueno, T. (2008). International technology-oriented agreements to address climate change. *Energy Policy*, *36*(1), 335–356. doi:10.1016/j.enpol.2007.09.030

Drexhage, J. (2008). *Global Environmental Governance (GEG) Briefing Paper # 2*. GEG.

Early, C. (2021). *Indigenous leaders' green state vision*. Ecologist. https://theecologist.org/2021/nov/08/indigenous-leaders-green-state-vision

Eleftheriadou, M. (2020). Fragmentation and Cooperation in the Jihadi International (Sub)System: 'Islamic State' vs. Al-Qaeda and Beyond. *Religions*, *11*(4), 168. doi:10.3390/rel11040168

Ellorin, B. (2011). *Big business into environmental destruction valid NPA targets*. Minda News.

EPL. (2023). *The Environment Is A Silent Victim Of The War In Ukraine Without Effective Legal Protection Mechanisms*. EPL.

Feliciano, D., Recha, J., Ambaw, G., MacSween, K., Solomon, D., & Wollenberg, E. (2022). Assessment of agricultural emissions, climate change mitigation and adaptation practices in Ethiopia. *Climate Policy*, *22*(4), 427–444. doi:10.1080/14693062.2022.2028597

Ferrer, M. C. R.-D. E. (2000). *Engaging Non-State Actors in a Landmine Ban, A Pioneering Conference*. ICBL. Www.Icbl.Org/Wg/Nsa

Fischer, C., Torvanger, A., Shrivastava, M. K., Sterner, T., & Stigson, P. (2012). How should support for climate-friendly technologies be designed? *Ambio*, *41*(S1, SUPPL.1), 33–45. doi:10.1007/s13280-011-0239-0 PMID:22314855

Fortin, K. (2015). *Education and Non-State Actors: Towards a Comprehensive Agenda*. Armed Groups and International Law. https://armedgroups-internationallaw.org/2015/09/30/education-and-non-state-actors-towards-a-comprehensive-agenda/

Furlan, M. (2020). Understanding Governance by Insurgent Non-State Actors : A Multi-Dimensional Typology Understanding Governance by Insurgent Non-State. *Civil Wars*, *00*(00), 1–34.

Gates, S., & Nordås, R. (2015). *Recruitment*. Retention, and Religion in Rebel Groups.

Gordon, N. (2022a, November 14). *How Climate Change Helps Violent Non-state Actors*. Carnegie Endowment for International Peace.

Gupta, J. (2023). *Interview: Myanmar insurgent groups key to forest and climate protection*. The Third Pole. https://www.thethirdpole.net/en/nature/interview-myanmar-insurgent-groups-key-to-forest-and-climate-protection/

Holmqvist, C. (2005). Engaging Armed Non-State Actors in Post-Conflict Settings. In A. Bryden & H. Hänggi (Eds.), Security Governance in Post-Conflict Peacebuilding. Geneva Centre for the Democratic Control of Armed Forces (DCAF).

Htoo, M. H. C., Steenhuisen, B., & Verschuuren, B. (2023). What Karen Perceptions of Forest Reveal about Nature Conservation in Indigenous Contexts. *Conservation & Society*, *21*(1), 28–37. https://www.jstor.org/stable/27206657. doi:10.4103/cs.cs_83_21

Huang, R., & Sullivan, P. L. (2020). Arms for education? External support and rebel social services. *Journal of Peace Research*, *20*(10), 1–15. doi:10.1177/0022343320940749

ICRC. (2011). *Strengthening legal protection for victims of armed conflicts*. ICRC.

Ide, T., Bruch, C., Carius, A., Conca, K., Dabelko, G. D., Matthew, R., & Weinthal, E. (2021). The past and future(s) of environmental peacebuilding. *International Affairs*, *97*(1), 1–16. doi:10.1093/ia/iiaa177

Jabareen, Y. (2015). The emerging Islamic State: Terror, territoriality, and the agenda of social transformation. In *Geoforum* (Vol. 58, pp. 51–55). Elsevier Ltd., doi:10.1016/j.geoforum.2014.10.009

Johnson, M. F., Ide, T., & Gonzalez Cruz, J. (2023). Conceptualising resilience within environmental peacebuilding. *Current Opinion in Environmental Sustainability*, *65*, 101362. doi:10.1016/j.cosust.2023.101362

Kasfir, N., Frerks, G., & Terpstra, N. (2018). Introduction: Armed Groups and Multi-layered Governance. In Civil Wars, 19(3), 257–278). Routledge. doi:10.1080/13698249.2017.1419611

KIC. (2016, October 11). *KNU and WWF sign the Environmental Conservation MOU*. Burma News International. https://www.bnionline.net/en/news/karen-state/item/2488-knu-and-wwf-sign-environmental-conservation-mou.html

Knox, J. (2018). *Report of the Special Rapporteur on the issue of human rights obligations relating to the enjoyment of a safe, clean, healthy and sustainable environment (A/HRC/31/53)* [Dataset]. Environmental Rights Database. www.environmentalrightsdatabase.org,

Le Billon, P. (2001a). The political ecology of war: Natural resources and armed conflicts. *Political Geography*, *20*(5), 561–584. doi:10.1016/S0962-6298(01)00015-4

Lenschow, A., Newig, J., & Challies, E. (2016). Globalisation's limits to the environmental state? Integrating telecoupling into global environmental governance. *Environmental Politics*, *25*(1), 136–159. doi:10.1080/09644016.2015.1074384

Lenshie, N. E., Okengwu, K., Ogbonna, C. N., & Ezeibe, C. (2021). Desertification, migration, and herder-farmer conflicts in Nigeria: rethinking the ungoverned spaces thesis. *Small Wars and Insurgencies, 32*(8), 1221–1251. doi:10.1080/09592318.2020.1811602

Lietzman, M. (1999). *Environment and Security in an International Context*.

Lillywhite, L. (2015). *Non-State Armed Groups, Health and Healthcare*. Chatam House. https://www.chathamhouse.org/sites/default/files/events/special/NSAGs Meeting Summary in the template - final edit from Jo - E.R.- PKA 27.10.15.pdf

Lochard, I. V. (2008). Understanding the Nexus of Governance, Intrastate Conflict and Non-State Armed Groups: Implications for Peace and Security in the Twenty-First Century. [Thesis, The Fletcher School of Law and Diplomacy].

Loyle, C. E., Cunningham, K. G., Huang, R., & Jung, D. F. (2021). New Directions in Rebel Governance Research. *Perspectives on Politics*, 1–13. doi:10.1017/S1537592721001985

McCullough, A. (2015). *The Legitimacy of States and Armed Non-State Actors*. GSDRC. www.gsdrc.org

Medina, L., Ensor, M. O., Schapendonk, F., Sieber, S., Pacillo, G., Laderach, P., Hellin, J., & Bonatti, M. (2023). Community voices on climate, peace and security: A social learning approach to programming environmental peacebuilding. *Environment and Security*.

Mia, I. (2023). *The Armed Conflict Survey*.

Mouratidi, Y. (2022, April 25). *Let us talk about policy: non-state armed groups and international environmental law*. Armed Groups and International Law.

Munive, J. S. F. (2023a). *How non-state armed groups engage in environmental protection*. Research Gate.

Munive, J. S. F. (2023b). *How non-state armed groups engage in environmental protection*. DIIS.

Nations, J. (2010). *The Ecology of the Zapatista Revolt*. Cultural Survival. https://www.culturalsurvival.org/publications/cultural-survival-quarterly/ecology-zapatista-revolt

Noriega, C. (2023, August 23). *The secret to Colombia's drop in deforestation?* Al Jazeera. https://www.aljazeera.com/news/2023/8/22/the-secret-to-colombias-drop-in-deforestation-armed-groups

NUI. (2021). *Climate*. Peace and Security Fact Sheet.

Pandey, C. (2015). Managing Climate Change: Shifting Roles for NGOs in the Climate Negotiations. In Environmental Values (6th ed., pp. 799–824). White Horse Press.

Pattberg, P., Kaiser, C., Widerberg, O., & Stripple, J. (2022). 20 Years of global climate change governance research: taking stock and moving forward. *International Environmental Agreements: Politics, Law and Economics, 22*(2), 295–315. doi:10.1007/s10784-022-09568-5

Paul, C. J., & Weinthal, E. (2019). The development of Ethiopia's Climate Resilient Green Economy 2011–2014: Implications for rural adaptation. *Climate and Development*, *11*(3), 193–202. doi:10.1080/17565529.2018.1442802

PAX. (2023). *Axed and Burned: How Conflict-caused Deforestation Impacts Environmental, Socio-economic and Climate Resilience in Syria - Syrian Arab Republic*. PAX.

Pegg, S. (1998). *International society and the de facto state*. Routledge.

Peters, G. (2010). *Governing in the Shadows*.

Pham, J. P. (2011). State collapse, insurgency, and famine in the Horn of Africa: Legitimacy and the ongoing Somali crisis. *Journal of the Middle East and Africa*, *2*(2), 153–187. doi:10.1080/21520844.2011.617238

Phillips, B. J. (2009). *How Terrorist Organizations Survive: Cooperation And Competition In Terrorist Group Networks.* Research Gate.

Phillips, B. J. (2014). Terrorist group cooperation and longevity. *International Studies Quarterly, 58*(2), 336–347. doi:10.1111/isqu.12073

Podder, S. (2013). Non-State Armed Groups and Stability: Reconsidering Legitimacy and Inclusion. *Contemporary Security Policy, 34*(1), 16–39. doi:10.1080/13523260.2013.771029

Podder, S. (2014). Mainstreaming the non-state in bottom-up state-building: Linkages between rebel governance and post-conflict legitimacy. *Conflict Security and Development, 14*(2), 213–243. doi:10.1080/14678802.2014.889878

Prescott, G. W. Sutherland (2017). Political transition and emergent forest-conservation issues in Myanmar. *Conservation Biology, 31*(6), 1257–1270. https://www.jstor.org/stable/44973665

Rapoport, D. C. (1992). "Terrorism," in Encyclopedia of Government and Politics (M. H. and M. Kogan, Ed.). Routledge.

ReliefWeb. (2014). *Islamic law and the rules of war.* ReliefWeb. https://reliefweb.int/report/world/islamic-law-and-rules-war

Repez, F., & Atanasiu, M. (2020). The Environment - a "Silent Victim" of Armed Conflicts: Array. *Acta Universitatis Danubius. Relations Internationales, 12*(2). https://dj.univ-danubius.ro/index.php/AUDRI/article/view/45

Rödder, S. (2020). The ambivalent role of environmental NGOs in climate communication. *JCOM, Journal of Science Communication, 19*(6), C03. doi:10.22323/2.19060303

Rodenhäuser, T. (2018). *Organising rebellion: Non-state armed groups under international humanitarian, human rights, and international criminal laws.* Oxford University. doi:10.1093/oso/9780198821946.001.0001

Ross, M. L. (2004a). How Do Natural Resources Influence Civil War? Evidence from Thirteen Cases. *International Organization, 58*(1). doi:10.1017/S002081830458102X

Ross, M. L. (2004b). What Do We Know about Natural Resources and Civil War? *Journal of Peace Research, 41*(3), 337–356. doi:10.1177/0022343304043773

Rubin, B. R. J. (2008). *Chronologies of modern terrorism* (1st ed., Vol. 1). M.E. Sharpe.

Rubin, M. A. (2019). Rebel Territorial Control and Civilian Collective Action in Civil War: Evidence from the Communist Insurgency in the Philippines. *The Journal of Conflict Resolution, 64*(2–3), 459–489.

Schlichte, K. (2009). *In the Shadow of Violence: The Politics of Armed Groups.* Campus Verlag.

Stanislawski, B. H. (2008). Para-States, Quasi-States, and Black Spots: Perhaps Not States, But Not "Ungoverned Territories," Either. *International Studies Review, 10*(2), 366–396. doi:10.1111/j.1468-2486.2008.00795.x

Stranadko, N. (2022). Global climate governance: Rising trend of translational cooperation. *International Environmental Agreement: Politics, Law and Economics, 22*(4), 639–657. doi:10.1007/s10784-022-09575-6 PMID:35370522

Terpstra, N., & Frerks, G. (2017). Rebel Governance and Legitimacy: Understanding the Impact of Rebel Legitimation on Civilian Compliance with the LTTE Rule. *Civil Wars, 19*(3), 279–307. doi:10.1080/13698249.2017.1393265

Theohary, C. A., & Rollins, J. (2011). *Terrorist Use of the Internet: Information Operations in Cyberspace*. CRS. www.crs.gov

Thomas, T. K. S. C. W. (2005). *Warlords Rising: Confronting Violent Non-State Actors*. Lexington Books.

UN. (2021, February 10). *ISIL Must Be Defeated in Cyberspace, Under-Secretary-General Tells Security Council, as Terrorist Group Takes Advantage of Pandemic-Related Disruptions*. U.N. Meetings Coverage and Press Releases. https://www.un.org/press/en/2021/sc14433.doc.htm

UNEP. (2009). *Protecting the Environment During Armed Conflict An Inventory and Analysis of International Law United Nations Environment Programme*. UNEP. https://www.unep.org/conflictsanddisasters

Vinci, A. (2007). "Like worms in the entrails of a natural man": A conceptual analysis of warlords. *Review of African Political Economy, 34*(112), 313–331. doi:10.1080/03056240701449711

Walch, C. (2018). Weakened by the storm: Rebel group recruitment in the wake of natural disasters in the Philippines. *Journal of Peace Research, 55*(3), 336–350. doi:10.1177/0022343317741535

Weinstein, J. (2003). *Inside Rebellion: The Political Economy of Rebel Organization*. Harvard University.

Young, O. (1997). *Global Governance*. MIT Press. https://mitpress.mit.edu/9780262740203/global-governance/

ZELIN. A. Y. (2016). The Islamic State's Territorial Methodology. The Washington Institute for Near East Policy, 29.

Zhukov, Y. M. (2012). Roads and the diffusion of insurgent violence. The logistics of conflict in Russia's North Caucasus. *Political Geography, 31*(3), 144–156. doi:10.1016/j.polgeo.2011.12.002

Zürn, M. (2010). *Handbook on Multi-level Governance. Global governance is multi-level governance*. Edward Elgar Publishing Limited.

Zürn, M. (2018). Contested Global Governance. *Global Policy, 9*(1), 138–145. doi:10.1111/1758-5899.12521

ENDNOTES

1 COP3, held in Kyoto, Japan, led to the formation of the Kyoto Protocol due to global cooperation in the fight against climate change. The Kyoto Protocol, adopted as a part of the United Nations Framework Convention on Climate Change (UNFCCC), is an international document that aims to

reduce greenhouse gases. The implementation rules of the protocol were accepted at COP7, which was held in Marrakesh and entered into force in 2005. The protocol is based on the principle of common but differentiated responsibilities. The Kyoto Protocol attempted to clarify the obligations of developed and developing countries.

2 Within this framework, the absence of a compelling state capability of governance (state collapse or decay) or being partially deprived of its governing capabilities (state failure or weakness) leads to many unlawful entities/actors within the state.

3 For more information, please visit https://ceobs.org/perac-principles-frequently-asked-questions/

4 They are also called non-state armed groups or armed groups, and they are used interchangeably in this study.

5 To see the report, please follow the link: http://www.diag.gov.af/diagproject.

6 They cause environmental degradation, including soil degradation, deforestation, and the pollution of water resources with heavy metals. Moreover, the extensive use of explosive weapons has the potential to bring about significant alterations to entire species' populations by degrading habitats and disrupting food chains.

7 According to the report "Action on Armed Violence", explosive weapons were used by 44 distinct non-state actors in 2019.

8 Click the link to reach the declaration: http://theirwords.org/media/transfer/doc/et_onlf_02-3c7a7281a188e37a9c88003e82188845.pdf.

9 Please find the complete statement https://www.ulmwp.org/benny-wenda-green-state-vision-our-pathway-to-saving-worlds-third-largest-rain-forest

Chapter 12
How the Productivist Welfare System Frames the Risks of Ageing During the COVID-19 Pandemic:
Insights From the Four Asian Tigers

Tauchid Komara Yuda
Department of Social Development and Welfare, Universitas Gadjah Mada, Indonesia

Zhen Tian
School of Graduate Studies, Lingnan University, Hong Kong

Zhiming Hu
Department of Sociology and Social Policy, Lingnan University, Hong Kong

ABSTRACT

COVID-19 presents a systemic social risk for the East Asian welfare system. This chapter focuses on global shocks and its policy responses targeted at older residents, which are East Asia's most pressing social policy issues before and during the COVID-19 pandemic. This review reveals that Taiwan and South Korea seem to combine the developmental-universalist and social democratic welfare state models, whereas Hong Kong and Singapore have followed a typical mix of development-universalist and facilitative approaches. Overall, they have successfully transitioned from an economic-driven preference to a more balanced protective-productive feature, but they have done so through multiple pathways, with the market-conforming role of social policy for the elderly remaining dominant. This study responds to the current debate on policy continuity and adaptation in East Asia and suggests a new perspective.

DOI: 10.4018/979-8-3693-1742-6.ch012

INTRODUCTION

In recent decades, newly industrialised East Asian countries have adopted a productivism strategy for social service provision. The productivism welfare principle under authoritarian governments combines growth-oriented policies and limited social rights to maintain human productivity with a representational character in which welfare policies are subordinated to economic development and employment maintenance (Holliday, 2000; Holliday & Wilding, 2003). As the 21st century began, socio-demographic shifts and "compressed modernity" changes posed new challenges to East Asia's productivism welfare state (Hudson et al., 2014). The context of political and economic change has, most notably, caused a social imbalance (Raymo et al., 2015). The support for unproductive groups, notably the growing older population, poses new challenges for the productivism welfare arrangements (Wen et al., 2021; Yeung & Thang, 2018).

Consequently, social policies in East Asian societies have undergone extensive reforms. On the one hand, regions, such as Taiwan and Mainland China, have intensified government intervention in unproductive populations through universal and redistributive policies (Fleckenstein & Lee, 2017), making them comparable to European welfare states (Abrahamson, 2017; Lin & Wong, 2013). On the other hand, structural changes and policy expansion did not produce significant regime changes. Rather, a large number of publications stated that the East Asia's welfare system remains to demonstrate a higher degree of continuity in productivism features (e.g. Ahn & Lee, 2012; Choi, 2012; Hwang, 2012; Yang, 2014; Yang & Kühner, 2020). This argument is parallel to the fact that the market-conforming policy approach—e.g., promoting active labour market policies, productive ageing programs, and other social investment policies—endures in Hong Kong, Singapore, and South Korea (Kim, 2020; Lai & Chui, 2014; Mok, 2013).

The persistence of the coronavirus disease 2019 (COVID-19) pandemic poses a systemic social shock for the East Asian welfare regime, which prioritises social investment over social protection. Existing social policy research has focused more on how these risks have affected working-age and school-age groups. The risks associated with ageing populations and public safety nets for older adults, which are the most pressing social policy issues in East Asia prior to and during COVID-19, have been overlooked (Choi et al., 2022; Mok et al., 2021; Soon et al., 2021; Yuda et al., 2021; Wong & Ho, 2022). As Holliday (2000) argued, the main difference between pure forms of productivism welfare types is the extent to which social rights extend beyond the productive elements of society. Thus, more detailed policy responses towards the unproductive population is required for the analysis of welfare regime continuity and adaptation.

This study focuses on the global shocks towards the old-age population and the related policy responses. The authors first review the literature on the relation between social risks and old-age population to show why social risk is crucial for analysing policy consistency and welfare regime. This study then uses the cross-case qualitative analysis to address two research questions: (1) how are welfare policies updated or adjusted in response to COVID-19 risks; and (2) how this has affected the welfare regime consistency? Through the analysis, this article explores whether the "Four Asian Tigers" (Global-Is-Asian Staff, 2021), namely, Hong Kong, Singapore, South Korea, and Taiwan, prioritise the social investment principle during the COVID-19 pandemic or adopt a protection-oriented type of policy. This study contributes to the contentious terrain that justifies or refutes the transition arguments of productivist welfare states in the literature by illustrating the policy responses to dealing with COVID-19 challenges.

NEW CHALLENGE FOR WELFARE STATES UNDER COVID-19 SHOCKS

Individuals have always been vulnerable to the possibility of losing welfare benefits due to social and economic changes, which is referred to as social risk. Hence, one of the primary reasons for the existence of the welfare state is to manage individual vulnerability while pooling unpredictable market risks (Harris, 2012). The term "welfare state" normally refers to a formally recognised network of political and governing institutions that protects and promotes the economic and social well-being of the inhabitants of a confined territorial entity, typically a nation state (Cook & Titterton, 2023). Many scholars have been devoted to categorising modern welfare states, considering the trajectories of policy responses and adaptation to social risks.

As Esping-Andersen (1999) pointed out, certain risks persist throughout history, whereas others ebb and flow. In the period between 1945 and the mid-1970s, industrialized welfare states dealt with the risk of earning ability loss caused by old age, illnesses, or unemployment (Huber & Stephens, 2001; Goodin, 2003; Bonoli, 2007). The transition to a post-industrial society, as well as the emergence of globalization in the 1970s, had a substantial impact on the risk structures of the modern welfare state (Esping-Andersen, 1990; Taylor-Gooby, 2004; Emmenegger et al., 2012). A vulnerable population of low-skilled and low-educated workers, atypical employees, single parents, and seniors deprived of family care has emerged (Bonoli, 2007; Lewis, 2002; Taylor-Gooby, 2004). Subsequently, new social policies, such as active labour market policies and social support for care services, were introduced (Yuda, 2021). The COVID-19 pandemic has exacerbated existing social risks while also introducing new risks for old-age groups (Feng & Gu, 2023; Reich, 2020). In the setting of economic downturn, abrupt job loss, physical and psychological disorders, as well as rising digitalization and deglobalization, an unpredictable and newly created lifestyle is presenting far-reaching societal repercussions (Choi et al., 2022; Hall et al., 2021). Moreover, a large amount of evidence suggests that COVID-19 infection and mortality are primarily confined to fragile individuals who are in their later years, with nursing home residents without adequate support being particularly at risk (Cohen & Tavares, 2020; Comas-Herrera et al., 2020; Irving, 2020; Landi et al., 2020; Morley & Vellas, 2020). Moreover, the increased social isolation caused by the high risk of infection leads to fewer personal interactions with others, which negatively impacts the older population's psychological and physical health (HelpAge International, 2020). Hence, the population structure is crucial in determining the potential risks of COVID-19 to welfare states. Therefore, rethinking the previous optimism regarding the challenges of population ageing during new social risks is necessary (Harper, 2021).

Compared with the western world, the rapid growing older adults in East Asia rely more on their familial network, owing to a less generous welfare system, underdeveloped welfare institutions, and a filial piety culture that values family care for the elderly (Chou et al., 2013; Peng & Chien, 2018; Shaw et al., 2020). As a result, most older individuals in East Asia rely on informal employment and family assistance for financial sustainability. Consequently, the impact of the COVID-19 on East Asia's familistic welfare regime was particularly severe (Chou et al., 2013; Peng & Chien, 2018). Therefore, the conceptualization of social rights of the disadvantaged groups has an impact on the identification of social risks, which in turn facilitates in understanding the long-standing welfare typology debate. The recognition of emerging social risks and the structure of policies to address them reveals key structure of its welfare system and challenges the existing theories of welfare regime typologies.

Welfare Characteristics and Old-Age Supports in East Asian Societies

The ability of modern welfare states to adapt to social risks, as well as the typology debate, have been heatedly discussed in the literature. Since Esping-Anderson's three types of welfare states were introduced, researchers have widened the debate in recent decades. Nordic welfare states have typically offered substantial support to disadvantaged communities facing social risks. Whereas in many corporatist-conservative and Southern European welfare states, the welfare system prioritises the interests of the working population through collective provision, responding to non-breadwinners who confront social risks is particularly challenging. Under a liberal welfare state, social risks are carefully defined and the role of the state is constrained. The market is preferred as the source of welfare benefits. Meanwhile, a productivist welfare system was introduced in the late 20th century to promote the economic growth in newly industrialised Asian economies, including Hong Kong, Singapore, Taiwan, Japan, and South Korea (Yang and Kühner, 2020). Social rights are therefore minimal, and welfare programmes aim to boost productivity (Mok et al., 2020). The East Asian welfare characteristics was then summarised as follows: adopt an economic growth-oriented development policy strategy and ensure that all areas of social policy are designed to facilitate labour market operation with appropriately qualified workforce (Holliday, 2005; Wen et al., 2022;Wilding, 2008). Scholars (e.g., Holliday, 2000; Peng & Wong, 2008; Yang, 2017; Yang & Kühner, 2020) further identified subtypes based on different policy beneficiaries and focuses: Development-Universalists (e.g., Korea and Taiwan) support the market and family through childcare and activation policies to rebalance existing social structures and enhance workers' employability in the face of new risks; Developmental-Particularistic Model (e.g., Singapore) gives more weight to social protection for workers in the formal sector and government employees, as well as encourages the family play to a larger role in social welfare; the Facilitative Model (e.g., Hong Kong) operates with the lowest level of social provision and a market-oriented approach.

Following the discussion on welfare regime typology and features, it is typically believed that policy responses to new social risks would proceed along the same route as in the past welfare arrangement due to the path dependency effect (Pierson, 1996; Esping-Andersen, 2010, p12; Mei, 2020; Yang, 2017). For instance, the welfare states in Europe cut welfare provision and entered "permanent austerity" in order to address the new social risks that emerged after the 1980s. In which they privatised social services, deregulated labour markets, and withdrew government from social sectors (Bonoli, 2007). While Krause et al. (2023) observed that a considerable number of United States cities have given increased attention and prioritised policy dimensions to economic development. However, with newly emerging demographic and socioeconomic crises, current welfare states cannot be viewed as frozen landscapes or solely path dependent, but rather as patchworks of old and new policies and institutions (Peng & Wong, 2008; Hemerijck, 2012). Recent scholarships reveal a path-breaking tendency in the expansion of family policy, albeit in various ways in the UK, Germany, and the Netherlands (Fleckenstein & Seeleib-Kaiser, 2011; Yerkes, 2014). In response to the COVID-19 issue, Europe and Russia are likewise showing a path-departing tendency by raising social expenditure and expanding welfare benefits (Cook & Titterton, 2023). Moreover, previous policy measurements place a strong emphasis on cluster analysis of income-maintenance programmes such as pensions and social expenditure, which are basically passive programmes that make it difficult to capture the mutations and explain changes in welfare institutions (Esping-Andersen, 2010).

Meanwhile, the governments in the East Asian region appear to be shedding their reputations as "growth at any cost" productivism in the face of population ageing risks (Peng & Wong, 2004; Kwon,

2005). Hong Kong, Singapore, South Korea, and Taiwan, as symbols of Asia's economic progress miracle in the last century, are all experiencing higher rates of population ageing and severe global shocks during the past decades (Yeung & Lee, 2022). From the implementation of universal health care to new social policy innovations in long term care for the elderly and in family care, universalism social protection has begun to grow out of the post-war productivist state model (Wong, 2004; Wong, 2019). Therefore, some authors have characterised East Asian societies, particularly South Korea and Taiwan, as post-productivist. The two countries have effectively implemented a variety of protective measures mostly focusing on care assistance and income protection to become more inclusive for supporting older citizens (Choi, 2012). While Singapore and Hong Kong have followed a policy consistency by continuing to develop welfare in a particularistic/productivist manner. The implementation and expansion of old-age support policies were specifically restricted and insignificant in the two economies (Abrahamson, 2017). The majority of the policy support promoted employment opportunities for older persons in line with a self-empowerment and self-reliance ideology. And the varied basic social programs expansion has been proved less successful, compounding the impact of stigmatisation and increasing the extent of marginalisation (Kühner & Chou, 2019; Yip et al., 2020).

Notably, in productive-oriented East Asian welfare states, where the older population are among the most disadvantaged groups, old-age security is still a significant problem. Due to the lack of adequate social protection and highly reliance on paid labour, the older individuals in East Asia were more vulnerable to COVID-19 risks than those living in welfare states with strong social safety nets. Meanwhile, the subjective and objective necessity and willingness of older people in East Asia to work longer has significantly grown due to diminishing old-age support ratios (Yeung & Lee, 2022). Nevertheless, studies on what constitutes "productive" welfare support are not always consistent. Strauss and Trommer (2018) have further argued that the degree of de-familization and the role which welfare states attribute to the family have a significant influence in senior people's engagement in productive activities. Hence, the demographic transition has necessitated a crowding-in approach to address the social risks related with population ageing, which is closely tied to the history and adaptation of certain welfare states. Existing literature on the degree of productivism in East Asian identified de-familization and old-age employment support as productive policies, whereas old-age income security and care supports were identified as protective factors. Chen et al. (2022) have also suggested that prioritisation of social policies is essential for distinguishing welfare characteristics and policy orientations in the East Asia region.

Therefore, further discussion is required in the context of East Asia on the claim that older people's wellbeing is categorised by traditional welfare debate as a protective policy orientation. The extent whereby the state protects marginalised populations such as the old-age is a key indicator for analysing the regime-shift and adaptation of the welfare system amid public crises, which remains overlooked by academia and policymakers (An & Tang, 2020; Rehm, 2016). As demonstrated in Table 1, although the four industrialised societies of East Asia provided a variety of social services to their senior citizens, there were variances in both the scope and complexity of each programme. The Hong Kong administration promoted the idea that "Money Can Solve Anything" by offering various benefits to senior citizens under stringent censorship. Whereas, South Korea places a strong focus on creating an environment with comprehensive "Age-Friendly" supports, expanding older worker benefits, and providing older individuals with living, healthcare and income assistance. On the other side, Singapore has been working hard to promote "Active Ageing" through strengthening community-based organisations and senior activity centres that may motivate seniors to engage in social activities. Taiwan relied on its national insurance system and long-term care policy scheme to provide welfare supports for the older population. While the programmes in the field of employment are extensive and active in four societies, the conditions of income subsidies and care services are rigorous and targeted at older persons with low and intermediate wealth.

In the face of the new risks under COVID-19, as well as population ageing without adequate social protection, whether a path-breaking will emerge and depart from East Asia's productivist orientation requires further discussion (Lue & Park, 2013). The policy consistency and adaptation tendencies of East Asian welfare systems could be reflected in the social policy initiatives implemented by various governments in response to population ageing challenges.

RESEARCH METHOD AND THEORETICAL FRAMEWORK

Taking into account the growing interest in analysing the response to the pandemic crisis, this study goes beyond the debate between protectionist and productivist measures. Instead, a social risk perspective was emphasised in this study. We focus on how growth-oriented welfare systems in East Asia are dealing with population ageing and redistribution of social capital to older people, who are among the most vulnerable groups facing new risks. Due to the COVID-19 challenges, several studies have examined policy instruments and institutional transformation in the East Asian area (An & Tang, 2020; Chen et al., 2022; Shaw et al., 2020). Hence, this study highlighted the role which welfare states attribute to the old-age support will be the key to justifying or refuting the policy adaptation and continuity argument. The analysis of a nations' underdeveloped social policies is also the key to explore their social policy expansion and adaptation (Hwang, 2012).

Against this backdrop, this study focuses on policy design and how it benefits the older population. It aims to determine whether redistributive measures in certain welfare systems have evolved or changed since the COVID-19 outbreak, and whether they are distinguishable from defined policy orientation. This study follows the institutional continuity discussion that has taken centre stage in the social and political sciences. Typically, the debate over institutional continuity has been split into three camps: path-dependency, punctuated equilibrium, and gradual shift. The institutional continuity debate concentrates on how actors gradually make changes inside a system that may have transformational implications.

The path dependence hypothesis recognises that early decisions can have a lasting impact on establishing the foundation or impetus for future decisions, particularly when institutional inertia is at play (Campbell, 2004; Pierson, 2000). Once policy institutionalisation has reached a certain level of maturity, the existing configuration and features are likely to persist. The punctuated equilibrium highlights the fragility of institutions when confronted with a brief interval of disruption (a critical juncture) that forces established principles and rules to be renegotiated in the short and long term (Capoccia, 2015). Moreover, gradual shift theory developed within institutionalist theory as a response to a critical view of punctuated equilibrium theory as underemphasizing endogenous factors as tacit drivers of change. Overviewed by Hogan, et.al (2022), the gradual shift hypothesis has connected institutional change by following methods through which institutions can adapt and adjust their features as a means of ensuring a policy's survival and advancement. Nevertheless, this is a mechanism that requires gradual changes over a relatively long period of time, which can be illustrated by examples of drift, conversion, and layering (Streeck & Thelen, 2005). In further discussion, Mahoney & Thelen (2010) have highlighted that one of the important causes of change will be a shifting of power balances within the system. Institutions change when individuals in positions of authority within them are allowed and encouraged to change or interpret rules in ways that further their interests.

Table 1. Old-age supports before COVID-19 among four Asian societies

Old-age supports	Hong Kong	Singapore	South Korea	Taiwan
(De)Familization support	Working Family Allowance	-	-	-
Care support	Health Care Voucher; Rehabilitation Care; Community Care Voucher; Home Maintenance Support; Residential Care Homes; Multi-disciplinary Outreaching Support Teams	Community Health Assist; Home Living and Care Support; ComCare Long Term Assistance; Disability Assistance; Enhancement for Active Living; Medical Care Scheme; Silver Volunteer Fund	Long-term Care Insurance	National Health Insurance; Long-term Care Plan; Medical and Rehabilitation Care; Community Care and Service Facilities Construction; Home Care and Services; Old Friends Hotline; Daily Care and Nutritional Meal Scheme
Income support	Old Age Living Allowance; Comprehensive Social Security Assistance; Rent Allowance; Occupational Retirement Schemes	Central Provident Fund; Supplementary Retirement Scheme	National Pension Scheme	Old-age Benefits and Allowance; National Pension; Special Care and Living Allowance for Middle or Low-income Senior Citizens; Welfare allowance for older farmers/fishermen
Employment support	Employment Training Programme; Interactive Employment Service	National Silver Academy; SkillsFuture Credit	Unemployment Benefits Scheme; Senior-Friendly Industry Promotion Act; Senior Employment Training; Social Service Employment Programs; Unemployment Benefits Scheme; Employment Stabilization Scheme; Job Skill Development Programme; Extended Old-age Employment Subsidy	Middle-aged and Elderly Employment Promotion Act; Old-age Learning College

To identify the characteristic of policy dynamics presented during COVID-19 situation, this study highlighted the characteristic discussion by considering the degree of policy consistency in East Asian as expanding old-age employment support (see APPENDIX 1). Taking Four representative Asian societies' policy development as illustration, a two-dimension framework was performed by identifying risk response patterns for evaluating the policy consistency and adaptation of old-age support. Policy innovation and institutional changes in old-age income security, care supports, and de-familization policies were identified as strong policy adaptation. Cross-case analyses were conducted to determine the policy adaptation and continuity in each case (George & Bennett, 2005). This analytical framework followed to map COVID social risks policies consists of two aspects: identification and generosity degree for risk pools. Multiple social policy domains, including employment, income protection, care support,

Figure 1. Research framework

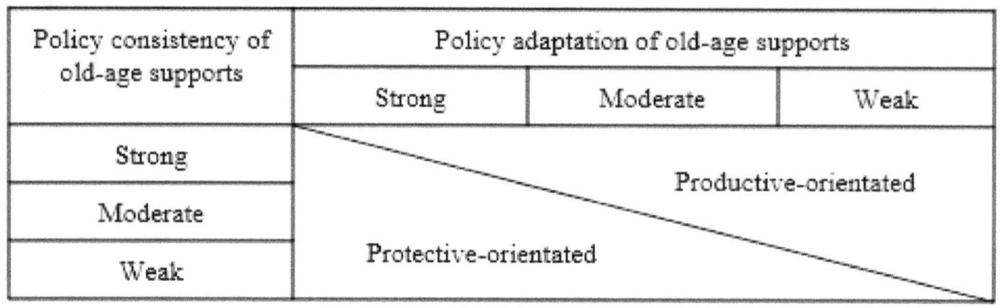

and de-familization schemes, were selected for context analysis. Public investment, service category, generosity, and accessibility were investigated to illustrate the policy strategies and instruments utilised by four case regions.

Qualitative analysis was adopted in this study to better explore the complicated policy transformation that varies among cases. Given the significance of qualitative and quantitative data in the discussion of social policy and welfare, qualitative research that emphasises in-depth and illustrative information comprehension offers a powerful tool for understanding the various dimensions of societal processes and phenomena that cannot be reduced to the operationalization of variables (Flanagan, 2013; Maxwell, 2013; Queirós et al., 2017). For data collection and analysis, case studies and document review were employed, investigating intricate situations with numerous aspects and providing a great opportunity for innovation and testing theoretical presumptions (Breuing & Ahlquist, 2014; Corbin & Strauss, 2008). Secondary data were obtained from open-access websites and international databases to support the qualitative research, and a descriptive technique was utilised to analyse the data.

POLICY RESPONSES RELATED TO AGEING RISKS DURING COVID-19

Given that the social insurance and welfare arrangements in four selected economies diverge, we searched in a variety of social policy areas, including employment, income protection, life support, and health care schemes, to determine whether any policy updates or readjustments emerged in response to population ageing risks during COVID-19. We adhere to existing classifications, specifically that employment policies represent measures of productive welfare, whereas social and medical care, income, and other old-age life support policies are more protective. Moreover, no policy was found for the education of older people in the Four Asian Tiger.

Hong Kong

Instead of a comprehensive pension system, Hong Kong has been implementing a residual old-age protection system, encompassing the social security system (Comprehensive Social Security Assistance CSSA, Old Age Allowance OAA, Old Age Living Allowance OALA and Disability Allowance DA), the contributory Manual Provident Fund (MPF) system, and public housing and healthcare services.

However, the effectiveness and sustainability of the aforementioned programs have been questioned since they require additional tax and income verification in order to preserve the older individuals with low incomes' fundamental subsistence sources. Therefore, in reaction to the global crisis, Hong Kong has been seen to promote both market-based initiatives and redistributive policies.

Following the COVID-19 outbreak, Hong Kong raised monthly allowances standards, including the Old Age Allowance and Comprehensive Social Security Assistance, by 2.6% per year to alleviate the financial burden on the older adults, their families, and residential care facilities. Meanwhile, the Hong Kong government launched a new old-age allowance scheme for older people who were stuck in the mainland and unable to return to Hong Kong due to the pandemic boundary control. Beginning January 1, 2020, the social welfare department in Hong Kong introduced the Old Age Living Allowance (OALA) for the Guangdong Scheme and Fujian Scheme on the basis of the Old Age Allowance program. The qualified elderly in Hong Kong who choose to remain in the provinces of Guangdong or Fujian rather than return to Hong Kong each year are provided with normal OALA (HK$2675) or higher OALA (HK$3585), and increased by about HK$200 per year after the outbreak of COVID-19. The social welfare department received nearly 10,600 applications for OALA under the Guangdong Scheme and the Fujian Scheme within two months of the application opening (The Government of the Hong Kong Special Administrative Region, 2020).

In response to the global economic downturn after 2020, Hong Kong has extended and reinforced the existing employment assistance programmes. The newly announced employment support programmes adhere to the prior policy principle of offering short-term unemployment allowances together with job training for skills. Notably, Hong Kong has extended its employment assistance strategy to encourage employers and companies to hire older workers through policy subsidies. Policy initiatives such as the Employment Programme for the Elderly, Support for Self-reliance scheme, Employment Support Services, and On-the-Job Training Allowance, were implemented to assist young-old (aged 60–64) in improving their employability and thus become self-sufficient. These projects not only provide young-old with short-term unemployment allowance and help them acquire job-specific skills through individual employment training covering "Vocational Skills," "Generic Skills," and "Innovation and Technology" of 28 trades. Meanwhile, to encourage the hiring of job seekers aged 60 or older, the Hong Kong Labour Department provides subsidies and actively encourages employers to implement friendly employment practices and extend the working lives of their employees, allowing older people who prefer to work to remain in the workforce.

Furthermore, Hong Kong has increased the old-age care services in light of the social isolation concern during COVID-19 pandemic. Hong Kong has one of the highest proportions of elderly in residential care facilities worldwide and places a strong priority on providing care and assistance for older individuals. As of September 2021, round 59,000 older individuals are living in various types of residential care homes, accounting for approximately 4.1% of the population aged 65 and above (Labor and Welfare Bureau, 2021). Meanwhile, living conditions are frequently cramped and antiquated in Hong Kong. Social restrictions under COVID-19 worsen senior housing issues. Besides the building maintains subsidies, the Hong Kong government announced pilot schemes in 2022 to provide vouchers for residential and community care services to the older people, allowing them to purchase care services that best meet their needs under the "money-following-the-user" model. Specifically, older people in need and their family's wealth are evaluated through the asset-test. Hence, it helps in the provision of better and more equal services to comparatively underserved senior citizens, as well as assists in the old-age individuals being able to get essential care services more quickly and typically at a lower cost.

Singapore

Following the COVID-19 outbreak in 2020, the Singaporean government released a variety of healthcare support programmes. Particularly, Singapore began reforming its old-age welfare system, taking over the administration of ElderlySheild from private insurers and creating the CareShield Life scheme, which provides monthly income support for the elderly on all fronts. These two programs are intended to cover the daily healthcare expenses of healthy and impaired older adults. The elderly will be covered for the remainder of their lives if they have paid all their premiums by the age of 65. Furthermore, Singapore has enhanced financial support for the elderly in 2022 by launching the Merdeka Generation Package and Pioneer Generation Package and renewing the Seniors' Mobility and Enabling Fund and Assistive Technology Fund. Moreover, policies named as "Assurance Package (AP) Senior's Bonus", "Assurance Package (AP) Medisave", "Cost-of-Living (COL) Seniors' Bonus" and, GST Voucher (GSTV) - Medisave" in 2023, which is going to provide cash benefits for low- and mid--income people who are aged 55 and above (SupportGoWhere, 2023). A growing tendency could be seen in Singapore's policy responses for financial assistance to the older population and protective support services.

Singapore, which has one of the greatest life expectancies, had a 26.8% employment rate for people aged 65 in 2018. In 2015, the employment rate for the elderly aged 65–69 was 40%, and by 2019, the employment rate for seniors aged 65 and above had risen to 27.6% and 28.5% in 2020. In July 2022, the retirement and re-employment ages will be raised to 63 and 68, respectively, with the goal of reaching 65 and 70 in 2030 (Ang, 2021; Han, 2021). Faced with an economic recession caused by the COVID-19 pandemic, Singapore has implemented new policy initiatives to encourage older people to continue working and to assist older people who have lost jobs to support themselves and return to the labour market. The Silver Support Scheme, Senior Worker Early Adopter Grant, Senior Worker Early Adopter Grant, and Part-time Re-employment Grant were enacted to provide cash benefits to older people who were left jobless during the pandemic and to encourage older adults to participate in the labour market as self-sufficient employees. Prior to the COVID-19, Singapore had comparatively few and less risk-resistant employment supports and programmes for the senior citizens. As of now, Singapore has been implementing numerous state-led policy initiatives to encourage older people to continue working and help older workers who have lost their jobs to become self-reliant.

Taiwan

Among the four Asian societies, Taiwan had established a well-structured national health insurance system and a well-developed labour pension programme before the outbreak of COVID-19. Moreover, Taiwan places a strong emphasis on the government's role in providing welfare supports to older people and accomplishes it via formal acts. After the outbreak of COVID-19 pandemic, this policy characteristic has persisted. By updating current legislation and welfare programmes, the Taiwanese government emphasises the responsibilities of the state and families for the care and assistance of older adults. In the 2020 update of the senior citizen welfare act, the government is responsible not only for providing direct institutional services and daily assistance to the elderly, but also for overseeing relatives' care responsibilities. Between 2017 and 2022, the government budget for long-term care 2.0 surged from NT$5 billion (US$167.3 million) to more than NT$60 billion (US$2 billion) and the number of care service locations has ballooned from over 700 sites to over 11,000 sites. The Long-Term Care Development Fund's funding then increased to $1.8 billion in 2022 (Ministry of health and welfare, 2023). Along with maintaining the state-led old-age support, Taiwan places a strong emphasis on the part that family support plays in old-age care services by releasing new care regulations.The newly issued 2021 Long-Term Care Services Act covers services for older people in their homes, communities, and institutions, as well as fixed-location and home-supportive services for family caregivers.

Meanwhile, the Taiwanese government has released new regulations that place a strong emphasis on the quality control over old-age services and care supports. The Ministry of health and welfare introduced the Residential Care Institutions Quality Improvement Plan in 2021 as a program to award subsidies to facilities that adhere to high service standards. Later in 2022, the government further promotes institutional development to supplement family care and protect the health and physical well-being of older individuals. The Establishment Standards of Senior Citizens' Welfare Institutions proposed the development of more individual-centered domiciliary care institutions with all-day services. Meanwhile, nursing homes for general and dementia-specific elderly have been segregated to provide high-quality care in accordance with various requirements.

Faced with the increased unemployment induced by the COVID-19 pandemic, Taiwan has enhanced employment supports and unemployment benefits for older individuals. To address the challenges of the COVID-19 pandemic, the government has launched new employment support initiatives rather than amending the Employment Promotion Act. Taiwan released four policy documents simultaneously at the end of 2020, focusing on compelling employers to hire old-age workers, providing temporary unemployment benefits and vocational training, and reducing loan interest rates. The policies promote older individuals entering the labour market in various ways, including encouraging employers to recruit older employees, providing temporary unemployment benefits, vocational training, and offering lower business loan interests. Aside from basic employment assistance strategies, Taiwan helped older individuals in obtaining employment by increasing social mobility. Subsidies for job search transportation, cross-region employment, relocation, and rent are all used to encourage the elderly to seek employment 30 kilometers away from their permanent residence. Taiwan's employment stimulation policies for older employees also include promoting intergenerational collaboration through new approaches, such as the sharing of experience, mentoring talents, and complementing abilities.

South Korea

Prior to the outbreak of COVID-19 epidemic, South Korea had already demonstrated a fairly clear path for the universal development of the welfare system, including the provision of pensions and health insurance for the old-age groups. As a result of impact of the pandemic on old-age population, the South Korean government is updating and amending current social policies rather than discarding them. In 2020 and 2021, South Korea's National Pension Act and Employment Insurance Act were amended separately, providing older people with basic employment and income protection. The South Korean government has further expanded the range of benefits beyond pension and medical care to enhanced benefits like housing and social entertainment. By 2020, 22.1 million individuals were covered by the National Pension Scheme, and the government planned to raise the Basic Pension amount from KRW 300,000 to KRW 400,000 (OECD, 2022). Moreover, the South Korean government introduced a new "living support" program in 2021 for low-income older individuals who already receive the national pension. Eligible individuals with income below a certain threshold and limited assets can receive up to KRW 250,000 per month to supplement their national pension. Hence, the amount of income support and pension coverage are both being increased by the South Korean government.

Meanwhile, South Korea has also updated its National Health Insurance Act and Long-Term Care Insurance Policy by increasing coverage and benefits to provide better supports for older people's daily living. For instance, the National Health Insurance further included mental health care such as cognitive-behavioral therapy and psychotherapy in 2021. In 2021, the government introduced a new long-term care insurance programme for older people with disabilities, which provides additional support for their care needs. Starting in January 2022, the maximum benefit amount increased from KRW 2.5 million to KRW 3 million per month. Meanwhile, the Korean government released a community-based integrated care plan based on the three proposed stage of the long-term care scheme, in order to satisfy the second phase, which is to build a comprehensive community care foundation (2023-2025), and the third phase, which is to universalize the community care. Moreover, the 2020 amendment to the Act on the Guarantee of Convenience Promotion of Senior Citizens also supported facility owners of public areas, multifamily housing, and telecommunication buildings in upgrading settings for a disadvantaged-friendly environment.

In regarding of older unemployment challenge during COVID-19 pandemic, the employment policies of South Korea has been tremendously revised. 40 trillion Korean won of budget and funds have been mobilized to cope with the resulting economic crisis and the deteriorating business and labour market situation. Through the revision of laws in 2020 and 2021, the unemployment benefit system appears to be evolving toward coverage of "all workers" by expanding the scope of the insured to include people working in the art industry and various types of dependent contractors who had not been previously covered. Other from consistently providing direct assistance to older people seeking employment opportunities, the Korean government has also broadened the employment supports to include companies and businesses by offering subsidies to encourage the hiring of older workers.

The newly issued employment supports in South Korea aims to promote employment stability and security for older employees. Recent changes were made to increase minimum benefit amounts, extend benefit periods, and provide special COVID-related job loss benefits. The Government-assisted Employment Programme directly provided job placement for the aged 65 and over. The Employment Insurance Act's Article 23 was revised on May 26, 2020, to give border assistance to business owners who employ or help senior citizens who have particular difficulty finding a job. Article 40 for the eligibility requirements for job-seeking benefits were also modified four times between January 15, 2019, and January 5, 2021, in order to motivate persons to find new employment (Korea Legislation Research Institute, 2022). Beginning January 1, 2022, a new Elderly Employment Promotion Subsidies System was implemented, providing partial funding to help cover the costs of hiring seniors at medium-sized businesses with a growing number of employees over the age of 60, which ensured that self-sufficiency and productive ageing are prioritised. Over a two-year period, a total of 300,000 won was awarded quarterly for each newly hired old-age employee (Ministry of Employment and Labor, 2022). In addition, South Korea government also relaxed the requirements for employment retention subsidy programme to support older employee retention during the COVID-19 challenges (OECD, 2020).

POLICY ADAPTATION OF THE FOUR ASIAN TIGERS

Despite regional disparities in social insurance and welfare arrangements, the Four Tigers' ageing policies in response to the COVID-19 pandemic were "age-friendly" policies guided by the basic principle of individual-reliance and self-sufficiency. Productive and protective welfare measures are intertwined.

Table 2. Welfare features of the four Asian tigers after COVID-19

Economies	Employment	Income protection	Life support	Healthcare
Hong Kong SAR	Government-funded employment training; Self-sufficient oriented provision	Multi-pillar Private Pension System	Public Saving Scheme; Ageing in Place Community and Housing Programme	Universal healthcare system
Republic of Singapore	State-funded senior employment and re-employment scheme	Three-pillar pension system	Mandatory saving schemes; Age-friendly city and senior-friendly community; Subsidies for assisting physical autonomy	Community-oriented healthcare
Republic of South Korea	State-funded senior employment and re-employment scheme; Social investment-oriented provision;	Multi-pillar pension system (without the four pillars) with mature enterprise-based contribution act	Basic livelihood benefits	National health insurance
Republic of China (Taiwan)	Universal insurance system for senior workers; employment act	Multi-pillar pension system, Labor-oriented pension insurance	National long-term care scheme; Market-oriented housing policy; Statutory family care obligations	Universal and mandatory healthcare insurance

As summarised in table 2, during the pandemic, all four economies have enacted market-oriented policy adaptations and new welfare programmes to encourage active employment of older people, by providing the necessary financial support to eradicate poverty and promoting employment opportunities. This is accomplished generally, for example, by raising the statutory retirement age instituting the notion of re-employment age, offering financial assistance to enterprise that employ the aged, and encouraging the elderly to start their own businesses Fundamentally, those newly emerging employment policies in Four Tigers are more of a measure of productive welfare rather than protecting older people's human right and wellbeing in the labour market.

Meanwhile, existing protective policies for health care, income protection, and social assistance are continuing and expanding, even though there are modest variances in benefits, such as budget and coverage across the Four Tigers. It is usually done by increasing the effectiveness of the pension pillar system, improving the health of the aged through long-term health care, providing basic livelihood aid, and developing "age-friendly" cities. Only Taiwan emphasizes the significant role of families as old-age welfare supports among the Four Tigers, whereas the other three societies mainly followed the old-age policy path and broaden the scope of protective services and financial assistance based on the current welfare framework.

Taking our review of data on policies to mitigate the risks associated with ageing into account, we can assume that COVID-19 arrangements have resulted in two variations in old-age policy adaptation across four economies. Hong Kong and Singapore have demonstrated a mix of developmental-universalist and facilitative features to mitigate ageing risks by strengthening their protective features to reactivate community function in tandem with expanded market-oriented self-reliance policies. Whereas South Korea and Taiwan appear to be on the verge of becoming a mix of developmental-universalist and protective feature, as evidenced by the implementation of individual-centered domiciliary care policies, universal health insurance, and efforts to provide temporary compensation to the unemployed older individuals and protective services for older employees during COVID-19 challenges. Hence, the four Asian societies demonstrated a dependence on their current welfare features, and the policy adaptation lays a strong emphasis on the employment of senior citizens. In the four economies, policy measures targeted at re-employment and active employment of older people mostly take the form of financial assistance and incentives, rather than strengthening older people's employability through the development of old-age educational policies. The juxtaposition of low living standards and a weak social safety net for the older population may complicate the future transition of East Asian welfare system transition.

Among the above-mentioned productive and protective measures, Hong Kong, as a "Tiger" with the least adequate safety net, has implemented the most diverse strategies to meet the fundamental living needs of its old-age residents. Following the emergence of the COVID-19 pandemic, the new policies enacted in the Hong Kong and Singapore focus mostly on stimulating old-age employment in the local labour market while also emphasizing the elderly's healthcare and community life. Given that income and health programs for older people are financed on the basis of grading and eligibility, auditing has hindered the establishment of a universal welfare system. When assessing the extent of participation of multiple welfare actors, Hong Kong and Singapore maintain market-oriented and community-based policies. Generally, evolving welfare provisions in the two cities prior to and during pandemics are linked by shared experiences and characteristics as extreme capitalist welfare states that distinguish them from their East Asian counterparts.

In contrast, South Korea may be the most generous of the Four Asian Tigers, with the implementation of updated pension, health care and employment insurance act. Both Singapore and Taiwan have issued new employment support policies to facilitate the protection of older workers. However, Taiwan has gradually placed more emphasis on the family's social duty while Singapore tends to hand over control and administration of social services to the government. Both South Korea and Taiwan place a strong emphasis on government support, with Taiwan highlighting families' responsibility in the field of old-age cares. Furthermore, features associated with the social democratic welfare feature appear in programs, such as government involvement in pre-emptive policy, to ensure that the labor market produces welfare while also addressing social risks. Despite this, our review above demonstrates that for welfare provision, families, communities, and markets are prioritized over the state. This arrangement, particularly the emphasis on the family, suggests that filial piety tradition remains paramount as the underlying motivation for these economies' minimal commitment to social welfare.

CONCLUSION

This article begins with a question: Are Hong Kong, Singapore, South Korea, and Taiwan updating or adjusting their ageing policies in response to COVID-19 risks? This study notes that although there were qualitative and quantitative updates on policy features ranging from targeting to universal coverage, or from workers to households as beneficiaries, the general ideas of productivism and developmentalism were retained as the framework to manage the risks associated with ageing during COVID-19. This can be seen from the emphasized approaches to welfare that encourage self-sufficiency and productive ageing rather than the protective or redistributive dimension (Mok et al., 2021).

Regarding the second question: what has been the impact of that configuration on the policy consistency within the four examined economies? Through an extensive review of wide-ranging policies related to ageing risk reduction, this paper suggests the diversity and changes in East Asian old-age supports during the COVID-19 challenges. Some East Asian economies such as South Korea and Taiwan have demonstrated an adaptation from productivist typologies to a more balanced protective-productive policy feature, but have utilized multiple pathways, with the market-conforming role of social policy retaining a dominant role. The reason for this can be hypothetically explained. Despite being one of the world's most affluent capitalist regions, inadequate welfare provisions for the elderly are not due to a lack of financial resources, but rather the result of an ideology that favors workfare, self-reliance, and familial piety. This can be seen in policies such as means-tested benefits, which require individuals to demonstrate their need for assistance before they can receive it, and the expectation that families will provide care for their elderly relatives, rather than the state.

Another hypothesis suggests that policymakers tend to adhere to what they know (e.g., the existing institutional settings, policy legacies, path dependency of ideas, and crisis routines) in times of emergency or uncertainty rather than trying out something new that may have unpredictable consequences (Starke et al., 2013). In this cognitive sense, the COVID-19 policy response is also related to the previous experience of institutional adaptation, developed through interactions, such as the 2008 financial crisis and the 2003 SARS outbreak, making East Asian nations more likely to pursue path-dependent productivist policies (Soon et al., 2021). Therefore, COVID-19 policy responses could have been interpreted as extensions of ongoing reform and development shaped by the urgency and the scale of the previous shock. Unlike the previous crisis which generated radical changes, these COVID-19 policy responses represent a minor adaptation to the system. Generally, what has been discussed here, to some extent, is similar to what has occurred in Southeast Asian social policy responses (Yuda et al., 2022)

Overall, this article demonstrates that the COVID-19 pandemic will not necessarily prompt East Asian societies to overhaul their social policies in the same way that previous economic crises have (Choi, 2012; Fleckenstein & Lee, 2018; Hwang, 2012). To weather the storm, the East Asian government instead employs balanced institutional complementarities between the protective and the productive via recalibration strategies (Mok et al., 2021; Soon et al., 2021). Despite that the COVID-19 poses a global health concern, East Asian economies primarily view it as an economic issue, with a focus on self-sufficiency and an active labor market. The strategy chosen was based on the fact that the proximity of East Asian economies to the global economy effectively allows them to think collectively about accelerating economic recovery during difficult times. We thus conclude that, despite the significant expansion of ageing-related policies, East Asian welfare supports are frequently based on and implemented in accordance with economic-prioritized strategies and filial piety values that affirm the role of family, community, and business rather than the state.

In a broader theoretical framework, our analysis demonstrates that produced policy responses and adaptations within the East Asia societies can be seen as politics for the market. This strategy is designed to prevent the most detrimental economic and social consequences of the COVID-19 pandemic. Thus, the economies under examination had to avoid excessive welfare reform. Most policy makers, instead, stick to what they know (Starke et al., 2013). In the case of East Asian countries, the focus on social policy adjustments as a form of adaptation to the COVID-19 crisis reflects historically ingrained strategies of adaptive governance in the face of crises. East Asian governments have a history of responding to crises (e.g., the SARS outbreak in 2003) with significant policy shifts, suggesting that their institutional frameworks are designed to accommodate rapid adjustments in response to external shocks.

Gradualism and punctuated equilibrium logic also play a role in this phenomenon. East Asian governments tend to favor gradual change over sudden, radical change. This means that they are more likely to make incremental adjustments to existing policies rather than introducing entirely new policies. The

COVID-19 crisis has forced these governments to make rapid changes to their policies, but they are still more likely to do so gradually rather than introducing sudden, radical changes.

In addition, rational choice institutionalists posit that actors within institutions are sensible and that their behavior aims to maximise their utility. From this perspective, the focus on social policy adjustments can be interpreted as strategic behaviour by East Asian governments to optimize outcomes in the face of the pandemic. Given the unprecedented nature of the COVID-19 crisis, maintaining policy consistency might not have been seen as the optimal choice. Instead, adjusting policies in real-time, based on new information and changing circumstances, could be viewed as a rational strategy to minimize the health and economic impacts of the pandemic. This argument holds true in other developed capitalist regions, such as the United States, Canada, and Europe, where the response to COVID-19 failed to generate a significant shift in policy direction, despite the new risks that were presented (Aidukaite et al., 2021; Béland et al., 2021; Cantillon et al., 2021; Hick & Murphy, 2021; Greve et al., 2021; Moreira & Hick, 2021).

Overall, the welfare state has strong path dependency effects that are difficult to overcome, and this process cannot be ignored even in the face of severe shocks. Therefore, in line with Castles (2010) and Starke et al. (2013), the authors conclude that external shocks in health field have a limited effect on path-departing changes.

Limitation

Although this qualitative study provides insight into how East Asian economies are dealing with population ageing in the context of the COVID-19 pandemic, the findings cannot be generalised. Other economies may experience the same or a different transformation in ageing policy than the four economies included in this study. More lessons may be learned to better understand social policy and welfare regime changes and developments in East Asia as time passes and other nations update their ageing policies.

The overall analysis presented here is limited to responses to COVID-19. In other words, out initial survey requires much scrutiny over the next few years, especially regarding whether COVID-19 will generate a 'critical juncture' that would complete an ongoing reform programme. Alternatively, another wave of reforms will be applied overlaid on top of an unfinished agenda of expansion-driven policy responses to the previous crisis, which accumulates in incremental system layers. As the global economic turmoil has remained constant in East Asia, this opens up a more comprehensive range of possibilities. There is only a reasonable likelihood that COVID-19 led to regime change if the changes implemented by different governments continue to be effective beyond the COVID-19 period.

REFERENCES

Abrahamson, P. (2017). East Asian welfare regime: Obsolete ideal-type or diversified reality. *Journal of Asian Public Policy*, *10*(1), 90–103. doi:10.1080/17516234.2016.1258524

Ahn, S.-H., & Lee, S. S.-y. (2012). Explaining Korean welfare state development with new empirical data and methods. *Asian Social Work and Policy Review*, *6*(2), 67–85. doi:10.1111/j.1753-1411.2012.00063.x

Aidukaite, J., Saxonberg, S., Szelewa, D., & Szikra, D. (2021). Social policy in the face of a global pandemic: Policy responses to the Covid-19 crisis in Central and Eastern Europe. *Social Policy and Administration*, *55*(2), 358–373. doi:10.1111/spol.12704 PMID:33821058

An, B. Y., & Tang, S.-Y. (2020). Lessons from covid-19 responses in East Asia: Institutional infrastructure and enduring policy instruments. *American Review of Public Administration*, *50*(6–7), 790–800. doi:10.1177/0275074020943707

Ang, R. (2021, December 1). *Employment rate of seniors rose at a faster pace to 31.7%: MOM. The Straits Times.* https://www.straitstimes.com/singapore/jobs/employment-rate-of-seniors-rose-at-a-faster-pace-to-317-mom

Béland, D., Dinan, S., Rocco, P., & Waddan, A. (2021). Social policy responses to COVID-19 in Canada and the United States: Explaining policy variations between two liberal welfare state regimes. *Social Policy and Administration*, *55*(2), 280–294. doi:10.1111/spol.12656 PMID:34230721

Bonoli, G. (2007). Time matters: Postindustrialization, new social risks, and welfare state adaptation in advanced industrial democracies. *Comparative Political Studies*, *40*(5), 495–520. doi:10.1177/0010414005285755

Breunig, C., & Ahlquist, J. S. (2014). Quantitative methodologies in public policy. In I. Engeli & C. R. Allison (Eds.), *Comparative Policy Studies: Conceptual and Methodological Challenges* (pp. 109–129). Palgrave Macmillan. doi:10.1057/9781137314154_6

Cantillon, B., Seeleib-Kaiser, M., & van der Veen, R. (2021). The COVID-19 crisis and policy responses by continental European welfare states. *Social Policy and Administration*, *55*(2), 326–338. doi:10.1111/spol.12715 PMID:34230722

Castles, F. G. (2010). Black swans and elephants on the move: The impact of emergencies on the welfare state. *Journal of European Social Policy*, *20*(2), 91–101. doi:10.1177/0958928709358793

Choi, Y. J. (2012). End of the era of productivist welfare capitalism? Diverging welfare regimes in East Asia. *Asian Journal of Social Science*, *40*(3), 275–294. doi:10.1163/156853112X650827

Choi, Y. J., Kühner, S., & Shi, S.-J. (2022). From "new social risks" to "COVID social risks": The challenges for inclusive society in South Korea, Hong Kong, and Taiwan amid the pandemic. *Policy and Society*, *41*(2), 260–274. doi:10.1093/polsoc/puac001

Chou, Y.-C., Nakano, T., Chang, H.-H., & Liang, L.-F. (2013). Parent-carers in Taiwan and Japan: Lifelong caring responsibilities within a familistic welfare system. In T. Kröger & S. Yeandle (Eds.), *Combining paid work and family care: Policies and experiences in international perspective* (pp. 143–159). Bristol University Press. doi:10.2307/j.ctt9qgp6n.14

Cohen, M. A., & Tavares, J. (2020). Who are the most at-risk older adults in the COVID-19 ERA? it's not just those in nursing homes. *Journal of Aging & Social Policy*, *32*(4–5), 380–386. doi:10.1080/08959420.2020.1764310 PMID:32418475

Corbin, J., & Strauss, A. (2008). Analyzing data for concepts. In Basics of Qualitative Research (3rd ed.): Techniques and Procedures for Developing Grounded Theory (pp. 159-194). SAGE Publications, Inc. doi:10.4135/9781452230153.n8

Emmenegger, P., Häusermann, S., Palier, B., & Seeleib-Kaiser, M. (2014). *The age of dualization: The changing face of inequality in deindustrializing societies.* Oxford University Press.

Esping-Andersen, G. (1993). *The three worlds of welfare capitalism*. Princeton University Press.

Esping-Andersen, G. (1999). *Social foundations of postindustrial economies*. Oxford University Press. doi:10.1093/0198742002.001.0001

Fleckenstein, T., & Lee, S. C. (2017). Democratization, post-industrialization, and East Asian welfare capitalism: The politics of welfare state reform in Japan, South Korea, and Taiwan. *Journal of International and Comparative Social Policy*, *33*(1), 36–54. doi:10.1080/21699763.2017.1288158

George, A. L., & Bennett, A. (2005). *Case studies and theory development in the social sciences*. MIT Press.

Global-is-Asian staff. (2021, July 8). *Reviewing a year of COVID-19 responses in the four 'Asian Tigers.'* LKYSPP. https://lkyspp.nus.edu.sg/gia/article/reviewing-a-year-of-covid-19-responses-in-the-four-asian-tigers

Goodin, R. E. (2003). The end of the welfare state? In *Terence Ball & Richard Bellamy edited by, The Cambridge History of 20th Century Political Thought* (pp. 202–216). Cambridge University Press.

Greve, B., Blomquist, P., Hvinden, B., & van Gerven, M. (2020). Nordic welfare states—Still standing or changed by the COVID-19 crisis? *Social Policy and Administration*, *55*(2), 295–311. doi:10.1111/spol.12675 PMID:33362319

Hall, G., Laddu, D. R., Phillips, S. A., Lavie, C. J., & Arena, R. (2021). A tale of two pandemics: How will covid-19 and global trends in physical inactivity and sedentary behavior affect one another? *Progress in Cardiovascular Diseases*, *64*, 108–110. doi:10.1016/j.pcad.2020.04.005 PMID:32277997

Han, G. Y. (2021, October 5). Employment rate of seniors aged 65 and above increased last year: Tan See Leng. *The Straits Times*. https://www.straitstimes.com/singapore/politics/employment-rate-of-seniors-aged-65-and-above-increased-last-year-tan-see-leng

Harper, S. (2021). The impact of the COVID-19 pandemic on global population ageing. *Journal of Population Ageing*, *14*(2), 137–142. doi:10.1007/s12062-021-09330-w PMID:34055101

Harris, J. (2012). The 'welfare state' in legal and social philosophy: Origins and controversies. In *Michael Lobban & Julia Moses edited by, The impact of ideas on legal development* (pp. 75–99). Cambridge University Press.

HelpAge International. (2020). *COVID-19 and older people in Asia Pacific 2020*. HelpAge. https://www.helpage.org/silo/files/covid19-and-older-people-in-asia-pacific-2020-in-review.pdf

Hemerijck, A. (2012). When changing welfare states and the eurocrisis meet. *Sociologica*. doi:10.2383/36887

Hick, R., & Murphy, M. P. (2021). Common shock, different paths? Comparing social policy responses to COVID-19 in the UK and Ireland. *Social Policy and Administration*, *55*(2), 312–325. doi:10.1111/spol.12677

Holliday, I. (2000). Productivist welfare capitalism: Social policy in East Asia. *Political Studies*, *48*(4), 706–723. doi:10.1111/1467-9248.00279

Holliday, I., & Wilding, P. (2003). *Welfare capitalism in East Asia: Social policy in the tiger economies*. Palgrave Macmillan., doi:10.1057/9780230597563

Huber, E., & Stephens, J. D. (2001). *Development and crisis of the welfare state*. University of Chicago Press Books. doi:10.7208/chicago/9780226356495.001.0001

Hudson, J., Kühner, S., & Yang, N. (2014). Productive welfare, the east Asian "model" and beyond: Placing welfare types in greater china into context. *Social Policy and Society, 13*(2), 301–315. doi:10.1017/S1474746413000572

Hwang, G. J. (2012). Explaining welfare state adaptation in East Asia: The cases of Japan, Korea and Taiwan. *Asian Journal of Social Science, 40*(2), 174–202. doi:10.1163/156853112X640134

Irving, J. (2020, October). COVID-19, older adults and long-term care in the Asia Pacific, Report prepared for HelpAge International Asia Pacific. *Analysis of variable COVID-19 mortality among older people in Asia Pacific, by forms of long-term care*. Ageing Asia. https://ageingasia.org/wp-content/uploads/2020/12/COVID_LTC_Report-Final-20-November-2020.pdf

Jefferies, S., French, N., Gilkison, C., Graham, G., Hope, V., Marshall, J., McElnay, C., McNeill, A., Muellner, P., Paine, S., Prasad, N., Scott, J., Sherwood, J., Yang, L., & Priest, P. (2020). Covid-19 in New Zealand and the impact of the national response: A descriptive epidemiological study. *The Lancet. Public Health, 5*(11), e612–e623. doi:10.1016/S2468-2667(20)30225-5 PMID:33065023

Kim, S. Y. (2020). Reappraisal of the developmental welfare state theory on the underdevelopment of state welfare in East Asian growth economies: The case of South Korea. *Journal of Asian and African Studies, 55*(4), 568–585. doi:10.1177/0021909619886679

Kühner, S., & Chou, K. L. (2019). Poverty alleviation, coverage and fiscal sustainability: Investigating the effect of a new social pension in Hong Kong. *International Journal of Social Welfare, 28*(1), 89–99. doi:10.1111/ijsw.12321

Kwon, H. (2005). Transforming the developmental welfare state in East Asia. *Development and Change, 36*(3), 477–497. doi:10.1111/j.0012-155X.2005.00420.x

Labour and Welfare Bureau. (2021). *Improvement in elderly care services (Chinese only)*. LWB. https://www.lwb.gov.hk/tc/blog/post_05092021.html#:~:text=%E7%8F%BE%E6%99%82%E9%A6%99%E6%B8%AF%E7%B4%84%E6%9C%89145,%E4%BB%A5%E4%B8%8A%E4%BA%BA%E5%8F%A3%E7%9A%84%E7%B4%844.1%25%E3%80%82

Lai, D., & Chui, E. (2014). A Tale of Two Cities: A comparative study on the welfare regimes of Hong Kong and Macao. *Social Policy and Society, 13*(2), 263–274. doi:10.1017/S1474746413000614

Landi, F., Barillaro, C., Bellieni, A., Brandi, V., Carfì, A., D'Angelo, M., Fusco, D., Landi, G., Lo Monaco, R., Martone, A. M., Marzetti, E., Pagano, F., Pais, C., Russo, A., Salini, S., Tosato, M., Tummolo, A., Benvenuto, F., Bramato, G., & Bernabei, R. (2020). The new challenge of geriatrics: Saving frail older people from the SARS-COV-2 pandemic infection. *The Journal of Nutrition, Health & Aging, 24*(5), 466–470. doi:10.1007/s12603-020-1356-x PMID:32346682

Lee, C. H., Huang, N., Chang, H. J., Hsu, Y. J., Wang, M. C., & Chou, Y. J. (2005). The immediate effects of the severe acute respiratory syndrome (SARS) epidemic on childbirth in Taiwan. *BMC Public Health*, *5*(1), 30. doi:10.1186/1471-2458-5-30 PMID:15804368

Lewis, J. (2002). Gender and welfare state change. *European Societies*, *4*(4), 331–357. doi:10.1080/1461669022000022324

Lin, K., & Wong, C. K. (2013). Social policy and social order in East Asia: An evolutionary view. *Asia Pacific Journal of Social Work*, *23*(4), 270–284. doi:10.1080/02185385.2013.778785

Lue, J.-D., & Park, C. (2013). Beyond productivist social policy–the East Asian Welfare–work Nexus in transition. *Journal of Asian Public Policy*, *6*(1), 1–9. doi:10.1080/17516234.2013.765182

Mamelund, S. E. (2012). Fertility fluctuations in times of war and pandemic influenza. *The Journal of Infectious Diseases*, *206*(1), 140–141. doi:10.1093/infdis/jis315 PMID:22535995

Maxwell, J. A. (2021). Why qualitative methods are necessary for generalization. *Qualitative Psychology*, *8*(1), 111–118. doi:10.1037/qup0000173

McBain, R. K., Wickett, E., Mugunga, J. C., Beste, J., Konwloh, P., & Mukherjee, J. (2016). The post-Ebola baby boom: Time to strengthen health systems. *Lancet*, *388*(10058), 2331–2333. doi:10.1016/S0140-6736(16)31895-5 PMID:27845079

Ministry of Employment and Labour. (2022). *Implementation of the elderly employment promotion subsidies system starting from 2022*. MOEL. https://www.moel.go.kr/english/news/moelNewsDetail.do?idx=3063

Mok, K. H., Ku, Y.-W., & Yuda, T. K. (2021). Managing the COVID-19 pandemic crisis and changing welfare regimes. *Journal of Asian Public Policy*, *14*(1), 1–12. doi:10.1080/17516234.2020.1861722

Mok, K. H., & Ramesh, M. (2014). After the regional and global financial crises: Social development challenges and social policy responses in Hong Kong and Macau. In K. H. Mok & M. K. W. Lau (Eds.), *Managing social change and social policy in greater China: Welfare regimes in transition* (pp. 12–30). Routledge. doi:10.4324/9781315887579

Moreira, A., & Hick, R. (2021). COVID-19, the great recession and social policy: Is this time different? *Social Policy and Administration*, *55*(2), 261–279. doi:10.1111/spol.12679

Morley, J. E., & Vellas, B. (2020). Editorial: COVID-19 and older adult. *The Journal of Nutrition, Health & Aging*, *24*(4), 364–365. doi:10.1007/s12603-020-1349-9 PMID:32242202

Peng, I., & Chien, Y.-C. (2018). Not all in the same family: Diverging approaches to family policy in East Asia. In G. B. Eydal & T. Rostgaard (Eds.), *Handbook of family policy* (pp. 236–248). Edward Elgar Publishing. doi:10.4337/9781784719340.00027

Peng, I., & Wong, J. (2004, September). Growing out of the developmental state: East Asian welfare reform in the 1990s. In Presented at the *RC19 Conference* (Vol. 2, p. 4). Research Gate.

Peng, I., & Wong, J. (2008). Institutions and institutional purpose: Continuity and change in East Asian social policy. *Politics & Society*, *36*(1), 61–88. doi:10.1177/0032329207312180

Population Reference Bureau. (2020). *World population data sheets*. PRB. https://www.prb.org/2020-world-population-data-sheet/

Queirós, A., Faria, D., & Almeida, F. (2017). Strengths and limitations of quelitative and quantitative research methods. *European Journal of Education Studies*, *3*(9), 369–387. doi:10.5281/zenodo.887089

Raymo, J. M., Park, H., Xie, Y., & Yeung, W. J. (2015). Marriage and Family in East Asia: Continuity and Change. *Annual Review of Sociology*, *41*(1), 471–492. doi:10.1146/annurev-soc-073014-112428 PMID:30078932

Reich, R. (2020, April 28). *The Remotes. The Essentials. The Unpaid. The Forgotten: Divided, but intertwined.* Berkely. https://blogs.berkeley.edu/2020/04/28/the-remotes-the-essentials-the-unpaid-the-forgotten-divided-but-intertwined/

Rui, L., Sirui, L., Xuebei, D., Xujun, Y., & Yanggan, W. (2020). Clinical observations in very elderly patients with COVID-19 in Wuhan. *Geriatrics & Gerontology International*, *20*(7), 709–714. doi:10.1111/ggi.13974 PMID:32634855

Shaw, R., Kim, Y. K., & Hua, J. (2020). Governance, technology and citizen behavior in pandemic: Lessons from COVID-19 in East Asia. *Progress in Disaster Science*, *6*, 100090. doi:10.1016/j.pdisas.2020.100090 PMID:34171010

Soon, S., Chou, C. C., & Shi, S. J. (2021). Withstanding the plague: Institutional resilience of the east Asian welfare state. *Social Policy and Administration*, *55*(2), 374–387. doi:10.1111/spol.12713 PMID:33821059

Starke, P., Kaasch, A., & van Hooren, F. (2013). *The welfare state as crisis manager explaining the diversity of policy responses to economic crisis*. Palgrave Macmillan.

Taylor-Gooby, P. (2004). *New risks, new welfare: The transformation of the European welfare state*. Oxford University Press. doi:10.1093/019926726X.001.0001

Taylor-Gooby, P. (2004). New social risks in postindustrial society: Some evidence on responses to active labour market policies from Eurobarometer. *International Social Security Review*, *57*(3), 45–64. doi:10.1111/j.1468-246X.2004.00194.x

The government of the Hong Kong Special Administrative Region. (2020). *LCQ14: Guangdong scheme and Fujian scheme*. INFO. https://www.info.gov.hk/gia/general/202001/08/P2020010800366.htm?fontSize=1

Van Mechelen, N., Verbist, G., & Van den Bosch, K. (2004). Evaluating welfare state efforts and the model family approach: problems and promises. *In 2004 ESPAnet conference*. Research Gate. https://www.researchgate.net/profile/Gerlinde-Verbist/publication/254827237_Evaluating_welfare_state_efforts_and_the_model_family_approach_problems_and_promises/links/00463537b4e62e8b93000000/Evaluating-welfare-state-efforts-and-the-model-family-approach-problems-and-promises.pdf

Wen, Z., Mok, K. H., & Amoah, P. A. (2021). Productive engagement and ageing in productivist welfare regimes: Questing for an age-friendly city in Hong Kong. *Ageing and Society*, 1–23. doi:10.1017/S0144686X21000167

Wilding, P. (2008). Is the East Asian welfare model still productive? *Journal of Asian Public Policy*, *1*(1), 18–31. doi:10.1080/17520840701835815

Wong, J. (2004). The adaptive developmental state in East Asia. *Journal of East Asian Studies (Seoul), 4*(3), 345–362. doi:10.1017/S1598240800006007

Wong, J. (2019). Healthy democracies and welfare politics in Taiwan: The arguments, refinements and limitations. In *Taiwan Studies Revisited* (pp. 141–159). Routledge. doi:10.4324/9780429259937-9

Wong, J. H., & Ho, G. W. (2022). Shielding without a Shield—Older People under COVID-19: A Comparison of Four Cities. *Social Sciences (Basel, Switzerland), 11*(11), 498. doi:10.3390/socsci11110498

Wood, G., & Gough, I. (2006). A comparative welfare regime approach to global social policy. *World Development, 34*(10), 1696–1712. doi:10.1016/j.worlddev.2006.02.001

Yang, J. (2014). Welfare states' policy response to new social risk: Sequence analysis for welfare policy. *Development and Society, 43*(2), 269–296. doi:10.21588/dns.2014.43.2.007

Yang, N. (2017). East Asia in transition: Re-examining the East Asian welfare model using fuzzy sets. *Journal of Asian Public Policy, 10*(1), 104–120. doi:10.1080/17516234.2016.1258525

Yang, N., & Kühner, S. (2020). Beyond the limits of the productivist regime: Capturing three decades of East Asian welfare development with fuzzy sets. *Social Policy and Society, 19*(4), 613–627. doi:10.1017/S147474641900054X

Yeung, W. J., & Thang, L. L. (2018). Long-term care for older adults in ASEAN plus Three: The roles of family, community, and the state in addressing unmet eldercare needs. *Journal of Aging and Health, 30*(10), 1499–1515. doi:10.1177/0898264318796345 PMID:30239253

Yeung, W. J. J., & Lee, Y. (2022). Aging in East Asia: New findings on retirement, health, and well-being. *The Journals of Gerontology. Series B, Psychological Sciences and Social Sciences, 77*(3), 589–591. doi:10.1093/geronb/gbab055 PMID:33788932

Yip, P., Chan, M., So, B. K., Wat, K. P., & Lam, K. F. (2021). A decomposition analysis to examine the change in the number of recipients in the comprehensive social security assistance (CSSA) system. *China Population and Development Studies, 4*(3), 284–297. doi:10.1007/s42379-020-00069-z PMID:33133735

Yuda, T. K. (2021). The evolving Korean childcare regime. *The International Journal of Sociology and Social Policy, 41*(9/10), 1089–1107. doi:10.1108/IJSSP-09-2020-0438

Yuda, T. K., Damanik, J., & Nurhadi. (2021). Examining emerging social policy during COVID-19 in Indonesia and the case for a community-based support system. *Asia Pacific Journal of Social Work, 31*(1–2), 13–22. doi:10.1080/02185385.2020.1829499

Chapter 13
Municipal Communication, Governance, and the Role of the Local Community:
A Case Study in Guimarães (Portugal)

Diana Salgado Pereira
Polytechnic Institute of Viana do Castelo, Portugal

Manuel José Serra da Fonseca
https://orcid.org/0000-0002-3290-8449
Applied Management Research Unit, Instituto Politécnico de Viana do Castelo, Portugal

Bruno Barbosa Sousa
https://orcid.org/0000-0002-8588-2422
Polytechnic Institute of Cávado and Ave (IPCA), Portugal & CiTUR and UNIAG, Portugal

ABSTRACT

Communication is a relevant process at the business level, but it also plays an important role in territorial contexts and in relation to the local community, citizens, and tourists. Territorial marketing is a set of strategic actions planned, aiming to improve the competitiveness of a territory, and consequently contributing to its development, promoting the satisfaction of the residents 'needs in each territory.' Municipalities tried to keep up with the evolution of the previous concepts, which resulted in their restructuring, emphasizing the search for the expansion of their effectiveness in society at the same time that they establish a bilateral relationship. This conjecture led to difficulties in the process of the message by the residents, especially in specific themes about the Autarchy itself, on the other hand, to the recognition of improvements by the entity under study. This chapter presents insights into territorial management, local development, and contributions to the tourist destination (i.e. Guimarães).

DOI: 10.4018/979-8-3693-1742-6.ch013

INTRODUCTION

People are motivated to visit some destinations for a wide range of purposes such as leisure, seeking for a novelty, experiencing specific objects within the different types of tourism, including special interest tourism or niche tourism trends (Atsız & Temiz, 2022). Among these, literary tourism has become a popular market segmentation over the past decades and has gained significant attention from tourism scholars (Atsız, & Temiz, 2022). Communication develops in a cycle from the sender to the receiver who sometimes encounters barriers that make it difficult to decode the message and change their perception, thus highlighting the relevance of analyzing all the processes suffered. In this sense, companies have been exploring this term in order to achieve better results in two aspects: intrinsic and extrinsic, fostering the relationship with their employees and enhancing the reinforcement of their image externally. It is clear, then, the significance that communication has in the daily life of the entire community, in its various aspects. Bearing in mind that Autarchy encompasses all residents, therefore varied desires and needs while operating with external audiences, in order to encourage local development, be it at an economic or other level, it can be affirmed as an organization. Therefore, communication in this area objectively helps to satisfy citizens, while establishing transparent relationships. Territorial marketing presents its relevance associated with the development of strategies in order to overcome the promotion of a given space to boost a relationship between the various stakeholders' present (Kotler & Haider, 1993; Sousa & Rocha, 2019; Silva, Sousa & Abreu, 2023). Countries, regions or cities must differentiate themselves from the others by creating a competitive advantage, which allows them to communicate and offer a unique image of the territory in question. Thus, it is crucial to be attentive to all opportunities with a view to establishing strategies that lead to the differentiation of geography and increased competitiveness (Eichinger Schreier & van Osselaer, 2022; Abreu, 2018). Therefore, municipal communication with the local community was defined as a context (i.e. Municipality of Guimarães, Portugal). The creation of an research, firstly in this county, recognized throughout the country as the "cradle of the nation" and the patriotism correlated to its citizens, aroused interest in understanding how its autarchy manages to successfully apply, or not, strategies naturally linked to communication and certain emotions aroused by residents from Guimarães. Furthermore, it becomes relevant to investigate this success in the line of culture and leisure, excluding other areas from the outset.

THEORETICAL BACKGROUNG

The tourism sector has been growing and deepening its diversity, becoming one of the fastest growing economic sectors in the world (Pimenta et al. fastest growing sectors in the world (Pimenta et al., 2021). According to the World Tourism Organization (UNWTO), this sector has become one of the largest elements of international trade. trade, representing one of the largest sources of income for many developing countries (Roseta et al., 2020). The growth of tourism in Portugal has made a positive contribution to the development of the national economy, generating employment and wealth, as well as enhancing the national heritage. It is responsible for almost 50 percent of service exports and close to 17 percent of total exports. In 2016 Portugal received, for the first time, more foreign tourists than the total Portuguese resident population (11.4 million). The revenue generated by tourism have also seen strong growth and, in the same year, the sector had a weight in GDP of almost 7 percent (Araújo, 2017). As the tourism sector is considered to be one of the largest economic sectors, it has the potential to create jobs, boost exports and generate prosperity around the world. According to Silva, Sousa & Abreu (2022), the development of a brand for a country, a city or a region is beneficial for the organizations present in that space, namely for companies. The territorial brand will be accompanied by useful competitive advantages for local businesses and products. Furthermore, it will add value to existing attributes, stimulate competitiveness and, consequently, attract people and investments (Méndez Prada, López Barraza, Ziritt Trejo, & Ruiz Escorcia, 2023). The aforementioned advantages will also be felt, as a consequence, by the residents, so the management of the territories must be carried out in a rigorous and delicate way with them, regularly communicating projects, cultural and artistic activities and, at the same time, seeking to develop a positive environment among residents, namely by extolling values, such as friendship, solidarity, security, respect, so that this results in an increase in affective commitment. For Caroli (1999), through territorial marketing it is possible to identify the competitive opportunity of a city, develop a strategy capable of meeting this opportunity, promote the necessary steps for the execution of the defined strategy and communicate with the city's public (current and potentials). Through this concept, local governments will feel obliged to create policies focused on attracting these different target audiences. These practices have been widely used with a view to increasing global competitiveness, as well as with the aim of positioning their cities as they wish (Ma, Jong, Hoppe & Bruijne, 2021). Place marketing is a strategic tool with an increasingly significant influence on the management of cities, and it is essential to develop a marketing strategy that is capable of positioning the city and giving it something differentiating. However, we cannot ignore the most recent events that have marked the year 2020 and the damaging effects caused by the new coronavirus pandemic (i.e. covid-19), breaking the curve that had been rising in previous years and consequently causing changes in local, regional and territorial areas.

The projection of an evolved society that saw the alteration of its own identity is associated with changes in the public and political space that began to take into account the equality of all through decision-making that, from the outset, are the most consensual possible (Azimovna, Ilkhomovna & Shokhrukhovich, 2022). In this regard, the communication developed by the municipalities continues with the same pattern of evolution described above, contributing to cooperation with citizens through an action plan that is more suited to their needs and desires, felt in the collective. In this way, the term municipal communication encompasses the aggregation of multiple activities, whether verbal or extraverbal, developed or supported by the municipality, whose purpose is to authenticate the values, goals and activities of the same, ensuring not only a good image but also the good relationship with those it operates (Hasanaj & Manxhari, 2017). Thus, it is understood that political communication is seen as an interactive medium, discussed between three parties, the media and the public, that is, in addition to the message, it is necessary to consider other symbols such as images and representations and, only with the interaction between all members there is a deliberate democracy. Bearing in mind that, for the proper functioning of any strategic plan, both concrete and specific objectives are defined, duly weighted, which assist the development of the projects themselves and contribute to the delineation of tasks. Thus, municipal communication follows this technique and develops goals that aim to achieve with its activities the solution of local dilemmas or to achieve objectives municipalities in particular Person Behnke & Jürgens (2023). Therefore, the established goals are relevant for the analysis and evaluation of the strategies, given that purposes related to the message, the public and even the most relevant means for dissemination are established and, after their implementation, the measures are rigorously evaluated. actions, understanding those that worked, but above all those that failed to understand where they failed and how this issue can be resolved (Frandsen & Johansen, 2009; Chen & Dwyer, 2017). Due to the growing interaction between people in the tourism activity, the support of residents has proved to be fundamental in tourism marketing, namely with regard to tourism planning and development, as well as their participation and involvement in it (Cheung & Hui, 2018). The importance of residents' behaviors is also mentioned by Litvin, Goldsmith & Pan (2008), as they influence tourists' travel experiences at all levels, from information seeking to consumption of tourist products (Litvin, Goldsmith & Pan, 2008).

CONTEXT AND METHODOLOGY

Guimarães is classified nationally as a medium-sized city, where its 242.32 km2 articulate between modernity and ancestors, thus belonging to the North of Portugal, more specifically the non-metropolitan conurbation of Vale do Ave. Therefore, the cradle city presents itself as a municipality in the district of Braga, incorporating both Nut II and Nut III of Ave, thus being surrounded in the North, Northwest and Southeast by Póvoa de Lanhoso, Braga and Santo Tirso, while in the The South and Southeast zone borders Vizela and Felgueiras, Fafe to the East and Famalicão to the West. Effectively, the trend of an increasingly aging country, as a result of the reduced birth rate and the increase in average life expectancy, is no exception to what is considered the Cradle of the Nation, as it presents, over the years, a rise in the birth rate. aging of around 88.9% of that registered since 2001, raising average life expectancy by 19.6 years, throughout mainland Portugal and islands. The case study confers the reality analysis procedure, providing the investigation with varied study perspectives, as well as understanding and improving the social and professional reality. In this way, it has two aspects associated with it, if on the one hand the objective is to describe and explain a certain situation based on a theory and its validation, on the other hand it allows the illustration and analysis of a real situation, which makes it possible to explore, describe, explain and evaluate the phenomenon. Here, the objective is to investigate the Municipality of Guimarães in a specific context, namely in municipal communication and its role in the local community. While content analysis, seen as a technique, allows a qualitative observation of the data, that is, descriptive of certain aspects, whenever the nature of the study allows it, quantitative analysis is carried out, such as the calculation of percentages (Amado, Costa & Crusoé, 2000; Hetenyi, Lengyel & Szilasi, 2019; Liberato, Limbado Sousa & Liberato, 2022). Despite these two perspectives differing, the combination of both can be very useful and suitable for the study, allowing the understanding, explanation and deepening of reality. The assumption of the complementarity of both leads this investigation to resort to the resource of the mixed approach, therefore it uses qualitative and quantitative techniques. In this follow-up, two studies are applied, one from the exploratory interview (qualitative method) and the other from the survey by questionnaire (quantitative method) which allow reaching broad results, avoiding bias in reality.

According to [3], this municipality is located in the sub-region NUT III – Ave. As of 2021, Guimarães is a municipality made up of 156,849 people, of which 19,587 are under 15 years of age and 31,329 are 65 years of age or older. Census data show that between 1940 and 2001, the number of inhabitants grew by around 43,304, however, since then, there has been a slight decrease of only 2,727 inhabitants until 2021. With regard to the number of young people, also shows a very significant downward trend, in the same way that the elderly increased from 21,568 to 31,329 in the last 10 years alone. Regarding birth rates, the values recorded do not show major fluctuations. In 2017, there were 1251 births, followed by 1262 in 2018, followed by the year 2019 with 1255 registered live births and in 2020 there is the highest value with 1280 births. With regard to the number of deaths, these have been experiencing exponential growth over the years. In 2017, there is the lowest value with 1165 deaths, in 2018 it increases slightly to 1200, in 2019 there is an increase again to 1268 and finally in 2020 the highest value is reached with 1418 deaths [3].

Regarding the licensing and completion of works in 2020, it appears that 410 works were licensed, which represents 34.5% of the NUT III subdivision. Of these, 342 are new constructions, while 68 are rehabilitations. With regard to completed works, in 2020 there were a total of 249, representing 29% of the NUT III subdivision, of which 27 were renovations and 222 were new constructions. As far as tourism is concerned, in 2020, the municipality had 41 hotel establishments, of which only 16 were hotels. There were 85,200 guests in a total of 143,684 overnight stays, which translated into €6,032.00 of revenue, representing 46% of the revenue of the NUT III subdivision.

During the development of the questionnaire survey, a pre-test was initially carried out with 15 possible respondents, with the aim of identifying possible gaps with the target audience. Subsequently, it moved on to the administration of surveys by questionnaire. Thus, from the 16th of December 2020, until the 19th of that same month, the pre-testing of the questionnaire on the theme of municipal communication and its role in the local community was available on digital platforms: Case study, Municipality of Guimarães. Considering the possible improvements exposed by those who initially performed it, namely spelling mistakes, doubts related to specific concepts and others that made it possible to change the order of the themes, moving the last theme, Socio-demographic information to the first section, demonstrating that small details make the difference and, mainly, that contributed to the conclusion of this stage.

PRELIMINARY ANALYSIS

The survey of this study brought fundamental results for obtaining concrete answers to the questions posed initially, for this it is necessary, at first, to understand who the respondents are and, if they really belong to the municipality of Guimarães, hence, in a first moment, it is essential to ask this question. Most respondents actually belong to the municipality in question, so 400, equivalent to 93.5% selected the option yes and only 28 (6.5%) "no". Therefore, these 400 people from Guimarães are dispersed across the various parishes that make up the city of Guimarães, however there is a greater number of responses in the village of São João de Ponte with 106 people, corresponding to 26.5%, on the other hand there are 6 parishes that had no respondents, namely Guardizela; Lordelo; Selho (S. Cristóvão); UF of Arosa and Castelões; UF of Briteiros S. Salvador and Briteiros Sta. Leocádia and UF de Selho S. Lourenço e Gominhães.

A large part of the sample neither agrees nor disagrees with the statement: "I consider myself well informed about the Autarchy of Guimarães" with precisely 148 responses, even so it is mentioned that there is a significant number of people who do not agree with it., the communication that is received by Vimaranenses is done mainly through social networks, followed by local newspapers and the website. Autarchy to be, mainly through the online medium. In general, the surveyed residents of Guimarães do not have an opinion on the statements made, especially those referring to the strategies and objectives of the departments and the Institution, which makes it difficult to explore their opinions. This "neither disagree nor agree" compromises the analysis, however it is possible to investigate the reason for this selection, possibly the work done by the Municipality in these aspects finds some noise in the communication cycle which prevents its proper reception by the residents. Consequently, the data referring to "totally agree" show significantly low numbers when compared to "totally disagree" or to the other option. Emphasis is given to information relating to the area of culture and leisure by the majority of respondents, matching 250 responses (62.5%), however, those belonging to education follow with 168 (42%) and health with 166 (41.5%), placing this possibility of choice even for the pandemic period in which this case study was prepared. It is noted that access to information related to competitions taking place in the city is not very relevant for a considerable majority of individuals, precisely 11.3%.

Considering the European capital of culture, as one of the events with great impact on this continent, Guimarães, as a candidate and selected in 2012 for this purpose, benefited from the increase in its tourist demand, making it necessary to create a multidimensional planning. Therefore, the absolute majority, in this case, fell on the positive response (75.3%) in what served as the impetus for the communication issued. In order to understand the most used communication channel that allows access to information issued about culture and leisure, the question was created, resulting in the superiority of answers in the "social networks" with 70.3%;| followed by "website" with 14.2%; "radio" with 6.3%; "local newspapers" with 4.7%; informal conversations" with 3.7%, while the sum of "events", "placards" and "billboards" do not appear with 1%. Throughout the results, there is a similarity between the agreement between the various options, with a large part defending that the sharing of information in the area addressed is positive for the numerous sectors, increasing in terms of the number of votes in "I totally agree". Briefly, this sharing helps to improve the relationship of the Municipality with residents, tourists and visitors, consequently increasing sales, making Guimarães a center for demand and supply of information.

FINAL CONSIDERATIONS AND NEXT STEPS

Tourists increasingly resort to the Internet, particularly websites, review channels and social networks, as their main source of information (Almeida-Santana and Moreno-Gil, 2017; Clark et al., 2023). Resultantly, all these platforms can influence the perception and image of a particular destination, business or brand (Foroudi et al., 2018; Vinyals-Mirabent et al., 2019). The concepts of Communication and Marketing go hand in hand in terms of needs and expectations, therefore, both become complex processes that face various barriers when they do not follow a linear and properly verified plan. In this perspective, the Municipalities, which function as entities operating internally and externally, resort to Communication in order to reach their target audience. It is true that changes have been made that alter the communicative paradigm itself, moving from a mass approach to a bilateral relationship between Autarchy - Target Public, as it is known that inclusion, in this case of citizens in projects linked to Autarchy, changes feelings negative effects that are often associated with it. Additionally, mutual work, when properly developed, generates a greater impact on what citizens' lives are, revealing positive content for potential markets. With regard to Territorial Marketing, it covers the value of the territory that aggregates various resources, together with the dynamics of network relationships, stimulated by territorial actors, making it crucial to deepen the true needs to create adequate solutions, reconciling the purposes of society and respective values. While, in an initial part, they are considered to be frequent themes and of high knowledge, the fact is that with the course of the research the study and the information are vast, however the theoretical part is not always easily planned and applied. Hence the relevance of introducing two methodological approaches, namely qualitative and quantitative, in order to make it possible to compare the issuing entity, as an Autarchy, and the receiver as a local community.

The European Capital of Culture brought recognition to the Municipality, creating the brand and all its surroundings even by including the citizens, despite the results the communication was made by external entities that, operating in the area, thus have greater specific knowledge and facilitated the arrival of the message to the public. Considering, the pandemic context experienced exposes the public's large online presence, but also its saturation at a certain stage in receiving too much content, resulting in a post-Covid-19 with actors less willing to interact with the Autarchy, therefore making it difficult to form how the Autarchy emanates its message, especially with regard to closed spaces, where a large part of the community still feels reticent. At this point, the simple and well-targeted message would result in bringing the public closer, for example through cultural content that generates a lot of interaction interspersed with the sharing of information about the municipality, as specific objectives of the sectors that involve the municipality.

The quantitative approach consisted of applying an online questionnaire survey, reaching 400 individuals residing in the city of Guimarães, a sample that, following the analysis of its results, is similar in social terms, for example in terms of age, level of education and others. observed. Although there is a large number of stakeholders who consider themselves informed by the Autarchy, it should be noted that the data relating to the lack of knowledge about topics associated with the Autarchy, such as the objectives of the departments and the Institution refers to a considerable percentage that cannot receive this information. The participants' responses showed an affective connection to the place, but it would be important to know their opinion about their identification with the municipal initiatives, as well as their availability to participate in campaigns led by the respective municipalities. Since the scope of the manuscript was not intended to address the issue of external evaluation by tourists, but the perception of residents, it will be necessary for their testimonies to confirm their opinion about the components of quality of life, in terms of housing, school infrastructure, economic activities, commerce and services, in a perspective of sustainable growth. In a general sense, the positive connotation of the questions addressed is really significant, covering the various themes represented in the pre-established objectives of the work, however it is necessary to understand the reasons that bring together several respondents in situations of denial in the face of them, because grouping the answers of "no" the numbers are very considerable, making it necessary to reformulate the Communication issued by the Municipality, not least because the majority of respondents have shown that the entity in question cannot reach the scope of the message issued, therefore, it does not comply with overall objective. Therefore, it is clear that the online medium is here to stay and, as it manages to be the most effective in transmitting information, it objectively reaches the largest number of people, due to the transformation of society itself. The contents with the greatest interaction relate to the Culture and Leisure area, where citizens can mainly process information about events, highlighting the European Capital of Culture event, as a lever for the Municipality's own communication. In addition to the attachment that residents may have to their territory, other variables will have to be included in the model, particularly those that unequivocally demonstrate the existence of quality of life and that are very important for the consolidation of the brand. This chapter presents insights for territorial management, local development and contributions to the tourist destination (i.e. Guimarães).

ACKNOWLEDGMENT

The authors are grateful to the Foundation for Science and Technology (FCT, Portugal) for financial support by national funds FCT/MCTES to UNIAG (UIDB/04752/2020 and UIDP/04752/2020).

REFERENCES

Abreu, J. (2018). *Inteligência Territorial – Governança, Sustentabilidade e Transparência*. Almedina.

Agnoletti, M., Conti, L., Frezza, L., & Santoro, A. (2015). Territorial analysis of the agricultural terraced landscapes of Tuscany (Italy): Preliminary results. *Sustainability (Basel)*, *7*(4), 4564–4581. doi:10.3390/su7044564

Almeida-Santana, A., & Moreno-Gil, S. (2017). New trends in information search and their influence on destination loyalty: Digital destinations and relationship marketing. *Journal of Destination Marketing & Management*, *6*(2), 150–161. doi:10.1016/j.jdmm.2017.02.003

Amado, J., Costa, A. P., & Crusoé, N. (2000). A técnica de análise de conteúdo. *Revista Referência*, *5*, 53–63.

Atsız, O., & Temiz, S. (2022). Literary tourism: A perspective of the visitor experience in the Museum of Innocence. In *Global Perspectives on Literary Tourism and Film-Induced Tourism* (pp. 37–52). IGI Global. doi:10.4018/978-1-7998-8262-6.ch003

Azimovna, M. S., Ilkhomovna, U. D., & Shokhrukhovich, U. F. (2022). The Concept of Marketing Policy in Trade and Service Enterprises. *Central Asian Journal Of Innovations On Tourism Management And Finance*, *3*(8), 1–5.

Caroli, M. (1999). *Il marketing territoriale. Lineamenti teorici e strumenti d'intervento* (F. Angeli, Ed.).

Chen, H. Y., Wang, L., Zhang, X., Wei, W., & Lyu, J. (2024). Does linguistic diversity make destinations more sophisticated? Exploring the effects on destination personality. *Journal of Destination Marketing & Management*, *31*, 100828. doi:10.1016/j.jdmm.2023.100828

Chen, N., & Dwyer, L. (2017). Residents' Place Satisfaction and Place Attachment on Destination Brand-Building Behaviors: Conceptual and Empirical Differentiation. *Journal of Travel Research*, *57*(8), 1026-1041. 004728751772976. doi:10.1177/0047287517729760

Cheung, L. T. O., & Hui, D. L. H. (2018). Influence of residents' place attachment on heritage forest conservation awareness in a peri-urban area of Guangzhou, China. *Urban Forestry & Urban Greening*, *33*(May), 37–45. doi:10.1016/j.ufug.2018.05.004

Clark, M., Kang, B., & Calhoun, J. R. (2023). Green meets social media: Young travelers' perceptions of hotel environmental sustainability. *Journal of Hospitality and Tourism Insights*, *6*(1), 36–51. doi:10.1108/JHTI-03-2021-0062

Eichinger, I., Schreier, M., & van Osselaer, S. M. (2022). Connecting to place, people, and past: How products make us feel grounded. *Journal of Marketing*, *86*(4), 1–16. doi:10.1177/00222429211027469

Frandsen, F., & Johansen, W. (2009). Institutionalizing crisis communication in the public sector: An explorative study in Danish municipalities. *International Journal of Strategic Communication*, *3*(2), 102–115. doi:10.1080/15531180902805460

Glyptou, K. (2024). Operationalising tourism sustainability at the destination level: A systems thinking approach along the SDGs. *Tourism Planning & Development*, *21*(1), 95–121. doi:10.1080/21568316.2022.2069150

Hasanaj, R., & Manxhari, A. M. (2017). Importance of communication during change: A case of the municipality of vlora. *European Journal of Multidisciplinary Studies*, *2*(1), 15–19. doi:10.26417/ejms.v4i1.p15-19

Hetenyi, G., Lengyel, A., & Szilasi, M. (2019). Quantitative analysis of qualitative data: Using voyant tools to investigate the sales-marketing interface. [JIEM]. *Journal of Industrial Engineering and Management*, *12*(3), 393–404. doi:10.3926/jiem.2929

Kotler, P., & Haider, D. R. (1993). *Marketing Places*. Free Press.

Liberato, D., Limbado, B., Sousa, B., & Liberato, P. (2022). Northern portugal tourism experiences management for the post-covid period: facing demand changes in tourism products and services. In *Advances in Tourism, Technology and Systems: Selected Papers from ICOTTS 2021* (Vol. 1, pp. 625–643). Springer Nature Singapore. doi:10.1007/978-981-19-1040-1_52

Litvin, S. W., Goldsmith, R. E., & Pan, B. (2008). Electronic word-of-mouth in hospitality and tourism management. *Tourism Management*, *29*(3), 458–468. doi:10.1016/j.tourman.2007.05.011

Ma, W., Jong, W. M., Hoppe, T., & Bruijne, M. (2021). From city promotion via city marketing to city branding: Examining urban strategies in 23 Chinese cities. *Cities*, *116*, 103269. doi:10.1016/j.cities.2021.103269

Méndez Prada, M. C., López Barraza, L. M., Ziritt Trejo, G. Y., & Ruiz Escorcia, R. R. (2023). Explanatory structural equation model validation for territorial branding tourism policies. *International Journal of Tourism Cities*, *9*(2), 377–393. doi:10.1108/IJTC-06-2021-0119

Nieves-Pavón, S., López-Mosquera, N., & Jiménez-Naranjo, H. (2024). The role emotions play in loyalty and WOM intention in a Smart Tourism Destination Management. *Cities (London, England)*, *145*, 104681. doi:10.1016/j.cities.2023.104681

Person, C., Behnke, N., & Jürgens, T. (2023). Effects of Territorial Party Politics on Horizontal Coordination among the German Länder–An Analysis of the COVID-19 Pandemic Management in Germany. *German Politics*, 1–26. doi:10.1080/09644008.2023.2187782

Roseta, P., Sousa, B. B., & Roseta, L. (2020). Determiners in the consumer's purchase decision process in ecotourism contexts: A Portuguese case study. *Geosciences*, *10*(6), 224. doi:10.3390/geosciences10060224

Sautter, E. T., & Leisen, B. (1999). Managing stakeholders a Tourism Planning Model. *Annals of Tourism Research*, *26*(2), 312–328. doi:10.1016/S0160-7383(98)00097-8

Silva, J., Sousa, B., & Abreu, J. (2023). Place Marketing and Destination Management: A Study in the "Quadrilátero do Minho". In *Advances in Tourism, Technology and Systems: Selected Papers from ICOTTS 2022* (Vol. 2, pp. 567–577). Springer Nature Singapore. doi:10.1007/978-981-19-9960-4_49

Sousa, B., & Rocha, A. T. (2019). The role of attachment in public management and place marketing contexts: A case study applied to Vila de Montalegre (Portugal). *International Journal of Public Sector Performance Management*, *5*(2), 189–205. doi:10.1504/IJPSPM.2019.099094

Spadaro, I., Pirlone, F., Bruno, F., Saba, G., Poggio, B., & Bruzzone, S. (2023). Stakeholder Participation in Planning of a Sustainable and Competitive Tourism Destination: The Genoa Integrated Action Plan. *Sustainability (Basel)*, *15*(6), 5005. doi:10.3390/su15065005

Vinyals-Mirabent, S., Kavaratzis, M., & Fernandez-Cavia, J. (2019). The role of functional associations in building destination brand personality: When official websites do the talking. *Tourism Management*, *75*, 148–155. doi:10.1016/j.tourman.2019.04.022

KEY TERMS AND DEFINITIONS

Communication: Communication is a process that involves the exchange of information between two or more interlocutors.

Loyalty: Consideration of the precepts that concern honor, decency, and honesty.

Place Dependence: Functional connection with a particular place or context. Place dependence is related to the perceived attachment power between the person and the specific place associated with the particular place quality and the other alternative places quality compared to the intended location.

Place Identity: Symbolic or emotional connection for a location or context. Place identity or place-based identity refers to a cluster of ideas about place and identity in the fields of geography, urban planning, urban design, landscape architecture, interior design, spatial design, environmental psychology, ecocriticism and urban sociology/ecological sociology. Place identity is sometimes called urban character, neighbourhood character or local character.

Relationship Marketing: Relationship marketing corresponds to marketing work focused on the relationship with customers and suppliers.

Territorial Brand: a territory brand is a combination of unique qualities, unfading universal values reflecting the originality, unique original consumer characteristics of a given territory and community.

Chapter 14
Navigating the Gap: Protecting Human Rights in the Era of Environmental Migration

Abhinash Mohanta
https://orcid.org/0000-0002-8732-3202
KIIT University, India

Akash Bag
https://orcid.org/0000-0001-8820-171X
Adamas University, India

Shreya
https://orcid.org/0009-0008-3533-797X
Soa University, India

Kumud Choudhary
Adamas University, India

ABSTRACT

Human migration has helped populations survive harsh environments. However, international law has mostly addressed migration caused by persecution, conflict, and war, leaving environmental migrants unprotected. This chapter critically evaluates four essential international human rights and environmental law tools to protect environmental refugees. These include the refugee convention, complementary protection, guiding principles on internal displacement, and UNFCCC. By carefully analyzing these instruments, it becomes clear that they cannot fully address environmental migration. This constraint highlights the need for a separate international mechanism to address environmental displacement. The instrument should strengthen affected populations' resilience and assist in relocation.

DOI: 10.4018/979-8-3693-1742-6.ch014

INTRODUCTION

A catastrophic magnitude-8 earthquake that rocked the Chinese Sichuan province in 2008 caused an incredible 15 million people to be displaced (Bernal & Procee, 2012). A' superstorm,' Hurricane Sandy pushed 1.2 million people from six countries—including the United States—to flee their homes three years later in 2011 (Burger et al., 2019). In 2018, 1.6 million people were forced to flee their homes due to the destructive effects of Typhoon Mangkhut in the Philippines (IDMC, 2020, p. 28). Even if these instances alone amount to a significant human tragedy, they only make up a small portion of the roughly 260 million people who were forced to from their homes due to various disaster-related incidents during the previous ten years (IDMC, 2020). The scientific community and international law have mostly focused on comprehending anthropogenic climate change and its influence on weather patterns and coastlines, notwithstanding the historical usage of human migration to cope with climatic changes. Unfortunately, very little thought has gone into how climate change would affect people's ability to move about. The legal system has primarily addressed migration brought about by persecution, war, and violence, therefore excluding environmental migrants from a complete system of protection (Brown, 2008). Furthermore, environmental migration strains already unstable governments and the international community, and it challenges the human rights of impacted communities. These issues have received little attention in international politics.

This lack of focus is alarming, particularly in light of the sporadic and selective character of international cooperation in migration. A prime illustration of this problem is the current "*crisis*" of refugees resulting from the civil war in Syria. Despite their shared commitment to the right to asylum under the 1951 Geneva Convention relating to the Status of Refugees, European Union (EU) Member States engaged in lengthy discussions over responsibility-sharing and allocation, while Middle Eastern states found it difficult to receive new arrivals (Brown, 2008). This crisis highlighted how inadequate ad hoc solutions are for handling mass migration. The issue of environmental migration is expected to worsen as the effects of climate change increase. As a result, it becomes urgently necessary to develop a global, legally obligatory protection framework for environmental migrants. Such a regime is required to guarantee collective responsibility within the international community and stop human rights breaches. This chapter investigates how current international legal tools might effectively protect environmental migrants' rights.

METHODOLOGY

The study reported in this chapter results from a careful and systematic review of the literature regarding the changing state of international human rights protection for people forced to migrate because of environmental circumstances. To attain accuracy in the definition of environmental migration, we combined resources from two reputable international organizations: the United Nations Environment Programme (UNEP) and the International Organisation for Migration (IOM). Academic articles delving into many aspects of the phenomenon supplemented these basic definitions. We used information from the Internal Displacement Monitoring Center's annual Global Report to calculate the scope of the problem (IDMC) quantitatively. We also examined international human rights conventions and the authoritative interpretations of those conventions found in the General Comments that corresponded with them, grounding our viewpoint in the human rights domain. We expanded our scope by including peer-reviewed books and journal papers that tackled the job of contrasting the relevance and appropriateness of current international legal frameworks in addressing the situation of environmental migrants. Resources like Google Scholar and the University of Vienna library repository made this extensive investigation possible.

To emphasize the need for international action, we used socio-scientific models, thought about flexible and robust approaches, and looked at current political discourse on migration and asylum. Potential future paradigms were projected as the result of these efforts. In addition, we examined official documents and guidelines regarding environmental migration and examined news articles explaining natural disasters and national governments' reactions. Wherever they were accessible, we took inspiration from national laws, international legal instruments, regional policy documents, and United Nations resolutions. We spoke with Dr. Margit Ammer, E.MA., a renowned Senior Researcher at the Ludwig Boltzmann Institute for Human Rights in Vienna, Austria, as a final and worthwhile attempt to deepen our investigation. Dr. Ammer is an expert in human rights and the environment, especially regarding migration and displacement. With Dr. Ammer's permission, we recorded an hour-long interview using a semi-structured interviewing technique. Unfortunately, our original plan to incorporate two more expert interviews was derailed since these experts could not be reached by the chapter deadline. However, no obstacles were found while attempting to get relevant secondary literature.

THE NEXUS BETWEEN MIGRATION AND THE ENVIRONMENT

Changes have significantly influenced human migration in the environment. It has been established that this occurrence is an adaptation mechanism to adverse environmental circumstances (Mcadam, 2011). German cartographer Ernst Ravenstein initially proposed that an "*unattractive climate*" could drive human migration in 1885 (Ravenstein, 1885). But in the early 20th century, environmental issues became less and less relevant in the migration debate; this was especially true in the 1980s regarding debates over man-made climate change. The Intergovernmental Panel on Climate Change (IPCC) publications have provided important new information about the connection between migratory patterns and environmental changes. The discourse on environmental migration has taken on new dimensions due to the threat of climate change. Climate change worsens environmental changes, making more people vulnerable to displacement (Faist & Schade, 2013). Because of this, conventional adaption techniques become less and less effective in the face of such swift environmental changes (Mcadam, 2011). There are two main schools of thought in the scholarly literature on this subject: alarmists and skeptics. To raise awareness of the problem of environmental migration, alarmists highlight environmental problems as the primary causes of migration (Faist & Schade, 2013). On the other hand, detractors contest the alarmists' estimations of the populations impacted, stating that various variables usually impact migration (Adamo, 2009). Ecologists and environmentalists who support environmental protection are typically alarmists; on the other hand, migration researchers who worry that the discussion will stigmatize migrants are known as skeptics (Faist & Schade, 2013).

Research shows that environmental changes can cause population shifts, notwithstanding disagreements in the debate. The choice to move or stay put is influenced by several intricately interacting elements, such as social, political, economic, demographic, and environmental aspects. Environmental factors are significant because they might reinforce these other determinants (Mcadam, 2011). Migration depends on the interplay among shifting climatic conditions, additional macro-level drives, pre-existing vulnerabilities, and other micro- and meso-level intervening or supporting variables. Since population migrations also affect the environmental conditions of locations along migratory routes, it is imperative to recognize that the relationship between the environment and migration is bidirectional (Foresight, 2011). The main topic of this essay is the idea of an "*environmental push*" that causes migration and is linked to weather fluctuations and the depletion of natural resources (European Parliament, 2011). In reaction to their declining environmental conditions, people and communities are compelled by this environmental urge to look for new homes and sources of income (European Parliament, 2011).

Defining Environmental Migration

Because human mobility due to environmental variables is complex and multifaceted, obtaining reliable numerical data regarding environmental migration is difficult. This is mainly due to the various causal elements at work and the controversial definitional aspects of environmental migration. In particular, rigorous official documentation of population migration caused by the negative consequences of progressive environmental changes—such as extended droughts, rising sea levels, and other environmental degradation—remains elusive (Faist & Schade, 2013). Due to this situation, estimating the future numbers of environmental migrants is an extremely difficult issue, in addition to determining the total number of people whom environmental factors have historically displaced. However, in academic debate, several estimates have emerged, the most well-known of which are from the works of Myers. Myers said, based on data related to internally displaced people (IDPs), that 25 million people could be categorized as "*environmental refugees*" in 1995 (Argos & Reeves, 2010). In addition, Myers conjectured that by 2010, this number would rise to at least 50 million; by 2050, environmental changes may put 200 million people at risk of being uprooted from their homes (Kent & Myers, 1995). These estimates, however, should be examined closely because they are predicated on several audacious assumptions and wild guesses (European Parliament, 2011).

Even with the lack of hard data, a more accurate estimate of the extent of environmental migration can be obtained by carefully analyzing the population displaced by sudden-onset disasters and the demographics living in areas disproportionately vulnerable to environmental degradation. Data on the number of people internally displaced by sudden-onset disasters has been released annually by the Internal Displacement Monitoring Centre (IDMC) since 2008. These numbers come from various sources, such as government disaster management organizations, non-governmental organizations, the International Federation of the Red Cross and Red Crescent Societies, and the United Nations. However, these numbers do not specify the displacement length, the migration scope, or the final resettlement locations. Most displaced people appear to stay inside their home countries' borders (Hinnawi, 1985). As such, internal displacement represents the majority of human mobility in this setting, even though it does not fully capture the entirety of movements made by environmental migrants. Because of this, it is used sparingly to estimate the total number of people displaced by sudden-onset disasters when more complete data is unavailable.

Between 2008 and 2017, an average of 24.7 million people worldwide were relocated for the first time due to natural disasters yearly (IDMC, 2020). Between 2010 and 2011, the number of internally displaced people caused by disasters varied from 15.0 million to a maximum of 42.4 million. Just one year later, in 2017, 18.8 million individuals in 135 countries were the victims of new internal displacements caused by sudden-onset catastrophes (IDMC, 2020). This accounted for 61 percent of all new internal displacements that year. Interestingly, only a small percentage of these displacements were caused by natural disasters like earthquakes; storms and floods are responsible for 7.5 million and 8.6

million, respectively. Just ten weather-related incidents accounted for over 10 million of the 18.8 million new displacements in 2017(IDMC, 2020). The most significant of these was Hurricane Irma, a natural disaster that in August and September uprooted over two million people in the Caribbean and the United States (IDMC, 2020).

Looking at the nations most affected by disaster displacement in 2017, China came first with 4.5 million newly displaced people. The Philippines came in second with 2.5 million, followed by the USA and Cuba with 1.7 million and India with 1.3 million. Interestingly, these five countries house over a million displaced individuals from sudden-onset disasters and reflect the regional dispersion of displaced persons worldwide. Historically, the Americas, the Pacific, and South and East Asia have been hardest hit by relocation brought on by natural disasters; this pattern persisted until 2017(Hiraide, 2023). Specifically, in 2017, more than 8.5 million people were displaced by disasters in East Asia and the Pacific, making up almost half of all internally displaced individuals caused by disasters in that region. China and the Philippines were found to be the most affected countries in this region (IDMC, 2020). This is mainly because around thirty percent of the world's population lives in this region, much of which is concentrated in coastal cities. The Americas area was second with about 24 percent of the world's total disaster displacement. The primary reason for this prominence is Hurricane Irma and the other storms during the 2017 Atlantic hurricane season. Smaller island developing nations in the Caribbean were disproportionately burdened with the burden of displacement caused by disasters, even though the United States and Cuba were clearly among the nations with the biggest numbers of displaced people in this region (IDMC, 2020).

Most of the 2.8 million people newly displaced in South Asia 2017 were affected by the monsoon season, a situation made worse by pre-existing vulnerabilities related to the region's poverty, inequality, and unsustainable growth. In contrast, Sub-Saharan Africa's population distribution provided a fair share of worldwide disaster displacements. On the other hand, the combined share of inhabitants displaced by disasters in Europe, Central Asia, North Africa, and the Middle East was less than two percent, indicating a comparatively lower frequency of such displacements in these regions (IDMC, 2020). This historical data highlights the extent of displacement caused by disasters, and projections show that this situation will only continue to worsen (Hiraide, 2023). The IDMC estimated in 2017 that 11 million people would experience internal displacement annually due to disasters; just a year later, this estimate was corrected to 13.9 million people annually (IDMC, 2020). The disaster displacement risk model developed by the IDMC predicts that floods will be the main cause of future displacements, with storm surges caused by cyclones uprooting an average of 2 million people yearly. With potential yearly displacements of 4.2 million and 5 million people, respectively, this projected risk mostly focuses on South Asia and the East Asia-Pacific area (Hiraide, 2023). Predictive models additionally pinpoint the nation's most vulnerable to future disaster-related relocation: India, China, Bangladesh, Vietnam, and the Philippines (IDMC, 2020). These projections, however cautious, do not account for people who might be evacuated ahead of time or those compelled to relocate as a result of slow environmental deterioration because they are based on estimates of the number of severely damaged or destroyed houses and average household sizes.

Compared to the comparatively well-researched displacement resulting from sudden-onset disasters, estimates about the number of people displaced by slow-onset disasters are controversial and difficult, as there is a shortage of historical data. However, it is generally accepted that many more people are anticipated to move due to slow environmental degradation instead of abrupt natural disasters. For the first time, the IDMC released data on drought-related displacement in 2017, estimating that at least 1.3 million people were displaced during the year (IDMC, 2020). Approximately 900,000 of these displacements took place inside Somalia. Drought-stricken areas are predicted to grow due to the current water constraint and the aggravating impacts of climate change. By 2025, 1.8 million people will live in afflicted countries, mostly Africa and Asia. Subsequently, a notable surge in water scarcity and drought-related displacements is anticipated (Hiraide, 2023). Approximations indicate that these gradual disasters may impact anywhere from 24 to 700 million people globally. Although it takes longer, rising sea level is still a serious environmental threat (IDMC, 2020). According to current climate change forecasts, coastal communities living in locations less than one meter above sea level would have negative outcomes in the next several decades. Currently, the prospect of flooding threatens about 40 million people living in large coastal cities in both developed and developing countries (IDMC, 2020). The rise in sea level is expected to affect over 40% of the world's population within 100 km of shoreline, particularly the approximately 150 million people who live in river deltas and tiny island states.

Even though these statistics offer insightful information about the scope of the issue, it's critical to recognize that most of these impacted groups are unlikely to relocate due to environmental factors. The decision to migrate in response to environmental changes is influenced by several factors (Hiraide, 2023). Notably, these changes disproportionately impact those who live in poverty since they frequently cannot afford to employ expensive environmental adaptation techniques. The data on disaster displacement shows that 61% of these displacements in 2014 happened in lower middle-income nations—home to around one-third of the world's population—reflecting this imbalance (Hiraide, 2023).

Human Rights at Stake and Protection Needs

The 'International Bill of Rights,' comprising the Universal Declaration of Human Rights (UDHR), the International Covenant on Civil and Political Rights (ICCPR), and the International Covenant on Economic, Social, and Cultural Rights (ICESCR), grants fundamental rights to every person, irrespective of their location of displacement—whether it is domestically or internationally, brought about by environmental factors or other migration-related causes, or not at all (Zetter, 2011a). These rights are applicable at every stage of migration. However, they fall into different categories of protection. First and foremost, there is the defence of life, personal safety, bodily integrity, and dignity. Protecting rights related to the bare needs of existence comes in second (Kolmes et al., 2022). The defence of additional economic, social, and cultural rights comes in third. The defence of additional civil and political rights comes last. When environmental migration results directly from either a slow-onset or sudden-onset disaster event, the first two categories of rights protection are given the highest priority as soon as the event occurs (Lyons & editor, 2020). These categories include the right to an adequate quality of living (as defined in Article 11 of the ICESCR) and the right to life (as stated in Article 6 of the ICCPR). The latter covers housing and shelter, food, and water rights, as General Comment No. 15 of the Economic and Social Council specified.

It is important to remember that, according to General Comment No. 6 of the Human Rights Council, a person's right to life and security is unalienable and cannot be renounced or restricted, not even in dire circumstances (Bradley & Cohen, 2015). This right is especially important when natural calamities like storms, floods, or droughts directly threaten people's lives and means of subsistence. In a larger sense, particularly regarding environmental migration, preserving other fundamental rights linked to necessities and the physical environment is intimately linked to realizing an individual's right to life and security (Bradley & Cohen, 2015). This includes the right, as stated in Article 1(2) of the ICCPR and ICESCR, to not have one's means of subsistence away from oneself. Future environmental changes are likely to significantly impact food production, with a notably negative effect on global food security, especially in areas presently experiencing extreme poverty (Freeland & Horn, 2009). Furthermore, the distribution of humanitarian food aid to those displaced due to natural catastrophes emphasizes the value of the right to food, which includes the right not to hunger and the necessity of guaranteeing fair access to relief.

Concurrently, water rights are being threatened by environmental changes, mainly because freshwater resources are running low. When one considers that natural disasters sometimes result in displacement, this worry intensifies further. In addition, the right to shelter becomes crucial in these situations, and the loss of dwellings brought on by both gradual and sudden-onset disasters, along with the subsequent relocations they need, puts the wider right to housing in jeopardy (Wu, 2021). Two more areas of rights protection become increasingly important when we go farther into the future, past the immediate aftermath of disaster occurrences and in scenarios where environmental migration occurs in response to or anticipation of worsening environmental deterioration (Bradley & Cohen, 2015). These include, on the one hand, voting rights, and political freedoms, and, on the other, access to jobs and educational possibilities. Furthermore, documentation is a major concern when it comes to environmental displacement. Catastrophic incidents frequently destroy personal property, challenging the establishment of one's identity and claims (Freeland & Horn, 2009). Article 17 of the Universal Declaration of Human Rights (UDHR) states that property rights come into play, as does protecting people against abuses concerning the return or compensation of their property, which is relevant for many environmental migrants (Cohen & Bradley, 2010).

The ability to own property and live in one's home area is closely linked to the possibility of moving back home. People may lose their prior property when returning becomes unrealistic or unreasonable, especially in the face of frequent calamities or livable regions. But even in cases where returning home is a practical option, temporary environmental migrants can still need assistance in reconstructing their lives and means of sustainable subsistence(Freeland & Horn, 2009). It's important to remember that while the rights listed above apply to all environmental migrants, abuses of these rights are more likely to affect women, children, and members of socially marginalized groups. The prejudice and gender inequality that are pervasive in many countries are the cause of this increased vulnerability (Freeland & Horn, 2009). In addition to being more vulnerable to the dangers associated with environmental changes, women may experience gender-based violence while migrating. In a similar vein, environmental changes provide unique difficulties for indigenous cultures. People with deep cultural attachments to their native lands and ways of life are frequently more vulnerable to environmental changes (Bradley & Cohen, 2015).

Apart from these susceptible populations, residents of states that risk losing their whole territory should also receive extra protection. Although international agreements cover the situation of stateless people, it's crucial to distinguish between *de facto* and *de jure* statelessness (being refused citizenship). Regarding environmental migration, some people might *de facto* become stateless if the country they belong to disappears (Jayawardhan, 2017). This is the case for small island governments that are becoming untenable by increasing sea levels. This chapter clarifies that although environmental migration is associated with several human rights, nations' obligations to protect these rights are not immediately apparent (Jayawardhan, 2017). Environmental migrants cannot base their claims on the explicit establishment of a right to a healthy environment under international law. Moreover, it rejects the idea that states have "*common but differentiated responsibilities*," which would hold them responsible for how they contribute to environmental changes.

Internal displacement laws may, in part, apply to environmental displacement inside the borders of the state of origin. On the other hand, other types of internal environmental migration show serious weaknesses in guaranteeing and protecting human rights, especially those linked to gradual degradation and viewed as more voluntary. Comparably, international environmental migrants experience shortcomings in international law even though they are entitled to the general protection of human rights in their destination state. As such, individuals might not have an inalienable right to admission into that state nor a manifest right to stay in the states where they take sanctuary (Karacasulu & Karakir, 2021). That is why the next chapter explores several current international legal mechanisms that either protect or have the capacity to protect the rights of different types of environmental migrants (Kaelin, 2019).

EXISTING LEGAL INSTRUMENTS AND THEIR POTENTIAL TO EXPAND TO ENVIRONMENTAL MIGRANTS

The ICCPR and ICESCR provide a baseline level of protection for all environmental migrants but do not fully guarantee their human rights. The next chapter examines the legality of altering or tailoring international refugee and environmental laws to address the difficulties of environmental migration better.

The Guiding Principles on Internal Displacement

Adopted by the UN General Assembly in 1998, the Guiding Principles on Internal Displacement are a type of soft law that serves to reaffirm and condense the duties already present in international humanitarian, refugee, and human rights law (Gemenne & Brucker, 2015). As such, they are not legally enforceable on nations. The idea of the responsibility to protect, which emphasizes that the sovereign state where internally displaced people (IDPs) are located bears the main responsibility for their protection and support, impacts these concepts (Cohen, 2004). The international community's participation becomes necessary when a state cannot offer this support and protection. These 30 Guiding Principles acknowledge the rights of internally displaced people and the obligations of states to protect them. They address protection against displacement, during displacement, and following displacement during repatriation or resettlement, among other stages of displacement. They notably contain clauses that forbid forced relocation, discriminatory aid, arbitrary displacement, and the defence of property rights. They also give a precise explanation of who is considered an IDP.

Coercion and staying inside national borders are the two key components of this definition. IDPs are people or groups who, without having crossed an internationally recognized state border, have been compelled to flee their homes because of armed conflict, widespread violence, breaches of human rights, or natural or man-made disasters. As long as they stay inside national borders, people internally displaced by natural disasters—including those with abrupt onsets like floods and earthquakes—are also covered by this definition (Omisore et al., 2020). The Guiding Principles also acknowledge internally displaced people (IDPs) who have been forced to flee their homes because of intentional environmental degradation and the effects of climate change. This group includes people from small island nations uprooted by increasing sea levels and those impacted by gradual environmental changes like desertification, so long as the latter are categorized as catastrophes and the uprooting is forced. The non-binding nature of the Guiding Principles restricts their practical application, even if they provide a viable model for managing environmental migration (Orchard, 2018). There are insufficient mechanisms for enforcement and accountability, and many governments limit the scope of their domestic IDP protection laws to relocation caused by conflict. Moreover, the definition's coercive component excludes those who relocate proactively because they anticipate environmental degradation and restricts protection to circumstances in which the area is completely unsuitable (Kaelin, 2019). Their application to international environmental migrants is further limited by the obligation to remain inside national borders.

Geneva Convention Relating to the Status of Refugees 1951

The 1951 Geneva Convention, specifically the "Convention Relating to the Status of Refugees," is pivotal in establishing the international rights and protections afforded refugees (Betts, 2010). This convention, born out of the aftermath of World War II, codifies the fundamental principle that individuals who face a genuine and well-founded fear of persecution for reasons such as race, religion, nationality, membership in a particular social group, or political opinion, and are unable or unwilling to receive protection from their home country, are entitled to seek asylum in another country. Importantly, the definition of a refugee under this convention hinges on the presence of persecution, which is often interpreted as serious harm resulting from human rights violations and a state's failure to protect the individual against such violations (Billings, 2008). This definition also encompasses violations of various civil, political, economic, social, and cultural rights, focusing on a state's fulfillment of its core obligations in these areas (Marcs, 2008).

The convention emphasizes that persecution is typically related to actions by state authorities, but it can also occur when a state fails to provide effective protection, even if there is no explicit intent to persecute. The convention lists five protected grounds for persecution: race, religion, nationality, membership in a particular social group, and political opinion. While the first four grounds are relatively straightforward, a "particular social group" is broader and can encompass groups with shared characteristics, whether immutable or socially defined (Zieck, 2015). Now, the chapter delves into whether the refugee definition can be extended to cover environmental migrants. It argues that the convention does not explicitly exclude environmental factors as a basis for persecution, leaving room for a broader interpretation. Environmental changes can lead to human rights violations, potentially amounting to persecution when state actions or omissions cause severe infringements. For instance, deliberate environmental harm, deprivation of cultural existence, food scarcity, or health issues resulting from environmental changes can all be seen as forms of persecution.

However, the chapter notes that while environmental changes can harm affected populations, it is challenging to establish a direct link to the convention grounds (race, religion, nationality, political opinion) or even a particular social group. Environmental changes tend to affect many people without necessarily targeting specific groups. Furthermore, the refugee convention is primarily designed to protect those who have already left their home countries, making it less suitable for environmental migrants who may be internally displaced or who have not yet crossed international borders.

Complementary Protection

The demands of international environmental migrants are not adequately met by the Refugee Convention, a crucial piece of the international legal framework for protecting refugees. This shortcoming forces one to think of supplementary defences. By definition, complementary protection functions as a substitute for the Refugee Convention, and its interpretation within the framework of international law differs. Currently, it's recognized as extending nations' protection duties beyond the conventional "refugee" classification (Mcadam, 2011). By doing away with the need for a protected ground and concentrating instead on the non-refoulement principle present in several international human rights treaties, complementary protection expands the eligibility requirements for international protection (McAdam, 2008). Non-refoulement is based on several international agreements, including the Convention against Torture (CAT) and the International Covenant on Civil and Political Rights (ICCPR), which forbid states from sending people under their jurisdiction back to a location where they could be subjected to torture or other serious human rights violations (Marcs, 2008).

Regional human rights documents like the American Convention on Human Rights (ACHR) and the European Convention on Human Rights (ECHR) have similar duties. Thus, these clauses broaden the scope of state protection obligations beyond individuals who are being persecuted to include those who may be arbitrarily deprived of their lives or subjected to torture and inhumane treatment. Compared to the Refugee Convention, complementary protection is not a lower calibre or length of protection (Bradley & Cohen, 2015). Rather, the national laws of each state determine the requirements for eligibility, status, and type of protection offered. States respond to specific asylum seekers who cannot be deported because of an expanded principle of non-refoulement under international law by implementing complementary protection systems (Lyons & editor, 2020).

Different nations have established national laws that permit people to stay in their country when it is neither practical nor wise to remove them. Examples of these policies include subsidiary protection in the European Union, temporary protection in the USA, and the status of "persons in need of protection" in Canada. Economic, social, and cultural rights, as well as civil and political rights, may be violated by environmental changes (Cohen, 2004). Thus, two possible ways exist to incorporate environmental migrants into complementary protection schemes. The first option is for foreign environmental migrants to claim protection based on civil or political rights, like the right to life. This includes people escaping sudden-onset natural disasters or armed conflicts brought on by shifting environmental conditions and the consequent scarcity of resources (Jayawardhan, 2017).

Severe abuses of economic, social, and cultural rights give rise to the second option; these violations may be construed as inhuman or humiliating treatment even when they are not directly connected to any particular safeguard. This would include circumstances in which people lose their means of subsistence and access to resources because environmental changes prevent them from receiving the fundamental services required for a dignified living. Nonetheless, a high bar remains for supplementary protection grounded in economic, social, and cultural rights (Wu, 2021). It only applies in dire situations—not just when there is widespread poverty or a lack of resources, but when environmental changes make survival in the place of origin impossible. Complementary protection is thus a cure for extreme environmental changes that make living conditions instantly intolerable; in other words, it acts as a haven when a state or region becomes completely untenable. However, because it requires the environment to reach extreme conditions, it can not account for movement that happens proactively, such as people departing small island states in preparation for increasing sea levels (Billings, 2008).

When calamities strike suddenly, humanitarian principles may warrant temporary protection; nevertheless, in most situations, supplemental protection is restricted to those already under another state's jurisdiction during the disaster (Lyons & editor, 2020). Furthermore, only a small number of states or regional organizations have implemented complementary protection, which results in the primarily regional application of the mechanism—particularly in the context of the ECHR and ACHR—even though it may be appropriate for some groups of environmental migrants (Burger et al., 2019).

United Nations Framework Convention on Climate Change

The United Nations Framework Convention on Climate Change (UNFCCC), ratified in 1992, is uniquely positioned among international legal treaties. In contrast to the Refugee Convention, the Guiding Principles on Internal Displacement, and other related protection measures that mainly deal with human rights law and particular types of human mobility, the UNFCCC is a foundational piece of international environmental law that focuses on climate change, one of the most important environmental factors (McAdam, 2008). The primary goal of the UNFCCC is to " stabilize greenhouse gas concentrations in the atmosphere at a level that would prevent dangerous anthropogenic interference with the climate system." It also outlines the global community's common interests concerning climate change. To achieve these goals and others outlined in the UNFCCC, state parties have set several guiding principles to direct their actions (Gemenne & Brucker, 2015). The idea of "common but differentiated responsibilities and respective capabilities" recognizes the worldwide effects of climate change. It acknowledges that industrialized nations have not only contributed more significantly to climate change—mainly through increased greenhouse gas emissions—but also have better resources and capacity to mitigate its effects (United Nations, 2021). As such, developed nations have an even greater obligation to combat climate change. Furthermore, the UNFCCC's Article 3 Paragraph 2 highlights the particular vulnerability of emerging nations, which bear a disproportionate amount of the brunt of environmental change (United Nations, 2021).

The UNFCCC requires states to adopt preventative or mitigating actions to avoid or lessen the negative effects of climate change. It says categorically that "lack of full scientific certainty should not be used as a reason for postponing such measures," especially when doing so could cause irreversible environmental harm. The treaty also requires developed governments to give financial support to developing countries to build appropriate systems for climate change adaptation, and it also requires states to implement facilitative measures in this regard. These UNFCCC-enshrined principles act as guidelines for worldwide collaboration in the fight against environmental migration (United Nations, 2021). As a major cause of environmental displacement, industrialized states are held responsible for their part in climate change, according to the "common but differentiated responsibilities" theory. This strategy recognizes that wealthy nations have benefited economically from their environmentally destructive actions, improving their ability to adapt to climate change and lowering the number of environmental migrants coming from their borders. On the other hand, environmental migrants tend to settle in industrialized nations (Cohen & Bradley, 2010).

The UNFCCC's Article 3, paragraph 2 emphasizes the needs of developing nations, underscoring their vulnerability to environmental migration. It also highlights the obligation to develop adaptive solutions collaboratively (United Nations, 2021). The United Nations Framework Convention on Climate Change (UNFCCC) identifies several regions as having a disproportionate need for efficient adaptation measures. These regions include tiny island states, low-lying coastal areas, and places susceptible to drought, desertification, or sudden-onset disasters. These areas align with where most environmental migrants are probably from (Cohen, 2004). Furthermore, the Cancun Agreement, which was negotiated in 2010 as part of the UNFCCC Conference of the Parties (COP), clearly recognizes the significance of state cooperation about migration, planned relocation, and displacement caused by climate change at all levels, including national, regional, and worldwide. The necessity to address displacement brought on by climate change is further highlighted by events such as the creation of the UNFCCC's Task Force on Displacement and the Warsaw International Mechanism for Loss and Damage in 2015 (Hiraide, 2023).

Although the UNFCCC's principles apply to environmental migration management, the treaty does not mention human mobility; its rules on adaptation strategies are general. The Cancun Agreement of 2010 was the first to explicitly include displacement caused by climate change, albeit in a relatively weakened form (Burger et al., 2019). While this component has been reinforced by the creation of the Task Force on Displacement, there is still a long way to go until state parties agree on real commitments (United Nations, 2021). This is because specific efforts to put the task force's recommendations into implementation have not yet been taken. It is also crucial to remember that the UNFCCC does not impose any particular state responsibilities, even while emphasizing shared responsibility (Cohen, 2004). As an alternative, it formalizes shared goals by characterizing climate change and its effects as a "common concern of humankind."

POLITICAL FEASIBILITY

Many moral grounds exist for states cooperating to create an effective environmental migrant protection device. First, the humanitarian case is strong. This perspective stresses protecting environmental change-affected populations. These people are typically displaced, lose their jobs, and must resettle. It's moral to defend and help them. The second is restorative justice. This argument suggests that environmental factors related to involuntary displacement, loss of income, and relocation require compensation. The goal is to restore justice and fairness to those impacted. Environmental migration raises security problems. Migration can cause regional strife and instability. This may affect world security. Thus, developing an international protection instrument may address these security issues. The political will to act on this issue might be low, especially in governments unaffected by environmental migration.

European Union

Since the 1990s, environmental migration—especially migration brought on by climate change—has received much attention and policy discussion inside the European Union (EU). The European Parliament first addressed the problem of "climate refugees" in a 1999 study titled "The Environment, Security, and Foreign Policy," which is when this focus first became apparent (Zetter, 2017). The potential effects of environmental migration were acknowledged in this report on several fronts, including immigration laws, global political stability, and EU development and humanitarian relief programs. About ten years later, in 2007, the European Commission published a Green Paper titled "Adapting to Climate Change in Europe," which went into additional detail on the subject (Zetter, 2011b). This agreement recognized that internal displacement or forced migration could occur due to natural resource conflicts and unforeseen disasters. Consequently, it suggested that the EU's policies regarding migration management take climate migration into account. The European Commission persisted in stressing security issues in a report titled "Climate Change and International Security," published in 2008. This analysis predicted environmental migrants would significantly increase the EU's migration demand (Zetter, 2010).

It warned that environmental migration may increase the likelihood of conflicts along migration routes, endangering European interests. The research also stressed the importance of the EU in tackling environmental migration by working with pertinent international organizations to build an all-encompassing European migration policy. Several research initiatives were funded to collect data on the relationship between environmental changes and forced migration, including the Environmental Change and Forced

Migration Scenarios (EACH-FOR). Remarkably, the matter also became more prominent within the European Refugee Fund, indicating the issue's importance. The conversation was advanced in 2011 by research on "Climate Refugees" by the European Parliament. The potential for integrating environmental migrants into current international mechanisms was investigated in this chapter. In the process, it exposed serious weaknesses in the legal frameworks of the EU and other countries that protect this particular category of migrants (Zetter, 2009).

The Member States of the European Union (EU) convened in 2013 to devise a climate change adaptation plan. A Commission Staff Working Document (CSWD) that addressed migration, environmental degradation, and climate change was released concurrently with this approach. The term "environmentally induced migrant" was used by the CSWD to refer to a broad category of people who migrate inside their nations or across borders because of environmental degradation or climate change (Zetter, 2011b). It also recognized the function of adaptation in migratory control. Interestingly, the paper emphasizes migration control as a practical way to deal with environmental displacement. But rather than migration towards the EU itself, the EU focused most of its emphasis on migration "between developing countries in the same region" and on migration within countries due to environmental reasons. As a result, environmental migration was primarily considered a problem under the jurisdiction of EU development cooperation and humanitarian aid policies within the external dimension of EU migration policy (Mayrhofer & Ammer, 2014).

Around 2015, as the Syrian civil conflict deepened and more migrants began to reach Europe, the European Commission reiterated the EU's international obligations. In the European Agenda for Migration, it underlined the EU's duty to provide a haven for people escaping persecution. The Agenda recognized the need to protect the EU's external borders and fight against irregular migration, human trafficking, and smuggling simultaneously (Scott, 2023). This call to action indicates a larger trend prevalent at the time: the growing politicization of migration in discourse. Due to this phenomenon, migration was considered a danger to European societies' sovereignty. Immigration ranked among the top ten concerns for European residents in 2015, a seven-percentage point increase since 2012. This securitization found resonance in popular opinion. This change in discourse also affected the vocabulary used by politicians and the media, who frequently used phrases like "wave of refugees," "refugee crisis," or "influx of refugees" about dangers or natural catastrophes—this purposeful use of language sought to link migration to chaos, terror, and unpredictable occurrences (Mayrhofer & Ammer, 2022).

The European Parliament discussed a viewpoint in 2017 that differed from the prior focus on a security-based strategy to handle migration-related issues. Rather, it emphasized the significance of not concentrating solely on security issues. The idea that development cooperation should persistently address climate change as a driver of migration was revitalized by this new viewpoint. It called on Member States to take the lead in identifying how climate change affects large-scale displacement, noting that these types of displacements are anticipated to increase in frequency and scope. In addition, the resolution served as a call to action for EU member states, imploring them to carry out the Paris Agreement's stated obligations regarding climate change mitigation (Zetter, 2010). It also audaciously pushed for creating a "special international protection status" considering the particular circumstances of those uprooted by climate change. This analysis of the documents demonstrates how environmental migration was presented as a security issue in the EU's early attempts. These worries eventually merged into a more comprehensive development-focused strategy for handling the external aspect of migration. This strategy entails incorporating the EU's immigration and asylum policy into its outward interactions with other nations (Mayrhofer & Ammer, 2014).

Nevertheless, it is important to remember that the ultimate goal of both strategies is to lower immigration to EU member states. By strengthening controls both inside and outside the EU, they hope to accomplish this. Regrettably, these methods have not sufficiently considered immigration to the EU and the defense of environmental migrants' human rights. The policies put into place so far have been, at most, cautious. Institutional responses have been cautious despite several documents calling for the EU and its Member States to take the lead in addressing environmental migration. This one has been assigned a low priority concerning other EU Agenda issues. Individual Member States have implemented a variety of measures to safeguard particular categories of environmental migrants under their asylum laws in the absence of a comprehensive EU-wide agreement. As an illustration, Sweden's asylum laws now include a new category of protected individuals (Scott, 2023). In addition to refugees and those needing subsidiary protection, this category also includes people who are "otherwise in need of protection." People impacted by sudden-onset disasters who cannot safely return to their native country fall under this larger category. There are restrictions on this clause, though. It is only relevant when the person's nation offers no protection choices. Moreover, if Sweden finds it difficult to accept newcomers, it may withdraw the protection offered by this clause. This clause has not been implemented in reality (Cohen & Bradley, 2010).

With two different types of protection available to those relocated due to natural disasters, Finland adopts an even more comprehensive strategy. First, a person may be awarded national temporary protection status for three years. This pertains to situations in which a significant number of individuals have been displaced within their nation of origin as a result of armed war, violent crimes, or natural disasters that render a safe return unfeasible. The second option, outlined in Finnish asylum legislation, is a humanitarian protection status that can be applied for by anyone who cannot return home because of a serious human rights violation, an environmental disaster, or inadequate security due to internal or external armed conflicts. These Finnish measures, like the Swedish provision, emphasize the availability of domestic protection choices. As such, they have not been used as of yet.

Humanitarian protection provisions that might apply to environmental migrants are also incorporated into the asylum rules of several other EU members. A few states have indicated that they are prepared to acknowledge environmental migrants as a separate group that needs to be protected. For example, in its policy declarations, Bulgaria's Ministry of Interior has identified natural disasters as migratory drivers. Belgium has initiated initiatives to support the UN and EU for an "environmental refugee" designation. But as of yet, no concrete policy advancement has occurred. Rather than committing to new legislative instruments on this topic, the EU and its Member States will likely make small tweaks to their development cooperation programs.

USA

In recent decades, the United States has experienced an important phenomenon called environmental migration. This phenomenon includes migration from other countries and mobility within the nation. Surprisingly, American immigration regulations do not specifically acknowledge this environmental migration (Ragheboom, 2017). There aren't many allusions to this important topic in the country's migration policies. In the 1990s, the United States, like many other nations, passed laws about temporary protection. People currently in the United States who are momentarily unable to safely return home because of an ongoing armed conflict, natural disasters, or other extraordinary and temporary conditions are granted protected status under this legislation (as indicated by the emphasis added). This clause distinguishes between natural calamities and hostilities (Martin, 2010). When an environmental disaster occurs, the government of the afflicted nation must apply for temporary protected status; in contrast, when there is an armed conflict, this status is automatically given. Interestingly, this clause is consistent with the notion of "refugees sur place," meaning it only applies to people already on US soil during the environmental calamity. As a result, it ignores the needs of those impacted by international environmental migration who are outside the United States but seeking entrance for humanitarian reasons (Klepp & Herbeck, 2016).

It's also critical to realize that, as its name implies, this tool provides transient protection. As such, it is not appropriate as a reaction to global environmental migration caused by long-term environmental changes like rising sea levels or progressive degradation. In addition, any protected status granted may be withdrawn if an environmental disaster has long-lasting impacts. Environmental considerations are noticeably missing from US immigration policy, even when temporary protected status is granted. Nonetheless, it is imperative to place the country's environmental migration policy in the larger perspective of President Donald J. Trump's strict immigration policies (Cohen & Bradley, 2010). Considering this situation in the global discourse on securitized migration, which emerged in reaction to the European refugee crisis beginning in 2015, becomes even more crucial. A 'zero-tolerance' policy was enforced at the US-Mexico border in 2018. This strategy aimed to classify crossing the border without the required authorization as an illegal entrance and penalize anyone who did so. The number of refugees allowed access into the United States for resettlement was significantly reduced due to this rigorous policy, being lowered by more than half (Hartmann, 2010).

Furthermore, hundreds of thousands of migrants who were already living in the United States were impacted when six countries' temporary protected status was ended the same year. It seems probable that restrictive regulations about environmental migration will persist. This is due to the growing narrative linking climate change to terrorism as a security danger to the United States. Consequently, tackling climate change is now a component of an all-encompassing national defense strategy, where development assistance is essential (Scott, 2023). In the context of environmental migration, for example, the US Agency for International Development has refocused on tactics meant to assist prospective countries of origin in adjusting to changing environmental conditions. They stress that violent confrontations or exploiting environmental changes for damaging ends are possible if political systems or governments do not support adaptation (Martin, 2010).

The focus on strengthening developing nations' ability to adapt suggests that US officials, like the European Union, believe that environmental migration—also known as South-South migration—occurs within or between nations in the same region. Responses to sudden-onset disasters that cause population displacement within the United States are likewise covered by this viewpoint. For instance, government representatives refrained from designating millions of Americans who had been displaced by Hurricane Katrina in 2005 as internally displaced persons (IDPs). The US's belief that internal displacement is a phenomenon that happens "elsewhere" and is predominantly caused by conflict led to this decision. As such, those internally displaced within the United States due to environmental disasters do not receive treatment based on their rights (Cohen & Bradley, 2010). Beyond the Trump period, it is critical to acknowledge that regular migration has long been considered economically beneficial and socially acceptable by the US in its national post-war goals. Establishing the country's ability to welcome immigrants was seen as essential to advancing innovation, creating economic development, and establishing favorable international relations throughout the administration of former President Barack Obama (Klepp & Herbeck, 2016).

Immigration reform has become a major goal in this scenario. This change attempted to achieve a compromise between giving individuals who fulfilled the requirements a route to citizenship and successfully enforcing immigration laws. Despite these goals, comprehensive immigration reform could not become law during the Obama administration due to strong political opposition. Still, it is possible that a new administration—especially one that supports the Democratic Party—will alter immigration and asylum laws (Hartmann, 2010). A change of this kind would align the US with its left-leaning neighbor, Canada. Following the Syrian civil war, Prime Minister Justin Trudeau skillfully negotiated Canada's convoluted political terrain to preserve the nation's welcoming and inclusive attitude toward refugees and migrants (Freeland & Horn, 2009).

DISCUSSION

The previous chapters stressed the need for a specialized environmental migration framework. This requirement stems from empirical data showing the impact on impacted populations and a legal analysis showing the limitations of international institutions in protecting environmental migrants. To illustrate this, we will imagine two scenarios: one with a worldwide instrument for environmental migration and one without. The following future depictions should not be taken as imaginative or based on statistical possibilities from existing understanding. Instead, these depictions are future-oriented theories that outline probable outcomes within current uncertainties. Before speculating on the future, depending on whether an international instrument governs environmental migration, we must determine the environmental elements affecting these scenarios. Both pessimistic and optimistic estimates assume a rise in Earth's average temperature. This increase in average temperature is not uniform across the world; temperatures are higher over landmasses and lower over the vast oceanic surface. Temperature rises correspondingly from coastal to continental interiors and lower to higher latitudes.

Our future includes rising sea levels, which harm sensitive coastal wetlands. This phenomenon causes local fisheries to suffer, seawater intrusion into groundwater reservoirs in low-lying coastal regions and islands, and increased storm surge and tsunami heights, wreaking havoc on exposed coastlines. Another important aspect of environmental changes creating our speculative terrain is precipitation patterns. Two main patterns are increased precipitation in tropical and high-latitude regions and decreased precipitation in subtropical and mid-latitude regions. These locations are more vulnerable to extended drought due to the latter tendency. Note that these environmental changes are purposely not quantified. This approach is made because the degree and timing of these changes are not crucial to the illustrated projections. We focus on imagining probable futures based on environmental dynamics, not quantitative precision.

Without a structure to control environmental migration, people move haphazardly without sufficient planning when needed. Unplanned migration affects vulnerable regions more than is organized and shared equally by the international community. Human mobility affects international security in both ways. Population movements promote violence and conflict, which causes additional migration. Changes in the environment also affect environmental migration. These changes worsen the cycle by increasing resource shortages and livable area shifts and magnifying the effects of human movement, sometimes intertwined with conflicts. Environmental changes exacerbate global inequality. As habitable land, food, and water grow scarcer, more people depend on and compete for them. Unorganized movements to reduce population pressure often result from this competition. Conflicts may arise when resource imbalances become significant, prompting migration again. This cycle restarts in migratory regions. Migration can also change the ethnic character of many countries by bringing diverse groups together and competing for resources. Pre-existing tensions may increase.

Environmental migration can destroy poorer cultures' habitats because environmental changes impact them hardest. This can make weak states fail and promote regional instability. Environmental migration and its effects are considered risks even in countries unaffected by these phenomena. Some regions view security measures like building barriers and strengthening border security as drastic responses to these perceived dangers. Rising sea levels are causing land loss in South and East Asia, which has many islands and low-lying coastlines. Bangladesh is an example of a country becoming uninhabitable due to rising sea levels, regular storms, and floods. This forces people to shift inside the country, away from susceptible coastal locations, or to neighboring countries. Rising global temperatures have also stressed regional agricultural and water resources. Due to environmental issues, locals and environmental refugees compete for these scarce resources. This competition causes instability in Bangladesh and political problems with neighboring countries, especially India. Many Bangladeshi migrants and residents of the small Bay of Bengal islands forced to flee to the mainland by rising sea levels go to India. On India's other side, Pakistan and China dispute Kashmir. Conflicts over water supplies exacerbate these disagreements. Due to glacier melting, the Indus River, which Pakistan relies on, floods in summer and decreases in winter as the region becomes more parched. These growing environmental changes and immigration undermine these countries' internal stability and exacerbate the Indian subcontinent's tensions.

Water shortages are also a problem in northern China. As monsoon rains fail, droughts worsen these shortages—migration trends from rural to urban areas pressure already overcrowded cities. People also move to areas with enough rain. As ethnic minority groups fight for these resources, conflicts arise. Africa has a large environmental migration pattern. Due to the unsustainable growth of agriculture, people leave rural areas in other countries. They prefer urban centers with alternate employment options and social services. However, internal migration puts great pressure on governments with limited resources and capacities. It increases the danger of state failures and prolongs political confrontations. Due to their instability, Nigeria and East Africa face the greatest geopolitical difficulties from Africa's environmental migration. Water issues between Syria, Israel, Lebanon, Jordan, the Palestinian territories, Iraq, Iran, and Turkey affect Middle East politics. The Jordan, Euphrates, and Tigris rivers are at stake in these disputes. Due to these issues, populations are fleeing to secure access to these vital water supplies or to avoid confrontation. Cross-border immigration increases tensions and instability in both regions, threatening world security.

Populations continue to flee conflict and deteriorating livelihoods, either south to South Africa or north to Europe, a haven. The negative effects of rising temperatures on food production in Mediterranean countries are compensated by better circumstances in the north of Europe. However, external pressure on Europe's frontiers has led to nationalism and strict border security. This pattern echoes the 2015 European migrant 'crisis' narrative. More environmental migrants are flocking to Europe than in the 2010s. Europe intensifies its border sealing by externalizing border control. Development policy is a preventative security measure to preserve 'Fortress Europe' from environmental changes. The southern US responds to environmental migration, especially from Central America and the Caribbean. The US is the main destination for environmental refugees from these locations. Extreme heatwaves in Central America cause water shortages and food scarcity, while more frequent and strong hurricanes and rising sea levels in the Caribbean islands cause people to travel north to North America, which is less affected and richer.

However, the US faces its issues. Southwest US droughts are becoming more regular and protracted. Droughts affect agricultural and fast-growing cities. Low-lying Gulf and mid-Atlantic coastal communities are also at risk of Hurricane Katrina-like catastrophes. The US prioritizes citizen well-being and implements costly adaptive measures to maintain internal stability. It also strictly restricts immigration. Negotiating an international environmental migration accord proved difficult. As the problem gained pace, the world community realized its importance. It was believed that environmental changes worsen resource distribution issues but do not threaten humanity. As a result, they can be fixed without compromising security. In pursuit of peace and stability, developed nations have helped poorer nations adapt to environmental changes. This strategy worked. Environmental migrants have declined in the years since the instrument's deployment. Comprehensive labor migration strategies and shorter displacement durations are used for unavoidable displacement. Integration of relocated people has also increased cultural diversity in host countries.

State parties contribute to a worldwide fund for environmental adaptation based on their economic capabilities under the instrument. Developed nations lead this endeavor, allowing less rich countries to get humanitarian aid for sudden-onset disaster displacement. This funding also assists adaption strategies to reduce environmental impacts on livelihoods and aid relocations. The environmental adaptation fund has successfully implemented initiatives in South and Southeast Asia, which were severely hit by environmental issues. These strategies reduce disaster risk. Offshore dykes protect long coasts from flooding and increasing sea levels. Thousands of kilometers of drainage channels have been built to prevent flooding. Countries like Bangladesh have started reforestation. These programs maintain coasts, minimize abrupt calamities, and provide economic opportunities for locals. Regionwide, good actions have been implemented. This reduces the number of environmental migrants from these places, which eases pressure on countries like India that were previously their destinations. States across the Pacific and Caribbean have taken similar steps. These include complete domestic and international relocation programs. The Maldives inspired some states to implement Safer Island Strategies. These tactics entail resettling communities from smaller, weaker islands to larger ones. Governments can focus on environmental adaptation with this method.

Food security programs and temperature-adaptive livelihoods have reduced environmental migration in China, Mexico, and Central America. These countries have also strengthened their social security systems to protect disadvantaged populations. Water management strategies have reduced the Middle East's Jordan River, Euphrates, and Tigris disputes. Efficient irrigation maximizes food output. These strategies prevent droughts, minimize resource pressures, and reduce migratory migrations. Similar irrigation and water management projects have helped across Africa. As environmental pressures decrease, countries in the region work together to protect pastoralists' historic movements inside or across borders during droughts and floods. Environmental issues can cause conflict. This collaboration includes conflict resolution. African cooperative initiatives enable temporary and permanent migration to locations with work possibilities, regardless of climate. This enables environmentally affected populations to earn a living and sustain their families, allowing them to stay in their homelands.

Environmental migration has a very mild influence on developed countries that can adjust to environmental changes. Due to greater temperatures, Europe, Australia, and New Zealand have longer growing seasons. As Global South countries become more resilient to environmental changes, pressure on developed nations' borders reduces. Develop countries now set aside adequate territory for groups that need to go abroad, creating a welcoming culture. Resettlement programs and inclusive participation and integration activities prepare migrants and host populations for planned relocations, guaranteeing a smooth transition and human rights protection. New labor migration policies allow low-income people to move to more economically stable countries. Since the 2019 EU elections, Green Parties have grown across Europe and the EU. This has led to widespread rejection of 'Fortress Europe' and political focus on ecological rights and climate action. As scientific and technical understanding increases, adaptation measures are created and implemented with affected populations. This ensures local requirements are met, and environmental migration policies are implemented to build resilience and support planned relocations. In addition to the steps outlined earlier, a global disaster response strategy provides effective support and protection for persons displaced by abrupt calamities, whether they migrate within or beyond borders. This approach guarantees displaced people's human rights through standardized temporary and permanent admittance schemes.

This disaster response plan is rarely used due to adaptation measures, advanced early warning systems, and regional evacuation plans. The instrument regulating environmental migration can reduce environmental changes to a certain amount, but it can only do so much. Environmental changes can overwhelm even industrialized nations, leaving them unable to cope. Populations can only adapt so much, and environmental migration may occur again when suitable destination regions become scarcer. Therefore, a tool for managing environmental migration can only be successful when combined with genuine measures to reduce human environmental damage. This means lowering environmental change-causing actions so the world community can better manage and cope with them.

CONCLUSION

Environmental migration has become a major global concern because of the increasing effects of climate change and its aftereffects. Natural disasters internally displaced 17.2 million people in their nations in 2018 alone. Given the tightening immigration laws in both the developed and developing worlds—the developed world's North and South—this occurrence presents complicated issues. As a result, environmental migrants frequently find themselves in a difficult scenario where they are forced to choose between living in hostile conditions and losing their source of income in their home countries. This situation begs the question of how international law might protect environmental migrants' human rights. There are two schools of thought in the discourse surrounding environmental migration: alarmists who maintain that environmental factors are the main forces behind population movements and skeptics who contend that migration is too complex to be caused exclusively by environmental factors. While socioeconomic, demographic, political, and environmental factors can all impact migration decisions, environmental changes are especially concerning since they tend to compound the effects of these other drivers.

Understanding environmental migration thoroughly is crucial, especially considering the disagreements regarding terminology and meanings. In this sense, the definition of environmental migrants is adopted from the International Organization for Migration, which describes them as people or groups forced to leave their country of origin or choose to do so because of unfavorable environmental changes, whether they occur suddenly or gradually. The scope of this problem indicates its global reach. 18.8 million people were internally displaced in 135 countries 2017 due to droughts and sudden-onset calamities. Notably, most environmental changes affect those who are poor or reside in developing nations. Because these communities' fundamental human rights are in jeopardy, they require the greatest protection. Protecting people's lives, their security, their bodily integrity, their dignity, and their access to basic requirements must be given top priority during emergencies. Additional economic, social, cultural, civil, and political rights become more significant the longer migration lasts, with property rights and citizenship concerns taking on a special importance.

This chapter addresses four international legal tools already in place and may be enhanced in the future to address environmental migrants' human rights. Despite their importance, the Guiding Principles on Internal Displacement are not frequently followed, and their emphasis on internal displacement provides room for cross-border movements. While still applicable, the Refugee Convention presents difficulties because environmental elements do not result in personal persecution, which makes it challenging to classify certain individuals as refugees. Complementary protection rules do not adequately address the severity of environmental causes, and migration is only briefly discussed in the United Nations Framework Convention on Climate Change (UNFCCC). As a result, a customized international instrument that fully addresses the protection of environmental migrants is desperately needed. This kind of agreement ought to cover prepared relocation, resilience-building, adaptive capacity development, and disaster response. To reduce environmental migration, negotiating such an instrument could avert future hostilities and encourage global collaboration.

But the reality of politics depicts a different picture. The European Union has explored environmental migration, mostly in national and regional contexts. While there are temporary protective statuses for individuals in the US after environmental disasters, no more comprehensive rules are in place. The securitization of the immigration debate worries about terrorism, and an emphasis on development initiatives in the Global South all contribute to this hesitation. Nonetheless, it seems more practical and consistent with Western security interests for international cooperation to fund adaptation and mitigation efforts in developing nations. Some little island nations, most impacted by environmental migration, advocate for increased awareness of the problem worldwide. Some want to add "climate refugees" to the Refugee Convention, while others want international cooperation to strengthen their adaptation efforts. A few states nationwide have implemented relocation plans to promote dignified migration and bought land.

Globally, initiatives like the Global Compact for Safe, Orderly, and Regular Migration and the Nansen Initiative have attempted to address cross-border migration brought on by environmental causes. However, the main focus of these initiatives is conversation, and it is more likely that these will advance at the regional or bilateral level. This chapter's conclusion emphasizes how inadequate international law protects environmental migrants' human rights. There isn't much political desire to negotiate a new document that closes this protection gap. For those who are unable to move because of vulnerability criteria like age, gender, or lack of social networks, there is an additional protection gap. Because of the particular difficulties these people experience, governments should concentrate on lowering obstacles to movement and supporting their attempts at adapting.

REFERENCES

Adamo, S. B. (2009). *Search of Shelter*. Mapping the Effects of Climate Change on Human Migration and Displacement.

Argos, C., & Reeves, H. (2010). Climate Refugees (First Edition first Printing). The MIT Press.

Bernal, V. A., & Procee, P. (2012, May 11). *Four years on: What China got right when rebuilding after the Sichuan earthquake*. World Bank Blogs. https://blogs.worldbank.org/eastasiapacific/four-years-on-what-china-got-right-when-rebuilding-after-the-sichuan-earthquake

Betts, A. (2010). Survival Migration: A New Protection Framework. *Global Governance, 16*(3), 361–382. https://www.jstor.org/stable/29764952. doi:10.1163/19426720-01603006

Billings, P. (2008). Complementary Protection in International Refugee Law – By Jane Mcadam. *Legal Studies, 28*(1), 143–148. doi:10.1111/j.1748-121X.2007.00082_2.x

Bradley, M., & Cohen, R. (2015). Disasters, Displacement and Protection: Challenges, Shortcomings and Ways Forward. *Disentangling Migration and Climate Change: Methodologies, Political Discourses and Human Rights*, 207–228. doi:10.1007/978-94-007-6208-4_9

Brown, O. (2008). The Numbers Game. *Forced Migration Review*, 8–9.

Burger, J., Gochfeld, M., & Lacy, C. (2019). Concerns and future preparedness plans of a vulnerable population in New Jersey following Hurricane Sandy. *Disasters, 43*(3), 658–685. doi:10.1111/disa.12350 PMID:30990925

Cohen, R. (2004). The Guiding Principles on Internal Displacement: An Innovation in International Standard Setting. *Global Governance, 10*(4), 459–480. https://www.jstor.org/stable/27800542. doi:10.1163/19426720-01004006

Cohen, R., & Bradley, M. (2010). Disasters and Displacement: Gaps in Protection. *Journal of International Humanitarian Legal Studies, 1*(1), 95–142. doi:10.1163/187815210X12766020139884

European Parliament. (2011). *"Climate Refugees"—Legal and Policy Responses to Environmentally Induced Migration*. Committee on Civil Liberties, Justice and Home Affairs. https://www.europarl.europa.eu/thinktank/en/document/IPOL-LIBE_ET(2011)462422

Faist, T., & Schade, J. (2013). The Climate-Migration Nexus: A Reorientation. *Disentangling Migration and Climate Change: Toward an Analysis of Methodologies, 7*. https://pub.uni-bielefeld.de/record/2582697

Foresight. (2011). *Migration and global environmental change: Future challenges and opportunities* (p. 11). The Government Office for Science. https://www.gov.uk/government/publications/migration-and-global-environmental-change-future-challenges-and-opportunities

Freeland, S., & Horn, L. S. (2009). More than hot air: Reflections on the relationship between climate change and human rights. *University of Western Sydney Law Review*. https://researchdirect.westernsydney.edu.au/islandora/object/uws%3A12506/

Gemenne, F., & Brucker, P. (2015). From the Guiding Principles on Internal Displacement to the Nansen Initiative: What the Governance of Environmental Migration Can Learn from the Governance of Internal Displacement. *International Journal of Refugee Law, 27*(2), 245–263. Advance online publication. doi:10.1093/ijrl/eev021

Hartmann, B. (2010). Rethinking climate refugees and climate conflict: Rhetoric, reality and the politics of policy discourse. *Journal of International Development, 22*(2), 233–246. doi:10.1002/jid.1676

Hinnawi, E. E. (1985). *Environmental refugees*. UNEP. https://digitallibrary.un.org/record/121267

Hiraide, L. A. (2023). Climate refugees: A useful concept? Towards an alternative vocabulary of ecological displacement. *Politics, 43*(2), 267–282. doi:10.1177/02633957221077257

IDMC. (2020). *Global Report on Internal Displacement 2019.* Internal Displacement Monitoring Centre. https://www.internal-displacement.org/global-report/grid2019/

Jayawardhan, S. (2017). Vulnerability and Climate Change Induced Human Displacement. *Consilience, 17*, 103–142. https://www.jstor.org/stable/26188784

Kaelin, W. (2019). International Responses to Climate-Related Migration. *Journal of International Affairs, 73*(1), 255–260. https://www.jstor.org/stable/26872797

Karacasulu, N., & Karakir, İ. A. (2021). Climate-Related Migration: Formulating a Contemporary Framework. *Journal of International and Area Studies, 28*(1), 99–118. https://www.jstor.org/stable/27210937

Kent, J., & Myers, N. (1995). *Environmental Exodus: An Emergent Crisis in the Global Arena*. Semantic Scholar. https://www.semanticscholar.org/paper/Environmental-Exodus%3A-An-Emergent-Crisis-in-the-Kent-Myers/17981f73b39684b7629e447c58ce59874517c88e

Klepp, S., & Herbeck, J. (2016). The politics of environmental migration and climate justice in the Pacific region. *Journal of Human Rights and the Environment, 7*(1), 54–73. doi:10.4337/jhre.2016.01.03

Kolmes, S. A., Kolmes, S. K., & Lin, P.-H. (2022). What Lies Ahead: How Aid for Climate Refugees Must Focus on Human Rights and Human Health. *Environment, 64*(3), 7–16. doi:10.1080/00139157.2022.2046455

Lyons, K. (2020, January 20). Climate refugees can't be returned home, says landmark UN human rights ruling. *The Guardian*. https://www.theguardian.com/world/2020/jan/20/climate-refugees-cant-be-returned-home-says-landmark-un-human-rights-ruling

Marcs, C. (2008). Spoiling Movi's River: Towards Recognition of Persecutory Environmental harm Within the Meaning of the Refugee Convention. *American University International Law Review, 24*(1). https://digitalcommons.wcl.american.edu/auilr/vol24/iss1/5

Martin, S. (2010). Climate Change, Migration, and Governance. *Global Governance, 16*(3), 397–414. https://www.jstor.org/stable/29764954. doi:10.1163/19426720-01603008

Mayrhofer, M., & Ammer, M. (2014). People Moving in the Context of Environmental Change: The Cautious Approach of the European Union. *European Journal of Migration and Law, 16*(3), 389–429. doi:10.1163/15718166-12342062

Mayrhofer, M., & Ammer, M. (2022). Climate mobility to Europe: The case of disaster displacement in Austrian asylum procedures. *Frontiers in Climate, 4*, 990558. https://www.frontiersin.org/articles/10.3389/fclim.2022.990558. doi:10.3389/fclim.2022.990558

McAdam, J. (2008). Introduction: Asylum and the Universal Declaration of Human Rights. *Refugee Survey Quarterly, 27*(3), 3–12. doi:10.1093/rsq/hdn041

Mcadam, J. (2011). Swimming against the Tide: Why a Climate Change Displacement Treaty is Not the Answer. *International Journal of Refugee Law, 23*(1), 2–27. doi:10.1093/ijrl/eeq045

Omisore, S. R., Abifarin, O., & Amana, A. R. (2020). Nigeria's Policy On Internally Displaced Persons. *World Affairs: The Journal of International Issues, 24*(3), 148–159. https://www.jstor.org/stable/48590649

Orchard, P. (2018). *Protecting the Internally Displaced: Rhetoric and Reality.* Routledge., doi:10.4324/9781315756189

Ragheboom, H. (2017). The International Legal Status and Protection of Environmentally-Displaced Persons: A European Perspective. In *The International Legal Status and Protection of Environmentally-Displaced Persons: A European Perspective.* Brill Nijhoff. https://brill.com/display/title/33176

Ravenstein, E. G. (1885). The Laws of Migration. *Journal of the Statistical Society of London, 48*(2), 167–235. doi:10.2307/2979181

Scott, M. (2023). Adapting to Climate-Related Human Mobility into Europe: Between the Protection Agenda and the Deterrence Paradigm, or Beyond? *European Journal of Migration and Law, 25*(1), 54–82. doi:10.1163/15718166-12340144

United Nations. (2021). *United Nations Framework Convention on Climate Change.* Good Press.

Wu, C.-F. (2021). Challenges to Protecting the Right to Health under the Climate Change Regime. *Health and Human Rights, 23*(2), 121–138. https://www.ncbi.nlm.nih.gov/pmc/articles/PMC8694293/ PMID:34966230

Zetter, R. (2009). *The role of legal and normative frameworks for the protection of environmentally displaced people.* RSC. https://www.rsc.ox.ac.uk/publications/the-role-of-legal-and-normative-frameworks-for-the-protection-of-environmentally-displaced-people

Zetter, R. (2010). *Protecting people displaced by climate change: Some conceptual challenges.* RSC. https://www.rsc.ox.ac.uk/publications/protecting-people-displaced-by-climate-change-some-conceptual-challenges

Zetter, R. (2011a). *Protecting environmentally displaced people Developing the capacity of legal and normative framework.* Refugee Studies Centre Oxford Department of International Development.

Zetter, R. (2011b). *Protecting environmentally displaced people: Developing the capacity of legal and normative frameworks.* RSC. https://www.rsc.ox.ac.uk/publications/protecting-environmentally-displaced-people-developing-the-capacity-of-legal-and-normative-frameworks

Zetter, R. (2017). Why they are not refugees – Climate change, environmental degradation and population displacement. *Siirtolaisuus-Migration Quarterly,* 23–28. https://www.rsc.ox.ac.uk/publications/why-they-are-not-refugees-2013-climate-change-environmental-degradation-and-population-displacement

Zieck, M. (2015). Guidelines on International Protection No. 11: Prima Facie Recognition of Refugee Status (UNHCR). *International Legal Materials, 54*(6), 1115–1129. doi:10.5305/intelegamate.54.6.1115

ADDITIONAL READING

de Sherbinin, A., Grace, K., McDermid, S., van der Geest, K., Puma, M. J., & Bell, A. (2022). Migration Theory in Climate Mobility Research. *Frontiers in Climate, 4,* 882343. https://www.frontiersin.org/articles/10.3389/fclim.2022.882343. doi:10.3389/fclim.2022.882343

Ghosh, R. C., & Orchiston, C. (2022). A systematic review of climate migration research: Gaps in existing literature. *SN Social Sciences*, *2*(5), 47. doi:10.1007/s43545-022-00341-8

Hoffmann, R., Šedová, B., & Vinke, K. (2021). Improving the evidence base: A methodological review of the quantitative climate migration literature. *Global Environmental Change*, *71*, 102367. doi:10.1016/j.gloenvcha.2021.102367

Khavarian-Garmsir, A. R., Hajian Hossein Abadi, M., Sadeghi, A., Rahimi, D., & Asadzadeh, A. (2023). Trends and future research in climate migration: A bibliometric analysis of forty years. *Environmental Hazards*, *0*(0), 1–24. doi:10.1080/17477891.2023.2265928

Liang, B., Shi, G., Sun, Z., Babul, H., & Zhou, M. (2023). Evolution trend and hot topic measurement of climate migration research under the influence of climate change. *Frontiers in Ecology and Evolution*, *11*, 1118037. https://www.frontiersin.org/articles/10.3389/fevo.2023.1118037. doi:10.3389/fevo.2023.1118037

Milán-García, J., Caparrós-Martínez, J. L., Rueda-López, N., & de Pablo Valenciano, J. (2021). Climate change-induced migration: A bibliometric review. *Globalization and Health*, *17*(1), 74. doi:10.1186/s12992-021-00722-3 PMID:34217341

KEY TERMS AND DEFINITIONS

Climate Change and Displacement Risks: The chapter links climate change to increasing risks of displacement. It underscores how climate change intensifies environmental changes, leading to higher vulnerability and displacement risks. This connection is crucial for understanding the growing scale of environmental migration and the urgent need for international action.

Disaster-Related Displacement Statistics: The chapter provides various statistics on displacement caused by environmental disasters, illustrating the magnitude of the issue. It mentions millions of people displaced by events like Hurricane Sandy, Typhoon Mangkhut, and other natural disasters, highlighting the global and increasing scale of disaster-related displacement.

Environmental Migration: This refers to the movement of people due to environmental changes, often exacerbated by climate change. The article highlights that environmental migration is multifaceted, involving both sudden-onset disasters (like hurricanes and earthquakes) and slow-onset events (like droughts and sea-level rise). It's a complex issue due to the interplay of various factors like social, political, and economic conditions.

Human Rights and Environmental Displacement: The chapter emphasizes the impact of environmental migration on human rights, particularly in the context of international law. It discusses the protection needs for environmental migrants, including rights to life, personal safety, adequate living conditions, and access to basic necessities. The article also notes the challenges in ensuring these rights, given the lack of a comprehensive legal framework specifically for environmental migrants.

International Legal Frameworks: This keyword relates to the examination of existing international legal tools and their effectiveness in protecting the rights of environmental migrants. The article suggests that current international laws are insufficient for addressing the unique challenges posed by environmental migration, indicating the need for a more robust and specific legal regime.

Chapter 15
Navigating the Grey Area: Can Cyber Warfare Trigger a State's Right to Self-Defense?

Anirudha Choudhury
KIIT University, India

Asif Iqubal Shah
St. Xavier's University, Kolkata, India

Shrabana Chattopadhyay
University of Engineering and Management, India

Akash Bag
https://orcid.org/0000-0001-8820-171X
Adamas University, India

ABSTRACT

The chapter examines the concept of self-defense in international law and cyber operations, focusing on when a cyber operation escalates to a cyber-attack and justifying a state's right to self-defense. The severity of a cyber operation is crucial, as it distinguishes between operations causing significant harm and those causing only economic damage. The chapter also explores the complexities surrounding the involvement of non-state actors in cyber operations, suggesting the 'unwilling or unable' doctrine for defensive actions against non-state actors. The legitimacy of self-defense is based on the necessity of the response as a last resort and its proportionality to the threat faced.

INTRODUCTION

The physical world has been significantly altered by the quick development of technology, changing both the civilian and military spheres. Cybersecurity requires ongoing attention because today's pervasive reliance on computers, systems, and networks. Numerous cyber threats, including infringements, as-

DOI: 10.4018/979-8-3693-1742-6.ch015

saults, and espionage, have given birth to this requirement. States are investing in cyber capabilities due to this technological boom, realizing that cyber warfare can take many forms, from small-scale online vandalism to large-scale strikes on government infrastructure. Cyber operations can now cause harm equivalent to that caused by physical (kinetic) force (Buchan, 2012). For example, in 2007, a controversy over a Soviet war memorial led Russian hackers to target Estonian institutions. Georgia saw comparable cyberattacks connected to the Russian-Georgian conflict the next year. Even though no one was physically harmed in these cases, the substantial financial losses show how seriously cyber operations may influence an organization.

The 2010 discovery of the Stuxnet worm is a prominent illustration of the physical harm cyber activities can wreak. This computer worm, which mostly affected Iran, attacked nuclear centrifuges, resulting in silent but devastating explosions and failures. It was a more stealthy and effective attack than using traditional explosives. These changes raise Critical legal concerns, particularly about international law and the use of force and self-defense (Boo, 2017). These ideas about physical force have traditionally been understood. But given the rise of cyber-technology, these ideas must be re-examined. The goal of the UN Charter is to uphold world peace and security. However, it is unclear how cyber operations fit into this framework and how they relate to the right to self-defense. Understanding when a cyber operation qualifies as an attack and what kinds of self-defense a targeted state is allowed to use is made possible by this investigation. Although armed cyberattacks are the main topic, related ideas like aggressiveness and the use of force are only mentioned in passing (Buchan, 2012). The UN Charter's necessity and proportionality standards are considered when discussing non-coercive measures. The intention is to provide precise rules for state behavior in cyberspace consistent with maintaining global security and peace.

METHODOLOGY

This chapter explores public international law, focusing on legal positivism and how legislation is formed and interpreted about its sources. Legal positivism emphasizes the formal position of a rule within a legal system as its legitimacy, rather than extrinsic elements like morality, and focuses on comprehending the law as it currently stands (lex lata). National legal systems and public international law are very different. It doesn't have a gold standard that establishes a hierarchy for its sources. Rather, the relevant sources fall under the purview of several international courts and tribunals. This can make figuring out the law difficult. The most authoritative source on these sources is the Statute of the International Court of Justice (ICJ Statute), specifically Article 38(1), which regards international treaties and customs as primary and general principles, judicial decisions, and doctrines as secondary or subsidiary.

After that, the chapter discusses how the term "armed attack" is defined in international law, beginning with Article 51 of the UN Charter. A nuanced understanding of the term "armed attack" requires a review of case law and doctrine because the Charter does not provide a full description of the term. However, this article acknowledges that interpretations may differ depending on the sources examined and their relative weighting. Instead, it aims to analyze how this term pertains to cyber operations rather than provide a definition. Regarding cyberattacks, there are difficulties because there isn't a common definition in international law, and there aren't any pertinent court cases. In this case, the chapter mostly relies on doctrine, especially the Tallinn Manuals, which are important sources of international law about cyberspace, even if they are not primary sources. These Manuals restate current rules that apply to cyber warfare and were created by international legal professionals. While admitting the risks of relying on subsidiary sources for defining lex lata, the chapter uses the more recent Tallinn Manual 2.0, using a 'lex posterior' approach where newer laws take precedence in case of conflicts.

The study also looks at the United Nations General Assembly's 2021 compilation of voluntary State contributions, representing different State viewpoints (opinio juris) on cyber operations and self-defense. In addition to these opinions, the Tallinn Manuals and other doctrines provide context for the debate about the nature and extent of cyberattacks. A deeper analysis of the right to self-defense based on treaty and customary law is done. To comprehend the concept's scope and legal application, one must examine the definition included in Article 51 of the UN Charter, international customary law, and case law and doctrine.

WHAT CONSTITUTES AN ARMED ATTACK?

The Nature of an Armed Attack

A state's right to self-defense is crucial under international law, especially in light of the UN Charter. Article 51, which recognizes a state's right to self-defense during an armed attack, outlines this right. The UN Charter's Article 2(4) generally forbids using force, with this clause as a noteworthy exception. The guiding premise is that one may only use force in self-defense in the event of an armed assault. To gain a deeper understanding of this, let us examine the 2003 Oil Platforms Case, in which Iran claimed that the US had destroyed its oil platforms. Self-defense against an Iranian onslaught served as the U.S. justification for its actions (Bethlehem, 2012). The International Court of Justice (ICJ) was tasked with deciding whether Iran had launched an armed attack on the United States in this particular instance. The Court underlined that a state must provide clear evidence that it was defending itself against an armed attack to assert self-defense. In this case, the United States' claim of self-defense was invalidated because it could not present enough proof of an attack of that kind by Iran (Hayward, 2017a).

The attack needs to involve transnational activity, which is another essential component. This indicates that internal disputes are not included in the definition of an armed attack as defined by international law. Unfortunately, the UN Charter leaves room for interpretation about what exactly qualifies as a "armed attack," making it difficult for governments to decide whether using force in self-defense is appropriate. Furthermore, the terms "threat or use of force" and "acts of aggression" are mentioned in the UN Charter, but it is unclear how these terms relate to the definition of "armed attack." For example, the definition of "aggression" in Article 39 is frequently seen as being more serious than a simple threat or breach of peace. By tackling these subtleties, the ICJ has tried to define "armed attack" more precisely. The Court considered whether the actions of armed groups supported by one state against another qualified as an armed attack in the Nicaragua Case 1986 (Wilmshurst & Wood, 2013a). The Court suggested a tight connection between aggression and armed attack using the General Assembly's definition of aggression. However, this interpretation isn't widely agreed upon, and differences are still made in reality, as evidenced by the various scenarios that organizations like the Security Council classify (Bethlehem, 2012).

The International Court of Justice has tried to discern between more and less serious uses of force, qualifying as armed attacks. However, this distinction has generated debate since it draws a line between what Article 2(4) prohibits using force and what Article 51 permits as self-defense. This criterion set by the ICJ has received broad recognition despite challenges. According to international law, one of the most important factors in deciding whether an act counts as an armed attack is the weaponry or tactics utilized in the fight (Hayward, 2017a). The International Court of Justice (ICJ) gave significant attention to this matter in its 1996 Advisory Opinion on the legality of nuclear weapons. The General Assembly requested the Court's decision on whether the United Nations Charter could be applied to the threat or use of nuclear weapons. After conducting an analysis, the International Court of Justice (ICJ) determined that the employment of a weapon in an assault—nuclear or not—does not decide whether the act qualifies as an armed attack (Hargrove, 1987). This viewpoint is consistent with the dominant understanding in international state practice, which acknowledges that attacks utilizing chemical, biological, and radiological weapons can be classified as armed attacks even though they do not include a physical impact or are not kinetic.

The UN Security Council's reaction to the September 11, 2001, terrorist attacks lend more credence to this interpretation. In this case, the Council recognized the attacks as an armed attack and upheld the United States' right to self-defense when they were carried out using hijacked aircraft. Furthermore, the United States asserted its right to self-defense in the Oil Platforms Case in reaction to several acts by Iranian forces, including assaults on neutral ships in the Persian Gulf (Ruys, 2014). The International Court of Justice (ICJ) deliberated over whether a series of smaller-scale strikes, none of which would qualify as an armed attack on its own, might be taken collectively into account as such. Even though the Court determined that the criterion was not satisfied in this specific case, it did not rule out the possibility that, in certain situations, a string of smaller attacks could come together to form an armed attack (Hayward, 2017a).

Temporal Element

In international law, pinpointing the exact instant an armed attack begins is difficult. Determining the precise moment, the UN Charter's right to self-defense takes effect is crucial. Since these are the effects of the attack, it is generally accepted that an armed attack starts before the victim state sustains casualties or damage. For example, when a missile locks onto an aircraft, rather than at the point of impact, the attack is said to have started in an armed scenario, including aircraft. This knowledge becomes more important in light of contemporary armament, which frequently enables quick attacks, giving the targeted state little time to react. One hotly debated topic is the legality of anticipatory self-defense—taking action before an impending attack (Boo, 2017). Whether preemptive or anticipatory self-defense is acceptable is a topic that neither state practice nor precedent has definitively agreed upon. The question of immediate threats was not addressed in the historic Nicaragua Case because the parties did not bring it up. As a result, the International Court of Justice (ICJ) specifically declined to comment on the legitimacy of taking military action in response to an impending danger (Shah, 2007a).

However, by recognizing the right to self-defense in the event of an immediate threat, the Caroline Case of 1837 established a precedent. In this case, American forces claimed the American warship Caroline was being used to support American revolutionaries, so they destroyed it. Subsequently, the U.S. Secretary of State outlined the requirements for self-defense, highlighting the need for an immediate and severe threat that leaves little room for hesitation or other options. Even though imminence was not specifically addressed in this case, the rules it set are now commonly recognized in customary international law. Practically speaking, it is impossible to expect a state to do nothing in the face of obvious plans to launch an armed attack against it (Schachter, 1987). The UN Charter's language, "an armed attack occurs," is generally understood to cover objectively verifiable and imminent attacks. However, under Article 51 of the UN Charter, a mere future threat is insufficient to justify the right to self-defense.

The meaning of "imminence" is still debatable, as it is not widely agreed upon. An unduly preventive self-defense action could go against the UN Charter's Article 2(4) ban on using force. There are differing opinions regarding imminence. Some support a narrow reading that considers self-defense to be appropriate just when an assault is about to occur, while others support a more expansive interpretation that views imminence as the final chance to stop an attack (Searles & Berger, 1987).

Pre-emptive self-defense is a theory by the US that justifies using force to avert future attacks rather than ones already underway. However, this interpretation is debatable and viewed by many as going beyond what is permissible under international law. The discussion surrounding proactive and anticipatory self-defense draws attention to the difficulty of understanding the right to self-defense in light of contemporary international relations and warfare and how this interpretation is always changing (Hathaway et al., 2012a).

Non-State Actors

The phrase "non-state actors" refers to a wide variety of organizations that are not sovereign nations in international law. Individuals, global organizations, terrorist groups, and multinational criminal organizations are all included in this. Notwithstanding states' complete legal ability under international law, non-state actors have a major impact. One noteworthy feature is the capacity of non-state actors to influence international judicial proceedings and conclusions (Mulford, 2016). This influence is clear in the reactions to acts by international terrorists or criminal groups, which have prompted the United Nations Security Council and other organizations to impose sanctions and pass resolutions. The United States 9/11 attacks brought to light the potential harm that non-state actors can inflict, as well as the capabilities of these actors and the global response to their activities. The link between non-state actors and a state's right to self-defense is crucial in this setting. This involves the issue of whether the state is accountable for acts committed by non-state actors (Wijninga et al., 2014). The International Court of Justice's (ICJ) decision in the Nicaragua Case sets a significant legal precedent. In determining that a state must have "effective control" over a non-state actor to be held legally liable for their acts, the International Court of Justice (ICJ) considered whether the United States could be held legally liable for its participation with an armed group in Nicaragua. The Court did not, however, specify the cutoff point for this kind of supervision (Wilmshurst & Wood, 2013a).

The International Criminal Tribunal for the former Yugoslavia (ICTY) offered an opposing perspective in the Tadic Case Appeals Chamber. A more expansive interpretation was proposed by the ICTY, which claimed that "overall control" over a non-state actor may be sufficient for state responsibility if it included assistance and coordination of military operations. The International Court of Justice (ICJ) reopened this case in 2007 in the Genocide Convention Case, looking primarily at Yugoslavia's role in the atrocities at Srebrenica. The Court reiterated its position on "effective control" as established in the Nicaragua Case and declined to accept the ICTY's lower level of control (Ruys, 2014). In conclusion, the International Law Commission (ILC) tackled this matter in its Draft Articles on the Responsibility of States, declaring that a state has accountability for the deeds of a non-state actor if the latter acts at the state's behest or under its supervision. However, the ILC made it clear that, in the Tadic Case, the ICTY's jurisdiction is largely related to individual criminal liability rather than state responsibility.

The concept of self-defense in international law—especially the legal difficulties in defending oneself against violent attacks by non-state actors—is the central concern of the matter. Article 51 of the United Nations Charter grants the right to employ force in self-defense, traditionally used in reaction to attacks by other states (Wilmshurst & Wood, 2013a). The surge in terrorist assaults, however, has called into question this comprehension. Because the UN Charter does not specifically provide that an attacker must be a provider, it is unclear whether terrorist organizations or other non-state actors can rightfully invoke a State's right to self-defense. After the terrorist attacks in the United States on September 11, 2001, this uncertainty became even more apparent (Trapp, 2007). The international community acknowledged the United States' right to self-defense against al-Qaeda, a non-State actor, in UN Security Council Resolutions 1368 and 1373. This answer raised the possibility of extending the reach of Article 51.

Despite this, the International Court of Justice (ICJ) took a conventional approach. The International Court of Justice (ICJ) stated in the Building of a Wall Advisory Opinion (2004) that the right to self-defense is only valid when a State attacks, not when non-state actors attack (Burkadze, 2020). This opinion pertained to Israel's building of a wall in occupied Palestinian land. But not every judge felt the same way, suggesting that opinions on this issue varied. Once more, the International Court of Justice had the chance to examine this matter in the Armed Activities on the Territory of the Congo Case (2005). Despite ruling that there was insufficient evidence linking the Democratic Republic of the Congo to non-state actors operating in Uganda, some judges voiced different views, arguing that it is irrational to deny a State the right to self-defense simply because the attacker is not a State (Trapp, 2007).

The fundamental contention is that restricting self-defense to only State actors may jeopardize the UN Charter's commitment to upholding global peace and security. This is due to the possibility that it would provide non-state actors impunity, allowing them to abuse State sovereignty and giving States the ability to wage war against these actors secretly (Aslan, 2020). The difficulty is in striking a balance between the necessity for States to protect themselves from grave threats, irrespective of the status of the assailant, and the possibility that this power would be abused, resulting in transgressions of international law and State sovereignty. The ability of non-state actors to commit serious violent acts is growing, and the international legal system is still having difficulty adjusting conventional ideas of war and self-defense to address modern security threats.

In international law, the question of whether terrorist groups and other non-state actors can carry out an armed attack on their own and, therefore, support a state's right to self-defense is a complicated and divisive one. Since several states have responded to terrorist acts with force, this subject has attracted attention. The interpretation of the United Nations Charter, in particular paragraphs 2(4) and 51, is a central theme of this discussion (Franck, 2001a). Article 51 acknowledges a state's inherent right to self-defense in the event of an armed attack, whereas Article 2(4) forbids the use of force in international affairs. Notably, Article 51 stipulates that the aggressor must be a state and the victim, but it leaves unclear if both requirements must be met. This omission has led to the inference that non-state actors could perpetrate armed attacks, triggering a state's right to self-defense (Bethlehem, 2012).

After the terrorist strikes against the United States on September 11, 2001, this perspective became increasingly popular. The UN Security Council adopted Resolution 1368 to counter these assaults, denouncing the attacks and recognizing the US right to self-defense. Resolution 1373, which upheld the right to self-defense against terrorist groups like al-Qaeda, served as more confirmation of this attitude. The right of the United government to employ force in self-defense against al-Qaeda has received broad backing from the international community, which includes governments and international organizations. Nonetheless, it is still unclear how these developments will affect how Article 51 of the UN Charter is interpreted (Bethlehem, 2012). According to some academics, Article 51 should be expanded to cover assaults by non-state actors in light of how the world reacted to the 9/11 attacks. Some argue that the 9/11 attacks were unique and do not represent a fundamental shift in how Article 51 is interpreted.

Therefore, the legal community is divided on the idea that non-state actors have the right to use force to defend states when attacked, even though this idea has some merit. The complicated and dynamic subject of whether self-defense extends to attacks by non-state actors in international law is still being debated. Two pending cases demonstrate this intricacy before the International Court of Justice (ICJ).

The first case dealt with Israel's construction of a wall in the West Bank and East Jerusalem and was the subject of an advisory opinion issued in 2004. Israel defended the wall by claiming that it was an essential precaution against terrorist assaults (Burra, 2020). However, the International Court of Justice (ICJ) decided that Article 51 of the UN Charter only grants the right to self-defense in cases where a state launches an armed attack on another. According to this understanding, a state's right to self-defense under international law is not activated by acts of non-state actors, such as terrorist organizations. Notably, not every judge shared this opinion. Judge Higgins, for instance, contended that since Article 51 does not specifically restrict the right to self-defense to attacks by states, self-defense may also be justified by acts of non-state actors (Boo, 2017). In the second case, the Armed Activities on the Territory of the Congo Case in 2005, the Democratic Republic of the Congo asserted that Uganda had attacked it. Uganda used the justification of self-defense against attacks by armed groups inside the Congo to justify its actions. The International Court of Justice (ICJ) ruled that Uganda's claim of self-defense was unjustified since there was insufficient evidence to connect these acts to the Congolese state. In contrast, Judge Kooijmans argued in a different decision that armed attacks carried out by non-state organizations with headquarters in another state nevertheless qualify as armed attacks (Cordesman & Khazai, 2014).

He claimed that nothing in the UN Charter supports restricting a state's ability to defend itself only because an aggressor is not a state and that doing so would be absurd. These cases highlight the continuous discussion concerning the limits of self-defense under international law, particularly regarding attacks by non-state actors. The ICJ's decisions, which emphasize state-to-state violence, indicate a more conventional approach. However, dissident views within the Court show an understanding of how international conflicts are evolving and how non-state players are becoming increasingly important. The UN Charter's core goal of preserving world peace and security may encounter difficulties if non-state entities are denied the ability to carry out military assaults. This exclusion may effectively grant this non-state actors' impunity, enabling them to hide under the shield of a territorial State's sovereignty. Furthermore, an exception of this kind might lead to a scenario in which States would fight one another while hiding their involvement behind non-state entities. There is a good case to be made against limiting the designation of "aggressor" in armed attacks to States alone, despite the appearance that the International Court does not readily accept that non-state actors might engage in armed attacks (Gleason & Shaihutdinov, 2005). The argument is based on the increasing quantity of non-state actors who can inflict severe violence on States. Under these circumstances, a victim State must protect itself from actions that surpass a particular severity level, whether committed by non-state or State actors. Furthermore, States are not the only entities that might be classified as aggressors in an armed attack due to common practice among them. As a result, it becomes clear that dealing with the changing nature of armed conflicts—where non-state actors are becoming increasingly important in undermining international peace and security—may require a sophisticated strategy (van der Meer, 2020).

Defining Cyber Attack

Cyber operations are a constantly changing field that includes a range of activities that have the potential to have a big impact on both the virtual and actual worlds. Recognizing that these activities have the potential to develop into cyberattacks, which are distinguished by unique tactics and outcomes, is essential to comprehend them (Buchan, 2012). Cyberattacks are primarily carried out in two ways: either by erasing software or hardware or by flooding systems with so much data that they eventually crash. For instance, denial of service (DoS) assaults overload a computer or network with data, failing. As demonstrated by the 2007 attack on Estonia, a more sophisticated variant, Distributed Denial of Service (DDoS), uses several computers to target bigger networks. Another often-used tactic is exploiting software weaknesses, usually via viruses and worms. While worms can move freely over networks, viruses connect to legal programs and replicate and modify them. Trojan horses, like the malware used in the Stuxnet attack against Iran's nuclear facility in Natanz, are especially cunning; they pose benign programs while concealing harmful content (Hathaway et al., 2012).

These attacks can cause data loss, corruption, or system disruption immediately. Nevertheless, they may also indirectly affect the physical infrastructure and the people who depend on it. Cyber operations are distinct from physical attacks due to their temporal aspect; they can be initiated and carried out nearly instantly or remain dormant until activated (Boo, 2017). This makes it difficult to determine when the "right moment" is for a defensive reaction. Legally speaking, "imminence" is central to the discussion, especially regarding self-defense. Conventional perspectives confine self-defense to the seconds immediately preceding an assault; however, this is difficult for cyber operations because of their sudden or gradual implementation. Most experts recommend the 'final window of opportunity' strategy because it provides preemptive defense when an attack appears certain and impending (Ball & Waters, 2013). This opinion is challenged, nevertheless, because of possible misuses brought on by arbitrary interpretations. Different countries have differing opinions about this matter. Australia favors the majority's larger understanding of imminence, whereas France supports a narrower definition, in line with the minority perspective. While they haven't clearly defined "imminence," other nations like Brazil, Singapore, the Netherlands, and Germany recognize the right to self-defense against immediate cyber threats.

Non-State Actors and State Responsibility

Attribution in the context of cyber operations is a multifaceted and intricate task, especially when carried out by non-state actors on behalf of a State. Establishing the originator of a cyber activity is naturally difficult due to the anonymous nature of the internet. An individual or group carrying out such actions can easily hide their identity, making finding and identifying them more difficult. The ability to perform many operations simultaneously from different locations, such as distributed denial-of-service (DDoS) attacks, exacerbates this further. The International Group of Experts underlines that State responsibility for cyber-attacks is equivalent to that for kinetic strikes. Should a State execute a cyberattack through a non-state actor, the State bears accountability if it maintains effective control over the non-state actor. This crucial concept of "effective control" was originally defined in the Nicaragua Case. Nations with a high threshold of effective control in attributing non-state actors' acts to a State include Brazil, the Netherlands, and Norway. They stress that determining a state's obligation in cyber operations is less of a legal issue and more of an evidentiary one. Whether non-state actors can carry out armed cyberattacks independently is a controversial question (Bethlehem, 2012). The International Group of Experts, which holds non-state actors accountable, is divided on whether or not non-state actors may carry out such attacks without the cooperation of the State. A minority, on the other hand, thinks that Article 51 of the UN Charter restricts the ability to launch such assaults on States or non-state actors that are effectively under the control of a State (Burkadze, 2020).

There is disagreement among nations over how to react to non-state actors cyberattacks. Brazil, for instance, contends that independent non-state actors cannot use self-defense as a defense against their cyberattacks. Conversely, nations such as the United States and the Netherlands assert that the right to self-defense against cyberattacks is legitimate, irrespective of the attackers' classification as non-state or State actors. However, according to France, for a cyber operation to be considered a cyber-attack, it must be directly or indirectly connected to a State. Germany admits that non-state actors' cyber actions may qualify as cyberattacks. However, many States still haven't taken a firm position on this issue. Because of the intricate interaction of technological, legal, and factual variables in the digital age, it isn't easy to attribute cyber operations to States, particularly when non-state actors carry them out. Due to its complexity, existing standards of state accountability and international law are called into question, requiring different nations and international organizations to interpret the rules in complex and sometimes divisive ways (Ball & Waters, 2013).

WHEN IS SELF-DEFENCE LEGAL?

Certain standards govern the use of force by a State in self-defense in the framework of international law, which are rooted in both the UN Charter and customary international law (Akande & Liefländer, 2013). The Caroline Case of 1837 established the fundamental tenet of this right: self-defense is lawful when there is an "instant and overwhelming threat," which leaves no time for consideration of other options or deliberate action. Though there has been disagreement about how to read it, Article 51 of the UN Charter likewise upholds this idea. The main point of contention is whether Articles 51 and 2(4) of the UN Charter recognize an intrinsic right to self-defense that results from customary international law or if they are exhaustive. This was made clear by the Nicaragua Case, which recognized that the right to self-defense is recognized by both treaty and customary law since Article 51 alludes to the pre-existing right of self-defense under customary international law (Franck, 2001b).

Although not specifically stated in Article 51, it is implied from this dual basis in customary and treaty law that the requirements of necessity and proportionality still apply to the right to self-defense. The established principles of international customary law are as follows. Article 51 also establishes certain obligations, including notifying the Security Council of self-defense actions and capping them until the Council takes action to preserve world peace and security (Wilmshurst & Wood, 2013b). Moreover, according to the UN Charter (Articles 2(3) and 33), issues potentially impacting international peace and security should be addressed peacefully, including diplomatic efforts and adjudication. While conciliation and negotiation are part of diplomatic procedures, adjudication entails using impartial third parties, such as arbitrations or court rulings, to settle conflicts (Spaight, 1932).

The UN Charter's Article 2(4) forbids using force; however, Article 51 exempts this rule. Therefore, legitimate self-defense is exempt from this restriction. According to Article 21 of the International Law Commission's (ILC) Draft Articles, self-defense is not limited to using force and can potentially justify other measures. These include failing to fulfill specific international responsibilities if they are directly connected to the attacking state. Countermeasures and retorsions are examples of non-violent self-defense tactics. Countermeasures would be illegal if they weren't implemented to force another State to stop violating its international responsibilities. Conversely, retorsions are non-legal actions that are politically or morally insensitive. Examples include calling ambassadors, stopping state visits, blocking port access, cutting diplomatic ties, or enacting economic sanctions (Oorsprong et al., 2023).

Under international law, the right to self-defense is based on the essential idea of need. This idea was emphasized in the Nicaragua Case when it was decided that self-defense is only allowed by law when it is required to repel an armed attack. According to this necessity requirement, a state has to show why using force in retaliation is imperative. The Legality of the Threat or Use of Nuclear-Weapons Advisory Opinion emphasized this issue even more by stating that using force in self-defense is only permissible when necessary. Recognizing that the definition of "necessary" action differs based on particular circumstances is critical (Shah, 2007b). Furthermore, for the state to assert self-defense, it must present strong proof that the specific armed attack warranted the use of force. In the Oil Platforms Case, for instance, the International Court of Justice (ICJ) determined that the United States had not provided enough proof to support its use of force against Iran. The International Court of Justice (ICJ) observed that the United States' formal complaint to Iran on its military operations on the oil platforms may have been enough to stop Iran's actions, obviating the necessity for a strong reaction (Reisman & Armstrong, 2006).

Moreover, according to the need criteria, one may only assert self-defense during an active armed attack. This immediate nature of self-defense emphasizes that its goal is to halt the attack, not to exact revenge on the assailant. From a forward-looking standpoint, the state must demonstrate that using force was the only way to thwart or repel the attack and that all other non-coercive measures had failed. This immediacy criterion is somewhat flexible, giving the victim state time to identify the attacker and be sure the attack wasn't an accident. Even if not every act is ongoing or impending, self-defense may still be used in multiple incidents (Mirza & Sajid, 2019). This demonstrates that the need criterion's use in self-defense is context-dependent and necessitates giving each particular circumstance considerable thought. Under customary international law, the legitimacy of self-defense is heavily influenced by the proportionality principle. The question of whether the defensive reaction should be commensurate to the total threat posed by the attack or the amount of force utilized in the first attack is raised by this notion (Oorsprong et al., 2023).

The victim state is limited to using no more force in retaliation than against them if proportionality is determined by the force employed in the initial attack. This could lead to impractical outcomes. An assaulting state might, for example, utilize a surprise attack to take territory with little force, making it challenging for the victim state to recover its territory without using more force than necessary. According to this situation, judging proportionality based on the severity of the initial attack may go against the fundamental principles of the right to self-defense. On the other hand, if the attack's threat level determines proportionality, the emphasis is more forward-looking. The amount of force required in this case to repel the attack successfully would determine how the victim state would respond. This strategy appears to align more with the realistic requirements of self-defense (Mirza & Sajid, 2019).

The question of how to quantify proportionality is still up for dispute. Nonetheless, the critique of employing the original attack as a benchmark emphasizes its likelihood of resulting in unjustifiable limitations on the status of the victim (Greig, 1991). The proportionality examination also considers the type of weaponry employed in self-defense. Proportionality does not automatically forbid the use of nuclear weapons in self-defense, as was covered in the Legality of the Threat or Use of Nuclear-Weapons Advisory Opinion. However, international humanitarian law and other more general restrictions on armed conflict law must be followed. This suggests that while the choice of weapons is not the primary consideration in evaluating proportionality, the results of the defensive acts and their adherence to international law greatly influence the admissibility of certain weapons or methods in self-defense circumstances (Greig, 1991).

Article 51 of the UN Charter defines the notion of collective self-defense, which gives states the right, under certain circumstances, to defend themselves and other states. The International Court of Justice (ICJ) expounded on this in the Nicaragua Case, clarifying the requirements for its legitimate implementation (Akande & Liefländer, 2013). Three prerequisites must be satisfied for a state to lawfully employ force in collective self-defense. First, at least one state attacked with weapons must have a legitimate case for individual self-defense. This establishes the fundamental need for a genuine armed attack against a state to serve as the basis for collective self-defense. Second, the state that is being attacked has to announce that it has been attacked with weapons legally. This criterion highlights the importance of having the circumstance officially recognized as one that calls for self-defense (Franck, 2001b).

Thirdly, the state that is being attacked needs to ask other states for help. This clause ensures that, as opposed to being an uninvited intervention, the use of force in collective self-defense directly reacts to a request from the state in question. It's important to note that neither an existing alliance between the participating governments nor a direct threat to the security of the supporting states are prerequisites for collective self-defense (Schachter, 1989). 'Unwilling or unable' states also became a notion, especially in counterterrorism. According to this theory, a nation unable or unwilling to stop non-state actors from attacking its territory may defend itself against those actors through self-defense. As long as it is proven that the host state is incapable or unwilling to handle the threat on its own, a state may employ force in self-defense against non-state actors on that state's territory without that state's agreement. This theory, which gained notoriety following the terrorist events on September 11, 2001, attempts to handle situations in which non-state actors, acting without state sponsorship or control, pose serious risks (Oorsprong et al., 2023).

The complicated and controversial doctrine permits governments to employ force against non-state actors on their territory if the other state is unable or unwilling to stop the actors from initiating assaults. This doctrine's debate arises mostly from two factors. It first contests the idea of territorial integrity and state sovereignty (Schachter, 1989). If another state determines that a state is either unwilling or incapable of controlling non-state actors, that state may be forced to submit to the use of force on its territory against its will. This evaluation frequently entails analyzing the state's policies, which are viewed as an infringement on its equality and sovereignty. Second, there is disagreement among academics as to whether this notion is a recognized standard in customary international law or if it is only a political idea with insufficient state practice to be considered customary law (Schachter, 1989). While some academics claim that self-defense against non-state actors might be legally justified in some specific instances, even without the requirement of attributing the conduct of non-state actors to the state, the broad acceptability and applicability of this concept remain contested. In practical terms, following the 2001 terrorist attacks on the United Nations, there have been multiple instances where nations have employed force against non-state entities. Israeli operations against Islamic Jihad in Syria and against Hezbollah in Lebanon are two notable examples of Russian actions against Chechen groups in Georgia (Greig, 1991).

The US military campaign in Iraq and Syria against the Islamic State of Iraq and Syria (ISIS) was one such instance. Iraq assented to these operations within its boundaries by establishing international legal principles (Schachter, 1989). The United States, however, justified its actions in Syria by using the natural right to self-defense against non-state actors acting from a state (in this case, Syria) that is judged incapable or unwilling to repel such attacks. The United States contended that Syria has shown itself incapable of acting against ISIS or unwilling to do so. As a result of this move, a coalition of states joined the American-led campaign against ISIS. This instance demonstrates the continuous conflict between new theories addressing the realities of contemporary asymmetric warfare and terrorism and established international law norms like state sovereignty. Intense discussion surrounds the morality and legality of using force under this international law and relations theory (Mirza & Sajid, 2019).

SELF-DEFENCE AGAINST CYBER ATTACKS?

In international law and cyber security, there are precise rules governing when and how a state may lawfully use force in retaliation for a cyberattack. Important concepts like necessity, urgency, and proportionality are the foundation for these recommendations. First, based on the need requirement, it is acknowledged that using force is only an extreme measure. A state must identify the attacker and ensure the cyberattack is deliberate rather than accidental before using force. The authorities must also investigate all other non-coercive alternatives, such as passive cyber defenses (firewalls, for example), which don't entail compulsion or intrusion (Kolton, 2017). Force must be used legally only if all other options have failed to avert an impending or ongoing cyberattack. The state being attacked is used to evaluate the necessity of immediacy. For instance, if State B uses force in response to an attack by State A, this action is deemed appropriate if State B was unaware that State A had already ceased its cyberattacks. In essence, evaluating a state's response depends on how well-informed it was during the attack (Tsagourias, 2012).

At last, the proportionality principle is applied. This principle considers the reaction's size, breadth, duration, and severity and restricts it to what is required to halt the cyberattack. Crucially, the nature or degree of force used in the response need not correspond to that of the initial attack. It implies that a state may respond to a cyberattack by using more cyber actions or physical (kinetic) force, depending on what is necessary to thwart the attack. It's important to remember that the response must be appropriate for preventing the attack, not just a reflection of it (Dorn, 2017). Regarding international law and cyber security, different governments have different perspectives on the appropriate ways for states to exercise self-defense in the event of cyberattacks. This comprehension centers on the concepts of proportionality and necessity and how these concepts relate to various response modes, including conventional (kinetic) and cyber (Chen & Taw, 2023). Several nations, including Estonia, Germany, Norway, and the United Kingdom, have agreed that self-defense against cyberattacks extends beyond online activities. Put differently, a state that is the target of a cyberattack has the right to defend itself with conventional military action or using cyber means. It is important that any response—regardless of its kind—must follow proportionality and necessity rules. This means the response must be critical to thwarting the attack and not go beyond what is required to neutralize the threat (Hayward, 2017b).

The Netherlands emphasizes the value of proportionality and stresses that defense should only be strictly essential to stop or avert impending assaults to avoid escalation. Similar to this viewpoint, Australia maintains that the extent, duration, and size of any force used in self-defense must be appropriate. The International Group of Experts concurs with the International Court of Justice's (ICJ) standards for collective self-defense in cyberspace (Chen & Taw, 2023). Legalizing collective self-defense against a cyber operation requires the attacked state to announce the cyberattack and request help openly. Any state offering assistance must do so within the request's parameters and with the attacking state's permission. The assisting state may even be restricted to non-kinetic actions at the victim state's request. The concept of sovereignty is a topic of much discussion, particularly in light of non-state actors' cyberattacks that are difficult to link to a specific state (Blaxland, 2020). Regarding recognizing the "unwilling or unable" theory as a component of international law (lex lata), the International Group of Experts is split. According to the majority opinion, using force in self-defense against a non-state actor conducting a cyberattack is acceptable if the state the actor is acting from is unable or unwilling to end the attack. Respecting the principle of sovereignty, the victim state must demand that the territory state address the attack and give it a chance to do so before using self-defense (Hayward, 2017b).

The victim state might be unable to wait in an emergency, though. A state cannot use self-defense against a non-state actor acting from another state without the approval of the territorial state or authorization from the Security Council, according to the minority opinion (Marrone & Sabatino, 2021). The legality and reaction protocols to cyberattacks, especially those carried out by non-state actors, are hotly contested issues that differ from country to country. For example, Brazil maintains that the concept of "unwilling or unable" is inapplicable under international law in the context of cyberattacks, particularly as the definition of a cyberattack is limited to actions that can be clearly attributed to States. According to Brazil, non-state actors' cyber activities are considered significant crimes, even if they resemble state-sponsored cyberattacks in their intent (Dorn, 2017). The territorial state where these actors are situated ought to handle these. If the territorial state does nothing, it will be viewed as an internationally wrongful act that calls for peaceful solutions but does not excuse the victim state from using force against the non-state actor or the territorial state (Mahmoud, 2013).

On the other hand, the Netherlands adopts a different stance, claiming that under international law, self-defense against non-state actors is legal provided the cyberattacks origin can be positively identified and the reaction satisfies the requirements of necessity and proportionality. This viewpoint makes it possible for a state to protect itself from cyberattacks by non-state actors, so long as the reaction is proportionate and well-founded (Blaxland, 2020). Operation Red October serves as a practical example to highlight this topic. Red October was an advanced cyber espionage network discovered in 2012 by the Russian cybersecurity company Kaspersky Lab. It had infiltrated over 350 governmental, diplomatic, and scientific research organizations across 39 states, including the Russian Embassy, and had compromised important documents from the EU and NATO. The operation was noteworthy for its size and sophistication, raising the possibility of a state actor being involved. Even though Red October's beginnings are still unknown, some experts think that a state may be behind this espionage network due to the network's engagement with Russian speakers and its primary targets being diplomatic organizations (Dorn, 2017).

The difficulties in assigning individual actors—whether states or non-state entities—to cyber activities are brought to light by the Red October case. It also demonstrates the dynamic character of cyber threats, which frequently conflate actions by states and non-state actors, complicating and escalating the application of established international law doctrines like the "unwilling or unable" theory (Kolton, 2017). The intricacy of the situation is exacerbated by the absence of prior legal precedent in global courts concerning cyberattacks, even though these operations have become more frequent and sophisticated in the last twenty years. The examination of the Red October cyber espionage operation, which mainly targeted Russia, provides valuable insights into how international law interprets situations of this nature, especially when considering the right to self-defense (Hayward, 2017b). It is important to analyze whether the Red October operation qualified as a cyberattack to determine whether Russia may claim the right to self-defense. When a cyber operation's scope and consequences are serious enough, it becomes a cyber-attack (Chen & Taw, 2023).

Although Russia suffered a large-scale operation in Red October, involving 35 distinct infections and substantial data theft, the nature of these cyberattacks was not harmful. Since the victims were unaware that they were being targeted, it was clear that cyber espionage, by its very nature, does not usually result in physical harm or interfere with vital infrastructure. Even if these data thefts have a significant impact, they do not have the same devastating impacts as using force in combat. According to the International

Group of Experts, cyber theft does not qualify as a cyberattack without negative or disruptive repercussions. Even considering the overall consequences of the Red October operations, the impact is not great enough to give rise to the right to self-defense (Chen & Taw, 2023). On the other hand, the cyberattacks against Estonia in 2007 paint a different picture. These actions, which included banks, political parties, and government institutions as targets for distributed denial-of-service (DDoS) assaults, severely disrupted Estonia's internal economy and profoundly affected society. Throughout the 22-day cyber operation, vital services, business ventures, and regular avenues of communication were all negatively impacted. There were significant financial losses (Marrone & Sabatino, 2021).

Early indications suggested that some machines may have belonged to Russian state organizations. The Estonian cyber activities originated on computers in 178 countries. Nevertheless, experts pointed out that there was little proof to connect the cyber operations to the Russian government, while Russian officials denied involvement (Dorn, 2017). Even if certain people and organizations took credit, their accounts only partially matched the cyber activities that Estonia was involved in. Important considerations concerning the application of international law are brought up by the investigation of cyber operations, including those against Estonia and the Stuxnet worm, especially regarding self-defense in the face of cyberattacks. While there were no physical injuries or property losses in Estonia due to the cyber activities, there was a major interruption to vital infrastructure, including the inability to access government websites and e-banking services (Dorn, 2017). The international legal community has not resolved whether such disruptions—absent physical harm or injury—qualify as a cyberattack that would support a state's right to self-defense. The severity and scope of such disruptions would have to be significant for them to be considered grounds for self-defense. In Estonia's case, there was a brief disruption that did not meet the standard for military force, even if there was significant economic harm. While some nations support it, not everyone agrees to include economic loss in the assessment (Hayward, 2017b).

On the other hand, a contrasting situation is presented by the Stuxnet cyber worm, which targets Iranian nuclear facilities. In contrast to the Estonian case, Stuxnet resulted in physical harm, albeit without any personal injury (Blaxland, 2020). Targeting nuclear centrifuges in particular, the worm caused malfunctions, breakdowns, and in some cases, explosions. The extent of physical harm inflicted upon vital infrastructure marks a notable divergence from the outcomes of the Estonian cyber operations. Given its complexity and the specialized expertise needed for it, only a small group of extremely skilled private individuals or state actors could have carried out Stuxnet's operation (Dorn, 2017). No official government has taken credit for the operation, despite extensive conjecture and media coverage linking it to a joint US-Israeli endeavor (Chen & Taw, 2023). The stark difference between these two incidents—the physical harm caused by Stuxnet and the interruption of Estonia's vital infrastructure—highlights the difficulties in extending the rules of international law to cyber operations. Because of the brief and non-physical character of the interruptions, the Estonian case did not meet the requirements for justifying self-defense; however, Stuxnet's direct physical harm to vital infrastructure makes a stronger argument for using self-defense. This discrepancy highlights how constantly changing cyber threats are and how difficult it is to judge whether a response is lawful under international law (Tsagourias, 2012).

A key example in the discussion of cyberattacks and international law is the Stuxnet case, which is separate from the Red October activities and the cyber operations against Estonia. Unlike the prior examples, Stuxnet delivered physical harm and destruction, notably to nuclear centrifuges, triggering failures and explosions. Its distinct physical effect begs the question of whether Stuxnet qualified as a cyberattack for purposes of international law (Mahmoud, 2013). Regarding this matter, the International Group of Experts is split. Some contend that because of Stuxnet's extreme effects, it qualifies as a cyberattack, drawing comparisons to the International Court of Justice's (ICJ) decision in the Oil Platforms Case, which deemed an attack on a lone military vessel to be an act of armament. This analogy implies that Stuxnet's physical harm might be categorized as a cyberattack. However, as Iran has not formally disclosed the details of the physical damages, it is unclear exactly how much harm has been done (Hayward, 2017b).

The question of lawful self-defense is made more difficult by the uncertainty surrounding Stuxnet's origin. Iran might have directed self-defense measures against these governments if the United governments and Israel were to blame, as long as the rules of necessity and proportionality were followed. This means Iran's response should have been strictly essential to cease the cyber-attacks and not excessively worry about the harm posed (Chen & Taw, 2023). Alternatively, Iran would have followed a different approach if Stuxnet had been the work of a non-state actor. Iran would have to locate the non-state actor's operating state and get in touch with it to demand that it take steps to put an end to the attack. Iran would also need to allow the occupying state to reply. Theoretically, Iran could have been allowed to employ force in self-defense against the non-state actor if the territorial state was unable or unwilling to intervene, once more according to the requirements of necessity and proportionality (Pryor et al., 2019).

DISCUSSION

The discourse explores the complex relationship between self-defence rights and cyber attacks in international law, particularly the UN Charter. It emphasizes the need to restrict the right to self-defense under Article 2(4) of the UN Charter to promote global peace and security. Cyberspace, a new area of public international law, requires strict interpretation. This discussion highlights state differences in cyber attack definition and consequences. This disagreement goes beyond academia to national interests, ideologies, and morals. Economic damages as a criterion for cyber activities that constitute force, which the UN Charter forbids, is a difficult issue. Some states now support considering economic damages in cyber attack assessments, a major move from earlier economic coercion perspectives. Identifying whether a cyber activity becomes an armed attack and triggers the right to self-defense is difficult. No unanimity on what constitutes an armed attack in cyberspace adds to this complication. States must agree on whether cyber activities that impair vital infrastructure without physical damage or casualties are cyber assaults. The growing identification of non-physical impacts in deciding armed attacks suggests a movement in state practice and jurisprudence toward a broader definition of internet armed attacks.

This discourse is further complicated by the changing role of non-State actors in international law, notably in cyberspace. Despite their lack of military power, non-state actors can initiate cyber operations that threaten national security. This issue raises questions about state responsibility and how to hold states accountable for non-State actor behavior, especially given the difficulties of attributing cyber attacks to states. States targeted by non-State cyber assaults have limited reaction options due to state sovereignty and the restriction of interfering in other states' domestic affairs. The notion of unwilling or unable allows self-defence under certain conditions to balance sovereignty and territorial integrity. The chapter concludes that cyber operations pose unprecedented issues to international law, including state liability, cyber attack attribution, and self-defence thresholds. As the digital domain evolves, international law and state practice will adapt to address the multifaceted challenges of cyber attacks and self-defence, highlighting the dynamic relationship between technological advancements and legal norms and principles aimed at preserving international peace and security.

CONCLUSION

This chapter clarifies the complexities and difficulties associated with the idea of self-defense against cyberattacks in the context of international law. As an exception to Article 2(4) of the United Nations Charter, which forbids the use of force, the right to self-defense must be construed strictly. Upholding international peace and security—the principal goal of the UN Charter—requires adherence to this view. In the context of jus ad bellum (the right to war) in cyberspace, where legal precedents and concerns are still developing within the framework of public international law, this becomes even more important. The differences between state definitions and responses to cyberattacks are an important factor to consider. Their differing national interests, philosophies, and ideals are frequently reflected in this disparity. States that once disregarded the possibility that using economic pressure could be considered an unlawful use of force are now pushing for including economic damages in the definition of a cyberattack. As a result, it's critical to acknowledge how state interests shape perceptions of what constitutes a political viewpoint vs. a recognized component of international law (lex lata).

The main difficulty is figuring out if a cyber operation qualifies as a cyber-attack and, in turn, activates the right to self-defense. This difficulty is exacerbated by the contentious definition of "armed attack" in this context. A cyber operation's scope and impact must be on par with that of a conventional military force for it to be classified as a cyberattack. However, determining this equivalency might be subjective and case-specific, resulting in the state drawing arbitrary judgments since it sees itself as the victim. Whether cyber activities that interfere with vital infrastructure without endangering people or property count as cyberattacks is particularly hotly debated. There is no agreement on this issue, even though some governments support a more expansive view that considers these non-physical impacts. But given how frequently cyber operations aimed against vital infrastructure occur, it's crucial to determine whether these occurrences qualify as cyberattacks. The definition of an armed attack in cyberspace is expected to grow due to changing state practices and opinio juris, which is the idea that some actions are required by international law. This could include actions that have major non-physical effects.

The dynamics of state security and accountability have been profoundly affected by the growing influence of non-state players in international law, especially in cyberspace. Even though they lack the armed power of governments, non-state actors have proven they are capable of causing significant harm. This presents complicated questions since there are gaps in accountability for serious operations that these players independently carry out, particularly given the high threshold needed to attribute their acts to states. There's a growing realization that non-state actors can carry out armed strikes as state behavior changes. Nonetheless, victim governments face numerous legal and diplomatic obstacles when utilizing their existing reaction tools. Respecting other states' sovereignty and territorial integrity is necessary, on the one hand. Self-defense in the face of a non-state actor operating on another state's territory may go against these values and inflame tensions because it may be interpreted as an infringement on the territorial state's sovereignty.

On the other hand, imbalance results from denying victim nations the resources they need to defend themselves against non-state actors. It might make it possible for nations to use non-state actors to cover indirect attacks on other states, evading responsibility and endangering global peace and security. This conundrum is especially apparent regarding cyberattacks since it is frequently hard to accurately determine attribution. I believe the 'unwilling or unable' notion provides a reasonable solution. It recognizes a victim state's right to self-defense against armed attacks by non-state entities while upholding sovereignty and territorial integrity. Several cases where states have employed force against non-state actors operating from another state's territory have already demonstrated how this theory is used. Nonetheless, considering the sovereignty and territorial integrity of the state where the non-state actor is based, the criteria of necessity and proportionality must be followed in such circumstances. Force should only be used as a final resort after more subdued tactics have failed to thwart the attack.

The distinct characteristics of cyber activities present novel obstacles for international law. Cyberattacks are stretching the limits of a severe threshold for armed attacks, as they can seriously disrupt a state's infrastructure without resulting in physical or human damage. The interpretation of an impending threat becomes more difficult due to the instantaneous nature of cyber operations, which can be initiated and result in damage virtually instantly. Additionally, the difficulty in tracing cyber activities to a specific state contradicts existing standards regarding using force in self-defense. In conclusion, international law and state practices will probably change to meet these new issues as cyberspace becomes important. To ensure that the regulations and standards governing cyberattacks and self-defense stay applicable in this quickly evolving field, the adaptation is expected to concentrate on improving them.

REFERENCES

Akande, D., & Liefländer, T. (2013). Clarifying Necessity, Imminence, and Proportionality in the Law of Self-Defense. *The American Journal of International Law*, *107*(3), 563–570. doi:10.5305/amerjintelaw.107.3.0563

Aslan, M. (2020). Hybrid Political Order in Libya: State, Non-State, and Armed Actors. *Insight Turkey*, *22*(4), 139–156. doi:10.25253/99.2020224.09

Ball, D., & Waters, G. (2013). Cyber Defence and Warfare. *Security Challenges*, *9*(2), 91–98.

Bethlehem, D. (2012). Self-Defense Against an Imminent or Actual Armed Attack by Nonstate Actors. *The American Journal of International Law*, *106*(4), 769–777. doi:10.5305/amerjintelaw.106.4.0769

Blaxland, J. (2020). Developing a new Plan B for the ADF: Implications from a Geostrategic SWOT Analysis for Australia. *Security Challenges*, *16*(2), 13–23.

Boo, H. (2017). An Assessment of North Korean Cyber Threats. *The Journal of East Asian Affairs*, *31*(1), 97–117.

Buchan, R. (2012). Cyber Attacks: Unlawful Uses of Force or Prohibited Interventions? *Journal of Conflict and Security Law*, *17*(2), 211–227. doi:10.1093/jcsl/krs014

Burkadze, K. (2020). A Shift in the Historical Understanding of Armed Attack and Its Applicability to Cyberspace. *The Fletcher Forum of World Affairs*, *44*(1), 33–48.

Burra, S. (2020). Use of Force as Self Defence against Non-State Actors and TWAIL Considerations: A Critical Analysis of India's State Practice. In S. Lee & H. E. Lee (Eds.), *Asian Yearbook of International Law, Volume 24 (2018)* (pp. 106–126). Brill. https://www.jstor.org/stable/10.1163/j.ctv1sr6j7f.9

Chen, S., & Taw, J. (2023). Conventional Retaliation and Cyber Attacks. *The Cyber Defense Review*, *8*(1), 67–86.

Cordesman, A. H., & Khazai, S. (2014). *Other Extremist Non-State Actors, Syria, and Iran* (Iraq in Crisis, pp. 193–215). Center for Strategic and International Studies (CSIS). https://www.jstor.org/stable/resrep36981.13

Dorn, W. (2017). Cyberpeacekeeping: A New Role for the United Nations? *Georgetown Journal of International Affairs, 18*(3), 138–146. doi:10.1353/gia.2017.0046

Franck, T. M. (2001a). Terrorism and the Right of Self-Defense. *The American Journal of International Law, 95*(4), 839–843. doi:10.2307/2674629

Franck, T. M. (2001b). Terrorism and the Right of Self-Defense. *The American Journal of International Law, 95*(4), 839–843. doi:10.2307/2674629

Gleason, G., & Shaihutdinov, M. E. (2005). Collective Security and Non-State Actors in Eurasia. *International Studies Perspectives, 6*(2), 274–284. doi:10.1111/j.1528-3577.2005.00206.x

Greig, D. W. (1991). Self-Defence and the Security Council: What Does Article 51 Require? *The International and Comparative Law Quarterly, 40*(2), 366–402. doi:10.1093/iclqaj/40.2.366

Hargrove, J. L. (1987). The Nicaragua Judgment and the Future of the Law of Force and Self-Defense. *The American Journal of International Law, 81*(1), 135–143. doi:10.2307/2202142

Hathaway, O. A., Crootof, R., Levitz, P., Nix, H., Nowlan, A., Perdue, W., & Spiegel, J. (2012a). The Law of Cyber-Attack. *California Law Review, 100*(4), 817–885.

Hathaway, O. A., Crootof, R., Levitz, P., Nix, H., Nowlan, A., Perdue, W., & Spiegel, J. (2012b). The Law of Cyber-Attack. *California Law Review, 100*(4), 817–885.

Hayward, R. J. (2017a). Evaluating the "Imminence" of a Cyber Attack for Purposes of Anticipatory Self-Defense. *Columbia Law Review, 117*(2), 399–434.

Hayward, R. J. (2017b). Evaluating the "Imminence" of a Cyber Attack for Purposes of Anticipatory Self-Defense. *Columbia Law Review, 117*(2), 399–434.

Kolton, M. (2017). Interpreting China's Pursuit of Cyber Sovereignty and its Views on Cyber Deterrence. *The Cyber Defense Review, 2*(1), 119–154.

Mahmoud, K. W. (2013). *Cyber Attacks: The Electronic Battlefield.* Arab Center for Research & Policy Studies. https://www.jstor.org/stable/resrep12651

Marrone, A., & Sabatino, E. (2021). *Cyber Defence in NATO Countries: Comparing Models.* Istituto Affari Internazionali (IAI). https://www.jstor.org/stable/resrep28807

Mirza, M. N., & Sajid, A. (2019). Use of Force in Self-Defence for Global Peace: A Conceptual Framework. *Strategic Studies, 39*(3), 1–21. doi:10.53532/ss.039.03.00102

Mulford, J. P. (2016). Non-State Actors in the Russo-Ukrainian War. *Connections, 15*(2), 89–107. doi:10.11610/Connections.15.2.07

Oorsprong, F., Ducheine, P., & Pijpers, P. (2023). Cyber-attacks and the right of self-defense: A case study of the Netherlands. *Policy Design and Practice, 6*(2), 217–239. doi:10.1080/25741292.2023.2179955

Pryor, C. D., Garcia-Millan, T., Gelman, J., Madan, T., Moore, S., Pryor, C., Reijula, L., Smolinske, N., Tensley, B., Weatherby, C., & Yang, J. (2019). *Taiwan's Cybersecurity Landscape and Opportunities for Regional Partnership* (Perspectives on Taiwan, pp. 10–15). Center for Strategic and International Studies (CSIS). https://www.jstor.org/stable/resrep22549.5

Reisman, W. M., & Armstrong, A. (2006). The Past and Future of the Claim of Preemptive Self-Defense. *The American Journal of International Law*, *100*(3), 525–550. doi:10.1017/S0002930000031043

Ruys, T. (2014). The Meaning of "Force" and the Boundaries of the Jus Ad Bellum: Are "Minimal" Uses of Force Excluded from Un Charter Article 2(4)? *The American Journal of International Law*, *108*(2), 159–210. doi:10.5305/amerjintelaw.108.2.0159

Schachter, O. (1987). Self-Defense. [American Society of International Law]. *Proceedings of the Annual Meeting (American Association of University Teachers of Insurance)*, *81*, 350–354.

Schachter, O. (1989). Self-Defense and the Rule of Law. *The American Journal of International Law*, *83*(2), 259–277. doi:10.2307/2202738

Searles, P., & Berger, R. J. (1987). The Feminist Self-Defense Movement: A Case Study. *Gender & Society*, *1*(1), 61–84. doi:10.1177/089124387001001004

Shah, N. A. (2007a). Self-defence, Anticipatory Self-defence and Pre-emption: International Law's Response to Terrorism. *Journal of Conflict and Security Law*, *12*(1), 95–126. doi:10.1093/jcsl/krm006

Shah, N. A. (2007b). Self-defence, Anticipatory Self-defence and Pre-emption: International Law's Response to Terrorism. *Journal of Conflict and Security Law*, *12*(1), 95–126. doi:10.1093/jcsl/krm006

Spaight, J. M. (1932). Self-Defence and International Air Power. *Journal of Comparative Legislation and International Law*, *14*(1), 20–29.

Trapp, K. N. (2007). Back to Basics: Necessity, Proportionality, and the Right of Self-Defence against Non-State Terrorist Actors. *The International and Comparative Law Quarterly*, *56*(1), 141–156. doi:10.1093/iclq/lei153

Tsagourias, N. (2012). Cyber attacks, self-defence and the problem of attribution. *Journal of Conflict and Security Law*, *17*(2), 229–244. doi:10.1093/jcsl/krs019

van der Meer, S. (2020). *How states could respond to non-state cyber-attackers*. Clingendael Institute. https://www.jstor.org/stable/resrep25677

Wijninga, P., Oosterveld, W. T., Galdiga, J. H., Marten, P., Chivot, E., Gehem, M., Knowles, E., Maas, M., Schellekens, M., Silveira, J., Yang, M. Y., Zelinska, O., de Jong, S., Kogut, P., & van Luit, E. (2014). *State and Non-State Actors: Beyond the Dichotomy*. Hague Centre for Strategic Studies. https://www.jstor.org/stable/resrep12608.8

Wilmshurst, E., & Wood, M. (2013a). Self-Defense Against Nonstate Actors: Reflections on the "Bethlehem Principles.". *The American Journal of International Law*, *107*(2), 390–395. doi:10.5305/amerjintelaw.107.2.0390

Wilmshurst, E., & Wood, M. (2013b). Self-Defense Against Nonstate Actors: Reflections on the "Bethlehem Principles.". *The American Journal of International Law*, *107*(2), 390–395. doi:10.5305/amerjintelaw.107.2.0390

ADDITIONAL READING

Aravindakshan, S. (2021). Cyberattacks: A look at evidentiary thresholds in International Law. *Indian Journal of International Law*, *59*(1–4), 285–299. doi:10.1007/s40901-020-00113-0

Choudhary, A. S., Choudhary, P. P., & Salve, S. (2018). A Study On Various Cyber Attacks And A Proposed Intelligent System For Monitoring Such Attacks. *2018 3rd International Conference on Inventive Computation Technologies (ICICT)*, (pp. 612–617). IEEE. 10.1109/ICICT43934.2018.9034445

Li, Y., & Liu, Q. (2021). A comprehensive review study of cyber-attacks and cyber security; Emerging trends and recent developments. *Energy Reports*, *7*, 8176–8186. doi:10.1016/j.egyr.2021.08.126

Madubuike-Ekwe, J. N. (2021). Cyberattack and the Use of Force in International Law. *Beijing Law Review*, *12*(2), 2. doi:10.4236/blr.2021.122034

Oorsprong, F., Ducheine, P., & Pijpers, P. (2023). Cyber-attacks and the right of self-defense: A case study of the Netherlands. *Policy Design and Practice*, *6*(2), 217–239. doi:10.1080/25741292.2023.2179955

Radziwill, Y. (2015). Cyber-Attacks and the Exploitable Imperfections of International Law. In *Cyber-Attacks and the Exploitable Imperfections of International Law*. Brill Nijhoff. https://brill.com/display/title/31492

Simmons, N. (2014). A Brave New World: Applying International Law of War to Cyber-Attacks. *Journal of Law & Cyber Warfare*, *4*(1), 42–108.

KEY TERMS AND DEFINITIONS

Armed Attack: In the context of international law, an armed attack is a severe form of aggression that justifies a state's right to self-defense. It usually implies a significant level of violence or force, beyond mere political or economic coercion.

Cyber Operations: These refer to the range of activities conducted through cyberspace, often involving computers, networks, and the internet. Cyber operations can range from benign activities to hostile ones like cyberattacks and espionage.

Non-State Actors: These are individuals or groups that are not affiliated with any national government. In cyber operations, they can play significant roles, ranging from independent hackers to groups indirectly supported by states.

Proportionality: This is a principle in international law, particularly in self-defense, where the response to an attack must be proportionate to the threat posed. It aims to prevent excessive or unnecessary use of force.

Self-Defense: Self-defense in international law is the right of a state to use appropriate force to defend itself against an armed attack. It's contingent on the principles of necessity (as a last resort) and proportionality (response commensurate with the threat).

Chapter 16
Pilgrimage Creative Tourism: A Gateway to Sustainable Development Goals in Bangladesh

Mohammad Badruddoza Talukder
https://orcid.org/0000-0001-7788-2732
International University of Business Agriculture and Technology, Bangladesh

Sanjeev Kumar
https://orcid.org/0000-0002-7375-7341
Lovely Professional University, India

Fahmida Kaiser
https://orcid.org/0009-0002-4113-207X
Daffodil Institute of IT, Bangladesh

Md. Nasir Mia
Islamic University, Bangladesh

ABSTRACT

This chapter investigates the possibility that creative tourism based on pilgrimage could serve as a driving force in achieving sustainable development goals (SDGs) in Bangladesh. By incorporating artistic components into pilgrimage experiences, this strategy not only improves the cultural and theological importance of the journey but also promotes economic growth, environmental conservation, and the empowerment of communities. The authors shed light on how pilgrimage sites can function as hubs for sustainable tourism development, thereby creating money for local communities, protecting cultural heritage, and fostering environmental stewardship. The authors employ secondary sources to compile the study. They examine techniques for collaboration between government agencies, non-governmental organizations (NGOs), and local stakeholders to possible socio-economic gains. The results of this research highlight the transformative power of pilgrimage creative tourism in Bangladesh, furthering the sustainable development goals (SDGs) for developing sustainable tourism in the context of the global community.

DOI: 10.4018/979-8-3693-1742-6.ch016

INTRODUCTION

The advent of the Creative Era heralds a new paradigm in economic growth, dubbed the "Creative Economy" (Scranton et al., 2021). This economic development approach focuses on knowledge, education, creativity, and intellectual property associated with culture, wisdom, technology, and innovation. As a result of its breadth, this notion is being promoted as a guideline for developing countries that need to establish economic prosperity and security for their people's living conditions (Dias et al., 2021). The Creative Economy movement has also contributed to developing an alternative tourist paradigm. The primary goals of travelers in the first era are leisure and entertainment. Second-generation tourism addresses cultural and environmental implications and community sustainability in tourist hotspots. The third period is characterized by creative tourism, a subset of cultural tourism that emphasizes and encourages active learning about the local arts, culture, and history through firsthand experience (Galvagno & Giaccone, 2019). The global community has recognized the significance of this shift in the tourism paradigm. It has begun employing local knowledge to foster tourism growth within communities through innovative approaches to the industry.

Tourism professionals, business owners, and representatives of local governments and their allied groups would help people educate themselves on the nature and application of local knowledge in creative tourism (Talukder et al., 2024). Those who like the arts and culture will find that creative tourism caters to their interests and needs. Customers or sightseers want to take part in imaginative endeavours themselves. Customers in the market for creative tourism want to "go where the creativity is" and get their hands dirty in making and sharing (Kumar et al., 2024). People are becoming more co-creators, offering information and expertise as experiences develop. In addition to their monetary value, creative tourism experiences can be transformative because of the potential for new ideas, products, and services to emerge through the exchanges, discussions, and collaborations among their participants (Das et al., 2024). A 'creative atmosphere' makes areas desirable not only for the creative class but also for others. Therefore, creative development policies are naturally connected to tourism (Akdemir et al., 2023).

On the other hand, attraction-based methods are linked to gentrification, exclusion, and serial reproduction, all leading to the loss of a place's unique character, initially the goal of these initiatives. This points to the importance of improving the design of inspirational locations to ensure people remain unique and inspiring throughout time. Grass-roots, endogenous processes may be more effective at stimulating sustainable creative development, although top-down planning activities may help steer the design process in the right direction (Zhou et al., 2023; Kumar et al., 2024).

Creative Tourism

It is commonly agreed that alternative forms of tourism, such as creative tourism, enhance more conventional forms of cultural tourism. Cultural tourism provides visitors with an opportunity to learn about a place's history and culture through visits to sites, both natural and artificial. In contrast, creative tourism encourages visitors to try new things while taking advantage of regional specialities (Leoti et al., 2023). The development of innovative tourism in countries like Brazil, New Zealand, and Thailand are more examples of success stories. In Brazil, visitors can participate in samba dance classes rather than witness a performance, and in New Zealand, there are many indigenous-themed programs led by experts in the field. Rural areas in Thailand also provide visitors with homestay options and culinary classes using authentic Thai foods. The creative tourism industry "is shifting towards a more extensive relationship between tourism and the creative industries," as noted in recent years (Arcos-Pumarola et al., 2023).

In recent years, there has been a greater emphasis on the relevance of co-creating processes in inventive interactions. Creative tourism must take into consideration how each location is experienced, how local identity can be bolstered, and how tourists can help to generate their own experience beyond simply making use of particular features, linking the locations with the territorial capital of the area, and challenging tourists to complete a specific task with the assistance of the local community (make a traditional craft, participate in an event, etc.) (Santos et al., 2022). To "interact, to learn, to do, to self-express" and to "shift the attention from the tourist's gaze to his all-being". Creative tourism must do more than provide possibilities for learning and self-expression, employ local resources, and ensure community involvement; it must also inspire participants' originality and passion. The essential elements are "active participation, creative self-expression, learning, and community engagement". The possibilities of creative tourism to solve the industry's problems and individual tourists' needs are discussed (Agapity & Mugobi, 2023).

Salient Features of Creative Tourism

a) Inviting visitors to try new things and learn from one another to immerse themselves in the local culture.
b) Encouraging visitors to collaborate with locals to make meaningful community contributions while expanding their creative capacities.
c) Exploring innovative ways to provide tourism products with significant added value.
d) Valuing one's intangible cultural and creative assets over one's material heritage. It may be argued that tiny and medium-sized private companies are more important than the government.
e) Encouraging long-term expansion of the tourism industry because:
    i. It breathes new life into tried-and-true products.
    ii. It helps traditional cultural tourism adapt to changes, like the proliferation of cheap knockoffs of famous landmarks.
    iii. It makes better use of cutting-edge technology to streamline service delivery (Ababneh, 2017).

Concentrations of Creative Tourism

Creative tourism is becoming increasingly popular as people seek to distinguish themselves via their experience consumption.

1. Creativity affords vacationers the chance to have more memorable trips.
2. Creative tourism may be an excellent way for hosts to promote local culture and talent while attracting visitors.
3. Small and medium-sized enterprises (SMEs) must be creative to provide novel and exciting tourism products (Kumar et al., 2024).
4. Creative tourism offers a way for locations to stand out in a crowd.

For survival in today's ever-competitive industry and for fostering mutually beneficial relationships between site visitors and the natives of the area (Tilburg University, The Netherlands & Richards, 2019)

Opportunities for Creative Tourism

People's well-being, cultural immersion, responsible travel, small-scale travel, networks, and domestic travel are just a few examples of how creative tourism can be a solution to today's problems, as revealed by an exploratory approach to the field based on the literature on tourism and the characteristics of creative travel.

Inspiring Happiness and Satisfying the Yearning for Feelings, Creative Tourism

The idea that visitors want to connect on an emotional level with the locations people visit is not new, but it is on the rise. "Entirely from their home lives and engage sincerely with a different way of living" by integrating with the locals is becoming increasingly popular among tourists (Paschinger, 2021). Conscious tourists place a premium on experiences that appeal to their ethics, spirituality, and authenticity. Conscientious travellers view travel as a call to action. When planning a trip, it is essential to consider the stories each location might tell, the feelings people might evoke, and the locals that call it home. After the pandemic, a specific type of traveller is more concerned with pursuing happiness and the value of their travel experiences.

Travelers care more about the "why" than the "what" when deciding where to go. Tourists gain the emotional connections people want as humans, as well as cognitive and affective benefits from their travels, not simply with locations but also with the development of emotional connections and the pursuit of more humane interactions between visitors and locals. Involvement and emotion are significant factors in leisure behaviour (Cabeça et al., 2021). Therefore, it is believed that the tourist industry and business owners should emphasise creating deep connections between people and places. This need presents an opening for the sector to promote travel as a form of self-expression. That is the idea behind creative tourism: connecting people and places so that every trip is different because of the people and the businesses involved. According to a recent study, participants in creative tourism activities seek more significant opportunities for social and emotional engagement with the local population and a sense of belonging to the location (Talukder & Hossain, 2021). In reality, visitors also anticipate opportunities to participate in the local community, a factor crucial to creative tourism's success (Ihamäki, 2012).

Participatory and Interactive Community Events

This type of traveller follows a trajectory of immersion and engagement and a quest for authenticity, meaning, and purpose in the culture of their destination. Travellers planning travels for 2022 are most interested in discovering off-the-beaten-path gems, fulfilling lifelong dreams, and participating in nature-centred activities (Talukder, 2020). In this case, it is not just the crucial assets unique to a territory; local communities and business owners are as people. Researchers recommend Community participation in decision-making and the design of authentic and engaging experiences to revitalize tourism in each region and enhance the quality of the tourist experience. Booming tourism that meets the demands of visitors should reflect the local culture in its offerings, be driven by a shared passion for cultural exchange, and be organized and operated by residents of the destination area themselves. Place-based tourism, which involves using each area's distinctive territorial capital and including residents in planning, is essential because it produces one-of-a-kind vacation spots (Duxbury et al., 2019).

Respect for Local Culture and Rules and Tourists' Obligations to Locals

Lately, it has been stated that "active participation, socially and environmentally responsible traveling" is what "can fulfil people's dreams and desires ". Sustainability concerns are no longer limited to suppliers and hosting communities; consumers now expect people. Travelers are committed to preserving the human, cultural, and physical environment and make ethical decisions while planning their trips (Tomaz et al., 2020). Vacationers now consider the effects of their trips on locals' lives and economies, as well as the possible harm people could do to a destination's historical and cultural landmarks. Possibilities for a new kind of tourism to arise, one that achieves social and economic aims while benefiting local communities, are expanded. That is why "responsible tourism combined with creative marketing needs to be integrated into tourism policies". Local communities must see tourism grow and prosper while protecting their natural and cultural heritage. For the sake of future generations, the tourism industry must likewise practice resourcefulness. Consumers can feel good about their impact on local economies when they partake in innovative tourism offers because they know that the local community will be involved and will profit from the experiences provided. Creative tourism presents a chance to reimagine the pre-pandemic tourism model as more sustainable and closer to the local community, helping preserve local identities, territories, and communities to the mutual benefit of locals, tourists, and businesses. Regulating the number of visitors to a destination can help lessen the damage people may have to the local environment. Highlight the potential for post-pandemic communities to develop innovative approaches to tourism management (Lebedova & Sapundzhiev, 2023).

A Substitute for Cluttered and Excessive Mass Tourism

Numerous authors are currently concentrating their efforts on finding ways to prevent the tourism industry from reviving its economy by employing the same antiquated methods that have brought about a decline in the living standards of locals, had a detrimental effect on their well-being, and led to an inferior spatial experience for tourists (Talukder et al., 2022). As a result of the excessive number of visitors, the locals experience negative social and environmental repercussions. Along with strategies such as crowd control, mitigation of visitor flows, investment in cultural tourism, and conservation and environmental practices, moderation of risks with a focus on sustainability is advised in studies of strategic techniques for reviving the tourism industry (Branstrator et al., 2023). Specific plans were put down before the outbreak that may now be executed to their full potential. These plans include creative tactics for specialization and marketing plans. The aims of protecting the environment, preserving culture, and maintaining one's health have joined the ranks of product and market diversity. It is believed that the proposed measures will be sufficient to make regions more competitive and attract visitors throughout the year, qualify the territory and the environment, reduce the seasonality of the tourism industry, and reduce the excessive concentration on a single tourism product (Mohammad et al., 2024). Expanding a place's attractiveness via diversification may help preserve the history of a region and its natural and economic resources. This is made possible through the preservation of the territory's resources. When the region's financial base is geared toward a particular product, the economic, social, demographic, and tourist differences existing across different places within the same area become much more pronounced (Cabeca et al., 2021). Visitors are being drawn to areas outside of traditional tourism circuits, such as rural and low-density territories, by creative tourism. This type of tourism allows visitors to interact with local communities. This meets the need to diversify the tourist range, develop tourism in small-scale places, use local resources, and boost local economies. Creative tourism enhances a region's appeal and sense of identity by putting local creativity and resourcefulness to use in the service of long-term economic development plans. It has the potential to improve the quality of life in rural areas that have not benefited much from tourism, lead to the discovery of destinations that were previously undiscovered, and provide tourists with unforgettable experiences, which increases the number of locations that are considered "worth going" at any time of year. However, for locations to realize the advantages of an increase in the number of visitors, they need to incentivise tourists so that they would remain for more extended periods. For locales to increase the number of overnight stays they get and the money they generate, it is necessary to create local networks that supply concentrated offers (Mastika et al., 2023).

Local Connections and Synergies

For people to be able to empower human resources, advertise items, educate customers, and raise demand, more robust networks are required. A network must have both size and vitality to sustain itself. It can increase the representation factor of its members, qualify its offer, teach its members, provide services, innovate, and trade resources with other organizations (Mohammad et al., 2023). A concerted effort from the general population, the corporate community, and the governmental sector is required for the tourist industry to thrive. The advantages of participating in creative endeavours with other people have been recognized and researched for quite some time. It has been shown that having a variety of actors participate in collaborative processes is beneficial to both the process of invention and the growth of communities. More than focusing on a particular regional effort, this new working approach supports the development of global value chains (Utami et al., 2023). Modern collaborative platforms take the shape of dynamic informational environments in which interactional practices produce new forms of social organization and new methods. This facilitates an increase in both the level of creative output and the likelihood of survival for all members. For instance, the formation of synergy in the tourist business enables partners to thrive while working toward a shared objective: promoting an economically beneficial region to local communities. The more we work together, the more we can accomplish. After studying the relationships between Destination Management Organizations and local agents, the authors concluded that conventional methods might help them achieve their objectives. According to Dias et al. (2021), improving a destination's competitiveness and innovation requires strategic planning and reinvention of networks that include local stakeholders (Shrestha &L'Espoir Decosta, 2023). It is vital to bridge inequalities by creating sustainable networks for development. This is because various areas have differing capacities to begin the development process. Local communities need to be able to use the resources available to them to make their regions sustainable. To do this, local communities need to be able to adapt to new conditions, behaviors, ways of communication, and so on. In light of this, it is clear how important it is to strengthen the resilience of local communities. Participation at the micro-level is necessary because of this. Once small businesses have established themselves in their respective communities, fostering the growth of their competitive base requires forging a connection between tourism offerings, territory, and the area's natural, social, and historical context. It should also include the locals if you believe that individuals will be influential in spreading the word about the location.

Local agents are responsible for promoting local economies by using their territorial capital. This involves bringing together local enterprises and individuals in collaborative networks that can transmit the destination's image to prospective tourists. Only in this manner is it feasible to provide one-of-a-kind, once-in-a-lifetime experiences for customers. Creative Tourism Networks are place-based networks that trigger creativity, linking creativity to places, improving tourism offers and the experiences of tourists, and contributing to sustainable development goals. All of these things have resulted in the establishment of such collaborations (Cabeca et al., 2021). The emphasis on tourism products must be placed on local and international markets. The creative tourist products are rooted in the economics of the host communities.

Home-Based Travel

Many people have no desire to travel large distances after the outbreak. Post-pandemic travel trends show that individuals are avoiding towns designed to attract tourists, as determined. People favor driving because it allows them to avoid close social interaction. Tourists are avoiding public transportation and opting to visit locations within driving distance. This is partly because some restrictions still exist but also because people view trips to nearby areas as safer because people know people can get back home quickly in an emergency.

Tourists considering taking a trip are more likely to do so if people can bring a loved one along. Much research has been done on the mobility of creative tourism participants, and the results are encouraging (Della Lucia & Pashkevich, 2023). According to a poll conducted in Portugal, most people who participate in creative tourist experiences make their way to the locations where people occur, which tend to be small cities and rural areas. Most people went for the sole aim of taking part in the event. These findings suggest that, first, visitors choose their destination based on the activities people can develop there rather than because of its exact geographical location, and second, that the activities to be carried out at the destination are decisive when choosing the goal itself. Even if visitors are not staying in the same place as the action, people will make their way there if they happen to be close. Participants in Portugal's creative tourism experiences did not travel to the activity site because people were accompanied by someone else or persuaded to do so by the event's organizers (Cabeça et al., 2021). In this way, unique tourist activities draw people to specific locations. Creative tourism experiences are generally located in low-density territories, which attracts people who, in the present day, seek out outdoor activities and socially distant excursions in addition to those who seek out culturally driven experiences. The growing enthusiasm among local groups to learn about their past and participate in local identity-building processes is another possibility for developing tourism experiences deeply rooted in communities and their territorial capital (Paschinger, 2021). People are actively constructing local cultural identities with territorial origins, which may also boost the number of domestic visitors ready to engage in creative tourism experiences tied to their shared history. (Gastronomy, festivities, traditional know-how and nature). Knowing and interacting with the setting where an activity occurs might make it much easier to carry it out.

Opportunity for Sustainable Tourism

The prospects for creative tourist development discussed above, and the definition of creative tourism itself makes it abundantly evident that there is a strong connection between creative activities and sustainable development. Sustainable tourism has the same potential as creative tourism, including making use of the destination's unique qualities (by connecting them to their territorial capital), emphasizing the importance of local culture, involving residents in the tourism industry, boosting economic growth in the area, protecting the environment, and fostering community. The tourism industry must reduce its adverse effects on the environment and the quality of life for locals and visitors alike, become less dependent on the seasons, and use resources more efficiently to ensure that future generations are not at risk. Communities, service providers, and governments worldwide seek ways to mitigate the tourism industry's increasingly detrimental effects (Vogl & Micek, 2023). Travelers with a higher level of mindfulness are more sensitive to the needs of others and more likely to make sustainable choices. People nowadays are increasingly aware of the climate crisis, worried about minimizing their impact, and open to alternative ways to celebrate the holidays. Sustainable development goals are "development that meets the needs of the present without compromising the living needs of future generations," a worldview that considers this crucial to the process. Researchers and professionals in the tourism industry see the industry's revival as a chance to improve sustainability: "The historical and social moment may lend itself to repositioning and redeveloping places and structures of the territories of tourism, bringing them more in line with international criteria of sustainability, ethics, and aesthetics". Some of the suggestions involve making certain areas more appealing (to stop their desertification), limiting the number of visitors to other sites (to keep them habitable), spending money on environmentally friendly vacation options, integrating tourism into local economies and communities, favouring locally produced goods and services, and so on. Sustainable development goals processes are in harmony with creative tourism initiatives. Sustainable development goals must be guided by local needs and opportunities, such as people, natural resources, cultural norms, and geographical features (An & Alarcón, 2020). Citizens' wants and a destination's unique characteristics motivate creative tourism.

OPPORTUNITIES FOR CREATIVE TOURISM IN BANGLADESH

Cultural Celebrations

Festivals are commonplace in Bangladesh, adding to the country's well-known reputation. Some festivals in Bangladesh have religious or cultural significance, some have historical or traditional roots, and others are commemorated nationally. Most Bangladeshi celebrations have deep roots in the country's past (Remoaldo et al., 2022).

The Symbolism of National Events and History

In 1971, Bangladesh gained its independence from Pakistan. Bangladesh's national holidays are March 26 (Independence Day) and December 16 (Victory Day). The Bangladeshi flag's primary colours, red and green, represent the country's vibrant culture and the sun's warmth, respectively. Bengali Bangla is widely spoken among the population of Bangladesh. Rabindranath Tagore, a globally renowned poet, is credited with penning the national song.

Ekushey February

Bangladesh celebrates Ekushey February, also known as Shaheed Dibas (Martyrs' Day), on February 21. Only one country in the world went to war to protect its indigenous tongue (Bangla). In the year 2000, the United Nations Educational, Scientific, and Cultural Organization (UNESCO) declared February 21 to be "International Mother Language Day" in recognition of the efforts that the people of Bangladesh have made to maintain their mother language (International Mother Language Day 2021). February 21 is one of the most significant days in Bangladesh's history (Travel-News, 2020). On this day, Bangladeshis take the day off work to remember the people who gave their lives during the Bengali Language Movement of 1952 to defend the status of "Bangla" as the country's official language (Talukder, 2021).

Pohela Falun

The first day of the Bengali month Falgun, which corresponds to spring, is called Pahela Falgun. This occurrence takes place during the much-anticipated springtime. Pahela Falgun gives the festivals customary in the Bengali language community a revitalizing boost. As the garden begins to spring back to life, new leaves grow on the trees, and butterflies and bees may be seen flitting from blooming to bloom. People are happy to see the end of a relatively calm winter, so they celebrate the day with various festivities (Li & Kovacs, 2022).

Nabanna Utsav

The celebration of the new harvest, called "Nabanna Utsab," is observed during the Bengali month of Agrahayan, which falls between November and December. It is a big occasion when the Bengali month of Agrahayan begins since this day denotes the beginning of the harvesting season for the nation's farmers. People from all walks of life, including poets, painters, musicians, and 'Bauls (traditional singers), gather annually at this event (Talukder et al., 2024a). The Nabanna Mela (fair) is traditionally staged in rural areas. The farmers bring back a large quantity of golden paddies. In many rural areas, this is a time of grand celebration.

PoushParban

'Poush Sankranti,' also known as 'Makar Sankranti,' marks the end of the Bengali month of 'Poush' (Sankranti means 'end' in Bengali) and is celebrated annually in Bangladesh. On January 15, the Gregorian calendar's first Bengali holiday, Poush Sankranti, climaxes.

Traditional Customs

The people of Bangladesh have their distinct styles when it comes to clothing. The 'Panjabi' is the traditional dress of the men of Bangladesh, while the 'Saree' is the significant and traditional dress of the women. Most importantly, each cloth has a unique role in evoking Bangladeshi heritage and customs. Traditional peopleavers of Sonargaon, Dhaka, are known for making excellent 'Dhakai Jamdani' sarees, and UNESCO has designated the 'Jamdani' as an intangible cultural heritage. The 'Jamdani' fabric is designed using the 'Muslin' fabric. Bangladesh (Sonargaon, the birthplace of Jamdani - Jamdani Festival 2019) celebrates the fabric's historical, cultural, and even religious significance by holding an annual festival dedicated to it. Jamdani is the name given to the lineage of Muslin that managed to live. In recent years, Bangladesh has worked to protect its unique 'Muslin' textile as a legally protected Geographical Indication (GI).

Traditional Foods

The sceneries of Bangladesh, as well as the products of its land, rivers, and ocean, profoundly impact the country's cuisine. The quantity of water, especially during the monsoon, and the country's relatively low elevation give it a unique character. Dhaka's historic trade routes and many dominant cultures have significantly impacted the development of Bangladeshi cuisine. The Mughals introduced Turkish and Persian arts and cuisine to the region. The cuisine of Bangladesh is unmistakably South Asian, and its dishes generally reflect the country's culinary past and rich legacy (Talukder et al., 2023). As a result, the cuisine is distinctive in its reliance on an abundance of fish and a wide range of pastes created from crushed roots, spices, and chiles. Dinner plates in Bangladesh always include rice and two or three other foods like vegetables, fish, meat, lentils, dry fish (locally called 'Shutki'), etc. Pantha (formed from the rice after putting water on it for some time) and Ilish (the 'Hilsa' fish, called 'Ilish' in Bengali) are the most traditional foods of Bangladesh, and no PahelaBoishakh festival would be complete without them (Chan et al., 2022).

Traditional Athletics

The history and traditions of a country are the best indicators of its ethnic makeup. Sports and other forms of cultural entertainment have a significant role in Bangladeshi society. Bangladesh is home to a wide variety of indigenous games. Cultural sports in Bangladesh include "Ha-Dudu" (Kabaddi), "Dariabandha," "Kanamachhi," "Gollachut," "Kho Kho," "Lathi Khela," "Boli Khela," "Nouka Baich," and "Sharer Lorai."

METHODOLOGY OF THE STUDY

According to the study's methodology, an all-encompassing approach that includes several steps is carried out. In the beginning, a comprehensive literature analysis is carried out to acquire information about creative tourism for pilgrimages and how it aligns with sustainable development goals, with a particular emphasis on Bangladesh. Immediately after this, a research design is developed, which outlines the study's objectives and scope. In the following step, data collection occurs, pulled from various sources, including academic publications, government reports, and online archives. Following that, considers aspects such as the cultural significance, the economic impact, and the engagement of different communities. The information acquired is subjected to a thorough analysis using appropriate methodologies, which enables the identification of patterns and insights into the connection between pilgrimage creative tourism and sustainable development objectives. The findings are evaluated within the context of the existing literature and theoretical frameworks, and the process culminates in the formulation of conclusions and suggestions to inform policy, practice, and future research endeavours linked to sustainable tourism development in Bangladesh.

FINDINGS OF THE STUDY

The study's findings provide vital insights into the relationship between creative tourism and pilgrimage in Bangladesh and the aims of sustainable development in the country. As a result of an exhaustive study, it was discovered that pilgrimage sites play a significant role in promoting sustainable tourism practices, economic growth, preserving cultural heritage, and empowering local people (Talukder et al., 2024). According to the study's findings, several essential aspects contribute to the success of creative tourism efforts involving pilgrimages. These characteristics include effective community engagement, infrastructure development, and sustainable resource management. Furthermore, the findings highlighted the significance of stakeholder engagement and policy assistance in maximising the socio-economic benefits of pilgrimage tourism while simultaneously reducing its adverse effects on the environment. Additionally, the research highlighted the potential for creative pilgrimage tourism to help the attainment of a variety of sustainable development goals, including the reduction of poverty, the promotion of gender equality, and the preservation of the environment. The findings, taken as a whole, highlight the significance of incorporating innovative approaches into pilgrimage tourism initiatives to strengthen the contribution these strategies should make to the sustainable development of Bangladesh.

The study's findings revealed additional information that highlighted the transformative potential of creative tourism in the pilgrimage sector in Bangladesh. It was observed that incorporating artistic components into pilgrimage experiences not only increases the satisfaction experienced by visitors but also promotes the sharing of cultural ideas and discourse between people of different faiths. In addition, the research demonstrated that pilgrimage tourism favours local economies, including creating jobs, generating income, and stimulating small enterprises. In addition, the findings highlighted the significance of implementing sustainability principles into tourism planning and management methods to guarantee the long-term viability of pilgrimage sites. In addition, the study highlighted the importance of implementing capacity-building activities and awareness campaigns to encourage responsible tourism behaviour among tourists and visitors to the area. The findings, taken as a whole, offer valuable insights that may be utilized by policymakers, tourism stakeholders, and local communities to fully exploit the potential of creative tourism as a driver of sustainable development in Bangladesh.

Further, the study's findings shed light on the complex dynamics within creative tourism for pilgrimages in Bangladesh. It was discovered that although pilgrimage sites have a tremendous potential to act as catalysts for sustainable development, significant obstacles must be overcome (Talukder and Kumar, 2023). These obstacles include inadequate infrastructure, environmental deterioration, and socio-cultural issues. In addition, the research revealed that there are inequities in the distribution of benefits that are derived from pilgrimage tourism. The study found that certain groups and areas can reap higher profits than others. This demonstrates the significance of tourist development strategies that are both inclusive and equitable and that put the well-being of all stakeholders at the forefront of their priorities. In addition, the findings highlighted the significance of technology and innovation in improving the overall experience of tourists, encouraging the preservation of the natural environment, and simplifying the procedures involved in tourism management. It is possible that holistically addressing these findings will result in the formulation of targeted interventions and policies that are intended to maximize the positive impacts of pilgrimage creative tourism while mitigating its negative consequences, which will ultimately result in the development of a tourism sector in Bangladesh that is more sustainable and resilient.

RECOMMENDATIONS FOR DEVELOPING CULTURAL TOURISM IN BANGLADESH

Creative tourism can be fostered within the innovative economy policy framework, which requires creating an integrated policy strategy.

Since the creative industries are a driving force behind the expansion of the national economy and the tourist sector, the government may play an instrumental role in bolstering them for sustainable development goals. The government, for instance, finances the development of television programs and provides loans to boost the exports of content and tourist businesses. It has also set up an agency specifically for fostering creative talent and fostering the expansion of creative industries.

a) Creative tourism can be developed under the policy framework of the creative economy's sustainable development goals.
b) Bolstering funding for tourism companies, including public-private partnerships, carefully chosen IT and cross-sector collaboration. Get funding to help with rent and the creation of unique tourist offerings. People also offer instruction on breaking into the tourism industry and bringing original concepts to the market.
c) The government can conduct broad campaigns for specific demographics, consumer segments, and sustainable development goals.

CONCLUSION AND FUTURE PROSPECTS

It is time for the tourist industry to take a step back and assess its progress to better plan its future for sustainable development goals. While tourism has been a critical contributor to economic prosperity in many areas of the world, its fast expansion has brought new challenges and worries even as it has created new opportunities. The unsustainable influx of tourists has damaged local ecosystems and harmed residents' livelihoods in some tourist hotspots. Thus, many studies (some

Figure 1. Creative tourism and its sustainability
(Authors compilation)

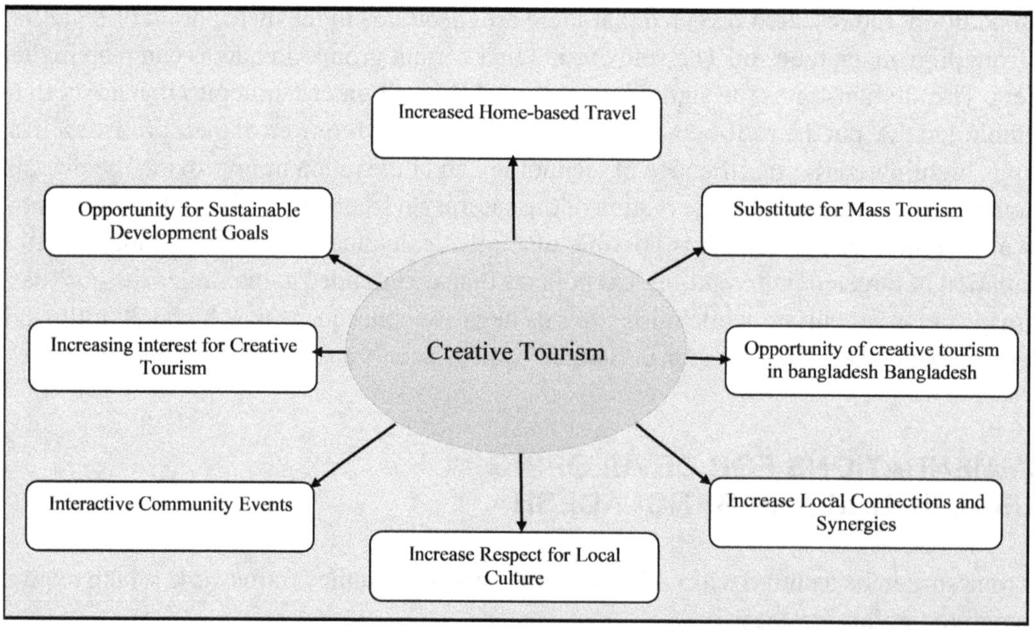

of which are described here) regard the tourism slump brought on by the pandemic as a chance to resume activity while rejecting its “old ways,” doing things in a novel way. This entails considering ways to ensure that small, local tourism businesses can continue to prosper and contribute to sustainable growth despite the repercussions of pre-pandemic tourism. It also necessitates thinking about how local communities might reap the rewards of resource conservation efforts (frequently, local value creation results in revenues not being redistributed to the area of origin) for sustainable development goals. The tourism industry is on the upswing because of fresh perspectives. Tourists are changing their habits, which presents new problems for the tourism business, such as creating more meaningful experiences and having a more positive influence. Sustainable development goals rely on a broad participation process that includes stakeholders and local actors. This new vision for tourism emphasizes a more environmentally and socially conscious approach to travel that is sensitive to the needs of locals and visitors alike, respectful of the land and its resources, community-driven, and open to new perspectives and experiences. One way to make tourism more sustainable is to encourage creative tourist practices that benefit local communities and visitors. Moreover, Creative Tourism, a niche tourism industry sector, can soothe visitors by limiting their isolation and lowering their exposure to danger in the context of sustainable development goals.

REFERENCES

Ababneh, M. M. A. (2017). Creative Tourism. *Journal of Tourism & Hospitality (Los Angeles, Calif.), 06*(02). doi:10.4172/2167-0269.1000282

Agapity, G., & Mugobi, T. (2023). Escapism Experience an Avenue for Tourism Development: Mapping the Test of Tanzania: Evidence from Arusha Region. *African Journal of Tourism and Hospitality Management, 2*(1), 1–18. doi:10.37284/ajthm.2.1.1204

AkdemirH.Sousa De São JoséJ. M.Rodrigues GonçalvesA. (2023). Empirical Research on Creative Tourism: A Systematic Review. Journal of Tourism & Development, 531-550 Páginas. doi:10.34624/RTD.V41I0.30537

An, W., & Alarcón, S. (2020). How Can Rural Tourism Be Sustainable? A Systematic Review. *Sustainability (Basel), 12*(18), 7758. doi:10.3390/su12187758

Arcos-Pumarola, J., Paquin, A. G., & Sitges, M. H. (2023). The use of intangible heritage and creative industries as a tourism asset in the UNESCO creative cities network. *Heliyon, 9*(1), e13106. doi:10.1016/j.heliyon.2023.e13106 PMID:36747939

Branstrator, J. R., Cavaliere, C. T., Day, J., & Bricker, K. S. (2023). Civic Reporting Indicators and Biocultural Conservation: Opportunities and Challenges for Sustainable Tourism. *Sustainability (Basel), 15*(3), 1823. doi:10.3390/su15031823

Cabeça, S. M., Gonçalves, A. R., Marques, J. F., & Tavares, M. (2021). Gastronomic creative tourism: Experiences in the Algarve region of Portugal. In N. Duxbury, S. Albino, & C. P. De Carvalho (Eds.), *Creative tourism: Activating cultural resources and engaging creative travellers* (1st ed., pp. 62–67). CABI. doi:10.1079/9781789243536.0009

Chan, C.-S., Chang, T. C., & Liu, Y. (2022). Investigating Creative Experiences and Environmental Perception of Creative Tourism: The Case of PMQ (Police Married Quarters) in Hong Kong. *Journal of China Tourism Research, 18*(2), 223–244. doi:10.1080/19388160.2020.1812459

Das, I. R., Talukder, M. B., & Kumar, S. (2024). Implication of Artificial Intelligence in Hospitality Marketing. *Utilizing Smart Technology and AI in Hybrid Tourism and Hospitality*. IGI Global, USA. doi:10.4018/979-8-3693-1978-9.ch014

Della Lucia, M., & Pashkevich, A. (2023). A sustainable afterlife for post-industrial sites: Balancing conservation, regeneration and heritage tourism. *European Planning Studies, 31*(3), 641–661. doi:10.1080/09654313.2022.2154141

Dias, Á., González-Rodríguez, M. R., & Patuleia, M. (2021). Developing poor communities through creative tourism. *Journal of Tourism and Cultural Change, 19*(4), 509–529. doi:10.1080/14766825.2020.1775623

Duxbury, N., Silva, S., & De Castro, T. V. (2019). Creative Tourism Development in Small Cities and Rural Areas in Portugal: Insights from Start-Up Activities. In D. A. Jelinčić & Y. Mansfeld, Creating and Managing Experiences in Cultural Tourism (pp. 291–304). WORLD SCIENTIFIC. doi:10.1142/9789813233683_0018

Galvagno, M., & Giaccone, S. C. (2019). Mapping Creative Tourism Research: Reviewing the Field and Outlining Future Directions. *Journal of Hospitality & Tourism Research (Washington, D.C.), 43*(8), 1256–1280. doi:10.1177/1096348019862030

Ihamäki, P. (2012). Geocachers: The creative tourism experience. *Journal of Hospitality and Tourism Technology, 3*(3), 152–175. doi:10.1108/17579881211264468

Kumar, S., Talukder, M. B., Kabir, F., & Kaiser, F. (2024). Challenges and Sustainability of Green Finance in the Tourism Industry: Evidence from Bangladesh. In S. Taneja, P. Kumar, S. Grima, E. Ozen, & K. Sood (Eds.), (pp. 97–111). Advances in Finance, Accounting, and Economics. IGI Global. doi:10.4018/979-8-3693-1388-6.ch006

Kumar, S., Talukder, M. B., & Kaiser, F. (2024). Artificial Intelligence in Business: Negative Social Impacts. In Demystifying the Dark Side of AI in Business (pp. 81-97). IGI Global. https://doi.org/doi:10.4018/979-8-3693-0724-3.ch005

Kumar, S., Talukder, M. B., & Pego, A. (Eds.). (2024). *Utilizing Smart Technology and AI in Hybrid Tourism and Hospitality*. IGI Global. doi:10.4018/979-8-3693-1978-9

Lebedova, R., & Sapundzhiev, M. (2023). *The teaching and research laboratory - an opportunity for intellectual and creative expression in the educational process*. EduLearn. doi:10.21125/edulearn.2023.0383

Leoti, A., Dos Anjos, F. A., & Costa, R. (2023). Creative Territory and Gastronomy: Cultural, Economic, and Political Dimensions of Tourism in Historic Brazilian Cities. *Sustainability (Basel), 15*(7), 5844. doi:10.3390/su15075844

Li, P. Q., & Kovacs, J. F. (2022). Creative tourism and creative spaces in China. *Leisure Studies, 41*(2), 180–197. doi:10.1080/02614367.2021.1948596

Mastika, I. K., Harsono, S. S., Khristianto, W., Oktawirani, P., & Hutama, P. S. (2023). Creative strategies of local resources in managing geotourism in the Ijen Geopark Bondowoso, East Java, Indonesia. *International Journal of Geoheritage and Parks*, *11*(1), 149–168. doi:10.1016/j.ijgeop.2023.01.002

Paschinger, E. (2021). Creative travellers in Austria. In N. Duxbury, S. Albino, & C. P. De Carvalho (Eds.), *Creative tourism: Activating cultural resources and engaging creative travellers* (1st ed., pp. 26–29). CABI., doi:10.1079/9781789243536.0003

Remoaldo, P., Matos, O., Freitas, I., Gôja, R., Araújo Alves, J., Ribeiro, V., Pereira, M., & Xavier, C. (2022). An International Overview of Certified Practices in Creative Tourism in Rural and Urban Territories. *Journal of Hospitality & Tourism Research (Washington, D.C.)*, *46*(8), 1545–1573. doi:10.1177/1096348020950792

Santos, C., Castanho, R. A., & Couto, G. (2022). Understanding Creative Tourism as a Potential Catalyst for Regional Economic Development in Ultra-Peripheral Territories: Highlighting Pilot-Projects in the Azores Islands. *WSEAS TRANSACTIONS ON BUSINESS AND ECONOMICS*, *20*, 295–306. doi:10.37394/23207.2023.20.28

Sarantou, M., Kugapi, O., & Huhmarniemi, M. (2021). Context mapping for creative tourism. *Annals of Tourism Research*, *86*, 103064. doi:10.1016/j.annals.2020.103064

Shrestha, R. K., & L'Espoir Decosta, P. (2023). Developing dynamic capabilities for community collaboration and tourism product innovation in response to crisis: Nepal and COVID-19. *Journal of Sustainable Tourism*, *31*(1), 168–186. doi:10.1080/09669582.2021.2023164

Talukder, M., Kumar, S., Misra, L., & Kabir, F. (2024). Determining the role of eco-tourism service quality, tourist satisfaction,and destination loyalty: A case study of Kuakata Beach. *Acta Scientiarum Polonorum. Administratio Locorum*, *23*(1), 133–151. doi:10.31648/aspal.9275

Talukder, M., Shakhawat Hossain, M., & Kumar, S. (2022). Blue Ocean Strategies in Hotel Industry in Bangladesh: A Review of Present Literatures' Gap and Suggestions for Further Study. SSRN Electronic Journal. doi:10.2139/ssrn.4160709

Talukder, M. B. (2020). An Appraisal of the Economic Outlook for the Tourism Industry, Specially Cox's Bazar in Bangladesh. *i-manager's Journal on Economics & Commerce*, *2*(1), 23-35. doi:10.26634/jecom.2.1.17285

Talukder, M. B. (2020b). The Future of Culinary Tourism: An Emerging Dimension for the Tourism Industry of Bangladesh. I-Manager's. *Journal of Management*, *15*(1), 27. doi:10.26634/jmgt.15.1.17181

Talukder, M. B. (2021). An assessment of the roles of the social network in the development of the Tourism Industry in Bangladesh. *International Journal of Business, Law, and Education*, *2*(3), 85–93. doi:10.56442/ijble.v2i3.21

Talukder, M. B. (2024). Implementing Artificial Intelligence and Virtual Experiences in Hospitality. In *Innovative Technologies for Increasing Service Productivity* (pp. 145–160). IGI Global., doi:10.4018/979-8-3693-2019-8.ch009

Talukder, M. B., & Hossain, M. M. (2021). Prospects of Future Tourism in Bangladesh: An Evaluative Study. I-Manager's. *Journal of Management, 15*(4), 1–8. doi:10.26634/jmgt.15.4.17495

Talukder, M. B., Kabir, F., Kaiser, F., & Lina, F. Y. (2024). Digital Detox Movement in the Tourism Industry: Traveler Perspective. In Business Drivers in Promoting Digital Detoxification (pp. 91-110). IGI Global. doi:10.4018/979-8-3693-1107-3.ch007

Talukder, M. B., & Kumar, S. (2023). *The Effect of Food Service Quality on Customer Satisfaction in the Hotel Industry: A Conceptual Paper*. ResearchGate. https://www.researchgate.net/publication/371503829_The_Effect_of_Food_Service_Quality_on_Customer_Satisfaction_in_the_Hotel_Industry_A_Conceptual_Paper

Talukder, M. B., & Kumar, S. (2023). *Revisit Intention in Hotel Industry of Bangladesh: A Critical Review of Present Literatures' Limitations and Suggestions for Further Study*. ResearchGate. https://www.researchgate.net/publication/371503587_Revisit_Intention_in_Hotel_Industry_of_Bangladesh_A_Critical_Review_of_Present_Literatures'_Limitations_and_Suggestions_for_Further_Study

Talukder, M. B., Kumar, S., & Das, I. R. (2024). *Food Wastage on the Economic Outcome: Evidence From the Hotel Industry. Sustainable Disposal Methods of Food Wastes in Hospitality Operations*. IGI Global. doi:10.4018/979-8-3693-2181-2.ch005

Talukder, M. B., Kumar, S., & Das, I. R. (2024). Mindfulness of Digital Detoxification: Healthy Lifestyle in Tourism. In *Contemporary Management and Global Leadership for Sustainability* (pp. 56–71). IGI Global. doi:10.4018/979-8-3693-1273-5.ch004

Talukder, M. B., Kumar, S., Sood, K., & Grima, S. (2023). Information Technology, Food Service Quality and Restaurant Revisit Intention. *International Journal of Sustainable Development and Planning, 18*(1), 295–303. doi:10.18280/ijsdp.180131

Tomaz, E., Costa, P., Gato, M. A., Cruz, A. R., & Perestrelo, M. (2020). *Discussing impact assessment on creative tourism: A theoretical and analytical model.* DINÂMIA'CET-ISCTE. doi:10.15847/dinamiacet-iul.wp.2020.05

Utami, D. D., Dhewanto, W., & Lestari, Y. D. (2023). Rural tourism entrepreneurship success factors for sustainable tourism village: Evidence from Indonesia. *Cogent Business & Management, 10*(1), 2180845. doi:10.1080/23311975.2023.2180845

Vogl, T., & Micek, G. (2023). Work-leisure concepts and tourism: Studying the relationship betpeopleen hybrid coworking spaces and the accommodation industry in peripheral areas of Germany. *World Leisure Journal, 65*(2), 276–298. doi:10.1080/16078055.2023.2208081

Zhou, L., Cheng, X., Wall, G., & Zhang, D. (2023). Entrepreneurial networks in creative tourism placemaking: Dali village, Wuhan, China. *Tourism Geographies, 25*(1), 220–242. doi:10.1080/14616688.2020.1866056

Chapter 17
Regulation of Transnational Corporations (TNCs) in International Law:
Exploring the Concept of Home and Host State

Krishangee Bhattacharyya
Symbiosis Law School, Symbiosis International University, India

Shaeyuq Ahmad Shah
Symbiosis Law School, Symbiosis International University, India

Abhilash Arun Sapre
https://orcid.org/0000-0002-7680-0894
Gujarat National Law University, Gandhinagar, India

Shalini Singh
Gujarat Maritime University, Gandhinagar, India

ABSTRACT

The regulation of companies (MNCs) in international law has become a significant concern in global governance. This study investigates the relationship between the countries where these companies are based and the countries where they operate in terms of regulating their activities. The exploration underscores the importance of balancing promoting economic growth through MNC activities and ensuring responsible corporate behaviour globally. By examining principles and mechanisms within international law such as state sovereignty, corporate responsibility, and jurisdiction beyond national borders, this research aims to shed light on the challenges and opportunities involved in balancing the interests of MNCs and the communities they affect. Through an approach that includes legal analysis case studies and theoretical frameworks this study contributes to the ongoing discussion on effective governance strategies, for MNCs within the context of globalization and economic interdependence.

DOI: 10.4018/979-8-3693-1742-6.ch017

INTRODUCTION

As globalisation progressed, economic development became increasingly important. The TNC's were the initial group to demonstrate to the world their status as major participants on a global scale and their importance to the development of humanity. Under the guise of promoting economic progress, it has widened disparities across countries—the affluent became wealthier while the poor kept becoming poorer—increased instances of prejudice against women, and posed a serious danger to human rights. The resource exploitation businesses helped the oppressive law enforcement agencies that were employed in Burma, Nigeria, and Colombia by providing monetary and operational support.

The governance of TNC has historically been challenging due to limitations on authority by the sovereign imposed by international legislation. The international legal system is primarily focused on how governments interact with one another. The degree to which international legislation explicitly puts duties on TNC's remains debatable. It is never sure if international legislation, as it is now designed, is adequately prepared to handle the issues given by global economic operations due to the state-centric nature of how it is applied. Additionally, since TNC's cross international borders, no sovereign has duties or rights regarding them. As a result, TNC's frequently evade the restrictions of international law. If a state doesn't take proper care in policing corporate activity within its borders, it may be held accountable for the actions of companies.

The idea of state accountability for human rights infringes by private entities like TNCs must thus be examined because nations bear the principal obligation for ensuring the safeguarding and advancement of human rights. TNCs are often not bound to international law statutes and regulations for liability, and if these companies are also covered by the principles of international legislation is an issue of contention among international legal experts in the field. A cornerstone of international legislation is the concept of state accountability, which establishes the responsibilities that states have to one another. The issue at hand is whether TNCs can be tacitly controlled by the law according to the notion of state accountability. For the international crimes and abuses carried out by TNCS, the idea of state responsibility is significant. According to the concept of state accountability, a state is responsible to the entire world for whatever global responsibilities it breaches.

Thus, the author will explore on how nations are required by global law to control corporate activity in order to uphold their commitment to defend human rights. Particularly, it demands that nations have a duty to monitor and oversee business overseas activity, as well as a duty to respond appropriately to violations of international legal standards. This kind of accountability frequently focuses on the host nation where company operations are conducted. However, it is regrettable that the current approach, which holds that the host nations are in charge of TNC governance, creates a number of difficulties. Thus, international legislation is increasingly heading closer to a need that the home nation to exert authority over company activity overseas.

Subjects of International Law

When regarding the legal ramifications of a TNC's human rights infringements, it is crucial to take into account its legal standing within international law. The global realm defines an actor's lawful standing by its status as an issue of international law. The concept of 'subject of international law 'refers to an-

'Entity which has the capability of owning international rights and obligation and has the ability to safeguard its rights by bringing international claims'.

The term legal person means an entity that is accepted by customary rule to be able to enjoying rights and obligations, as well as pursuing international claims and obtaining those rights.

States as Subjects

The State has all the rights and privileges that qualify a body as an element of international law. It has the power to ratify foreign conventions and accords, bring claims for violations of international law, and benefit from advantages and immunity from national legal systems. This is true even though occasionally specific entities might possess these abilities and immunities. States are the main centres of formally recognised power over individuals and regions. The fundamental priority of the State as an element of international connections and the law may solely be established in the context of States authority, privileges, jurisdictional restrictions, and legislation capacities. These factors also affect the boundaries of territories and jurisdictions, accountability for legally binding acts, as well as a variety of additional issues of interaction among countries.

Individuals as a Subject of International Law

As stated by Professor Brownlie, there's no universal principle stating that a person cannot be considered an element of international law, and under certain circumstances, the human can be seen as a legal person operating on an international level. However, if they are categorised as elements, it could suggest that they have abilities that others do not. Individuals cannot sign treaties or gain the same rights and exemptions as states. Despite this, people are granted to file allegations for violations of international human rights legislation, through the regulatory mechanisms created therewith. The court has authority over natural people who perpetrate crimes under its purview and who are directly accountable and punished. In light of the aforementioned changes, it is acceptable to say that people are now considered 'subjects' rather than 'objects' of international law.

Corporations as a Subject of International Law

1. Legal Personality of Corporations under Municipal Law

The issue regarding if companies have distinct legal personalities continues to be up for debate. Several legal minds believe that companies are 'persons' with unique legal personalities. The House of Lords have established the idea of a company as an 'independent legal entity'. The 'real' and 'fictitious' personalities of companies are analysed by John Dewey in his work. He asserts that 'person' means whatever the law allows it to mean, which means that 'societal circumstances, political goals, and several other extra-legal considerations have unavoidably slipped into a conceptual investigation of the essence of corporate personality'. When applied to local laws, these counterclaims are more persuasive.

2. Legal Personality of Corporations under International law

States where companies are established, the corporations under municipal legislation operate in several additional states. These types of companies are capable of and frequently enter into arrangements with other governments, especially concession deals. Since 'legal persons' were expressly excluded from the Act, it solely recognised the legal duties of people under international criminal law. On the other hand, Article 23 sub-clauses 5 and6 of the particularly addressed the criminal liability of legal entities. Additionally, while Article 99, which dealt with the execution of penalties and confiscation regulations equally, was binding on legal persons, Article 76 specified fines that were enforceable against legal persons. Due to strong opposition from nations like the US, the duty for legal entities was deleted within the Final legislation. Therefore, it does not indicate that TNCs should not be held accountable pursuant to international legislation.

It is argued that TNCs might end up being governed by international legislation. TNCs should be thought of as subjects of international legislation for certain reasons. Firstly, by expanding the rights of people to become subjects, TNCs are virtually nothing more than a collection of people working together to establish a company with a collective legal identity. In addition to corporate personality can also be applied to international legislation. Lastly, a comparison among the functions of states and TNCs might be made, for instance, if the TNCs operate on the instruction of the state. Connections among nations are no more the main focus of the global landscape. Transnational corporations are only one example of non-state entities whose behaviours have a significant influence on countless individuals every day. TNCs now occupy a significant part of the economy by working on infrastructures as well as essential assignments, which were formerly thought to be largely the province of the government.

Doctrine of State Responsibility

Traditionally, the doctrine of state responsibility has been used in international law to protect the rights of aliens (Danwood M Chirwa, 2004). It defines states' accountability for crimes committed on a global scale and offers a structure for assessing the repercussions of these offenses. Whenever a state violates an international law, that State is responsible.Conventions and other international treaties, in addition to traditional international legislation, are the main foundation of the concept of state responsibility.This concept states that a state has a legal obligation and can potentially be made liable for its conduct whenever it engages in a globally unlawful activity. The infringement of an international agreement, an infraction of conventional international regulations, or the conduct of an internationally recognized offense are just a few examples of what constitutes a globally unlawful activity.

A broad concept of international justice has recently been raised to the stature of state accountability (Danwood M Chirwa, 2004). According to the Permanent Court of International Justice, it is a more comprehensive theory concerning the law that entails responsibility for establishing remedies for any violation of an agreement (Germany v. Poland (Chorzow Factory Case), 1928). State responsibility may result in diplomatic or political repercussions, including demonstrations, penalties, or severing diplomatic ties. It could also include legal relief, including the payment of compensation or reparation, an end to the wrongdoing, or assurances that it won't happen again. State autonomy and equal treatment by the State are the foundations of state accountability. State responsibility is established by the ILC Draft on State Responsibility when two requirements are met (Danwood M Chirwa, 2004). Then there has to be an international agreement which the behaviour of the involved State has broken. One can conclude that the degree to which the State is accountable for wrongdoing depends on that relationship. One can conclude that the degree to which the State is responsible for wrong doing depends on that relationship. The actions of private actors must meet the criteria for an "act of a state" for governments to be held accountable for a personal act.

The Responsibility of States for Human Rights Violations Committed by TNCs: Analysing the Doctrine of State Responsibility

Before addressing the query of whether TNCs' had any accountability for human rights violations, it is significant to initially glance at the responsibility of States for human rights violations, as the State has the primary duty to safeguard human rights according to international conventions. According to the framework of international law, States are obligated to two types of responsibilities:

1. Direct Responsibility
2. Indirect Responsibility

Every time the State violates human rights, it bears direct responsibility. Every State has an unquestionable responsibility for upholding human rights, as the human rights treaties clearly show. The responsibility to prevent infringements by their organizations or residents against others and their fellow people arises clearly from this requirement. The tenets of state responsibility—either the primary principles or the secondary principles—are the foundation for this. The primary principles are the states' fundamental commitments. Secondary principles define precisely what it implies for a state to be held legally liable for violating these legal responsibilities. Therefore, a State has a global duty to restrict human rights offences perpetrated by its TNCs towards its people, foreign residents in the country, and the people of other nations. These are the 'indirect' duties that the States have. Even though these indirect responsibilities are entirely within the bounds of international law, there haven't been many assertions that corporations also have direct responsibilities. According to the conventional approach, international law is divided into two categories: the sole direct responsibilities placed on its citizens by the law. Using the State, the subjects of the legal framework are indirectly responsible (James Crawford, 2001). Therefore, TNCs operate in the private realm and are not often governed by international laws; as a result, they are not bound to any explicit legal duties at the moment. The issue is whether or not international human rights legislation applies to the Draft Articles on State Responsibility. The concept of lex specialis covers this situation. The doctrine of state responsibility holds that nations have a universal duty to safeguard individuals who break international laws and to take appropriate action. Therefore, a universal requirement may be stipulated by international human rights legislation and is regularly mentioned in the practice of such entities.

States' Duty to Combat Atrocities Committed by TNCs'

International human rights law establishes three degrees of responsibility to the State (Jordan J. Paust, 2021). They have a responsibility to safeguard, defend, and uphold human rights. The state parties must take action to ensure that the people can exercise their human rights despite being violated. The obligation of the state parties comprises the need to take proactive measures to ensure that additional states or individuals have committed no offenses. A thorough investigation of the different human rights treaties and regulations must be conducted to determine the origin and extent of the State's responsibility regarding violations perpetrated by private parties. State signatories must protect and maintain all rights recognized in the Covenant for people living on their soil. The commitment to assure indicates that nations are responsible for defending citizens' human rights by taking appropriate action (UN Human Rights Committee, 1982). States have the ultimate responsibility to avert conflicts, actions of genocide, as well as additional instances of widespread bloodshed that result in the senseless sacrifice of life. The ICESCR Committee makes it clear that member states are required, according to the Convention, to guarantee the prevention of rights infringements by private organizations (ICESCR,2002). The Maastricht Guidelines follow the same pattern in that they specify duties for nations in situations where private enterprises violate international law. According to this argument, states would be held accountable if they failed to regulate private parties carefully (The Maastricht Guidelines, 1997). Countries must ensure every individual under their authority knows the rights they recognize (The European Convention on Human Rights, 1960). It is the State's responsibility to uphold the various rights it recognizes and ensure that each individual has the right to exercise these freedoms and rights within its boundaries (The American Convention on Human Rights, 1969). Lastly, it might be stated that it is settled in the international community that states are responsible for defending individuals or entities against human rights infringements by corporations or other entities that do not state. Even though a state is not liable for every personal act, it may be held accountable for failing to control its behaviour.

National Regulation Through Host State

States are generally recognized as having duties under international law (Sarah Joseph, 1999). Hence, prior international bodies and courts, TNCs, and other similar entities cannot be held accountable for breaking international rules and regulations. However, private organizations can't use this flexibility. States are, therefore, responsible for failing to implement the necessary precautions to prevent infringement by private actors and TNCs. According to international conventions, the host state is responsible for ensuring that TNCs don't infringe on human rights. Only if a state is a signatory to the international agreements, if there is conventional international law in force, or where *jus cogens* apply to the situation can states become responsible for infringements of norms (Mark Gibney et.al, 1999). Usually, actors with connections to and activity in many states are referred to as being in the host state. It is the State where the alleged infractions occur, and the actor is located in a different state known as its home state (Danwood M Chirwa, 2004). The host state's judiciary may be incapable of holding TNCs accountable for breaking local laws. The host state might not have enough assets to investigate the violations adequately.

Additionally, those affected may lack the resources to file and pursue accusations of corporate wrongdoing. Ironically, the TNCs could be in a more robust situation to protect themselves in court against legal claims. If the State plays a role in the infringement or is engaged in it with TNCs, the circumstances will be worsened. As a result, proceedings against TNCs might not be possible in such states' court systems. The principle of host state accountability depends on having a solid national legal framework to ensure those violating human rights are held responsible. Regulating TNCs is exceedingly tricky for underdeveloped states due to corporations' financial clout. TNCs may readily obstruct legislation and shoulder responsibility with these abilities (Mark Gibney et al., 1999). If diverse legal frameworks are offered in various country states, it would be advantageous for TNCs to migrate to a nation with an inadequate legislative framework. It is hard for a state to implement strict controls and regulations on TNCs due to the absence of universal worldwide regulation norms. As a result, host state accountability would have less impact. Even when an enforcement structure is in effect, states could hesitate to enforce the provisions against TNCs properly. There are additional circumstances in which various TNCs get together to conduct commercial operations. Since each of these businesses has its own legal identity, it would be challenging for those affected to hold the TNC's parent corporation accountable. This would give the parent firm the power to escape responsibility for the actions of its affiliates that were carried out with its consent. Even if those affected succeed in getting a court ruling in these situations, the subsidiary business may not have sufficient funds to pay them adequate damages. There are several restrictions on the host states. As a result, host countries frequently do little to stop TNCs from abusing human rights within their borders. Although it is possible in principle for TNCs to be regulated within the national jurisdiction of host governments, this cannot be depended upon; hence, additional methods of implementing human rights legislation against TNCs must be sought after.

National Regulation Through Home State

The majority of TNCs' parent corporations are situated in developed countries (Robert J. Fowler, 1995). TNCs might be effectively governed by the states' laws where they are based. The justification for home state regulation is based on the notion that developed nations are responsible for regulating TNCs and are equipped to do so. Principles of state responsibility under international law give home states the authority to exert extraterritorial jurisdiction over TNCs and other commercial entities formed there for conduct done in the host state's territory that violates human rights (Elisa Morgera, 2009).

To ensure that TNCs and other entities preserve and refrain from infringing on the human rights of individuals in developing nations where legal frameworks and channels for getting redress are weak, the mechanism of home state responsibility can be very useful. The Nicaragua Case supports this assertion (Republic of Nicargua V. United States of America,1986). A rebel group in Nicaragua perpetrated the infractions, but the lawsuit focused on the US's role in the transgressions. It is also noteworthy to consider that several domestic legal systems now acknowledge the importance of home states in ensuring corporation nationals uphold human rights overseas (The Alien Tort Claims Act, 1789). However, the importance of the home state's accountability theory cannot be overstated at this time. The successful supervision of company nationals overseas presents difficulties for the home-state supervision of TNCs. The corporate veil doctrine adds a significant barrier to successful home-state control.

Challenges in Home State Control

TNCs are conceived of as one distinct entity but are a collection of interrelated companies with a shared corporate identity. The numerous corporations hidden beneath a TNC are constitutionally separate corporations with unique legal existence. They are distinct corporate entities autonomous from their parent firm and different legal individuals. These companies may occasionally be incorporated in the nation where the underlying TNC is based. TNCs adopt the legal status of the host country, and all subsidiaries are brought under the control of the host state (Barcelona Traction case, 1970). Therefore, the host state's national sovereignty would be interfered with when the home state exercises jurisdiction beyond its borders.

It should be remembered that widely accepted human rights standards constrain the notions of the state authority and local authority, which is a crucial issue to recognize in this situation (Elisa Morgera, 2009). These standards are regarded as jus cogens because they have evolved into customary international law. All governments are required under international law to uphold human rights. No home state would be mindful of exercising close control over their corporate nationals, thereby creating disadvantages for the TNCs incorporated within their territory. Therefore, there is no longer a local jurisdiction's examination of human rights abuses. Home states have the authority to impose human rights standards on TNCs, and doing so would not contradict the host state's sovereignty. Home governments are not required by international law to exercise extraterritorial jurisdiction over TNCs, which presents another challenge for home state governance. It is essential to highlight that governance of TNCs by home states might be considered substantially more stringent if the International Court of Justice had not rejected the notion of control and the idea of successfully penetrating the barrier in the Barcelona Traction Case. Therefore, home states cannot bring charges against its TNC for actions that involve human rights breaches. No home state would consciously exercise strict oversight over its corporate individuals and disfavor its TNCs established on its soil. Hence, it may be concluded that the home state can only effectively regulate TNCs in specific situations when the host state's autonomy is not violated. The notion of *forum non conveniens* presents an additional barrier to the successful home-state governance of TNCs. According to this approach, courts may refuse to address matters because the proper tribunals in the host states may hear the dispute.

Challenges in Making TNCs Responsible under International Law

TNCs might be more likely to abuse human rights as a result of their more significant clout on the global scale.10 It was effectively noted that because of their worldwide presence, TNCs frequently conduct business in countries where infringements of human rights take place, gain and profit from subsidized agreements with authorities that contravene human rights, offer services and products that cause human rights violationsor organize manufacturing in methods that infringe employees human rights. While these possible hazards exist, there is presently no efficient international system for prosecuting TNCs responsible under the framework of international law (Elisa Morgera, 2009).The discussion for an agreement on corporations with human rights is currently taking shape amid a favorable backdrop as the topic regarding company accountability for human rights breaches generates a variety of significant difficulties or challenges. Some considerable challenges include company human rights breaches, poor state administration, complicated business structures, and problems with victims' rights to remedy.

- **Corporations as Duty Bearers**

The issue concerning company human rights duties was first mentioned. TNCs frequently abuse human rights when they act, particularly in areas with poor administration. All of a person's innate rights are acknowledged as human rights by international human rights conventions. Even thoughthe appropriate international agreements protect such rights, the duties arising from them have only been addressed about the function of governments. Although corporation actions significantly influence the exercise of human rights, it is unclear under international legislation if corporations have any duties that directly stem from personal human rights. However, global trading and trade laws frequently defend businesses and their monetary goals before considering how these actions affect human rights.

- **Weak Administration in State**

Another factor favoring company responsibility is the issue of poor state administration, as current statutory remedies concentrate on the recognized state accountability to shield people from TNCs' infringements of their human rights. States may occasionally be complicit in crimes, especially in the case of developing nations; states frequently make frantic attempts to entice investors from abroad and are hesitant to take action against TNCs (James Crawford, 2001). Furthermore, the State's institutional framework is sometimes too frail and faulty to take any steps to defend rights or deliver remedies.

- **Complex Corporate Structure**

The third concern regarding the control of TNC operations is the question of company architecture. Every company is a distinct legal person. The complicated corporate group frameworks and establishing several branches increase complexity. Therefore, it would be challenging to retain the parent firms with headquarters in developed nations, who are the real decision-makers. Several people have a role across boundaries due to the world's economic system's intricate supply chain structures, making it challenging to assign blame or identify the actual power brokers. Even though financial systems are interrelated, companies are nonetheless regarded as independent legal entities under the law.

- **Challenge for Victims' Right to Effective Remedy**

The issue of accessibility to remedies is defined as all the issues highlighted above that ultimately make it hard for those impacted by corporate human rights infringements to get adequate redress. Legal compensation for those targeted is not accessible until specified inside a particular jurisdiction since corporate legal duties are not explicitly recognized. The same limitations on having access to remedies apply to complicated business structures and inadequate governance. Further issues with victim accessibility to justice and the preservation of human rights are also noted. Individuals may look for redress abroad if insufficient administration of the State hinders a claim in a specific jurisdiction. However, forum non-conveniens and extraterritorial authority theories may make it extremely difficult for sufferers to pursue lawsuits against transnational corporate wrongdoing.A strategy for recognizing extraterritorial authority for the home states for representing TNCs to local tribunals of diverse national judicial systems was devised in the 1980s. TNCs have been the target of several prominent lawsuits alleging transnational human rights breaches.

- **Challenges in the Global Supply Chain**

The COVID 19 pandemic has brought to vulnerabilities in supply chains. Large multinational corporations have faced disruptions leading to a reassessment of their strategies for supply chains to improve resilience and reduce reliance on regions.

- **Increased Scrutiny of Tech Giants**

Major technology companies are facing growing scrutiny regarding concerns such as data privacy, antitrust issues and their impact on society. Governments and regulatory bodies worldwide are exploring measures to address these concerns and ensure behaviour by tech companies.

- **Focus on Ethical Business Practices**

There is an emphasis on sustainability and ethical conduct in business. Multinational corporations are increasingly expected to integrate social and governance (ESG) considerations into their operations. Investors are also placing importance on practices.

- **Acceleration of Digital Transformation**

The adoption of technologies has been accelerated by corporations playing a significant role in digital transformation. This includes intelligence, cloud computing and other innovations that reshape industries and economies globally.

- **Evolving Trade Policies**

Changes in global trade policies and geopolitical dynamics have impacted the strategies of corporations. Issues like trade tensions between economies and the emergence of trade agreements have implications for how these companies operate internationally.

- **How Corporations Respond to Climate Change**

Climate change has become a focus, for TNCs with many committing to sustainability goals. Companies are aligning their operations with the Paris Agreement. Taking actions to reduce carbon emissions reflecting a global effort to combat climate change.

CONCLUSION AND SUGGESTIONS

States are required under international law to defend citizens against human rights infringements. Nations should take caution when enacting legislation and other actions to regulate company behaviour and stop companies from violating human rights. The host and the home states are accountable for corporations' human rights violations. According to international legislation, host states have to take reasonable steps to supervise and regulate private entities to avoid human rights abuses. States must investigate and prosecute those responsible for violating human rights while offering appropriate redress to the aggrieved. Home states must ensure their citizens and others have authority over upholding human rights overseas. State accountability for corporate actions on the soil of a different state could occur, requiring a home state to enact laws regulating TNCs' international operations. According to the territoriality concept, host states are in charge of protecting human rights against TNC actions. The host states would also find it challenging to adequately control TNCs operating on their soil since, on the one hand, they want the TNCs' capital and, on the contrary, they are aware of their influence. The conversations indicate that the TNCs' home states can more successfully assist survivors of human rights neglect because they are more prepared to handle investigations and court proceedings. However, it is also evident that home jurisdiction in a state is restricted to a specific subset of situations because of barriers like the veil of corporate ownership, state autonomy, *forum non conveniens*, and the distinctive makeup of TNCs.

Therefore, it may be inferred that neither the host state nor its home nation could resolve the issue of jurisdiction during instances of human rights violations by TNCs outside of their geographical boundaries. It is better to let the native state exercise authority. However, corporate responsibility through municipal courts is still a hazard and an unknown. As a result, there is a perceived requirement for international company activity control. A global responsibility framework is preferred to ensure a uniform fulfilment of human rights. When it comes to regulating Transnational Corporations (TNCs) within the field of law, understanding the concepts of Home State and Host State reveals a complex network of relationships, challenges, and possible solutions. The relationship between Home States and Host States is crucial in regulating TNCs. It is essential to recognize that these entities have interests and responsibilities. Home States, which are where TNCs are incorporated initially or headquartered, must delicately balance be promoting their corporation's interests while ensuring corporate behaviour. On the other hand, Host States need to protect their national interests and sovereignty while creating an environment conducive to TNC operations. Throughout history, TNCs have faced criticism for taking advantage of loopholes and engaging in practices that can have adverse social, economic, and environmental consequences. The need for a regulatory framework becomes evident when considering how some actions by TNCs go beyond individual national jurisdictions. The push for corporate behaviour, as highlighted by international initiatives such as the United Nations Guiding Principles on Business and Human Rights (UNGPs), aims to establish a universal standard for multinational companies' operations. This standard emphasizes the responsibility to uphold rights and promote sustainable practices. Regulating companies poses challenges due to the diverse nature of industries, corporate structures, and economic contexts (Adam McBeth,2004). It is impractical to adopt a one-size-fits-all approach; instead, a customized framework that considers the characteristics of different sectors is needed. The paper explores various case studies to examine real-world implications and provides insights into the strengths and limitations of existing regulations. This analysis underscores the importance of flexibility and adaptability in crafting rules that can effectively address the unique challenges posed by multinational companies across industries. International organizations, the United Nations, and its specialized agencies are vital in fostering cooperation between nations and establishing guidelines for regulating multinational companies. Regional initiatives and agreements also contribute to developing a framework that recognizes the complexities associated with global operations within specific geographical areas. The community's collaborative efforts and principles, like UNGPs, demonstrate a shared commitment to tackling challenges related to multinational activities. Understandably, individual states want to protect their autonomy, and any regulatory framework should respect their right to create and enforce laws within their borders. Finding a balance between regulating TNCs while respecting national sovereignty is a delicate task that requires ongoing dialogue and cooperation between the states where these companies are based and where they operate. Through a joint effort to balance the interests of home countries, host countries, and multinational companies, we can create a fair and sustainable regulatory framework for transnational business in the 21st century.

REFERENCES

Barbara A Frey, *The Legal and Ethical Responsibilities of TNCs in the Protection of International Human Rights*, 6 Minnesota Journal of Global Trade (1997).

Carlos Manuel Vázquez, *Direct v. Indirect Obligations for Corporations under International Law*, 43 Colum. J. Transnat'l L. 927, 943 (2005), https://scholarship.law.georgetown.edu/cgi/viewcontent.cgi?article=1987&context=facpub&httpsredir=1&referer=

Carlos Manuel Vázquez, *Direct v. Indirect Obligations for Corporations under International Law*, 43 Colum. J. Transnat'l L. 927, 943 (2005), https://scholarship.law.georgetown.edu/cgi/viewcontent.cgi?article=1987&context=facpub&httpsredir=1&referer

Chirwa, D. M. *The Doctrine of State Responsibility as a Potential Tool Means of Holding Private Actors Accountable for Human Rights*, 5 MEL J. INT'L 1, 5(2004), https://law.unimelb.edu.au/__data/assets/pdf_file/0005/1680422/Chirwa.pdf

Chirwa, D. M. *The Doctrine of State Responsibility as a Potential Tool Means of Holding Private Actors Accountable for Human Rights*, 5 MEL J. INT'L 1, 5(2004),https://law.unimelb.edu.au/__data/assets/pdf_file/0005/1680422/Chirwa.pdf

Crawford, J. (2001). *Responsibility to the International Community as a Whole*, 8. *Indiana Journal of Global Legal Studies.*

Fowler, R. J. (1955). International Environmental Standards for Transnational Corporations. Environmental Law.

Germany v. Poland (Chorzow Factory Case), (1928) PCIJ (ser A) No.13.

Gibney, M., Tomasevski, K., & Hansen, J. V. (1999). Transnational State Responsibility for Violations of Human Rights. Harvard Human Rights Journal.

Gibney, M., Tomasevski, K., & Hansen, J. V. (1999). *Transnational State Responsibility for Violations of Human Rights*, 12. *Harvard Human Rights Journal.*

Joseph, S. (1999). Taming the Leviathans: Multinational Enterprises and Human Rights. Netherlands International Law Review.

McBeth, A. (2004). *Privatising Human Rights: What Happens to the State's Human Rights Duties When Services are Privatised?* 5. *Melbourne Journal of International Law.*

Morgera, E. (2009). *Corporate Accountability in International Environmental Law*. Oxford University Press. doi:10.1093/acprof:oso/9780199558018.001.0001

Paust, J. J. (2021). *Human Rights Responsibilities of Private Corporations,* 35 VAND. *J. Transnat'l, L,* 801. https://scholarship.law.vanderbilt.edu/vjtl/vol35/iss3/3

UN Human Rights Committee, General Comment 6, Report of the Human Rights Committee, UN Doc. A/37/40 (1982) Id., in General Comment 16, Report of the Human Rights Committee, UN Doc. A/43/40 (1988)

Vasques, C. M. (2005). *Direct Vs. Indirect Obligations of Corporations under International Law*, 43. *Columbia Journal of Transnational Law.*

Chapter 18
Santals, Sal, and Forest Policy of Bangladesh:
Reminiscence of Ethnographic Experience

Parimal Kumar Roy
https://orcid.org/0000-0002-0461-2587
Universiti Malaya, Malaysia

Haris Abd Wahab
https://orcid.org/0000-0001-9834-3797
Universiti Malaya, Malaysia

Mashitah Binti Hamidi
Universiti Malaya, Malaysia

Pias Kumar Das
EXIM Bank Limited, Bangladesh

ABSTRACT

This chapter reflects on the Ph.D. journey within the Santals of Bangladesh, followed by an ethnographic method at Birganj in Dinajpur, Bangladesh. The Government of Bangladesh formulated diverse forest policies, acts, and rules and either ratified or approved international treaties/documents to preserve, guide, and nurture the forests. However, when the author entered the remote Santals hamlet, they talked about their grief regarding the Sal Forest. Before starting the academic journey, the first author was born and developed in a village where the Indigenous research methodology was embedded informally in his mind as a consciousness part; moreover, as a student spent with Santals neighbours in the agri-field, school, colleges, and even the common playground in the countryside. As a result, it is decorated with field experiences and deals with the "capability approach" while the PhD candidate stayed in the research field for a long time and observed an intricate relationship between Santals and the international legal frameworks to ratify in Bangladesh.

DOI: 10.4018/979-8-3693-1742-6.ch018

INTRODUCTION

It is a popular discursive discourse amid Santals' *jol, jongal, and bhumi'* (water, forest, and land) are interconnected parts of life to understand their lifeworld. Against this backdrop, this study highlighted the Santals community living adjacent to northern Bangladesh's Sal (*shorea robusta*) Forest. The Sal Forest and the Santals relationship needs to be explored with an ethnographic journey because "Research on forest ownership has received growing attention in recent years "(Weiss, p. 99, 2019). This quotation is important also for another reason: there is no ethnographic study on the relationship between Santals and Sal in Bangladesh the authors had gathered the best information. Apart from these, as global socio-economic and political rhetoric and reality have changed, but we have social research techniques. The 21st century has seen a rise in the study of social research techniques because of its different experiences and trials based on the topic, environment, and area (Uddin, 2023).

For this reason, fieldwork differs throughout disciplines and regions. As a student of Anthropology, I followed the ethnographic method to study the customary law of the Santals with Sal Forest as a part of the unique narrative tone, and every tone has its unique social, political, historical, and environmental context. The journey of PhD research entails my interaction with the study subject and interpersonal connections with their lifeworld for a long time— here are embedded my thoughts, feelings, and actions for contextualization of the research community (Roy, 2024). Indeed, rebuilding models and modules of social research methods and techniques requires new since we are not limited to only four paradigms of Thomas Kuhn; rather, fresh fieldwork experiences of Social Research and its methodologies tended to alter and evolve like the Indigenous Research Paradigm— is another added paradigm to know the Indigenous' lifeworld (Linda, 2021; Chilisa, 2019; Nakata, 2004). As an upshot, this novel approach considered the researcher's political, social, cultural, emotional, and personal beliefs that have been established throughout the researcher's life settings. Hence, I have applied the personal knowledge and experiences straightforwardly as part of academic practice while staying in the research field that adheres to a virtuous professional and Research practice to use the instruments, strategies, concepts, and methodologies in a specific Sal Forest area (Sing, 2022; Uddin, 2023).

However, the precise number of ethnic groups in the 55 thousand 598 square Kilometre nation is contested in the official documentation like 25, 45, 27, 55, or higher? Santal is, without a doubt, one of them, regardless of the exact number. They are mostly found in Bangladesh's northern regions, particularly in Rajshahi and Dinajpur. Nonetheless, their little existence is also discernible in other areas. "This dispute has its genesis in the dispute over ownership and property of the state and the Adivasis, foregrounding the historic conflict between law and custom as the basis of right and empowerment" (Sing, 2022, p.3).

GLANCING BACK

Scholars and thinkers argue that the East India Company and the Permanent Settlement Act of 1793 are to blame for the Santal people's presence in today's Bangladesh (Mamun, eds, 2021; Doshi, 1990). This law led to a lack of agricultural labourers in Bengal and a concentration of land in the hands of zamindars. Thus, they were brought in as labourers for agriculture. They were then compelled to seek safety in the north by the Santals Rebellion and the Sepoy Mutiny. As a result, we may assume that the claims made by people living in the modern-day Indian regions of Rajshahi and Dinajpur are reliable. Therefore, it is believed that political motivations played a role in the Santals people's migration to this nation-state. As such, they were compelled to reside close to woodlands or forest regions. The forest or the region around it still serves as the Santals community's place of habitation. With this Forest, the vita-soil relationship of their ancestors, gods and goddesses, and devotion rituals. They consider their right of residency and forest clearance to be proof of ownership.

Nevertheless, why does the contemporary state accept it? The state is modern, but they got there slowly. As a result, the state and the Santal community are at odds over ownership concerns because they believe they are customary landowners, known as Adivasi.

Contrariwise, the state established and implemented several policies, laws, and rules to promote industry, remove animals from their natural habitats, designate places as eco-parks, or designate Forests as protected areas. The government of Bangladesh formulated laws and regulations that quickly caused the people who had authority, freedom of movement, ancestor-spiritual relationships, social cohesiveness, and cultural centers to vanish. Due to these factors, Santals' society is experiencing an existential crisis, which they frequently try to overcome by battling the government or the general populace. The primary goal of this chapter is to examine how the public life of the Santals community in the Sal (*shorea robusta*) Forest of the Dinajpur region is shaped by legal frameworks that prioritize situations.

SELF-POSITION IN THE FIELD

Academic and societal meanings are attached to personal experience (Uddin, 2023). Before beginning data collecting, I went to the Caritas office in the research field to explain the purpose of each interview and assured the respondents that they might examine the data obtained and leave the session at any moment. After explaining the study objectives to the participants, they put their signatures on the consent form. Every participant voluntarily signed the document. I obtained consent by outlining the methods of data collecting and demonstrated that they were completely aware of the Universiti Malaya's code of research ethics. When I travelled to the research area on the day after receiving an ethics approval letter from Universiti Malaya, the experience is described below.

"I roamed here and there instead of going directly to the Caritas office; by riding in local transport, called Van, for several hours. While riding in the Van as a passenger, the conversation between the Van puller and the researcher indeed was irrelevant. Nevertheless, this process worked great for understanding a specific society, culture, and its people; it was also worthwhile. Again, it is not entirely irrelevant, but the researcher tried to understand the overall situation by its interventions in the Research in its own way."

Eventually, after some aimless wandering, I made my way to the Caritas office, where the branch manager was prepared to assist in any way he could. I started on May 5, 2022, with a beautiful sky and pleasant afternoon temperatures. Following the branch manager's advice, we all set out to travel to the chosen village. As previously said, reporting that six employees were present in the office is excellent. Together, I determined that Kadampur (Pseudonym), a hamlet, would be a suitable study location. However, after a preliminary discussion and review of the available data, the researcher visited three villages, from which Kadampur was ultimately chosen. The Santal community predominates in Kadampur and other populations, including the Hindu, Muslim, and Christian faiths. In the Santal community of that hamlet, Caritas established several amenities (a collection of human-like relationships), and the researcher, the branch manager, and other employees made contact with one of these amenities. Because the investigation was overt, they eventually learned that the researcher was a PhD student after initially believing them to be a high-ranking Caritas official. The villagers strongly desired to work together on this project and shared mobile phone numbers so that those involved could stay in touch and develop a casual friendship. To demonstrate that the researcher is a sympathetic member of the community, the researcher eventually organized an unofficial get-together next to a market. Despite the researcher's strange smoking habit, they shared tea and brought local Handi—a wine produced by the Santals—as well. When he learned that the researcher resided in a little guest house, one of the van pullers extended an invitation for the researcher to stay at his home. During the visit, I gathered data by entering the community one at a time. The facts were instantly written on Chirkut (a little piece of paper).

After sitting at a table at the end of the day, the Chirkut system—a tiny piece of paper—worked efficiently to help people recollect the whole day's events. Subsequently, every detail is documented in the field journal. In order to ensure appropriate reflection in the thesis, the researcher composed any material that they had thought was important in the field in detail late at night in their room. This study was usually difficult as field research is, but it was made feasible by Caritas's genuineness, the local authorities, and the research community. For instance, the researcher first found it difficult to deal with the lack of housing, dietary customs, disparate cultures, and social mores, but everything eventually worked out with the kind assistance of all parties involved. The load-shedding and eating habits made life miserable at night when the researcher was out and about throughout the Santal hamlet, thinking about the various problems that were there. In this way, the process of gathering data is finished, and the associated documents are collected and securely kept under the researcher's supervision.

FOREST POLICY IN BANGLADESH: SALIENT FEATURE

The following table (Table 1) contains almost two hundred years of major acts, policies, and rules from the colonial period to today's Bangladesh. The table is highly significant for understanding Forest policy and its impact on ethnic people's lives. In a nutshell, our forest management policy originated from the British period, and it bears the colonial legacy. But today's ethnic people are not satisfied by the policy when they feel catastrophic consequences, particularly with Forest.

SAL FOREST AND INTERNATIONAL DOCUMENTS WITHIN SANTALS

UNDRIP is an effective strategy for conveying minorities into mainstreaming. However, 144 out of 195 countries ratified the agreement, and Bangladesh is one of the eleven non-signed countries, neither opposed nor agreed. The salient features prioritized in UNDRIP have been discussed in detail in the discussion section on how these features are associated with the unregulated rights of the Santal community. As a point of referral and severing them to assuming human rights, UNDRIP believes that achieving or ensuring these significant features would provide the desired self-determination of the Santal community or SEGs.This thesis has considered the following Figure 1 to contemplate the relationships between UNDRIP and the Santal community of Bangladesh to foster human rights situations.

Figure 1 demonstrates the paramount components of UNDRIP 2007. The agreement stipulates that the Santals community can be given self-determination if these are achieved with the help of triparty relationships. This means that to ensure self-determination, it is now essential to verify the mentioned

Table 1. Different policies, acts, rules (1927 to 2017)

Act / Policy / Rules	Year	Salient Features
The Forest Act	1927	i. Declaration of Protected Area and Forest. ii. Village and Social Forest iii. Governance & Management of Forest Department.
Asam Forest Regulation	1891	A regulation to revise the legislation dealing with Forests. Product and the duty leviable on timber in Assam.
Private Forest Ordinance	1959	An ***Ordinance*** to provide for the conservation of ***private forests*** and the afforestation in certain cases of wastelands in Bangladesh.
Preparation of brick and kiln establishment (control) Act	2013	The Act imposes a prohibition on the establishment of brick kilns within the boundaries of several areas, like public or privately owned forests, agricultural land; and Ecologically Critical Area.
Wildlife (Conservation and Protection) Law	2012	By dint of the Act, the government can declare any area as a sanctuary, community conservation area, safari park, eco park, botanical garden, wildlife reproduction centre, landscape zone, buffer zone, or core zone in relation to wildlife and plant preservation, protection, and their smooth growth.
Attia Forest (Protection) Ordinance	1982	An ***Ordinance*** to make provision for the ***protection*** of the ***Attia Forest*** in the districts of Dhaka and Tangail.
Chittagong Hill Tracts Transit Rules; Forest Forest Product Transit Rule	1973; 2011	These were enacted to govern sawpit and wood depot regions within the districts of CHT, as well as the transit of timber and other forest products across land or sea.
Revision of Social Forestry Rules 2004	2010 (Amendment)	This Rule for social forestry is to help people experiencing poverty become self-reliant by creating employment opportunities and meet their food, fodder, fuel, furniture, and capital needs.
Protected Area Management Rules	2017 (Amendment)	This rule for biodiversity conservation often provides habitat and protection from hunting for threatened and endangered species. Further helps to maintain ecological processes that cannot survive in the most intensely managed landscapes and seascapes.

Source: compiled from Roy, 2024

Figure 1. Salient features of UNDRIP

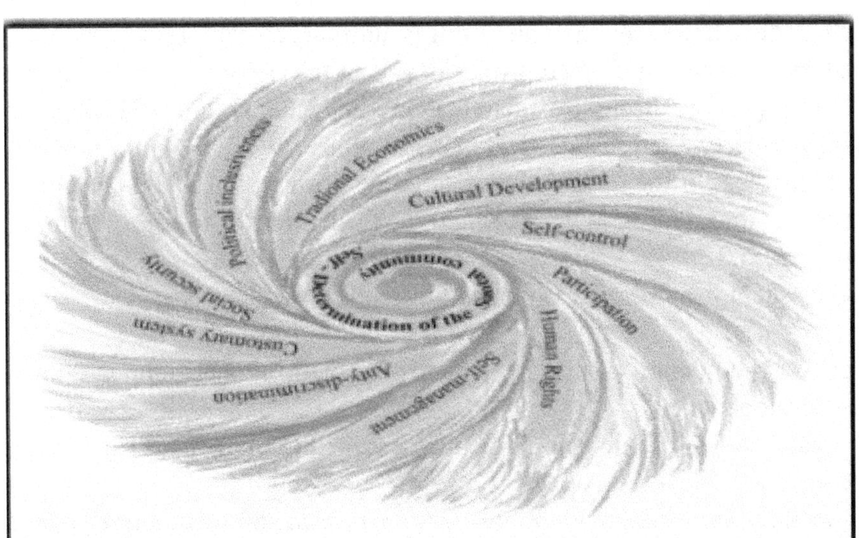

Figure 2. Salient features of ILO-169 convention

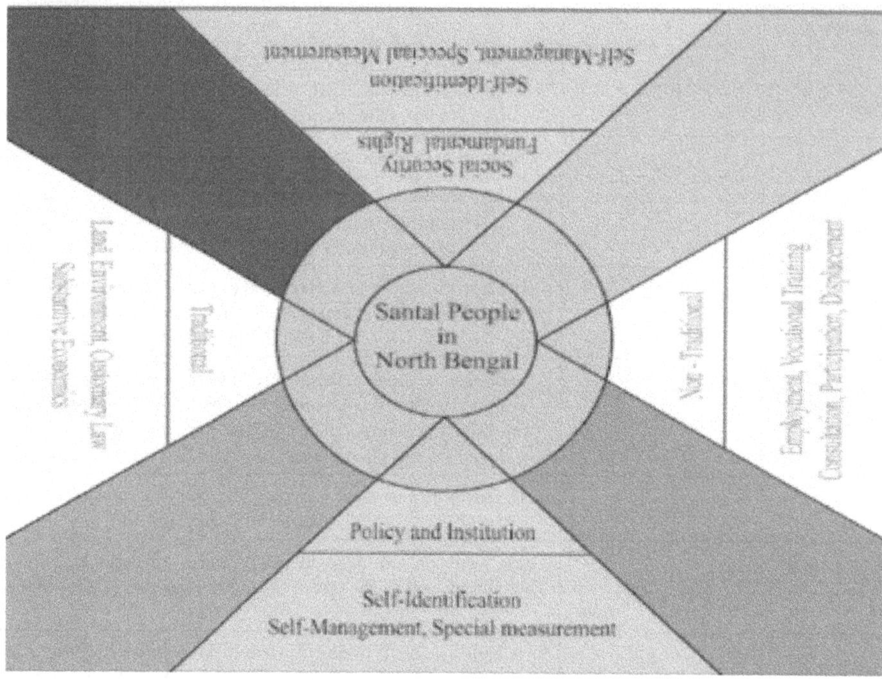

features in the UNDRIP guidelines in the context of the Santal people and Bangladesh (Chowdhury, eds, 2014). Are the rights described under UNDRIP primarily enjoyed by the people of the Santal community living in the north? The researcher investigated and presented those rights in the following research, and in determining yes or no, the information obtained from the common law (The Permanent Settlement Regulation 1793; The State Acquisition and Tenancy Act 1950; The Enemy Property Act 1965; The Acquisition of Immovable Property Act 1982; The Vested Property Act 1974; BiodiversityAct 2017; Education Policy,2010), news published in newspapers, articles (Debnath, 2010; 2020; Sarker et al., 2016; Shafie & Kilby, 2003), and different kinds of academic texts (Barkat, 2016; Chowdhury, eds., 2014; Tripura, 2020) have been used. But the result is alarming (Roy, 2024).

ILO 169 stands with some consequential ways to ensure the rights of minority groups, the elements we presented in a figure before discussing them in detail in the next section. However, the ILO convention-169 stipulates a triparty relationship amid of *Government, Workers, and Employers* to implement this convention. Regardless of the form and structure, the government is the principal accountable for this type of relationship (convention of ILO) to continue further results to keep community development sustainable (Roy et al., 2022).

At a glance, the salient features of ILO convention-169.

i. Social security and fundamental rights belong to peace, governance, human rights, and sustainable community development;
ii. Non-traditional features include employment, vocational training, consultation, participation, and displacement,
iii. Traditional features are land, environment, customary law, and substantive economics—finally,

iv. Policy and Institution belong to Self-determination, self-management, and particular measurement by the government. ILO claims that the government is responsible and accountable for implementing these convention articles. For ethnic welfare, but GoB still now did not heed this issue after demanding the ethnic population (Chowdhury, ed., 2014).

A Pace of Sustainable Collaboration: Global Treaties but Local Activities

UNDRIP and ILO are directive documents that work to protect and enhance the quality of ethnic lifeworld. The Sustainable Development Goals (SDGs) are one of the steps the United Nations has taken to make the enduring endeavour of Sustainable Development. Since 2015, this is an ongoing international program. Among the SDGs, 'Sustainable Communities' is the eleventh goal out of 17 in the sustainable initiatives by the UN, which, along with others, obviously address the people's issues. While implementing sustainable development goals from 2015, like other states, the Government of Bangladesh needs to ensure also sustainable communities (Goals-11), which UNDRIP and ILO—169 have advocated for a long time worldwide.

To sustain the Santals community, allow them to go their customary way because the SDGs, UNDRIP, and ILO are not even a hundred years old, but the sustainability mechanism practised in this community has been time-tested. To scholars, this is the key to a Sustainable Community or actual development without creating a predicament for future generations like the Brundtland Report 1987 or Club of Rome (Meadows et al., 2018[1972]), but the fact is to deny the local history and customs (Roy, 2010; Sen, 2009; Tobin, 2014). Taking the local customs into legal participation is seeded in the Community Resource Pool, Common Property Resources, and Political Participation. When customary leadership is involved in either decision-making at the community level or in the case of directing policies by the government of Bangladesh, then two direct outcomes are revealed in the Santal community. 'One is 'no human rights violation', and another one is 'inclusion within the legal framework', i.e., adopted self-determination. Nevertheless, in light of UNDRIP-2007 and ILO-169, as said, are legal dimensions to incorporate the peoples' knowledge, then the community [Santals] must continue to move towards political rights for sustainable community development.

All over the world, the ethnic community has a lifelong relationship with land and forests. Historically, the Santal had taken from West Bengal, India, to cultivate land in this Bengal (Ali, 2002; Mamun eds, 2021). The Santal community is not exceptional in Bangladesh. To grasp their land in Phulbari, Nawabganj, and Gobindoganj by State agency showed the disrespectful and inhumane relationship.! "God gives the earth to men.! Where the kings brought war, bring concord! Take it, not for the cannon but the plough! Not for the service but for commerce! Not for battle but for the industry! Not for conquest but for fraternity! Go on, do it! Make roads, make ports, make towns! Grow, cultivate, colonize , multiply! And on this land, ever clearer of priests and princes, may the divine spirit assert itself through peace and the human spirit through liberty! (Cited in Paul, 2008, p.51)." While discussing the concept of Sustainability, we need to look at the back of Western history. The New Science or the society of the West has made a significant contribution to the flourishing of Sustainable Development; how advanced are to measure developing countries like Bangladesh to measure the Santal people by Western standards? The meaning of the Development, for example, to the key informant or married woman mentioned in this study, will be calculated on the scale of this new science or by Western-determined indicators – GDP, Per capita income; how far will they go to make progress within the SDGs strategy? For the meaning of this paragraph or in this backdrop, this thesis discussed international treaties to protect human rights, security, and capability power as of the principles of neoliberalism. But, here is a question: when the treaties are still not ratified by the GoB, then what are the benefits to discuss in this thesis? Let them explain in the following paragraphs.

UNDRIP and ILO-169, GoB's Denial and Its Resonance

It is a question of why this thesis will work with the Sustainable Community Development Framework in light of these international treaties. When the Government of Bangladesh did not ratify them yet, then the following rejoinders to the beginning question in this paragraph—

First, this academic exploration will determine the course of action for future ethnic development in Bangladesh regarding legal actions. This backdrop for understanding the international relationship amid the nations' ethnic interventions — treaties, customary laws, traditions, cultural traits, ethnic peoples, and its communities- is the subject matter of this academic knowledge practice to comprehend their development strategy.

Second, the Government of Bangladesh did not officially announce yet that GoB will not ratify the treaties in the future; instead, the GoB is still now monitoring it. Because Bangladesh is a member country of International Labour Organizations and the United Nations, it has an opportunity to ratify those when the time befitting would come in front of the state. In this regard, the researcher discussed with ethnic leaders, human rights activists, and government officials to understand the attitude toward these treaties. According to the interview with civil bureaucrats of Bangladesh, the researcher can assert that the Government can thinks it is time to consider the two treaties. For examples of the Government interventions— one is that ILO-107 has been ratified (also it is arguable), and another one is one accord has been accomplished on 2nd December 1997 between GoB, and the Ethnic People of Chittagong Hill Tracts area; by dint of this treaty GoB formed a ministry to look after the ethnic people in CHT area (specifically three districts are—Khagrachari, Rangamati, and Bandarban; details see Roy et al., 2022). Therefore, this project would have helpful in comprehending the Government's adherence to ratifying the internal treaties soon.

Third, international organizations (ILO, UN, WFO, IMF, WB) have been claiming that these treaties have significant roles (respective websites) in developing the ethnic peoples' security, human rights, and economic upgradation at the community level; however, all are to be investigated to motivate the Government of Bangladesh to ratify those accords? But how? Yes, the logical relationship mentioned in the ILO-169 as a tripartite relation is also has been investigated in this Research using the ethnic lens. This lens —"Finding references to Santal's accession in Bengal is difficult since the sources are few. Numerous researchers, however, argue that the advent of Aryans forced Santals into the Bengal bushes. They did not accept Aryan superiority and clashed. Later, when Muslims and the British arrived, they were more dispersed and defenseless. A further theory seems to be that the Santals settled in Bangladesh from the Indian state of Bihar, particularly Santal Pargana, from 1840 to 1940 (Shamsuddoha & Jahan, 2016). However, colonisation laws forced them to work as bonded labourers during the British era. Santals found it impossible to repay debts, which finally turned them into generations-long enslaved people. Throughout this era, the British's land reforms and land rights legislation, such as the Permanent Settlement Regulation of 1793, the Bengal Tenancy Act 1885, and the State Acquisition and Tenancy Act 1950, all worked against the Santals' interests (Roy et al.,2021, 2022; Sarker et al.,2016). This deprivation eventually drove the Santals to revolt to reclaim their privileges. Numerous acts of abuse and torture resulted in the Santal insurrection formation, also called 'Santal Hul' in their native tongue. Tilka Murmu launched a rebellion against British persecution in 1784. Later, he and a follower were apprehended and condemned to death (Drong, 2019).

A Santal scare began on June 30, 1855; the Santals swore to build a free country for themselves under Sidhu and Kanu's leadership. Approximately 50,000 Santals started their long march into Kolkata. They are thought to have originated the concept of the long march as a form of protest. The rest of several of them led to the Santals / British fight. The insurgent gang murdered 19 soldiers. However, the Santals' archaic weaponry did not match the British's superior ones. Also, it inspired subsequent events like the Sepoy Revolution in 1857 and the rise of nation-states in 1947. Sadly, after 1947, the Santals were stripped of their land rights owing to a lack of legal documents. Many Muslims resorted to brutality, land grabs, and sophisticated legal manoeuvring when confronted with a small quantity of legal danger. In the Pakistan period, ethnic land almost completely evaporated from the documentation. The Santals engaged in the battle for independence in Bangladesh. They operated locally with their weapons, taking on the Pakistan army fearlessly. They were born to rebel, and they fought and died for the prospect of a better future. Sadly, Bangladesh was unable to fulfil its loan. The Santals began to become the prey of unlawful land grabs, inequality, and injustice after independence. The life of poverty went on. A similar tragedy occurred in Gaibandha recently when at least three Santal men were slain while claiming ancestral land rights. The land-grabbing how the Santal community was experiencing issues. Socio-ethnic cohesion and homogeneity among the ethnic groups' Santal are dissipating and eroding" (Roy et al., 2022, p.210).

Fourth, to imply any bridging policy for the Santal community and GoB, there requires a pleasant atmosphere so that the public sentiment goes positively; otherwise, as happened during the birth of Bangladesh in 1971(Roy et al.,2022), it would have an inverse result. For that reason, this thesis is a whistle-bowler in the state to create a positive environment for the ratification because this thesis is the ab initio of knowledge practice in the academic text of Bangladesh along with the Santal community, including UNDRIP and ILO-169. To connote this point, and according to GoB Constitution, article 27 says, "All citizens are equal before the law and are entitled to equal protection of law", which guarantees the equality of citizens before the law, and article 28/1 ('the State shall not discriminate against any citizen or grounds only of religion, race, caste, sex, or place of birth') prohibits discrimination on the grounds of religion, sex, caste, race, and place of birth. Nevertheless, the GoB defended the civil rights of ethnic people by giving them privileges; all ethnic people, including Santal, are vulnerable and stringent people in their homeland, and the 'Small Ethnic Group Cultural Institutions Act-2010' is one of the tools to analyse the impoverished conditions.

On October 4, 2018, the government abolished reservations for indigenous peoples and other quota categories for first and second-class government services through a gazette notification. Since its inception in 1985, the indigenous or "tribal" quota of 5% has failed to ensure proper indigenous participation. Bangladesh Public Services Commission recruited only 271 indigenous persons (0.66%) out of 2,051 candidates. Two ILO studies conducted by Ferdous and Islam (IWGIA-2017 report) between the 24th and 33rd BCS (2005-2014) exams for civil service recruitment in Bangladesh. Even though the required percentage has never been allocated in any given year, the quota has allowed some indigenous candidates to work in the public sector. The quota abolition puts indigenous job seekers in direct competition with everyone else, creating an unstable and unequal situation. Indigenous peoples in Bangladesh face numerous socio-economic and political disadvantages. As a result, they cannot compete with their "mainstream" peers. The lack of a quota will further reduce indigenous peoples' representation in the state bureaucracy. In this scenario, UNDRIP and ILO 169 can contribute to relieving the ethnic tension in Bangladesh (Roy et al.,2022 pp, 214-215).

JOURNEY WITH SANTALS: METHODOLOGICAL POSITION

In anthropological Research, participants' observation is a core matter in collecting and analyzing any social facts belonging to a community. The Santal is a marginal and minority community in Bangladesh; naturally, they fear disclosing sensitive information if it is a political issue. In this context, the thesis subject is customary law, and the countryside people always want to avoid legal matters or discussions. The researcher mingled with the villagers and talked formally and informally even though whether they offered any Handia or smoking did not matter to, then, researcher. The facts revealed are the top priority to the author. Sometimes, the researcher was present at their local meeting, marriage ceremonies, and religious festivals to get new facts that could enrich the research report. Sometimes, the researcher rented a Van, roaming here and there aimlessly to see the Santal people in the field, where they worked for crops. The researcher sat beside them and talked about any issues. However, in the village market, there is a tea-teal stall conventionally; the Santals people gather here and pass their time by gossiping and taking tea. When the first-day researcher rode a van, Van-puller was offered a cup of tea.

Interestingly, the Van puller did not enter any tea stall but took the researcher to a specific tea stall. The researcher was astonished, but it brought a blessing to the researcher. When the researcher got time, he took a cup of tea in that specific tea stall and noticed their discussion points and trends. The Santal people talked about their own society and culture and diversified topics to talk about their societal awareness. Furthermore, the researcher explored one more spots like this tea stall. Indeed, this is informal talking, and nothing happens in society. But to understand the Great traditions, and whether Sanskritaization or westernisation, this type of talk all are important. Political discussion on a cup of tea is not political science, but comprehending the political grasp is meaningful to the researcher.

DESCRIPTION: STUDY AREA AND LOCATION

The primary residence Santal community in Bangladesh is Dinajpur district. Taking this into account, the Dinajpur district is to be selected as the research area of this study. Birganj is one of the sub-districts of this District, and *Singra* is the Sal forest near to the Santal villages of this sub-district. This is a remote village and far from the town with a lack of urban amenities.

"In Bangladesh, Sal forests cover an area of about 121,000 ha, which is about 32% of the total forest land. Sal forests have a fairly wide but interrupted distribution in the drier central and northern part of the mainland, mostly occurring in Gazipur, Tangail, Mymensingh, Jamalpur, Comilla, Dinajpur, Thakurgaon, Rangpur and Rajshahi districts."

(https://en.banglapedia.org/index.php/Sal_Forest; accessed on 10 October 2023 at 12.45 pm)

The Singra Sal Forest: A Landscape

Singra National Park is a protected forest area of Bangladesh in the Dinajpur district of North Bengal. Locally, it is known as Singra Shalbon. 40 km from Dinajpur district city by road. North and 15 km from Birganj Upazila. Its location is far away in Bhognagar Union. The total area of this forest land is 355 hectares; out of it, the national park (conservation) is 305.69 hectares. Singra National Park is spread

Figure 3. Location of the study
Source: District administration website

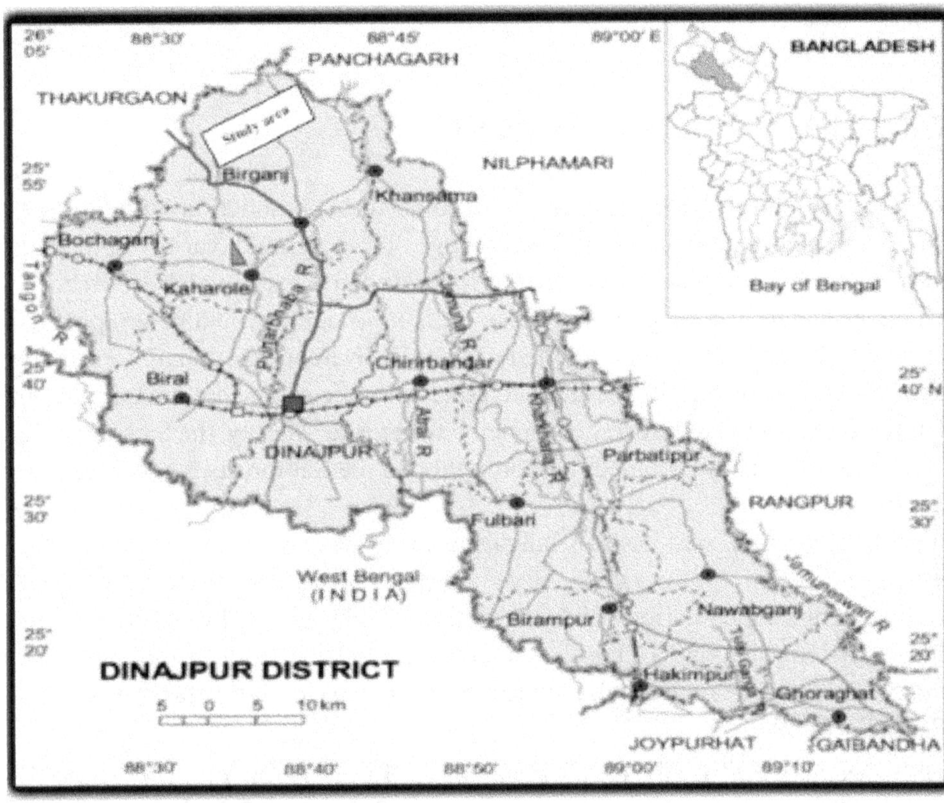

over 4 mauzas: Dalagram, Chaulia, Singra and Norta nadi (river). It was declared a National Park by the Forest Department on 10 October 2010 to improve the natural environment, conserve wildlife and develop tourism facilities.

Narta River flows through Singra National Park. There is a small rest house and two picnic spots for the convenience of tourists. In the winter season, the tourist traffic increases in this forest. A co-management committee consisting of local people's representatives is working in collaboration with NGO (RDRS) Bangladesh to conserve the biodiversity of Singra Shalbon.

As noted, Dinajpur is a district located in the country's northwestern region. It covers an area of 3450 square kilometres. The Santal people have a distinct identity. Birganj is

One of the subdistricts amidst thirteen. It has an area of 413 square kilometres and is located on the Dinajpur-Thakurgaon Highway. The study community is 8-10 kilometres far from Birganj Police Station in the Santal hamlet. For nine months May 2022 to January 2023, the researcher engaged in Research in a Santal community. The communication infrastructure is adequate, and Rickshaws and Vans function as vehicles. Numerous men and women work in a variety of factories, farms, brick kilns, rickshaws, and as labourers. Numerous non-governmental organisations (for example, Caritas, RDRS, BRAC, Grameen Bank, Supoth) and the Christian Missionaries in that community are working to improve their quality of life. Nevertheless, the state and NGOs remain entirely silent on the political empowerment they need. Although, seeing some academic works on how the state denies them as denial politics (Jahan, 2020) or how missionaries are converting them to Christianity (Debnath, 2020) as civilizing. Therefore, this study will work on customary law within the traditional power structure of the Santal community to compare it with the statute.

THE SANTALS LIVING WITH SAL FOREST

Although over 500 understory species have been documented in conjunction with Sal trees, Sal is the most significant tree species in Sal forests. The vast range of undergrowth variety in the Sal Forest ecosystem is made possible by a unique microclimate. However, Sal forests, which are rich in Phyto diversity, have been under threat for a long time because of their topography and geographic location (they are on a plateau), which has led to a rapid reduction through overexploitation, deforestation, excessive leaf litter collection, encroachment, indiscriminate collection of certain economically significant plant species (fodder, medicine), and other forms of human interference. Mainly, the Santal ethnic group lives in Bangladesh's Sal woods. These people rely thoroughly on the Sal forests for their social, ecological, and economic subsistence.

This ethnic minority group has its own language, norms, customary laws, property inheritance rules, marriage system, totems, political judiciary system, and gender order (Roy, 2024 [PhD Thesis]). The current study examines the relationship between the Santals and Sal Forest changes in acceptance towards customary systems among 'Santals communities', somewhat under a national legal dominated framework, and typical mainstream Bengali culture aligning the discussion with international documents like UNDRIP and ILO-169.

Local wisdom is a noble value that applies in the life of the community to, among other things, protect and manage the environment sustainably. Local wisdom is very influential in forest conservation because the community around the forest has a sustainable function, both in the economic field and even in the socio-cultural field; thus, they always maintain and manage the forest even though there are people who cannot care less about the function of the forest. Influences of Indigenous People on Sal Forest. An ethnic community named Santals, associated with a few Bengali communities, lives close to the Sal Forest. They are more or less dependent on the forest for their livelihood.

Local people collect fuel wood and dried leaves from the forest, which sometimes disturbs the regeneration of the forest and causes nutrient deficiency in the soil if the extraction is so high. Because we know that debris and leaves play a significant role in forest nutrient dynamics,

Ethnic communities are dependent mostly on hunting wild animals, making Sal forest severely lose the diversity of wild animals, "Indigenous community people are gathering food, fruits, medicinal plants from the forest which cause the extinction of some precious medicinal plants, Sometimes, seedlings are collected to make roof together with other thatching materials from the forest that adversely affects the regeneration. Due to some conflict between the Forest Department and Santals, Santals are illegally felling trees and collecting non-wood forest products. Local people need to be aware of the consequences of forest loss for a long time, making them use forest products unconsciously and leaving the idea of sustainable management of Sal forest. Forest firing also changes the structure of the forest, which ethnic people mainly do for some traditions.

"Scientific forest management in this sub-continent was started during British rule by the appointment of Sir D. Brandis as the Inspector General of Forest in 1865. A separate forest department was created for Bengal in 1876. In those days, forests were managed primarily for revenue collection under the control of the Revenue Department. Only valuable trees were extracted from the forest to get more revenue; keeping in mind the importance of the forest, a forest management plan or work plan is prepared for each forest division. This management plan guides forest managers to manage the forest or to perform day-to-day work in the forest."

CONCLUSION AND POLICY RECOMMENDATIONS

This concept of citizenship was heightened more in the 1990s when the UNO disseminated its prominent Charter of Human Rights, which thrived the global mobilisation of the indigenes. The charter adopted later by the GoB considered the displacement of people from their land a violation of their basic human rights, but unfortunately, this process persisted in the forced displacement of the Santals. For the Adivasis of Dinajpur, their human right was linked to their landscape and its protection and utilisation. Sergio Saurer (2012) argues that traditional communities' territory and territorial rights acquired new meanings through these 'land struggle (s)'. This way, self-definition or self-recognition as a socially differentiated group with an identity of its own and a close relation to a particular region and land' was strongly proclaimed.

Due to its abundance of medicinal plants, its importance as a natural habitat for endangered species like the Hoolock gibbon (Hylobates hoolock), and its worldwide significance as a dry, plainland tropical deciduous forest ecosystem, this disturbed but ecologically and socioeconomically significant forest ecosystem necessitates a thorough development of the entire ecosystem.

In the suggested framework for advancing the SDGs' implementation. The structure's principal parts are:

- Making financial and technical resources available for effective and accountable governance for strong institutions (SDGs-16).
- Pay attention to infrastructure, the environment, health, education, and human resources as significant forces behind economic Development;
- Emphasizing the customary laws to settle land issues as a fundamental need for life settings.

Long-Term Integrated Approach

The SDGs localization level should determine a methodology to understand the linkages between mandates of line ministries and sector governance within the country. This determining level should be flexible and operational with adaptive strategies to national variations by targeting SDGs11 and 16 at the most appropriate level. In this connection, we recommend ratifying UNDRIP and ILO-169 purposively to localize the SDGs to concentrate on local capacity development, building ownership, and responsibility. The cost of localizing, however, is still not addressed. But, the success of SDGs implementation depends on each country's social and economic capability for social development. That is why our long-term recommendation is—

The Government should take the initiative to ratify the UNDRIP-2007 and ILO Convention 169 for comprehensive development in the ethnic-centric area.

REFERENCES

Ali, M. (2002). *Dinajpurer Adivasi*. Dinajpur Adivasi Academy.

Chilisa, B. (2019). *Indigenous research methodologies*. Sage publications.

Chowdhury, M. S. (Ed.). (2014). *Survival Under Threat: Human Rights Situation of Indigenous Peoples in Bangladesh*. Asia Indigenous People Pact.

Debnath, M. (2020). A community under siege: Exclusionary education policies and indigenous Santals* in the Bangladeshi context. *Third World Quarterly*, *41*(3), 453–469. doi:10.1080/01436597.2019.1660634

Debnath, M. K. (2010). *Living on the Edge: The predicament of a rural indigenous Santal community in Bangladesh* [Doctoral dissertation, University of Toronto].

Doshi, S. L. (1990). *Tribal Ethnicity, Class and Integration*. Rawat Publications.

Drong, S. (2019). *Does God forget the Santals?* Suchipatra.

Jahan, F. (2020). *The issue of identity: state denial, local controversies and everyday resistance among the Santal in Bangladesh*, [PhD Thesis, Hale University].

Karim, R., Habib, T. Z., Arefin, S., Rahman, H., Rahman, S., & Swahnberg, K. (2020). Differences in the acceptance of wife abuse among ethnic minority Garo and Santal and mainstream Bengali communities in rural Bangladesh. *PLoS One*, *15*(7), e0236733. doi:10.1371/journal.pone.0236733 PMID:32722707

Mamun, M. (Ed.). (2021). *Subaltern, Revolt and Armed Resistance in Bangladesh (1763-1950)*. Kothaprokash.

Meadows, D. H., Meadows, D. L., Randers, J., & Behrens, W. W. (2018). The limits to growth. In *Green planet blues*. Routledge. doi:10.4324/9780429493744-3

Nakata, M. (2004). Indigenous knowledge and the cultural interface. *Disrupting preconceptions: Postcolonialism and Education*. Research Gate.

Paul, B. D. (2008). A history of the concept of sustainable development: Literature review.The Annals of the University of Oradea. *Economic Sciences Series*, *17*(2), 576–580.

Roy, P., Chowdhury, J. S., Abd Wahab, H., Saad, M. R. B., & Parahakaran, S. (2021). Christianity, COVID-19, and marginal people of Bangladesh: An experience from the Santal Community. In Handbook of Research on the Impact of COVID-19 on Marginalized Populations and Support for the Future (pp. 65-82). IGI Global.

Roy, P., Chowdhury, J. S., Abd Wahab, H., & Saad, R. B. M. (2022). Ethnic Tension of the Bangladeshi Santal: A CDA of the Constitutional Provision. In Handbook of Research on Ethnic, Racial, and Religious Conflicts and Their Impact on State and Social Security (pp. 208-226). IGI Global. doi:10.4018/978-1-7998-8911-3.ch013

Roy, P. K. (2024). *Customary Law and Sustainable Community Development: A Study of the Santals of Bangladesh*, [PhD Thesis, Universiti Malaya].

Roy, R. D., & Chakma, P. (2010). The Chittagong Hill Tracts Accord & Provisions on Lands, Territories, Resources and Customary Law. *Hope and Despair: Indigenous Jumma Peoples Speak on the Chittagong Hill Tracts Peace Accord.* Baguio City: Tebtebba Foundation. http://tebtebba. org/index.php/all-resources/category/8-books

Sarker, M. A. R., Khan, N. A., & Musarrat, K. M. (2016). Livelihood and vulnerability of the Santals community in Bangladesh. *The Malaysian Journal of Social Administration, 12*(1), 38–55. doi:10.22452/mjsa.vol12no1.2

Sauer, S. (2012). Land and Territory: Meanings of Land between Modernity and Tradition. *Agrarian South - the Journal of Political Economy, 1*(1), 85–107. doi:10.1177/227797601200100106

Sen, A (2009). *The Idea of Justice.* Allan lane Penguin Books.

Shafie, H., & Kilby, P. (2003). *Including the excluded: ethnic inequality and Development in Northwest Bangladesh.*

Singh, A. (2022). State, forest, and Adivasis at crossroads: Netarhat field firing range and contestations over rights. In *At the Crossroads of Rights* (pp. 6–22). Routledge. doi:10.4324/9781003269458-2

Smith, L. T. (2021). *Decolonizing methodologies: Research and indigenous peoples.* Bloomsbury Publishing. doi:10.5040/9781350225282

Tobin, B. (2014). *Indigenous peoples, customary law and human rights-why living law matters.* Routledge. doi:10.4324/9781315778792

Tripura, P. (2020). *Colonial Shadow in Bangladesh (Bangla books).* Sangbed.

Uddin, N. (2023). Methodological Issues in Social Research: Experience from the Twenty-First Century. In *The Palgrave Handbook of Social Fieldwork* (pp. 1–20). Springer International Publishing. doi:10.1007/978-3-031-13615-3_1

Weiss, G., Lawrence, A., Lidestav, G., Feliciano, D., Hujala, T., Sarvašová, Z., Dobšinská, Z., & Živojinović, I. (2019). Research trends: Forest ownership in multiple perspectives. *Forest Policy and Economics, 99*, 1–8. doi:10.1016/j.forpol.2018.10.006

ADDITIONAL READINGS

Ali, A. (1998). *Santals of Bangladesh.* Institute of Social Research & Applied Anthropology.

Chowdhury, J. S., Wahab, H. A., Mohd, R. M. S., Hamidi, M., Roy, P. K., & Ahmad, M. M. (2022). Constitutional Provision in Protecting and Managing Indigenous Knowledge Systems: A Case From Rakhain Community in Bangladesh. In Handbook of Research on Protecting and Managing Global Indigenous Knowledge Systems. IGI Global. doi:10.4018/978-1-7998-7492-8.ch011

Roy, P. (2023, February). *Reciprocity and Its Practice in Social Research.* IGI Global.

Roy, P. K., Abd Wahab, H., & Hamidi, M. (2023). A Philosophical Discussion of Sustainable Development: A Case From the Bangladeshi Santal Community. In *Handbook of Research on Implications of Sustainable Development in Higher Education* (pp. 97–114). IGI Global. doi:10.4018/978-1-6684-6172-3.ch005

Roy, P. K., Abd Wahab, H., & Hamidi, M. (2023). Achieving the Sustainable Development Goals: A Case Study of the Ministry of Chittagong Hill Tracts Affairs, Bangladesh. In Positive and Constructive Contributions for Sustainable Development Goals(pp. 161-180). IGI Global.

KEY TERMS AND DEFINITIONS

Adivasi: A popular discursive that out-of-mainstream people think of themselves as the person of Adivasi, i.e. indicating it means they are inhabitants from the beginning of the earth. In this term, all fifty ethnic groups are Adivasi, but the government of Bangladesh denied this term. Adivasi is similar to Indigenous, Primitive or Tribal, but GoB formulated a Policy as "Small Ethnic Groups Cultural Institute Acts 2010." So, they are a small ethnic group according to law and policy.

ILO 169: Convention 169 recognizes Indigenous peoples' right to self-determination within a nation-state while setting standards for national governments regarding Indigenous peoples' economic, socio-cultural and political rights, including the right to a land base. It is based on recognising indigenous and tribal peoples' aspirations to exercise control over their own institutions, ways of life and economic development and to maintain and develop their identities, languages and religions within the framework of the States in which they live.

Santals: The Santal is one of the officially declared 50 ethnic groups in Bangladesh. They live mainly northern part of Bangladesh—either greater Rajshahi or Dinajpur.

UNDRIP: The United Nations Declaration on the Rights of Indigenous Peoples (UNDRIP) was adopted by the General Assembly on Thursday, 13 September 2007. The Declaration is the most comprehensive international instrument on the rights of Indigenous peoples. Indigenous peoples have the collective right to live in freedom, peace and security as distinct peoples and shall not be subjected to any act of genocide or any other act of violence, including forcibly removing children of the group from another group.

Chapter 19
State Security Agent:
A Study on the Interaction Between State Sovereignty and Private Security Companies

Meng Yang
https://orcid.org/0009-0007-0480-4806
Nanjing University, China

Yuhong Li
https://orcid.org/0000-0002-3544-4475
Nanjing University, China

ABSTRACT

This chapter attempts to explore the interaction between national sovereignty and private security companies, taking Myanmar and Cambodia as examples. After the end of the cold war, some countries are still in the process of State-building. To ensure domestic and international security, the authorities decided to take their security off the border and entrust it to PSC. Among them, the adaptability of shared security sovereignty and the demand for security interests jointly determine the practice of shared security sovereignty of the state over PSC. During the military government period, Myanmar faced significant international pressure, but maintained a certain degree of national stability. the state and PSC had an unstable alliance relationship. After the democratization process began, overall international pressure weakened, and the two parties tended to be stable alliances or potential alliances. As for Cambodia, the lack of national capacity has led it to actively accept international norms and to strengthen cooperation with PSC. After a solid political authority was build, Cambodia began to reduce cooperation with PSC. Whether it is Myanmar or Cambodia, it has been shown that the disembedding of security is a last resort for transitional countries whose state construction has not yet been completed. Once a solid-state authority is established and it meets the needs of international norms, the state will often monopolize security supply. It does not allow private security companies to share security sovereignty.

DOI: 10.4018/979-8-3693-1742-6.ch019

INTRODUCTION

National security has always been an important research field in international relations. It is not only related to State-building and national sovereignty, but also the stability of national security is an important feature of whether a country can survive in the international community. On the one hand, a country should strive to maintain its interests in the international community, and on the other hand, ensure the stability of its internal security order. The state, therefore, needs to ensure the highest authority of its own within its jurisdiction, which depends on the state exercising control over the social system within its jurisdiction and relying on military violence over all members of society (Poggi, 1977). It can be said that in an ideal situation, a country is an international actor that relies entirely on its capabilities to ensure security. However, not all countries can rely on their abilities to ensure their highest authority in the international community for survival and control. Countries are more likely to form alliances with major powers to ensure survival or internal legitimacy, such as South Korea's alliance with the United States during the Cold War to ensure its survival and national stability on the Korean Peninsula. From this point of view, the survival (security) and State-building (sovereignty) of a country do not seem to be inseparable and so absolute.

When a country tries to survive in the international community, it is difficult for domestic stability to accept the unconditional monopoly of violence by the state. Therefore, after the Cold War, most countries focused on internal stability and to some extent entrusted survival issues to various regional security mechanisms. As more and more security mechanisms fail, countries are unable to effectively address security sovereignty issues both domestically and externally. A special type of actor has emerged in the international community, namely private security companies. Private security companies, as groups that share security governance within the scope of national sovereignty, are still not accepted by the international community. Some countries rely on private security companies to stabilize security both domestically and internationally. The Director of the Cambodian National Police praised the work of private security companies in maintaining social security and order, as well as their efforts in combating crime (Cambodian Chinese Network, July 30, 2022). This incident demonstrates that national security can be outsourced, rather than being solely provided by national/international organizations. In other words, the emergence of private security companies after the Cold War challenged the sovereignty norms centered around the state.

So why can private security companies share national security and sovereignty? If private security companies are seen as an armed force, what kind of initiative do they have to enable them to flow in the international community? This is the issue that this article focuses on the most. Especially for Southeast Asian countries, the construction of a nation-state (sovereign capacity) is not completely stable, and countries should not believe in any actors that will divide sovereign capacity. However, the reality is that private security companies can also maintain their initiative in Southeast Asian countries and share security and sovereignty with them. Therefore, this paper compares Myanmar and Cambodia as cases to illustrate the relationship between State-building in Southeast Asia and private security companies.

Research Objective

This paper will start with Giddens' theory of "Disembedding theory", compare the relationship between State-building and private security companies in Myanmar and Cambodia, and find the causal mechanism of interaction between state and non-state actors. The reason we chose these two countries is that

Myanmar and Cambodia were not considered stable states after the end of the Cold War, but they both cooperated with private security companies to some extent.

1. Discuss how private security companies can share the state capacity of security as sovereignty with the country (State-building is still in progress).
2. Examine how the (State-building is still in progress) state secedes itself from its security domain and entrusts it to private security companies.
3. Discuss how the two tensioned behaviors of national security interests and shared security interact? How does this interaction feedback to State-building?

RESEARCH METHOD

This article adopts the method of agreement in J.S.Mill's five methods of searching causal connections. Through empirical induction and comparative analysis of several consecutive facts, the researchers found that as long as factor A appears in the previous event, factor a must appear in the subsequent phenomenon, Moreover, each pair of facts has the characteristic of factor A and factor a appearing one after another, thus proving the existence of a corresponding or covariant relationship between factor A and factor a.

1. Comparing the interaction process between national security and private security companies in Myanmar and Cambodia
2 Pursue the interaction between Myanmar and Cambodia's security disembedding mechanism and State-building
3 Comparing the interaction between State-building and autonomy of private security companies in Myanmar and Cambodia

Research Hypothesis

Giddens' Modernization theory points out that one of the characteristics of modernization is disembedding. Disembedding refers to the cognitive differences caused by modernity, where people no longer rely on the connections of time and space to live, but rely on symbolic tokens and expert systems to overcome the differences in time and space. In modern society, there will no longer be cognitive differences in values, history, and culture due to regional limitations, and the media that carry these values, history, and culture (such as currency) can also have cross-regional limitations. In short, even if you are unaware or do not reside in a certain region, you can still learn about the values and culture of that region by consulting an encyclopedia and using the cultural media of that region (Giddens, 1981 & 1999).

According to Giddens' viewpoint, for the international community, we can view symbolic tokens as security interests (views), while expert systems are seen as security cooperation between countries. National security interests transcend time and space, allowing countries to understand each other's security interests even if they are not in the same region. As a medium for carrying security interests, security regime also promotes mutual understanding of security interests between countries when they interact with other countries or non-international actors across regions. International private security companies, as a new type of security regime, not only coordinate with the national security interests but also share the national capabilities of sovereignty and internal and external security governance with the

Table 1. Benefit-Security disembedding interaction hypothesis

	High adaptability to shared security	Low adaptability to shared security
High demand for security benefits	**(Stable alliance)**	**(Unstable alliance)**
Low need for security benefits	(Potential alliance)	(Unable to ally)

country. In short, even if the security interests between countries match, the choice of security regime between countries is no longer limited to countries or international organizations, but rather to engage in security cooperation with private security companies. Based on this scenario assumption, we can set assumptions about the interaction mechanism:

1. When the country has a high adaptability for shared security and a high demand for security benefits, it presents a strong autonomy of private security companies, and the state and private security companies share the sovereignty of security governance. (Stable alliance)
2. When countries have high adaptability to shared security and low demand for security benefits, that is, private security companies have greater autonomy, and countries can form alliances with them when necessary. (Potential alliances)
3. When the adaptability of national shared security is low and the demand for security benefits is high, that is, the autonomy of private security companies is small, and the state still holds most of the sovereignty of security governance. (Unstable alliance)
4. When the adaptability of national shared security is low and the demand for security interests is low, it presents a hostile relationship between private security companies and the state, and the state cannot accept the division of its security governance sovereignty. (Unable to ally)

RESULT

Myammar

Phase One (1989-2010): Unstable Alliance

In terms of national stability, the military government during this period held power and controlled all aspects of the country. In September 1988, the Burmese army took over power and established the State Law and Order Restoration Council (SLORC) (later changed to the State Peace and Development Council), and changed the name of the country to "Union of Myanmar". On May 27, 1990, Myanmar held its first multi-party system general election. The National League for Democracy led by Aung San Suu Kyi won 396 of the 485 seats, but the military government refused to transfer power. Later, a large number of political parties dissolved or were banned.

To this end, the Democratic League and the military government engaged in a series of arduous struggles, with both sides experiencing multiple outbreaks of conflict. In 2003, during a speech by Aung San Suu Kyi in the town of Dipeyin in northern Myanmar, there was a fierce conflict between supporters of the Democratic League and the military government, resulting in many casualties (*BBC NEWS*, July 4, 2011). In August 2007, the Saffron Revolution broke out in Myanmar, and Buddhist monks as the main crowd launched a Procession against the military government (Selth 2008). In terms of economy, although the military government claims to implement a "market economy policy", there are many restrictions in the economic field, and the degree of opening up to the outside world is not significant. There is a strong artificial color, such as the military government handing over the huge profit of importing palm oil to a company closely related to the government for monopoly management (Hayes&Weber 2021).

The multiple resistance actions of the anti-government camp in Myanmar did not shake the ruling foundation of the military government, but objectively prompted the military government to accelerate the process of democratization and reform. In 2003, then-military government leader Than Shwe proposed a seven-step democratic roadmap and gradually implemented it. In 2008, Myanmar passed a new constitution that ensured the special status of the military. In 2010, Myanmar held a new general election, marking the gradual transition from a military regime to a democratically elected regime.

In terms of international structural pressure, during the 23 years from 1988 to 2010, due to the suppression of the democratic movement by the Burmese military government, the international community continued to impose sanctions on it. Among them, the United States and Europe often unite to exert pressure on Myanmar. In the early 1990s, the sanctions imposed by the United States and Europe on Myanmar were relatively light. The main measures taken by the United States were the recall of its ambassador to Myanmar, the revocation of preferential economic and tax systems for Myanmar, etc. The main measures taken by the European Union were the cancellation of military cooperation. As the struggle between the National League for Democracy led by Aung San Suu Kyi and the military government continues to deepen, the sanctions imposed by the United States and Europe on Myanmar are also escalating. On May 20, 1997, the Clinton administration issued Executive Order 13047, restricting new investments by US companies in Myanmar (*Cato Institute*, March 26, 1998).

The European Commission also issued the first Common Position on Myanmar/Myanmar document in October 1996, prohibiting the issuance of visas to senior officials of the Burmese military government and those closely related to the military government, and canceling high-level government visits to Myanmar. The United States increased its sanctions on Myanmar three times in 2003, 2007, and 2008, and also designated Myanmar as an "Outpost of Tyranny" in 2005. The European Union further escalated its sanctions by freezing the assets of relevant personnel, prohibiting EU companies from investing in Myanmar and expanding the scope of visa bans for personnel (European Commission 2004). The difference between the sanctions imposed by the United States and Europe on Myanmar lies in the fact that the main purpose of the United States is to promote American-style democracy, while the main focus of the European Union is to remove democracy, as well as human rights.

Despite Myanmar's formal accession to ASEAN in 1997, ASEAN has maintained constructive engagement with Myanmar. But also due to the political and diplomatic pressure exerted by the West on Myanmar's democratic process and human rights issues, such as ASEAN countries agreeing to Myanmar's abandonment of the 2006 ASEAN rotating presidency. China emphasizes the principle of non-interference in internal affairs in its relations with Myanmar, but often cautiously proposes some political and economic reform suggestions to Myanmar (Egreteau 2008). At this stage, Myanmar is under significant external pressure, resulting in the military government being unable to obtain sufficient material resources from abroad to control the country's dependence. Although the military government plays a leading role in the Politics of Myanmar's political structure, the lack of external support still makes it need huge security interests.

The military government did not pay much attention to private security companies, and their development was in its early stages. According to the State-Owned Economic Enterprises Law of 1989, private security companies do not belong to the type of enterprise that is exclusively operated by the government or jointly operated with the government, which means that the Myanmar government has weak restrictions on the ownership of private security companies, to some extent, it is beneficial for the development of private security companies. But this cooperative relationship is unstable, and once external structural pressure weakens, the motivation for the alliance between the two sides will weaken.

The Burmese government vigorously developed state building, hoping to build a true national state. The core tasks of Myanmar's national construction include political transformation and national reconciliation. The former refers to the "demilitarization" of national politics and the gradual transition from a military government to a democratically elected government; The latter mainly involves the relationship between the main ethnic group Burmese and other minority groups, as well as the distribution of power between the central and local governments. As a result, the Myanmar government leaves less space for private security companies, which have less autonomy and the state still holds most of the sovereignty over security governance.

Phase Two (2011-2020): Potential Alliance

In terms of national stability, during the reign of Thein Sein, the Burmese government carried out a series of institutional reforms, which began to loosen the political pattern of military dictatorship. In terms of the political system, a series of measures have been taken to implement liberalization and democratization reforms, including releasing opposition leader Aung San Suu Kyi and allowing the National League for Democracy to register as a legitimate political party. In terms of public opinion control, relax the censorship of news media, such as narrowing the scope of publication censorship and opening up previously banned websites such as Skype, Yahoo, and YouTube (*BBC NEWS*, August 20, 2012).

On ethnic issues, the Thein Sein government has initiated a peace process and advocated for political solutions to ethnic issues. The Myanmar government began to hold peace talks with the Karen, Kachin, Shan, and other ethnic minorities in November 2011 and signed a ceasefire agreement with the Karen National Liberation Army in early 2012 (*BBC NEWS*, January 12, 2012). The reason why the Burmese government seeks reconciliation with ethnic armed groups is not only to create a peaceful environment for domestic reform but also because ending domestic armed violence is a condition for the West to lift sanctions against Myanmar.

After the Democratic League took office, there was no substantive breakthrough in the domestic conflict and national reconciliation process. Although the NLD government hosted the 21st Century Panglong Conference and reached some consensus, Myanmar's national reconciliation is far from being achieved (Ganesan 2018). The Kokang Allied Army, the Rakhine National Army, the Kachin Independence Army, and other armed forces have been fighting with the government forces for years, and it is difficult to reconcile the differences and contradictions between the central and local authorities on the issue of interest distribution.

In 2017, serious conflicts broke out between Rohingya people and government forces in Rakhine State, causing hundreds of thousands of Rohingya people to flee to neighboring Bangladesh (Trihartono 2018). It is disappointing that the NLD government led by Aung San Suu Kyi has done nothing on the human rights issues of ethnic minorities and has remained silent about the military's atrocities.

In addition, Myanmar's civil society has developed rapidly. Through social media, people have deepened their understanding of democracy and enhanced their willingness to participate in politics. In the face of unfair and illegal policies of the government, people have begun to take to the streets to express their positions through Procession, forcing the government to pay more attention to public opinion. Due to the lack of binding legal measures for NGOs in Myanmar, the growth and management of NGOs have been rampant. The influence of NGOs on Myanmar's society and public opinion has rapidly expanded, with a strong tendency to "kidnap" public opinion and interfere with government decision-making. One of the main tasks of NGOs is to replace the government in meeting the basic living needs of the public, which will weaken people's loyalty to the country (Holm 2019).

In terms of international structural pressure, Myanmar's relations with Western countries have eased. After the democratization process in Myanmar began, the West gradually lifted sanctions on Myanmar and continuously increased contact with Myanmar. In September 2009, Obama's policy towards Myanmar began to loosen. On November 30, 2011, US Secretary of State Hillary Clinton made a historic visit to Myanmar, becoming the first US Secretary of State to visit Myanmar in over 50 years. Since then, relations between the two countries have begun to improve. With the advancement of Myanmar's democratization process, the US government has gradually relaxed sanctions on Myanmar and allowed US companies to invest in Myanmar.

On November 19, 2012, US President Obama visited Myanmar, becoming the first US President to visit Myanmar during his tenure (*The White House*, November 19, 2012). In May 2013, Thein Sein, then President of Myanmar, visited the United States, becoming the first head of state of Myanmar to visit the United States in 47 years. In November 2014, US President Obama went to Myanmar to attend a series of East Asian Cooperation Leaders' Meetings. In 2012 and 2015, the United States and Myanmar held two human rights dialogues, and the Myanmar military made compromises on local minority human rights issues. On May 2, 2015, the Myanmar Consulate General in Los Angeles officially opened, with U Aung Kyaw Zan as the first Consul General.

In September 2016, Myanmar's Senior Minister Aung San Suu Kyi visited the United States. On October 7 of the same year, US President Obama issued a decree announcing the termination of the implementation of the National Emergencies Act against Myanmar (which came into effect on May 20, 1997, prohibiting US companies and individuals from engaging in investment, trade, and other business dealings with specific Myanmar companies and individuals) (*Executive Office of the President*, October 7, 2016). On the same day, the US Treasury Department issued a statement stating that the economic and financial sanctions imposed by the Office of Foreign Assets Control of the US Treasury Department on Myanmar were subsequently invalidated (*The U.S. Embassy in Burma*, October 7, 2016). After Trump took office, the United States' emphasis on Myanmar decreased, but the United States remains committed to promoting Myanmar's "democratization" transformation. In 2017, after the Rohingya crisis, there was a certain regression in US-Myanmar relations. At the same time, countries such as China, Japan, and India are also actively developing relations with Myanmar. Taking China as an example, China and Myanmar jointly build "the Belt and Road" cooperation and the China-Myanmar Economic Corridor. ASEAN is also willing to include Myanmar in the fast lane of ASEAN development, by helping Myanmar achieve modernization goals and reducing the security threats posed by humanitarian crises and armed conflicts to the entire region.

In terms of interaction between the state and private security companies, during this period, the Myanmar government supported the introduction of private security companies to protect foreign investment security and maintain social stability, and private security companies had greater autonomy. In 2015, experts predicted that mining projects and other large industries would drive demand for private security in the coming years, as Myanmar's richest economic resources are located in the most dangerous areas. Private security companies can protect the interests of foreign investors, but the lack of government regulation of private security companies can also lead to legal and human rights-related issues (*Business&Human Rights Resource Centre*, January 6, 2015).

To this end, in February 2015, the Myanmar Ministry of the Interior, the Ministry of Planning and Economic Development, and the Ministry of Commerce jointly discussed the development of the Private Security Services Law with private security companies to improve Myanmar's security standards through coordination between the government and private security companies (*Myanmar Business Today*, February 13, 2015).

In 2019, the Myanmar government issued a security license to Frontier Services Group, formerly known as Blackwater, whose business in Myanmar mainly provides security and logistics services to investors from Japan, China, and Thailand in Myanmar (*AFP*, March 21, 2019). In addition, according to Article 90 of the 2016 Myanmar Investment Law, the Myanmar government has the authority to command and manage private security companies in emergencies to maintain stability (Myanmar Investment Law 2016).

Phase Three (2021-Present): Stable Alliance

In terms of national stability, Myanmar's political situation is in a state of continuous turmoil. In the early morning of February 1, 2021, the Tatmadaw overthrew the National League for Democracy government that won the election in the 2020 parliamentary elections in Myanmar. A few hours after the coup, the Tatmadaw declared that Myanmar had entered a one-year state of emergency, and said that power had been transferred to Min Aung Hlaing, the commander-in-chief of the Tatmadaw. At the same time, the State Counselor Aung San Suu Kyi, President Win Myint, members of the central government cabinet, and leaders of 14 provinces and states (*BBC News*, April 1, 2021) were arrested.

Subsequently, protests against the military coup broke out throughout Myanmar, and the Myanmar military used direct shooting and other means to suppress the protests against the protesters. The government has also strengthened its control over the media. During the period from February to September 2021 after the military coup, 9 media institutions relocated from the country and another 9 media moved to ethnic minority armed control areas. Eight media organizations have had their licenses revoked, and over 100 journalists have been detained (*Myanmar Centre for Responsible Business*, Febuary, 2022).

The National Unity Government of Myanmar, formed by the Democratic League and elites from various ethnic political parties, serves as a "parallel government" to resist the rule of the military government and officially declared war on the military government on September 7, 2021. Armed conflicts have occurred in several provinces of Myanmar, including PDF (People's Defense Forces), KIA (Kachin Independence Army), KNU (Karen National Union), and other national armed forces cooperated with the unity governments (*The Washington Post*, September 7, 2021).

In addition, after nearly a decade of democratic practice, the level of political participation of Burmese citizens has significantly improved. Some supporters of the Democratic League government have expressed their dissatisfaction with the military government through strikes. Affected by the epidemic and armed conflict, Economy of Myanmar's economy is not strong, and a large number of unemployed people have begun to express their interests. In short, although the Burmese military overthrew the democratically elected government, its ruling foundation is not stable, the military government's control over society is limited, and it has brought about a series of humanitarian problems. For the ruling military government, when its strength is limited, the adaptability of sharing security sovereignty has increased, and it also holds a high tolerance towards private security companies participating in maintaining domestic order.

In terms of international structural pressure, the international community's response to the Myanmar coup has been mixed. Among them, Western countries such as the United States and Europe strongly condemned and reacted fiercely. China, Russia, India, and other countries emphasize the need to end the bloody conflict as soon as possible and call for a negotiated solution to the problem. The United Nations, as well as international and regional organizations such as ASEAN, hold a wait-and-see attitude. Specifically, the Myanmar Bureau of the United Nations International Cooperation and Coordination Agency stated after the coup, stating that the sudden changes in Myanmar's political situation were internal affairs of sovereign countries and calling for the peaceful resolution of differences through dialogue to avoid violence and internal strife (UN International Collaboration and Coordination Agency 2021).

On April 24, 2021, ASEAN leaders and Myanmar military leader Min Aung Hlaing reached a five-point consensus at the ASEAN Leaders' Special Meeting on Myanmar, which includes the need for all parties to immediately stop violent activities and exercise maximum restraint; All parties should engage in constructive dialogue, starting from the interests of the people, and seek peaceful solutions to problems; The special envoy of the ASEAN (rotating) presidency should promote the dialogue process with the assistance of the ASEAN Secretary-General; ASEAN should provide humanitarian assistance through the ASEAN Disaster Management Humanitarian Assistance Coordination Center; ASEAN envoys and delegations should visit Myanmar and hold meetings with relevant parties (ASEAN Secretariat 2021).

However, the consensus has not yet been implemented, resulting in Myanmar's military government leader Min Aung Hlaing not being invited to participate in the ASEAN summit in 2021 and 2022 for two consecutive years. After the coup, China expressed its hope that all parties in Myanmar can properly handle their differences within the constitutional and legal framework, and maintain political and social stability (*Xinhuanet*, February 1, 2021).

Afterward, at a meeting of the United Nations Security Council for internal consultations on the situation in Myanmar, China further stated that the international community should create a good external environment for properly handling the Myanmar issue, and Security Council resolutions should avoid exacerbating conflicts and further complicating the situation (*Xinhuanet*, February 3, 2021). It can be seen that China does not interfere in Myanmar's internal affairs, and at the same time does not want external forces to interfere in the situation in Myanmar, to avoid the escalation of conflicts as much as possible. China is an important external investor in Myanmar, and the stability of Myanmar is in China's interest.

Unlike the flexible positions of the aforementioned parties, Europe and the United States have a more hawkish attitude towards the Myanmar coup. After the coup, the United States condemned it. Afterward, the US government officially recognized a military coup in Myanmar and began imposing sanctions on military leaders, mainly including visa bans and asset freezes, while suspending some aid to Myanmar (Dietz&Hammond 2021).

By February 2023, the United States had sanctioned 80 individuals and 32 entities in Myanmar in an attempt to cut off the source of resources for the military government of Myanmar to commit violence. In addition, the United States continued to provide important Humanitarian aid to the people of Myanmar and strongly supported the pro-democracy movement in Myanmar (Blinken 2023). In general, Myanmar is faced with high external structural pressure, especially under the adverse background of the COVID-19 crisis, the Russia-Ukraine conflict, the game between China and the United States, and many other major countries, Myanmar's external support has significantly decreased, which seriously affects its national functions, and its demand for security interests is high.

In terms of the interaction between the state and private security companies, during this period, the government had a high demand for security interests, but its capabilities were insufficient to cope. Utilizing private security companies to maintain domestic order became one of the more reliable choices. Private security companies had greater autonomy and shared the sovereignty of security governance with the state.

For example, a research report released by the Myanmar Centre for Responsible Business pointed out that since the military took over power on February 1, 2021, there has been an increase in safety risks for workers, customers, and communities related to the private security industry, due to increased interaction between private security companies and the public safety department, The military government relies heavily on private security companies to jointly maintain the stability of the domestic political situation (*Myanmar Centre for Responsible Business*, Febuary, 2022).

Cambodia

Phase One (1991-2005): Potential Alliance

In October 1991, the four parties involved in the Cambodian conflict signed the 1991 Paris Peace Agreements in Paris, under which Cambodia began the process of national reconciliation (The United Nations 1991). In 1993, under the auspices and supervision of the United Nations, Cambodia held its first national election. The FUNCINPEC became the largest party in the National Assembly, and the People's Party led by Hun Sen became the second largest party. To coordinate the power competition between the two parties, Cambodia implements a dual prime minister system, with Norodom Ranariddh as the first prime minister of the Royal Government of Cambodia and Hun Sen as the second prime minister.

In 1997, the conflict between Hun Sen and Ranariddh intensified, and the two sides engaged in military warfare, forcing Ranariddh to step down and flee overseas. In 1998, Ranariddh returned to Cambodia to shake hands with Hun Sen and form a coalition government. In 2004, in the third national election, the People's Party and the FUNCINPEC compromised after a year of deadlock. Hun Sen and Ranariddh continued to serve as the Prime Minister and the President of the National Assembly respectively, and the bipartisan coalition government was re-established. It can be said that the stability of Cambodia's political situation and the legitimacy of Hun Sen's government during this period mainly depended on the relationship between the People's Party and the FUNCINPEC because the latter has a broad political foundation in Cambodia. As Hun Sen gradually took control of the Cambodian political situation, he also took various measures to strengthen social control. To maintain social order, the Royal Government led by Hun Sen established the Cambodian National Arms and Explosives Improvement Management Committee and began nationwide activities to collect and destroy illegal weapons at the end of 1998 (Wille 2006).

The Hun Sen government also attaches great importance to the reorganization of the military and disarmament. In November 1998, the People's Party and the FUNCINPEC reached an agreement that the armed forces of the two parties were reunited into a unified government army, and more than 30000 people were successively disarmed after 2000 (Whalan 2012). In addition, the Hun Sen government also focuses on legal construction and has formulated multiple laws to safeguard social stability and economic development. On the whole, at this stage, Cambodia is still in the initial stage of State-building, and the degree of national stability is not high.

In 1992, the United Nations Transitional Authority in Cambodia began post-war reconstruction work, and the United Nations dispatched 22000 staff, spending nearly 2.8 billion US dollars to help Cambodia implement the peace agreement (Abuza 1995). After the signing of the 1991 Paris Peace Agreements,

18 countries and some international institutions pledged to assist Cambodia in its reconstruction. But Cambodia must accept the supervision of donor countries and the dialogue meeting between donor countries and Cambodia is held once a year. During the two annual meetings, the Cambodian government is required to report to donor countries and receive inquiries every three months. Afterward, countries such as the United States, the European Union, and Japan (international organizations) provided economic and humanitarian assistance to Cambodia, with a large number of non-governmental organizations operating in Cambodia.

In 1997, the Cambodian Civil War did not break the contract policy of European and American countries with Hun Sen's government. In addition, Cambodia actively participates in regional and global organizations. On April 30, 1999, Cambodia joined ASEAN and became the 10th member state of ASEAN. Afterward, Cambodia actively participated in the political cooperation mechanism and economic integration process of ASEAN and continuously strengthened its ties with ASEAN countries.

In 1994, Cambodia applied to join the WTO. On April 18, 2003, it completed the task of multilateral negotiations at the WTO held in Geneva, Switzerland, and was officially admitted as a member of the WTO in September 2003 (Hill&Menon 2014). Overall, during this period, Cambodia actively introduced international norms, at least superficially following the values and requirements of European and American countries in terms of democracy, human rights, and other aspects, and established relatively good relations with the international community, with less pressure on the international structure.

In terms of the interaction between the state and private security companies, during this period, the Cambodian government held an open attitude towards private security companies, recognizing their role as auxiliary law enforcement agencies. In 1995, MPA INTERNATIONAL LTD. was founded as the first legitimate private security company in Cambodia (Muller 2023).

In the event of an emergency, private security companies have the right to participate in emergency response. For example, in a public Procession, private security companies cooperated with the police to suppress strikers and maintain order and stability (ICG Asia Report 2000). In other words, Cambodian private security companies have greater autonomy when Cambodian officials share security sovereignty with high adaptability and low demand for security interests, and the country is willing to form alliances with private security companies when necessary.

Phase Two (2005-2015): Unable to Ally

After the new century, the FUNCINPEC gradually split and declined, and the People's Party's one-party dominance trend became increasingly evident. The Cambodian People's Party led by Hun Sen has won successive general elections in Cambodia, forming a political structure dominated by one party. In the fourth Cambodian national election in 2008, the People's Party won 90 parliamentary seats (Giry 2015). However, with the rise of the National Rescue Party (CNRP) formed by the opposition Sam Rainsy Party and the Human Rights Party in the 2013 general election, Cambodian domestic politics has entered into a partisan dispute in election issues. In 2013, the CNRP led by Sam Rainsy won 55 of the 123 parliamentary seats, only 13 behind the People's Party, which won 68 seats, and became the largest opposition party in Cambodia in one fell swoop (*Reuters*, August 12, 2013).

Since then, the CNRP led by Sam Rainsy has launched hundreds of large-scale demonstrations with tens of thousands of people, which has brought enormous pressure to the Hun Sen government, but it has never changed the pattern that People's Party as the dominant force in Cambodian politics. On the one hand, the Hun Sen government is seeking domestic and foreign support, and on the other hand, it has stepped up the pace of domestic political and economic reforms to enhance the government's ruling legitimacy. For example, on April 17, 2010, Cambodia's first Anti-Corruption Law was voted by the National Assembly, marking a major progress in the Cambodian government's legal basis for combating corruption (Sihamoni 2010). In short, during this period, the People's Party led by Hun Sen dominated the political situation in Cambodia, and the country was relatively stable.

In terms of international structural pressure. During this period, the policy of the US towards Cambodia has undergone adjustment and reconstruction. Beginning in 2006, the US began to restore military ties and direct economic assistance to Cambodia, and the US Peace Corps also returned to Cambodia. In the first term of the Obama administration, the average annual aid amount was US$95.5 million; in the second term, the average annual aid amount was US$121 million (*Open Development Cambodia*, June 1, 2020). In January 2006, the new US embassy in Phnom Penh was completed, and US Assistant Secretary of State Hill and former President Clinton visited Cambodia successively. In November 2010 and July 2012, US Secretary of State Hillary Clinton visited Cambodia twice. In November 2012, US President visited Cambodia to participate in the East Asia Summit (EAS). The United States attaches great importance to Cambodia, which has something to do with the United States' return to the Asia-Pacific to balance China's influence.

China has been maintaining its influence over Cambodia in the political and economic spheres. In 2009, China became the largest investor in Cambodia, and provided Cambodia with 1.2 billion US dollars of non-refundable aid and preferential loans, becoming Cambodia's largest aid country (*Foreign Policy*, December 22, 2009). Cambodia is very important to China, especially its geopolitics in the South China Sea and the Greater Mekong Subregion. In terms of foreign relations, Cambodia has gradually become a "geo-leverage" stage for external political power games.

As for ASEAN again, Cambodia is also actively carrying out multilateral and bilateral cooperation with ASEAN countries to promote the construction of the ASEAN community. In 2012, Cambodia served as the rotating chair of ASEAN and successfully hosted the 21st ASEAN Summit. In addition, Cambodia is also actively developing economic, trade and political relations with Japan, the European Union, India and other countries. In short, during this period, Cambodia implemented a foreign policy of balance between major powers, maintained friendly relations with major world powers, and had less external structural pressure.

As far as the interaction between the state and private security companies is concerned, during this period, the growing national capacity of the Cambodian government has reduced its adaptability to sharing security sovereignty. At the same time, Cambodia has positive interactions with the international community. Major European and American countries, as well as China and Japan, are committed to strengthening ties with Cambodia, and the demand for security interests is relatively low. The Cambodian government adopts a policy of strict supervision of private security companies. In 2013, the Royal Government of Cambodia promulgated Sub-Decree No. 289, stipulating the rules and regulations for the establishment of private security companies. The decree stipulates that the Ministry of the Interior, assisted by the National Police Directorate, is appointed to control and manage these private security companies. A company can only be licensed by the Ministry of the Interior after it has been officially registered with the Ministry of Commerce. In addition, a letter of permission from the local administration is required when appointing a guard or security officer (Chhay & Wee 2013).

Phase Three (2015-present): Unstable Alliance

In terms of national stability, although the Hun Sen government still dominates, it faces many internal challenges. The opposition party, the National Rescue Party, has emerged, especially in rural areas, continuously eroding the influence of the People's Party. The National Rescue Party often incites the masses to organize large-scale Procession against the ruling party's rule. In June 2017, Cambodia held township and district grassroots council elections, and the gap in the number of grassroots council members won by the two parties narrowed, indicating the expansion of the influence of the Rescue Party (*The Phnom Penh Post*, June 5, 2017).

In addition, because the Internet, media, and non-governmental organizations have not been effectively managed for a long time, the Western "liberal democracy" ideology has become popular among the Cambodian people, and the people's sense of resistance has increased. Firstly, the rapid growth of non-governmental organizations has played an increasingly important role in Cambodia's development process and has had a significant impact on government decision-making, social development, and civil society formation in Cambodia. Secondly, a large number of youth groups began to participate in politics, changing the traditional pattern of particracy in Cambodia. Finally, social media has narrowed the distance between political parties and voters, playing an important role in Politics of Cambodia's politics. Faced with a series of challenges, the Hun Sen government has also proposed many countermeasures.

On September 3, 2017, Kem Sokha, chairman of the National Rescue Party, was arrested on suspicion of treason. On November 16, the Cambodian authorities dissolved the Cambodian opposition National Rescue Party and banned 118 members of the party from participating in politics for five years. Secondly, the Hun Sen government began actively using social media to interact with netizens, explaining policy concepts and clarifying policy implementation (*AP News*, March 28, 2022). Finally, the People's Party strengthened its control over non-governmental organizations and media, such as shutting down the domestic English language media The Cambodia Daily, revoking the licenses of several independent radio stations, and closing non-governmental organizations such as the National Democratic Institute (NDI) associated with the United States (*The Phnom Penh Post*, February 2, 2015). In short, during this period, the ruling party faced many challenges, but Hun Sen remained firmly in control of the regime.

In terms of international structure, there were some twists and turns in the interaction between Cambodia and the international community during this period. In 2017, the relationship between Cambodia and the United States rapidly declined. On January 17th, Cambodia unilaterally canceled the 2017 "Angkor Sentinel" Cambodia-US joint exercise. The Cambodian government has also filed a complaint with the United Nations, demanding that the chemical bombs left by the United States in Cambodia during the Cold War be resolved following the Chemical Weapons Act. In April, the Cambodian government terminated a US Navy Military aid project that had been implemented for nine consecutive years.

After Cambodia National Rescue Party was disbanded and its leader Kem Sokha was arrested on suspicion of treason, the United States implemented a series of sanctions against Cambodia. On September 13, the United States announced that it would stop issuing business and travel visas to officials and family members at or above the level of the Director General of the Ministry of Foreign Affairs of Cambodia, stop some aid to Cambodia, and threatened to reassess preferential tariffs on Cambodian imports. The Cambodian side retaliated and immediately announced the cessation of cooperation with the United States to search for the remains of American soldiers who died in Cambodia during the Vietnam

War, and the closure of pro-American media outlets (Heng 2022). On July 29, 2018, Cambodia held its sixth parliamentary election, and the People's Party led by Hun Sen won a majority of seats. Hun Sen was re-elected as Prime Minister, but the United States refused to recognize the election results.

At the same time, the EU accused the Hun Sen government of "human rights", "democracy", and "freedom", and even threatened to interrupt aid. In contrast, China and Japan have less involvement in Cambodia's internal affairs, and their cooperation has maintained stable development. In 2017, the total bilateral trade between Cambodia and China reached 5.8 billion US dollars, an increase of 22% compared to the previous year (*Xinhuanet*, June 21, 2018). In 2016, Japan's investment in Cambodia reached as high as 0.822 billion US dollars, making it the second largest investor after China (*Fresh News*, August 21, 2019). In short, during this period, Cambodia faced significant international structural pressure.

In terms of the interaction between the state and private security companies, during this period, the ruling authorities in Cambodia regarded private security companies as supplementary force in security governance. According to statistics, out of 49 foreign private security companies in Cambodia and Myanmar, 24 belong to China (Zheng 2021). Private security companies in Cambodia must be registered with the National Police. According to a sub-decree on private security management, noncompliant business, and institutional owners may be fined 10 million Riels ($2500), and security companies that hire guards without registration with the Ministry of the Interior may be fined 20 million Riels ($5000) (*Khmer Times*, September 7, 2022). In addition, the Cambodian police department emphasizes the importance of private security in assisting the police in protecting and maintaining safety and public order but does not allow any company or enterprise to hire foreigners as security personnel (*Cambodianess*, May 1, 2019).

This indicates that the Cambodian government has recognized the role of private security companies in maintaining stability, but on the other hand, it also hopes that private security companies can recruit more Cambodians, which can not only attract employment but also help constrain the illegal and irregular behavior of private security companies.

For example, the Department National Police chief claims that private security companies are the backup force of the police, and private security personnel should strengthen cooperation with the resident police and local authorities. When illegal or criminal activities are discovered, they should immediately report to the authorities (*The Phnom Penh Post*, July 29, 2022). Of course, with the easing of international structural pressure, Cambodia's demand for security interests will decrease, and the government can maintain national stability through its efforts. The dependence on private security companies will also decrease accordingly.

DISCUSSION

We discuss the interaction between national sovereignty and private security companies from two aspects. From the perspective of adaptability to shared security sovereignty, although Myanmar's military government has always been in a dominant position, domestic opposition forces and local minority groups have long been in a state of confrontation with the military government. National stability has become the primary concern of the ruling authorities, and the overall adaptability of the country to shared security sovereignty is relatively high; Cambodia is led by the Hun Sen government, but Hun Sen is willing to share power with the opposition, and there is a certain consensus among various forces, which is conducive to promoting various reforms of the country. The overall adaptability of the country to shared security sovereignty is on the decline.

	Myanmar	Cambodia
International Structural Pressure	Overall Larger	Overall Smaller
Domestic Stability	Lower and Lower	Higher and Higher
The Need for Security Benefits	Bigger	Smaller
Adaptability of Shared Security Sovereignty	Higher and Higher	Lower and Lower
State Attitudes towards Private Security Companies	High Tolerance	Less Inclusive
Autonomy of Private Security Companies	Overall Higher	Overall Lower

From the perspective of the demand for security interests, European and American countries are the largest External variable of Myanmar and Cambodia. At the same time, ASEAN and China have played an important hedging role, easing the international pressure faced by the two countries. However, overall, the Burmese military government does not allow external forces to threaten its decisive role in Myanmar, and is more resistant to the standardized localization practices implemented by European and American countries, resulting in its continued high structural pressure; Cambodia, on the other hand, began a process of national transformation on the ruins, with a high tolerance for international norms by a national authority. The structural pressure faced by the Hun Sen government has always been relatively low.

From the above two aspects, we can find that the interaction between national sovereignty and private security companies has a lot to do with the ability of national authority and its view on its role in State-building. When the state has strong authority and is not inclusive to the outside world, the ruling authorities are more inclined to not accept the normative construction imposed by both internal and external factors.

However, to maintain the stability of the domestic political situation, they have to disembedding national security and establish a relatively stable alliance with private security companies. Myanmar is an example of this situation. When the national authority is weak and has a high degree of inclusivity towards the outside world, the ruling authorities are willing to accept the construction of internal and external norms under certain conditions and are also willing to entrust national security to private security companies. However, as they gradually establish a stable national authority, the ruling authorities will gradually restrict the autonomy of private security companies to demonstrate that the state is still the owner of monopolistic violence, and Cambodia is an example of this situation.

In summary, the interaction between Myanmar, Cambodia, and private security companies is closely related to international structural pressure, domestic stability, and the country's demand for security interests. As shown in the following table:

CONCLUSION

By comparing the interaction process between national sovereignty and private security companies in Myanmar and Cambodia, we found that the adaptability of shared security sovereignty and the demand for security interests by the state largely determine how the state can disembed its security and delegate it to private security companies. In general, both Myanmar and Cambodia, as countries in transition that have not yet completed State-building, rely heavily on private security companies. However, the difference is that Myanmar's private security companies are becoming more and more autonomous, while Cambodia's private security companies are becoming less and less autonomous. The reason is that Cambodia's elite, represented by Hun Sen, is good at compromise at home, which has safeguarded national stability to the greatest extent, expanded opening up to the outside world, focused on establishing friendly and cooperative relations with many major countries, and has opened up Cambodia's international Lebensraum to the greatest extent.

In this case, Cambodia has built a "benevolent authoritarian" government, whose people have a high degree of acceptance of the government, and the government's ability to control society has gradually increased. In contrast, Myanmar has been condemned by the international community for its domestic minority issues. Strong local forces threaten the central authority, and the military government has limited control over society. Therefore, Myanmar has always been highly dependent on private security companies and is willing to share security sovereignty with private security companies.

We believe that both Myanmar and Cambodia indicate that the transition countries that have not yet completed the State-building are forced to deal with security disembedding. Once a solid national authority is established and meets the needs of international norms, the state tends to monopolize security supply, rather than allowing private security companies to share security sovereignty, this is fundamentally different from the top-down security privatization process guided by the concept of neoliberalism in countries such as Europe and America. What Southeast Asian countries need to do is, on the one hand, to actively rely on private security companies to meet security needs, thereby improving national survival security and State-building; on the other hand, to strictly supervise private security companies to prevent their illegal acts from damaging national authority.

REFERENCES

Abrahamsen, R., & Williams, M. (2005). *The Globalisation of Private Security: Country Report: Sierra Leone*. University of Wales. https://users.aber.ac.uk/rbh/privatesecurity/country%20report-sierra%20leone.pdf,

Abuza, Z. (1995). *Cambodia: The Legacy and Lessons of UNTAC*. Oxford University Press.

AFP. (2019). *Former Blackwater contractor in Myanmar security venture*. France24. https://www.france24.com/en/20190321-former-blackwater-contractor-myanmar-security-venture

AP News Staff. (2022). Cambodian leader says officials must master mobile internet. *AP News*. (https://apnews.com/article/technology-media-social-media-smartphones-cambodia-b19df581b637fe72d-366d24c9db3cf23

BBC News Staff. (2011). *Aung San Suu Kyi makes the first trip since her release*. BBC. https://www.bbc.com/news/world- Asia-pacific-14011850

BBC News Staff. (2012). *Burma abolishes media censorship*. BBC. https://www.bbc.com/news/world-asia-19315806

BBC News Staff. (2012). *Burma government signs ceasefire with Karen rebels*. BBC. https://www.bbc.com/news/world-asia-16523691

Blinken, A. J. (2023). *Marking Two Years Since the Military Coup in Burma*. U.S. Department of State. https://www.state.gov/marking-two-years-since-the-military-coup-in-burma/

Business & Human Rights Resource Centre. (2015). *Myanmar: Growing use of private security firms to guard businesses gives rise to rights concerns*. Business and Human Rights Resource Center. https://www.business-humanrights.org/en/latest-news/myanmar-growing-use-of-private-security-firms-to-guard-businesses-gives-rise-to-rights-concerns/

Cambodian Chinese Network. (2022). *Cambodian National Police: Private security needs to work closely with the police to fight crime*. CCN. https://www.boyoushe.com/65881.html,

Cambodianess. (2019). *National Police says won't allow the employment of foreigners in private security*. Cambodianess. https://cambodianess.com/article/national-police-says-wont-allow-employment-of-foreigners-in-private-security

Chesterman, S., & Lehnardt, C. (2007). *From Mercenaries to Market: The Rise and Regulation of Private Military Companies*. Oxford University Press. doi:10.1093/acprof:oso/9780199228485.001.0001

Chhay, H., & Wee, D. (2013). Sub-Decree No. 289 on private security management. *Lexology*. https://www.lexology.com/library/detail.aspx?g=99c6cf06-c361-478d-ba28-0930bb17165b

Cuddy, A. (2021). Myanmar coup: What is happening and why? *BBC News*. https://www.burmalibrary.org/sites/burmalibrary.org/files/obl/2021-04-01-Myanmar-coup-BBC-en-red.pdf,

Dietz, K., & Hammond, C. (2021). Three months on from the military coup, what should the international community do to support the people of Myanmar? *Global Witness*.

Egreteau, R. (2008). India and China Vying for Influence in Burma – A New Assessment. *India Review*, *7*(1), 38–72. doi:10.1080/14736480801901170

European Commission. (2004). *The EU's relations with Burma / Myanmar*. EC. https://www.europarl.europa.eu/meetdocs/2004_2009/documents/fd/dase20050419_003/dase20050419_003en.pdf

Executive Office of the President. (2016). *Termination of Emergency Concerning the Actions and Policies of the Government of Burma*. Federal Register. https://www.federalregister.gov/documents/2016/10/12/2016-24847/termination-of-emergency-with-respect-to-the-actions-and-policies-of-the-government-of-burma

Ganesan, N. (2018). Taking Stock of Myanmar's Ethnic Peace Process and the Third Twenty-First Century Panglong Conference. *Asian Journal of Peacebuilding*, *6*(2), 379–392. doi:10.18588/201811.00a072

Garmon, T. (2003). Domesticating International Corporate Responsibility: Holding Private Military Firms Accountable Under the Alien Tort Claims Act. *Tulane Journal International and Comparative Law, 11*, 325-354. https://heinonline.org/HOL/License

Giddens, A. (1981). Modernism and Post-Modernism. *New German Critique, NGC*, *22*(22), 15–18. doi:10.2307/487860

Giddens, A. (1999). Risk and Responsibility. *The Modern Law Review*, *62*(1), 1–10. https://courses.washington.edu/sales09/Handouts/Giddens_Risk_Responsibility.pdf. doi:10.1111/1468-2230.00188

Giry, S. (2015). Autopsy of a Cambodian Election: How Hun Sen Rules. *Foreign Affairs, 94*(5), 144–159. https://www.jstor.org/stable/24483746

Global Policy Forum. (2014). *Regulation and Oversight of PMSCs*. Global Policy Forum. https://archive.globalpolicy.org/pmscs/50211-regulation-and-oversight-of-pmscs.html

Hadar, L. T. (1998). U.S. Sanctions Against Burma: A Failure on All Fronts. *Cato Institute*. https://www.cato.org/trade-policy-analysis/us-sanctions-against-burma-failure-all-fronts

Hayes, J., & Weber, K. (2021). Globalization, deglobalization, and human security: The case of Myanmar. *International Affairs, 97*(5), 1469–1488. doi:10.1093/ia/iiab110

Heng, K. (2022. Mending Cambodia-US relations: A Cambodian Perspective. *Kyoto Review of Southeast Asia*. https://kyotoreview.org/issue-32/mending-cambodia-us-relations-a-cambodian-perspective/

Hill, H., & Menon, J. (2014). Cambodia: Rapid growth in an open, post-conflict economy. *World Economy, 37*(12), 1649–1668. doi:10.1111/twec.12206

Holm, E. (2019). *The NGO–state relationship and SRHR in Myanmar.* Department of Government, Uppsala University. https://www.diva-portal.org/smash/get/diva2:1299328/FULLTEXT01.pdf

Holmqvist, C. (2005). *Private Security Companies: The Case for Regulation*. SIPRI Policy Paper. http://www.guillaumenicaise.com/wp-content/uploads/2014/08/private-security-companies.pdf

Keating, J. (2009). China: We just gave Cambodia $1.2 billion because we're nice. *Foreign Policy*. https://foreignpolicy.com/2009/12/22/china-we-just-gave-cambodia-1-2-billion-because-were-nice/

Khmer Times. (2022). 4 Things to Consider Before Hiring a Security Company in Cambodia. *Khmer Times*. https://www.khmertimeskh.com/501146361/4-things-to-consider-before-hiring-a-security-company-in-cambodia/, accessed July 1, 2023.

Mahtani, S. (2021). Myanmar shadow government declares war on military junta, escalating crisis. *The Washington Post*. https://www.washingtonpost.com/world/asia_pacific/myanmar-military-war/2021/09/07/46c14ca2-0f93-11ec-baca-86b144fc8a2d_story.html

Muller, J. (2023). *Security Services Asia' Management*. SSA. http://www.securityservicesasia.com/security_services_asia_management_john_muller.htm,

Nebehay, S. (2020). *Trump's pardon of Blackwater Iraq contractors violates international law – UN.* Reuters. https://www.reuters.com/article/us-iraq-blackwater-un-idUSKBN294108,

Open Development Cambodia. (2020). *United States aid*. Open Development Cambodia. https://opendevelopmentcambodia.net/topics/united-states-aid/

Poggi, G. (1977). The Constitutional State of The Nineteenth Century: An Elementary Conceptual Portrait. *Sociology, 11*(2), 311–332. doi:10.1177/003803857701100204

Private Security Governance Observatory. (2009). *Mapping of National Private Security Sectors: regulation and overview: Sierra Leone*. Private Security Governance Observatory. https://observatoire-securite-privee.org/en/content/sierra-leone

Ryngaert, C. (2008). Litigating Abuses Committed by Private Military Companies. *European Journal of International Law*, *5*(19), 1035–1053. doi:10.1093/ejil/chn056

Schreier, F., & Caparini, M. (2005). *Privatising Security: Law, Practice, and Governance of Private Military and Security Companies,* Occasional Paper No.6, Geneva: The Democratic Control of Armed Forces. https://www.files.ethz.ch/isn/14077/occasional_6.pdf,.

Selth, A. (2008). Burma's 'saffron revolution and the limits of international influence. *Australian Journal of International Affairs*, *62*(3), 281–297. doi:10.1080/10357710802286742

Sihamoni, N. (2010). *Anti-Corruption Law Full Text*. CDC. https://cdc.gov.kh/wp-content/uploads/2022/05/ANTI-CORRUPTION-LAW-FULL-TEXT-.pdf

Sokheng, V., & Sokchea, M. (2015). CPP leadership sees an influx of new blood. *The Phnom Penh Post*. https://www.phnompenhpost.com/cpp-leadership-sees-influx-new-blood,

The United Nations. (1991). *Framework for a Comprehensive Political Settlement of the Cambodia Conflict*. UN. https://peacemaker.un.org/sites/peacemaker.un.org/files/KH_911023_FrameworkComprehensivePoliticalSettlementCambodia.pdf, accessed June 24, 2023.

The U.S. Embassy in Burma. (2016). *Treasury Implements Termination of Burma Sanctions Program.* U.S. Treasury Department Office of Public Affairs. https://mm.usembassy.gov/termination-burma-sanctions-program/

The White House. (2012). *President Obama Promises Support for the People of Burma*. The White House. https://obamawhitehouse.archives.gov/blog/2012/11/19/president-obama-promises-support-people-burma

Thul, P. C. (2013). *Cambodia election crisis deepens as opposition rejects results*. Reuters. https://www.reuters.com/article/us-cambodia-election-count-idUSBRE97B02I20130812

Trihartono, A. (2018). *Myanmar's Worsening Rohingya Crisis: A Call for Responsibility to Protect and ASEAN's Response. Sustainable Future for Human Security*. Springer. doi:10.1007/978-981-10-5433-4_1

UN International Collaboration and Coordination Agency. (2021). *A solemn statement on the situation in Myanmar by the Myanmar Bureau of the United Nations International Collaboration and Coordination Agency*. UN.

Weber, M. (1964). *The Theory of Social and Economic Organization*. Free Press.

Whalan, J. (2012). Evaluating peace operations: The case of Cambodia. *Journal of International Peacekeeping*, *16*(3-4), 226–251. doi:10.1163/18754112-1604003

Wille, C. (2006). *How many weapons are there in Cambodia?* Graduate Institute of International Studies. https://citeseerx.ist.psu.edu/document?repid=rep1&type=pdf&doi=eb4d6814f92bf11c5748e63381db7e719cf070fb

Xinhuanet. (2018). *Cambodia-China trade volume jumps to 5.8 bln USD last year: minister*. Xinhuanet. http://www.xinhuanet.com/english/2018-06/21/c_137270877.htm,

Xinhuanet. (2021). *Ministry of Foreign Affairs: China hopes that all parties in Myanmar will properly handle differences and maintain political and social stability*. Xinhuanet. http://www.xinhuanet.com/2021-02/01/c_1127050935.htm

Xinhuanet. (2021). *Ministry of Foreign Affairs: The international community should create a favorable external environment for Myanmar to properly resolve differences*. Xinhuanet. http://www.xinhuanet.com/world/2021-02/03/c_1127060947.htm,

Zhang, J. (2015). Study of Law and Regulation on the Overseas Business Development of Chinese Security Companies. *Journal of Chongqing University*, *21*(2), 116–121.

Zheng, S. (2021). *China turns to unregulated private security firms to protect interests along the Mekong*. SCMP. https://www.scmp.com/news/china/diplomacy/article/3138628/china-turns-unregulated-private-security-firms-protect

Chapter 20
The European Union Development Policy and Achieving Sustainable Development Goals (SDGs) of the United Nations

Mukesh Shankar Bharti
https://orcid.org/0000-0002-3693-7247
Jawaharlal Nehru University, India

ABSTRACT

The purpose of this study is to describe the European Union's (EU) developing approach and governance in the implementation of the sustainable development agenda of the United Nations (UN). UN's sustainable development goals are more vibrant to maintain peace and stability in the world. The EU's Global Gateway and Asia-Europe connectivity programme are supporting other nations to work on the SDGs. As a regional organisation, the EU shows enormous intention to eliminate poverty, malnutrition and famine, establish peace, respect for human rights and minority rights, and maintain global warming, biodiversity and the climate. Moreover, the EU also formed bilateral and multilateral level cooperation across the world for the establishment of democratic rule, peace, and prosperity. The EU's policy formulation keeps working on economic, social, and environmental development issues at the global level and supporting the UN mission across the world in different sectors. This research is based on qualitative analysis using primary and secondary literature. In addition, this study also uses the empirical method to discuss the main research gaps and answer major questions related to the SDGs. As a result, the EU has started significant work to achieve the objectives of the SDGs of the UN. The EU has also launched various development programs for the implementation of the SDGs in its member states. In conclusion, the EU's other institutions have been providing funds in different sectors in the Asian, African, Latin American, and Pacific countries under the SDGs.

DOI: 10.4018/979-8-3693-1742-6.ch020

INTRODUCTION

The SDGs were established by the UN General Assembly in September 2015 and the global community supported this initiative which is part of the United Nations (UN) 2030 Agenda. The UN's SDGs agenda is associated with poverty alleviation, protecting the planet, and inclusive human development with sustainable solutions. The world communities collectively pledged to poverty eradication and malnutrition across the world. The prime objective of this agenda is to ensure every person's human rights and other social development by 2030. The EU as a regional organisation had started work on the SDGs with like-minded global partners. The EU also initiated bilateral, trilateral, quadrilateral and multilateral partnerships with its global partners to achieve success in the area of development and well-being of people around the world. The agenda of the SDGs is a top priority of the EU from design to proper implementation. EU Member States have also enthusiastically participated in the implementation of the EU agenda and have led donors to accelerate the SDGs programmes. The EU and its twenty-eight members are key donors of official development assistance (ODA) at the global level (European Commission, n.d.-c).

The EU has initiated a positive and constructive contribution to developing countries for a complete transformation in the field of social prosperity, human support, education & and health, political reformation and economic development within the framework of the UN 2030 agenda. The 17 principal areas are found and encouraged to work together by the world community. These sectors are involved in completing a social revolution to make the balance between people and different governments for environmental sustainability, end poverty, fight against starvation, social justice, and work for the removal of gender discrimination. The EU and its Member States always show enormous interest in supporting inside and outside the EU, therefore, the EU's policies gain mileage in the comparison of other economies in the continent of Africa, Asia, Latin America and the Pacific region as well. The EU Member States work towards developing countries of the world with as shared vision (Prada, 2013). The concept of sustainable development is associated with the EU's Treaties and it has been the central policy for a long time for social and economic development.

The EU has a broad range of developing program for developing countries and its policy fosters the settlement of proper democratic institutions, sustainable development, social awareness and stability, with the ultimate goal of poverty eradication. The EU has also been providing funds under projects for the betterment of the education system and the improvement of health facilities in developing countries. Which is the key component of the UN's 17-point agenda of sustainable development. The EU's key external pillar is development assistance to the suffering countries worldwide under the EU's different treaties, alongside security support, infrastructural development programmes, and the establishment of education and health institutions (European Commission, n.d.-a). The EU development policy is based on easing human life in the world and has been successfully implemented in Europe for a long time.

Theoretical Background and Literature Review

The theory of development is explained according to Amartya Sen, who has provided paths for a broader range of development with a deeper interpretation of the underdeveloped regions of the world through a capabilities approach. Sen's development theory broadly discusses the concept of development in the context of human capital and social capital (Bali Swain & Yang-Wallentin, 2020; Sen, 2001, 2010). There is current literature that defines Sustainable Development is helpful as the elimination of social disparity and talks about inclusive growth. Many literatures also praise the well-being of the society at a global level to solve the socio-economic problems. The UN development policy seems to provide all kinds of help to the people of the developing world. It is also focuses on the need for developed countries to start working with a constructive approach in developing countries' betterment with social harmony (Arrow et al., 2012). The SDGs have multiple kinds of development targets across world, these targets don't have clear priorities and the theoretical approach is unable to assess the proper goal of the world community (Swain, 2018). The SDGs of the UN focus on the main five sectors: Prosperity, People, Peace, Planet, and Partnerships are core areas of cooperation under this policy of the UN (Szymańska & Zalewska, 2021).

Modernization theory encourages the development process, which is a ladder metaphor to frame the transformation to achieve the ultimate development agenda. This is a conceptual framework of development in terms of poverty alleviation and aims to achieve sustainable development in developing countries. In this context, the EU has been continuously working within and outside its Member States to the implementation of the UN's development agenda (Weber, 2017). Organizational theory is deeply elaborated in global governance that has paved the way for sustainable development. This theoretical debate further discusses that there is a nexus between global players for geopolitical stability and competition to grab more partner countries across the world. The new liberal world order has also provided geostrategic competition and in the name of development and establishing peace and prosperity, major global players have established themselves as strongholds in developing countries. This is the right justification for organizational theory, the EU Member States together working under a constructive policy for the achievement of the UN's Sustainable Development Agenda of 2030 (Bexell & Jönsson, 2019). In the theoretical debate, policy formulation is a key instrument to meet the criteria of any type of development that is adequate for the eradication of poverty and social disparity.

(Rahimifard & Trollman, 2018) describe how the UN has been accelerating global peace and cooperation in solving social problems worldwide to eradicate economic disparity, illiteracy, and disputes between countries, and ultimate goals are the establishment of social harmony, institutional development, democratic institutions, and social justice. These are also core values of the EU in Europe which has been working since the establishment of the European Steel and Coal Community in 1951. In October 2016, during the UN-HABITAT 3rd Conference in Quito (Japan) initiated the formation of the New Urban Agenda (NUA). The UN's key concept is related to global sustainability and resilience for a better tomorrow with a common future. In this connection, the EU seems to work inside the Member States and the continental level as well (Agyeman, 2020). Prominent leaders around the world have been supporting appropriate United Nations frameworks for the elimination of poverty and the well-being of people in developing countries and regional development under the SDGs (Immler & Sakkers, 2022).

The EU is working to maintain environmental issues, which is also the key focus of the United Nations 2030 SDGs Agenda. Thus, the increasing cases of health-related problems have been spreading rapidly due to the changing nature of environmental issues and the need to maintain Biodiversity is important for human life. The UN is concerned about global warming and its effect on nature and natural disasters around the world (Udeagha & Ngepah, 2023). Since 2015, the EU has been continuously working towards the UN SDGs and its Member States have been implementing the union's goals. Before 2015, EU countries were suffering from an economic crisis due to the recession that began in 2007-2008. Despite the economic crisis in Europe, the EU and its Member States have been enthusiastic in working on the United Nations Sustainable Development Agenda for 2030 (Gracia-de-Rentería et al., 2023; Lafortune et al., 2021). The Paris Climate Agreement has also paved the way for more sustainable development with a high rate of growth mainly in three sectors, i.e., economic, social and environmental. In this context, the EU Member States from Central and Eastern Europe (CEE) have also been implementing the EU norms for regional development. Thus, the EU has been focusing on better infrastructure development in the developing world to meet the UN's Sustainable Development Agenda of 2030. Moreover, they have been aware of reformation in healthcare, decent job opportunities for the young generation, and provision to get higher education for early bird meritorious students (M. S. Bharti, 2023b, 2023d; M. S. Bharti & Bharti, 2022).

Methods and Data

The empirical analysis is part of this study and is based on qualitatively discussing the research problems. This chapter utilises the techniques and methods of an empirical analysis using search results with suitable objectives which is related to the United Nations' Sustainable Development Goals (SDGs). The approach mentioned involves constructing aggregate indicators calculated as the simple average of normalized indicators to measure progress in SDGs, both collectively and individually. This study is aimed at analysing patterns in sustainable development across 28 European Union (EU) Member States from 2011 to 2023. The study involves monitoring the progress of several indicators categorised under economic, social, and environmental dimensions. The three main objectives of the research are:

Evaluate Sustainable Development Progress and Regional Differences

The first objective involves assessing the direction and magnitude of sustainable development progress in the selected EU Member States. Additionally, the study aims to explore potential variations or differences in sustainable development among different European regions.

Investigate Dynamics of SDGs

The second objective is to delve into the dynamics of the Sustainable Development Goals (SDGs) over the specified time period. This likely involves analysing trends, fluctuations, or shifts in the performance of the several indicators related to economic, social, and environmental aspects.

Explore Differences Among Sustainability Dimensions

The third objective is to explore potential variations among the three dimensions of sustainability-economic, social, and environmental. This could involve understanding how progress in one dimension may relate to or influence progress in the other dimensions.

This study implies data from the European Commission published reports, Eurostat indicator on SDGs, Europa.EU and UN reports on various projects under SDGs. Apart from these data, this research also gathered data from published primary and secondary resources from books, articles, working papers, newspapers, and public institutions' reports. The study utilizes data from the archival of Eurostat database and has chosen indicators based on their availability for all countries. The study to use data from the year 2015 is explained, and the list of initially selected indicators for analyzing the goal of the UN's Sustainable development of 2030.

European Union and Development Goals

It's encouraging that the EU has made significant progress toward three Sustainable Development Goals (SDGs): decent work and economic growth, reducing poverty, and improving gender equality. Let's briefly explore each of these following areas: This goal focuses on promoting sustained, inclusive, and sustainable economic growth, full and productive employment, and decent work for all. Progress in this area could involve initiatives to create more job opportunities, improve labor productivity, and ensure fair and safe working conditions. EU's aims to end poverty in all its forms everywhere. Achieving this goal involves implementing social protection systems, ensuring equal access to resources and opportunities, and addressing the needs of those living in poverty. Progress in reducing poverty is a fundamental aspect of sustainable development. Gender equality is a key component of sustainable development. Moreover, it seeks to achieve gender equality and empower all women and girls. Progress in this area could involve addressing gender-based discrimination, promoting equal access to education and healthcare, and ensuring women's participation in decision-making processes (Bharti, 2022, 2023a, 2023c; S. S. Bharti, 2020, 2022).

Major Sector of Significant Progress in the SDGs

Decent Work and Economic Growth (SDG 8): Achieving inclusive and sustainable economic growth, full employment, and decent work. Reducing Poverty (SDG 1): Efforts toward ending poverty in all its forms. Gender Equality (SDG 5): Advancements in promoting gender equality and empowering women and girls. Reducing Inequalities (SDG 10): Progress made in addressing and reducing inequalities. Quality Education (SDG 4): Advances in ensuring access to quality education for all. Peace, Justice, and Strong Institutions (SDG 16): Improvements in fostering peace, personal security, and access to justice. The EU has been getting success in the area of Health and Well-being (SDG 3): Progress despite setbacks caused by the COVID-19 pandemic. Innovation and Infrastructure (SDG 9): Advancements in fostering innovation and developing infrastructure. The EU has achieved moderate success in the sectors of Climate Action (SDG 13): Significant reduction in net greenhouse gas emissions, but additional efforts are needed for ambitious 2030 targets. Life on Land (SDG 15): Efforts needed to reverse the degradation of ecosystems. Global Partnerships (SDG 17): Trend partially influenced by cyclical effects, including the impact of the COVID-19 crisis (Eurostat, 2023).

The COVID-19 pandemic caused a decline in life expectancy in Europe, marking the first time such a decrease had been observed in 70 years. This underscores the severity of the public health crisis and its impact on mortality rates. The pandemic led to delays in health interventions, which could have implications for the timely treatment of various health conditions. These delays may have contributed to challenges in maintaining overall population health. The pandemic has been associated with an increase in mental health issues. The stress and uncertainty related to the virus, as well as the social and economic disruptions caused by lockdowns and other measures, have contributed to mental health challenges. Material deprivation and unemployment rates in the EU27 remained above pre-pandemic levels. This suggests ongoing economic challenges and difficulties for certain segments of the population in recovering from the economic impact of the pandemic. In 2021, there were indications of recovery, including reductions in the share of young people not in employment, education, or training (NEET). This suggests some improvement in the labor market and educational opportunities for young people. Various external factors pose threats to the recovery. These include the Russian aggression in Ukraine, an energy crisis, inflation, and budgetary constraints. These challenges have the potential to slow down or even reverse the progress made in 2021 (SDSN, 2022).

The challenges related to differences in Sustainable Development Goals (SDG) performance across European countries and regions highlight the concept of "convergence" as acknowledged by EU leaders. Here are key points based on the information regarding SDGs:

Convergence in SDG Performance

There are persisting differences in SDG performance across European countries and regions, with the term "convergence" being used to describe the goal of narrowing these gaps. Northern Europe, EFTA countries (European Free Trade Association), and Western Europe perform above the EU27 average on the SDG Index score, indicating relatively higher levels of achievement in sustainable development goals. In contrast, Baltic States, Southern Europe, and Central and Eastern European countries perform slightly below the average EU27 score. Despite performing below the average, these subregions have shown significant progress over the past decade. Candidate countries perform well below the EU27 average, particularly driven by poorer performance on socio-economic goals and SDG 16 (Peace, justice, and strong institutions). The pace of convergence is slow, indicating that the disparities in SDG performance are not diminishing rapidly. This could be attributed to various factors, including differing levels of economic development, historical contexts, and policy priorities. The information suggests that better performance is often concentrated in capital regions or urban agglomerations, while other regions and rural areas lag behind. This urban-rural disparity may contribute to the slow overall convergence in SDG performance.

The fourth challenge outlined pertains to negative international spillovers, particularly those embedded in trade and financial flows. European countries, through various practices such as unsustainable consumption, exports of toxic pesticides, plastic waste, unfair tax competition, and profit shifting, contribute to negative impacts on other countries' ability to achieve the Sustainable Development Goals (SDGs). Unsustainable consumption patterns, along with the export of environmentally harmful products such as toxic pesticides and plastic waste, can have detrimental effects on the environment and socio-economic development in other regions. Unfair tax competition and profit shifting by European countries can contribute to financial challenges in other countries, potentially hindering their ability to mobilize resources for sustainable development initiatives. The EU and its member states are recognized as the largest providers of official development assistance (ODA) globally. ODA plays a crucial role in supporting sustainable development initiatives in developing countries. The multiple crises faced by the EU and its member states may put additional pressures on concessional finance. This refers to financial assistance provided on terms more generous than market loans, typically in the form of grants or low-interest loans. The challenges faced by the EU could impact its ability to provide such concessional finance for global sustainable development efforts (Eurostat, 2023; Papadopoulos, 2016).

The International Spillover Index is likely a tool or metric used to assess and quantify the negative impacts generated by the EU abroad. It may help identify areas where interventions are needed to minimize adverse effects on other countries' sustainable development efforts. The mention of policy priorities suggests that there may be discussions or recommendations on how to address these negative international spillovers. This could involve implementing regulations, fostering sustainable trade practices, and promoting responsible business conduct on a global scale (Bharti & Bharti, 2022).

Figure 1 shows that SDG 10 specifically focuses on reducing inequalities. This goal recognizes the importance of creating more inclusive societies by addressing disparities in income, wealth, access to resources, and opportunities. SDG 17 emphasizes the need for partnerships to achieve the SDGs. In the context of inequalities, it calls for collaboration and cooperation among countries, organizations, and stakeholders to collectively work towards reducing disparities and fostering sustainable development. In Europe, the goal of reducing inequalities is often referred to as 'convergence.' This term is used to express the aspiration for a more balanced and equitable development across European countries and regions. Geopolitical tensions and climate change pose additional threats to global stability and development. Rising energy and food prices, exacerbated by climate change, disproportionately affect the most vulnerable countries and populations.

The 2022 European Leave No One Behind (LNOB) Index, emphasizing disparities in LNOB performance across European countries. Northern European countries, including Norway, Finland, and Iceland, have obtained the highest scores on the 2022 European LNOB Index. These top performers achieved scores ranging from 85.6 to 87.7 points, driven mainly by low levels of income inequality and material deprivation within these countries. The high scores in these Northern European countries are attributed to low levels of income inequality and material deprivation. This suggests that these nations have made significant progress in ensuring a more equal distribution of resources and reducing material deprivation among their populations. In contrast, stark within-country inequalities are observed in the Baltic States and Central and Eastern European countries, which appear at the bottom of the 2022 European LNOB Index. The average scores for these regions are around 70 points, indicating higher levels of inequality and challenges in achieving LNOB objectives. EU candidate countries face difficulties in catching up with Europe in terms of the LNOB Index. The challenges for these countries are primarily linked to higher rates of material deprivation and poverty, indicating that efforts are needed to address these socio-economic disparities. The mention of much higher rates of material deprivation and poverty in EU candidate countries underscores the significance of addressing basic needs and economic well-being as key components of LNOB (SDSN, 2022).

International Spillover Effects From EU Member States

SDG 17 emphasizes the need for partnerships to achieve the SDGs. The concept of "policy coherence" is mentioned, suggesting that aligning policies across various sectors is crucial for the effective implementation of sustainable development goals. SDG 12 stresses the importance of responsible consumption and production. This goal recognizes the need for sustainable practices in how goods and services are produced and consumed, which can have implications for global environmental and social impacts. SDG 8 focuses on decent work and economic growth. The goal includes the eradication of child labor and modern slavery as part of the broader agenda for promoting fair and just economic practices. The EU has taken a strong stance against child labor, advocating for 'zero tolerance' of this issue. This indicates a commitment to ensuring that products and services traded internationally do not involve the exploitation of children. The proposal to use trade to export European values throughout the world suggests that the EU sees trade as a mechanism to influence global practices positively. This could involve promoting ethical and sustainable standards in international trade relations (European Commission, 2023b).

Figure 1. For specific information on European countries and sub-regions of 2022 SDG dashboard
Source:*https://eu-dashboards.sdgindex.org/chapters/part-1-performance-of-european-countries-against-the-sdgs#figure-1-7-the-2022-sdg-dashboards-by-country-and-sub-regions*

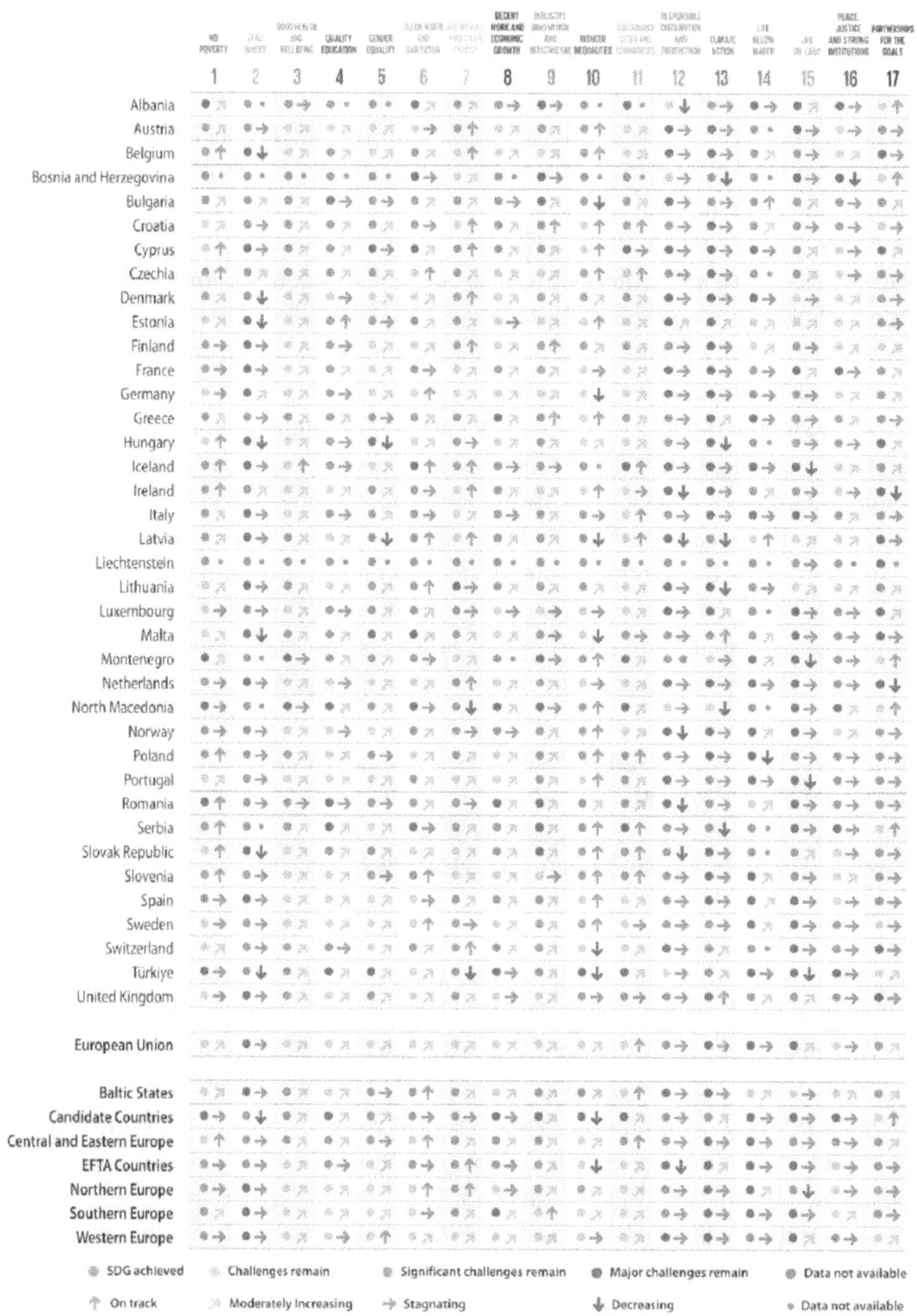

EU Development Aid

In 2022, Europe elevated its development aid to EUR 93 billion, showing a substantial increase of 30% compared to the previous year. This demonstrates a heightened commitment to supporting global development efforts. Europe's contribution now accounts for over 40% of global assistance. This signifies a substantial portion of the total aid being directed toward international development initiatives. The statement acknowledges Europe's recognition of its obligations in contributing to global development. This suggests a commitment to fulfilling international responsibilities and promoting sustainable development goals. While public funding is essential, the statement emphasizes the need to explore additional avenues to attract new funding for developing countries. This recognition indicates a commitment to innovation and diversification in financing mechanisms. The mention of the reform of MDBs highlights a focus on improving the effectiveness and efficiency of these institutions. Reforming of Multilateral Development Banks (MDBs) is seen as a crucial step in enhancing their capacity to address global development challenges. The statement indicates that Europe is responding to the Secretary-General's call for increased efforts in addressing global challenges. This aligns with broader international initiatives and collaborations to achieve sustainable development goals. The statement hints at a more detailed exploration of two specific ways in which Europe is answering the call for increased development efforts. This suggests that there are targeted strategies or initiatives in place to address global development challenges (European Commission, 2023b; SDSN, 2022).

Governments are urged to increase their capacity to measure how their societies impact the progress of other countries in achieving the SDGs. This involves assessing the positive or negative externalities generated by a country's actions. The benefits or costs incurred by other countries due to a nation's actions are referred to as positive or negative externalities. Positive externalities may contribute positively to other countries' progress on the SDGs, while negative externalities can hinder these efforts. The passage highlights those countries cannot achieve the SDGs if negative externalities from other countries counteract their efforts. This underscores the interconnected nature of global challenges and the need for collaborative and responsible actions on a global scale. International spillovers occur when one country's actions generate benefits or impose costs on another country, and these effects are not reflected in market prices. These spillovers are not internalized by the actions of consumers and producers, indicating a gap in market mechanisms. The concept of externalities implies that the impact of certain actions is not fully considered or internalized by market prices (Pradhan et al., 2017). As a result, the true costs or benefits are not reflected in economic transactions, potentially leading to suboptimal outcomes.

Europe is set to invest EUR 300 billion in developing economies over the next five years. This substantial investment reflects a commitment to supporting development initiatives on a significant scale. The investment plan targets key areas, including renewable energy, stronger health systems, quality education, green transport, and digital solutions. These sectors are crucial for sustainable development and align with the broader goals of advancing economic, social, and environmental well-being. The objective is to equip partner countries with resources, technologies, and skills to move up the value chains. This approach is aimed at fostering economic development, creating jobs, and protecting the environment. The investment plan involves using a portion of the public budget to de-risk private investments. This public-private partnership model aims to leverage both public and private resources for sustainable development initiatives. In addition to direct investments, Europe is supporting developing and emerging economies in creating their own green bond markets. This initiative is designed to attract more fresh capital toward the Sustainable Development Goals (SDGs). The ultimate goal is to attract capital toward the SDGs, emphasizing the importance of financial resources in achieving sustainable development objectives. Creating green bond markets is seen as a strategic way to mobilize additional funds for impactful projects. The investment plan is framed in the context of promoting economic growth, job creation, and environmental protection. It reflects a holistic approach to development, recognizing the interplay between economic, social, and environmental factors (European Commission, 2023b).

The EU, a Leading Global Partner for the SDGs

The EU engages in international partnerships to make progress toward relevant SDGs. This approach suggests a collaborative and cooperative effort involving multiple stakeholders, both within and outside the EU. The EU's pursuit of progress on SDGs is aligned with its priorities. This integration ensures that efforts related to sustainable development are coherent with the broader objectives and strategies of the EU. The EU's involvement in SDGs spans the entire process, from design to implementation and reporting. This comprehensive approach signifies a commitment to addressing sustainable development challenges at every stage, ensuring a holistic and integrated strategy. The EU, along with its Member States, holds a prominent position as the leading donors of official development assistance (ODA) globally. This underscores the financial commitment and support provided by the EU to address development challenges in various regions. By being a leading donor globally, the EU contributes significantly to international development efforts. This financial support can be instrumental in addressing issues related to poverty, health, education, and other key areas outlined in the SDGs.

DISCUSSION AND RESULTS

The successful implementation of the SDG agenda is portrayed as essential for addressing the global sustainability challenge. The SDGs are described as a system of interacting cogwheels, suggesting that each goal is interdependent and contributes to moving the global system toward a safe and just operating space. The passage emphasizes that no individual SDG can achieve the overarching goals of human well-being, economic prosperity, and environmental protection on its own. Instead, all SDGs are viewed as part of a holistic system that collectively works towards achieving sustainable development. The SDGs are characterized not as an additive structure but as a system of synergistic reinforcement. This implies that the goals are interconnected in a way that their combined efforts can have a greater impact than the sum of their individual contributions. The success of SDG attainment is suggested to depend on the ability to leverage synergies among goals and identify and address trade-offs. This highlights the importance of understanding the complex relationships between different goals and finding ways to navigate potential conflicts. The passage introduces a statistical formulation of SDG synergies and trade-offs based on correlation analysis of development. This suggests a data-driven approach to understanding the relationships between different SDGs and assessing their collective impact. The statistical formulation is presented as a contribution to making the SDG agenda a success. This aligns with the idea that data-driven insights can inform decision-making and policy development, leading to more effective strategies for achieving sustainable development (Jakob & Steckel, 2016).

The potential synergies or trade-offs between the goals contribute to the complexity of SDG interactions. This complexity arises from the fact that the goals are not independent of each other, and their outcomes may be interconnected. The mention of pursuing progress "together with EU priorities" suggests a coordinated and cohesive approach. This implies that the EU integrates its development assistance efforts with its broader policy objectives and strategies for a more effective and impactful outcome. Effective reporting mechanisms enable the EU to track and communicate the outcomes of its efforts in alignment with the SDGs. the EU's commitment to international cooperation, the alignment of SDG efforts with EU priorities, and the significant role the EU plays as a leading donor in official development assistance. This underscores the EU's dedication to addressing global challenges and contributing to sustainable development on a global scale. According to preliminary OECD figures. This financial contribution represents a substantial amount and accounts for 43% of global assistance, underscoring the EU's leading role in supporting global development. The EU's contribution constitutes 43% of global assistance, showcasing its substantial financial commitment to addressing development challenges worldwide (European Commission, n.d.-b). This reinforces the EU's position as a major player in international development efforts. The EU has rolled out the Global Gateway strategy, which focuses on sustainable investments in infrastructure on a global scale. This strategy reflects a proactive approach to addressing development challenges through strategic and sustainable investments. Global Gateway is positioned as a strategy that will directly contribute to progress on a range of interlinked Sustainable Development Goals (SDGs). The emphasis is on investments in key areas such as transport, energy, digitalization infrastructure, as well as health and education.

The Agenda 2030 signifies a paradigmatic shift toward a more participatory model of multi-stakeholder governance. This shift suggests a move away from traditional top-down approaches to a more inclusive and collaborative approach involving various stakeholders. The Multi-Stakeholder Platform set up by the Commission in 2017 played a role in facilitating engagement with stakeholders, including the European Economic and Social Committee (EESC). However, it is noted that this platform was not renewed. The passage highlights calls, including those from the European Parliament, for the re-launch of a platform or forum on the SDGs. This platform is envisioned to facilitate structured engagement with a diverse set of stakeholders, including civil society, youth organizations, businesses, trade unions, and scientists. The process of re-launching an SDG platform is expected to examine best practices from other relevant multi-stakeholder forums, such as the European Circular Economy Stakeholder Platform. Learning from these experiences is seen as valuable for organizing and structuring the new SDG platform.

The success of SDG implementation is noted to rely on the local level. Therefore, the proposed platform is expected to incorporate the views and input of local communities, recognizing their role in achieving sustainable development objectives. The envisioned platform is not only expected to facilitate engagement but also to play a role in policy development and monitoring related to the SDGs. This indicates a comprehensive approach that involves stakeholders throughout the policy cycle. The EU is urged to develop a comprehensive strategy on the SDGs with the objective of enhancing coherence and synergies across various policy areas and tools. While acknowledging the existence of the European Green Deal and other relevant EU strategies that contribute partially to SDG implementation, the passage emphasizes the need for stronger linkages between these strategies. The aim is to move away from a siloed approach and promote collaboration across sectors. here is a call to reinforce linkages between different strategies to move away from a siloed approach. The aim is to foster collaboration across sectors, with a particular emphasis on the social dimension and the principle of "leaving no one behind."

The strategy should have a clear focus on the social dimension of sustainable development, ensuring that social considerations are integrated into policies and initiatives. This aligns with the broader commitment to address social inequalities and inclusivity. The strategy is recommended to be accompanied by a clear and detailed implementation plan. This plan should include specific targets, timelines, and roadmaps for addressing both environmental and social issues. It also highlights the need to cover aspects not captured in the European Green Deal. The implementation plan should outline how the entire 2030 Agenda will be translated into practice within the EU context. This implies a commitment to concrete actions that align with the SDGs, and it emphasizes the importance of turning commitments into practical measures. The passage underscores the importance of considering the external dimension of SDG implementation. This involves addressing how the EU's actions impact partner countries, ensuring that domestic policies do not have negative consequences on external partners. The EU expresses its commitment to cooperative solutions in providing support to Ukraine. This indicates a collaborative and solidarity-based approach in addressing geopolitical challenges and supporting countries in need. Cooperative solutions are seen as essential for achieving sustainability goals both within the EU and globally. This aligns with the broader commitment to address environmental, social, and economic aspects of sustainability (European Commission, 2023a).

The cooperative solutions are framed in the context of promoting the Sustainable Development Goals (SDGs). This highlights the alignment of collaborative efforts with the broader global agenda for sustainable development. The EU's commitment to cooperative solutions in addressing economic, geopolitical, and sustainability challenges. It emphasizes the need for collaboration among diverse stakeholders to find solutions and promote the SDGs both within the EU and on the global stage. The Swedish EU Presidency, with the support of Member States, prepared a Presidency Report by December 2009. This report likely outlined the status and priorities related to sustainable development within the EU during that time. Following the submission of the Presidency Report, the European Council confirmed in December 2009 that sustainable development would remain one of the EU's fundamental objectives. This reaffirmation likely took place within the context of discussions and decisions made at the European Council meeting during that period. The European Council's confirmation underscored that sustainable development would continue to be considered one of the EU's fundamental objectives. This commitment indicates the importance attached to sustainability within the EU's overarching goals. The European Council affirmed that sustainable development would be a fundamental objective within the framework of the Lisbon Treaty. The Lisbon Treaty, also known as the Treaty of Lisbon, is an important legal framework that defines the functioning and objectives of the EU. The strategy for sustainable development was acknowledged to continue serving as the overarching policy framework for all EU policies and strategies. This implies that sustainability considerations would be integrated into and guide various aspects of EU policymaking and strategy development (Federal Ministry Republic of Austria, n.d.).

During the Swedish EU Presidency in December 2009, there was a reaffirmation of the EU's commitment to sustainable development. This commitment was reflected in the European Council's confirmation that sustainable development would remain a fundamental objective within the framework of the Lisbon Treaty, with the overarching strategy continuing to guide EU policies and strategies.

CONCLUSION

This study is highlighting the complex interplay of public health, economic, and geopolitical factors underscore the need for comprehensive and adaptive strategies to address the ongoing consequences of the pandemic and related challenges in Europe. It also emphasizes the importance of monitoring and responding to emerging threats to ensure a sustainable and inclusive recovery. Addressing these regional disparities in SDG performance requires targeted and context-specific interventions. Policymakers may need to focus on inclusive development strategies that address the unique challenges faced by different regions and populations. Additionally, efforts to improve socio-economic goals and strengthen institutions, particularly in candidate countries, could contribute to a more balanced and equitable progress across the European continent. The challenges faced by EU candidate countries underscore the need for tailored strategies to uplift their populations and improve overall LNOB performance. The study traced that the EU is a key donor to developing countries' development under the EU provision to address global challenges. the SDGs require collaboration and consideration of the broader impacts of actions beyond national borders. It emphasizes the shared responsibility of countries to ensure that their actions contribute positively to global sustainable development. The European Union (EU), enhancing their capacity to measure the impact of their societies on the ability of other countries to progress on the Sustainable Development Goals (SDGs).

Finally, this study finds that the SDG Summit in 2023 is seen as a crucial occasion for the global community to review the state of progress towards the SDGs. It is viewed as an opportunity to reinvigorate political commitment and accelerate efforts to meet the SDG targets. The SDG Summit is positioned as a platform to advance proposals from the UN Secretary-General's Our Common Agenda. These proposals aim to expedite the implementation of the 2030 Agenda, aligning with the broader global vision for sustainable development. The passage notes that the 2024 Summit of the Future, proposed by the UN Secretary-General, shares the same overall objective as the SDG Summit. Both aim to create conditions for a sustainable, equitable, and inclusive future, utilizing the 2030 Agenda as a shared roadmap. The overarching objective of both summits is to create conditions for a sustainable, equitable, and inclusive future. This indicates a commitment to fostering positive global outcomes aligned with the principles of sustainability and fairness. The 2030 Agenda is highlighted as a shared roadmap for the envisioned sustainable, equitable, and inclusive future. This underscores the central role of the SDGs in guiding collective efforts toward global development goals. The EU expresses its anticipation for a successful SDG Summit, emphasizing the importance of bringing together countries and stakeholders. The goal is to reach agreements on ambitious concrete actions to expedite the implementation of the 2030 Agenda. The EU reaffirms its commitment to accelerating the implementation of the 2030 Agenda. This commitment is framed as a common direction for enhanced efforts across the globe, emphasizing sustainable development, fairness, and prosperity. The pivotal role of the SDG Summit in 2023, highlighting its potential to galvanize political momentum, advance proposals for global development, and foster a sustainable and inclusive future. The shared objectives with the 2024 Summit of the Future underscore a unified commitment to the principles outlined in the 2030 Agenda. The EU expresses readiness to contribute to the success of the SDG Summit and advance efforts toward sustainable development globally.

This research also highlights the role of EU's other institutions to accelerate the UN's sustainable development (SDGs). The European Commission has introduced a new Circular Economy Action Plan. This plan is recognized as a positive step forward in contributing to a circular, clean, and green economy within the EU. Circular economy principles focus on minimizing waste and promoting the sustainable use of resources. The Commission has proposed legislation on Corporate Sustainability Due Diligence, which would impose supply chain oversight obligations on companies operating in the EU. The passage suggests that this legislation, if appropriately addressed in the ongoing legislative process, could be a meaningful step in promoting sustainability. There is an acknowledgment that the effectiveness of the legislation on Corporate Sustainability Due Diligence will depend on the outcome of the ongoing legislative process. It is important that the final legislation addresses any gaps in the initial proposal to ensure its meaningful impact.

REFERENCES

Agyeman, J. (2020). Local Environment and the UN Sustainable Development Goals. *Local Environment, 25*(5), 336–337. doi:10.1080/13549839.2020.1751444

Arrow, K. J., Dasgupta, P., Goulder, L. H., Mumford, K. J., & Oleson, K. (2012). Sustainability and the measurement of wealth. *Environment and Development Economics, 17*(3), 317–353. doi:10.1017/S1355770X12000137

Bali Swain, R., & Yang-Wallentin, F. (2020). Achieving sustainable development goals: Predicaments and strategies. *International Journal of Sustainable Development and World Ecology, 27*(2), 96–106. doi:10.1080/13504509.2019.1692316

Bexell, M., & Jönsson, K. (2019). Country Reporting on the Sustainable Development Goals—The Politics of Performance Review at the Global-National Nexus*. *Journal of Human Development and Capabilities, 20*(4), 403–417. doi:10.1080/19452829.2018.1544544

Bharti, M. S. (2022). The Economic Integration of the Central and Eastern European Countries into the European Union: Special Reference to Regional Development. *Copernicus Political and Legal Studies, 1*(2), 11–23. https://doi.org/doi.org/10.15804/CPLS.20222.01

Bharti, M. S. (2023a). China's Belt and Road Initiative (BRI) in Central and Eastern European Countries: The Role of '17+1' Framework for Extensive Economic Partnership. In D. W. Kim (Ed.), *Silk Road: Transnational Transmission of Sacred Thoughts and Literature*. Vernon Press.

Bharti, M. S. (2023b). Global Development and International Order Transition: The Role of China. In M. O. Dinçsoy & H. Can (Eds.), *Optimizing Energy Efficiency During a Global Energy Crisis* (pp. 200–212). IGI Global. doi:10.4018/979-8-3693-0400-6.ch013

Bharti, M. S. (2023c). The Geo-Economics Approach to the European Union Strategic Partnership in the Indo-Pacific Region: Challenges and Opportunities. In R. A. Castanho (Ed.), *Handbook of Research on Current Advances and Challenges of Borderlands, Migration, and Geopolitics*. IGI Global. doi:10.4018/978-1-6684-7020-6.ch015

Bharti, M. S. (2023d). The Sustainable Development and Economic Impact of China's Belt and Road Initiative in Ethiopia. *East Asia (Piscataway, N.J.), 40*(2), 175–194. doi:10.1007/s12140-023-09402-y PMID:37065271

Bharti, M. S., & Bharti, S. S. (2022). The EU Public Diplomacy in the Time of Virtual Reality: Political, Social and Economic Implications. In B. Olbrych (Ed.), *Life in Virtual Reality, Chances and dangers* (Vol. 2, pp. 13–25). Akademia Handlowa Nauk Stosowanych w Radomiu.

Bharti, S. S. (2020). Strengthening the Development Partnership between the EU and South Asia: A Contemporary Analysis. *Slovak Journal of Political Sciences, 20*(2), 278–298. doi:10.34135/sjps.200205

Bharti, S. S. (2022). Confronting Afghanistan's Security and Development Challenges: A Contribution of the European Union. *Geopolitics Quarterly, 18*(4), 151–176. 20.1001.1.17354331.1401.18.68.7.9

European Commission. (2023a, May). *EU Voluntary Review on the Implementation of the 2030 Agenda for Sustainable Development*. EC. https://commission.europa.eu/system/files/2023-06/SDG-Report-WEB.pdf

European Commission. (2023b, September 18). *Statement by President von der Leyen at the 2023 Sustainable Development Goals Summit*. EC. https://ec.europa.eu/commission/presscorner/detail/en/STATEMENT_23_4504

European Commission. (n.d.-a). *European development policy*. EC. https://international-partnerships.ec.europa.eu/policies/european-development-policy_en#:~:text=European%20development%20policy%20fosters%20sustainable,%2C%20security%2C%20and%20trade%20policies

European Commission. (n.d.-b). *International Partnerships*. EC. https://international-partnerships.ec.europa.eu/policies/sustainable-development-goals_en

European Commission. (n.d.-c). *Sustainable Development Goals*. EC.

Eurostat. (2023, May 24). *How has the EU progressed towards the SDGs?* Europa.Eu. https://ec.europa.eu/eurostat/web/products-eurostat-news/w/wdn-20230524-1#:~:text=EU%20made%20significant%20progress%20toward,gender%20equality%20(SDG%205)

Federal Ministry Republic of Austria. (n.d.). *European Sustainable Development Strategy*. BMK. https://www.bmk.gv.at/en/topics/climate-environment/sustainable-development/eu-sds.html#:~:text=The%20EU%20Strategy%20for%20Sustainable,present%20and%20for%20future%20Generations

Gracia-de-Rentería, P., Ferrer-Pérez, H., & Drabik, D. (2023). Sustainable development goals in the European Union and its regions: Are we moving forward in economic, social, and environmental dimensions? *Sustainable Development (Bradford)*, *31*(5), 3540–3552. doi:10.1002/sd.2609

Immler, N. L., & Sakkers, H. (2022). The UN-Sustainable Development Goals going local: Learning from localising human rights. *International Journal of Human Rights*, *26*(2), 262–284. doi:10.1080/13642987.2021.1913411

Jakob, M., & Steckel, J. C. (2016). Implications of climate change mitigation for sustainable development. *Environmental Research Letters*, *11*(10), 104010. doi:10.1088/1748-9326/11/10/104010

Lafortune, G., Puch, M. C., Mosnier, A., Fuller, G., Diaz, M., Riccaboni, A., Kloke-Lesch, A., Zachariadis, T., Carli, E., & Oger, A. (2021). *Europe sustainable development report 2021: transforming the European Union to achieve the sustainable development goals*. SDSN Europe and IEEP.

Papadopoulos, A. M. (2016). Forty years of regulations on the thermal performance of the building envelope in Europe: Achievements, perspectives and challenges. *Energy and Building*, *127*, 942–952. doi:10.1016/j.enbuild.2016.06.051

Prada, G. M. (2013). Meeting of the General Assembly Open Working Group on Sustainable Development Goals. *European Union and Its Member States - Speaking Points on "Means of Implementation/Global Partnership for Achieving Sustainable Development*. SDGS. https://sdgs.un.org/sites/default/files/statements/4663eu.pdf

Pradhan, P., Costa, L., Rybski, D., Lucht, W., & Kropp, J. P. (2017). A Systematic Study of Sustainable Development Goal (SDG) Interactions. *Earth's Future*, *5*(11), 1169–1179. doi:10.1002/2017EF000632

Rahimifard, S., & Trollman, H. (2018). UN Sustainable Development Goals: An engineering perspective. *International Journal of Sustainable Engineering, 11*(1), 1–3. doi:10.1080/19397038.2018.1434985

SDSN. (2022). *Peformance of European Countries against the SDGs*. Sustainable Development Solutions Network. https://eu-dashboards.sdgindex.org/chapters/part-1-performance-of-european-countries-against-the-sdgs

Sen, A. (2001). *Development as freedom*. Oxford University Press.

Sen, A. (2010). Equality of what? In S. M. MacMurrin (Ed.), *The Tanner lectures on human* (2nd ed., pp. 195–220). Cambridge University Press.

Swain, R. B. (2018). A Critical Analysis of the Sustainable Development Goals. In W. Leal Filho (Ed.), *Handbook of Sustainability Science and Research* (pp. 341–355). Springer International Publishing. doi:10.1007/978-3-319-63007-6_20

Szymańska, A., & Zalewska, E. (2021). Education in the light of sustainable development goals – The case of the European Union countries. *Globalisation, Societies and Education, 19*(5), 658–671. doi:10.1080/14767724.2021.1878010

Udeagha, M. C., & Ngepah, N. (2023). Towards climate action and UN sustainable development goals in BRICS economies: Do export diversification, fiscal decentralisation and environmental innovation matter? *International Journal of Urban Sustainable Development, 15*(1), 172–200. doi:10.1080/19463138.2023.2222264

Weber, H. (2017). Politics of 'Leaving No One Behind': Contesting the 2030 Sustainable Development Goals Agenda. *Globalizations, 14*(3), 399–414. doi:10.1080/14747731.2016.1275404

ADDITIONAL READINGS

Bilsky, E., Moreno, A. C., & Fernández Tortosa, A. (2021). Local Governments and SDG Localisation: Reshaping Multilevel Governance from the Bottom up. *Journal of Human Development and Capabilities, 22*(4), 713–724. doi:10.1080/19452829.2021.1986690

Carbone, M. (2021). Making a difference in multilateral negotiations: The European Union and the global agenda on aid effectiveness. *Global Affairs, 7*(4), 453–470. doi:10.1080/23340460.2021.1967183

Graute, U. (2016). Local Authorities Acting Globally for Sustainable Development. *Regional Studies, 50*(11), 1931–1942. doi:10.1080/00343404.2016.1161740

Hadfield, A., & Lightfoot, S. (2021). Shifting priorities of the EU as a development actor: Context and consequences. *Global Affairs, 7*(4), 487–504. doi:10.1080/23340460.2021.1985400

Missingham, R. (2021). A New Lens for Evaluation – Assessing Academic Libraries Using the UN Sustainable Development Goals. *Journal of Library Administration, 61*(3), 386–401. doi:10.1080/01930826.2021.1883376

Rodriguez-Anton, J. M., Rubio-Andrada, L., Celemín-Pedroche, M. S., & Alonso-Almeida, M. D. M. (2019). Analysis of the relations between circular economy and sustainable development goals. *International Journal of Sustainable Development and World Ecology*, *26*(8), 708–720. doi:10.1080/13504509.2019.1666754

Sama, L. M., Stefanidis, A., & Horak, S. (2020). Business ethics for a global society: Howard Bowen's legacy and the foundations of United Nations' Sustainable Development Goals. *International Studies of Management & Organization*, *50*(3), 201–208. doi:10.1080/00208825.2020.1811526

Steingass, S., Carbone, M., & Winand, P. (2021). The European Union and the evolving requirements of international development: Aid, policies, partnerships. *Global Affairs*, *7*(4), 425–436. doi:10.1080/23340460.2021.1999174

Winand, P. (2021). The European Union and India: From donor-recipient relations to partners in development. *Global Affairs*, *7*(4), 579–595. doi:10.1080/23340460.2021.1961597

Zhu, D. (2017). Research from global Sustainable Development Goals (SDGs) to sustainability science based on the object-subject-process framework. *Zhongguo Renkou Ziyuan Yu Huanjing*, *15*(1), 8–20. doi:10.1080/10042857.2017.1286147

KEY TERMS AND DEFINITIONS

Enforcing EU law: The Commission monitors member states' compliance with EU law and can take legal action against countries that fail to fulfill their obligations.

European Commission: The European Commission is one of the main institutions of the European Union (EU). It serves as the executive branch of the EU and is responsible for proposing legislation, implementing decisions, upholding EU treaties, and managing the day-to-day operations of the Union. The Commission operates independently of national governments and represents the interests of the EU as a whole. The primary functions of the European Commission include:

European Union (EU): The EU is a political and economic union of 27 member states located primarily in Europe. It was established by the Treaty of Maastricht in 1993 and is the result of decades of cooperation among European countries following the devastation of World War II. The EU operates through a system of supranational institutions and intergovernmental decision-making, which include the European Commission, the European Parliament, the Council of the European Union, the European Council, the Court of Justice of the European Union, and the European Central Bank, among others. The EU has a wide range of competencies, including the single market, customs union, competition policy, agricultural policy, trade policy, and monetary policy (for the Eurozone countries). It also promotes co-operation in areas such as justice and home affairs, energy, environment, and foreign policy. Additionally, the EU plays a significant role in global affairs, representing its member states in international negotiations and advocating for common positions on issues such as climate change, human rights, and trade.

Implementing EU policies: The Commission is responsible for implementing EU policies and decisions, ensuring that member states comply with EU law.

Managing the EU budget: The Commission is responsible for managing the EU budget and allocating funds to various programs and projects.

Proposing new legislation: The Commission has the sole right to initiate legislation in most policy areas, although the European Parliament and the Council of the European Union must approve it.

Representing the EU internationally: The Commission represents the EU in international negotiations and agreements, including trade negotiations and climate change talks.

Sustainable Development Goals (SDGs): The Sustainable Development Goals (SDGs) are a set of 17 interconnected global goals adopted by the United Nations (UN) in September 2015. These goals are designed to address a wide range of social, economic, and environmental challenges facing the world, with the aim of achieving a more sustainable and equitable future for all by the year 2030.

United Nations (UN): The United Nations (UN) was founded in 1945 with the primary objectives of maintaining international peace and security, promoting cooperation among nations to solve global problems, and fostering economic and social development. The UN promotes the rule of law and adherence to international legal norms as a basis for resolving disputes and preventing conflicts. The UN promotes gender equality and women's empowerment as fundamental principles for achieving peace, development, and human rights. The UN promotes sustainable development practices that balance economic growth, social inclusion, and environmental protection. This includes efforts to eradicate poverty, ensure access to education and healthcare, promote gender equality, and protect natural resources. The UN responds to humanitarian crises caused by natural disasters, armed conflicts, and other emergencies by providing lifesaving aid, such as food, water, shelter, and medical care, to affected populations. It also coordinates relief efforts and supports long-term recovery and rebuilding efforts.

Chapter 21
Assimilative Potentials in Planning and Public Policy Analysis:
Critical Pragmatic Perspective

Noe John Joseph Endencio Sacramento
https://orcid.org/0000-0002-7099-7673
Chiang Mai University, Thailand & University of the Philippines Cebu, Philippines

ABSTRACT

This chapter builds on the argument that assimilative formulas to policy analysis are essential to mending the debate between the technocratic paradigms and the critical approaches to policy analysis. In real-world policy practice at the height of the COVID-19 pandemic, addressing public problems demands an innovative direction to advance policy initiatives that are both inclusive and transformative. The chapter's discussion reimagined the characteristics and role of the assimilative practitioner spanning across issues on social injustices, high inequalities, professionalization, and micropolitics. Critical insight from Chiang Mai City, Thailand suggests that a sound policy analysis goes beyond the hectic technical systems or a messy deliberative process. Lessons direct us to go beyond these boundaries and limitations and seek a creative reimagination of policy analysis that is both assimilative and critically pragmatic.

INTRODUCTION

At a time when developing regions of the world face uncertain and complex public problems, scholars rethink the need to navigate the criticality and practicality of policy processes, options, and alternatives. Looking back into the evolutions of paradigms in public policy, we can see and trace the dominance of technical approaches where experts and those in authority have a hand in finding solutions for society's concerns (Dunn, 2015; Gilley, 2017). The leanings toward the role of expertise is preferred in a society where knowledge comes with authority and power (Thissen & Walker, 2013). However, critical scholars may have shaken this dominance by asserting a precarious direction to the policy process. The deliberative

DOI: 10.4018/979-8-3693-1742-6.ch021

element in an argumentative turn has also become pivotal to democratic and citizen-centered advancement in policy analysis (Fischer & Gottweis, 2012; Hajer, 2003; Wagenaar, 2014). Here, the public gets to amplify their voices, actively participate, and get to decide on policy alternatives that authentically correspond to their needs. Hearing that both paradigms have clashing stances, strategies, and approaches to dealing with public problems is crucial. Hence, it is essential to ask whether we limit the discussion of instrumentalizing strategies and tools within the purview of these two clashing camps.

This chapter revisits the discussion on the technocratic and critical debate in policy analysis, emphasizing the forgoing clash over the 'best fit' or 'soundest' approach in dealing with public problems (Boossabong & Fischer, 2018; Dunn, 2015; Fischer & Miller, 2007; Sacramento & Boossabong, 2023). From these debates, there are two premises that the chapter embarks on before providing an extensive discussion over the assimilative potentials in planning and policy analysis backed by critical pragmatism as a lens. The first premise points to the idea of complexity and uncertainty; that is, there are public problems that are too complex and dynamics that the 'one-way best solution' is insufficient to address (Geyer & Rihani, 2012; Hartley et al., 2019; Stark & Taylor, 2014). Some public problems are too scientific that it demands a more technical-oriented process. At the same time, others are highly critically oriented and would need the people (among other stakeholders) to discuss and address them collectively. However, the question being raised here is whether these dichotomized stances are still relevant today, with all the evolving public problems our society faces. The second premise focuses on navigating the 'contextual' appropriateness of the forgoing mainstream approaches that societies adopt and implement (Béné et al., 2018; Boossabong & Chamchong, 2019; Clarke, 2007). Viewing the process of policy analysis more holistically (including inclusivity, authentic elements, and culturally sensitive features) allows for making policy alternatives and addressing public problems that are accepted by society and the public. The foregoing discussion and literature in the field have missed that the unique features and elements (e.g., culture, tradition, power, respect, and social structures) are fundamental base considerations in forwarding policy agendas and solutions (Curato et al., 2018; Durnová, 2015, 2018; Durnová et al., 2022; Fung & Wright, 2003).

Critical to the exploration, the chapter answers the question: how can the assimilative potentials in planning and policy analysis respond to the need to tailor an approach that is sensitive to the contextual realities in non-western contexts, especially to those societies with massive influence of authority and power and evidence of high inequalities? The discussion will then fundamentally assert the position of the 'public' in policy and governance as it navigates along the critical pragmatic direction and the role of a critical-pragmatist practitioner, which this chapter highlights as a contribution. Moreover, the lessons in the case of Thailand will shed light on how planners and policy analysts navigated the complexities brought by uncertain and erupting public problems in a pandemic to address critical yet pragmatic alternatives necessary in 'real-time.' Based on the researcher's anecdotal accounts, the study draws from an autoethnographic lens as to how critical yet pragmatic policymaking has informed the assimilative potentials of doing policy analysis in the face of complex and uncertain threats during the pandemic. From November 2020 up until July 2022, the autoethnographic accounts of this study are based on the direct observation and immersion of the researcher in the policy analysis and implementation in Chiang Mai, Thailand[1]. Drawing from the lessons in the developing world, such as the case of Thailand, will definitely speak to the mainstream public policy paradigm as to why it is so feasible to consider the critical and pragmatic compromise that assimilates the highly technical strategies and subjectively critical approach in dealing with authority and power, norms and values, and culture and traditions greatly rooted in Asian practices, which also influenced public policy.

Tensed debate: Technocratic and Critical Approaches to Policy Analysis

It is crucial to revisit then how the discipline has grown and the debates embedding the technocratic and critical debate in policy analysis, emphasizing the forgoing clash over the 'best fit' or 'soundest' approach in dealing with public problems (Fischer & Miller, 2007; Wagenaar, 2014). Of course, the growth of the public policy discipline, in particular, has not emerged as independent from other established and highly guarded disciplines. Public policy first emerged and known as 'policy science' that sprung from the strategies, approaches, and paradigms inspired by hard science— natural and physical science, economics, and engineering (Dunn, 2015, 2018; Thissen & Walker, 2013). At that time of the aftermath of the world wars in the early 1900s, there were a lot of public problems that needed to be addressed, including economic, health, physical structures, and rebuilding initiatives, among others, which led to considering the scientific method of decision making to address these pressing issues (Bächtiger et al., 2018; Dye, 1978). However, the last quarter of the century has made various scholars rethink and see the argumentative turn in doing policy analysis (Fischer & Forester, 1993; Fischer & Gottweis, 2012; Forester, 1999, 2009; Hajer, 2003). Here, the likes of Majone, Fischer, and Forester, among other critical scholars, have reiterated that public policy should be people-centered and democratic in its processes, which is necessary for bringing the public to understand the issues they face and consider a sound alternative that is more genuinely oriented to their concerns and practically feasibly for implementation.

Borrowing from the observations of Sacramento and Boossabong (2023) in their project on smart city planning at the Fah Ham municipality in Chiang Mai, Thailand, amid the COVID-19 pandemic, their work has understood the existing debates of the clashing paradigms on the approach to policy analysis. Examples in their article pointed out various advantages and limitations as we consider both approaches in application to policy analysis. On the one hand, the technocratic policy analysis or TPA tends to favor supreme empiricist traditions and strategies that instrumentalize statistics, quantifiable observations, expert advice, and scientific knowledge in addressing public problems (however, it may fall short of not considering the structural and systemic elements that stir public problems and influences policy making). The critical approach to public policy, such as the deliberative policy analysis or the DPA, is more democratic and people-centered and values the public's voices and participation in the policy process and in speaking to power. However, the progressive approach to policy analysis may often face criticism as being messy, lengthy, and too idealistic, as some societies may value and take high regard for the disparities in socio-economic and political status and the imbalance in the distribution of power.

The exclusivist view over these approaches has taken shape in how policy analysts and practitioners have addressed public problems over the past decades. To note and not turn a blind eye, the way these approaches have taken the score over addressing various issues of the past has been very successful. However, we need to acknowledge that society is evolving and that uncertain and complex situations are inevitable, such as the COVID-19 pandemic that has shaken the social-political-economic status quo in which we have been living. In doing policy analysis in the midst of a crisis like COVID-19, policy practitioners have rethought this debate and navigated along the grey line that rather than staying within the limits of binary thinking of having pros and cons over the dominant approaches to policy analysis, facilitators of the smart city (Sacramento & Boossabong, 2023), for example, rather chose to understand the grounds for compromise. Though the very idea of smart city planning is highly technical in nature, the study has elevated the thought that it is even more productive to consider an assimilative practice of strategies in policy analysis rather than sticking with one-way design. The concept of an assimilative practice in planning and policy practice stems from a recognition of the critical and pragmatic understanding that to see public problems from the perspective of feasibility and practicability, and thus solutions are critically well-thought for the benefit of and centered on the public's interest. Moreover, the whole idea of the assimilative practice has been borne out from the equivocal forces of complexities and uncertainties and that of the critical consideration of context, norms, and belief systems.

An Equivocal Force: Complexity and Uncertainty

Undeniably, policy scholars have identified and critically reflected on the pressing challenge to society in contemporary times. The very nature of public problems is no longer the same as previously assumed to be predictable, and that can be concretely defined by policy experts and be provided by 'expert advice' (Fowler, 2021; Heazle, 2012; Howlett et al., 2015). We cannot dismiss the fact that the very expert-centered approach to understanding and providing solutions to public problems may have been proven effective in addressing some issues of the past, which is of urgent demand and needs, especially in the aftermath of wars and the emergence of globalization and further industrialization of societies. However, the global situations are also changing, and the landscapes on how we approach the issues attached to these changes also demand a progressive paradigm and strategies.

Complexities in public problems denote that there are intricate puzzles to understanding and making sense of their interconnectedness (Cairney, 2012; Head & Alford, 2015; Schwartz & Meltzer, 2019). Hence, public problems are to be understood as something that transcends the social, economic, political, and environmental aspects— and as they are complex, they cannot be solved by easily thought solutions. The complex nature of public problems often involves conflicting values and even extends to more cluttered networked dimensions that make one problem entangled and influence the other. According to the book of Geyer & Rihani (2012), complexities do infect our politics and the way we go with our daily transactions. Hence, the very essence of decentralization and flexibility is much needed in understanding that everything is connected, that there are different perspectives, and that it necessitates policy practitioners to navigate the complexities of public opinions and interest groups. Dealing with public problems requires a thoughtful and flexible approach, recognizing that there's no one-size-fits-all solution.

On the other hand, the uncertain nature of public problems is best exemplified by their unpredictability as they are ever-changing and irregularly appearing from time to time. One best-case scenario to illustrate is the emergence of crises that bring uncertainties to the public as to what urgent public problems they might be facing. As a biological disaster or crisis, the pandemic in itself posed uncertainty and distress to economic activities, political dynamics, and social well-being of the society (both locally and globally). There have been other popping public problems all over secondary to the pandemic, which became a result of the forced precarious measure that some decision-makers consider containing the spread of the virus without holistically looking at the causal nature of the action. Other than the pandemic, disasters are also examples of uncertain times that pose public problems to society that are difficult to navigate and are unprecedented. Disasters may open a window of opportunity for other public problems to occur or to unravel. In turn, this puts communities in distress when navigating solutions that are feasible and practical to apply as remedies to urgent issues they face.

The common denominator that the elements in the first premise elevate is the understanding that there is no such thing as a 'one-way best solution' to a public problem that is too complex and dynamic. A scientific approach to addressing an issue may be found necessary for the highly technical nature of public problems. At the same time, a critically oriented issue needs the public to participate in providing alternatives. But in the premise that was presented, the dichotomized or binary thinking towards evolving, complex, and uncertain public problems can be a bit problematic in real-world applications today. In making policy analysis more productive and practical, the move towards the assimilation of technical strategies and the critical approach is yet a conducive and promising direction for policy practitioners to consider. The flexibility of designing a policy analysis process leads to an open window for a creative and pragmatic consideration of potential alternatives to public problems.

Critical Consideration: Context, Norms, and Belief Systems

While a big consideration towards the turn to an assimilative strategy to policy analysis links to the very nature of a public problem, it is also equally relevant to underscore the realities of the society that a public problem occurs as an element, too. The second premise pays important attention to the contextual realities, social norms, and belief systems that also influence the policy process and contribute to how the public sees the situations and decides on a plausible alternative. These critical considerations provide more holistic perspectives (not to mention for policy practitioners to see better the bigger picture of inclusivity, authentic indigenous local knowledge, and culturally sensitive features) that allow a policy process that is more sensitive to people's realities. In turn, this railroad is a path towards crafting policy alternatives that are not parachute solutions and alien to public problems of communities but are informed by practices, local knowledge, and cultural sensitivity in the hopes of efficiency, practicability, and effectiveness.

Contextual realities, or better yet, contextualization in public policy, encompasses the historical backgrounds and cultural contests where public issues arise. Undeniably, these factors shape problems and, at the same time, manifest influence over the feasibility and acceptance of a proposed policy alternative. According to Torgerson (1985), even Harold Lasswell has considered contextualization as significant to policy analysis despite his positivist orientation and a strong focus on the professionalization of the field. In critical policy studies, the role of contextual realities holds significance in the process of policy analysis. For Taylor (1997), context is particularly crucial towards the notion of thinking relationally in unraveling social inequalities, realities on the ground, and the socio-political situations crucial to coming up with policy alternatives. On the other hand, social norms are the unwritten rules that govern society, which also play an important role in shaping public policy from a critical standpoint. In the Asian context, for example, there are some societies that have very high regard for social norms, and policies align with these existing norms. People tend most likely to embrace policies that align with their existing norms, while those that do not may face resistance (De Groot & Schuitema, 2012). Understanding social norms is also helpful to policymakers to prevent the public's reaction to the proposed solution that is linked to and resonates with the values of the community. Finally, belief systems also play a significant role as they encompass cultural, religious, and ideological perspectives in shaping the impact on public opinion and policy reception (Jenkins-Smith et al., 2014; Rein, 1971). In providing alternatives to public problems, some societies are keen on aligning respects to the prevailing belief system in forging policy support and legitimacy to succeed in implementations.

Ignoring the elements on the second premise (contextual realities, social norms, and belief systems) can lead to policies that are impractical, face opposition, or fail to address the root causes of public problems (Curato et al., 2018; De Groot & Schuitema, 2012). Therefore, an effective policy analysis involves a deep understanding of the local context, an awareness of prevailing social norms, and a respectful consideration of diverse belief systems (Buheji & Sisk, 2020; Jenkins-Smith et al., 2014). Integrating these elements ensures that policies are not only well-informed but also culturally sensitive and more likely to garner public acceptance and support. Especially in Asia, the unique features and elements of culture, tradition, power, respect, and social structures hinge strongly on decision-making and are fundamental grounds for consideration in forwarding policy agendas and solutions in most cases (Boossabong & Chamchong, 2019; Sacramento & Boossabong, 2023).

Bringing the 'Public' in Public Policy and Governance: The Role of a Critical Pragmatic 'Assimilative' Practitioner

Stemming from the previous work of Sacramento and Boossabong (2023), the critical observation from the smart city planning in Chiang Mai, Thailand, underscores the role of considerable assimilation of various strategies or approaches in doing policy analysis. This kind of approach to policy analysis moves away from a diagrammatic picture to a nature of nexus that illustrates what is claimed as a 'pragmatic' direction. The concern of the previous work is about the interface of two traditions (TPA as technical-positivist and DPA as subjectivist post-positivist) that become more adaptive and open to a pragmatic understanding that policy analysis is not a linear activity. However, the work may need to be substantially found in its theoretical clutches despite pointing out the productive potential of pragmatic direction to policy analysis. Holistically looking at the assimilative practice goes beyond integrating the practical strategies of assimilations as it is fundamentally founded on the critical reflections and discernment of actors in navigating the public problem. Moreover, the foregoing may have fallen short of clarifying the role of the policy practitioner in the assimilative process. To renavigate the previous work of Fischer and Forester (1993) on the '*Argumentative turn in policy analysis and planning*' and that of Forester (1999) on the '*Deliberative practitioner*' is a critical consideration to understanding the role of a facilitator in the assimilative process of policy analysis.

Needless to say, this writing has excessively pointed out the term 'critical pragmatism' as a crucial thread to policy analysis and to the whole development of the assimilative practice. The use of the concept of critical pragmatism refers much to that of John Forester, where he factored in the role of a policy analyst or planner that is way beyond the 'ideal' technocratic policy analysis who see themselves as experts, and at the same time neutralizes how critical theories take shape (Crane & Weber, 2012; Forester, 2013, 2017; Wagenaar, 2011). Forester turned to the argument that there is a need for both communicative planning and facilitative leadership to blend in order to surface critical pragmatism in planning and policy analysis (Crane & Weber, 2012; Forester, 2017). Critical pragmatism disregards the usual notion of knowledge coming first and that action comes second or that our actions depend heavily on our intentions. What it encourages is to see the broader picture of spatial diversity and help manage interdependence. Hence, critical pragmatism helps reimagine the usual structured and idealistic planning and policy analysis that help us thoroughly evaluate the processes and goals and at the same time in both its action and desired result.

Forester puts attention on the idea that supra-critical approaches tend to overlook productively speaking to power, fall short of acting, and may lack undertaking responsibilities to answer unanswered questions (Forester, 2017; Haselsberger, 2017). At the end of the day, regardless of how critical and harsh policy actors deal with certain policy issues, there has to be someone who needs to work towards providing alternatives anyway (Forester, 2017). Forester's take on the matter lies along the line that regardless of the political orthodoxies and lingering domination of whatever preferred approach, there is still and will always be someone who needs to act, especially in situations that necessitate urgent action. In this vein, what he mentioned as a critical pragmatic planner relates to what the forgoing assimilative discussion in policy analysis thought as the assimilative practitioner. We heed what Forester points out as the core task of a planner or practitioner, which is to "safeguard the participation of those normally excluded from decision-making by institutionalized inequalities" (Wagenaar, 2011, p. 293).

In the previous decades, critical scholars have set forth the understanding of a deliberative practitioner, which eventually differentiated from the mainstream technical policy analyst. This attempt to surface the role of an assimilative practitioner does not negate any of the two. The attempt is to substantiate what could be the role of the assimilative facilitator as a compromise to respond to the productive direction of the assimilation of both camps in policy analysis. Particularly, what this work observed to be of utmost importance is to refer back to Forester's conception of the critical pragmatic theory and the becoming of a critical pragmatist planner. In a way, this complements the study's understanding of an assimilative practitioner and facilitator borne out from critical pragmatic thought.

In detail, an assimilative practitioner or facilitator is viewed as a three-fold characteristic. First, it refers back to the concept of communicative planning, which Wagenaar noted in his reviews as "a new view of public planning as the restructuring of communication between stakeholders with divergent and conflicting interests and large inequalities in power and influence" (Wagenaar, 2011, p. 293). Since the assimilative agenda centers on connecting TPA and DPA strategies, assimilative practitioners are expected to renavigate the usual modes of communication (that of the technical experts and that of the deliberative arena). Of course, the two camps have always seen their opinions themselves to be divergent and conflicted over what is demanded as the 'best' approach to addressing public problems. The assimilative facilitator needs to navigate this divergence in communication among stakeholders and find a compromise to keep the policy analysis going and address the issue. To think of the space for policy analysis as not just absolute but as something that is dynamic gives the practitioner more venues to creatively think of a strategy that is, of course, (a) sensitive to the situation of inequalities and power conflict and (b) that maintains the communicative aspect of facilitation and planning.

Secondly, the redefinition of the role of the policy analyst from the critical-pragmatic conception of Forester is crucial as we consider the assimilative potentials in policy analysis. Forster goes beyond the Lasswellian notion of professionalization of the policy planner or analyst that stemmed from an orthodox assumption that, as experts, they hold power. Instead, though professionals (or rather, some experts) still take the role, they are expected to be more hands-on in fostering inclusivity, collaborative environment, and other forms of participatory and collective action (Wagenaar, 2011). Similarly, an assimilative practitioner is also expected to practice the same, where their handful professional background (or at the very least, practitioner-based experience that is conscious of technical strategies and highly scientific approaches) integrates into the characteristic of a deliberative facilitator that values public participation and opinion, as well as sensitivity to cultural norms and belief system.

Finally, what is critical to the role of an assimilative practitioner is to embody the capability to discern and encourage a deliberative discussion on micropolitical concerns in societies. With the long tradition of technocrat domination and expert-centrism, it is fair that the practitioners are cautious in utilizing technical analysis strategies as it may overlook the probability of a hegemonic overtake rather than identifying the balance between efficiency and urgency in addressing concerns and ethics, as well as, values in addressing public problems. Deliberating the concerns in a micro-level space enables various stakeholders to expand their potential and comprehensively cover the enduring inequalities of power domination in problem identification, thinking of alternatives, and making decisions (Forester, 2013; Wagenaar, 2011). Hence, it is then proper to underscore that the role of an assimilative practitioner demands a certain level of precautions and consciousness in steering the whole policy analysis dynamics with an assimilative practice.

Then, how can the critical pragmatic role of the planner or practitioner support the idea of bringing in and genuinely engaging the 'public' in policy and governance? From the previous discussion, twofold manifestation is at the centerpiece:

a. The policy analysis process is not only delimited to whatever camp or approach is deemed fit to address a public problem best. We cannot deny the fact that a certain strategy from technical analysis and the participation of scientist-expert can be well demanded. But to balance the policy analysis through a critical pragmatic assimilative process, factors in public participation and their genuine involvement are needed. The assimilative practitioner's intervention is critical to making a judgment in integrating various approaches,
b. The assimilative practitioner is instrumental in the reform of the dynamics in policy analysis as they take the balance on how actors get involved in the policy process. Creatively designing the assimilative dynamics in policy analysis is fundamental in order to empower those who are under-represented to leverage their opinions about the problem and potential alternatives based on local knowledge.

Hence, we clarify that positioning the policy practitioner as an actor who embodies wisdom and fair judgment in making the policy process more inclusive is critical in the assimilative considerations to policy analysis. By critically pointing out the role of the assimilative practitioner, we hope to ensure and safeguard that the policy process hears all sides of the spectrum of decision-making (regardless of the technocrat or politician's expertise or that of the wisdom of the public from contextual and local knowledge). However, at some point, the practitioner needs to navigate the process as several critical junctures may necessitate prioritizing 'some' sound options (regardless of whether it is highly technical or progressively public-oriented) depending on what the context necessitates. Hence, the assimilative practitioners still need to appease their positionality of factoring in the publicness of policymaking and governance by going back to global values of inclusivity, people's participation, and transformation.

A Critical Pragmatic Juncture of Policy Analysis in Chiang Mai, Thailand, During COVID-19

The preceding discussion clarified the role and characteristics of an assimilative practitioner that takes off from a critical pragmatic lens. In this section, the essay will illustrate how critical pragmatism is considered the centerpiece of the COVID-19 policy response and, better yet said, "considerations for compromise," while delineating some critical points where policy practitioners and even the public have integrated the assimilative formula. From my personal notes, I will be illustrating Chiang Mai City's (Thailand) COVID-19 response in general and some specific illustrative instances during the pandemic that showcased flexibility in practitioners and local communities as they critically and pragmatically responded to the needs of the time.

Of course, the pandemic has posed tensions and abrupt shifts in public health policies, particularly during the first quarter of 2020, where the government's aspiration was to contain the spread of the virus (prior to finding and rollout of the vaccine) (V. Q. T. Li et al., 2022). I traveled to Chiang Mai at the height of the pandemic in November 2020 and have first-hand experience with how the Thai government has dealt with the situation (and, of course, with a brief comparative background from my experience in the Philippines). Also, note the purpose of the succeeding illustrations is not to romanticize the sufferings of the people from the pandemic situation but to draw lessons and insights from experiences on how society has adapted and adjusted to the circumstances brought by the pandemic by pointing out some of the assimilative junctures in doing policy analysis amid the crisis.

While there has been a global mandate from the international community that we in the Global South are boxed to adopt and follow due to the uncertainty and complexity of the situation, some policy practitioners (in some countries) have navigated the decision-making and implementation based on contextual realities. For once, Thailand, in general, draws a big chunk of its economy from tourism industries. COVID-19 has closed down tourism spots, travel, hotels, and resorts, among others, and has shaken local economies and communities (Sin et al., 2021). To put it in my words, Thailand experienced a 'tourism hangover' at that time, where the most artificially built environment where tourists used to flock was closed down and vacated. I also briefly remember going to a supposed 'indigenous long neck village' somewhere in the northern part of Chiang Mai City, but to a surprise, it turned out into a ghost town when indigenous hill tribe people flew back to the mountains (Suratana et al., 2021). Of course, social science has a lot to discuss on this matter, but from a policy perspective, it is interesting to see the links and how policy practitioners have navigated obstacles and attempts to resuscitate the local economy amid the pandemic.

Policy practitioners in Thailand have navigated the contextual realities, local situations in communities, as well as inequalities. Thais have demanded better treatment and conditions from the policymakers and implementors of the COVID-19 response, specifically on the decline of local economies where informal entrepreneurs and workers have been highly affected (especially those from the service and tourism industry). With all these considerations, COVID-19 response policies are observed to be a 'bit looser' compared to the supposed hard scientific informed strategies as applied by neighboring Vietnam, Singapore, and the Philippines (Djalante et al., 2020). As early as August to October 2020, Thailand navigated incessant efforts to open its doors to tourists due to the demand, feelings of despair, and pressure from the public, while at the same time weighing in some technically informed evidence and statistics from the COVID-19 situation. Personally, I have benefited from that compromising policy on entry of foreign nationals to Thailand in the middle of the pandemic. Hence, making such a decision is an example of an assimilative formula that not only understands the hard empirical evidence but also takes a handful of consideration of the contextual realities, situations, and social justice for those who are in need (Sacramento & Boossabong, 2023).

Expanding a bit on Thailand's measures during COVID-19, local tourism and travel are much encouraged, and travel expenses (plane tickets) are even subsidized by the government. Taking a flight from Chiang Mai City to Bangkok City and even to Phuket City is very encouraging due to low fares, which have eventually helped locals travel and spend in other provinces. The clamor for subsidies during the pandemic has made the government decide to implement further assistance to Thais in the high hopes of peddling local economies. Informed by discourses among the public (emotions, narratives, incessant efforts of the people to demand accountability from the government) (Djalante et al., 2020; Fakhruddin et al., 2020), policymakers made necessary compromises and adjustments by launching the *Kon La Krung* policy initiative (government subsidizing 50% of the price of purchase), which eventually have helped small business going and supported the local economy. This policy is so encouraging that it made the public pursue travel plans to different locations in Thailand. Looking at the assimilative formula in this policy initiative, *Kon La Krung* is even coupled with technical and innovative tools such as the use of a unified app for smooth implementation and regulation.

Linked to the initiative of resuscitating the local economy, of course, the COVID-19 situation and public health need not be compromised. Another effort of policymakers in Thailand is the launch of the *Thai Chana* tracing system via QR code scanning that allows people's mobility while keeping records for contact tracing. Deliberately, the public has also welcomed the idea of tracing their movements as it is imperative to public health, and at the same time, it has allowed them to move freely to different places and continue everyday life despite the pandemic. The *Thai Chana* initiative is an important conduit to steering local economies amid the pandemic, which eventually allowed tourism businesses and industries to gradually re-open for as long as there is religious compliance with the contract tracing policy.

On a similar page, the opening of schools and universities as early as November 2020 came from pressure when students clamored about the differences between online and onsite instructions. Thailand's pandemic policy on education has navigated along compromises and decentering agenda, which made practitioners aware of critical and pragmatic interventions should there be a breakout of the virus (Boossabong & Chamchong, 2020). For example, the deliberate tracking of COVID-19 statistics nationwide and in the city and province of Chiang Mai has informed the most pragmatic measures that education policy practitioners should consider. There was a time when academic activities inside and outside university engagements students brought the surge of COVID-19 cases and the most practical action that made policy practitioners respond to refer to contact tracing databases and utilize available resources and facilities such as university dormitories to become quarantine and isolation centers.

The pandemic has also decentered the way policy practitioners see their role as professionals (Boossabong & Chamchong, 2020). This has led to making them more hands-on in crafting and implementing inclusive, collective, and participatory policies. Drawing from Chiang Mai, Thailand's case, the rollout of vaccines has navigated not only the scientific advice but has also become a matter of deliberation and critical pragmatism. Thai people and even some foreigners living in Thailand have manifested whether or not they are getting the vaccine, what brand of vaccine to take, and whether the schedule is conducive, among other factors that also shaped the vaccine rollout policy. Of course, the dilemma over the brand of the vaccine has been a matter of public deliberation (Suphanchaimat et al., 2021). Because of the popular preference of some for a specific brand, there was a peculiar point where public health policy practitioners have also adjusted and adopted popular demand, which has led to organizing the purchase of a vaccine brand for people who would want it at their own cost (Mueangpoon et al., 2022). Regarding the rollout of the vaccine, the contact system that is linked to the Thai National IDs has made the process easier. The registered publics were contacted for their schedule for vaccination through their cellular numbers. The rollout of the vaccines was also almost available in all public spaces, such as university auditoriums and malls, beyond the supposed administration in professional healthcare centers. Of course, there are some flexibilities on schedules in consideration of several factors; while some would also opt out due to the unavailability of vaccine options, others would consider walking in during instances where they feel it is convenient.

Another aspect of the pandemic landscape in Chiang Mai City is the continuous delivery of social and economic development services and projects. While the public health sector has been focusing mainly on the effective and efficient rollout of COVID-19 response, vaccination, and recovery measures, the rest of the public service arm of the local government has, at the same time, become invested in addressing emergent policy issues of the time (especially in the middle of the pandemic). This discussion builds on what Boossabong and Chamchong (2020) highlighted in their work on "*Coping with*

COVID-19 in a non-democratic system: Policy lessons from Thailand's centralized government." They have argued that in a critical and uncertain situation like the COVID-19 pandemic, decentralizing and re-democratizing the systems of politics and governance is imperative for 'safety participation' in policy analysis and decision-making. The desired dynamics in decentralized and re-democratize policy analysis and decision-making are attributed to the essential relationship between science, politics, and the public (Boossabong & Chamchong, 2020), which is better exemplified and drawn from an assimilative formula that this work articulates.

In essence, being sensitive to the micropolitics (Forester, 2013, 2017; Wagenaar, 2011) within the dynamics of science, politics, and the public is an imperative consideration for practitioners amid the pandemic and for navigating a more practical yet critical policy analysis and alternatives (Boossabong & Chamchong, 2020; Sacramento & Boossabong, 2023). Some of the most familiar policy initiatives that local Chiang Mai City practitioners have implemented during the pandemic, to which I have direct access, illustrate two most important lessons. For once, planning and policy designing have reshaped their direction and approach of bringing people (among various stakeholders) together and closely to deliberate on matters concerning a public problem. The smart city planning in Fah Ham district in Chiang Mai, Thailand, has integrated an assimilative approach through linking strategies with what the situations would demand (Sacramento & Boossabong, 2023). At points, the planning necessitates integrating and assimilating various strategies in arriving at sound deliberation and policy alternatives that can practically address a concern without going too idealistic and, at the same time, sensitive to the resources and situational realities on the ground. The second lesson illustrates the role of policy practitioners in the process, especially in navigating the unique and dynamic micropolitical aspects of policy analysis. As already reiterated, decentralizing and re-democratizing the policy process is crucial to a productive policy process in Thailand during COVID-19. Of course, the assimilative practitioner, as the way we call it in this article, carefully looks into the dynamics of the policy analysis process that has navigated the diversity of stakeholders' opinions, knowledge, and power (Boossabong & Chamchong, 2023; Fung & Wright, 2003; Hoppe, 2011; Y. Li, 2015; Sacramento, 2023a, 2023b), and the varying policy arenas available and convenient during a turbulent time.

The illustration of (a) how policy analysis works through the lens of an assimilative agenda and (b) how assimilative practitioners navigated along the complexities of public problems made sense in the context of the developing country, specifically on how Thailand has faced the COVID-19 situation. How John Forester puts the characteristics of critical pragmatic planning resonates with how an assimilative practitioner works on the ground. What is much needed to underline here is how the assimilative potentials have worked in the non-democratic context. How the strategies of practitioners have navigated the complexities of situations and the diversities of actors in the face of authority and power manifests critical pragmatism in dealing with policy initiatives. While the illustrations may have presented interesting ground for engaging discourse on the assimilative strategy, critical pragmatic perspective, and the role of an assimilative practitioner, there is still much room to extend and clarify its advantages and limitations in application across contexts.

CONCLUSION

The chapter responds to the existing attempt to mend the debate between the two camps in policy analysis— the technocratic strategies in policy analysis (TPA) and the role of the critical and citizen-centered approach of critical policy analysis (i.e., DPA). The discussions contributed to how we imagine the role of an assimilative practitioner in policy analysis that links to existing discussions of John Forester on critical pragmatism in planning, as well as to critical scholars on deliberation like Frank Fischer and Hendrik Wagenaar who are open to flexibility, however, apprehensive about technical overtake and domination.

The role of assimilative agenda in policy analysis keenly showcased how critical pragmatism looks at the height of the COVID-19 pandemic. The illustration of the role of policy practitioners and the policy processes in Chiang Mai City, Thailand, manifested support for the direction of the study. The chapter highlights that the assimilative nature of policy analysis and the role of an assimilative practitioner can be drawn along the lines of critical pragmatism. In a time where society is shaken by the impending threats of the pandemic, many have suffered much in distress due to social injustices, high inequalities (of political power, resources, and social status), and pressing contextual realities. A sound policy analysis does not require a hectic and technical system or a very messy and lengthy deliberative process. Nevertheless, discussions (while necessary to give credit to both sides of the approaches) direct us to go beyond the boundaries and limitations and seek a creative reimagination of policy analysis that is both assimilative and critically pragmatic.

ACKNOWLEDGMENT

The author would like to extend his big appreciation to Dr. Piyapong Boossabong for constantly supporting and helping with the direction of his doctoral research and academic papers. Also, thanks to Dr. Frank Fischer and Dr. John Forester for the encouragement and for giving valuable insights to the theoretical debates and on the arguments surrounding planning and policy analysis, that have inspired and led the author to proceed with writing this chapter. The points presented are based on the author's observations and critical reflections.

REFERENCES

Bächtiger, A., Dryzek, J. S., Mansbridge, J., & Warren, M. E. (Eds.). (2018). *The Oxford handbook of deliberative democracy*. Oxford University Press.

Béné, C., Mehta, L., McGranahan, G., Cannon, T., Gupte, J., & Tanner, T. (2018). Resilience as a policy narrative: Potentials and limits in the context of urban planning. *Climate and Development*, *10*(2), 116–133. doi:10.1080/17565529.2017.1301868

Boossabong, P., & Chamchong, P. (2019). The practice of deliberative policy analysis in the context of political and cultural challenges: Lessons from Thailand. *Policy Studies*, *40*(5), 476–491. doi:10.1080/01442872.2019.1618815

Boossabong, P., & Chamchong, P. (2020). Coping with COVID-19 in a non-democratic system: Policy lessons from Thailand's centralized government. *International Review of Public Policy*, *2*(3), 358–371. doi:10.4000/irpp.1382

Boossabong, P., & Chamchong, P. (2023). Hope, fear and public policy: Towards empathetic policy process. *Critical Policy Studies*, •••, 1–19. doi:10.1080/19460171.2023.2247048

Boossabong, P., & Fischer, F. (2018). Deliberative policy analysis. In A. Bächtiger & ... (Eds.), *The Oxford handbook of deliberative democracy* (pp. 584–594)., doi:10.1093/oxfordhb/9780198747369.013.39

Buheji, D. M., & Sisk, F. C. W. (2020). *You and the new normal: Jobs, pandemics, relationship, climate change, success, poverty, leadership, and belief in the emerging new world.* Author House.

Cairney, P. (2012). Complexity theory in political science and public policy. *Political Studies Review, 10*(3), 346–358. doi:10.1111/j.1478-9302.2012.00270.x

Clarke, S. E. (2007). Context-sensitive policy methods. In F. Ficher & G. Miller (Eds.), *Handbook of public policy analysis*. Routledge.

Crane, R., & Weber, R. (2012). *The Oxford handbook of urban planning*. OUP USA.

Curato, N., Hammond, M., & Min, J. B. (2018). *Power in deliberative democracy: Norms, forums, systems*. Springer.

De Groot, J. I. M., & Schuitema, G. (2012). How to make the unpopular popular? Policy characteristics, social norms and the acceptability of environmental policies. *Environmental Science & Policy, 19–20*, 100–107. doi:10.1016/j.envsci.2012.03.004

Djalante, R., Nurhidayah, L., Van Minh, H., Phuong, N. T. N., Mahendradhata, Y., Trias, A., Lassa, J., & Miller, M. A. (2020). COVID-19 and ASEAN responses: Comparative policy analysis. *Progress in Disaster Science, 8*, 100129. doi:10.1016/j.pdisas.2020.100129

Dunn, W. N. (2015). *Public policy analysis*. Routledge.

Dunn, W. N. (2018). Public policy analysis: An integrated approach (Sixth Edition). Routledge, Taylor & Francis Group.

Durnová, A. (2015). Lost in translation: Expressing emotions in policy deliberation. In F. Fischer & ... (Eds.), *Handbook of Critical Policy Studies* (pp. 222–238).

Durnová, A. (2018). Understanding emotions in policy studies through Foucault and Deleuze. *Politics and Governance, 6*(4), 95–102. doi:10.17645/pag.v6i4.1528

Durnová, A., Formánková, L., & Hejzlarová, E. (2022). Empowered or patronized? The role of emotions in policies and professional discourses on birth care. *Critical Social Policy, 42*(1), 129–149. doi:10.1177/02610183211001494

Dye, T. R. (1978). *Policy analysis: What governments do, why they do it, and what difference it makes.* University of Alabama Press.

Fakhruddin, B. (Shm), Blanchard, K., & Ragupathy, D. (2020). Are we there yet? The transition from response to recovery for the COVID-19 pandemic. *Progress in Disaster Science, 7*, 100102. doi:10.1016/j.pdisas.2020.100102

Fischer, F., & Forester, J. (1993). *The argumentative turn in policy analysis and planning*. Duke University Press.

Fischer, F., & Gottweis, H. (2012). *The Argumentative turn revisited: Public policy as communicative practice*. Duke University Press.

Fischer, F., & Miller, G. J. (2007). *Handbook of public policy analysis: Theory, politics, and methods*. CRC Press.

Forester, J. (1999). *The deliberative practitioner: Encouraging participatory planning processes*. MIT Press.

Forester, J. (2009). Policy analysis as critical listening. In R. Goodin, M. Moran, & M. Rein (Eds.), The Oxford Handbook of Public Policy (pp. 124–151). Oxford University Press. https://doi.org/ doi:10.1093/oxfordhb/9780199548453.003.0006

Forester, J. (2013). On the theory and practice of critical pragmatism: Deliberative practice and creative negotiations. *Planning Theory*, *12*(1), 5–22. doi:10.1177/1473095212448750

Forester, J. (2017). On the evolution of a critical pragmatism. In B. Haselsberger (Ed.), *Encounters with Planning Thought* (pp. 280–296). Routledge.

Fowler, L. (2021). How to implement policy: Coping with ambiguity and uncertainty. *Public Administration*, *99*(3), 581–597. doi:10.1111/padm.12702

Fung, A., & Wright, E. O. (2003). *Deepening Democracy: Institutional Innovations in Empowered Participatory Governance*. Verso.

Geyer, R., & Rihani, S. (2012). *Complexity and public policy: A new approach to 21st century politics, policy and society*. Routledge., doi:10.4324/9780203856925

Gilley, B. (2017). Technocracy and democracy as spheres of justice in public policy. *Policy Sciences*, *50*(1), 9–22. doi:10.1007/s11077-016-9260-2

Hajer, M. (2003). Policy without polity? Policy analysis and the institutional void. *Policy Sciences*, *36*(2), 175–195. doi:10.1023/A:1024834510939

Hartley, K., Kuecker, G., & Woo, J. J. (2019). Practicing public policy in an age of disruption. *Policy Design and Practice*, *2*(2), 163–181. doi:10.1080/25741292.2019.1622276

Haselsberger, B. (2017). *Encounters in planning thought: 16 autobiographical essays from key thinkers in spatial planning*. Taylor & Francis.

Head, B. W., & Alford, J. (2015). Wicked problems: Implications for public policy and management. *Administration & Society*, *47*(6), 711–739. doi:10.1177/0095399713481601

Heazle, M. (2012). *Uncertainty in policy making*. Routledge., doi:10.4324/9781849776691

Hoppe, R. (2011). Institutional constraints and practical problems in deliberative and participatory policy making. *Policy and Politics*, *39*, 163–186. doi:10.1332/030557310X519650

Howlett, M., Ramesh, M., & Wu, X. (2015). Understanding the persistence of policy failures: The role of politics, governance and uncertainty. *Public Policy and Administration*, *30*(3–4), 209–220. doi:10.1177/0952076715593139

Jenkins-Smith, H., Silva, C. L., Gupta, K., & Ripberger, J. T. (2014). Belief system continuity and change in policy advocacy coalitions: Using cultural theory to specify belief systems, coalitions, and sources of change. *Policy Studies Journal: the Journal of the Policy Studies Organization*, *42*(4), 484–508. doi:10.1111/psj.12071

Li, V. Q. T., Ma, L., & Wu, X. (2022). COVID-19, policy change, and post-pandemic data governance: A case analysis of contact tracing applications in East Asia. *Policy and Society*, *41*(1), 129–142. doi:10.1093/polsoc/puab019

Li, Y. (2015). Think tank 2.0 for deliberative policy analysis. *Policy Sciences*, *48*(1), 25–50. doi:10.1007/s11077-014-9207-4

Mueangpoon, K., Inchan, C., Kaewmuneechoke, P., Rattana, P., Budsratid, S., Japakiya, S., Ngamchaliew, P., & Vichitkunakorn, P. (2022). Self-reported COVID-19 vaccine hesitancy and willingness to pay: A cross-sectional survey in thailand. *Vaccines*, *10*(4), 627. doi:10.3390/vaccines10040627

Rein, M. (1971). Social policy analysis as the interpretation of beliefs. *Journal of the American Institute of Planners*, *37*(5), 297–310. doi:10.1080/01944367108977836

Sacramento, N. J. J. E. (2023a). Grassroots involvement on Global South policy narratives and deliberative action on climate change loss and damage. *Public Administration and Policy*, *26*(2), 156–168. doi:10.1108/PAP-12-2022-0146

Sacramento, N. J. J. E. (2023b). How can informal discursive arenas complement deliberative policy analysis? *Journal of Public Administration, Public Affairs, and Management*, *21*(1), 1.

Sacramento, N. J. J. E., & Boossabong, P. (2023). Technocratic and deliberative nexus in policy analysis: Learning from smart city planning in Chiang Mai, Thailand. *Journal of Asian Public Policy*, *16*(3), 271–287. doi:10.1080/17516234.2021.2007210

Schwartz, A. F., & Meltzer, R. (2019). *Policy analysis as problem solving: A flexible and evidence-based framework*. Taylor and Francis.

Sin, H. L., Mostafanezhad, M., & Cheer, J. M. (2021). Tourism geographies in the 'Asian century.'. *Tourism Geographies*, *23*(4), 649–658. doi:10.1080/14616688.2020.1826571

Stark, A., & Taylor, M. (2014). Citizen participation, community resilience and crisis-management policy. *Australian Journal of Political Science*, *49*(2), 300–315. doi:10.1080/10361146.2014.899966

Suphanchaimat, R., Tuangratananon, T., Rajatanavin, N., Phaiyarom, M., Jaruwanno, W., & Uansri, S. (2021). Prioritization of the target population for coronavirus disease 2019 (COVID-19) vaccination program in Thailand. *International Journal of Environmental Research and Public Health*, *18*(20), 10803. doi:10.3390/ijerph182010803

Suratana, S., Tamornpark, R., Apidechkul, T., Srichan, P., Mulikaburt, T., Wongnuch, P., Kitchanapaibul, S., Yeemard, F., & Udplong, A. (2021). Impacts of and survival adaptations to the COVID-19 pandemic among the hill tribe population of northern Thailand: A qualitative study. *PLoS One*, *16*(6), e0252326. doi:10.1371/journal.pone.0252326

Taylor, S. (1997). Critical policy analysis: Exploring contexts, texts and consequences. *Discourse (Abingdon), 18*(1), 23–35. doi:10.1080/0159630970180102

Thissen, W. A. H., & Walker, W. E. (2013). *Public policy analysis: New developments*. Springer., doi:10.1007/978-1-4614-4602-6

Torgerson, D. (1985). Contextual orientation in policy analysis: The contribution of Harold D. Lasswell. *Policy Sciences, 18*(3), 241–261. doi:10.1007/BF00138911

Wagenaar, H. (2011). "A beckon to the makings, workings and doings of human beings": The critical pragmatism of John Forester. *Public Administration Review, 71*(2), 293–298. doi:10.1111/j.1540-6210.2011.02341.x

Wagenaar, H. (2014). *Meaning in action: Interpretation and dialogue in policy analysis*. Routledge., doi:10.4324/9781315702476

ENDNOTE

1 The researcher positions as both as an insider experiencing the whole process of policy making and implementation in Chiang Mai, Thailand during the COVID-19 pandemic. In addition, the research also has participated in various project implementation initiatives of the policy think tank within the same timeframe. As outsider, the research gives a third-eye view of the policy implementation process, that is to see from another perspective influenced by different government and regimes, cultural background, and beliefs.

Compilation of References

Ababneh, M. M. A. (2017). Creative Tourism. *Journal of Tourism & Hospitality (Los Angeles, Calif.), 06*(02). doi:10.4172/2167-0269.1000282

Abbott, K. W., & Snidal, D. (1998). Why states act through formal international organizations. *The Journal of Conflict Resolution, 42*(1), 3–32. doi:10.1177/0022002798042001001

Abdullahi, A. M. (2007). The Ogaden National Liberation Front (ONLF): The Dilemma of Its Struggle in Ethiopia. *Review of African Political Economy, 34*(113), 556–562. https://www.jstor.org/stable/20406430

Abrahamsen, R., & Williams, M. (2005). *The Globalisation of Private Security: Country Report: Sierra Leone*. University of Wales. https://users.aber.ac.uk/rbh/privatesecurity/country%20report-sierra%20leone.pdf,

Abrahamson, P. (2017). East Asian welfare regime: Obsolete ideal-type or diversified reality. *Journal of Asian Public Policy, 10*(1), 90–103. doi:10.1080/17516234.2016.1258524

Abreu, J. (2018). *Inteligência Territorial – Governança, Sustentabilidade e Transparência*. Almedina.

Abuza, Z. (1995). *Cambodia: The Legacy and Lessons of UNTAC*. Oxford University Press.

Acharya, A. (2003). Democratisation and the prospects for participatory regionalism in Southeast Asia. *Third World Quarterly, 24*(2), 375–390. doi:10.1080/0143659032000074646

Acharya, A. (2014). *Constructing a security community in Southeast Asia: ASEAN and the problem of regional order* (3rd ed.). Routledge. doi:10.4324/9781315796673

Adamo, S. B. (2009). *Search of Shelter*. Mapping the Effects of Climate Change on Human Migration and Displacement.

Adams, C. A., & Frost, G. R. (2008). Integrating sustainability reporting into management practices. *Accounting Forum, 32*(2), 1–15. doi:10.1016/j.accfor.2008.05.002

Adams, D., & Adams, J. (1968). Education and Social Development. *Review of Educational Research, 38*(3), 243–263. doi:10.2307/1169396

AFP. (2019). *Former Blackwater contractor in Myanmar security venture*. France24. https://www.france24.com/en/20190321-former-blackwater-contractor-myanmar-security-venture

Afsar, B., Badir, Y. F., & Bin Saeed, B. (2014). Transformational leadership and innovative work behavior. *Industrial Management & Data Systems, 114*(8), 1270–1300. doi:10.1108/IMDS-05-2014-0152

Agapity, G., & Mugobi, T. (2023). Escapism Experience an Avenue for Tourism Development: Mapping the Test of Tanzania: Evidence from Arusha Region. *African Journal of Tourism and Hospitality Management, 2*(1), 1–18. doi:10.37284/ajthm.2.1.1204

Agnoletti, M., Conti, L., Frezza, L., & Santoro, A. (2015). Territorial analysis of the agricultural terraced landscapes of Tuscany (Italy): Preliminary results. *Sustainability (Basel)*, *7*(4), 4564–4581. doi:10.3390/su7044564

Aguilera, R. V., Rupp, D. E., Williams, C. A., & Ganapathi, J. (2007). Putting the S Back in Corporate Social Responsibility: A Multi-Level Theory of Social Change in Organizations. *Academy of Management Review*, *32*(3), 836–863. doi:10.5465/amr.2007.25275678

Agyeman, J. (2020). Local Environment and the UN Sustainable Development Goals. *Local Environment*, *25*(5), 336–337. doi:10.1080/13549839.2020.1751444

Ahmadi, B. (2023, December 07). *How the Taliban Enables Violence Against Women*. United States Institute of Peace. https://www.usip.org/publications/2023/12/how-taliban-enables-violence-against-women

Ahmadi, B., & Ebadi, A. (2022, April 01). *Taliban's Ban on Girls' Education in Afghanistan*. United States Institute of Peace. https://www.usip.org/publications/2022/04/talibans-ban-girls-education-afghanistan

Ahn, S.-H., & Lee, S. S.-y. (2012). Explaining Korean welfare state development with new empirical data and methods. *Asian Social Work and Policy Review*, *6*(2), 67–85. doi:10.1111/j.1753-1411.2012.00063.x

Aidukaite, J., Saxonberg, S., Szelewa, D., & Szikra, D. (2021). Social policy in the face of a global pandemic: Policy responses to the Covid-19 crisis in Central and Eastern Europe. *Social Policy and Administration*, *55*(2), 358–373. doi:10.1111/spol.12704 PMID:33821058

Akande, D., & Liefländer, T. (2013). Clarifying Necessity, Imminence, and Proportionality in the Law of Self-Defense. *The American Journal of International Law*, *107*(3), 563–570. doi:10.5305/amerjintelaw.107.3.0563

AkdemirH.Sousa De São JoséJ. M.Rodrigues GonçalvesA. (2023). Empirical Research on Creative Tourism: A Systematic Review. Journal of Tourism & Development, 531-550 Páginas. doi:10.34624/RTD.V41I0.30537

Al-Debei, M., & Avison, D. (2010). Developing a unified framework of the business model concept. *European Journal of Information Systems*, *19*(3), 359–376. doi:10.1057/ejis.2010.21

AlHares, A. (2020). Corporate governance mechanisms and R&D intensity in OECD courtiers. *Corporate Governance (Bradford)*, *20*(5), 863–885.

Ali, M. (2002). *Dinajpurer Adivasi*. Dinajpur Adivasi Academy.

al-Jeratli, K., Fansa, M., & Khattab, B. (2024, January 19). *Who stops the destruction of vegetation in Syria?* Enab Baladi. https://english.enabbaladi.net/archives/2024/01/who-stops-the-destruction-of-vegetation-in-syria/

Allison, L., & Taylor, M. (2017). ASEAN's 'people-oriented' aspirations: Civil society influences on non-traditional security governance. *Australian Journal of International Affairs*, *71*(1), 24–41. doi:10.1080/10357718.2015.1135870

Almeida-Santana, A., & Moreno-Gil, S. (2017). New trends in information search and their influence on destination loyalty: Digital destinations and relationship marketing. *Journal of Destination Marketing & Management*, *6*(2), 150–161. doi:10.1016/j.jdmm.2017.02.003

Amado, J., Costa, A. P., & Crusoé, N. (2000). A técnica de análise de conteúdo. *Revista Referência*, *5*, 53–63.

Ameyaw-Brobbey, T. (2023). THE U.S. WITHDRAWAL, TALIBAN TAKEOVER, AND ONTOLOGICAL (IN)SECURITY IN AFGHANISTAN. *World Affairs*, *186*(1), 105–134. doi:10.1177/00438200221125800

Amoah, P. A. (2020). Examining attitudes towards welfare in an in/security regime: Evidence from Ghana. *Social Policy and Society*, *19*(4), 1–16. doi:10.1017/S1474746420000172

An, B. Y., & Tang, S.-Y. (2020). Lessons from covid-19 responses in East Asia: Institutional infrastructure and enduring policy instruments. *American Review of Public Administration*, *50*(6–7), 790–800. doi:10.1177/0275074020943707

Anbumozhi, V. (2017). Ensuring ASEAN's sustainable and resilient future. In A. Baviera & L. Maramis (Eds.), *ASEAN@50 Building ASEAN community: political–security and socio-cultural reflections* (Vol. 4, pp. 309–323). Economic Research Institute for ASEAN and East Asia.

Anderson, E. S., & Jessen, S. A. (2003). Project maturity in organisations. *International Journal of Project Management*, *21*(6), 457–461. doi:10.1016/S0263-7863(02)00088-1

Andonova, L. B., Betsill, M. M., & Bulkeley, H. (2009). Transnational climate governance. *Global Environmental Politics*, *9*(2), 52–73. doi:10.1162/glep.2009.9.2.52

Andreou, P. C., Antoniou, C., Horton, J., & Louca, C. (2016). Corporate governance and firm specific stock price crashes. *European Financial Management*, *22*(5), 916–956. doi:10.1111/eufm.12084

Ang, R. (2021, December 1). *Employ*ment rate of seniors rose at a faster pace to 31.7%: MOM. *The Straits Times*. https://www.straitstimes.com/singapore/jobs/employment-rate-of-seniors-rose-at-a-faster-pace-to-317-mom

Anshari, M., Almunawar, M. N., & Masri, M. (2020). An overview of financial technology in Indonesia. *Financial technology and disruptive innovation in ASEAN*, (pp. 216-224). IEEE.

Anshari, M., Almunawar, M. N., & Masri, M. (2022). Digital twin: Financial technology's next frontier of robo-advisor. *Journal of Risk and Financial Management*, *15*(4), 163. doi:10.3390/jrfm15040163

Anshari, M., Almunawar, M. N., Masri, M., & Hamdan, M. (2019). Digital marketplace and FinTech to support agriculture sustainability. *Energy Procedia*, *156*, 234–238. doi:10.1016/j.egypro.2018.11.134

Anshari, M., Almunawar, M. N., Masri, M., & Hrdy, M. (2021). Financial technology with AI-enabled and ethical challenges. *Society*, *58*(3), 189–195. doi:10.1007/s12115-021-00592-w

An, W., & Alarcón, S. (2020). How Can Rural Tourism Be Sustainable? A Systematic Review. *Sustainability (Basel)*, *12*(18), 7758. doi:10.3390/su12187758

AP News Staff. (2022). Cambodian leader says officials must master mobile internet. *AP News*. (https://apnews.com/article/technology-media-social-media-smartphones-cambodia-b19df581b637fe72d366d24c9db3cf23

Aras, G., & Crowther, D. (2009). Corporate sustainability reporting: A study in disingenuity? *Journal of Business Ethics*, *87*(1), 279–288. doi:10.1007/s10551-008-9806-0

Arcos-Pumarola, J., Paquin, A. G., & Sitges, M. H. (2023). The use of intangible heritage and creative industries as a tourism asset in the UNESCO creative cities network. *Heliyon*, *9*(1), e13106. doi:10.1016/j.heliyon.2023.e13106 PMID:36747939

Ares, M., Bürgisser, R., & Häusermann, S. (2021). Attitudinal polarization towards the redistributive role of the state in the wake of the COVID-19 crisis. *Journal of Elections, Public Opinion, and Parties*, *31*(sup1, S1), 41–55. doi:10.1080/17457289.2021.1924736

Argos, C., & Reeves, H. (2010). Climate Refugees (First Edition first Printing). The MIT Press.

Arino, Y., Prabhakar, S. V. R. K., Lee, Y.-Y., Ikeda, M., & Zusman, E. (2021). *ASEAN State of Climate Change Report*. ASEAN Secretariat.

Arjona, A., Kasfir, N., & Mampilly, Z. (2015). Rebel governance in civil war. In *Rebel Governance in Civil War*. Cambridge University Press., doi:10.1017/CBO9781316182468.009

Arrow, K. J., Dasgupta, P., Goulder, L. H., Mumford, K. J., & Oleson, K. (2012). Sustainability and the measurement of wealth. *Environment and Development Economics, 17*(3), 317–353. doi:10.1017/S1355770X12000137

Arts, W., & Gelissen, J. (2001). Welfare states, solidarity and justice principles: Does the type really matter? *Acta Sociologica, 44*(4), 283–299. doi:10.1177/000169930104400401

Asensio-López, D., Cabez-García, L., & González-Álvarez, N. (2019). Corporate governance and innovation: A theoretical review. *European Journal of Management and Business Economics, 28*(3), 266–284.

Ashford, S. J., Wellman, N., Sully de Luque, M., De Stobbeleir, K. E. M., & Wollan, M. (2018). Two roads to effectiveness: CEO feedback seeking, vision articulation, and firm performance. *Journal of Organizational Behavior, 39*(1), 82–95. doi:10.1002/job.2211

Ashurst, C., Doherty, N. F., & Peppard, J. (2008). Improving the impact of IT developments projects: The benefits realization capability model. *European Journal of Information Systems, 17*(4), 352–370. doi:10.1057/ejis.2008.33

Aslan, M. (2020). Hybrid Political Order in Libya: State, Non-State, and Armed Actors. *Insight Turkey, 22*(4), 139–156. doi:10.25253/99.2020224.09

Aspinall, E. (2014). Health care and democratization in Indonesia. *Democratization, 21*(5), 803–823. doi:10.1080/13510347.2013.873791

Atkinson, R. (1999). Project management: Cost, time and quality, two best guesses and a phenomenon, it's time to accept other success criteria. *International Journal of Project Management, 17*(6), 337–342. doi:10.1016/S0263-7863(98)00069-6

Atsız, O., & Temiz, S. (2022). Literary tourism: A perspective of the visitor experience in the Museum of Innocence. In *Global Perspectives on Literary Tourism and Film-Induced Tourism* (pp. 37–52). IGI Global. doi:10.4018/978-1-7998-8262-6.ch003

Avolio, B. J. (2007). Promoting more integrative strategies for leadership theory-building. *The American Psychologist, 62*(1), 25–33. doi:10.1037/0003-066X.62.1.25 PMID:17209677

Azimovna, M. S., Ilkhomovna, U. D., & Shokhrukhovich, U. F. (2022). The Concept of Marketing Policy in Trade and Service Enterprises. *Central Asian Journal Of Innovations On Tourism Management And Finance, 3*(8), 1–5.

Aziz, K. (2019). Why is humility so relevant for leaders and can it be developed through coaching? *Strategic HR Review, 18*(1), 30–33. doi:10.1108/SHR-10-2018-0088

Institucional. (2022). Uma das principais empresas de infraestrutura de mercado financeiro do mundo. Disponível em: < https://www.b3.com.br/pt_br/b3/institucional/quem-somos/>. Acesso em: 7 Ago. 2022.

Ba, A. D. (2016). Institutionalization of Southeast Asia: ASEAN and ASEAN centrality. In A. D. Ba, C.-C. Kuik, & S. Sudo (Eds.), *Institutionalizing East Asia: Mapping and reconfiguring regional cooperation* (pp. 11–34). Routledge. doi:10.4324/9781315709130-12

Baccarini, D. (1999). The logical framework method for defining project success. *Project Management Journal, 30*(4), 25–32. doi:10.1177/875697289903000405

Bächtiger, A., Dryzek, J. S., Mansbridge, J., & Warren, M. E. (Eds.). (2018). *The Oxford handbook of deliberative democracy*. Oxford University Press.

Backzo, A. (2023, November 14). *The Taliban Courts in Afghanistan: Waging War by Law.* Oxford Academic.

Bajra, U., & Cadez, S. (2018). The impact of corporate governance quality on earnings management: Evidence from European companies Cross-listed in the US. *Australian Accounting Review, 28*(2), 152–166. doi:10.1111/auar.12176

Baker, B. N., Murphy, D. C., & Fisher, D. (1998). Factors affecting project success. In D. I. Cleland & W. R. King (Eds.), *Project Management Handbook* (2nd ed., pp. 902–909). Van Nostrand Reinhold.

Bali Swain, R., & Yang-Wallentin, F. (2020). Achieving sustainable development goals: Predicaments and strategies. *International Journal of Sustainable Development and World Ecology, 27*(2), 96–106. doi:10.1080/13504509.2019.1692316

Ball, D., & Waters, G. (2013). Cyber Defence and Warfare. *Security Challenges, 9*(2), 91–98.

Bansal, P. (2001). Building Competitive Advantage and Managing Risk through Sustainable Development. *Ivey Business Journal, 66*, 47–52.

Baporikar, N. (2017). Corporate Leadership and Sustainability. In Collective Creativity for Responsible and Sustainable Business Practice (pp. 160-179). IGI Global. doi:10.4018/978-1-5225-1823-5.ch009

Baporikar, N. (2018). Critical success factors for executives in global economy. In *Geopolitics and Strategic Management in the Global Economy* (pp. 40–56). IGI Global. doi:10.4018/978-1-5225-2673-5.ch003

Baporikar, N. (2021). Innovative Systems Structure for Real Corporate Governance. [IJSDA]. *International Journal of System Dynamics Applications, 10*(4), 1–20. doi:10.4018/IJSDA.20211001.oa1

Baporikar, N. (2023b). Millennial Leadership in Global Society and Future Prospects. In T. Graham (Ed.), *Considerations and Characteristics of the Millennial Leader in Today's Global Society* (pp. 1–21). IGI Global. doi:10.4018/978-1-6684-4711-6.ch001

Baporikar, N. (2023c). Leadership for Sustainable Development in Emerging Economies. In B. Dutta & P. Chaudhuri (Eds.), *EDUCATION IN SUSTAINABLE DEVELOPMENT* (pp. 1–16). MTC Global.

Baporikar, N. (Ed.). (2023a). *Leadership and Governance for Sustainability*. IGI Global. doi:10.4018/978-1-6684-9711-1

Barbara A Frey, *The Legal and Ethical Responsibilities of TNCs in the Protection of International Human Rights*, 6 Minnesota Journal of Global Trade (1997).

Barcevičius, M., Cibaitė, E., Codagnone, G., Gineikytė, C., Klimavičiūtė, V., Liva, L., Matulevič, G., & Vanini, G. (2019). *Exploring Digital Government transformation in the EU - Analysis of the State of the art and review of literature.* Publications Office of the European Union., doi:10.2760/17207

Bartolini, G. P. M. (2016a, November). *The work of the ILC on the environment and armed conflicts: Enhancing protection for the 'silent victim of warfare'?* Questions of International Law.

Bass, B. M. (1985). Leadership: Good, better, best. *Organizational Dynamics, 13*(3), 26–40. doi:10.1016/0090-2616(85)90028-2

Baysinger, B. D., Kosnik, R. D., & Turk, T. A. (1991). Effects of board and ownership structure on corporate R&D strategy. *Academy of Management Journal, 34*(1), 205–214.

Baysinger, B., & Hoskisson, R. (1990). The Composition of Boards of Directors and Strategic Control: Effects on Corporate Strategy. *Academy of Management Review, 15*(1), 72–87. doi:10.2307/258106

Baysinger, B., & Hoskisson, R. E. (1990). The composition of boards of directors and strategic control: Effects on corporate strategy. *Academy of Management Review, 15*(1), 72–87.

BBC News Staff. (2011). *Aung San Suu Kyi makes the first trip since her release.* BBC. https://www.bbc.com/news/world- Asia-pacific-14011850

BBC News Staff. (2012). *Burma abolishes media censorship.* BBC. https://www.bbc.com/news/world-asia-19315806

BBC News Staff. (2012). *Burma government signs ceasefire with Karen rebels.* BBC. https://www.bbc.com/news/world-asia-16523691

BBC. (2016). *I.S. oil wells set on fire as Iraqi troops approach Mosul - BBC News.* BBC News. https://www.bbc.com/news/av/world-middle-east-37891389

BBCNews. (2017). *Taliban leader urges Afghans to plant more trees.* BBC. https://www.bbc.com/news/world-asia-39094578

Béland, D., Foli, R., & Kpessa-Whyte, M. (2018). Social Policy as Nation-building: Identity Formation, Policy Feedback, and Social Citizenship in Ghana. *Canadian Journal of African Studies / Revue Canadienne des études Africaines, 52*(1), 19 - 36.

Béland, D., Cantillon, B., Hick, R., & Moreira, A. (2021). Social policy in the face of a global pandemic: Policy responses to the COVID-19 crisis. *Social Policy and Administration, 55*(2), 249–260. doi:10.1111/spol.12718 PMID:34230721

Béland, D., & Cox, R. H. (2010). Introduction: Ideas and politics. In D. Béland & R. H. Cox (Eds.), *Ideas and politics in social science research* (pp. 3–20). Oxford University Press. doi:10.1093/acprof:oso/9780199736430.003.0001

Béland, D., & Cox, R. H. (2016). Ideas as coalition magnets: Coalition building, policy entrepreneurs, and power relations. *Journal of European Public Policy, 23*(3), 428–445. doi:10.1080/13501763.2015.1115533

Béland, D., & Cox, R. H. (Eds.). (2011). *Ideas and Politics in Social Science Research.* Oxford University Press.

Béland, D., Dinan, S., Rocco, P., & Waddan, A. (2021). Social policy responses to COVID-19 in Canada and the United States: Explaining policy variations between two liberal welfare state regimes. *Social Policy and Administration, 55*(2), 280–294. doi:10.1111/spol.12656 PMID:34230721

Belassi, W., & Tukel, O. (1996). A new framework for determining critical success/failure factors in project. *International Journal of Project Management, 14*(3), 141–151. doi:10.1016/0263-7863(95)00064-X

Belloc, F. (2012). Corporate Governance an Innovation: A Survey. *Journal of Economic Surveys, 26*(5), 835–864.

Béné, C., Mehta, L., McGranahan, G., Cannon, T., Gupte, J., & Tanner, T. (2018). Resilience as a policy narrative: Potentials and limits in the context of urban planning. *Climate and Development, 10*(2), 116–133. doi:10.1080/17565529.2017.1301868

Benedict, K. (2001). Global Governance. In N. J. Smelser & P. B. Baltes (Eds.), *International Encyclopedia of the Social & Behavioral Sciences* (pp. 6232–6237). Pergamon. doi:10.1016/B0-08-043076-7/04499-5

Benmira, S., & Agboola, M. (2021). Evolution of leadership theory. *BMJ Leader, 5*(1), 3–5.

Berghout, E., Nijland, M., & Grant, K. (2005). Seven ways to get your favoured IT project accepted-politics in IT evaluation. *The Electronic Journal of Information System Evaluation, 8*(1), 31–40.

Bernal, V. A., & Procee, P. (2012, May 11). *Four years on: What China got right when rebuilding after the Sichuan earthquake.* World Bank Blogs. https://blogs.worldbank.org/eastasiapacific/four-years-on-what-china-got-right-when-rebuilding-after-the-sichuan-earthquake

Berssaneti, F., & Carvalho, M. (2015). Identification of variables that impact project success in Brazilian companies. *International Journal of Project Management, 33*(3), 638–649. doi:10.1016/j.ijproman.2014.07.002

Bethlehem, D. (2012). Self-Defense Against an Imminent or Actual Armed Attack by Nonstate Actors. *The American Journal of International Law, 106*(4), 769–777. doi:10.5305/amerjintelaw.106.4.0769

Betts, A. (2010). Survival Migration: A New Protection Framework. *Global Governance*, *16*(3), 361–382. https://www.jstor.org/stable/29764952. doi:10.1163/19426720-01603006

Bexell, M., & Jönsson, K. (2019). Country Reporting on the Sustainable Development Goals—The Politics of Performance Review at the Global-National Nexus*. *Journal of Human Development and Capabilities*, *20*(4), 403–417. doi:10.1080/19452829.2018.1544544

Bezhan, F. (2020, October 02). *Is The Taliban Seeking A 'Sunni Afghan Version' Of Iran?* Radio Liberty. https://www.rferl.org/a/is-the-taliban-seeking-a-sunni-afghan-version-of-iran-/30870998.html

Bharti, M. S. (2022). The Economic Integration of the Central and Eastern European Countries into the European Union: Special Reference to Regional Development. *Copernicus Political and Legal Studies, 1*(2), 11–23. https://doi.org/doi.org/10.15804/CPLS.20222.01

Bharti, M. S. (2023a). China's Belt and Road Initiative (BRI) in Central and Eastern European Countries: The Role of '17+1' Framework for Extensive Economic Partnership. In D. W. Kim (Ed.), *Silk Road: Transnational Transmission of Sacred Thoughts and Literature*. Vernon Press.

Bharti, M. S. (2023b). Global Development and International Order Transition: The Role of China. In M. O. Dinçsoy & H. Can (Eds.), *Optimizing Energy Efficiency During a Global Energy Crisis* (pp. 200–212). IGI Global. doi:10.4018/979-8-3693-0400-6.ch013

Bharti, M. S. (2023c). The Geo-Economics Approach to the European Union Strategic Partnership in the Indo-Pacific Region: Challenges and Opportunities. In R. A. Castanho (Ed.), *Handbook of Research on Current Advances and Challenges of Borderlands, Migration, and Geopolitics*. IGI Global. doi:10.4018/978-1-6684-7020-6.ch015

Bharti, M. S. (2023d). The Sustainable Development and Economic Impact of China's Belt and Road Initiative in Ethiopia. *East Asia (Piscataway, N.J.)*, *40*(2), 175–194. doi:10.1007/s12140-023-09402-y PMID:37065271

Bharti, M. S., & Bharti, S. S. (2022). The EU Public Diplomacy in the Time of Virtual Reality: Political, Social and Economic Implications. In B. Olbrych (Ed.), *Life in Virtual Reality, Chances and dangers* (Vol. 2, pp. 13–25). Akademia Handlowa Nauk Stosowanych w Radomiu.

Bharti, S. S. (2020). Strengthening the Development Partnership between the EU and South Asia: A Contemporary Analysis. *Slovak Journal of Political Sciences*, *20*(2), 278–298. doi:10.34135/sjps.200205

Bharti, S. S. (2022). Confronting Afghanistan's Security and Development Challenges: A Contribution of the European Union. *Geopolitics Quarterly*, *18*(4), 151–176. 20.1001.1.17354331.1401.18.68.7.9

Bierman, F. (2014). Global governance and the environment. In M. Betsill, K. Hochstetler, & D. Stevis (Eds.), *Advances in international environmental politics* (2nd ed., pp. 245–270). Palgrave Macmillan.

Billings, P. (2008). Complementary Protection in International Refugee Law – By Jane Mcadam. *Legal Studies*, *28*(1), 143–148. doi:10.1111/j.1748-121X.2007.00082_2.x

Binsar, F., & Mauritsius, T. (2020). Mining of Social Media on Covid-19 Big Data Infodemic in Indonesia. *Journal of Computational Science*, *16*(11), 1598–1609. doi:10.3844/jcssp.2020.1598.1609

Blaxland, J. (2020). Developing a new Plan B for the ADF: Implications from a Geostrategic SWOT Analysis for Australia. *Security Challenges*, *16*(2), 13–23.

Blekesaune, M., & Quadagno, J. (2003). Public Attitudes toward Welfare State Policies: A Comparative Analysis of 24 Nations. *European Sociological Review*, *19*(5), 415–427. doi:10.1093/esr/19.5.415

Blinken, A. J. (2023). *Marking Two Years Since the Military Coup in Burma*. U.S. Department of State. https://www.state.gov/marking-two-years-since-the-military-coup-in-burma/

Bojicic, V., Turkmani, D., & Turkmani, R. (2018). War economy, governance and security in Syria's opposition-controlled areas. *Stability*, *7*(1), 1–17.

Bonoli, G. (2007). Time matters: Postindustrialization, new social risks, and welfare state adaptation in advanced industrial democracies. *Comparative Political Studies*, *40*(5), 495–520. doi:10.1177/0010414005285755

Boo, H. (2017). An Assessment of North Korean Cyber Threats. *The Journal of East Asian Affairs*, *31*(1), 97–117.

Boossabong, P., & Chamchong, P. (2019). The practice of deliberative policy analysis in the context of political and cultural challenges: Lessons from Thailand. *Policy Studies*, *40*(5), 476–491. doi:10.1080/01442872.2019.1618815

Boossabong, P., & Chamchong, P. (2020). Coping with COVID-19 in a non-democratic system: Policy lessons from Thailand's centralized government. *International Review of Public Policy*, *2*(3), 358–371. doi:10.4000/irpp.1382

Boossabong, P., & Chamchong, P. (2023). Hope, fear and public policy: Towards empathetic policy process. *Critical Policy Studies*, ●●●, 1–19. doi:10.1080/19460171.2023.2247048

Boossabong, P., & Fischer, F. (2018). Deliberative policy analysis. In A. Bächtiger & ... (Eds.), *The Oxford handbook of deliberative democracy* (pp. 584–594)., doi:10.1093/oxfordhb/9780198747369.013.39

Börzel, T. A., & Risse, T. (2010). Governance without a state: Can it work? *Regulation & Governance*, *4*(2), 113–134. doi:10.1111/j.1748-5991.2010.01076.x

Bousdekis, A., & Dimitris, K. (2020). *Digital transformation of local government: A case study from Greece*. In Proceedings IEEE 22nd Conference on Business Informatics, Antwerp, Belgium. 10.1109/CBI49978.2020.10070

Bradley, M., & Cohen, R. (2015). Disasters, Displacement and Protection: Challenges, Shortcomings and Ways Forward. *Disentangling Migration and Climate Change: Methodologies, Political Discourses and Human Rights*, 207–228. doi:10.1007/978-94-007-6208-4_9

Bradley, G. (2010). *Benefit Realization Management: A Practical Guide for Achieving Benefits through Change* (2nd ed.). Gower Publishing.

Branstrator, J. R., Cavaliere, C. T., Day, J., & Bricker, K. S. (2023). Civic Reporting Indicators and Biocultural Conservation: Opportunities and Challenges for Sustainable Tourism. *Sustainability (Basel)*, *15*(3), 1823. doi:10.3390/su15031823

Braun, S., & Peus, C. (2018). Crossover of work–life balance perceptions: Does authentic leadership matter? *Journal of Business Ethics*, *149*(4), 875–893. doi:10.1007/s10551-016-3078-x

Brennan, D. (2018). *Al-Shabab Bans Plastic Bags to Protect People and Livestock*. Newsweek.

Breslin, S., & Nesadurai, H. E. S. (2017). Who governs and how?: Non-State actors and transnational governance in Southeast Asia. *Journal of Contemporary Asia*, *48*(2), 187–203. doi:10.1080/00472336.2017.1416423

Breunig, C., & Ahlquist, J. S. (2014). Quantitative methodologies in public policy. In I. Engeli & C. R. Allison (Eds.), *Comparative Policy Studies: Conceptual and Methodological Challenges* (pp. 109–129). Palgrave Macmillan. doi:10.1057/9781137314154_6

Brookes, N., & Clark, A. (2009). *Using Maturity Models to Improve Project Management Practice*. In Proceedings of the *20th Annual Conference - Production and Operations Management Society (POMS)*, Orlando, Florida, USA.

Brossard, O., Lavigne, S., & Erdem Sakinç, M. (2013). Ownership structures and R&D in Europe: The good institutional investors, the bad and ugly impatient shareholders. *Industrial and Corporate Change, 22*(4), 1031–1068.

Brown, O. (2008). The Numbers Game. *Forced Migration Review*, 8–9.

Bruch, C., Jensen, D., Nakayama, M., & Unruh, J. (2019).. . *The Changing Nature of Conflict, Peacebuilding, and Environmental Cooperation., 49*, 10134–10154.

Brundtland, G. H., Khalid, M., Agnelli, S., Al-Athel, S., & Chidzero, B. J. N. Y. (1987). *Our common future*. New York. https://sustainabledevelopment.un.org/content/documents/5987our-common-future.pdf

Buchan, R. (2012). Cyber Attacks: Unlawful Uses of Force or Prohibited Interventions? *Journal of Conflict and Security Law, 17*(2), 211–227. doi:10.1093/jcsl/krs014

Buera, F. J., Kaboski, J. P., & Shin, Y. (2011). Finance and development: A tale of two sectors. *The American Economic Review, 101*(5), 1964–2002. doi:10.1257/aer.101.5.1964

Buheji, D. M., & Sisk, F. C. W. (2020). *You and the new normal: Jobs, pandemics, relationship, climate change, success, poverty, leadership, and belief in the emerging new world*. Author House.

Bulkeley, H., & Mol, A. P. (2003). Participation and environmental governance: Consensus, ambivalence and debate. *Environmental Values, 12*(2), 143–154. doi:10.3197/096327103129341261

Burger, J., Gochfeld, M., & Lacy, C. (2019). Concerns and future preparedness plans of a vulnerable population in New Jersey following Hurricane Sandy. *Disasters, 43*(3), 658–685. doi:10.1111/disa.12350 PMID:30990925

Burkadze, K. (2020). A Shift in the Historical Understanding of Armed Attack and Its Applicability to Cyberspace. *The Fletcher Forum of World Affairs, 44*(1), 33–48.

Burke, R. J., & Mattis, M. C. (Eds.). (2013). *Women on corporate boards of directors: International challenges and opportunities* (Vol. 14). Springer Science & Business Media.

Burniske, J. S., Modirzadeh, N. K., & Lewis, D. A. (2017). *Armed Non-State Actors and International Human Rights Law: An Analysis of the Practice of the U.N. Security Council and U.N. General Assembly*. Research Gate.

Burra, S. (2020). Use of Force as Self Defence against Non-State Actors and TWAIL Considerations: A Critical Analysis of India's State Practice. In S. Lee & H. E. Lee (Eds.), *Asian Yearbook of International Law, Volume 24 (2018)* (pp. 106–126). Brill. https://www.jstor.org/stable/10.1163/j.ctv1sr6j7f.9

Business & Human Rights Resource Centre. (2015). *Myanmar: Growing use of private security firms to guard businesses gives rise to rights concerns*. Business and Human Rights Resource Center. https://www.business-humanrights.org/en/latest-news/myanmar-growing-use-of-private-security-firms-to-guard-businesses-gives-rise-to-rights-concerns/

Busse, N. (1999). Constructivism and Southeast Asian Security. *The Pacific Review, 12*(1), 39–60. doi:10.1080/09512749908719277

Buysse, K., & Verbeke, A. (2003). Proactive environmental strategies: A stakeholder management perspective. *Strategic Management Journal, 24*(5), 453–470. doi:10.1002/smj.299

Caballero-Anthony, M. (2018). *Negotiating governance on non-traditional security in Southeast Asia and beyond*. Columbia University Press. doi:10.7312/caba18300

Cabeça, S. M., Gonçalves, A. R., Marques, J. F., & Tavares, M. (2021). Gastronomic creative tourism: Experiences in the Algarve region of Portugal. In N. Duxbury, S. Albino, & C. P. De Carvalho (Eds.), *Creative tourism: Activating cultural resources and engaging creative travellers* (1st ed., pp. 62–67). CABI. doi:10.1079/9781789243536.0009

Cairney, P. (2012). Complexity theory in political science and public policy. *Political Studies Review, 10*(3), 346–358. doi:10.1111/j.1478-9302.2012.00270.x

Calvert, K. (2018). Collaborative leadership: Cultivating an environment for success. *Collaborative Librarianship, 10*(2), 79.

Cambodian Chinese Network. (2022). *Cambodian National Police: Private security needs to work closely with the police to fight crime*. CCN. https://www.boyoushe.com/65881.html,

Cambodianess. (2019). *National Police says won't allow the employment of foreigners in private security.* Cambodianess. https://cambodianess.com/article/national-police-says-wont-allow-employment-of-foreigners-in-private-security

Campbell, J. L. (2004). *Institutional Change and Globalization*. Princeton University Press. doi:10.1515/9780691216348

Cantillon, B., Seeleib-Kaiser, M., & van der Veen, R. (2021). The COVID-19 crisis and policy responses by continental European welfare states. *Social Policy and Administration, 55*(2), 326–338. doi:10.1111/spol.12715 PMID:34230722

Caralli, R., Knight, M., & Montgomery, A. (2012). Maturity Models 101: A Primer for Applying Maturity Models to Smart Grid Security, Resilience, and Interoperability. CERT, Software Engineering Institute, Carnegie Mellon University. doi:10.21236/ADA610461

Carey, S. C., Mitchell, N. J., & Lowe, W. (2013). States, the security sector, and the monopoly of violence: A new database on pro-government militias. *Journal of Peace Research, 50*(2), 249–258. doi:10.1177/0022343312464881

Carlos Manuel Vázquez, *Direct v. Indirect Obligations for Corporations under International Law*, 43 Colum. J. Transnat'l L. 927, 943 (2005), https://scholarship.law.georgetown.edu/cgi/viewcontent.cgi?article=1987&context=facpub&https redir=1&referer

Carlos Manuel Vázquez, *Direct v. Indirect Obligations for Corporations under International Law*, 43 Colum. J. Transnat'l L. 927, 943 (2005), https://scholarship.law.georgetown.edu/cgi/viewcontent.cgi?article=1987&context=facpub&https redir=1&referer=

Caroli, M. (1999). *Il marketing territoriale. Lineamenti teorici e strumenti d'intervento* (F. Angeli, Ed.).

Carr, T (2018). *Supporting the Transition: Understanding Aid to Myanmar Since 2011.*

Carrasqueiro, S., Monteiro, M., Pereira, R., Pereira, C., & Martins, H. (2018). Dematerialization of the medical certificate for driving license in Portugal: a case study of success factors of whole-of-Government e-Government initiatives. In Proceedings of the *11th International Conference on Theory and Practice of Electronic Governance*, Galway, Ireland. 10.1145/3209415.3209510

Carr, N. G. (2003). It doesn't matter. *Harvard Business Review, 81*(5), 41–49. PMID:12747161

Carroll, A. B. (1979). A Three-Dimensional Conceptual Model of Corporate Performance. *Academy of Management Review, 4*(4), 497–505. doi:10.2307/257850

Carvalho Júnior, V. D. O. C., de Araujo, M. B. V., Lima, V. S., Corrar, L. J., & de Lima, G. A. S. F. (2010). Representatividade do valor de marcas no valor de mercado da empresa no Brasil. In Anais do Congresso Brasileiro de Custos-ABC.

Castles, F. G. (2010). Black swans and elephants on the move: The impact of emergencies on the welfare state. *Journal of European Social Policy, 20*(2), 91–101. doi:10.1177/0958928709358793

Chams, N., & Garcıa-Blandon, J. (2019). Sustainable or not sustainable? The role of the board of directors. *Journal of Cleaner Production, 226*, 1067–1081. doi:10.1016/j.jclepro.2019.04.118

Chan, K., Chen, H., Hong, L., & Wang, Y. (2015). Stock market valuation of R&D expenditures—The role of corporate governance. Pacific-Basin finance jornal, 31(1), 78-93.

Chan, C.-S., Chang, T. C., & Liu, Y. (2022). Investigating Creative Experiences and Environmental Perception of Creative Tourism: The Case of PMQ (Police Married Quarters) in Hong Kong. *Journal of China Tourism Research, 18*(2), 223–244. doi:10.1080/19388160.2020.1812459

Chandler, D., & Thomas, J. (2015). Does executive sponsorship matter for realizing project management value. *Project Management Journal, 46*(5), 46–61. doi:10.1002/pmj.21521

Chandra, A. C., Abdulrahim, R., & Almuttaqi, A. I. (2017). Non-state actors' engagement with ASEAN: Current state of play and way forward. In A. Baviera & L. Maramis (Eds.), *ASEAN@50 Building ASEAN community: Political–security and socio-cultural reflections* (Vol. 4, pp. 221–246). Economic Research Institute for ASEAN and East Asia.

Changchit, C., Joshi, K. D., & Lederer, A. L. (1998). Process and reality in information systems benefits analysis. *Information Systems Journal, 8*(2), 145–162. doi:10.1046/j.1365-2575.1998.00031.x

Chan, Y., & Reich, B. (2007). IT alignment: What have we learned? *Journal of Information Technology, 22*(4), 297–315. doi:10.1057/palgrave.jit.2000109

Chen, N., & Dwyer, L. (2017). Residents' Place Satisfaction and Place Attachment on Destination Brand-Building Behaviors: Conceptual and Empirical Differentiation. *Journal of Travel Research, 57*(8), 1026-1041. 004728751772976. doi:10.1177/0047287517729760

Cheng, Q., & Ngok, K. (2020). Welfare Attitudes Towards Anti-poverty Policies in China: Economical Individualism, Social Collectivism and Institutional Differences. *Social Indicators Research, 15*(2), 679–694. doi:10.1007/s11205-020-02313-y

Chen, H. Y., Wang, L., Zhang, X., Wei, W., & Lyu, J. (2024). Does linguistic diversity make destinations more sophisticated? Exploring the effects on destination personality. *Journal of Destination Marketing & Management, 31*, 100828. doi:10.1016/j.jdmm.2023.100828

Chen, S., & Taw, J. (2023). Conventional Retaliation and Cyber Attacks. *The Cyber Defense Review, 8*(1), 67–86.

Chen, Y., Liu, B., Zhang, L., & Qian, S. (2018). Can leader "humility" spark employee "proactivity"? The mediating role of psychological empowerment. *Leadership and Organization Development Journal, 39*(3), 326–339. doi:10.1108/LODJ-10-2017-0307

Chesbrough, H. (2011). *Open Services Innovation: Rethinking Your Business to Grow and Compete in a New Era* (1st ed.). Jossey-Bass.

Chesterman, S., & Lehnardt, C. (2007). *From Mercenaries to Market: The Rise and Regulation of Private Military Companies*. Oxford University Press. doi:10.1093/acprof:oso/9780199228485.001.0001

Cheung, L. T. O., & Hui, D. L. H. (2018). Influence of residents' place attachment on heritage forest conservation awareness in a peri-urban area of Guangzhou, China. *Urban Forestry & Urban Greening, 33*(May), 37–45. doi:10.1016/j.ufug.2018.05.004

Chhay, H., & Wee, D. (2013). Sub-Decree No. 289 on private security management. *Lexology*. https://www.lexology.com/library/detail.aspx?g=99c6cf06-c361-478d-ba28-0930bb17165b

Chiarini, A., & Vagnoni, E. (2017). TQM implementation for the healthcare sector: The relevance of leadership and possible causes of lack of leadership. *Leadership in Health Services, 30*(3), 210–216. doi:10.1108/LHS-02-2017-0004 PMID:28693393

Chilisa, B. (2019). *Indigenous research methodologies*. Sage publications.

Chirwa, D. M. *The Doctrine of State Responsibility as a Potential Tool Means of Holding Private Actors Accountable for Human Rights*, 5 MEL J. INT'L 1, 5(2004), https://law.unimelb.edu.au/__data/assets/pdf_file/0005/1680422/Chirwa.pdf

Chirwa, D. M. *The Doctrine of State Responsibility as a Potential Tool Means of Holding Private Actors Accountable for Human Rights*, 5 MEL J. INT'L 1, 5(2004),https://law.unimelb.edu.au/__data/assets/pdf_file/0005/1680422/Chirwa.pdf

Chivers, D. (2021). *West Papua: A Green State Vision*. New Internationalist. https://newint.org/features/2021/11/04/west-papua-green-state-vision-cop26

Choi, Y. J. (2012). End of the era of productivist welfare capitalism? Diverging welfare regimes in East Asia. *Asian Journal of Social Science*, *40*(3), 275–294. doi:10.1163/156853112X650827

Choi, Y. J., Kühner, S., & Shi, S. J. (2022). From "new social risks" to "COVID social risks:" the challenges for inclusive Society in South Korea, Hong Kong, and Taiwan amid the pandemic. *Policy and Society*, *41*(2), 260–274. doi:10.1093/polsoc/puac001

Chourabi, H., Nam, T., Walker, S., Gil-Garcia, J., Mellouli, S., Nahon, K., Pardo, T., & Scholl, H. (2012). *Understanding Smart Cities: An Integrative Framework*. In proceedings of the 45th Hawaii International Conference on System Sciences, Maui, HI, USA.

Chou, Y.-C., Nakano, T., Chang, H.-H., & Liang, L.-F. (2013). Parent-carers in Taiwan and Japan: Lifelong caring responsibilities within a familistic welfare system. In T. Kröger & S. Yeandle (Eds.), *Combining paid work and family care: Policies and experiences in international perspective* (pp. 143–159). Bristol University Press. doi:10.2307/j.ctt9qgp6n.14

Chowdhury, M. S. (Ed.). (2014). *Survival Under Threat: Human Rights Situation of Indigenous Peoples in Bangladesh*. Asia Indigenous People Pact.

Chu, W. K., Yang, N. T., & Yang, S. Y. (2016). Corporate governance'impact on research and development. *Journal of Business Research*, *69*(6), 2239–2243.

Clark, K., & Shapour, R. (2023). *WHAT DO THE TALEBAN SPEND AFGHANISTAN'S MONEY ON? Government expenditure under the Islamic Emirate*. Afghanistan Analyst Network. https://www.afghanistan-analysts.org/en/reports/economy-development-environment/what-do-the-taleban-spend-afghanistans-money-on-government-expenditure-under-the-islamic-emirate/

Clarke, S. E. (2007). Context-sensitive policy methods. In F. Ficher & G. Miller (Eds.), *Handbook of public policy analysis*. Routledge.

Clark, M., Kang, B., & Calhoun, J. R. (2023). Green meets social media: Young travelers' perceptions of hotel environmental sustainability. *Journal of Hospitality and Tourism Insights*, *6*(1), 36–51. doi:10.1108/JHTI-03-2021-0062

Cleland, D. L., & Ireland, L. R. (2002). *Project Management: Strategic Design and Implementation* (4th ed.). McGraw-Hill.

Cochran, P., & Wood, R. (1984). Corporate social responsibility and financial performance. *Academy of Management Journal*, *27*(1), 42–56. doi:10.2307/255956

Cockerham, G. B. (2010). Regional integration in ASEAN: Institutional design and the ASEAN way. *East Asia (Piscataway, N.J.)*, *27*(2), 165–185. doi:10.1007/s12140-009-9092-1

Código das Melhores Práticas de Governança Corporativa. (2023). 6. ed. São Paulo: Instituto Brasileiro de Governança Corporativa (IBGC).

Cohen, M. A., & Tavares, J. (2020). Who are the most at-risk older adults in the COVID-19 ERA? it's not just those in nursing homes. *Journal of Aging & Social Policy, 32*(4–5), 380–386. doi:10.1080/08959420.2020.1764310 PMID:32418475

Cohen, R. (2004). The Guiding Principles on Internal Displacement: An Innovation in International Standard Setting. *Global Governance, 10*(4), 459–480. https://www.jstor.org/stable/27800542. doi:10.1163/19426720-01004006

Cohen, R., & Bradley, M. (2010). Disasters and Displacement: Gaps in Protection. *Journal of International Humanitarian Legal Studies, 1*(1), 95–142. doi:10.1163/187815210X12766020139884

Collier, D., & Munck, G. L. (Eds.). (2022). *Critical Juncture and Historical Legacies: Insights and Methods.* The Rowman and Littlefield Publishing Group, Inc.

Collins, A. (2013). *Building a People-Oriented Security Community the ASEAN Way.* Routledge. doi:10.4324/9780203104842

Collins, A., & Baccarini, D. (2004). Project Success - A Survey. *Journal of Construction Research, 5*(2), 211–231. doi:10.1142/S1609945104000152

Collins, J. (2023). Armed Groups as Forest Protectors in Colombia: A Risky Dynamic. *Sierra.*

Conger, J. A., & Kanungo, R. N. (1994). Charismatic leadership in organizations: Perceived behavioral attributes and their measurement. *Journal of Organizational Behavior, 15*(5), 439–452. doi:10.1002/job.4030150508

Congressional Research Service. (2021, November 02). *Taliban Government in Afghanistan: Background and Issues for Congress.* CRS. https://crsreports.congress.gov/product/pdf/R/R46955

Cooke-Davies, T., Schlichter, J., & Bredillet, C. (2001). Beyond the PMBOK® guide. Paper presented at *Project Management Institute Annual Seminars & Symposium.* Newtown Square, PA: Project Management Institute.

Cooke-Davies, T. (2002). The "real" success factors on projects. *International Journal of Project Management, 20*(3), 185–190. doi:10.1016/S0263-7863(01)00067-9

Corbin, J., & Strauss, A. (2008). Analyzing data for concepts. In Basics of Qualitative Research (3rd ed.): Techniques and Procedures for Developing Grounded Theory (pp. 159-194). SAGE Publications, Inc. doi:10.4135/9781452230153.n8

Cordella, A., & Tempini, N. (2015). E-government and organizational change: Reappraising the role of ICT and bureaucracy in public service delivery. *Government Information Quarterly, 32*(3), 279–286. doi:10.1016/j.giq.2015.03.005

Cordesman, A. H., & Khazai, S. (2014). *Other Extremist Non-State Actors, Syria, and Iran* (Iraq in Crisis, pp. 193–215). Center for Strategic and International Studies (CSIS). https://www.jstor.org/stable/resrep36981.13

Cordis, A. S., & Kirby, C. (2017). Capital expenditures and firm performance: Evidence from a cross-sectional analysis of stock returns. *Accounting and Finance, 57*(4), 1019–1042.

Corrêa, E. D. L., Silva, W. A. C., Pinheiro, J. L., & Melo, A. A. O. (2015). Estrutura de propriedade e criação de valor em companhias brasileiras. *Tourism & Management Studies, 11*(2), 130–137.

Crane, R., & Weber, R. (2012). *The Oxford handbook of urban planning.* OUP USA.

Crawford, L., Cooke-Davies, T., Hobbs, B., Labuschagne, L., Remington, K., & Chen, P. (2008). Governance and Support in the Sponsoring of Projects and Programs. *Project Management Journal, 39.* doi:10.1002/pmj.20059

Crawford, J. (2001). *Responsibility to the International Community as a Whole,* 8. *Indiana Journal of Global Legal Studies.*

Crawford, L. H. (2003). Assessing and Developing the Project Management Competence of Individuals. In J. R. Turner (Ed.), *People in Project Management.* Grower.

Crawford, L. H. (2005). Senior Management Perceptions of Project Management Competence. *International Journal of Project Management*, *23*(1), 7–16. doi:10.1016/j.ijproman.2004.06.005

Crawford, L., Pollack, J., & England, D. (2006). Uncovering the trends in project management: Journal emphases over the last 10 years. *International Journal of Project Management*, *24*(2), 175–184. doi:10.1016/j.ijproman.2005.10.005

Cruz, C. V. O. A., & de Lima, G. A. S. F. (2010). Reputação corporativa e nível de disclosure das empresas de capital aberto no Brasil. *Revista Universo Contábil*, *6*(1), 85–101.

Cuddy, A. (2021). Myanmar coup: What is happening and why? *BBC News*. https://www.burmalibrary.org/sites/burmalibrary.org/files/obl/2021-04-01-Myanmar-coup-BBC-en-red.pdf,

Cullen, M. M., & Brennan, N. M. (2017). Differentiating control, monitoring and oversight. *Accounting, Auditing & Accountability Journal*, *30*(8), 1867–1894. doi:10.1108/AAAJ-12-2015-2345

Curato, N., Hammond, M., & Min, J. B. (2018). *Power in deliberative democracy: Norms, forums, systems*. Springer.

Currie, W. (2012). Institutional Isomorphism and Change: The National Programme for IT – 10 Years On. *Journal of Information Technology*, *27*(3), 236–248. doi:10.1057/jit.2012.18

Currie, W., & Guah, M. (2007). Conflicting institutional logics: A national programme for IT in the organizational field of healthcare. *Journal of Information Technology*, *22*(3), 235–247. doi:10.1057/palgrave.jit.2000102

D'Souza, S. M. (2016). Taliban: The Rebels Who Aspire to be Rulers. *Journal of Asian Security and International Affairs*, *3*(1), 20–40. https://www.jstor.org/stable/48602132. doi:10.1177/2347797015626043

Daigneault, P.-M. (2014). Reassessing the concept of policy paradigm: Aligning ontol- ogy and methodology in policy studies. *Journal of European Public Policy*, *21*(3), 453–469. doi:10.1080/13501763.2013.834071

Dal Mas, L. O., & Barac, K. (2018). The influence of the chief audit executive's leadership style on factors related to internal audit effectiveness. *Managerial Auditing Journal*, *33*(8-9), 807–835. doi:10.1108/MAJ-12-2017-1741

Dănescu, T., Prozan, M., & Prozan, R. D. (2015). Perspectives regarding accounting – corporate governance – internal control. *Procedia Economics and Finance*, *32*, 588–594. doi:10.1016/S2212-5671(15)01436-7

Daniel, D. R. (1961). Management Information Crisis. *Harvard Business Review*, *39*(5), 111–116.

Daniel, E., & Wilson, H. (2003). The role of dynamic capabilities in e-business transformation. *European Journal of Information Systems*, *12*(4), 282–296. doi:10.1057/palgrave.ejis.3000478

Das, I. R., Talukder, M. B., & Kumar, S. (2024). Implication of Artificial Intelligence in Hospitality Marketing. *Utilizing Smart Technology and AI in Hybrid Tourism and Hospitality*. IGI Global, USA. doi:10.4018/979-8-3693-1978-9.ch014

Das, M. B., Fisiy, C. F., & Kyte, R. (2013, October 18). *Inclusion Matters: The Foundation for Shared Prosperity*. New Frontiers of Social Policy Washington, D.C.: World Bank Group. https://documents1.worldbank.org/curated/en/114561468154469371/pdf/Inclusion-matters-the-foundation-for-shared-prosperity.pdf

Datta, P., Walker, L., & Amarilli, F. (2020). Digital transformation: Learning from Italy's public administration. *Journal of Information Technology Teaching Cases*, 1-18. . doi:10.1177/2043886920910437

Dawi, A. (2022, August 04). *Will US Hit Most-Wanted Haqqanis in Afghanistan?* VOA. https://www.voanews.com/a/will-us-hit-more-most-wanted-haqqanis-in-afghanistan-/6687402.html

Dawi, A. (2023, March 28). *Unseen Taliban Leader Wields Godlike Powers in Afghanistan*. VOA. https://www.voanews.com/a/unseen-taliban-leader-wields-godlike-powers-in-afghanistan-/7026112.html

Dawi, A. (2023, September 28). *Taliban Undertake Speedy Overhaul of Afghanistan's Justice System.* VOA. https://www.voanews.com/a/taliban-undertake-speedy-overhaul-afghanistan-justice-system/7289101.html

de Coninck, H., Fischer, C., Newell, R. G., & Ueno, T. (2008). International technology-oriented agreements to address climate change. *Energy Policy*, *36*(1), 335–356. doi:10.1016/j.enpol.2007.09.030

De Giovanni, P. (2012). Do internal and external environmental management contribute to the triple bottom line? *International Journal of Operations & Production Management*, *32*(3), 265–290. doi:10.1108/01443571211212574

De Groot, J. I. M., & Schuitema, G. (2012). How to make the unpopular popular? Policy characteristics, social norms and the acceptability of environmental policies. *Environmental Science & Policy*, *19–20*, 100–107. doi:10.1016/j.envsci.2012.03.004

Debnath, M. K. (2010). *Living on the Edge: The predicament of a rural indigenous Santal community in Bangladesh* [Doctoral dissertation, University of Toronto].

Debnath, M. (2020). A community under siege: Exclusionary education policies and indigenous Santals* in the Bangladeshi context. *Third World Quarterly*, *41*(3), 453–469. doi:10.1080/01436597.2019.1660634

Deichmann, D., & Stam, D. (2015). Leveraging transformational and transactional leadership to cultivate the generation of organization-focused ideas. *The Leadership Quarterly*, *26*(2), 204–219. doi:10.1016/j.leaqua.2014.10.004

Della Lucia, M., & Pashkevich, A. (2023). A sustainable afterlife for post-industrial sites: Balancing conservation, regeneration and heritage tourism. *European Planning Studies*, *31*(3), 641–661. doi:10.1080/09654313.2022.2154141

Demirjian, K., & Schmitt, E. (2023, April 25). Taliban Kill Head of ISIS Cell That Bombed Kabul Airport. *The New York Times*. https://www.nytimes.com/2023/04/25/us/politics/isis-leader-killed-kabul-airport-bombing.html

Deng, G., Zhao, D., Lio, J., Chen, X., Ma, X., Liang, L., & Feng, C. (2019). Strategic elements of residency training in China: Transactional leadership, self-efficacy, and employee orientation culture. *BMC Medical Education*, *19*(1), 1–8. doi:10.1186/s12909-019-1792-7 PMID:31521148

Devaraj, S., & Kohli, R. (2003). Performance Impacts of Information Technology: Is Actual Usage the Missing Link? *Management Science*, *49*(3), 273–289. doi:10.1287/mnsc.49.3.273.12736

Di Vito, J., Laurin, C., & Bozec, Y. (2010). R&D activity in Canada: Does corporate ownership structure matter?. Canadian Journal of Administrative Sciences/Revue Canadienne des Sciences de l'Administration, 27(2), 107-121.

Dias, Á., González-Rodríguez, M. R., & Patuleia, M. (2021). Developing poor communities through creative tourism. *Journal of Tourism and Cultural Change*, *19*(4), 509–529. doi:10.1080/14766825.2020.1775623

Dietz, K., & Hammond, C. (2021). Three months on from the military coup, what should the international community do to support the people of Myanmar? *Global Witness.*

Ding, D. K., & Beh, S. E. (2022). Climate change and sustainability in ASEAN countries. *Sustainability (Basel)*, *14*(2), 999. doi:10.3390/su14020999

Dinh, J. E., Lord, R. G., Gardner, W. L., Meuser, J. D., Liden, R. C., & Hu, J. (2014). Leadership theory and research in the new millennium: Current theoretical trends and changing perspectives. *The Leadership Quarterly*, *25*(1), 36–62. doi:10.1016/j.leaqua.2013.11.005

Djalante, R., Nurhidayah, L., Van Minh, H., Phuong, N. T. N., Mahendradhata, Y., Trias, A., Lassa, J., & Miller, M. A. (2020). COVID-19 and ASEAN responses: Comparative policy analysis. *Progress in Disaster Science*, *8*, 100129. doi:10.1016/j.pdisas.2020.100129

Dobbin, F., & Sutton, R. C. (1998). The Strength of a Weak State: The Rights Movement and the Rise of the Human Resources Management Divisions. *American Journal of Sociology.*

Doering, D. S., Cassara, A., Layke, C., Ranganathan, J., Revenga, C., Tunstall, D., & Vanasselt, W. (2002). *Tomorrow's Markets: Global Trends and their Implications for Business.* World Resources Institute.

Donaldson, T., & Dunfee, T. W. (1994). Toward a Unified Conception of Business Ethics: Integrative Social Contract Theory. *Academy of Management Review, 19*(2), 252–284. doi:10.2307/258705

Donaldson, T., & Dunfee, T. W. (1995). *Integrative Social Contracts Theory.* Economics and Philosophy. doi:10.1017/S0266267100003230

Donaldson, T., & Dunfee, T. W. (1999). *Ties That Bind. A Social Contracts Approach to Business Ethics.* Harvard Business School Press.

Dorfman, R., & Steiner, P. O. (1954). Optimal Advertising and Optimal Quality. *The American Economic Review, 44*, 826–836.

Dorn, W. (2017). Cyberpeacekeeping: A New Role for the United Nations? *Georgetown Journal of International Affairs, 18*(3), 138–146. doi:10.1353/gia.2017.0046

Doshi, S. L. (1990). *Tribal Ethnicity, Class and Integration.* Rawat Publications.

Drexhage, J. (2008). *Global Environmental Governance (GEG) Briefing Paper # 2.* GEG.

Driscoll, J. C., & Kraay, A. C. (1998). Consistent covariance matrix estimation with spatially dependent panel data. *The Review of Economics and Statistics, 80*(4), 549–560.

Driver, C., & Guedes, M. J. C. (2012). Research and development, cash flow, agency and governance: UK large companies. *Research Policy, 41*(9), 1565–1577.

Drong, S. (2019). *Does God forget the Santals?* Suchipatra.

Dryer, C. (2018). Leadership. *Teaching and Learning in Nursing, 13*(3), A7–A8. doi:10.1016/j.teln.2018.04.002

Duit, A., & Galaz, V. (2008). Governance and Complexity – Emerging issues for governance theory. *Governance: An International Journal of Policy, Administration and Institutions, 21*(3), 311–335. doi:10.1111/j.1468-0491.2008.00402.x

Dunlop, C., & Radaelli, C. (2018). The lessons of policy learning: Types, triggers, hindrances and pathologies. *Policy and Politics, 46*(2), 255–272. doi:10.1332/030557318X15230059735521

Dunn, W. N. (2018). Public policy analysis: An integrated approach (Sixth Edition). Routledge, Taylor & Francis Group.

Dunn, W. N. (2015). *Public policy analysis.* Routledge.

Durnová, A. (2015). Lost in translation: Expressing emotions in policy deliberation. In F. Fischer & ... (Eds.), *Handbook of Critical Policy Studies* (pp. 222–238).

Durnová, A. (2018). Understanding emotions in policy studies through Foucault and Deleuze. *Politics and Governance, 6*(4), 95–102. doi:10.17645/pag.v6i4.1528

Durnová, A., Formánková, L., & Hejzlarová, E. (2022). Empowered or patronized? The role of emotions in policies and professional discourses on birth care. *Critical Social Policy, 42*(1), 129–149. doi:10.1177/02610183211001494

Duthey, B. (2013). *Hearing Loss.* World Health Organization. https://www.who.int/medicines/areas/priority_medicines/BP6_21Hearing.pdf

Duxbury, N., Silva, S., & De Castro, T. V. (2019). Creative Tourism Development in Small Cities and Rural Areas in Portugal: Insights from Start-Up Activities. In D. A. Jelinčić & Y. Mansfeld, Creating and Managing Experiences in Cultural Tourism (pp. 291–304). WORLD SCIENTIFIC. doi:10.1142/9789813233683_0018

Düztaş, S. (2008). *Corporate governance: The effects of board characteristics, information technology maturity and transparency on company Performance.*

Dvir, D., Lipovetskey, S., Shenhar, A., & Tishler, A. (1998). In search of project classification: A non-uniform mapping of project success factors. *Research Policy*, *27*(9), 915–935. doi:10.1016/S0048-7333(98)00085-7

Dye, T. R. (1978). *Policy analysis: What governments do, why they do it, and what difference it makes.* University of Alabama Press.

Early, C. (2021). *Indigenous leaders' green state vision.* Ecologist. https://theecologist.org/2021/nov/08/indigenous-leaders-green-state-vision

Ebbinghaus, B., Lehner, L., & Naumann, E. (2022). Welfare state support during the COVID- 19 pandemic: Change and continuity in public attitudes towards social policies in Germany. *European Policy Analysis,* 1–15. https://doi.org/. doi:10.1002/epa2.11523118

Edrisi Muñoz, E., Capón-García, E., Laínez, J. M., Espuña, A., & Puigjaner, L. (2013). Considering environmental assessment in an ontological framework for enterprise sustainability. *Journal of Cleaner Production*, *47*, 149–164. doi:10.1016/j.jclepro.2012.11.032

Egreteau, R. (2008). India and China Vying for Influence in Burma – A New Assessment. *India Review*, *7*(1), 38–72. doi:10.1080/14736480801901170

Ehikioya, B. I. (2009). Corporate governance structure and firm performance in developing economies: Evidence from Nigeria. *Corporate Governance (Bradford)*, *9*(3), 231–245. doi:10.1108/14720700910964307

Eichinger, I., Schreier, M., & van Osselaer, S. M. (2022). Connecting to place, people, and past: How products make us feel grounded. *Journal of Marketing*, *86*(4), 1–16. doi:10.1177/00222429211027469

Eisenhardt, K. M. (1989). Agency theory: An assessment and review. *Academy of Management Review*, *14*(1), 57–74.

Eleftheriadou, M. (2020). Fragmentation and Cooperation in the Jihadi International (Sub)System: 'Islamic State' vs. Al-Qaeda and Beyond. *Religions*, *11*(4), 168. doi:10.3390/rel11040168

Eliot, J. L. (2020). Resilient Leadership: The Impact of a Servant Leader on the Resilience of their Followers. *Advances in Developing Human Resources*, *22*(4), 404–418. doi:10.1177/1523422320945237

Elkington, J. (1997). *Cannibals with Forks: The Triple Bottom Line of the 21st Century Business.* Capstone Publishing.

Elliott, L. (2003). ASEAN and environmental cooperation: Norms, interests and identity. *The Pacific Review*, *16*(1), 29–52. doi:10.1080/0951274032000043235

Elliott, L. (2012). ASEAN and environmental governance: Strategies of regionalism in Southeast Asia. *Global Environmental Politics*, *12*(3), 38–57. doi:10.1162/GLEP_a_00122

Elliott, L. (2017). Environmental regionalism: Moving in from the policy margins. *The Pacific Review*, *30*(6), 952–965. doi:10.1080/09512748.2017.1303534

Ellorin, B. (2011). *Big business into environmental destruction valid NPA targets.* Minda News.

Emmenegger, P., Häusermann, S., Palier, B., & Seeleib-Kaiser, M. (2014). *The age of dualization: The changing face of inequality in deindustrializing societies*. Oxford University Press.

EPL. (2023). *The Environment Is A Silent Victim Of The War In Ukraine Without Effective Legal Protection Mechanisms*. EPL.

Esping-Andersen, G. (1993). *The three worlds of welfare capitalism*. Princeton University Press.

Esping-Andersen, G. (1999). *Social foundations of postindustrial economies*. Oxford University Press. doi:10.1093/0198742002.001.0001

European Commission. (2004). *The EU's relations with Burma / Myanmar*. EC. https://www.europarl.europa.eu/meetdocs/2004_2009/documents/fd/dase20050419_003/dase20050419_003en.pdf

European Commission. (2020a). eGovernment Benchmark 2020: eGovernment that works for the people. Luxembourg: Publications Office of the European Union.

European Commission. (2020b). *Digital Economy and Society Index: Digital public services*. EC. https://ec.europa.eu/digital-single-market/en/news/digital-economy-and-society-index-desi-2020

European Commission. (2023a, May). *EU Voluntary Review on the Implementation of the 2030 Agenda for Sustainable Development*. EC. https://commission.europa.eu/system/files/2023-06/SDG-Report-WEB.pdf

European Commission. (2023b, September 18). *Statement by President von der Leyen at the 2023 Sustainable Development Goals Summit*. EC. https://ec.europa.eu/commission/presscorner/detail/en/STATEMENT_23_4504

European Commission. (n.d.-a). *European development policy*. EC. https://international-partnerships.ec.europa.eu/policies/european-development-policy_en#:~:text=European%20development%20policy%20fosters%20sustainable,%2C%20security%2C%20and%20trade%20policies

European Commission. (n.d.-b). *International Partnerships*. EC. https://international-partnerships.ec.europa.eu/policies/sustainable-development-goals_en

European Commission. (n.d.-c). *Sustainable Development Goals*. EC.

European Parliament. (2011). *"Climate Refugees"—Legal and Policy Responses to Environmentally Induced Migration*. Committee on Civil Liberties, Justice and Home Affairs. https://www.europarl.europa.eu/thinktank/en/document/IPOL-LIBE_ET(2011)462422

Eurostat. (2023, May 24). *How has the EU progressed towards the SDGs?* Europa.Eu. https://ec.europa.eu/eurostat/web/products-eurostat-news/w/wdn-20230524-1#:~:text=EU%20made%20significant%20progress%20toward,gender%20equality%20(SDG%205)

Executive Office of the President. (2016). *Termination of Emergency Concerning the Actions and Policies of the Government of Burma*. Federal Register. https://www.federalregister.gov/documents/2016/10/12/2016-24847/termination-of-emergency-with-respect-to-the-actions-and-policies-of-the-government-of-burma

Faheem, M., & Khan, M. M. (2022). Recognition of the Taliban Government in Afghanistan and International Community. *Strategic Studies, 42*(1), 81–96. https://www.jstor.org/stable/48732345

Faist, T., & Schade, J. (2013). The Climate-Migration Nexus: A Reorientation. *Disentangling Migration and Climate Change: Toward an Analysis of Methodologies*, *7*. https://pub.uni-bielefeld.de/record/2582697

Fakhruddin, B. (Shm), Blanchard, K., & Ragupathy, D. (2020). Are we there yet? The transition from response to recovery for the COVID-19 pandemic. *Progress in Disaster Science*, *7*, 100102. doi:10.1016/j.pdisas.2020.100102

Fama, E. F. (1970). Efficient capital markets: A review of theory and empirical work. *The Journal of Finance*, *25*(2), 383–423.

Fang, Y., Chen, J., Wang, M., & Chen, C. (2019). The impact of inclusive leadership on employees' innovative behaviors: The mediation of psychological capital. *Frontiers in Psychology*, *10*, 1803. doi:10.3389/fpsyg.2019.01803 PMID:31447740

Fealy, G. (2020). Jokowi in the Covid-19 Era: Repressive Pluralism, Dynasticism and the Overbearing State. *Bulletin of Indonesian Economic Studies*, *56*(3), 301–323. doi:10.1080/00074918.2020.1846482

Federal Ministry Republic of Austria. (n.d.). *European Sustainable Development Strategy*. BMK. https://www.bmk.gv.at/en/topics/climate-environment/sustainable-development/eu-sds.html#:~:text=The%20EU%20Strategy%20for%20Sustainable,present%20and%20for%20future%20Generations

Feliciano, D., Recha, J., Ambaw, G., MacSween, K., Solomon, D., & Wollenberg, E. (2022). Assessment of agricultural emissions, climate change mitigation and adaptation practices in Ethiopia. *Climate Policy*, *22*(4), 427–444. doi:10.1080/14693062.2022.2028597

Ferdowsian, M. C. (2016). Total business excellence – a new management model for operationalizing excellence. *International Journal of Quality & Reliability Management*, *33*(7), 942–984. doi:10.1108/IJQRM-08-2014-0109

Fernando, Y., Jabbour, C. J. C., & Wah, W. X. (2019). Pursuing green growth in technology firms through the connections between environmental innovation and sustainable business performance: Does service capability matter? *Resources, Conservation and Recycling, 141*, 8–20.

Ferrer, M. C. R.-D. E. (2000). *Engaging Non-State Actors in a Landmine Ban, A Pioneering Conference*. ICBL. Www.Icbl.Org/Wg/Nsa

Figueiredo, P. C. (2022). Leader Competence Effectiveness. In F. Ince (Ed.), *International Perspectives and Strategies for Managing an Aging Workforce* (pp. 115–143). IGI Global. doi:10.4018/978-1-7998-2395-7.ch006

Firmansyah, E. A., Masri, M., Anshari, M., & Besar, M. H. A. (2022). Factors affecting fintech adoption: A systematic literature review. *FinTech*, *2*(1), 21–33. doi:10.3390/fintech2010002

Firmansyah, E. A., Masri, M., Anshari, M., & Besar, M. H. A. (2024). Innovation in finance: A bibliometric and content-analysis study. *Nankai Business Review International*. Advance online publication. doi:10.1108/NBRI-08-2023-0071

Fischer, C., Torvanger, A., Shrivastava, M. K., Sterner, T., & Stigson, P. (2012). How should support for climate-friendly technologies be designed? *Ambio*, *41*(S1, SUPPL.1), 33–45. doi:10.1007/s13280-011-0239-0 PMID:22314855

Fischer, F., & Forester, J. (1993). *The argumentative turn in policy analysis and planning*. Duke University Press.

Fischer, F., & Gottweis, H. (2012). *The Argumentative turn revisited: Public policy as communicative practice*. Duke University Press.

Fischer, F., & Miller, G. J. (2007). *Handbook of public policy analysis: Theory, politics, and methods*. CRC Press.

Fithriyah, M., Masri, M., Almunawar, M. N., & Anshari, M. (2022). Financial Inclusion and Mobile Payment to Empower Small and Medium-Sized Enterprises: Post-COVID-19 Business Strategy. In FinTech Development for Financial Inclusiveness (pp. 50-59). IGI Global.

Fleckenstein, T., & Lee, S. C. (2017). Democratization, post-industrialization, and East Asian welfare capitalism: The politics of welfare state reform in Japan, South Korea, and Taiwan. *Journal of International and Comparative Social Policy*, *33*(1), 36–54. doi:10.1080/21699763.2017.1288158

Foli, R., Béland, D., & Fenwick, T. B. (2018). How Instrument Constituencies Shape Policy Transfer: A Case Study from Ghana. *Policy and Society*, *37*(1), 108–124. doi:10.1080/14494035.2017.1377987

Fombrun, C., & Shanley, M. (1990). What's in a Name? Reputation Building and Corporate Strategy. *Academy of Management Journal*, *33*(2), 233–258. doi:10.2307/256324

Ford, J. D., Cameron, L., Rubis, J., Maillet, M., Nakashima, D., Willox, A. C., & Pearce, T. (2016). Including indigenous knowledge and experience in IPCC assessment reports. *Nature Climate Change*, *6*(4), 349–353. doi:10.1038/nclimate2954

Foresight. (2011). *Migration and global environmental change: Future challenges and opportunities* (p. 11). The Government Office for Science. https://www.gov.uk/government/publications/migration-and-global-environmental-change-future-challenges-and-opportunities

Forester, J. (2009). Policy analysis as critical listening. In R. Goodin, M. Moran, & M. Rein (Eds.), The Oxford Handbook of Public Policy (pp. 124–151). Oxford University Press. https://doi.org/ doi:10.1093/oxfordhb/9780199548453.003.0006

Forester, J. (1999). *The deliberative practitioner: Encouraging participatory planning processes.* MIT Press.

Forester, J. (2013). On the theory and practice of critical pragmatism: Deliberative practice and creative negotiations. *Planning Theory*, *12*(1), 5–22. doi:10.1177/1473095212448750

Forester, J. (2017). On the evolution of a critical pragmatism. In B. Haselsberger (Ed.), *Encounters with Planning Thought* (pp. 280–296). Routledge.

Fortin, K. (2015). *Education and Non-State Actors: Towards a Comprehensive Agenda.* Armed Groups and International Law. https://armedgroups-internationallaw.org/2015/09/30/education-and-non-state-actors-towards-a-comprehensive-agenda/

Fortunato, G., Funchal, B., & Motta, A. P. (2012). Impacto dos investimentos no desempenho das empresas brasileiras. *Rev. Adm. Mackenzie*, *13*(4), 75–98.

Foster, S., & Macleod, J. (2003). Deaf people at work: Assessment of communication among deaf and hearing persons in work settings. *International Journal of Audiology*, *42*(sup1), 128–139. doi:10.3109/14992020309074634

Fowler, R. J. (1955). International Environmental Standards for Transnational Corporations. Environmental Law.

Fowler, L. (2021). How to implement policy: Coping with ambiguity and uncertainty. *Public Administration*, *99*(3), 581–597. doi:10.1111/padm.12702

Franck, T. M. (2001a). Terrorism and the Right of Self-Defense. *The American Journal of International Law*, *95*(4), 839–843. doi:10.2307/2674629

Franco, C., & Giustozzi, A. (2016). Revolution in the Counter-Revolution: Efforts to Centralize the Taliban's Military Leadership. *Central Asian Affairs*, *3*(3), 249–286. doi:10.1163/22142290-00303003

Franco-Santos, M., Nalick, M., Rivera-Torres, P., & Gomez-Mejia, L. (2017). Governance and Wellbeing in academia: Negative consequences of applying agency theory logic in higher education. *British Journal of Management*, *28*(4), 711–730. doi:10.1111/1467-8551.12249

Frandsen, F., & Johansen, W. (2009). Institutionalizing crisis communication in the public sector: An explorative study in Danish municipalities. *International Journal of Strategic Communication*, *3*(2), 102–115. doi:10.1080/15531180902805460

Freeland, S., & Horn, L. S. (2009). More than hot air: Reflections on the relationship between climate change and human rights. *University of Western Sydney Law Review*. https://researchdirect.westernsydney.edu.au/islandora/object/uws%3A12506/

Freeman, C. (2008). Systems of Innovation Selected Essays in Evolutionary Economics. Cheltenham, UK: Edward Elgar Publishing. doi:10.4337/9781035306176

Freeman, M., & Beale, P. (1992). Measuring Project Success. *Project Management Journal*, *23*(1), 8–17.

Fung, A., & Wright, E. O. (2003). *Deepening Democracy: Institutional Innovations in Empowered Participatory Governance*. Verso.

Furlan, M. (2020). Understanding Governance by Insurgent Non-State Actors : A Multi-Dimensional Typology Understanding Governance by Insurgent Non-State. *Civil Wars*, *00*(00), 1–34.

Fu, W., & Su, H. C. (2020). Take actions or outsource? An empirical examination of strategic environmental options of greenhouse gas emissions. *International Journal of Operations & Production Management*, *40*(6), 753–776. doi:10.1108/IJOPM-02-2020-0088

Gabriel Marcelo, L. D. (2019). Sustainability as a Key Component of Marketing Strategy. In P. Atul & S. Rajendra (Eds.), *Handbook of Advances in Marketing in an Era of Disruptions – Essays in Honour of Jagdish N. Sheth* (pp. 119–124). Sage.

Galbreath, J. (2013). ESG in focus: The Australian evidence. *Journal of Business Ethics*.

Galliers, R. D., & Sutherland, A. R. (2008). Information systems management and strategy formulation; the stages of growth' model revisited. *Information Systems Journal*, *1*(2), 89–114. doi:10.1111/j.1365-2575.1991.tb00030.x

Galvagno, M., & Giaccone, S. C. (2019). Mapping Creative Tourism Research: Reviewing the Field and Outlining Future Directions. *Journal of Hospitality & Tourism Research (Washington, D.C.)*, *43*(8), 1256–1280. doi:10.1177/1096348019862030

Ganesan, N. (2018). Taking Stock of Myanmar's Ethnic Peace Process and the Third Twenty-First Century Panglong Conference. *Asian Journal of Peacebuilding*, *6*(2), 379–392. doi:10.18588/201811.00a072

Gannon, K. (2022, March 24). Taliban Break Promise on Higher Education for Afghan Girls. *The Diplomat*. https://thediplomat.com/2022/03/taliban-break-promise-on-higher-education-for-afghan-girls/

Gao, P., & Zhang, G. (2019). Accounting manipulation, peer pressure, and internal control. *The Accounting Review*, *94*(1), 127–151. doi:10.2308/accr-52078

García, J., & Pardo, T. (2005). E-government success factors: Mapping practical tools to theoretical foundations. Government, IT implementation, Information Technology, Relevance, Success factors. *Government Information Quarterly*, *22*(2), 187–216. doi:10.1016/j.giq.2005.02.001

García-Sánchez, I., Rodríguez-Domínguez, L., & Frías-Aceituno, J. (2015). Board of directors and ethics codes in different corporate governance systems. *Journal of Business Ethics*, *131*(3), 681–698. doi:10.1007/s10551-014-2300-y

Gardberg, N. A., & Fombrun, C. J. (2006). Corporate Citizenship: Creating Intangible Assets Across Institutional Environments. *Academy of Management Review*, *31*(2), 329–346. doi:10.5465/amr.2006.20208684

Garmon, T. (2003). Domesticating International Corporate Responsibility: Holding Private Military Firms Accountable Under the Alien Tort Claims Act. *Tulane Journal International and Comparative Law*, *11*, 325-354. https://heinonline.org/HOL/License

Garriga, A. C. (2016). Human Rights Regimes, Reputation, and Foreign Direct Investment. *International Studies Quarterly*, *60*(1), 160–172. https://www.jstor.org/stable/43868314. doi:10.1093/isq/sqw006

Gates, S., & Nordås, R. (2015). *Recruitment*. Retention, and Religion in Rebel Groups.

Gemenne, F., & Brucker, P. (2015). From the Guiding Principles on Internal Displacement to the Nansen Initiative: What the Governance of Environmental Migration Can Learn from the Governance of Internal Displacement. *International Journal of Refugee Law*, *27*(2), 245–263. Advance online publication. doi:10.1093/ijrl/eev021

George, A. L., & Bennett, A. (2005). *Case studies and theory development in the social sciences*. MIT Press.

Gerard, K. (2014). ASEAN and civil society activities in 'created spaces': The limits of liberty. *The Pacific Review*, *27*(2), 265–287. doi:10.1080/09512748.2014.882395

Gerard, K. (2015). Explaining ASEAN's engagement of civil society in policymaking: Smoke and mirrors. *Globalizations*, *12*(3), 365–382. doi:10.1080/14747731.2015.1016304

Germany v. Poland (Chorzow Factory Case), (1928) PCIJ (ser A) No.13.

Gerstl, A., & Helmke, B. (2012). The Association of Southeast Asian Nations (ASEAN) and climate change: A threat to national, regime, and human security. In B. C. G. Teh (Ed.), *Human security securing East Asia's future* (pp. 135–156). Springer Netherlands. doi:10.1007/978-94-007-1799-2_7

Geyer, R., & Rihani, S. (2012). *Complexity and public policy: A new approach to 21st century politics, policy and society*. Routledge., doi:10.4324/9780203856925

Ghasabeh, M. S., Soosay, C., & Reaiche, C. (2015). The emerging role of transformational leadership. *Journal of Developing Areas*, *49*(6), 459–467. doi:10.1353/jda.2015.0090

Ghosh, P. (2021, September 17). Afghanistan had a ministry for women affairs. Taliban replace it with 'vice and virtue'. *Hindustan Times*. https://www.hindustantimes.com/world-news/afghanistan-had-women-ministry-taliban-replace-it-with-vice-and-virtue-101631887569231.html

Gibney, M., Tomasevski, K., & Hansen, J. V. (1999). Transnational State Responsibility for Violations of Human Rights. Harvard Human Rights Journal.

Gibney, M., Tomasevski, K., & Hansen, J. V. (1999). *Transnational State Responsibility for Violations of Human Rights*, 12. *Harvard Human Rights Journal*.

Giddens, A. (1981). Modernism and Post-Modernism. *New German Critique, NGC*, *22*(22), 15–18. doi:10.2307/487860

Giddens, A. (1999). Risk and Responsibility. *The Modern Law Review*, *62*(1), 1–10. https://courses.washington.edu/sales09/Handouts/Giddens_Risk_Responsibility.pdf. doi:10.1111/1468-2230.00188

Gilley, B. (2017). Technocracy and democracy as spheres of justice in public policy. *Policy Sciences*, *50*(1), 9–22. doi:10.1007/s11077-016-9260-2

Giry, S. (2015). Autopsy of a Cambodian Election: How Hun Sen Rules. *Foreign Affairs*, *94*(5), 144–159. https://www.jstor.org/stable/24483746

Gleason, G., & Shaihutdinov, M. E. (2005). Collective Security and Non-State Actors in Eurasia. *International Studies Perspectives*, *6*(2), 274–284. doi:10.1111/j.1528-3577.2005.00206.x

Glinski, S. (2022, February 28). Taliban Struggle to Maintain Unity Six Months into Their Reign. *Foreign Policy*. https://foreignpolicy.com/2022/02/28/taliban-divisions-afghanistan-government-resistance/

Global Policy Forum. (2014). *Regulation and Oversight of PMSCs*. Global Policy Forum. https://archive.globalpolicy.org/pmscs/50211-regulation-and-oversight-of-pmscs.html

Global-is-Asian staff. (2021, July 8). *Reviewing a year of COVID-19 responses in the four 'Asian Tigers.'* LKYSPP. https://lkyspp.nus.edu.sg/gia/article/reviewing-a-year-of-covid-19-responses-in-the-four-asian-tigers

Glyptou, K. (2024). Operationalising tourism sustainability at the destination level: A systems thinking approach along the SDGs. *Tourism Planning & Development*, *21*(1), 95–121. doi:10.1080/21568316.2022.2069150

Godinho, M. (2013). Inovação em Portugal. Fundação Francisco Manuel dos Santos.

Goel, R., & Sharma, R. (2021). Studying leaders & their concerns using online social media during the times of crisis - A COVID case study. *Social Network Analysis and Mining*, *11*(46), 1–12. doi:10.1007/s13278-021-00756-w

Góis, A. D., Parente, P. H. N., & Ponte, V. M. R. (2015). Estrutura de Propriedade e Investimentos em P&D: uma análise nas companhias abertas do Brasil. Revista Base (Administração e Contabilidade) da UNISINOS, 12(1), 2-14.

Gomes, J., & Romão, M. (2015). *Maturity, Benefits and Project Management shaping Project Success.* Springer. doi:10.1007/978-3-319-16486-1_43

Gomes, J., Romão, M., & Caldeira, M. (2013). *Linking Benefits to Maturity Models.* In Proceedings of the 15th International Conference of Academy of Management and Business, ISEG, Lisboa.

Gomes, J., & Romão, M. (2012). How benefits management helps Balanced Scorecard to deal with business dynamic environments. *Tourism & Management Studies*, *9*(1), 129–138. https://www.tmstudies.net/index.php/ectms/article/view/558

Gomes, J., & Romão, M. (2014). Advantages and Limitations of Performance Measurement Tools: The Balanced Scorecard. In *Proceedings of the 7th IADIS International Conference (IS 2014)*, Madrid, Spain.

Gomes, J., & Romão, M. (2016). Improving Project Success: A Case Study Using Benefits and Project Management. *Procedia Computer Science*, *100*, 489–497. doi:10.1016/j.procs.2016.09.187

Gomes, J., & Romão, M. (2017). Aligning Information Systems and Technology with Benefit Management and Balanced Scorecard. In S. De Haes & W. Van Grembergen (Eds.), *Strategic IT Governance and Alignment in Business Settings* (pp. 112–131). IGI Global. doi:10.4018/978-1-5225-0861-8.ch005

Gomes, J., Romão, M., & Caldeira, M. (2013). The Benefits Management and Balanced Scorecard Strategy Map: How They Match. *International Journal of IT/Business Alignment and Governance*, *4*(1), 44–54. doi:10.4018/jitbag.2013010104

Gompers, P., Ishii, J., & Metrick, A. (2003). Corporate governance and equity prices. *The Quarterly Journal of Economics*, *118*(1), 107–155. doi:10.1162/00335530360535162

Goodin, R. E. (2003). The end of the welfare state? In *Terence Ball & Richard Bellamy edited by, The Cambridge History of 20th Century Political Thought* (pp. 202–216). Cambridge University Press.

Gordon, N. (2022a, November 14). *How Climate Change Helps Violent Non-state Actors.* Carnegie Endowment for International Peace.

Gracia-de-Rentería, P., Ferrer-Pérez, H., & Drabik, D. (2023). Sustainable development goals in the European Union and its regions: Are we moving forward in economic, social, and environmental dimensions? *Sustainable Development (Bradford)*, *31*(5), 3540–3552. doi:10.1002/sd.2609

Graham-Harrison, E., & Makoii, A. M. (2021, September 07). Taliban name all-male Afghan cabinet including minister wanted by FBI. *The Guardian.* https://www.theguardian.com/world/2021/sep/07/taliban-name-afghanistans-new-government

Grant, K. P., & Pennypacker, J. S. (2006). Project Management Maturity: An assessment of Project Management Capabilities Among and between Selected Industries. *IEEE Transactions on Engineering Management*, *53*(1), 59–68. doi:10.1109/TEM.2005.861802

Greig, D. W. (1991). Self-Defence and the Security Council: What Does Article 51 Require? *The International and Comparative Law Quarterly*, *40*(2), 366–402. doi:10.1093/iclqaj/40.2.366

Greve, B., Blomquist, P., Hvinden, B., & van Gerven, M. (2021). Nordic welfare states – still standing or changed by the COVID-19 crisis. *Social Policy and Administration*, *55*(2), 295–311. doi:10.1111/spol.12675 PMID:33362319

Gul, A. (2021, September 28). *Taliban Say They Will Use Parts of Monarchy Constitution to Run Afghanistan for Now*. VOA. https://www.voanews.com/a/taliban-say-they-will-use-parts-of-monarchy-constitution-to-run-afghanistan-for-now/6248880.html

Gul, A. (2022, June 18). *Taliban Say US Is 'Biggest Hurdle' to Diplomatic Recognition*. VOA. https://www.voanews.com/a/taliban-say-us-is-biggest-hurdle-to-diplomatic-recognition/6623070.html

Guler, B. (2021, August 24). *6 major figures to lead Taliban through critical process*. Anadolu Agency. https://www.aa.com.tr/en/asia-pacific/6-major-figures-to-lead-taliban-through-critical-process-/2343771

Güler, A., & Crowther, D. (2009). *The Durable Corporation: Strategies for Sustainable Development*. Gower.

Gul, F. A., Kim, J. B., & Qiu, A. A. (2010). Ownership concentration, foreign shareholding, audit quality, and stock price synchronicity: Evidence from China. *Journal of Financial Economics*, *95*(3), 425–442.

Güller, A., & Crowther, D. (2008). Governance and sustainability: An investigation into the relationship between corporate governance and corporate sustainability. *Management Decision*, *46*(3), 433–448. doi:10.1108/00251740810863870

Gupta, J. (2023). *Interview: Myanmar insurgent groups key to forest and climate protection*. The Third Pole. https://www.thethirdpole.net/en/nature/interview-myanmar-insurgent-groups-key-to-forest-and-climate-protection/

Haas, E. (1980). Why collaborate? Issue-linkage and international regimes. *World Politics*, *32*(3), 357–405. doi:10.2307/2010109

Haas, P. (2000). International institutions and social learning in the management of global environmental risks. *Policy Studies Journal: the Journal of the Policy Studies Organization*, *28*(3), 558–575. doi:10.1111/j.1541-0072.2000.tb02048.x

Hadar, L. T. (1998). U.S. Sanctions Against Burma: A Failure on All Fronts. *Cato Institute*. https://www.cato.org/trade-policy-analysis/us-sanctions-against-burma-failure-all-fronts

Hajer, M. (2003). Policy without polity? Policy analysis and the institutional void. *Policy Sciences*, *36*(2), 175–195. doi:10.1023/A:1024834510939

Hakimi, S., & Fair, C. (2022, September 09). *The Taliban's Amir on the "Victory" in Afghanistan*. Hudson Institute. https://www.hudson.org/node/45218

Hall, G., Laddu, D. R., Phillips, S. A., Lavie, C. J., & Arena, R. (2021). A tale of two pandemics: How will covid-19 and global trends in physical inactivity and sedentary behavior affect one another? *Progress in Cardiovascular Diseases*, *64*, 108–110. doi:10.1016/j.pcad.2020.04.005 PMID:32277997

Hamdan, M., & Anshari, M. (2020). Paving the Way for the Development of FinTech Initiatives in ASEAN. In *Financial technology and disruptive innovation in ASEAN* (pp. 80–107). IGI Global. doi:10.4018/978-1-5225-9183-2.ch004

Hamdan, M., Besar, M. H. A., Salleh, N. A. H., & Anshari, M. (2021, December). Small and Medium Enterprises & International Financial Reporting Standards (IFRS): Evidence from Emerging Economy. In *2021 International Conference on Sustainable Islamic Business and Finance* (pp. 109-118). IEEE. 10.1109/IEEECONF53626.2021.9686347

Han, G. Y. (2021, October 5). Employment rate of seniors aged 65 and above increased last year: Tan See Leng. *The Straits Times.* https://www.straitstimes.com/singapore/politics/employment-rate-of-seniors-aged-65-and-above-increased-last-year-tan-see-leng

Hanelt, A., Bohnsack, R., Marz, D., & Marante, C. (2020). A Systematic Review of the Literature on Digital Transformation: Insights and Implications for Strategy and Organizational Change. *Journal of Management Studies.* doi:10.1111/joms.12639

Hankins, R. (2015). *Social Interaction Between Deaf And Hearing People.* CORE. https://core.ac.uk/download/pdf/148695046.pdf

Hargrove, J. L. (1987). The Nicaragua Judgment and the Future of the Law of Force and Self-Defense. *The American Journal of International Law, 81*(1), 135–143. doi:10.2307/2202142

Haris, S. M., Mustafa, F. B., & Ariffin, R. N. R. (2020). Systematic literature review of climate change governance activities of environmental nongovernmental organizations in Southeast Asia. *Environmental Management, 66*(5), 816–825. doi:10.1007/s00267-020-01355-9 PMID:32893336

Harper, S. (2021). The impact of the COVID-19 pandemic on global population ageing. *Journal of Population Ageing, 14*(2), 137–142. doi:10.1007/s12062-021-09330-w PMID:34055101

Harris, J. (2012). The 'welfare state' in legal and social philosophy: Origins and controversies. In *Michael Lobban & Julia Moses edited by, The impact of ideas on legal development* (pp. 75–99). Cambridge University Press.

Hartley, K., Kuecker, G., & Woo, J. J. (2019). Practicing public policy in an age of disruption. *Policy Design and Practice, 2*(2), 163–181. doi:10.1080/25741292.2019.1622276

Hartmann, B. (2010). Rethinking climate refugees and climate conflict: Rhetoric, reality and the politics of policy discourse. *Journal of International Development, 22*(2), 233–246. doi:10.1002/jid.1676

Hart, S. L. (1995). *A Natural-Resource-based View of the Firm.* Academy of Management Journal. doi:10.2307/258963

Hart, S. L., & Milstein, M. B. (2003). Creating sustainable value. *The Academy of Management Perspectives, 17*(2), 56–67. doi:10.5465/ame.2003.10025194

Hasanaj, R., & Manxhari, A. M. (2017). Importance of communication during change: A case of the municipality of vlora. *European Journal of Multidisciplinary Studies, 2*(1), 15–19. doi:10.26417/ejms.v4i1.p15-19

Haselsberger, B. (2017). *Encounters in planning thought: 16 autobiographical essays from key thinkers in spatial planning.* Taylor & Francis.

Hathaway, O. A., Crootof, R., Levitz, P., Nix, H., Nowlan, A., Perdue, W., & Spiegel, J. (2012a). The Law of Cyber-Attack. *California Law Review, 100*(4), 817–885.

Hawn, O., Chatterji, A., & Mitchell, W. (2014). *How Firm Performance Moderates the Effect of Changes in Status on Investor Perceptions: Additions and Deletions by the Dow Jones Sustainability Index.* (Working paper).

Hayes, J., & Weber, K. (2021). Globalization, deglobalization, and human security: The case of Myanmar. *International Affairs, 97*(5), 1469–1488. doi:10.1093/ia/iiab110

Hayward, R. J. (2017a). Evaluating the "Imminence" of a Cyber Attack for Purposes of Anticipatory Self-Defense. *Columbia Law Review*, *117*(2), 399–434.

Hazy, J. K., & Uhl-Bien, M. (2015). Towards operationalizing complexity leadership: How generative, administrative and community-building leadership practices enact organizational outcomes. *Leadership*, *11*(1), 79–104. doi:10.1177/1742715013511483

Head, B. W., & Alford, J. (2015). Wicked problems: Implications for public policy and management. *Administration & Society*, *47*(6), 711–739. doi:10.1177/0095399713481601

Heazle, M. (2012). *Uncertainty in policy making*. Routledge., doi:10.4324/9781849776691

HelpAge International. (2020). *COVID-19 and older people in Asia Pacific 2020*. HelpAge. https://www.helpage.org/silo/files/covid19-and-older-people-in-asia-pacific-2020-in-review.pdf

Hemerijck, A. (2012). When changing welfare states and the eurocrisis meet. *Sociologica*. doi:10.2383/36887

Henfridsson, O., & Yoo, Y. (2013). The Liminality of Trajectory Shifts in Institutional Entrepreneurship. *Organization Science*. doi:10.1287/orsc.2013.0883

Heng, K. (2022. Mending Cambodia-US relations: A Cambodian Perspective. *Kyoto Review of Southeast Asia*. https://kyotoreview.org/issue-32/mending-cambodia-us-relations-a-cambodian-perspective/

Hetenyi, G., Lengyel, A., & Szilasi, M. (2019). Quantitative analysis of qualitative data: Using voyant tools to investigate the sales-marketing interface. [JIEM]. *Journal of Industrial Engineering and Management*, *12*(3), 393–404. doi:10.3926/jiem.2929

Hick, R., & Murphy, M. (2021). Common shock, different paths? Comparing social policy responses to COVID-19 in the UK and Ireland. *Social Policy and Administration*, *55*(2), 312–325. doi:10.1111/spol.12677

Hill, H., & Menon, J. (2014). Cambodia: Rapid growth in an open, post-conflict economy. *World Economy*, *37*(12), 1649–1668. doi:10.1111/twec.12206

Hillman, A. J., & Keim, G. D. (2001). Shareholder Value, Stakeholder Management, and Social Issues: What's the Bottom Line? *Strategic Management Journal*, *22*(2), 125–139. doi:10.1002/1097-0266(200101)22:2<125::AID-SMJ150>3.0.CO;2-H

Hillson, D. (2003). *Effective Opportunity Management for Projects*. Marcel Decker. doi:10.1201/9780203913246

Hinnawi, E. E. (1985). *Environmental refugees*. UNEP. https://digitallibrary.un.org/record/121267

Hiraide, L. A. (2023). Climate refugees: A useful concept? Towards an alternative vocabulary of ecological displacement. *Politics*, *43*(2), 267–282. doi:10.1177/02633957221077257

Hoffman, A. J. (2005). Climate Change Strategy: The Business Logic behind Voluntary Greenhouse Gas Reductions. *California Management Review*, *47*(3), 21–46. doi:10.2307/41166305

Hogan, J., Howlett, M., & Murphy, M. (2022). Re-thinking the coronavirus pandemic as a policy punctuation: COVID-19 as a path-clearing policy accelerator. *Policy and Society*, *41*(1), 40–52. doi:10.1093/polsoc/puab009

Holliday, I. (2000). Productivist welfare capitalism: Social policy in East Asia. *Political Studies*, *48*(4), 706–723. doi:10.1111/1467-9248.00279

Holliday, I., & Wilding, P. (2003). *Welfare capitalism in East Asia: Social policy in the tiger economies*. Palgrave Macmillan., doi:10.1057/9780230597563

Holm, E. (2019). *The NGO–state relationship and SRHR in Myanmar.* Department of Government, Uppsala University. https://www.diva-portal.org/smash/get/diva2:1299328/FULLTEXT01.pdf

Holm, F., & Fairhurst, G. T. (2018). Configuring shared and hierarchical leadership through authoring. *Human Relations*, *71*(5), 692–721. doi:10.1177/0018726717720803

Holmqvist, C. (2005). Engaging Armed Non-State Actors in Post-Conflict Settings. In A. Bryden & H. Hänggi (Eds.), Security Governance in Post-Conflict Peacebuilding. Geneva Centre for the Democratic Control of Armed Forces (DCAF).

Holmqvist, C. (2005). *Private Security Companies: The Case for Regulation.* SIPRI Policy Paper. http://www.guillaumenicaise.com/wp-content/uploads/2014/08/private-security-companies.pdf

Honkonen, T. (2009). The principle of common but differentiated responsibility in post-2012 climate negotiations. *Review of European Community & International Environmental Law*, *18*(3), 257–267. doi:10.1111/j.1467-9388.2009.00648.x

Honoré, F., Munari, F., & de La Potterie, B. V. P. (2015). Corporate governance practices and companies' R&D intensity: Evidence from European countries. *Research Policy*, *44*(2), 533–543.

Hoppe, R. (2011). Institutional constraints and practical problems in deliberative and participatory policy making. *Policy and Politics*, *39*, 163–186. doi:10.1332/030557310X519650

Hort, S. E. O., & Kuhnle, S. (2000). The coming of east and south-east Asian welfare states. *Journal of European Social Policy*, *10*(2), 162–184. doi:10.1177/a012488

Howlett, M., & Cashore, B. (2009). The dependent variable problem in the study of policy change: Understanding policy change as a methodological problem. *Journal of Comparative Policy Analysis*, *11*(1), 33–46. doi:10.1080/13876980802648144

Howlett, M., Ramesh, M., & Wu, X. (2015). Understanding the persistence of policy failures: The role of politics, governance and uncertainty. *Public Policy and Administration*, *30*(3–4), 209–220. doi:10.1177/0952076715593139

Hozoori, S. (2022). Comparing the Foreign Relations of Emirate I and Emirate II: Has Anything Changed? *India Quarterly*, *78*(4), 585–601. doi:10.1177/09749284221127806

Hsieh, J. Y., & Liou, K. T. (2018). Collaborative leadership and organizational performance: Assessing the structural relation in a public service agency. *Review of Public Personnel Administration*, *38*(1), 83–109. doi:10.1177/0734371X15623619

Hsu, C. Y., Hsiao, H. F., & Li, C. A. (2009). Effect of board monitoring on corporate investment and firm performance: Taiwan evidence. *Investment Management and Financial Innovations*, *6*(3), 84–93.

Htoo, M. H. C., Steenhuisen, B., & Verschuuren, B. (2023). What Karen Perceptions of Forest Reveal about Nature Conservation in Indigenous Contexts. *Conservation & Society*, *21*(1), 28–37. https://www.jstor.org/stable/27206657. doi:10.4103/cs.cs_83_21

Huang, R., & Sullivan, P. L. (2020). Arms for education? External support and rebel social services. *Journal of Peace Research*, *20*(10), 1–15. doi:10.1177/0022343320940749

Huang, Z., & Gao, W. (2022). The effects of formal and informal CEO power on debt policy persistence. *The North American Journal of Economics and Finance*, *62*, 101748.

Huber, E., & Stephens, J. D. (2001). *Development and crisis of the welfare state.* University of Chicago Press Books. doi:10.7208/chicago/9780226356495.001.0001

Hudson, J., Kühner, S., & Yang, N. (2014). Productive welfare, the east Asian "model" and beyond: Placing welfare types in greater china into context. *Social Policy and Society*, *13*(2), 301–315. doi:10.1017/S1474746413000572

Hull, C. E., & Rothenberg, S. (2008). Firm performance: The interactions of corporate social performance with innovation and industry differentiation. *Strategic Management Journal, 29*(7), 781–789. doi:10.1002/smj.675

Hulme, M., & Mahony, M. (2010). Climate change: What do we know about the IPCC? *Progress in Physical Geography, 34*(5), 705–718. doi:10.1177/0309133310373719

Husted, B. W., & de Sousa-Filho, J. M. (2017). The impact of sustainability governance, country stakeholder orientation, and country risk on environmental, social, and governance performance. *Journal of Cleaner Production, 155*, 93–102. doi:10.1016/j.jclepro.2016.10.025

Hwang, G. J. (2012). Explaining welfare state adaptation in East Asia: The cases of Japan, Korea and Taiwan. *Asian Journal of Social Science, 40*(2), 174–202. doi:10.1163/156853112X640134

Iannacci, F., Seepma, A., Blok, C., & Resca, A. (2019). Reappraising maturity models in e-Government research: The trajectory-turning point theory. *The Journal of Strategic Information Systems, 28*(3), 310–329. doi:10.1016/j.jsis.2019.02.001

Iansiti, M., & Levien, R. (2004). Strategy as ecology. *Harvard Business Review, 82*(3), 68–81. PMID:15029791

Ibbs, C. W., & Kwak, Y. H. (2000). Assessing project management maturity. *Project Management Journal, 31*(1), 32–43. doi:10.1177/875697280003100106

Ibrahimi, S. Y. (2022). False negotiations and the fall of Afghanistan to the Taliban. *International Journal (Toronto, Ont.), 77*(2), 168–187. doi:10.1177/00207020221135299

ICRC. (2011). *Strengthening legal protection for victims of armed conflicts.* ICRC.

Ide, T., Bruch, C., Carius, A., Conca, K., Dabelko, G. D., Matthew, R., & Weinthal, E. (2021). The past and future(s) of environmental peacebuilding. *International Affairs, 97*(1), 1–16. doi:10.1093/ia/iiaa177

IDMC. (2020). *Global Report on Internal Displacement 2019.* Internal Displacement Monitoring Centre. https://www.internal-displacement.org/global-report/grid2019/

Ihamäki, P. (2012). Geocachers: The creative tourism experience. *Journal of Hospitality and Tourism Technology, 3*(3), 152–175. doi:10.1108/17579881211264468

Immler, N. L., & Sakkers, H. (2022). The UN-Sustainable Development Goals going local: Learning from localising human rights. *International Journal of Human Rights, 26*(2), 262–284. doi:10.1080/13642987.2021.1913411

Ingold, J. O., & Stuart, M. (2015). The demand-side of active labour market policies: A regional study of employer engagement in the work programme. *Journal of Social Policy, 44*(3), 443–462. doi:10.1017/S0047279414000890

Irving, J. (2020, October). COVID-19, older adults and long-term care in the Asia Pacific, Report prepared for HelpAge International Asia Pacific. *Analysis of variable COVID-19 mortality among older people in Asia Pacific, by forms of long-term care.* Ageing Asia. https://ageingasia.org/wp-content/uploads/2020/12/COVID_LTC_Report-Final-20-November-2020.pdf

Ishfaq, S. (2019, December 31). South Asia's Most Notorious Militant Groups. *The Diplomat.* https://thediplomat.com/2019/12/south-asias-most-notorious-militant-groups/

Jabareen, Y. (2015). The emerging Islamic State: Terror, territoriality, and the agenda of social transformation. In *Geoforum* (Vol. 58, pp. 51–55). Elsevier Ltd., doi:10.1016/j.geoforum.2014.10.009

Jahan, F. (2020). *The issue of identity: state denial, local controversies and everyday resistance among the Santal in Bangladesh,* [PhD Thesis, Hale University].

Jakob, M., & Steckel, J. C. (2016). Implications of climate change mitigation for sustainable development. *Environmental Research Letters, 11*(10), 104010. doi:10.1088/1748-9326/11/10/104010

James, B. E., & McGuire, J. B. (2016). Transactional-institutional fit: Corporate governance of R&D investment in different institutional contexts. *Journal of Business Research, 69*, 3478–3486.

Janowski, T. (2015). Digital government evolution: From transformation to contextualization. *Government Information Quarterly, 32*(3), 221–236. doi:10.1016/j.giq.2015.07.001

Jayawardhan, S. (2017). Vulnerability and Climate Change Induced Human Displacement. *Consilience, 17*, 103–142. https://www.jstor.org/stable/26188784

Jefferies, S., French, N., Gilkison, C., Graham, G., Hope, V., Marshall, J., McElnay, C., McNeill, A., Muellner, P., Paine, S., Prasad, N., Scott, J., Sherwood, J., Yang, L., & Priest, P. (2020). Covid-19 in New Zealand and the impact of the national response: A descriptive epidemiological study. *The Lancet. Public Health, 5*(11), e612–e623. doi:10.1016/S2468-2667(20)30225-5 PMID:33065023

Jenkins-Smith, H., Silva, C. L., Gupta, K., & Ripberger, J. T. (2014). Belief system continuity and change in policy advocacy coalitions: Using cultural theory to specify belief systems, coalitions, and sources of change. *Policy Studies Journal: the Journal of the Policy Studies Organization, 42*(4), 484–508. doi:10.1111/psj.12071

Jensen, M. C. (1993). The modern industrial revolution, exit, and the failure of internal control systems. the Journal of Finance, 48(3), 831-880.

Jensen, C., Cline, O., & Owen, M. (2011). *Combining Business Process Management and Enterprise Architecture for Better Business Outcomes* (1st ed.). IBM Redbooks.

Jensen, M. C., & Meckling, W. H. (1976). Theory of firm – managerial behaviour, agency costs and ownership structure. *Journal of Financial Economics, 3*(4), 305–360.

Jia, G., Chen, Y., Xue, X., Chen, J., Cao, J., & Tang, K. (2011). Program management organization maturity integrated model for mega construction programs in China. *International Journal of Project Management, 29*(7), 834–845. doi:10.1016/j.ijproman.2011.03.003

Johnson, M. F., Ide, T., & Gonzalez Cruz, J. (2023). Conceptualising resilience within environmental peacebuilding. *Current Opinion in Environmental Sustainability, 65*, 101362. doi:10.1016/j.cosust.2023.101362

Johnston, A. I. (2003). Socialization in international institutions: The ASEAN way and international relations theory. In G. J. Ikenberry & M. Mastanduno (Eds.), *International relations theory and the Asia-Pacific* (pp. 107–162). Columbia University Press.

Jones, B., & Baumgartner, F. (2012). From There to Here: Punctuated Equilibrium to the General Punctuation Thesis to a Theory of Government Information Processing. *The Policy Studies Journal, 40*(1).

Jones, D. M., & Jenne, N. (2016). Weak states' regionalism: ASEAN and the limits of security cooperation in Pacific Asia. *International Relations of the Asia-Pacific, 16*(2), 209–240. doi:10.1093/irap/lcv015

Jones, D. M., & Smith, M. L. (2007). Making process, not progress: ASEAN and the evolving East Asian regional order. *International Security, 32*(1), 148–184. doi:10.1162/isec.2007.32.1.148

Jordan, J. D. (2018). 'Welfare grunters and workfare monsters? An empirical review of the operation of two UK 'work programme' centres'. *Journal of Social Policy, 47*(3), 583–601. doi:10.1017/S0047279417000629

Jørgensen, F., Bor, A., Lindholt, M. F., & Petersen, M. B. (2021). Public support for government responses against COVID-19: Assessing levels and predictors in eight Western democracies during 2020. *West European Politics*, *44*(5–6), 1129–1158. doi:10.1080/01402382.2021.1925821

Jorgenson, D. W., & Stiroh, K. J. (2000). Raising the speed limit: US economic growth in the information age. In Jorgenson (eds) Economic growth in the information age, 1-146, Cambridge, Massachusetts: MIT Press

Joseph, S. (1999). Taming the Leviathans: Multinational Enterprises and Human Rights. Netherlands International Law Review.

Joshi, M., & Jha, S. (2017). Choice of an authoritative style when implementing a survival urgency-based strategic change. *Journal of Strategy and Management*, *10*(2), 168–186. doi:10.1108/JSMA-06-2014-0041

Judgev, K., & Müller, R. (2005). A Retrospective Look at our Evolving Understanding of Project Success. *Project Management Journal*, *36*(4), 19–31. doi:10.1177/875697280503600403

Jugdev, K., & Thomas, J. (2002). Project management maturity models: The silver bullets of competitive advantage? *Project Management Journal*, *33*(4), 4–14. doi:10.1177/875697280203300402

Kaelin, W. (2019). International Responses to Climate-Related Migration. *Journal of International Affairs*, *73*(1), 255–260. https://www.jstor.org/stable/26872797

Kakar, A. W. (2022, April 25). In Afghanistan, Vice and Virtue Are Front and Center. *New Lines Magazine*. https://newlinesmag.com/reportage/in-afghanistan-vice-and-virtue-are-front-and-center/

Kamaludin, N. K., Nurmandi, A., & Salahudin. (2022). How Does the Local Government Provide Official Website and Twitter Quality? Case Study of Three Local Governments of Indonesia. *Lecture Notes in Networks and Systems*, *216*, 137–147. doi:10.1007/978-981-16-1781-2_14

Kanwal, I., Lodhi, R. N., & Kashif, M. (2019). Leadership styles and workplace ostracism among frontline employees. *Management Research Review*, *42*(8), 991–1013. doi:10.1108/MRR-08-2018-0320

Kaplan, R. S., & Norton, D. P. (1996). *The Balanced Scorecard: Translating Strategy into Action*. Harvard Business School Press.

Karacasulu, N., & Karakir, İ. A. (2021). Climate-Related Migration: Formulating a Contemporary Framework. *Journal of International and Area Studies*, *28*(1), 99–118. https://www.jstor.org/stable/27210937

Karim, R., Habib, T. Z., Arefin, S., Rahman, H., Rahman, S., & Swahnberg, K. (2020). Differences in the acceptance of wife abuse among ethnic minority Garo and Santal and mainstream Bengali communities in rural Bangladesh. *PLoS One*, *15*(7), e0236733. doi:10.1371/journal.pone.0236733 PMID:32722707

Kasfir, N., Frerks, G., & Terpstra, N. (2018). Introduction: Armed Groups and Multi-layered Governance. In Civil Wars, 19(3), 257–278). Routledge. doi:10.1080/13698249.2017.1419611

Kastberg, G., & Siverbo, S. (2016). The role of management accounting and control in making professional organizations horizontal. *Accounting, Auditing & Accountability Journal*, *29*(3), 428–451. doi:10.1108/AAAJ-03-2014-1632

Keating, J. (2009). China: We just gave Cambodia $1.2 billion because we're nice. *Foreign Policy*. https://foreignpolicy.com/2009/12/22/china-we-just-gave-cambodia-1-2-billion-because-were-nice/

Kent, J., & Myers, N. (1995). *Environmental Exodus: An Emergent Crisis in the Global Arena*. Semantic Scholar. https://www.semanticscholar.org/paper/Environmental-Exodus%3A-An-Emergent-Crisis-in-the-Kent-Myers/17981f73b39684b7629e447c58ce59874517c88e

Kerzner, H. (2001). *Applied Project Management: Best Practices on Implementation.* John Wiley & Sons, Inc.

Kerzner, H. (2019). *Using the Project Management Maturity Model: Strategic Planning for Project Management* (3rd ed.). John Wiley and Sons.

Kerzner, H. (2022). *Project Management: a systems approach to planning, scheduling and controlling* (13th ed.). John Wiley and Sons.

Ketkar, S., & Ratha, D. (Eds.). (2008). *Innovative financing for development.* World Bank Publications. doi:10.1596/978-0-8213-7685-0

Khan, S. K. (2021, September 21). *Taliban bring new faces to fill Cabinet positions in Afghanistan.* Anadolu Agency. https://www.aa.com.tr/en/asia-pacific/taliban-bring-new-faces-to-fill-cabinet-positions-in-afghanistan/2370524

Khmer Times. (2022). 4 Things to Consider Before Hiring a Security Company in Cambodia. *Khmer Times.* https://www.khmertimeskh.com/501146361/4-things-to-consider-before-hiring-a-security-company-in-cambodia/, accessed July 1, 2023.

KIC. (2016, October 11). *KNU and WWF sign the Environmental Conservation MOU.* Burma News International. https://www.bnionline.net/en/news/karen-state/item/2488-knu-and-wwf-sign-environmental-conservation-mou.html

Kim, B., Burns, M. L., & Prescott, J. E. (2009). The Strategic Role of the Board: The Impact of Board Structure on Top Management Team Strategic Action Capability. *Corporate Governance, 17*(6), 728–743.

Kim, M. H. (2011). Theorizing ASEAN integration. *Asian Perspective, 35*(3), 407–435. doi:10.1353/apr.2011.0005

Kim, S. Y. (2020). Reappraisal of the developmental welfare state theory on the underdevelopment of state welfare in East Asian growth economies: The case of South Korea. *Journal of Asian and African Studies, 55*(4), 568–585. doi:10.1177/0021909619886679

Klassen, R. D., & Whybark, D. C. (1999). The Impact of Environmental Technologies on Manufacturing Performance. *Academy of Management Journal, 42*(6), 599–615. doi:10.2307/256982

Klepp, S., & Herbeck, J. (2016). The politics of environmental migration and climate justice in the Pacific region. *Journal of Human Rights and the Environment, 7*(1), 54–73. doi:10.4337/jhre.2016.01.03

Knox, J. (2018). *Report of the Special Rapporteur on the issue of human rights obligations relating to the enjoyment of a safe, clean, healthy and sustainable environment (A/HRC/31/53)* [Dataset]. Environmental Rights Database. www.environmentalrightsdatabase.org,

Koh, K. L., & Robinson, N. (2002). Regional environmental governance: examining the Association of Southeast Asian Nations (ASEAN) model. In D. C. Esty & M. H. Ivanova (Eds.), *Global environmental governance: Options & opportunities* (Vol. 8, pp. 101–120). Yale School of Forestry and Environmental Studies., https://elischolar.library.yale.edu/fes-pubs/8

Kohli, R., & Johnson, S. (2011). Digital Transformation in Latecomer Industries: CIO and CEO Leadership Lessons from Encana Oil & Gas (USA) Inc. *MIS Quarterly Executive, 10*(4), 141–156.

Koi-Akrofi, G. (2020). Justification of, and benefits realization beyond IT investments: Analysis from literature. *International Journal of Managing Value and Supply Chains, 11*(3), 1–16. doi:10.5121/ijmvsc.2020.11301

Kolk, A. (2008). Sustainability, accountability and corporate governance: Exploring multinationals' reporting practices. *Business Strategy and the Environment, 17*(1), 1–15. doi:10.1002/bse.511

Kolmes, S. A., Kolmes, S. K., & Lin, P.-H. (2022). What Lies Ahead: How Aid for Climate Refugees Must Focus on Human Rights and Human Health. *Environment, 64*(3), 7–16. doi:10.1080/00139157.2022.2046455

Kolton, M. (2017). Interpreting China's Pursuit of Cyber Sovereignty and its Views on Cyber Deterrence. *The Cyber Defense Review*, *2*(1), 119–154.

Komatsuzaki, T. (2019). Improving public infrastructure in the Philippines. *Asian Development Review*, *36*(2), 159–184. doi:10.1162/adev_a_00135

Koremenos, B., Lipson, C., & Snidal, D. (2001). The rational design of international institutions. *International Organization*, *55*(4), 761–799. doi:10.1162/002081801317193592

Kor, Y. Y. (2006). Direct and interaction effects of top management team and board compositions on R&D investment strategy. *Strategic Management Journal*, *27*(11), 1081–1099.

Kothari, A., Foisey, L., Donelle, L., & Bauer, M. (2021). How do Canadian public health agencies respond to the COVID-19 emergency using social media: A protocol for a case study using content and sentiment analysis. *BMJ Open*, *11*(4), e041818. doi:10.1136/bmjopen-2020-041818 PMID:33888527

Kotler, P., & Haider, D. R. (1993). *Marketing Places*. Free Press.

Krasner, S. (1982). Structural causes and regime consequences: Regimes as intervening variables. *International Organization*, *36*(2), 185–205. doi:10.1017/S0020818300018920

Kregel, J. A. (2004). *External financing for development and international financial instability* (Vol. 32). Geneva: UN.

Krishnankutty, P. (2023, June 10). UN report says Taliban showing no signs of 'bending' to pressure for reform, has split leadership. *The Print*. https://theprint.in/world/un-report-says-taliban-showing-no-signs-of-bending-to-pressure-for-reform-has-split-leadership/1622069/

Krog, C. L., & Govender, K. (2015). The relationship between servant leadership and employee empowerment, commitment, trust and innovative behaviour: A project management perspective. *SA Journal of Human Resource Management*, *13*(1), 1–12. doi:10.4102/sajhrm.v13i1.712

Kühner, S. (2015). Analysing the productive and protective dimensions of welfare in the Asia-Pacific: Pathways towards human development and income equality? *Journal of International and Comparative Social Policy*, *31*(2), 151–173. doi:10.1080/21699763.2015.1047395

Kühner, S., & Chou, K. (2020). The Politics of MPF Reform: Lessons from Public Attitudes in Hong Kong. *Social Policy and Society*, *19*(3), 414–430. doi:10.1017/S1474746420000020

Kühner, S., & Chou, K. L. (2019). Poverty alleviation, coverage and fiscal sustainability: Investigating the effect of a new social pension in Hong Kong. *International Journal of Social Welfare*, *28*(1), 89–99. doi:10.1111/ijsw.12321

Kumar, S., Talukder, M. B., & Kaiser, F. (2024). Artificial Intelligence in Business: Negative Social Impacts. In Demystifying the Dark Side of AI in Business (pp. 81-97). IGI Global. https://doi.org/ doi:10.4018/979-8-3693-0724-3.ch005

Kumari, A. Sharma, A. (2016). *Infrastructure financing and development: A bibliometric review*.

Kumar, S., Talukder, M. B., Kabir, F., & Kaiser, F. (2024). Challenges and Sustainability of Green Finance in the Tourism Industry: Evidence from Bangladesh. In S. Taneja, P. Kumar, S. Grima, E. Ozen, & K. Sood (Eds.), (pp. 97–111). Advances in Finance, Accounting, and Economics. IGI Global. doi:10.4018/979-8-3693-1388-6.ch006

Kumar, S., Talukder, M. B., & Pego, A. (Eds.). (2024). *Utilizing Smart Technology and AI in Hybrid Tourism and Hospitality*. IGI Global. doi:10.4018/979-8-3693-1978-9

Kurawa, J. M., & Abdulrahman, S. (2014). Effect of corporate governance on corporate social responsibility of listed firms in the Nigerian petroleum marketing industry. In *Proceedings of International Conference on Humanities, Science and Sustainable Development*. Research Gate.

Kuruppuarachchi, P., Mandal, P., & Smith, R. (2002). IT project implementation strategies for effective changes: A critical review. *Logistics Information Management, 15*(2), 126–137. doi:10.1108/09576050210414006

Kusujiarti, S. (2012). Pluralistic and informal welfare regime: The roles of Islamic institution in the Indonesian welfare regime. In T. Keskin (Ed.), *The sociology of Islam: Secularism, economy, and politics* (pp. 419–452). Itacha Press.

Kusumasari, B., Fauzi, F. Z., & Santoso, A. D. (2023). Amplifying Local Leadership: A Twitter Analysis of Indonesian Responses to the COVID-19 Pandemic. *BISNIS & BIROKRASI: Jurnal Ilmu Administrasi Dan Organisasi, 30*(1). doi:10.20476/jbb.v30i1.1385

Kusumasari, B., Munajat, M. E., & Fauzi, F. Z. (2022). Measuring global pandemic governance: How countries respond to COVID-19. *The Journal of Management and Governance, 0*(0), 1–27. doi:10.1007/s10997-022-09647-4

Kwak, Y. H., & Ibbs, C. W. (2002). Project management process maturity $(PM)^2$ model. *Journal of Management Engineering, 18*(3), 150–155. doi:10.1061/(ASCE)0742-597X(2002)18:3(150)

Kwon, H. (2005). Transforming the developmental welfare state in East Asia. *Development and Change, 36*(3), 477–497. doi:10.1111/j.0012-155X.2005.00420.x

La Porta, R., Lopez-de-Silanes, F., Shleifer, A., & Vishny, R. (2000). Investor protection and corporate governance. *Journal of Financial Economics, 58*(1-2), 3–27.

Labour and Welfare Bureau. (2021). *Improvement in elderly care services (Chinese only)*. LWB. https://www.lwb.gov.hk/tc/blog/post_05092021.html#:~:text=%E7%8F%BE%E6%99%82%E9%A6%99%E6%B8%AF%E7%B4%84%E6%9C%89145,%E4%BB%A5%E4%B8%8A%E4%BA%BA%E5%8F%A3%E7%9A%84%E7%B4%844.1%25%E3%80%82

Lacatus, C., & Meibauer, G. (2022). 'Saying it like it is': Right-wing populism, international politics, and the performance of authenticity. *British Journal of Politics and International Relations, 24*(3), 437–457. doi:10.1177/13691481221089137

Lafortune, G., Puch, M. C., Mosnier, A., Fuller, G., Diaz, M., Riccaboni, A., Kloke-Lesch, A., Zachariadis, T., Carli, E., & Oger, A. (2021). *Europe sustainable development report 2021: transforming the European Union to achieve the sustainable development goals*. SDSN Europe and IEEP.

Lai, D., & Chui, E. (2014). A Tale of Two Cities: A comparative study on the welfare regimes of Hong Kong and Macao. *Social Policy and Society, 13*(2), 263–274. doi:10.1017/S1474746413000614

Lain, T. (2019). A picture is worth a thousand words: the evidentiary promise of emoji-based sentiment analysis. 1–14.

Landi, F., Barillaro, C., Bellieni, A., Brandi, V., Carfì, A., D'Angelo, M., Fusco, D., Landi, G., Lo Monaco, R., Martone, A. M., Marzetti, E., Pagano, F., Pais, C., Russo, A., Salini, S., Tosato, M., Tummolo, A., Benvenuto, F., Bramato, G., & Bernabei, R. (2020). The new challenge of geriatrics: Saving frail older people from the SARS-COV-2 pandemic infection. *The Journal of Nutrition, Health & Aging, 24*(5), 466–470. doi:10.1007/s12603-020-1356-x PMID:32346682

Lawrence, R. L. (2017). Understanding collaborative leadership in theory and practice. *New Directions for Adult and Continuing Education, 17*(156), 89–96. doi:10.1002/ace.20262

Le Billon, P. (2001a). The political ecology of war: Natural resources and armed conflicts. *Political Geography, 20*(5), 561–584. doi:10.1016/S0962-6298(01)00015-4

Lebedova, R., & Sapundzhiev, M. (2023). *The teaching and research laboratory - an opportunity for intellectual and creative expression in the educational process*. EduLearn. doi:10.21125/edulearn.2023.0383

Lee, B., & Barua, A. (1999). An integrated assessment of productivity and efficiency impacts of information technology investments: Old data, new analysis and evidence. *Journal of Productivity Analysis*, *121*(1), 21–43. doi:10.1023/A:1007898906629

Lee, C. H., Huang, N., Chang, H. J., Hsu, Y. J., Wang, M. C., & Chou, Y. J. (2005). The immediate effects of the severe acute respiratory syndrome (SARS) epidemic on childbirth in Taiwan. *BMC Public Health*, *5*(1), 30. doi:10.1186/1471-2458-5-30 PMID:15804368

Lee, L. S., & Anderson, R. M. (2006, Fall). An Exploratory investigation of the Antecedents of the IT Project Management Capability. *e-Service Journal*, *5*(1), 27–42. doi:10.2979/esj.2006.5.1.27

Lee, M. (2015). Impact of corporate governance on research and development investment in the pharmaceutical industry in South Korea. *Osong Public Health and Research Perspectives*, *6*(4), 249–255.

Lenschow, A., Newig, J., & Challies, E. (2016). Globalisation's limits to the environmental state? Integrating telecoupling into global environmental governance. *Environmental Politics*, *25*(1), 136–159. doi:10.1080/09644016.2015.1074384

Lenshie, N. E., Okengwu, K., Ogbonna, C. N., & Ezeibe, C. (2021). Desertification, migration, and herder-farmer conflicts in Nigeria: rethinking the ungoverned spaces thesis. *Small Wars and Insurgencies*, *32*(8), 1221–1251. doi:10.1080/09592318.2020.1811602

Leoti, A., Dos Anjos, F. A., & Costa, R. (2023). Creative Territory and Gastronomy: Cultural, Economic, and Political Dimensions of Tourism in Historic Brazilian Cities. *Sustainability (Basel)*, *15*(7), 5844. doi:10.3390/su15075844

Leroy, H., Anseel, F., Gardner, W. L., & Sels, L. (2015). Authentic leadership, authentic followership, basic need satisfaction, and work role performance: A cross-level study. *Journal of Management*, *41*(6), 1677–1697. doi:10.1177/0149206312457822

Lewis, J. (2002). Gender and welfare state change. *European Societies*, *4*(4), 331–357. doi:10.1080/1461669022000022324

Liberato, D., Limbado, B., Sousa, B., & Liberato, P. (2022). Northern portugal tourism experiences management for the post-covid period: facing demand changes in tourism products and services. In *Advances in Tourism, Technology and Systems: Selected Papers from ICOTTS 2021* (Vol. 1, pp. 625–643). Springer Nature Singapore. doi:10.1007/978-981-19-1040-1_52

Lietzman, M. (1999). *Environment and Security in an International Context*.

Lieven, A. (2021, May 15). An Afghan Tragedy: The Pashtuns, the Taliban and the State. *Survival*, *63*(3), 7–35. doi:10.1080/00396338.2021.1930403

Lillywhite, L. (2015). *Non-State Armed Groups, Health and Healthcare*. Chatam House. https://www.chathamhouse.org/sites/default/files/events/special/NSAGs Meeting Summary in the template - final edit from Jo - E.R.- PKA 27.10.15.pdf

Lim, C. S., & Mohamed, M. Z. (1999). Criteria of project success: An explanatory re-examination. *International Journal of Project Management*, *17*(4), 243–248. doi:10.1016/S0263-7863(98)00040-4

Ling, Q., Liu, F., & Wu, X. (2017). Servant versus authentic leadership: Assessing effectiveness in China's hospitality industry. *Cornell Hospitality Quarterly*, *58*(1), 53–68. doi:10.1177/1938965516641515

Lin, K., Lin, C., & Tsao, H. (2005). IS/IT Investment Evaluation and Benefit Realization Practices in Taiwanese SMEs. *Journal of Information Science and Technology*, *2*(4), 44–71. http://hdl.handle.net/20.500.11937/38113

Lin, K., & Wong, C. K. (2013). Social policy and social order in East Asia: An evolutionary view. *Asia Pacific Journal of Social Work, 23*(4), 270–284. doi:10.1080/02185385.2013.778785

Li, P. Q., & Kovacs, J. F. (2022). Creative tourism and creative spaces in China. *Leisure Studies, 41*(2), 180–197. doi:10.1080/02614367.2021.1948596

Litvin, S. W., Goldsmith, R. E., & Pan, B. (2008). Electronic word-of-mouth in hospitality and tourism management. *Tourism Management, 29*(3), 458–468. doi:10.1016/j.tourman.2007.05.011

Li, V. Q. T., Ma, L., & Wu, X. (2022). COVID-19, policy change, and post-pandemic data governance: A case analysis of contact tracing applications in East Asia. *Policy and Society, 41*(1), 129–142. doi:10.1093/polsoc/puab019

Li, Y. (2015). Think tank 2.0 for deliberative policy analysis. *Policy Sciences, 48*(1), 25–50. doi:10.1007/s11077-014-9207-4

Locatelli, G., Mariani, G., Sainati, T., & Greco, M. (2017). Corruption in public projects and megaprojects: There is an elephant in the room! *International Journal of Project Management, 35*(3), 252–268. doi:10.1016/j.ijproman.2016.09.010

Lochard, I. V. (2008). Understanding the Nexus of Governance, Intrastate Conflict and Non-State Armed Groups: Implications for Peace and Security in the Twenty-First Century. [Thesis, The Fletcher School of Law and Diplomacy].

Lombardi, C., & March, A. (2022, February 28). *Afghan Taliban Views on Legitimate Islamic Governance*. United States Institute of Peace. https://www.usip.org/publications/2022/02/afghan-taliban-views-legitimate-islamic-governance

Loyle, C. E., Cunningham, K. G., Huang, R., & Jung, D. F. (2021). New Directions in Rebel Governance Research. *Perspectives on Politics*, 1–13. doi:10.1017/S1537592721001985

Lueg, R., & Lu, S. (2012). Improving efficiency in budgeting: An interventionist approach to spreadsheet accuracy testing. *Problems and Perspectives in Management, 10*, 32–41. https://ssrn.com/abstract=2156164

Lueg, R., & Lu, S. (2013). How to improve efficiency in budgeting: The case of business intelligence in SMEs. *European Journal of Management, 13*(2), 109–120. https://ssrn.com/abstract=2463828. doi:10.18374/EJM-13-2.13

Lue, J.-D., & Park, C. (2013). Beyond productivist social policy–the East Asian Welfare–work Nexus in transition. *Journal of Asian Public Policy, 6*(1), 1–9. doi:10.1080/17516234.2013.765182

Lu, J., & Wang, W. (2015). Board independence and corporate investments. *Review of Financial Economics, 24*, 52–64.

Lv, D. D., Chen, W., Zhu, H., & Lan, H. (2019). How does inconsistent negative performance feedback affect the R&D investments of firms? A study of publicly listed firms. *Journal of Business Research, 102*, 151–162.

Lyer, K. C., & Jha, K. N. (2005). Factors affecting cost performance: Evidence from Indian Construction Projects. *International Journal of Project Management, 22*(4), 283–295. doi:10.1016/j.ijproman.2004.10.003

Lyons, K. (2020, January 20). Climate refugees can't be returned home, says landmark UN human rights ruling. *The Guardian*. https://www.theguardian.com/world/2020/jan/20/climate-refugees-cant-be-returned-home-says-landmark-un-human-rights-ruling

Ma, W., Jong, W. M., Hoppe, T., & Bruijne, M. (2021). From city promotion via city marketing to city branding: Examining urban strategies in 23 Chinese cities. *Cities, 116*, 103269. doi:10.1016/j.cities.2021.103269

Machmud, M., Fatimah, J. M., Sultan, M. I., & Farid, M. (2024). Social media as communication tools for anti-corruption campaign in Indonesia. *International Journal of Data and Network Science, 8*(1), 357–368. doi:10.5267/j.ijdns.2023.9.018

Madeira, B., Gomes, J., & Romão, M. (2017). Applying Benefits Management to the Implementation of a Copy Point: A Case Study. *International Journal of Strategic Decision Sciences, 8*(1), 13–26. doi:10.4018/IJSDS.2017010102

Mahmoud, K. W. (2013). *Cyber Attacks: The Electronic Battlefield.* Arab Center for Research & Policy Studies. https://www.jstor.org/stable/resrep12651

Mahoney, J., & Thelen, K. (2010). A Theory of Gradual Institutional Change. In J. Mahoney & K. Thelen (Eds.), *Explaining Institutional Change: Ambiguity, Agency, and Power* (pp. 1–37). Cambridge University Press.

Mahon, J. F., & Waddock, S. A. (1992). Strategic Issues Management: An Integration of Issue Life Cycle Perspectives. *Business & Society, 31*(1), 19–33. doi:10.1177/000765039203100103

Mahtani, S. (2021). Myanmar shadow government declares war on military junta, escalating crisis. *The Washington Post.* https://www.washingtonpost.com/world/asia_pacific/myanmar-military-war/2021/09/07/46c14ca2-0f93-11ec-baca-86b144fc8a2d_story.html

Maier, S. (2005). *How global is good governance?* Ethical Investment Research Services.

Malejacq, R., & Terpstra, N. (2023, July 30). *Why International Leverage Has Failed with the Taliban.* Lawfare. https://www.lawfaremedia.org/article/why-international-leverage-has-failed-with-the-taliban

Mamelund, S. E. (2012). Fertility fluctuations in times of war and pandemic influenza. *The Journal of Infectious Diseases, 206*(1), 140–141. doi:10.1093/infdis/jis315 PMID:22535995

Mamun, M. (Ed.). (2021). *Subaltern, Revolt and Armed Resistance in Bangladesh (1763-1950).* Kothaprokash.

Manescu, C. (2011). Stock returns in relation to environmental, social and governance performance: Mispricing or compensation for risk? *Sustainable Development (Bradford), 19*(2), 95–118. doi:10.1002/sd.510

Marcs, C. (2008). Spoiling Movi's River: Towards Recognition of Persecutory Environmental harm Within the Meaning of the Refugee Convention. *American University International Law Review, 24*(1). https://digitalcommons.wcl.american.edu/auilr/vol24/iss1/5

Marrone, A., & Sabatino, E. (2021). *Cyber Defence in NATO Countries: Comparing Models.* Istituto Affari Internazionali (IAI). https://www.jstor.org/stable/resrep28807

Martino, P., D'Onza, G., & Melville, R. (2019). The relationship between CAE leadership and the IAF's involvement in corporate governance. *Journal of Accounting, Auditing & Finance, 34*(4), 1–19.

Martin, S. (2010). Climate Change, Migration, and Governance. *Global Governance, 16*(3), 397–414. https://www.jstor.org/stable/29764954. doi:10.1163/19426720-01603008

Mastika, I. K., Harsono, S. S., Khristianto, W., Oktawirani, P., & Hutama, P. S. (2023). Creative strategies of local resources in managing geotourism in the Ijen Geopark Bondowoso, East Java, Indonesia. *International Journal of Geoheritage and Parks, 11*(1), 149–168. doi:10.1016/j.ijgeop.2023.01.002

Mata, J., & Woerter, M. (2013). Risky innovation: The impact of internal and external R&D strategies upon the distribution of returns. *Research Policy, 42*(2), 495–501.

Mathew, S., Ibrahim, S., & Archbold, S. (2018). Corporate governance and firm risk. *Corporate Governance (Bradford), 18*(1), 52–67. doi:10.1108/CG-02-2017-0024

Matt, C., Hess, T., & Benlian, A. (2015). Digital Transformation Strategies. *Business & Information Systems Engineering, 57*(5), 339–343. doi:10.1007/s12599-015-0401-5

Maxwell, J. A. (2021). Why qualitative methods are necessary for generalization. *Qualitative Psychology, 8*(1), 111–118. doi:10.1037/qup0000173

Mayrhofer, M., & Ammer, M. (2014). People Moving in the Context of Environmental Change: The Cautious Approach of the European Union. *European Journal of Migration and Law*, *16*(3), 389–429. doi:10.1163/15718166-12342062

Mayrhofer, M., & Ammer, M. (2022). Climate mobility to Europe: The case of disaster displacement in Austrian asylum procedures. *Frontiers in Climate*, *4*, 990558. https://www.frontiersin.org/articles/10.3389/fclim.2022.990558. doi:10.3389/fclim.2022.990558

McAdam, J. (2008). Introduction: Asylum and the Universal Declaration of Human Rights. *Refugee Survey Quarterly*, *27*(3), 3–12. doi:10.1093/rsq/hdn041

Mcadam, J. (2011). Swimming against the Tide: Why a Climate Change Displacement Treaty is Not the Answer. *International Journal of Refugee Law*, *23*(1), 2–27. doi:10.1093/ijrl/eeq045

McBain, R. K., Wickett, E., Mugunga, J. C., Beste, J., Konwloh, P., & Mukherjee, J. (2016). The post-Ebola baby boom: Time to strengthen health systems. *Lancet*, *388*(10058), 2331–2333. doi:10.1016/S0140-6736(16)31895-5 PMID:27845079

McBeth, A. (2004). *Privatising Human Rights: What Happens to the State's Human Rights Duties When Services are Privatised?* 5. *Melbourne Journal of International Law*.

McCullough, A. (2015). *The Legitimacy of States and Armed Non-State Actors*. GSDRC. www.gsdrc.org

Meadows, D. H., Meadows, D. L., Randers, J., & Behrens, W. W. (2018). The limits to growth. In *Green planet blues*. Routledge. doi:10.4324/9780429493744-3

Medina, L., Ensor, M. O., Schapendonk, F., Sieber, S., Pacillo, G., Laderach, P., Hellin, J., & Bonatti, M. (2023). Community voices on climate, peace and security: A social learning approach to programming environmental peacebuilding. *Environment and Security*.

Megheirkouni, M., Amaugo, A., & Jallo, S. (2018). Transformational and transactional leadership and skills approach: Insights on stadium management. *International Journal of Public Leadership*, *14*(4), 245–259. doi:10.1108/IJPL-06-2018-0029

Melville, N., Kraemer, K. L., & Gurbaxani, V. (2004). Information Technology and Organizational Performance: An Integrative Model of IT Business Value. *Management Information Systems Quarterly*, *28*(2), 283–321. doi:10.2307/25148636

Méndez Prada, M. C., López Barraza, L. M., Ziritt Trejo, G. Y., & Ruiz Escorcia, R. R. (2023). Explanatory structural equation model validation for territorial branding tourism policies. *International Journal of Tourism Cities*, *9*(2), 377–393. doi:10.1108/IJTC-06-2021-0119

Menz, M., & Barnbeck, F. (2017). Determinants and consequences of corporate development and strategy function size. *Strategic Organization*, *15*(4), 481–503. doi:10.1177/1476127017711070

Mercer Investment Consulting. (2006). *Fearless Forecast*. Mercer Investment Consulting.

Meredith, J., & Mantel, S. J. (2009). *Project Management: A managerial approach* (7th ed.). John Wiley and Sons, Inc.

Mergel, I., Edelmann, N., & Haug, N. (2019). Defining digital transformation: Results from expert interviews. *Government Information Quarterly*, *36*(4), 101385. doi:10.1016/j.giq.2019.06.002

Mesquita, R., Fernandes, A. A. T., & Figueiredo Filho, D. B. (2020). Uma introdução à regressão com dados de painel. *Revista Política Hoje*, *29*(1), 434–507.

Mesu, J., Sanders, K., & van Riemsdijk, M. (2015). Transformational leadership and organisational commitment in manufacturing and service small to medium-sized enterprises: The moderating effects of directive and participative leadership. *Personnel Review*, *44*(6), 970–990. doi:10.1108/PR-01-2014-0020

Mettler, T., & Rohner, P. (2009). Situational Maturity Models as Instrumental Artifacts for Organizational Design. In Proceedings of the *4th International Conference on Design Science Research in Information Systems and Technology (DESRIST'09),* Malvern, PA, USA. 10.1145/1555619.1555649

Meuser, J. D., Gardner, W. L., Dinh, J. E., Hu, J., Liden, R. C., & Lord, R. G. (2016). A network analysis of leadership theory: The infancy of integration. *Journal of Management*, *42*(5), 1374–1403. doi:10.1177/0149206316647099

Mia, I. (2023). *The Armed Conflict Survey.*

Milgrom, P., & Roberts, J. (1986). Price and Advertising Signals of Product Quality. *Journal of Political Economy*, *94*(4), 796–821. doi:10.1086/261408

Ministry of Employment and Labour. (2022). *Implementation of the elderly employment promotion subsidies system starting from 2022.* MOEL. https://www.moel.go.kr/english/news/moelNewsDetail.do?idx=3063

Mir, A. (2023, August 15). *Two Years Under the Taliban: Is Afghanistan a Terrorist Safe Haven Once Again?* United States Institute of Peace. https://www.usip.org/publications/2023/08/two-years-under-taliban-afghanistan-terrorist-safe-haven-once-again

Mirza, M. N., & Sajid, A. (2019). Use of Force in Self-Defence for Global Peace: A Conceptual Framework. *Strategic Studies*, *39*(3), 1–21. doi:10.53532/ss.039.03.00102

Mithas, S., Tafti, A., Bardhan, T., & Goh, J. M. (2012). Information Technology and Firm Profitability: Mechanisms and Empirical Evidence. *Management Information Systems Quarterly*, *36*(1), 205–224. doi:10.2307/41410414

Moghaddam, A. T., Massihabadee, A., Shorvarzi, M., & Mehrazeen, A. (2018). Board of directors and general manager role in organization governance and attention to board of directors' characteristics components. *International Journal of Organizational Leadership*, *7*(2), 143–152. doi:10.33844/ijol.2018.60213

Mohammadi, G. H. (2024, January 24). The Plight of Hazaras Under the Taliban Government. *The Diplomat.* https://thediplomat.com/2024/01/the-plight-of-hazaras-under-the-taliban-government/

Mok, K. H., Ku, Y.-W., & Yuda, T. K. (2021). Managing the COVID-19 pandemic crisis and changing welfare regimes. *Journal of Asian Public Policy*, *14*(1), 1–12. doi:10.1080/17516234.2020.1861722

Mok, K. H., & Ramesh, M. (2014). After the regional and global financial crises: Social development challenges and social policy responses in Hong Kong and Macau. In K. H. Mok & M. K. W. Lau (Eds.), *Managing social change and social policy in greater China: Welfare regimes in transition* (pp. 12–30). Routledge. doi:10.4324/9781315887579

Montabon, F., Sroufe, R., & Narasimhan, R. (2007). An examination of corporate reporting, environmental management practices and firm performance. *Journal of Operations Management*, *25*(4), 998–1014. doi:10.1016/j.jom.2006.10.003

Montagna, J. (2005). A framework for the assessment and analysis of electronic government proposals. *Electronic Commerce Research and Applications*, *4*(3), 204–219. doi:10.1016/j.elerap.2005.01.003

Moravcsik, A. (1993). Preferences and power in the European Community: A liberal intergovernmentalist approach. *Journal of Common Market Studies*, *31*(4), 473–524. doi:10.1111/j.1468-5965.1993.tb00477.x

Moreira, A., & Hick, R. (2021). COVID-19, the great recession and social policy: Is this time different? *Social Policy and Administration*, *55*(2), 261–279. doi:10.1111/spol.12679

Morgenthau, H. (1962). A political theory of foreign aid. *The American Political Science Review*, *56*(2), 301–309. doi:10.2307/1952366

Morgera, E. (2009). *Corporate Accountability in International Environmental Law*. Oxford University Press. doi:10.1093/acprof:oso/9780199558018.001.0001

Morley, J. E., & Vellas, B. (2020). Editorial: COVID-19 and older adult. *The Journal of Nutrition, Health & Aging*, *24*(4), 364–365. doi:10.1007/s12603-020-1349-9 PMID:32242202

Moskowitz, M. (1972). Choosing socially responsible stocks. *Business and Society Review*, *1*(1), 71–75.

Mouratidi, Y. (2022, April 25). *Let us talk about policy: non-state armed groups and international environmental law*. Armed Groups and International Law.

Mueangpoon, K., Inchan, C., Kaewmuneechoke, P., Rattana, P., Budsratid, S., Japakiya, S., Ngamchaliew, P., & Vichitkunakorn, P. (2022). Self-reported COVID-19 vaccine hesitancy and willingness to pay: A cross-sectional survey in thailand. *Vaccines*, *10*(4), 627. doi:10.3390/vaccines10040627

Muhammad, H., Migliori, S., & Consorti, A. (2024). Corporate governance and R&D investment: Does firm size matter? *Technology Analysis and Strategic Management*, *36*(3), 518–532.

Muhammad, H., Migliori, S., & Mohsni, S. (2022). Corporate governance and R&D investment: The role of debt financing. *Industrial and Corporate Change*, *31*(3), 628–653.

Mulford, J. P. (2016). Non-State Actors in the Russo-Ukrainian War. *Connections*, *15*(2), 89–107. doi:10.11610/Connections.15.2.07

Mullaly, M. (2006). Longitudinal Analysis of Project Management Maturity. *Project Management Journal*, *36*(3), 62–73. doi:10.1177/875697280603700307

Muller, J. (2023). *Security Services Asia' Management*. SSA. http://www.securityservicesasia.com/security_services_asia_management_john_muller.htm,

Munive, J. S. F. (2023a). *How non-state armed groups engage in environmental protection*. Research Gate.

Munive, J. S. F. (2023b). *How non-state armed groups engage in environmental protection*. DIIS.

Murphy, J. (2019). The historical development of Indonesian social security. *Asian Journal of Social Science*, *47*(2), 255–279. doi:10.1163/15685314-04702005

Muuri, A. (2010). The Impact of the Use of the Social Welfare Services or Social Security Benefits on Attitudes to Social Welfare Policies. *International Journal of Social Welfare*, *19*(2), 182–193. doi:10.1111/j.1468-2397.2009.00641.x

Naciti, V., Cesaroni, F., & Pulejo, L. (2021). Corporate governance and sustainability: A review of the existing literature. *The Journal of Management and Governance*, *26*(1), 1–20. doi:10.1007/s10997-020-09554-6

Nagamine, Y. (2015). *The Legitimization Strategy of the Taliban's Code of Conduct*. Palgrave Macmillan. doi:10.1007/978-1-137-53088-2

Nahum, N., & Carmeli, A. (2019). Leadership style in a board of directors: Implications of involvement in the strategic decision-making process. *The Journal of Management and Governance*, *7*(19), 1–29.

Nakata, M. (2004). Indigenous knowledge and the cultural interface. *Disrupting preconceptions: Postcolonialism and Education*. Research Gate.

Nandwani, P., & Verma, R. (2021). A review on sentiment analysis and emotion detection from text. *Social Network Analysis and Mining*, *11*(1), 1–19. doi:10.1007/s13278-021-00776-6 PMID:34484462

Nassaji, H. (2015). Qualitative and descriptive research: Data type versus data analysis. *Language Teaching Research*, *19*(2), 129–132. doi:10.1177/1362168815572747

Nations, J. (2010). *The Ecology of the Zapatista Revolt*. Cultural Survival. https://www.culturalsurvival.org/publications/cultural-survival-quarterly/ecology-zapatista-revolt

Navarro, A., & Llanto, G. M. (2014). Financing infrastructure in the Philippines: Fiscal landscape and resources mobilization. *Philippine Institute for Development Studies.*

Navarro, P. (1988). Why do corporations give to charity? *The Journal of Business*, *61*(1), 65–93. doi:10.1086/296420

Nebehay, S. (2020). *Trump's pardon of Blackwater Iraq contractors violates international law – UN*. Reuters. https://www.reuters.com/article/us-iraq-blackwater-un-idUSKBN294108,

Nekhili, M., Boubaker, S., & Lakhal, F. (2012). Ownership structure, voluntary R&D disclosure and market value of firms: the French case. International journal of business, 17(2), 126.

Nelson, M. J. (2021, November 03). *Taliban Constitutionalism in Comparative Perspective*. Berkeley Center for Religion, Peace, and World Affairs https://berkleycenter.georgetown.edu/responses/taliban-constitutionalism-in-comparative-perspective

Nesadurai, H. E. (2009). ASEAN and regional governance after the Cold War: From regional order to regional community? *The Pacific Review*, *22*(1), 91–118. doi:10.1080/09512740802651169

Newig, J., Challies, E., Jager, N. W., Kochskaemper, E., & Adzersen, A. (2018). The environmental performance of participatory and collaborative governance: A framework of causal mechanisms. *Policy Studies Journal: the Journal of the Policy Studies Organization*, *46*(2), 269–297. doi:10.1111/psj.12209 PMID:30034065

Newman, A., Schwarz, G., Cooper, B., & Sendjaya, S. (2017). How servant leadership influences organizational citizenship behavior: The roles of LMX, empowerment, and proactive personality. *Journal of Business Ethics*, *145*(1), 49–62. doi:10.1007/s10551-015-2827-6

Ng, K. (2023, April 18). *Afghan economic hopes threatened by Taliban – UN*. BBC. https://www.bbc.com/news/world-asia-65307858

Ng, I. Y. H. (2015). Welfare Attitudes of Singaporeans – Ambiguity in Shifting Socio-Political Dynamics. *Social Policy and Administration*, *49*(7), 946–965. doi:10.1111/spol.12107

Nieuwenkamp, R. (2017). *Ever Heard of SDG Washing? The Urgency of SDG Due Diligence*. OECD Development Matters. https://oecd-development-matters.org/2017/09/25/ever-heard-of-sdg-washing-the-urgency-of-SDG-due-diligence/

Nieves-Pavón, S., López-Mosquera, N., & Jiménez-Naranjo, H. (2024). The role emotions play in loyalty and WOM intention in a Smart Tourism Destination Management. *Cities (London, England)*, *145*, 104681. doi:10.1016/j.cities.2023.104681

Nokes, S. (2007). *The Definitive Guide to Project Management: The Fast Track to Getting the Job Done on Time and on Budget* (2nd ed.). Pearson Education Limited.

Noriega, C. (2023, August 23). *The secret to Colombia's drop in deforestation?* Al Jazeera. https://www.aljazeera.com/news/2023/8/22/the-secret-to-colombias-drop-in-deforestation-armed-groups

Northouse, P. G. (2019). *Leadership, theory and practice* (8th ed.). SAGE.

NUI. (2021). *Climate*. Peace and Security Fact Sheet.

Nurmandi, A., Almarez, D., & Roengtam, S. (2018). To what extent is social media used in city government policy making? Case studies in three asean cities. *Public Policy and Administration, 17*(4), 600–618. doi:10.13165/VPA-18-17-4-08

O'Connor, M., Rafferty, M., & Sheikh, A. (2013). Equity compensation and the sensitivity of research and development to financial market frictions. *Journal of Banking & Finance, 37*(7), 2510–2519.

OECD. (2014). *Recommendation of the Council on Digital Government Strategies.* Public Governance Committee. https://www.oecd.org/gov/digital-government/Recommendation-digital-government-strategies.pdf

Omisore, S. R., Abifarin, O., & Amana, A. R. (2020). Nigeria's Policy On Internally Displaced Persons. *World Affairs: The Journal of International Issues, 24*(3), 148–159. https://www.jstor.org/stable/48590649

Ongkittikul, S. (2014). Thailand country report. *Financing ASEAN Connectivity: ERIA Research Project Report FY2013, 15*, 355-400.

Oorsprong, F., Ducheine, P., & Pijpers, P. (2023). Cyber-attacks and the right of self-defense: A case study of the Netherlands. *Policy Design and Practice, 6*(2), 217–239. doi:10.1080/25741292.2023.2179955

Open Development Cambodia. (2020). *United States aid.* Open Development Cambodia. https://opendevelopmentcambodia.net/topics/united-states-aid/

Orchard, P. (2018). *Protecting the Internally Displaced: Rhetoric and Reality.* Routledge., doi:10.4324/9781315756189

Ortas, E., Álvarez, I., Jaussaud, J., & Garayar, A. (2015). The impact of institutional and social context on corporate environmental, social and governance performance of companies committed to voluntary corporate social responsibility initiatives. *Journal of Cleaner Production, 108*, 673–684. doi:10.1016/j.jclepro.2015.06.089

Ortiz, S. L., & Oubiña, C. P. (2021). The informative coverage of tragic events into television channels. A case study: The Pedrógão Grande fires in Portugal and the disappearance of Julén Roselló in Spain. *Observatorio (OBS*), 15*(4), 19–39. doi:10.15847/obsOBS15420211963

Osborne, H., & Parkinson, H. (2018, March 22). Cambridge Analytica scandal: The biggest revela- tions so far. *The Guardian.* https://www.theguardian.com/uk- news/2018/mar/22/cambridge-analytica-scandal-the-biggest-revelations-so-far

Osma, B. G. (2008). Board independence and real earnings management: The case of R&D expenditure. *Corporate Governance, 16*(2), 116–131.

Osterwalder, A., & Pigneur, Y. (2010). *Business Model Generation: Handbook for Visionaries, Game Changers, and Challengers.* John Wiley & Sons, Inc.

Otter, K., & Paxton, D. (2017). A journey into collaborative leadership: Moving toward innovation and adaptability: A journey into collaborative leadership. *New Directions for Adult and Continuing Education, 2017*(156), 33–42. doi:10.1002/ace.20248

Overland, I., Sagbakken, H. F., Chan, H.-Y., Merdekawati, M., Suryadi, B., Utama, N. A., & Vakulchuk, R. (2021). The ASEAN climate and energy paradox. *Energy and Climate Change, 2*, 100019. doi:10.1016/j.egycc.2020.100019

Padamsee, T. (2009). Culture in connection: Re-contextualizing ideational processes in the analysis of policy development. *Social Politics, 16*(4), 413–445. doi:10.1093/sp/jxp018

Palier, B., & Martin, C. (2007). From a 'frozen landscape' to structural reforms: The sequential transformation of Bismarckian welfare systems. *Social Policy and Administration, 41*(6), 535–554. doi:10.1111/j.1467-9515.2007.00571.x

Panagiotopoulos, P., Al-Debei, M., Fitzgerald, G., & Elliman, T. (2012). A business model perspective for ICTs in public engagement. *Government Information Quarterly, 29*(2), 192–202. doi:10.1016/j.giq.2011.09.011

Pande, S., & Ansari, V. A. (2014). A theoretical framework for corporate governance. Indian. *Journal of Corporate Governance*, *7*(1), 56–72.

Pandey, C. (2015). Managing Climate Change: Shifting Roles for NGOs in the Climate Negotiations. In Environmental Values (6th ed., pp. 799–824). White Horse Press.

Pankaj, A. K. (2005). Revisiting foreign aid theories. *International Studies*, *42*(2), 103–121. doi:10.1177/002088170404200201

Papadopoulos, A. M. (2016). Forty years of regulations on the thermal performance of the building envelope in Europe: Achievements, perspectives and challenges. *Energy and Building*, *127*, 942–952. doi:10.1016/j.enbuild.2016.06.051

Parguel, B., Benoît-Moreau, F., & Larceneux, F. (2011). How Sustainability Ratings Might Deter "Greenwashing": A Closer Look at Ethical Corporate Communication. *Journal of Business Ethics*, *102*(1), 15–28. doi:10.1007/s10551-011-0901-2

Parsons, C. (2007). *How to Map Arguments in Political Science*. Oxford University Press. doi:10.1093/oso/9780199286676.001.0001

Paschinger, E. (2021). Creative travellers in Austria. In N. Duxbury, S. Albino, & C. P. De Carvalho (Eds.), *Creative tourism: Activating cultural resources and engaging creative travellers* (1st ed., pp. 26–29). CABI., doi:10.1079/9781789243536.0003

Pattberg, P., Kaiser, C., Widerberg, O., & Stripple, J. (2022). 20 Years of global climate change governance research: taking stock and moving forward. *International Environmental Agreements: Politics, Law and Economics, 22*(2), 295–315. doi:10.1007/s10784-022-09568-5

Paul, B. D. (2008). A history of the concept of sustainable development: Literature review.The Annals of the University of Oradea. *Economic Sciences Series*, *17*(2), 576–580.

Paul, C. J., & Weinthal, E. (2019). The development of Ethiopia's Climate Resilient Green Economy 2011–2014: Implications for rural adaptation. *Climate and Development*, *11*(3), 193–202. doi:10.1080/17565529.2018.1442802

Paust, J. J. (2021). *Human Rights Responsibilities of Private Corporations,* 35 VAND. *J. Transnat'l, L*, 801. https://scholarship.law.vanderbilt.edu/vjtl/vol35/iss3/3

PAX. (2023). *Axed and Burned: How Conflict-caused Deforestation Impacts Environmental, Socio-economic and Climate Resilience in Syria - Syrian Arab Republic*. PAX.

Pegg, S. (1998). *International society and the de facto state*. Routledge.

Peng, I., & Wong, J. (2004, September). Growing out of the developmental state: East Asian welfare reform in the 1990s. In Presented at the *RC19 Conference* (Vol. 2, p. 4). Research Gate.

Peng, I., & Chien, Y.-C. (2018). Not all in the same family: Diverging approaches to family policy in East Asia. In G. B. Eydal & T. Rostgaard (Eds.), *Handbook of family policy* (pp. 236–248). Edward Elgar Publishing. doi:10.4337/9781784719340.00027

Peng, I., & Wong, J. (2008). Institutions and institutional purpose: Continuity and change in East Asian social policy. *Politics & Society*, *36*(1), 61–88. doi:10.1177/0032329207312180

Peppard, J., Ward, J., & Daniel, E. (2008). Managing the realization of business benefits from IT investments. *MIS Quarterly Executive*, *6*(1), 15–25. https://aisel.aisnet.org/misqe/vol6/iss1/3

Person, C., Behnke, N., & Jürgens, T. (2023). Effects of Territorial Party Politics on Horizontal Coordination among the German Länder–An Analysis of the COVID-19 Pandemic Management in Germany. *German Politics*, 1–26. doi:10.1080/09644008.2023.2187782

Peters, G. (2010). *Governing in the Shadows*.

Pham, J. P. (2011). State collapse, insurgency, and famine in the Horn of Africa: Legitimacy and the ongoing Somali crisis. *Journal of the Middle East and Africa*, *2*(2), 153–187. doi:10.1080/21520844.2011.617238

Phang, S. Y. (2003). Strategic development of airport and rail infrastructure: The case of Singapore. *Transport Policy*, *10*(1), 27–33. doi:10.1016/S0967-070X(02)00027-6

Phillips, B. J. (2009). *How Terrorist Organizations Survive: Cooperation And Competition In Terrorist Group Networks*. Research Gate.

Phillips, B. J. (2014). Terrorist group cooperation and longevity. *International Studies Quarterly*, *58*(2), 336–347. doi:10.1111/isqu.12073

Pierson, P. (1994). *Dismantling the Welfare State? Reagan, Thatcher, and the Politics of Retrenchment*. Cambridge University Press. doi:10.1017/CBO9780511805288

Pierson, P. (1996). The new politics of the welfare state. *World Politics*, *48*(1), 143–179. doi:10.1353/wp.1996.0004

Pierson, P. (2000). Increasing returns, path dependence, and the study of politics. *The American Political Science Review*, *94*(1), 251–267. doi:10.2307/2586011

Pihir, I., Tomičić-Pupek, K., & Tomičić, M. (2019). Digital transformation playground - literature review and framework of concepts. *Journal of Information and Organizational Sciences*, *43*(1), 33–48. doi:10.31341/jios.43.1.3

Pindado, J., de Queiroz, V., & De la Torre, C. (2015). How do country-level governance characteristics impact the relationship between R & D and firm value? *R & D Management*, *45*(5), 515–526.

Pittaway, J., & Montazemi, A. (2020). Know-how to lead digital transformation: The case of local governments. *Government Information Quarterly*, *37*(4), 101474. doi:10.1016/j.giq.2020.101474

Piwowar-Sulej, K. (2021). Organizational culture and project management methodology: Research in the financial industry. *International Journal of Managing Projects in Business*, *14*(6), 1270–1289. doi:10.1108/IJMPB-08-2020-0252

Poddar, A., Narula, S. A., & Zutshi, A. (2019). A study of corporate social responsibility practices of the top Bombay Stock Exchange 500 companies in India and their alignment with the Sustainable Development Goals. *Corporate Social Responsibility and Environmental Management*, *26*(6), 1184–1205. doi:10.1002/csr.1741

Podder, S. (2013). Non-State Armed Groups and Stability: Reconsidering Legitimacy and Inclusion. *Contemporary Security Policy*, *34*(1), 16–39. doi:10.1080/13523260.2013.771029

Podder, S. (2014). Mainstreaming the non-state in bottom-up state-building: Linkages between rebel governance and post-conflict legitimacy. *Conflict Security and Development*, *14*(2), 213–243. doi:10.1080/14678802.2014.889878

Poggi, G. (1977). The Constitutional State of The Nineteenth Century: An Elementary Conceptual Portrait. *Sociology*, *11*(2), 311–332. doi:10.1177/003803857701100204

Pollack, J. (2017). Change management as an organizational project capability. In Sankaran, S., Müller, R., Drouin, N. (eds.) Cambridge Handbook of Organizazonal Project Management. Cambridge University Press. doi:10.1017/9781316662243.021

Population Reference Bureau. (2020). *World population data sheets*. PRB. https://www.prb.org/2020-world-population-data-sheet/

Portal da Industria. (2022). Apenas 10% das empresas usam recursos públicos para inovação, diz sondagem da CNI. agência de notícias da indústria. Disponível em: <https://noticias.portaldaindustria.com.br/noticias/inovacao-e-tecnologia/apenas-10-das-empresas-usam-recursos-publicos-para-inovacao-diz-sondagem-da-cni/#:~:text=Apenas%2010%25%20das%20empresas%20usam%20recursos%20p%C3%BAblicos%20para,entrevistados%20disseram%20usar%20apenas%20recursos%20pr%C3%B3prios%20para%20inovar>. Acesso em: 31 Jul. 2022.

Porter, M. E., & Kramer, M. R. (2006). Strategy and Society: The Link between Competitive Advantage and Corporate Social Responsibility. *Harvard Business Review, 84*, 78–92. PMID:17183795

Prada, G. M. (2013). Meeting of the General Assembly Open Working Group on Sustainable Development Goals. *European Union and Its Member States - Speaking Points on "Means of Implementation/Global Partnership for Achieving Sustainable Development.* SDGS. https://sdgs.un.org/sites/default/files/statements/4663eu.pdf

Pradhan, P., Costa, L., Rybski, D., Lucht, W., & Kropp, J. P. (2017). A Systematic Study of Sustainable Development Goal (SDG) Interactions. *Earth's Future, 5*(11), 1169–1179. doi:10.1002/2017EF000632

Prescott, G. W. Sutherland (2017). Political transition and emergent forest-conservation issues in Myanmar. *Conservation Biology, 31*(6), 1257–1270. https://www.jstor.org/stable/44973665

Private Security Governance Observatory. (2009). *Mapping of National Private Security Sectors: regulation and overview: Sierra Leone*. Private Security Governance Observatory. https://observatoire-securite-privee.org/en/content/sierra-leone

Pryor, C. D., Garcia-Millan, T., Gelman, J., Madan, T., Moore, S., Pryor, C., Reijula, L., Smolinske, N., Tensley, B., Weatherby, C., & Yang, J. (2019). *Taiwan's Cybersecurity Landscape and Opportunities for Regional Partnership* (Perspectives on Taiwan, pp. 10–15). Center for Strategic and International Studies (CSIS). https://www.jstor.org/stable/resrep22549.5

Pullen, W. (2007). A public-sector HPT maturity model. *Performance Improvement, 46*(4), 9–15. doi:10.1002/pfi.119

Pynnönen, A., & Takala, T. (2018). The discursive dance: The employee co-operation negotiations as an arena for management-by-fear. *Journal of Business Ethics, 147*(1), 165–184. doi:10.1007/s10551-015-2991-8

Qiao-Franco, G. (2021). ASEAN's role expectations and the diffusion of common but differentiated responsibilities principle in the climate change context. *The Pacific Review, 34*(6), 1079–1107. doi:10.1080/09512748.2020.1797860

Queirós, A., Faria, D., & Almeida, F. (2017). Strengths and limitations of quelitative and quantitative research methods. *European Journal of Education Studies, 3*(9), 369–387. doi:10.5281/zenodo.887089

Rafhanah, M. (2020). *Social Interaction Between Non Hearing and Hearing Employees in the Workplace* [Unpublished thesis, Universiti Brunei Darussalam].

Raghavan, S. (2021, November 01). The Taliban is trying to win over Afghanistan's Shiites with a 33-year-old Hazara emissary. But many question the group's sincerity. *The Washington Post.* https://www.washingtonpost.com/world/asia_pacific/taliban-afghanistan-hazaras/2021/11/01/096c9690-3775-11ec-9662-399cfa75efee_story.html

Raghavan, S. (2021, September 11). The U.S. branded the Haqqanis terrorists and issued $5 million bounties. Now they're in power in the Taliban government. *The Washington Post.* https://www.washingtonpost.com/world/asia_pacific/haqqanis-afghanistan-taliban/2021/09/10/71f82620-123b-11ec-baca-86b144fc8a2d_story.html

Ragheboom, H. (2017). The International Legal Status and Protection of Environmentally-Displaced Persons: A European Perspective. In *The International Legal Status and Protection of Environmentally-Displaced Persons: A European Perspective.* Brill Nijhoff. https://brill.com/display/title/33176

Rahimifard, S., & Trollman, H. (2018). UN Sustainable Development Goals: An engineering perspective. *International Journal of Sustainable Engineering, 11*(1), 1–3. doi:10.1080/19397038.2018.1434985

Rajamani, L. (2000). The principle of common but differentiated responsibility and the balance of commitments under the climate regime. *Review of European Community & International Environmental Law*, *9*(2), 120–131. doi:10.1111/1467-9388.00243

Raj, H. W., & Balachandran, S. (2020). Future emoji entry prediction using neural networks. *Journal of Computational Science*, *16*(2), 150–157. doi:10.3844/jcssp.2020.150.157

Ramia, G., & Perrone, L. (2021). Crisis Management, Policy Reform, and Institutions: The Social Policy Response to COVID-19 in Australia. *Social Policy and Society*, *0*(0), 1–15. doi:10.1017/S1474746421000427

Randa, I. O., & Baporikar, N. (2022). Collaborative Governance Contribution for Improving Post-Crash Responsiveness at Motor Vehicle Accident Fund. [IJSEM]. *International Journal of Sustainable Economies Management*, *11*(1), 1–25. doi:10.4018/IJSEM.304875

Ranganathan, C., Goode, V., & Ramaprasad, A. (2003). Managing the transition to bricks and clicks. *Communications of the ACM*, *46*(12), 308–316. doi:10.1145/953460.953515

Rao, K., & Tilt, C. (2016). Board composition and corporate social responsibility: The role of diversity, gender, strategy and decision making. *Journal of Business Ethics*, *138*(2), 327–347. doi:10.1007/s10551-015-2613-5

Rapoport, D. C. (1992). "Terrorism," in Encyclopedia of Government and Politics (M. H. and M. Kogan, Ed.). Routledge.

Rasyid, S. B. A., Nurmandi, A., Suswanta, Mutiarin, D., & Salahudin. (2021). Public Communication of Local Government Leaders: A Case Study of Three Major Governors in Indonesia. *Advances in Intelligent Systems and Computing*, *1352*, 487–497. doi:10.1007/978-3-030-71782-7_43

Ravenstein, E. G. (1885). The Laws of Migration. *Journal of the Statistical Society of London*, *48*(2), 167–235. doi:10.2307/2979181

Ray, S. (2015). *Infrastructure finance and financial sector development*. Research Gate.

Raymo, J. M., Park, H., Xie, Y., & Yeung, W. J. (2015). Marriage and Family in East Asia: Continuity and Change. *Annual Review of Sociology*, *41*(1), 471–492. doi:10.1146/annurev-soc-073014-112428 PMID:30078932

Reeskens, T., Muis, Q., Sieben, I., Vandecasteele, L., Luijkx, R., & Halman, L. (2021). Stability or change of public opinion and values during the coronavirus crisis? Exploring Dutch longitudinal panel data. *European Societies*, *23*(sup1, S1), S153–S171. doi:10.1080/14616696.2020.1821075

Reich, R. (2020, April 28). *The Remotes. The Essentials. The Unpaid. The Forgotten: Divided, but intertwined.* Berkely. https://blogs.berkeley.edu/2020/04/28/the-remotes-the-essentials-the-unpaid-the-forgotten-divided-but-intertwined/

Rein, M. (1971). Social policy analysis as the interpretation of beliefs. *Journal of the American Institute of Planners*, *37*(5), 297–310. doi:10.1080/01944367108977836

Reisman, W. M., & Armstrong, A. (2006). The Past and Future of the Claim of Preemptive Self-Defense. *The American Journal of International Law*, *100*(3), 525–550. doi:10.1017/S0002930000031043

ReliefWeb. (2014). *Islamic law and the rules of war*. ReliefWeb. https://reliefweb.int/report/world/islamic-law-and-rules-war

Remoaldo, P., Matos, O., Freitas, I., Gôja, R., Araújo Alves, J., Ribeiro, V., Pereira, M., & Xavier, C. (2022). An International Overview of Certified Practices in Creative Tourism in Rural and Urban Territories. *Journal of Hospitality & Tourism Research (Washington, D.C.)*, *46*(8), 1545–1573. doi:10.1177/1096348020950792

Repez, F., & Atanasiu, M. (2020). The Environment - a "Silent Victim" of Armed Conflicts: Array. *Acta Universitatis Danubius. Relations Internationales*, *12*(2). https://dj.univ-danubius.ro/index.php/AUDRI/article/view/45

Reymenyi, D., Sherwood-Smith, M., & White, T. (1997). *Achieving Maximum Values from Information Systems: A Process Approach*. John Wiley & Sons.

Ricart, J. E., & Rey, C. (2021). Purpose in Corporate Governance: The Path towards a More Sustainable World. *Sustainability (Basel)*, *14*(8), 4384. doi:10.3390/su14084384

Rich, A. (2010). Ideas, expertise, and think tanks. In D. Béland & R. H. Cox (Eds.), *Ideas and politics in social science research* (pp. 191–208). Oxford University Press. doi:10.1093/acprof:oso/9780199736430.003.0010

Rillo, A. D. (2017). *Public financing of infrastructure in Asia: In search of new solutions*. Research Gate.

Risse, T., & Sikkink, K. (1999). The socialization of international human rights norms into domestic practices: Introduction. In T. Risse, S. C. Ropp, & K. Sikkink (Eds.), *The power of human rights: International norms and domestic change* (pp. 1–38). Cambridge University Press. doi:10.1017/CBO9780511598777.002

Ritchie, J., Spencer, L., & O'Connor, W. (2003). Carrying out qualitative analysis. In J. Ritchie & J. Lewis (Eds.), *Qualitative research practice* (pp. 219–262). Sage Publications.

RobertsD. J.Van den SteenE. (2000). Shareholder interests, human capital investment and corporate governance. Stanford GSB Working. doi:10.2139/ssrn.230019

Rödder, S. (2020). The ambivalent role of environmental NGOs in climate communication. *JCOM, Journal of Science Communication*, *19*(6), C03. doi:10.22323/2.19060303

Rodenhäuser, T. (2018). *Organising rebellion: Non-state armed groups under international humanitarian, human rights, and international criminal laws*. Oxford University. doi:10.1093/oso/9780198821946.001.0001

Rodrigues, R., Samagaio, A., & Felício, T. (2020). Corporate governance and R&D investment by European listed companies. *Journal of Business Research*, *115*, 289–295.

Rogers, D. (2016). *The digital transformation playbook: rethink your business for the digital age*. Columbia University Press. doi:10.7312/roge17544

Roseta, P., Sousa, B. B., & Roseta, L. (2020). Determiners in the consumer's purchase decision process in ecotourism contexts: A Portuguese case study. *Geosciences*, *10*(6), 224. doi:10.3390/geosciences10060224

Rosli, S. N., Anshari, M., Almunawar, M. N., & Masri, M. (2022). Digital wallet ecosystem in promoting financial inclusion. In *FinTech development for financial inclusiveness* (pp. 31–49). IGI Global. doi:10.4018/978-1-7998-8447-7.ch003

Ross, J., Beath, C., & Mocker, M. (2019). *Designed for Digital How to Architect Your Business for Sustained Success*. MIT Press. doi:10.7551/mitpress/12188.001.0001

Ross, M. L. (2004a). How Do Natural Resources Influence Civil War? Evidence from Thirteen Cases. *International Organization*, *58*(1). doi:10.1017/S002081830458102X

Ross, M. L. (2004b). What Do We Know about Natural Resources and Civil War? *Journal of Peace Research*, *41*(3), 337–356. doi:10.1177/0022343304043773

Roy, P. K. (2024). *Customary Law and Sustainable Community Development: A Study of the Santals of Bangladesh*, [PhD Thesis, Universiti Malaya].

Roy, P., Chowdhury, J. S., Abd Wahab, H., & Saad, R. B. M. (2022). Ethnic Tension of the Bangladeshi Santal: A CDA of the Constitutional Provision. In Handbook of Research on Ethnic, Racial, and Religious Conflicts and Their Impact on State and Social Security (pp. 208-226). IGI Global. doi:10.4018/978-1-7998-8911-3.ch013

Roy, P., Chowdhury, J. S., Abd Wahab, H., Saad, M. R. B., & Parahakaran, S. (2021). Christianity, COVID-19, and marginal people of Bangladesh: An experience from the Santal Community. In Handbook of Research on the Impact of COVID-19 on Marginalized Populations and Support for the Future (pp. 65-82). IGI Global.

Roy, R. D., & Chakma, P. (2010). The Chittagong Hill Tracts Accord & Provisions on Lands, Territories, Resources and Customary Law. *Hope and Despair: Indigenous Jumma Peoples Speak on the Chittagong Hill Tracts Peace Accord.* Baguio City: Tebtebba Foundation. http://tebtebba. org/index. php/all-resources/category/8-books

Royal National Institute for Deaf People. (n.d.). *Persons with a hearing loss in the Workplace*. RNID. https://rnid.org.uk/wp-content/uploads/2020/05/Employers-Guide.pdf

Rubin, B. R. J. (2008). *Chronologies of modern terrorism* (1st ed., Vol. 1). M.E. Sharpe.

Rubin, M. A. (2019). Rebel Territorial Control and Civilian Collective Action in Civil War: Evidence from the Communist Insurgency in the Philippines. *The Journal of Conflict Resolution*, *64*(2–3), 459–489.

Rui, L., Sirui, L., Xuebei, D., Xujun, Y., & Yanggan, W. (2020). Clinical observations in very elderly patients with COVID-19 in Wuhan. *Geriatrics & Gerontology International*, *20*(7), 709–714. doi:10.1111/ggi.13974 PMID:32634855

Rüland, J. (2014). The limits of democratizing interest representation: ASEAN's regional corporatism and normative challenges. *European Journal of International Relations*, *20*(1), 237–261. doi:10.1177/1354066112445289

Russo, M. V., & Fouts, P. A. (1997). A Resource-Based Perspective on Corporate Environmental Performance and Profitability. *Academy of Management Journal*, *40*(3), 534–559. doi:10.2307/257052

Ruys, T. (2014). The Meaning of "Force" and the Boundaries of the Jus Ad Bellum: Are "Minimal" Uses of Force Excluded from Un Charter Article 2(4)? *The American Journal of International Law*, *108*(2), 159–210. doi:10.5305/amerjintelaw.108.2.0159

Ryngaert, C. (2008). Litigating Abuses Committed by Private Military Companies. *European Journal of International Law*, *5*(19), 1035–1053. doi:10.1093/ejil/chn056

Sacramento, N. J. J. E. (2023a). Grassroots involvement on Global South policy narratives and deliberative action on climate change loss and damage. *Public Administration and Policy*, *26*(2), 156–168. doi:10.1108/PAP-12-2022-0146

Sacramento, N. J. J. E. (2023b). How can informal discursive arenas complement deliberative policy analysis? *Journal of Public Administration, Public Affairs, and Management*, *21*(1), 1.

Sacramento, N. J. J. E., & Boossabong, P. (2023). Technocratic and deliberative nexus in policy analysis: Learning from smart city planning in Chiang Mai, Thailand. *Journal of Asian Public Policy*, *16*(3), 271–287. doi:10.1080/17516234.2021.2007210

Sadatsafavi, H., & Walweski, J. (2011). Study of organizational change management in project-driven organizations using maturity models. Paper presented at *PMI® Global Congress 2011—North America*. Newtown Square, PA: Project Management Institute

Safitri, Y., Angeline, M., & Wibowo, D. (2021). *Tweeps and their tweeting behavior during natural disaster. 729*(1). doi:10.1088/1755-1315/729/1/012083

Sahraie, M. (2011). The ASEAN actions on climate change: Recognizing or pro-actively addressing the issue. *Sustainable development law on climate change: Working paper series.* International Development Law Organization (IDLO) and the Centre for International Sustainable Development Law (CISDL).

Sakhi, N. (2022). The Taliban Takeover in Afghanistan and Security Paradox. *Journal of Asian Security and International Affairs*, *9*(3), 383–401. doi:10.1177/23477970221130882

Salas, V. (2002). El gobierno de la empresa: Presentación. Ekonomiaz. *Revista Vasca de Economía*, *50*, 10–27.

Sánchez, L. P. C., Guerrero-Villegas, J., & Hurtado Gonzalez, J. M. (2017). The influence of organizational factors on board roles. *Management Decision*, *55*(5), 842–871.

Sankranti, S. (2023, September 28). *Under Taliban, Afghan currency tops global rankings amid turmoil.* WION. https://www.wionews.com/business-economy/under-taliban-afghan-currency-tops-global-rankings-amid-turmoil-640145

Santos, C., Castanho, R. A., & Couto, G. (2022). Understanding Creative Tourism as a Potential Catalyst for Regional Economic Development in Ultra-Peripheral Territories: Highlighting Pilot-Projects in the Azores Islands. *WSEAS TRANSACTIONS ON BUSINESS AND ECONOMICS*, *20*, 295–306. doi:10.37394/23207.2023.20.28

Sarantou, M., Kugapi, O., & Huhmarniemi, M. (2021). Context mapping for creative tourism. *Annals of Tourism Research*, *86*, 103064. doi:10.1016/j.annals.2020.103064

Sarker, M. A. R., Khan, N. A., & Musarrat, K. M. (2016). Livelihood and vulnerability of the Santals community in Bangladesh. *The Malaysian Journal of Social Administration*, *12*(1), 38–55. doi:10.22452/mjsa.vol12no1.2

Sauer, S. (2012). Land and Territory: Meanings of Land between Modernity and Tradition. *Agrarian South - the Journal of Political Economy*, *1*(1), 85–107. doi:10.1177/227797601200100106

Saunders, M., Thornhill, A., & Lewis, P. (2019). *Research methods for business students* (8th ed.). Pearson Education Limited. ISBN.

Sautter, E. T., & Leisen, B. (1999). Managing stakeholders a Tourism Planning Model. *Annals of Tourism Research*, *26*(2), 312–328. doi:10.1016/S0160-7383(98)00097-8

Schachter, O. (1987). Self-Defense. [American Society of International Law]. *Proceedings of the Annual Meeting (American Association of University Teachers of Insurance)*, *81*, 350–354.

Schachter, O. (1989). Self-Defense and the Rule of Law. *The American Journal of International Law*, *83*(2), 259–277. doi:10.2307/2202738

Schaltegger, S., & Wagner, M. (2006). Integrative management of sustainability performance, measurement and reporting. *International Journal of Accounting. Auditing and Performance Evaluation*, *3*(1), 1–19. doi:10.1504/IJAAPE.2006.010098

Schlichte, K. (2009). *In the Shadow of Violence: The Politics of Armed Groups*. Campus Verlag.

Schmidt, V. A. (2011). Reconciling ideas and institutions through discursive institu- tionalism. In D. Béland & R. H. Cox (Eds.), *Ideas and Politics in Social Science Research* (pp. 47–64). Oxford University Press.

Schreier, F., & Caparini, M. (2005). *Privatising Security: Law, Practice, and Governance of Private Military and Security Companies,* Occasional Paper No.6, Geneva: The Democratic Control of Armed Forces. https://www.files.ethz.ch/isn/14077/occasional_6.pdf,.

Schreurs, M. A. (2010). Multi-level governance the ASEAN Way. In H. Enderlein, S. Wälti, & M. Zürn (Eds.), *Handbook on multi-level governance* (pp. 308–320). Edward Elgar. doi:10.4337/9781849809047.00029

Schwab, K. (2016). *The Fourth Industrial Revolution*. Geneve, Switzerland: World Economic Forum.

Schwartz, A. F., & Meltzer, R. (2019). *Policy analysis as problem solving: A flexible and evidence-based framework.* Taylor and Francis.

Science and Technology Options Assessment. (n.d.). *Assistive technologies for people with disabilities Part II: Current and emerging technologies STUDY*. European Parliament. https://www.europarl.europa.eu/RegData/etudes/IDAN/2018/603218/EPRS_IDA(2018)603218(ANN2)_EN.pdf

Scott, M. (2023). Adapting to Climate-Related Human Mobility into Europe: Between the Protection Agenda and the Deterrence Paradigm, or Beyond? *European Journal of Migration and Law*, *25*(1), 54–82. doi:10.1163/15718166-12340144

SDSN. (2022). *Peformance of European Countries against the SDGs*. Sustainable Development Solutions Network. https://eu-dashboards.sdgindex.org/chapters/part-1-performance-of-european-countries-against-the-sdgs

Seah, S., & Martinus, M. (2021). *Gaps and opportunities in ASEAN's climate governance*. ISEAS-Yusof Ishak Institute. doi:10.1355/9789814951609

Searles, P., & Berger, R. J. (1987). The Feminist Self-Defense Movement: A Case Study. *Gender & Society*, *1*(1), 61–84. doi:10.1177/089124387001001004

Selth, A. (2008). Burma's 'saffron revolution and the limits of international influence. *Australian Journal of International Affairs*, *62*(3), 281–297. doi:10.1080/10357710802286742

Sen, A (2009). *The Idea of Justice*. Allan lane Penguin Books.

Sen, A. K. (2022, October 27). *Missteps and Missed Opportunities for Peace in Afghanistan*. United States Institute of Peace. https://www.usip.org/publications/2022/10/missteps-and-missed-opportunities-peace-afghanistan

Sen, A. (2001). *Development as freedom*. Oxford University Press.

Sen, A. (2010). Equality of what? In S. M. MacMurrin (Ed.), *The Tanner lectures on human* (2nd ed., pp. 195–220). Cambridge University Press.

Sen, S., & Bhattacharya, C. B. (2001). Does Doing Good Always Lead to Doing Better? Consumer Reactions to Corporate Social Responsibility. *JMR, Journal of Marketing Research*, *38*(2), 225–243. doi:10.1509/jmkr.38.2.225.18838

Shafie, H., & Kilby, P. (2003). *Including the excluded: ethnic inequality and Development in Northwest Bangladesh*.

Shah, N. A. (2007a). Self-defence, Anticipatory Self-defence and Pre-emption: International Law's Response to Terrorism. *Journal of Conflict and Security Law*, *12*(1), 95–126. doi:10.1093/jcsl/krm006

Shaw, R., Kim, Y. K., & Hua, J. (2020). Governance, technology and citizen behavior in pandemic: Lessons from COVID-19 in East Asia. *Progress in Disaster Science*, *6*, 100090. doi:10.1016/j.pdisas.2020.100090 PMID:34171010

Shenhar, A. J., Levy, O., & Dvir, D. (1997). Mapping the dimensions of project success. *Project Management Journal*, *28*(2), 5–13.

Shenhar, A., Dvir, D., Levy, O., & Maltz, A. C. (2001). Project success: A multidimensional strategic concept. *Long Range Planning*, *34*(6), 699–725. doi:10.1016/S0024-6301(01)00097-8

Shrestha, R. K., & L'Espoir Decosta, P. (2023). Developing dynamic capabilities for community collaboration and tourism product innovation in response to crisis: Nepal and COVID-19. *Journal of Sustainable Tourism*, *31*(1), 168–186. doi:10.1080/09669582.2021.2023164

Siew, R. Y. J. (2014). Evaluating and enhancing the impact of sustainability reporting tools (SRTs) [Doctoral dissertation, Ph. D. thesis, School of Civil and Environmental Engineering, University of New South Wales, Sydney].

Sihamoni, N. (2010). *Anti-Corruption Law Full Text*. CDC. https://cdc.gov.kh/wp-content/uploads/2022/05/ANTI-CORRUPTION-LAW-FULL-TEXT-.pdf

Silva, A. L. C. (2014). *Governança corporativa e sucesso empresarial: melhores práticas para aumentar o valor da firma* (2nd ed.).

Silva, J., Sousa, B., & Abreu, J. (2023). Place Marketing and Destination Management: A Study in the "Quadrilátero do Minho". In *Advances in Tourism, Technology and Systems: Selected Papers from ICOTTS 2022* (Vol. 2, pp. 567–577). Springer Nature Singapore. doi:10.1007/978-981-19-9960-4_49

Singh, Y. (2023, February 15). Afghanistan remains primary source of terrorist threat for Central and South Asia UN report. *The Week*. https://www.theweek.in/wire-updates/international/2023/02/15/fgn9-un-afghan.html

Singh, A. (2022). State, forest, and Adivasis at crossroads: Netarhat field firing range and contestations over rights. In *At the Crossroads of Rights* (pp. 6–22). Routledge. doi:10.4324/9781003269458-2

Sin, H. L., Mostafanezhad, M., & Cheer, J. M. (2021). Tourism geographies in the 'Asian century.'. *Tourism Geographies*, *23*(4), 649–658. doi:10.1080/14616688.2020.1826571

Skjold, S., & Lundberg, K. (2022). Accountability in personalised Supported Employment-based activation services. *Journal of Social Policy*, 1–17. doi:10.1017/S0047279422000915

Skulmoski, G. (2001). Project maturity and competence interface. *Cost Engineering (Morgantown, W. Va.)*, *43*(6), 1–18.

Sliż, P. (2018). Concept of the organization process maturity assessment. *Journal of Economics and Management*, *33*(3). . oi:10.22367/jem.2018.33.05

Smith, L. T. (2021). *Decolonizing methodologies: Research and indigenous peoples*. Bloomsbury Publishing. doi:10.5040/9781350225282

Sokheng, V., & Sokchea, M. (2015). CPP leadership sees an influx of new blood. *The Phnom Penh Post*. https://www.phnompenhpost.com/cpp-leadership-sees-influx-new-blood,

Soon, S., Chou, C. C., & Shi, S. J. (2021). Withstanding the plague: Institutional resilience of the East Asian welfare state. *Social Policy and Administration*, *55*(2), 374–387. doi:10.1111/spol.12713 PMID:33821059

Sousa, B., & Rocha, A. T. (2019). The role of attachment in public management and place marketing contexts: A case study applied to Vila de Montalegre (Portugal). *International Journal of Public Sector Performance Management*, *5*(2), 189–205. doi:10.1504/IJPSPM.2019.099094

Sowden, R. (2010). *OGC´s Portfolio, Programme and Project Management Maturity Model (P3M3): Introduction Guide to P3M3*. AXELOS Limited.

Spadaro, I., Pirlone, F., Bruno, F., Saba, G., Poggio, B., & Bruzzone, S. (2023). Stakeholder Participation in Planning of a Sustainable and Competitive Tourism Destination: The Genoa Integrated Action Plan. *Sustainability (Basel)*, *15*(6), 5005. doi:10.3390/su15065005

Spaight, J. M. (1932). Self-Defence and International Air Power. *Journal of Comparative Legislation and International Law*, *14*(1), 20–29.

Spector, B. A. (2016). Carlyle, Freud, and the great man theory more fully considered. *Leadership*, *12*(2), 250–260. doi:10.1177/1742715015571392

Srivastav, A., & Hagendorff, J. (2016). Corporate governance and bank risk-taking. *Corporate Governance*, *24*(3), 334–345.

Srivastava, A. K., & Sushil. (2017). Alignment: The foundation of effective strategy execution. *International Journal of Productivity and Performance Management*, *66*(8), 1043–1063. doi:10.1108/IJPPM-11-2015-0172

Stalley, P. (2018). Norms from the periphery: Tracing the rise of the common but differentiated principle in international environmental politics. *Cambridge Review of International Affairs*, *31*(2), 141–161. doi:10.1080/09557571.2018.1481824

Stanislawski, B. H. (2008). Para-States, Quasi-States, and Black Spots: Perhaps Not States, But Not "Ungoverned Territories," Either. *International Studies Review*, *10*(2), 366–396. doi:10.1111/j.1468-2486.2008.00795.x

Stark, A., & Taylor, M. (2014). Citizen participation, community resilience and crisis-management policy. *Australian Journal of Political Science*, *49*(2), 300–315. doi:10.1080/10361146.2014.899966

Starke, P., Kaasch, A., & van Hooren, F. (2013). *The welfare state as crisis manager explaining the diversity of policy responses to economic crisis*. Palgrave Macmillan.

Steckler, E., & Clark, C. (2019). Authenticity and corporate governance. *Journal of Business Ethics*, *155*(4), 951–963. doi:10.1007/s10551-018-3903-5

Steurer, R., Langer, M. E., Konrad, A., & Martinuzzi, A. (2005). Corporations, Stakeholders and Sustainable Development I: A Theoretical Exploration of Business-Society Relations. *Journal of Business Ethics*, *61*(3), 263–281. doi:10.1007/s10551-005-7054-0

Stranadko, N. (2022). Global climate governance: Rising trend of translational cooperation. *International Environmental Agreement: Politics, Law and Economics*, *22*(4), 639–657. doi:10.1007/s10784-022-09575-6 PMID:35370522

Strassmann, P. (1997). Will big spending on computers guarantee profitability? Maybe. But maybe not. In Paul Strassmann's book The Squandered Computer. Datamation-Highlands Ranch.

Stubbs, R. (2019). ASEAN sceptics versus ASEAN proponents: Evaluating regional institutions. *The Pacific Review*, *32*(6), 923–950. doi:10.1080/09512748.2019.1611627

Suikki, R., Tromsted, R., & Haapasalo, H. (2002). Project management competence development framework in turbulent business environment. *Tecnovation*, 1-16. doi:10.1016/j.technovation.2004.11.003

Suphanchaimat, R., Tuangratananon, T., Rajatanavin, N., Phaiyarom, M., Jaruwanno, W., & Uansri, S. (2021). Prioritization of the target population for coronavirus disease 2019 (COVID-19) vaccination program in Thailand. *International Journal of Environmental Research and Public Health*, *18*(20), 10803. doi:10.3390/ijerph182010803

Suratana, S., Tamornpark, R., Apidechkul, T., Srichan, P., Mulikaburt, T., Wongnuch, P., Kitchanapaibul, S., Yeemard, F., & Udplong, A. (2021). Impacts of and survival adaptations to the COVID-19 pandemic among the hill tribe population of northern Thailand: A qualitative study. *PLoS One*, *16*(6), e0252326. doi:10.1371/journal.pone.0252326

Sutiyo, S. (2022). A neo-institutional analysis of social protection: Insights from Indonesia. *Global Social Policy*, *0*(0), 1–18.

Swain, R. B. (2018). A Critical Analysis of the Sustainable Development Goals. In W. Leal Filho (Ed.), *Handbook of Sustainability Science and Research* (pp. 341–355). Springer International Publishing. doi:10.1007/978-3-319-63007-6_20

Swanepoel, D. W., & Laurent, C. (n.d.). *Open Access Guide to Audiology and Hearing Aids for Otolaryngologists' Classification of hearing Loss*. Research Gate.

Sydow, J., & Staber, U. (2002). The Institutional Embeddedness of Project Networks: The Case of Content Production in German Television. *Regional Studies*, *36*(3), 215–227. doi:10.1080/00343400220122034

Szymańska, A., & Zalewska, E. (2021). Education in the light of sustainable development goals – The case of the European Union countries. *Globalisation, Societies and Education*, *19*(5), 658–671. doi:10.1080/14767724.2021.1878010

Taderdoost, H., & Keshavarzsaleh, A. (2016). *Critical Factors that lead to Projects' Success/Failure in Global Marketplace.* In Proceedings of the 9th International Conference Interdisciplanary in Engineering (INTER-ENG 2015), Tirgu-Mures, Romania.

Tadesse, S. (2004). The allocation and monitoring role of capital markets: Theory and international evidence. *Journal of Financial and Quantitative Analysis, 39*(4), 701–730. doi:10.1017/S0022109000003185

Taliban announces new government in Afghanistan . (2021, September 07). Al Jazeera. https://www.aljazeera.com/news/2021/9/7/taliban-announce-acting-ministers-of-new-government

Talukder, M. B. (2020). An Appraisal of the Economic Outlook for the Tourism Industry, Specially Cox's Bazar in Bangladesh. *i-manager's Journal on Economics & Commerce, 2*(1), 23-35. doi:10.26634/jecom.2.1.17285

Talukder, M. B., & Kumar, S. (2023). *Revisit Intention in Hotel Industry of Bangladesh: A Critical Review of Present Literatures' Limitations and Suggestions for Further Study.* ResearchGate. https://www.researchgate.net/publication/371503587_Revisit_Intention_in_Hotel_Industry_of_Bangladesh_A_Critical_Review_of_Present_Literatures'_Limitations_and_Suggestions_for_Further_Study

Talukder, M. B., & Kumar, S. (2023). *The Effect of Food Service Quality on Customer Satisfaction in the Hotel Industry: A Conceptual Paper.* ResearchGate. https://www.researchgate.net/publication/371503829_The_Effect_of_Food_Service_Quality_on_Customer_Satisfaction_in_the_Hotel_Industry_A_Conceptual_Paper

Talukder, M. B., Kabir, F., Kaiser, F., & Lina, F. Y. (2024). Digital Detox Movement in the Tourism Industry: Traveler Perspective. In Business Drivers in Promoting Digital Detoxification (pp. 91-110). IGI Global. doi:10.4018/979-8-3693-1107-3.ch007

Talukder, M., Shakhawat Hossain, M., & Kumar, S. (2022). Blue Ocean Strategies in Hotel Industry in Bangladesh: A Review of Present Literatures' Gap and Suggestions for Further Study. SSRN Electronic Journal. doi:10.2139/ssrn.4160709

Talukder, M. B. (2020b). The Future of Culinary Tourism: An Emerging Dimension for the Tourism Industry of Bangladesh. I-Manager's. *Journal of Management, 15*(1), 27. doi:10.26634/jmgt.15.1.17181

Talukder, M. B. (2021). An assessment of the roles of the social network in the development of the Tourism Industry in Bangladesh. *International Journal of Business, Law, and Education, 2*(3), 85–93. doi:10.56442/ijble.v2i3.21

Talukder, M. B. (2024). Implementing Artificial Intelligence and Virtual Experiences in Hospitality. In *Innovative Technologies for Increasing Service Productivity* (pp. 145–160). IGI Global., doi:10.4018/979-8-3693-2019-8.ch009

Talukder, M. B., & Hossain, M. M. (2021). Prospects of Future Tourism in Bangladesh: An Evaluative Study. I-Manager's. *Journal of Management, 15*(4), 1–8. doi:10.26634/jmgt.15.4.17495

Talukder, M. B., Kumar, S., & Das, I. R. (2024). *Food Wastage on the Economic Outcome: Evidence From the Hotel Industry. Sustainable Disposal Methods of Food Wastes in Hospitality Operations.* IGI Global. doi:10.4018/979-8-3693-2181-2.ch005

Talukder, M. B., Kumar, S., & Das, I. R. (2024). Mindfulness of Digital Detoxification: Healthy Lifestyle in Tourism. In *Contemporary Management and Global Leadership for Sustainability* (pp. 56–71). IGI Global. doi:10.4018/979-8-3693-1273-5.ch004

Talukder, M. B., Kumar, S., Sood, K., & Grima, S. (2023). Information Technology, Food Service Quality and Restaurant Revisit Intention. *International Journal of Sustainable Development and Planning, 18*(1), 295–303. doi:10.18280/ijsdp.180131

Talukder, M., Kumar, S., Misra, L., & Kabir, F. (2024). Determining the role of eco-tourism service quality, tourist satisfaction,and destination loyalty: A case study of Kuakata Beach. *Acta Scientiarum Polonorum. Administratio Locorum, 23*(1), 133–151. doi:10.31648/aspal.9275

Tastan, N. (2023, November 15). *Afghan refugees returning from Pakistan in 'very bad condition,' says UN official.* Anadolu Agency. https://www.aa.com.tr/en/asia-pacific/afghan-refugees-returning-from-pakistan-in-very-bad-condition-says-un-official/3054109

Taylor-Gooby, P. (2004). *New risks, new welfare: The transformation of the European welfare state.* Oxford University Press. doi:10.1093/019926726X.001.0001

Taylor-Gooby, P. (2004). New social risks in postindustrial society: Some evidence on responses to active labour market policies from Eurobarometer. *International Social Security Review, 57*(3), 45–64. doi:10.1111/j.1468-246X.2004.00194.x

Taylor-Gooby, P., Chung, H., & Leruth, B. (2018). The contribution of deliberative forums to studying welfare state attitudes: A United Kingdom study. *Social Policy and Administration, 52*(4), 914–927. doi:10.1111/spol.12405

Taylor, S. (1997). Critical policy analysis: Exploring contexts, texts and consequences. *Discourse (Abingdon), 18*(1), 23–35. doi:10.1080/0159630970180102

Terpstra, N., & Frerks, G. (2017). Rebel Governance and Legitimacy: Understanding the Impact of Rebel Legitimation on Civilian Compliance with the LTTE Rule. *Civil Wars, 19*(3), 279–307. doi:10.1080/13698249.2017.1393265

The government of the Hong Kong Special Administrative Region. (2020). *LCQ14: Guangdong scheme and Fujian scheme.* INFO. https://www.info.gov.hk/gia/general/202001/08/P2020010800366.htm?fontSize=1

The U.S. Embassy in Burma. (2016). *Treasury Implements Termination of Burma Sanctions Program.* U.S. Treasury Department Office of Public Affairs. https://mm.usembassy.gov/termination-burma-sanctions-program/

The United Nations. (1991). *Framework for a Comprehensive Political Settlement of the Cambodia Conflict.* UN. https://peacemaker.un.org/sites/peacemaker.un.org/files/KH_911023_FrameworkComprehensivePoliticalSettlementCambodia.pdf, accessed June 24, 2023.

The White House. (2012). *President Obama Promises Support for the People of Burma.* The White House. https://obamawhitehouse.archives.gov/blog/2012/11/19/president-obama-promises-support-people-burma

Theohary, C. A., & Rollins, J. (2011). *Terrorist Use of the Internet: Information Operations in Cyberspace.* CRS. www.crs.gov

Thissen, W. A. H., & Walker, W. E. (2013). *Public policy analysis: New developments.* Springer., doi:10.1007/978-1-4614-4602-6

Thomas, T. K. S. C. W. (2005). *Warlords Rising: Confronting Violent Non-State Actors.* Lexington Books.

Thul, P. C. (2013). *Cambodia election crisis deepens as opposition rejects results.* Reuters. https://www.reuters.com/article/us-cambodia-election-count-idUSBRE97B02I20130812

Tobin, B. (2014). *Indigenous peoples, customary law and human rights-why living law matters.* Routledge. doi:10.4324/9781315778792

Toigo, L. A., Hein, N., & Kroenke, A. (2018). Características predominantes dos mecanismos de governança corporativa e desempenho pós-fusões e aquisições no Brasil. Enfoque. *Reflexão Contábil, 37*, 85–104.

Tomaz, E., Costa, P., Gato, M. A., Cruz, A. R., & Perestrelo, M. (2020). *Discussing impact assessment on creative tourism: A theoretical and analytical model.* DINÂMIA'CET-ISCTE. doi:10.15847/dinamiacet-iul.wp.2020.05

Too, E., & Weaver, P. (2014). The management of project management: A conceptual framework for project governance. *International Journal of Project Management*, *32*(8), 1382–1394. doi:10.1016/j.ijproman.2013.07.006

Torfing, J. (2009). Rethinking path dependence in public policy research. *Critical Policy Studies*, *3*(1), 70–83. doi:10.1080/19460170903158149

Torgerson, D. (1985). Contextual orientation in policy analysis: The contribution of Harold D. Lasswell. *Policy Sciences*, *18*(3), 241–261. doi:10.1007/BF00138911

Trapp, K. N. (2007). Back to Basics: Necessity, Proportionality, and the Right of Self-Defence against Non-State Terrorist Actors. *The International and Comparative Law Quarterly*, *56*(1), 141–156. doi:10.1093/iclq/lei153

Trihartono, A. (2018). *Myanmar's Worsening Rohingya Crisis: A Call for Responsibility to Protect and ASEAN's Response. Sustainable Future for Human Security*. Springer. doi:10.1007/978-981-10-5433-4_1

Tripura, P. (2020). *Colonial Shadow in Bangladesh (Bangla books)*. Sangbed.

Tsagourias, N. (2012). Cyber attacks, self-defence and the problem of attribution. *Journal of Conflict and Security Law*, *17*(2), 229–244. doi:10.1093/jcsl/krs019

Turban, D. B., & Greening, D. W. (1997). Corporate social performance and organizational attractiveness to prospective employees. *Academy of Management Journal*, *40*(3), 658–672. doi:10.2307/257057

Turner, J. R. (2008). *The Handbook of Project-Based Management: Leading Strategic Chance in Organisations* (3rd ed.). McGraw-Hill.

Turner, J. R., & Müller, R. (2005). The Project Manager's Leadership Style as a Success Factor on Projects: Literature Review. *Project Management Journal*, *36*(1), 46–61. doi:10.1177/875697280503600206

Uddin, N. (2023). Methodological Issues in Social Research: Experience from the Twenty-First Century. In *The Palgrave Handbook of Social Fieldwork* (pp. 1–20). Springer International Publishing. doi:10.1007/978-3-031-13615-3_1

Udeagha, M. C., & Ngepah, N. (2023). Towards climate action and UN sustainable development goals in BRICS economies: Do export diversification, fiscal decentralisation and environmental innovation matter? *International Journal of Urban Sustainable Development*, *15*(1), 172–200. doi:10.1080/19463138.2023.2222264

UN Human Rights Committee, General Comment 6, Report of the Human Rights Committee, UN Doc. A/37/40 (1982) Id., in General Comment 16, Report of the Human Rights Committee, UN Doc. A/43/40 (1988)

UN International Collaboration and Coordination Agency. (2021). *A solemn statement on the situation in Myanmar by the Myanmar Bureau of the United Nations International Collaboration and Coordination Agency*. UN.

UN. (2021, February 10). *ISIL Must Be Defeated in Cyberspace, Under-Secretary-General Tells Security Council, as Terrorist Group Takes Advantage of Pandemic-Related Disruptions*. U.N. Meetings Coverage and Press Releases. https://www.un.org/press/en/2021/sc14433.doc.htm

UNEP. (2009). *Protecting the Environment During Armed Conflict An Inventory and Analysis of International Law United Nations Environment Programme*. UNEP. https://www.unep.org/conflictsanddisasters

United Nations. (2021). *United Nations Framework Convention on Climate Change*. Good Press.

Utami, D. D., Dhewanto, W., & Lestari, Y. D. (2023). Rural tourism entrepreneurship success factors for sustainable tourism village: Evidence from Indonesia. *Cogent Business & Management*, *10*(1), 2180845. doi:10.1080/23311975.2023.2180845

Valarino, I., Meil, G., & Rogero-García, J. (2018). Family or state responsibility? Elderly- and childcare policy preferences in Spain. *The International Journal of Sociology and Social Policy*, *38*(11/12), 1101–1115. doi:10.1108/IJSSP-06-2018-0086

Vale, G., Margolin, D., & Akbari, F. (2023). *Repeating the Past or Following Precedent? Contextualising the Taliban 2.0's Governance of Women*. International Centre for Counter - Terrorism. https://www.icct.nl/sites/default/files/2023-01/Taliban%202.0%E2%80%99s%20Governance%20of%20Women%20-%20Vale%2C%20Margolin%20Akbari%20final.pdf

Van Aarde, A. (2017). 'By faith alone' (undivided loyalty) in light of change agency theory: Jesus, Paul and the Jesus-group in Colossae. *Hervormde Teologiese Studies*, *73*(3). Advance online publication. doi:10.4102/hts.v73i3.4355

van der Meer, S. (2020). *How states could respond to non-state cyber-attackers*. Clingendael Institute. https://www.jstor.org/stable/resrep25677

Van Mechelen, N., Verbist, G., & Van den Bosch, K. (2004). Evaluating welfare state efforts and the model family approach: problems and promises. *In 2004 ESPAnet conference*. Research Gate. https://www.researchgate.net/profile/Gerlinde-Verbist/publication/254827237_Evaluating_welfare_state_efforts_and_the_model_family_approach_problems_and_promises/links/00463537b4e62e8b93000000/Evaluating-welfare-state-efforts-and-the-model-family-approach-problems-and-promises.pdf

Van Veenstra, A. F., Klievink, B., & Janssen, M. (2011). Barriers and impediments to transformational government: Insights from literature and practice. *Electronic Government. International Journal (Toronto, Ont.)*, *8*(2/3), 226–241. doi:10.1504/EG.2011.039838

Vasques, C. M. (2005). *Direct Vs. Indirect Obligations of Corporations under International Law*, 43. *Columbia Journal of Transnational Law*.

Vinci, A. (2007). "Like worms in the entrails of a natural man": A conceptual analysis of warlords. *Review of African Political Economy*, *34*(112), 313–331. doi:10.1080/03056240701449711

Vinyals-Mirabent, S., Kavaratzis, M., & Fernandez-Cavia, J. (2019). The role of functional associations in building destination brand personality: When official websites do the talking. *Tourism Management*, *75*, 148–155. doi:10.1016/j.tourman.2019.04.022

Vogl, T., & Micek, G. (2023). Work-leisure concepts and tourism: Studying the relationship betpeopleen hybrid coworking spaces and the accommodation industry in peripheral areas of Germany. *World Leisure Journal*, *65*(2), 276–298. do i:10.1080/16078055.2023.2208081

Volden, G., & Welde, M. (2022). Public project success? Measuring the nuances of success through ex post evaluation. *International Journal of Project Management*, *40*(6), 703–714. doi:10.1016/j.ijproman.2022.06.006

Waddock, S. A., & Graves, S. B. (1997). The corporate social performance-financial performance link. *Strategic Management Journal*, *18*(4), 303–319. doi:10.1002/(SICI)1097-0266(199704)18:4<303::AID-SMJ869>3.0.CO;2-G

Wagenaar, H. (2011). "A beckon to the makings, workings and doings of human beings": The critical pragmatism of John Forester. *Public Administration Review*, *71*(2), 293–298. doi:10.1111/j.1540-6210.2011.02341.x

Wagenaar, H. (2014). *Meaning in action: Interpretation and dialogue in policy analysis*. Routledge., doi:10.4324/9781315702476

Walch, C. (2018). Weakened by the storm: Rebel group recruitment in the wake of natural disasters in the Philippines. *Journal of Peace Research*, *55*(3), 336–350. doi:10.1177/0022343317741535

Waldman, D. A., Siegel, D. S., & Javidan, M. (2006). Components of CEO Transformational Leadership and Corporate Social Responsibility. *Journal of Management Studies*, *43*(8), 1703–1725. doi:10.1111/j.1467-6486.2006.00642.x

Wan Halim, W. M. A., & Desa, R. (2022). Analysis of Hifz al-Nafs' (Protection of Life) Achievements on the Shariah Criminal Offenses Enactment in Malaysia Based on the Fuzzy Delphi Method. *International Journal of Academic Research in Business & Social Sciences, 12*(5). doi:10.6007/IJARBSS/v12-i5/13239

Wang, H., & Rosenau, J. N. (2001). Transparency International and Corruption as an Issue of Global Governance. *Global Governance, 7*(1), 25–49. https://www.jstor.org/stable/27800285. doi:10.1163/19426720-00701005

Ward, J., & Daniel, E. (2006). *Benefits Management - Delivering Value from IS & IT Investments*. John Wiley and Sons Ltd.

Ward, J., & Elvin, R. (1999). A New Framework for Managing IT-enabled Business Change. *Information Systems Journal, 9*(3), 197–222. doi:10.1046/j.1365-2575.1999.00059.x

Ward, J., & Griffiths, P. (1996). *Strategic Planning for Information Systems* (2nd ed.). John Wiley.

Ward, J., Hertogh, S. D., & Viaene, S. (2007). *Managing Benefits from IS/IT Investments: An Empirical Investigation into Current Practice. Proceedings of 40th Hawaii International Conference on Information Systems*, Waikoloa, Big Island, HI, USA. 10.1109/HICSS.2007.330

Ward, J., Taylor, P., & Bond, P. (1996). Evaluation and Realization of IS/IT Benefits: An Empirical Study of Current Practice. *European Journal of Information Systems, 4*(4), 214–225. doi:10.1057/ejis.1996.3

Wateridge, J. (1995). IT projects: A basis for success. *International Journal of Project Management, 13*(3), 169–172. doi:10.1016/0263-7863(95)00020-Q

Weber, H. (2017). Politics of 'Leaving No One Behind': Contesting the 2030 Sustainable Development Goals Agenda. *Globalizations, 14*(3), 399–414. doi:10.1080/14747731.2016.1275404

Weber, M. (1964). *The Theory of Social and Economic Organization*. Free Press.

Weerakkody, V., Omar, A., El-Haddadeh, R., & Al-Busaidy, M. (2016). Digitally-enabled service transformation in the public sector: The lure of institutional pressure and strategic response towards change. *Government Information Quarterly, 33*(4), 658–668. doi:10.1016/j.giq.2016.06.006

Weinstein, J. (2003). *Inside Rebellion: The Political Economy of Rebel Organization*. Harvard University.

Weiss, G., Lawrence, A., Lidestav, G., Feliciano, D., Hujala, T., Sarvašová, Z., Dobšinská, Z., & Živojinović, I. (2019). Research trends: Forest ownership in multiple perspectives. *Forest Policy and Economics, 99*, 1–8. doi:10.1016/j.forpol.2018.10.006

Weisstanner, D. (2022). COVID-19 and welfare state support: The case of universal basic income. *Policy and Society, 41*(1), 96–110. doi:10.1093/polsoc/puab015

Wen, Z., Mok, K. H., & Amoah, P. A. (2021). Productive engagement and ageing in productivist welfare regimes: Questing for an age-friendly city in Hong Kong. *Ageing and Society*, 1–23. doi:10.1017/S0144686X21000167

Werner, M., & Gehrke, N. (2019). Identifying the absence of effective internal controls: An alternative approach for internal control audits. *Journal of Information Systems, 33*(2), 205–222. doi:10.2308/isys-52112

Whalan, J. (2012). Evaluating peace operations: The case of Cambodia. *Journal of International Peacekeeping, 16*(3-4), 226–251. doi:10.1163/18754112-1604003

Wheeldon, T. (2021, August 19). Who are the Taliban leaders ruling Afghanistan? *France 24*. https://www.france24.com/en/asia-pacific/20210819-who-are-the-taliban-leaders-ruling-afghanistan

Wijninga, P., Oosterveld, W. T., Galdiga, J. H., Marten, P., Chivot, E., Gehem, M., Knowles, E., Maas, M., Schellekens, M., Silveira, J., Yang, M. Y., Zelinska, O., de Jong, S., Kogut, P., & van Luit, E. (2014). *State and Non-State Actors: Beyond the Dichotomy*. Hague Centre for Strategic Studies. https://www.jstor.org/stable/resrep12608.8

Wilding, P. (2008). Is the East Asian welfare model still productive? *Journal of Asian Public Policy*, *1*(1), 18–31. doi:10.1080/17520840701835815

Willcocks, L., & Lester, S. (1999). Information Technology: Transformer or Sink Hole. In L. Willcocks & S. Lester (Eds.), *Beyond the IT Productivity Paradox*. John Wiley and Sons Ltd.

Wille, C. (2006). *How many weapons are there in Cambodia?* Graduate Institute of International Studies. https://citeseerx.ist.psu.edu/document?repid=rep1&type=pdf&doi=eb4d6814f92bf11c5748e63381db7e719cf070fb

Wilmshurst, E., & Wood, M. (2013a). Self-Defense Against Nonstate Actors: Reflections on the "Bethlehem Principles.". *The American Journal of International Law*, *107*(2), 390–395. doi:10.5305/amerjintelaw.107.2.0390

Wilsford, D. (1994). Path dependency, or why history makes it difficult but not impossible to reform health care systems in a big way. *Journal of Public Policy*, *14*(3), 285–309. doi:10.1017/S0143814X00007285

Wilson, M., & Lombardi, R. (2001). Globalisation and its Discontents. *Ivey Business Journal*, *66*, 69–72.

Wolfe, R., & Aupperle, K. (1991). Introduction to Corporate Social Performance: Methods for Evaluating an Elusive Construct. *Research in Corporate Social Performance and Policy*, *12*, 265–268.

Wong, J. (2004). The adaptive developmental state in East Asia. *Journal of East Asian Studies (Seoul)*, *4*(3), 345–362. doi:10.1017/S1598240800006007

Wong, J. (2019). Healthy democracies and welfare politics in Taiwan: The arguments, refinements and limitations. In *Taiwan Studies Revisited* (pp. 141–159). Routledge. doi:10.4324/9780429259937-9

Wong, J. H., & Ho, G. W. (2022). Shielding without a Shield—Older People under COVID-19: A Comparison of Four Cities. *Social Sciences (Basel, Switzerland)*, *11*(11), 498. doi:10.3390/socsci11110498

Wood, D. (1991). Corporate Social Performance Revisited. *Academy of Management Review*, *16*(4), 691–718. doi:10.2307/258977

Wood, G., & Gough, I. (2006). A comparative welfare regime approach to global social policy. *World Development*, *34*(10), 1696–1712. doi:10.1016/j.worlddev.2006.02.001

World Bank. (2023, August 31). *Afghan Economic Monitor*. World Bank. https://thedocs.worldbank.org/en/doc/8cd4001da4ac981a9d239f5536b173ea-0310012023/original/Afghanistan-Economic-Monitor-31-August-2023.pdf

World Development Report 1994. (1994). Oxford University Press. https://documents1.worldbank.org/curated/en/535851468336642118/pdf/131840REPLACEMENT0WDR01994.pdf

Wu, C.-F. (2021). Challenges to Protecting the Right to Health under the Climate Change Regime. *Health and Human Rights*, *23*(2), 121–138. https://www.ncbi.nlm.nih.gov/pmc/articles/PMC8694293/ PMID:34966230

Xinhuanet. (2018). *Cambodia-China trade volume jumps to 5.8 bln USD last year: minister*. Xinhuanet. http://www.xinhuanet.com/english/2018-06/21/c_137270877.htm,

Xinhuanet. (2021). *Ministry of Foreign Affairs: China hopes that all parties in Myanmar will properly handle differences and maintain political and social stability*. Xinhuanet. http://www.xinhuanet.com/2021-02/01/c_1127050935.htm

Xinhuanet. (2021). *Ministry of Foreign Affairs: The international community should create a favorable external environment for Myanmar to properly resolve differences.* Xinhuanet. http://www.xinhuanet.com/world/2021-02/03/c_1127060947.htm,

Yang, J. (2014). Welfare states' policy response to new social risk: Sequence analysis for welfare policy. *Development and Society*, *43*(2), 269–296. doi:10.21588/dns.2014.43.2.007

Yang, N. (2017). East Asia in transition: Re-examining the East Asian welfare model using fuzzy sets. *Journal of Asian Public Policy*, *10*(1), 104–120. doi:10.1080/17516234.2016.1258525

Yang, N., & Kühner, S. (2020). Beyond the limits of the productivist regime: Capturing three decades of East Asian welfare development with fuzzy sets. *Social Policy and Society*, *19*(4), 613–627. doi:10.1017/S147474641900054X

Yeh, C.-Y., & Ku, Y. W. (2021). Welfare attitude and economic developmentalism in new democratic developmental welfare state: An examination of the Taiwanese case. *Journal of Asian Public Policy*, *14*(1), 13–29. doi:10.1080/17516234.2020.1790729

Yeung, W. J. J., & Lee, Y. (2022). Aging in East Asia: New findings on retirement, health, and well-being. *The Journals of Gerontology. Series B, Psychological Sciences and Social Sciences*, *77*(3), 589–591. doi:10.1093/geronb/gbab055 PMID:33788932

Yeung, W. J., & Thang, L. L. (2018). Long-term care for older adults in ASEAN plus Three: The roles of family, community, and the state in addressing unmet eldercare needs. *Journal of Aging and Health*, *30*(10), 1499–1515. doi:10.1177/0898264318796345 PMID:30239253

Yin, R. (2018). *Case Study Research and Applications: Design and Methods* (6th ed.). Sage Publications, Inc.

Yip, P., Chan, M., So, B. K., Wat, K. P., & Lam, K. F. (2021). A decomposition analysis to examine the change in the number of recipients in the comprehensive social security assistance (CSSA) system. *China Population and Development Studies*, *4*(3), 284–297. doi:10.1007/s42379-020-00069-z PMID:33133735

Yoshimatsu, H. (2005). From distrust to mutual interests?: Emerging cooperation in Northeast Asia. *East Asia (Piscataway, N.J.)*, *22*(4), 18–38. doi:10.1007/s12140-005-0002-x

Young, O. (1997). *Global Governance*. MIT Press. https://mitpress.mit.edu/9780262740203/global-governance/

Young, O. R. (2017). *Governing complex systems: Social capital for the anthropocene*. The MIT Press. doi:10.7551/mitpress/9780262035934.001.0001

Yu, A. G., Fleett, P. D., & Bowers, J. A. (2005). Developing a value-cantered proposal for assessing project success. *International Journal of Project Management*, *23*(6), 428–436. doi:10.1016/j.ijproman.2005.01.008

Yuda, T. K. (2021). The evolving Korean childcare regime. *The International Journal of Sociology and Social Policy*, *41*(9/10), 1089–1107. doi:10.1108/IJSSP-09-2020-0438

Yuda, T. K. (2022). Who should care? Exploring the views and experiences of individuals in negotiating solutions for health security. *The International Journal of Sociology and Social Policy*, *42*(11-12), 1109–1128. doi:10.1108/IJSSP-09-2021-0246

Yuda, T. K. (forthcoming). Comparing Social Policy Responses Between Separate Crises: Taking the Case of Indonesia. In C. Aspalter (Ed.), *The Covid-19 Pandemic: Problems Arising* (pp. xx–xx). Springer Verlag.

Yuda, T. K., Damanik, J., & Nurhadi. (2021). Examining emerging social policy during COVID-19 in Indonesia and the case for a community-based support system. *Asia Pacific Journal of Social Work*, *31*(1–2), 13–22. doi:10.1080/02185385.2020.1829499

Yuda, T. K., Kim, M., Pholpark, A., & Bin Aedy Rahman, H. N. (2022). Unmasking the social policy responses of COVID-19 in four southeast Asian nations: Institutional patterns and policy adjustment. *Asia Pacific Journal of Social Work*, *0*(0), 1–22. doi:10.1080/02185385.2022.2136234

Yuda, T. K., & Kühner, S. (2022). Bringing Indonesia into the global welfare regime debate: A literature review and future research agenda. *Asian Social Work and Policy Review*, *0*(0), 1–12.

Yuda, T. K., & Pholpark, A. (2022). Healthcare expansion in Indonesia and Thailand: A causal mechanism and its implications for welfare regimes. *Journal of International and Comparative Social Policy*, *38*(2), 111–129. doi:10.1017/ics.2022.6

Yuda, T. K., & Qomariyah, N. (2022). Ideas and Policy Response to the COVID-19 Crisis: Evidence from Jakarta, Indonesia. *Social Policy and Society*, *0*(0), 1–20. doi:10.1017/S1474746422000616

Yuda, T. K., & Rezza, M. (2021). The forms of decommodification and (de)familisation measures during COVID-19: What is the impact on female's welfare? *Public Administration and Development*, *41*(3), 135–141. doi:10.1002/pad.1955 PMID:34539025

Yusufzai, A. (2019, January 25). Taliban appoint Mullah Baradar as head of political office in Doha. *Arab News*. https://www.arabnews.com/node/1441536/amp

Zadek, S. (2001). *Third-generation corporate citizenship*. The Foreign Policy Centre.

Zelin, A. (2015). *Full Text Statement Delivered By the Delegation of the Political Office in the International Pugwash Research Conference*. Jihadology. https://jihadology.net/2015/05/05/new-re-lease-from-the-islamic-emirate-of-afghanistan-full-text-of-statement-delivered-by-the-delegation-of-the-political-office-in-the-international-pugwash-research-conference

ZELIN. A. Y. (2016). The Islamic State's Territorial Methodology. The Washington Institute for Near East Policy, 29.

Zetter, R. (2009). *The role of legal and normative frameworks for the protection of environmentally displaced people*. RSC. https://www.rsc.ox.ac.uk/publications/the-role-of-legal-and-normative-frameworks-for-the-protection-of-environmentally-displaced-people

Zetter, R. (2010). *Protecting people displaced by climate change: Some conceptual challenges*. RSC. https://www.rsc.ox.ac.uk/publications/protecting-people-displaced-by-climate-change-some-conceptual-challenges

Zetter, R. (2011b). *Protecting environmentally displaced people: Developing the capacity of legal and normative frameworks*. RSC. https://www.rsc.ox.ac.uk/publications/protecting-environmentally-displaced-people-developing-the-capacity-of-legal-and-normative-frameworks

Zetter, R. (2017). Why they are not refugees – Climate change, environmental degradation and population displacement. *Siirtolaisuus-Migration Quarterly*, 23–28. https://www.rsc.ox.ac.uk/publications/why-they-are-not-refugees-2013-climate-change-environmental-degradation-and-population-displacement

Zetter, R. (2011a). *Protecting environmentally displaced people Developing the capacity of legal and normative framework*. Refugee Studies Centre Oxford Department of International Development.

Zhang, J. (2015). Study of Law and Regulation on the Overseas Business Development of Chinese Security Companies. *Journal of Chongqing University*, *21*(2), 116–121.

Zheng, S. (2021). *China turns to unregulated private security firms to protect interests along the Mekong*. SCMP. https://www.scmp.com/news/china/diplomacy/article/3138628/china-turns-unregulated-private-security-firms-protect

Zhou, L., Cheng, X., Wall, G., & Zhang, D. (2023). Entrepreneurial networks in creative tourism place-making: Dali village, Wuhan, China. *Tourism Geographies*, *25*(1), 220–242. doi:10.1080/14616688.2020.1866056

Zhukov, Y. M. (2012). Roads and the diffusion of insurgent violence. The logistics of conflict in Russia's North Caucasus. *Political Geography*, *31*(3), 144–156. doi:10.1016/j.polgeo.2011.12.002

Zieck, M. (2015). Guidelines on International Protection No. 11: Prima Facie Recognition of Refugee Status (UNHCR). *International Legal Materials*, *54*(6), 1115–1129. doi:10.5305/intelegamate.54.6.1115

Zürn, M. (2010). *Handbook on Multi-level Governance. Global governance is multi-level governance.* Edward Elgar Publishing Limited.

Zürn, M. (2018). Contested Global Governance. *Global Policy*, *9*(1), 138–145. doi:10.1111/1758-5899.12521

About the Contributors

Muhammad Anshari is a Senior Assistant Professor in Business Information Systems at the Universiti Brunei Darussalam School of Business and Economics (UBDSBE), and currently serves as Deputy Director for the Institute of Policy Studies. He has been named on the Stanford University List of Top 2% World Researchers since 2022 for the categories of ICT, Business & Management. Together with colleagues from UBDSBE and IPS, winning the Outstanding Paper award at the Emerald Literati Awards 2023 for two published papers. Patent Impact: His research has also been referenced in two patents, US Patent 10,999,416, 2021, and US Patent 11,489,906, 2022. Following the completion of his PhD at FBEPS UBD, Dr. Anshari worked as a research fellow at National Taiwan University. Before that, in 2009, he was a research fellow at King Saud University, Saudi Arabia.

Emil Ali is a lecturer and researcher at the Institute of Policy Studies (IPS), Universiti Brunei Darussalam. Prior to this, he started his career as an Education Officer working with the Ministry of Education. He obtained his first degree in Business Economics and Finance from the University of Loughborough; and his Master's degree in Public Administration (MPA) with distinction from the University of York, United Kingdom. His research interests are in the areas of public-sector finance with a special interest in Public-Private Partnerships. His recent publications include "Public Private Partnerships in Small States: The Case of Brunei Darussalam"; "COVID-19, Artificial Intelligence, Ethical Challenges and Policy Implications". AI & Soc. He currently works on his PhD research with a topic on "Evaluating Risk in the Management of UK Waste Public-Private Partnerships."

***

Sridharan A. is a Professor in the School of Business and Management at Christ (deemed to be a University). He has done his Ph.D. in Marketing. After serving the industry for 30 years, his last assignment being Vice President-Supply Chain, he joined academics in the year 2009. During the last 13 years, he has published research papers in national and international journals and was twice awarded for best paper in two international conferences.

Lili Yulyadi Arnakim is a senior faculty member in the Department of International Relations, Faculty of humanities, BINUS University, Jakarta. He was a visiting professor at Asia Europe Institute (AEI), University of Malaya, 2016-2019. His current research projects are on Financing for development in Southeast Asian Countries (2023), and Belt and Road Initiative's (BRI) influence towards Chinese Enterprises in Southeast Asia. (2022), China's State Capitalism and Economic Development in Southeast

Asia (2021), funded by BINUS University, and a team member of H2020 Global governance research funded by European Commission. His latest works have published in Intellectual Discourse, AEI Insights: An International Journal of Asia-Europe Relations, Transylvanian Review, Revista De Cercetare Si Interventie Sociala, Sejarah, CCPS and Jati (Journal of Southeast Asian Studies). Lili Yulyadi Arnakim holds Ph.D from University of Malaya.

Siti Nur Rafhanah Binti Awang Masri hails from the beautiful land of Brunei Darussalam. In 2020, she completed her Bachelor of Arts degree with a focus on Sociology and Anthropology, marking the beginning of her academic journey into the intricacies of human society and culture. Passionate about understanding social dynamics and driven by a deep interest in Islamic governance, she is currently pursuing her Master's degree in Islamic Governance through dedicated research. Rafhanah's academic pursuits are not only a testament to her intellectual curiosity but also reflect her commitment to exploring the intersection of societal structures, culture, and Islamic principles. Her academic endeavors aim to contribute meaningful insights into the governance systems within an Islamic context. Beyond academia, Rafhanah finds joy in various interests, cherishing moments of leisure through hobbies like reading, engaging in community activities, and actively seeking opportunities to broaden her perspectives through diverse cultural exchanges. As she continues her academic journey and research, Rafhanah remains dedicated to deepening her understanding of societal frameworks, aspiring to make meaningful contributions that align with her passion for societal improvement and Islamic principles.

Neeta Baporikar is currently Professor/Director(Business Management) at Harold Pupkewitz Graduate School of Business, Namibia University of Science and Technology, Namibia. Prior to this, she was Head-Scientific Research, with the Ministry of Higher Education CAS-Salalah, Sultanate of Oman, Professor (Strategy and Entrepreneurship) at IIIT Pune and BITS India. With a decade-plus of experience in the industry, consultancy, and training, she made a lateral switch to research and academics in 2000. Prof Baporikar holds D.Sc. (Management Studies) USA, Ph.D. (Management), SP Pune University, INDIA with MBA (Distinction) and Law (Hons.) degrees. Apart from this, she is an external reviewer, Oman Academic Accreditation Authority, an Accredited Management Teacher, a Qualified Trainer, an FDP from EDII, a Doctoral Guide, and a Board Member of the Academic Advisory Committee in accredited B-Schools. She has to her credit many conferred doctorates, 350+ scientific publications, and authored 30+ books in the areas of Strategy, Entrepreneurship, Management, and Higher Education. She is also a member of the international and editorial advisory board, and reviewer for Emerald, IGI, Inderscience, Wiley, etc.

Mukesh Shankar Bharti is a research scholar with a research background in foreign policy analysis and social science research. The author holds a PhD degree in International Relations with a specialization in East and Central Europe. His research area includes democracy, political institutions, European Union and South Asia.

Krishangee Bhattacharyya has completed her Master's degree in Business and Corporate Law from Symbiosis Law School, Hyderabad Campus, Symbiosis International (Deemed University), Pune.

Fadhli Zul Fauzi is a Lecturer at Faculty of Politics and Government, Institut Pemerintahan Dalam Negeri, Sumedang, Indonesia. His areas of research expertise are in governance and public policy.

Manuel José Serra da Fonseca played professional activities such as marketing communications technician and professor of higher education. He is currently Coordinating Professor at the Polytechnic Institute of Viana do Castelo (Portugal). He is a researcher at UNIAG (Applied Management Research Unit, since 2014). He acts in the Social Sciences field with an emphasis in Communication and Marketing Sciences.

Jorge Gomes is Professor of Strategy and Management at Universidade Lusófona and researcher at ADVANCE/CSG/ISEG - University of Lisbon. He holds a PhD in Management from ISEG and a Master's in Management Sciences from ISCTE-IUL, a postgraduate degree in Project Management from INDEG / ISCTE and a degree in Geographic Engineering from the Faculty of Sciences of the University of Lisbon. For the last 35 years he has worked as an engineer, project manager, quality auditor and consultant. His research interests include Strategy and Operations, Benefits Management, Project Management, Project Success, Maturity Models, IS/IT Investment Management.

Zhiming Hu is research assistant at Lingnan University, Hong Kong SAR. His current research interests are Comparative Social Policy, Welfare Regime, Confucianism, Neo-Confucianism, and Chan Buddhism.

Fahmida Kaiser is a distinguished academic figure in the field of tourism and hospitality management. As a Lecturer at the Department of Tourism and Hospitality Management at Daffodil Institute of IT, she has dedicated her career to advancing knowledge in the intersection of tourism and sustainability. With a passion for exploring the multifaceted relationship between tourism and sustainable practices, Her research has not only contributed to the academic community but also holds significant implications for the global tourism industry. Her commitment to shedding light on the importance of responsible and eco-conscious tourism practices has garnered recognition from both peers and students alike.

Muhammed Karakuş, PhD, is a specialist in Middle East and Africa geopolitics, security and strategic affairs. His studies mainly focused on Violent Non-State Armed Actors and their governance and resilience capacities. He is currently instructor in Adiyaman University, Turkey. He has several book translations (best known with Arab Uprising The Story of Arab National Movement- George Antonius) and several researches.

Jovito Jose P. Katigbak is a lecturer at the Department of Political Science and Development Studies, College of Liberal Arts, of De La Salle University Manila located in the Philippines.

Sadaf Khan has extensive teaching experience of more than ten years. A core academician and a prolific researcher, she has done incredible work in the domain of English Literature, Cultural Studies, and Afghanistan Studies. Having an international teaching experience, she has been felicitated multiple times as 'Best Teacher' by various academic institutions in which she had worked. Besides, she has also served as the Joint Editor of Women's College Annual magazine of Aligarh Muslim University for the session 2007-2008.

Saad Ullah Khan has more than a decade long extensive experience at university level teaching and research. Currently he is working at Amity School of Communication, Amity University Rajasthan

(India). He has authored various research papers in Journals of national as well as international repute. He was awarded 'Rajat Jayanti Vigyan Sancharak Fellowship-2009' by DST, Ministry of Science and Technology(Government of India) for his contribution to the field of communication and its social implications. Further he was bestowed with MANF Fellowship 2011 by UGC to carry out his research work. A PhD from prestigious Aligarh Muslim University, Dr. Saad Ullah Khan has presented 90 Research Papers in various National and International Conferences. He was awarded 'Best Researcher Award' twice (2020 & 2023) and 'Best Journalism Teacher Award' in 2021.

Sanjeev Kumar is an accomplished expert in Food and Beverage. He currently holds the positions of Professor at the Lovely Professional University, Punjab, India. With over a decade of experience in the field, food Service Industry, his research focuses on Alcoholic beverages, Event management and Sustainable Management Practices, Metaverse and Artificial Intelligence. He has published more than 35 research papers, articles and chapters in Scopus Indexed, UGC Approved and peer reviewed Journals and books. Dr. Sanjeev Kumar participated and acted as resource person in various National and International conferences, seminars, research workshops and industry talks and his work has been widely cited.

Sunita Kumar is an Associate Professor in the School of Business and Management at CHRIST University, Banerghatta Road, Bengaluru, India. Her doctoral thesis was on brand strategies in retail marketing. She has published articles in various international and national refereed journals. Her areas of research interest include social media marketing, branding, Advertising and neuromarketing.

Yuhong Li is a doctoral student at Nanjing University in China. His main research interests include global governance, international relations theory, and international society research. He has published articles in the Asia-Pacific Journal of Humanities and Social Sciences (Australia), Jebat: Malaysian Journal of History, Politics & Strategic Studies (Malaysia), Asian Political Science Review (Thailand), Macao Academic Journal (Macao), Macedonian Political Science Forum (Macedonia), Journal of ASEAN-China Studies (Thailand), Rajabhat Chiang Mai Research Journal (Thailand), Journal of South China Sea Studies (China) Russian Law Journal (Russia), Masyarakat, Kebudayaan dan Politik (Indonesia), and so on.

Nasir Mia is a prominent figure in tourism and hospitality management. As a Lecturer in the Department of Tourism and Hospitality Management at Islamic University, he has devoted his professional life to advancing knowledge concerning the junction of tourism and sustainability. His study has made a substantial contribution to the academic community and has significant consequences for the tourism sector worldwide. He has a lifelong interest in investigating the complex relationship between tourism and environmentally responsible practices. He has received praise from both his contemporaries and younger students because of his dedication to bringing awareness to the significance of ethical and environmentally conscientious tourist practices.

Hizkia Putra Purnomo is a research assistant in the Department of International Relations Department, Bina Nusantara University. His research focus is on International Political Economy, particularly on foreign aid.

Mário José Batista Romão is an Associate Professor of Information Systems at ISEG – University of Lisbon. He is Director of the Master's program in Computer Science and Management. He holds a

PhD in Management Sciences by ISCTE-IUL and by Computer Integrated Manufacturing at Cranfield University (UK). He also holds a MsC in Telecommunications and Computer Science, at IST - Instituto Superior Técnico, University of Lisbon. He is Pos-Graduated in Project Management and holds the international certification Project Management Professional (PMP), by PMI – Project Management International. He has a degree in Electrotecnic Engineer by IST.

Parimal Roy worked in the project management sector for ten years (2006-2015). Then, paced in academia from 2015; before that, he had started a career in 2006 in the Development sector, collaborating with international development partners like ADB, DFID, UNFPA, SIDA, PKSF, and Orbis International. Nevertheless, he is immensely inquisitive about the affinity between theory, policy, and practice amid ethnic groups; to this end, he dissected several policies and int'l frameworks that have been published. He is an undergraduate and post-graduated in Anthropology and another Master's in Business Administration, and now pursuing a PhD in Community[Indigenous-Santals] Development at Universiti Malaya, Malaysia. Furthermore, he satisfied the "FinTech & Regulator Innovation"; and "Digital Assets for Regulator" at the University of Cambridge, UK, by getting ADBI scholarship. He also obtained two PGDs in Project Management and Criminology.

Noe John Joseph E. Sacramento is an assistant professor of political science (public policy and administration) at the College of Social Sciences, University of the Philippines Cebu. He is also a Doctor of Philosophy in Public Policy candidate at the School of Public Policy, Chiang Mai University, Thailand under the CMU Presidential Scholarship and the University of the Philippines Doctoral Fellowship. His research interest is on critical policy studies, deliberations, narratives, and emotions. He has published articles in scientific indexed academic journals like the Journal of Asian Public Policy, Public Administration and Policy, Agrarian South, and Thammasat Review, among others.

Virgemarie Salazar is an assistant professor at the Department of Political Science of the University of the Philippines Diliman. She is a graduate of the International Doctoral Program in Asia-Pacific Studies of the National Chengchi University in Taipei, Taiwan. She also holds a master's degree in public policy and management from the Institute of Policy Studies at Universiti Brunei Darussalam. Before pursuing her PhD, she worked as a Senior Foreign Affairs Research Specialist at the Center for International Relations and Strategic Studies of the Foreign Service Institute in the Philippines.

Asif Iqubal Shah is presently working as an Assistant Professor in Law at the Xavier Law School, St. Xavier's University, Kolkata. Prior to that he was associated with Aligarh Muslim University, Centre Murshidabad as an Assistant Professor in the Department of law. A Graduate and Post-Graduate in Law from the Department of Law, University of Calcutta, Dr. Asif has been awarded Ph.D in Law from KIIT (Deemed to be) University. He has prime interest in Criminology, Penology and Criminal Justice Administration and has published articles in renowned national and international journals including Scopus (UGC-Care Group-II) and other peer-reviewed journals.

Shaeyuq Ahmad Shah is an Assistant Professor of Law at Symbiosis Law School, Hyderabad Campus, Symbiosis International (Deemed University) Pune

Adriana Silva is Adjunct Professor in Management Accounting at the Polytechnic Institute of Santarém. Integrated member researcher of the CICF, School of Management, IPCA, Barcelos, Portugal. Member researcher of the Laboratory of Critical and Interpretive Studies in Accounting (LECIC) at the Federal University of Pará (UFPA). Associated Editor of journal "Revista Contemporânea de Economia e Gestão". PhD in Accounting from the University of Minho. Research interest focuses on critical and interpretative accounting and accounting history, specifically on themes that give prominence to subordinated voices.

Bruno Barbosa Sousa is Adjunct Professor of Marketing at Polytechnic Institute of Cávado and Ave (IPCA), Portugal and PhD in Marketing and Strategy in Universidade do Minho, Portugal. Head of Masters Program - Tourism Management and Marketing Tourism (IPCA); CiTUR – Center for Tourism Research, Development and Innovation and UNIAG research member. He has published in the Journal of Enterprising Communities, Tourism Management Perspectives, Current Issues in Tourism, Journal of Organizational Change Management, World Review of Entrepreneurship, Management and Sust. Development, among others.

Miranda Paulina Tahalele is a faculty member in the Department of International Relations, Faculty of Humanities, Bina Nusantara (BINUS) University. She received her PhD in Anthropology (Development Studies) from the Australian National University (ANU). Her main research topics are the political economy of international development cooperation and the globalised world of foreign aid, with a focus on Indonesia's South–South Cooperation and North - South Relations. She has previously worked as, among others, consultant for G20 Empower – Indonesia Presidency at the Ministry of Women Empowerment and Child Protection (2021-2022), development practitioner with the United Nations Development Programme (UNDP) and at the Ministry of National Development Planning (BAPPENAS).

Mohammad Badruddoza Talukder is an Associate Professor, College of Tourism and Hospitality Management, International University of Business Agriculture and Technology, Dhaka, Bangladesh. He completed PhD. in Hotel Management, School of Hotel Management and Tourism, Lovely Professional University, India. He holds a bachelor's and a master's degree in Hotel Management from India. He has been teaching various courses in the Department of Tourism and Hospitality at various universities in Bangladesh since 2008. His research areas include tourism management, hotel management, hospitality management, food & beverage management, and accommodation management, where he has published research papers in well-known journals in Bangladesh and abroad. Mr. Talukder is one of the executive members of the Tourism Educators Association of Bangladesh. He has led training and counseling for a wide range of hospitality organizations in Bangladesh. As an administrator, Mr. Talukder served as a debate advisor at the University, coordinator for courses and exams in the Department of Tourism and Hotel Management. He has experience as a manager in various business class hotels in Bangladesh. He is one of the certified trainers for the food and beverage service department of the SEIP project from Bangladesh. He just become an honorary facilator at Bangladesh Tourism Board's Bangabandhu international tourism and hospitality training institution.

Zhen Tian is Lecturer of Sociology and Social Policy at Lingnan University, Hong Kong. Her research focuses on integrated service delivery and community care for older people in China. Her research interests include ageing studies, comparative policy, welfare regime, city governance, and higher education

Omar Vargas-González is a professor, research assistant and former Head of Computer Systems Department at Tecnologico Nacional de Mexico Campus Ciudad Guzman, professor at Telematic Engineering at Centro Universitario del Sur Universidad de Guadalajara with a master degree in Computer Systems. Has been trained in Innovation and Multidisciplinary Entrepreneurship at Arizona State University (2018) and a Generation of Ecosystems of Innovation, Entrepreneurship and Sustainability for Jalisco course by Harvard University T.H. Chan School of Health. At present conduct research on diverse fields such as Entrepreneurship, Economy, Statistics, Mathematics and Information and Computer Sciences. Has colaborated in the publication of many scientific articles and conducted diverse Innovation and Technological Development projects.

Tauchid Komara Yuda is Assistant Professor at the Department of Social Development & Welfare, Gadjah Mada University (UGM), Indonesia and concurrently R&D Director of Wiraanggaran Indonesia Policy Consultant Ltd. His areas of research expertise are in policies and politics of welfare state and social innovation with reference to Indonesia and Democratic Middle-Income Countries (DMICs). The range of his publications includes papers in Social Policy & Administration, Social Policy & Society [Cambridge University Press], International Journal of Social Welfare, International Social Work, Journal of International and Comparative Social Policy [Cambridge University Press], Public Administration & Development, Political Studies Review and others.

Index

E

F

G

H

I

L

M

N

O

P

R

S

T

U

W

www.ingramcontent.com/pod-product-compliance
Lightning Source LLC
LaVergne TN
LVHW062107300926
849161LV00010B/2391